A CATALOGUE OF THE PRE-1500 WESTERN MANUSCRIPT BOOKS AT THE NEWBERRY LIBRARY

MS 83, fol. 1. Prayer Book of Anne of Brittany

A CATALOGUE OF THE PRE-1500 WESTERN MANUSCRIPT BOOKS AT THE NEWBERRY LIBRARY

Paul Saenger

THE UNIVERSITY OF CHICAGO PRESS CHICAGO AND LONDON

PAUL SAENGER is the George A. Poole III Curator of Rare Books at the Newberry Library

THE UNIVERSITY OF CHICAGO PRESS, CHICAGO 60637
THE UNIVERSITY OF CHICAGO PRESS, LTD., LONDON

Printed in the United States of America
98 97 96 95 94 93 92 91 90 89 5 4 3 2 1

This publication has been supported by a grant from the National Endowment for the Humanities, an independent federal agency.

⊗The paper used in this publication meets the minimum requirements of the American National Standard for Information Sciences—Permanence of Paper for Printed Library Materials, ANSI Z39.48-1984.

LIBRARY OF CONGRESS CATALOGING-IN-PUBLICATION DATA

Saenger, Paul Henry, 1945-
A catalogue of the pre-1500 western manuscript books at the Newberry Library / Paul Saenger.
p. cm.
Bibliography: p.
Includes index.
ISBN 0-226-73350-5 (alk. paper)
1. Manuscripts, Medieval—Catalogs. 2. Manuscripts, Renaisance—Catalogs. 3. Manuscripts, Medieval—Library resources—Illinois—Chicago—Catalogs. 4. Manuscripts, Renaissance—Library resources—Illinois—Chicago—Catalogs. 5. Civilization, Occidental—Manuscripts—Library resources—Illinois--Chicago—Catalogs. 6. Newberry Library—Catalogs. I. Newberry Library. II. Title.
Z6621.N66S23 1989
011′.31—dc19 88-36581
CIP

For N. M. S.

CONTENTS

INTRODUCTION

The Newberry Library collection of medieval and Renaissance manuscripts falls into four major divisions. At the end of the nineteenth century and in the early twentieth century, the Newberry acquired through purchase and donation two major private collections, those of Henry Probasco (1890) and Edward E. Ayer (1920). These two collections combined account for about 25 percent of the Library's pre-1500 books. From the early 1930s to the early 1950s, the selection of manuscripts rested with the Committee on Collections on which Professor B. L. Ullman of the University of Chicago played a prominent role. Under his influence the Library acquired materials documenting the history of paleographic evolution from the eleventh to the fourteenth century. From the 1950s through the mid 1960s, the collection fell under the tutelage of the Newberry's Distinguished Research Bibliographer and noted historian of the Italian Renaissance, Dr. Hans Baron. In 1964, Library Director Lawrence W. Towner arranged for the purchase of the collection of Louis H. Silver, which included manuscripts important for illumination and text. In addition, since its founding the Newberry has received gifts of individual volumes from private midwestern collectors who thus played an important role, complementing the careful and meticulous selection of the professional curators. Both these sorts of acquisitions, together, have given the collection its special strength. It should also be noted that from time to time the funds of the John M. Wing Foundation for the History of Printing have been used to purchase fifteenth-century manuscript books which, either because of production techniques or because of text, were judged to be pertinent to the history of the early printed book.

The oldest manuscripts in the Newberry's collections were acquired when the collection was under the stewardship of the Committee on Collections. The oldest book is MS f1, a book of homilies from southern France, probably from the abbey of Saint Pierre of Moissac and dating from the first half of the eleventh century. Another very old codex is a patristic collection including the works of Julian of Toledo written in southern France in the first half of the eleventh century. A third unquestionably pre-1100 manuscript is MS f3, an eleventh-century manuscript copied at Novalesa in northern Italy. Because of the nature of the sources of the book trade in the twentieth century, pre-1100 manuscripts are rarities in American libraries, and the Newberry's holdings give students the invaluable opportunity of examining the kinds of early medieval manuscripts, written without complete word separation, which constitute major *fonds* in the national and provincial libraries of Europe.

Among the other early codices is MS f9, a copy of Boethius's *De musica,* written in Austria probably very late in the eleventh century. The partial dissolution of Austrian monastic manuscript holdings between the two world wars felicitously corresponded with the zenith of Professor Ullman's influence at Newberry. Newberry obtained the *De musica* from Admont via London in 1939. Eight years before, in 1931, the Library acquired from bookseller E. P. Goldschmidt in London an early twelfth-century copy of Isidore of Seville's *Sententiae* which originated in the abbey of Lambach. In 1936, the Newberry obtained also from Goldschmidt a twelfth-century Admont collection of patristic texts, and in 1937, the Admont copy of Isidore of Seville's *Etymologiarum.* In 1938, the Library purchased MS +23, a fourteenth-century collection of Aristotle texts, formerly in the abbey of Melk, and after the Second World War, the Newberry added to its strength of Austrian holdings by acquiring MS 31.1, an important collection of moralized texts, copied in Bohemia and formerly in the library of the abbey of Admont. Most of these manuscripts are in the original or at least late medieval bindings, and it is fair to state that as a consequence of these purchases Newberry is one of the nation's most important centers for the study of medieval Austrian codices.

The period between the wars witnessed the acquisition of other important twelfth- and thirteenth-century manuscript books by the Library. In 1936, MS −10, an eleventh-century copy of Boethius's *De consolatione philosophiae,* one of the rare surviving books from the library of the Augustinian Canons of Hammersleve, was obtained from H. P. Kraus, then still located in Vienna, and in 1937 the Library purchased an important set of seven codices containing the collected works of Saint Augustine copied during the twelfth century in the Benedictine monastery of Reading. Directly after the Second World War, the strength in early German manuscripts was augmented with an evangelistary, MS f4, copied in the late eleventh century in a south German or Swiss monastery affiliated with Saint Gall. In 1951, the Newberry obtained a Cistercian missal, MS +7, copied in the diocese of Würzburg before 1173. This missal had made its way to Hohenfurt in Bohemia and emendations in it indicate that it was in regular use there through the fifteenth century.

Between the two great European wars, the Library also made important acquisitions of vernacular materials. In 1939, an early *Lancelot du Lac* manuscript, copied in about 1300, was obtained through Bernard Quaritch. This manuscript has the longest uninterrupted genealogy of any Newberry codex, for its owners can be traced from the second half of the fifteenth century to the present day. In 1937, a still unstudied codex of works of Jean de Meun was purchased. In 1932, the Library acquired MS 31, a fourteenth-century codex from the library of Whitechurch (Hants) including English vernacular texts which were subsequently studied by R. H. Robbins in an important article in the 1940 *Modern Language Review.* In 1938, the Library acquired from William H. Robinson in London an English literary roll dating from about 1400 containing the vernacular text of the *Stations of Rome* accompanied by a Latin rubric, which makes it a significant source for the history of late medieval reading technique. Another codex important for its texts, MS f36, containing the works of Alain Chartier and subsequently studied at the Newberry by Curt Bühler and edited by M. S. Blayney, was obtained from William H. Robinson in March 1937. In 1938, the Library obtained from Maggs Brothers MS f37, a critically important manuscript of Froissart's *Chroniques* which Leopold Delisle knew from an eighteenth-century sales catalogue, but which he failed to locate during his lifetime. Again and again the careful judgment exercised by the Library in its selections has been vindicated by acquisitions which subsequently stirred significant scholarly interest.

Like other American collections of medieval and Renaissance manuscripts, the Newberry's has its share of late medieval Bibles, breviaries, and books of hours. The majority of these manuscripts entered the Library in 1890 and 1920, first as part of the collection of the Cincinnati hardware magnate and bibliophile Henry Probasco and later from the collection of Newberry Trustee Edward E. Ayer of Chicago, who made his fortune manufacturing and selling railroad ties. The Probasco collection is an important instance of the diffusion of the artifacts of medieval and Renaissance European culture in the American Midwest. In 1873 Probasco commissioned the Librarian of the Cincinnati Public Library, William Frederick Poole, to prepare the *Catalogue of the Collection of Books, Manuscripts and Works of Art Belonging to Mr. Henry Probasco.* This work was privately printed at Harvard University Press in seventy-five copies. Poole, whose primary interest was printed books, described Probasco's manuscripts so briefly that at times it is difficult to assign the unnumbered articles to a specific Newberry codex. Fourteen years later, W. F. Poole became Newberry's first Librarian and bought the entire Probasco collection for $52,000. On the average, individual volumes cost less than Probasco often paid for his mosaic bindings which he generally reserved for printed books and placed on only one manuscript, MS −18, a thirteenth-century Latin Bible copied in France.

Probasco's collection and its catalogue tell us much about the style of collecting in late nineteenth-century midwestern America. In many instances Probasco and his librarian were ignorant of the correct identification of the codices which were acquired during two extended voyages to Europe in 1856 and 1866. Without correctly identifying their origins, the Probasco collection brought to the Newberry three thirteenth-century French portable Bibles and a Spanish portable Bible dating from about 1300. A fourth thirteenth-century French portable Bible arrived later with the Ayer collection. These five Bibles form a rich source for investigating the production methods of the first books produced on a relatively large scale in the medieval world. Indeed, thirteenth-century Bibles were still so numerous in fifteenth-century France that the early printing of Bibles was discouraged, and significantly, the Newberry Bibles show signs of use through at least the early sixteenth century.

The Probasco acquisition also brought the Library its entire holdings of breviaries, including MS 24, a Franciscan breviary with musical notation dating from about 1230 which has been made famous by S. J. P. Van Dijk's studies on Haymo of Faversham and the origins of the modern Roman liturgy. Franciscan capitulary MS +88, another Probasco liturgical manuscript studied by Van Dijk, is one of the few identified examples of a genre of choir book related in its origins to the breviary. Other breviaries from the Probasco collection include fifteenth-century Italian manuscripts for the use of the Congregation of Saint Justina, the Camaldolese Order, and the Hieronymite Order. Among related codices are a Spanish fifteenth-century Carthusian missal and a lectionary of the Charterhouse of San Lorenzo in Florence.

Here one might ask the question, did Henry Probasco know the origin and understand the liturgical function of these books? The conclusive evidence from the privately printed catalogue of his library is that he did not. Judging from the books themselves, it seems that Probasco, who was fundamentally self-educated, collected, like many of his peers, with an eye chiefly to physical beauty. All of his volumes shared the common traits of illuminated miniatures and border decorations and attractive bindings. When the collection arrived in Chicago, it was the printed books and early modern manuscripts that drew the attention of Poole and the Newberry Trustees, and probably as a result, the manuscript holdings were curiously ignored by the Chicago press.

Over one-third of Probasco's manuscripts were prayer books and books of hours. Among these were eight French books of hours and three books of hours of the use of Rouen, one of which, from the library of Count Potocki of Vilna, was later to catch the eye of Erwin Panofsky. Without being aware of it, Probasco possessed a prayer book, MS 83, which had been prepared especially for Anne of Brittany as queen of France. In contrast to the celebrated Hours of Anne of Brittany in the Bibliothèque Nationale in Paris (which contains prayers in masculine form), this book was personalized for the queen by adjusting prayers to feminine form and inserting her name in red ink into two of them. Copied in Florence, it was likely a gift made by King Louis XII during the Italian wars to his pregnant wife. The book contains a special royal prayer to Saint Leonard to be recited during childbirth. Unfortunately, we do not know where in Europe Probasco acquired this volume or any other of his manuscripts, for he left no archival record of his collecting activities. Probasco also possessed a fragment of a book of hours with Catalan rubrics, copied and decorated in Bruges and probably intended for export. Two other portions of this manuscript are preserved today in the Bibliothèque Royale in Brussels. A second Probasco *horae* from the Low Countries was Geert Groote's vernacular hours with inserted miniatures, a typical example of the books intended for private devotion which were mass-produced in the late Middle Ages. In addition to liturgical and devotional manuscripts, the collection included four calligraphic textual manuscripts, two of which by chance were to correspond particularly well with the later collecting interests of the Newberry. MS +92, an Italian copy of the incunable edition of Rodrigo Sánchez de Arévalo's *Compendiosa historia hispanica,* was copied from an incunable printed in Rome in 1470. MS +97, copied in the mid-fifteenth century for the library of King Alfonso the Magnanimous of Naples, contains a still unedited neo-Latin translation of Plato's *Republic*. The former is an important document for the history of printing; the latter is important for the study of Italian Renaissance humanism.

Edward E. Ayer is most famous for his rich collection on the discovery and exploration of the New World, which he presented to the Newberry along with a generous endowment in 1911. As part of this truly vast collection, the Library received five medieval Western manuscripts of importance for the study of medieval astronomy and the textual history of Ptolemy. These codices are designated by their Ayer shelf numbers in this catalogue. Far less well known is Ayer's collection of medieval manuscripts which he gave in 1920. This collection was approximately one-third the size of the Probasco collection, which it resembles in bibliophilic taste. Most of the Ayer codices were books of hours. These, by felicitous happenstance, included two *horae* from western France and one from eastern France, both regions unrepresented among the Probasco manuscripts. Historically the most important book of hours is MS 56, a composite codex of which the second half was written for Margaret of Croy, daughter of Antoine of Croy, chamberlain of Philip the Good. This manuscript, of exceptional length for a book of private devotion (it contains over one hundred discrete texts), was personalized for Margaret's use by altering the gender of its prayers and inserting her name into four of them. Just as Probasco in the case of MS 83 had no knowledge of the original owner, so too was Ayer unaware of the patron of this illuminated manuscript. The Ayer manuscripts also brought the Newberry MS 35, the Library's only book of hours written for English use. Like the Probasco Catalan Hours, MS 35 was manufactured in Bruges for exportation abroad. In addition, Ayer provided the Newberry with two of its four Italian books of hours, one of which, MS 82, contains sixty-seven discrete texts. Ayer's manuscripts thus included two especially rich collections of late medieval prayers. He, like Probasco, collected textual manuscripts only when they were examples of beautiful calligraphy and decoration, and undoubtedly Ayer purchased MS f95 because of its visual allure. However, its contents made it a precursor of the Newberry collecting of the 1950s and 1960s. MS f95 preserves a recension of Petrarch's *De vita solitaria* of which the variants would be extensively studied half a century later by B. L. Ullman in his *Studies in the Italian Renaissance*.

The religious persecution of the Third Reich, a source of then unimaginable human suffering, created a class of refugee scholars which had a profound and beneficial effect on the study in America of the Middle Ages and the Renaissance. This tragedy had an equally profound effect on the growth of the Newberry's collection of pre-1500 manuscripts, for in 1948 Hans Baron, already internationally recognized as a leading scholar of Leonardo Bruni, became the Library's principal selector of European manuscripts. He brought to this task a passion for the unknown which placed questions of textual content in the forefront. During his tenure, and especially from 1954 to 1964, Baron scoured catalogues of American and European antiquarian bookdealers in his quest for codices containing unidentified or unedited texts or texts with significant variants to editions already printed. In 1954 he bought MS f57, an important volume originating in the diocese of Liège, which included an unidentified selection of northern humanistic material. In 1961, he chose from Bernard Rosenthal MS 78.1, a humanistic miscellany, modest in its appearance but rich in the kind of unidentified materials which piqued Baron's interest in the textually unexplored. In 1959, another acquisition from Bernard Rosenthal brought to the Library MS 90.1, a curious mélange of religious and humanistic texts from the Franciscan convent of Tuscanella. In 1967, Baron selected from William H. Schab in New York a French volume, MS 93.1, which contained twenty-one texts, most unidentified, including several humanistic *inedita*. These and more than a score of similar Baron purchases have made the Newberry the premier collection in America for the study of the diffusion of Italian humanism.

Like all truly great collectors, Baron did not

narrowly confine his selections to his own personal interests, but building on them he abstracted criteria broadly applicable to the books of medieval Europe. In 1963 he obtained, again from Schab in New York, an important collection of Burgundian political texts from the epoch of Philip the Good, and in 1957 he chose from Ifan Kyrle Fletcher of London MS −14.1, a diverse collection of unidentified French twelfth-century sermons. In 1958 he acquired from Lathrop Harper in New York MS 105, which included over 40 unidentified prayers. The same year, again from Fletcher, he selected an unidentified compilation of German Saints' Lives, MS f65.1, and in 1960 he led the Library to bid successfully at the Dyson Perrins Sale in London for MS 102.2, a codex of the letters of Saint Jerome which included over 183 unidentified texts. In 1955, Baron acquired from Nebehay in Vienna MS 54.1, a collection of rare musical texts, two of which were subsequently published in the *Corpus scriptorum de musica,* and in 1959 he obtained, again from Fletcher, MS 67.3, a Carthusian codex containing extracts from over 55 different works. This volume has now been identified as an autograph of Johannes Hagen.

When choosing manuscripts of classical Latin and Greek authors Baron favored books with unidentified fifteenth-century commentaries such as those found in a fragmentary copy of Aristotle's *Ethics* obtained in Milan from R. Rizzi. In 1959 he obtained from Bernard Rosenthal a fifteenth-century copy of Lucan's *Pharasalia* with unidentified glosses and notes, and in 1962 he recommended for purchase from H. P. Kraus a fifteenth-century manuscript *Aeneid,* copied in Rome. This volume contains an unidentified humanist's gloss which continues to fascinate Newberry research fellows. Baron also built the collection of Latin grammars by selecting a codex of Priscian from Bernard Weinreb in London in 1963 and, in 1953 and 1959, three of the Library's four Latin glossaries, two from Bernard Rosenthal and one from Hamill and Barker, Chicago bookdealers. Baron also bought a number of dated manuscripts and, building on previous strength, made the Newberry's collection distinguished in this area, particularly for the late medieval period.

Just as the early collecting had been fundamentally shaped by the acquisition of the Probasco and Ayer collections, the more recent history of the collection has been in part molded by two block acquisitions, the C. L. Ricketts Collection in 1942 and the Silver Collection in 1964. The Ricketts collection, acquired by librarian Stanley Pargellis with funds from the Wing Foundation, brought to the Newberry a group of fifteenth-century Italian Renaissance manuscripts similar in character to those subsequently selected by Baron. It also included three extremely rare alphabet model books. The Silver collection has a more complicated history. Louis H. Silver of Wilmette, a Chicago hotel magnate and Newberry trustee, favored handsome English and French vernacular books and generally all books of interesting and distinguished provenance. In 1960 he gave the Library MS 59.1, a missal from the Church of Saint Michael in Ghent, and before his death in 1963 he gave the Library MS 32.5, one of its two Barrois codices. Silver had intended to leave his entire library to the Newberry, but circumstances did not permit him to do so. Librarian Lawrence W. Towner arranged for its purchase in 1964. This block acquisition brought the Newberry seven additional pre-1500 manuscripts, including two deluxe illustrated codices prepared at the Burgundian court during the fifteenth century. These represented a class of book hitherto not consultable in the Library's collection. One of these Burgundian manuscripts was the copiously illustrated French translation of the *Speculum humanae salvationis,* recorded in the 1467 and 1485 inventories of the library of Philip the Good. It is identifiable by the incipit of its second folio. The other Burgundian manuscript is Jacques Legrand's *Livre de bonnes moeurs,* from the library of Wolfart de Borsele, knight of the Order of the Golden Fleece. Both are written in *lettre bâtarde,* the script of the French-speaking aristocracy; while *hybrida,* represented by MS 59.1, was the script of the Flemish-speaking townsmen of the Low Countries. Acquiring MSS +33.3, +33.5, and f33.7 strengthened the Library's holdings in English vernacular texts. The Silver collection included as well MS 102.5, a second Dyson Perrins codex of Saint Jerome's treatises and letters related closely in content as in provenance to the volume of Jerome's letters which Hans Baron had led the Library to acquire four years earlier.

A final important source for the Library's collection has been the gifts of individual volumes by private donors and institutions. In 1889 B. F. Stevens of the celebrated London book firm gave the Newberry its first medieval manuscript, a missal written in the Rhine Valley c. 1250, and still the only representative of its type in the Library's collections. In 1935 Philip Hofer, later of Harvard, gave the Library Sallust's *Histories* copied in Brescia in 1477 by a known humanist scribe. In 1949 Librarian Emeritus George B. Utley presented MS f68, a still unidentified commentary on the *Decretales*. In 1950 the Chicago Historical Society presented the Newberry with a manuscript of English rhetorical treatises, and in 1969 the Chicago collector Chester D. Tripp gave a fourth book of hours of the use of Rouen.

From this brief survey it is clear that the Library's manuscript collections have been built from a broad variety of interests, and it is precisely this fact that gives it its unique character. The two great private collections which entered the Library early in its history as block acquisitions represent the typical tastes of nineteenth-century private collectors. In some American rare-book libraries, these interests have dominated, sometimes to the virtual exclusion of all other criteria of selection, creating a beautiful but profoundly false image of a medieval world populated in every century exclusively by deluxe decorated codices. The Newberry has its fair share of beautiful books, both liturgical and secular. However, it also has a wide variety of visually modest books collected for their textual, paleographical, and codicological interest. It is this special mixture which makes the Newberry collection a rare pedagogical tool for the art historian, the editor of texts, the paleographer, and especially the student of the history of written and printed communication.

* * *

Catalogues are not only an important means of access to important collections of artifacts, they also offer lessons on how these objects are to be viewed and understood. Medieval manuscripts are so complex that it is doubtful that any cataloguing format will forever answer every inquiry which scholars might pose. Rather, each generation of cataloguers, building on the insights of its predecessors, aspires to incorporate its own peculiar insights into previously unnoted details in order to cast light on a manuscript's contents, manufacture, and modes of use. It is in this way that the science of manuscript studies is advanced. The format of the notices in this catalogue is based on Neil Ker's monumental *Medieval Manuscripts in British Libraries* (Oxford, 1969–83). To it, I have made modifications principally in regard to the nomenclature of script, which has been largely borrowed from the system expounded by the late Julian Brown. I have modified Professor Brown's system in one respect. The term *hybrida* has been reserved for the gothic hybrid writing of central Europe and the Low Countries; the term *lettre bâtarde* has been used to denote the analogous French script. The plate on page 2 illustrating selected scripts is complemented by the plates at the end of the volume. I have also departed from Ker by recording certain codicological details and data concerning liturgical texts. Specifically, I have recorded for manuscripts of the fifteenth century whether or not the scribe began to write on the first ruled line. This practice is important because it indicates conscious or unconscious imitation of pre-thirteenth-century codices. It is usually, but not always, found in the presence of humanistic script. In MS 54.5, writing on the first ruled line is a unique sign of humanistic influence in an otherwise gothic French codex. A second innovation which I have made is to record variations from the ten standard short prayers that follow the litany in books of hours, breviaries, and other private liturgical books. Particularly in the fifteenth century, the patterns of inclusions and omissions are important, not only for local use, but as subtle indications of the political proclivities which scribes imputed to prospective owners. In an age of schism and conciliarism, the absence or presence of the prayer for the pope in the use of Rome is of considerable import. The scribe's choice of Roman or other use may also indicate either political or third-order religious affiliations.

In general each notice contains the following elements:

1. *Heading, including shelf number, summary title, place of origin, and date.* The number within parentheses is the Newberry acquisition number. The designation Ry denotes books purchased with the Edward L. Ryerson Book Fund. In reading the dates it should be noted that s. X/XI denotes a codex of which major elements have been written separately in both the tenth and the eleventh centuries. The notation s. X–XI indicates a codex copied either in the late tenth or the early eleventh century for which a more precise date is not at present possible.
2. *Textual content.* Where possible (and no format can ever preserve a complete similitude to the complex vagaries of the handwritten page) the use of arabic numerals corresponds in textual manuscripts to the divisions made by the scribe. When, because of uncertain textual tradition or through scribal error, two or more texts have been conflated, the second text has been denoted as *bis*. This convention has been observed to respect the integrity of the manuscript and also to facilitate the identification of Newberry codices in old library catalogues. The designation "in red" is used, rather than italics, in order to aid the reader in distinguishing the text of the scribe from that of the rubricator, who was often a different individual. In certain instances, humanist texts for example, the choice of color is closely linked to the content of the book. In this catalogue, all terms denoting color (red, violet, etc.) apply to all preceding text beginning from the previous full stop. It is the author's hope to provide in this manner a precise and unambiguous verisimilitude of the manuscript page. Texts contained on flyleaves and pastedowns and the primary texts of palimpsests are recorded and listed subsequent to the numbered items. The incipits have been given to aid the reader to identify the texts contained in these codices and elsewhere. The // indicates that the incipit or explicit is incomplete as a result of the physical removal of a folio or a portion thereof. Brackets indicate text not present and provided by the author of the catalogue; parentheses indicate references given by the author of the catalogue. Text within brackets preceded by a minus sign indicates a deletion by the scribe. Original spelling, including the use of the cedilla, double initial consonants, and Anglo-Saxon characters, has been preserved because of its philological significance. However, no attempt has been made to replicate either original word separation, capitalization, and punctuation, or the use of alternate letterforms (e.g., u or v, i or j, short s or long s) because of the impossibility of doing all these things accurately given the constraints of modern type fonts. In Latin, the u has been used in words, the v in numbers. Where the presence of *traits d'union* and accents has been deemed significant, they have been included in the physical description. The exact transcription of two signs of punctuation, however, has been respected: the parenthesis, present only in MS f96, and the question mark. All other punctuation has been standardized according to modern conventions. No accents or other diacritical marks have been added to vernacular texts, but apostrophes have been used to clarify word boundaries in French and Italian. In MS f65.1, the umlaut was written by the scribe. In summaries of liturgical contents the usual Latin or English forms of saints' names have been used, whereas in calendars the names are given in Latin or in French exactly as they appear in the manuscript. Texts noted as additions without a specific date appear to be written within a half century of the main texts of the book. The "changed Office of the Virgin" is that form of the Office which provides specific prayers for days of the week. Pages described as blank are ruled, unless noted as blank and unruled.
3. *Art historical content.* All illustration and major decoration including illuminated minia-

tures, border decoration, and major initials are described in this section. Routine rubricating and related minor decoration is considered in the section for physical description.

4. *Physical description.* The collations given are, unless otherwise qualified, for the medieval book. Modern flyleaves and pastedowns are not included. A full collation has been given for all manuscripts where the binding permits reasonable accuracy. In the measurements height precedes width. The first dimensions are those of the leaves; the dimensions that follow in parentheses are of the written space. In the latter instance, height is taken from the top of the ascenders on the first written line to the feet of the minim strokes on the last written line. The measurements are not of the ruled space, the dimensions of which may or may not be the same. For the early manuscript, such data, when interpreted in the light of similar information from other related books, may yet offer clues to the identification of scriptoria. For the later manuscripts, this information is important for elucidating general and regional patterns of book-making techniques. The presence of original or medieval foliation or signatures is recorded for its obvious importance for the history of reading and book production. The absence of regular word separation is noted for its importance for the history of reading and as an element for dating certain manuscripts of the tenth and eleventh centuries. Separation by vertical terminal strokes as an adjunct to space is noted for certain late gothic scripts, e.g., MS 104.5. Aspects of punctuation significant for the history of reading, such as the use of the acute accent and *traits d'union,* have also been recorded.
5. *Binding.*
6. *Origin and provenance.* Illuminated coats of arms have been described with the other aspects of provenance. All references to geographical units, e.g., eastern France, Belgium, Switzerland, reflect political borders as they exist today. Flanders denotes western Belgium and adjacent northern France. The numbers given to Probasco manuscripts refer to those written in the books; Poole's privately printed summary catalogue is without numbers. For books of hours and prayer books, the presence of prayers altered into feminine form has been noted in this section. In all, nineteen manuscripts indicate gender, and of these, ten indicate feminine use.
7. *Second folio.* Since the first words of the second folio were sometimes included in some late medieval catalogues of ecclesiastic and more particularly secular libraries, they have been recorded here for all manuscripts, excepting those liturgical books and books of hours in which the second folio incipit is invariable. A correspondence in second folio incipits has been crucial for establishing the provenance of a single manuscript, MS f40. It would be fair to state that the author is less convinced of the utility of recording second folios than he was at the onset of this project.
8. *Bibliography.* References to De Ricci and Faye-Bond precede references to all other works, which are arranged by date of publication. This section is reserved for studies and catalogues not cited elsewhere in the description.

⋆ ⋆ ⋆

The author wishes to thank the following individuals for their important aid in preparing this catalogue. To Nadine Saenger fell the heavy burden of typing all the draft descriptions. I am indebted to her for her careful performance of this difficult task. I am indebted too to Richard Rouse and Consuelo Dutschke, who read all the descriptions in draft form. Their generosity in sharing their time, expertise, and great familiarity with manuscript scholarship was invaluable. Paul Gehl read each of the descriptions against the manuscripts, thus providing invaluable assistance in detecting errors and inserting corrections. Armando Petrucci offered his expertise for the Italian manuscripts and was particularly helpful in problems of dating and localization. Denis Dutschke read the descriptions of the Italian manuscripts against the manuscripts and corrected numerous errors. Gino Corti and Giuseppe Billanovich offered invaluable aid in transcribing difficult-to-read passages. The French manuscript descriptions were read by Sylvia Huot. Bernard and Ségolène Barbiche aided in the deciphering of difficult flyleaf and pastedown notes. Dutch and Low Country manuscript descriptions were corrected by Peter Obbema. The German descriptions were corrected by Martin Steinmann. The late Anthony Petti helped greatly with the English vernacular manuscripts, and Kathleen Scott resolved important problems relating to the illustrations of these same books. Mark D. Johnston corrected the descriptions of the Spanish manuscripts. W. Braxton Ross provided a draft description of MS f2 and read the descriptions of other early books. Michael Masi's draft descriptions of the Latin Bibles were an invaluable aid. In addition François Avril, J. H. Baker, Julian Brown, Paolo Cherchi, William J. Courtenay, John Patrick Donnelly, Douglas Farquhar, Astrik Gabriel, Pierre Gasnault, Michael Gullick, Geneviève Hasenohr, Jeffrey Huntsman, Thomas Izbicki, Robert Lerner, Robert E. Lewis, the late Edward E. Lowinsky, Robert Maloy, James H. Marrow, Michel Pastoureau, Svato Schutzner, Jean Vezin, Ruth F. Vyse, and Chrysogonus Waddell aided with specific manuscripts. Anne D. Hedeman and Sandra Hindman read all the descriptions of books of hours against the manuscripts. M. B. Parkes generously gave his opinion on the place of origin of the thirteenth-century Latin Bibles. Don Jacques and Eleanor Roach performed an invaluable service by reading the description of the Latin manuscripts against the codices and thereby corrected numerous errors, and I am grateful to them and to Rolf Achilles and Richard Brown for reading the introduction. Finally, Paul Oskar Kristeller, Lilian Randall, and Mario Trovato read the entire manuscript and made numerous invaluable emendations and suggestions.

The author is especially indebted to Richard H. Brown, Academic Vice President at the Newberry, who encouraged this project at every stage and who provided administrative support through numerous difficulties. Without his guidance, this catalogue could not have been completed. The Newberry's Center for Renaissance Studies through three Summer Institutes in the Archival Sciences made possible consultation with leading manuscript scholars from western Europe and North America, who otherwise would not have been available. I am indebted too to John Tedeschi, formerly Curator of Rare Books at the Newberry, who invited me to begin this project and offered crucial encouragement in its early stages. The staff of the Institute de Recherche et d'Histoire des Textes, especially Jeannine Fohlen, were most helpful in the identification of numerous texts, scribes, and provenances. A generous grant from the Division of Research Programs of the National Endowment for the Humanities was crucial for the completion of this catalogue. I would like to thank Charles Cullen, President and Librarian of the Newberry, and Mark Mickelberry for their generous help in preparing the indices, and Bernard Rosenthal and James Wells for identifying a number of the antiquarian book dealers of the first half of this century who are either deceased or no longer active in the trade. I would also like to thank President Emeritus Lawrence W. Towner, who provided invaluable moral support throughout the entire project. Finally, the author is deeply indebted to Jeffrey Auld, Marilyn DeBerry, and Rose Marie White for their careful typing of the final manuscript draft of this volume.

ABBREVIATIONS AND REFERENCES

ADB
Allgemeine deutsche Biographie (Leipzig, 1875–1912)

AHDLM
Archives d'histoire doctrinale et littéraire du Moyen-Age (Paris, 1926/27–)

AL
G. Lacombe, *Aristoteles latinus* (Rome, 1939–55)

Achery, *Spicilegium*
Luc d'Achery, *Spicilegium sive collectio veterum aliquot scriptorum qui in Galliae bibliothecis delituerant* (Paris, 1723; reprinted, Hants, 1967)

Achten, *Die lateinischen Gebetbuchhandschriften*
G. Achten, L. Eizenhöfer, and H. Knaus, *Die lateinischen Gebetbuchhandschriften der hessischen Landes- und Hochschulbibliothek Darmstadt* (Wiesbaden, 1972)

Achten and Knaus, *Deutsche und niederländische Gebetbuchhandschriften*
G. Achten and H. Knaus, *Deutsche und niederländische Gebetbuchhandschriften der hessischen Landes- und Hochschulbibliothek Darmstadt* (Darmstadt, 1959)

Acta sanctorum
Acta sanctorum quotquot toto orbe coluntur (Antwerp, 1643–1940)

Alexander and de la Mare, *Italian Manuscripts*
J. J. A. Alexander and A. C. de la Mare, *Italian Manuscripts in the Library of J. R. Abbey* (London, 1969)

Allen, *Writings Ascribed to Richard Rolle*
H. E. Allen, *Writings Ascribed to Richard Rolle and Materials for His Biography* (New York, 1927)

Analecta franciscana (Quaracchi, 1885–1926)

Analecta hymnica
Analecta hymnica medii aevi (Leipzig, 1886–1922)

Andrieu, *Ordines romani*
M. Andrieu, *Les "Ordines romani" du haut Moyen Age* (Louvain, 1931–56)

Anselme
Anselme de Sainte Marie, *Histoire généalogique et chronologique de la maison royale de France,* 3d ed. (Paris, 1726–33)

Assemanus, *Ephraemi Syri opera omnia*
J. S. Assemanus and S. E. Assemanus, *Ephraemi Syri opera omnia* (Rome, 1732–46)

BGPTM
Beiträge zur Geschichte der Philosophie und Theologie des Mittelalters. Texte und Untersuchungen (Münster, 1891–)

BHL
Bibliotheca hagiographica latina (Brussels, 1898–1901)

BHM
B. Lambert, *Bibliotheca hieronymiana manuscripta: la tradition manuscrite des oeuvres de Saint Jérome* (Steenbergen, 1969–72)

BL
Bodleian Library

BM
Bibliothèque Municipale; British Museum (today British Library)

BN
Bibliothèque Nationale

BR
Bibliothèque Royale

B. M. Cat. of 15th-Century Books
Catalogue of Books Printed in the Fifteenth Century Now in the British Museum (London, 1908–71)

Baluze-Mansi, *Miscellanea*
E. Baluze, *Miscellanea,* ed. J. D. Mansi (Lucca, 1761–64)

Bandini, *Catalogus codicum latinorum*
A. M. Bandini, *Catalogus codicum latinorum bibliothecae Mediceae Laurentianae* (Florence, 1774–78)

Barfield, "Lord Fingall's Cartulary"
S. Barfield, "Lord Fingall's Cartulary of Reading Abbey," *English Historical Review* 3 (1888): 113–25

Barlow, *Opera omnia*
C. W. Barlow, *Martini episcopi bracarensis opera omnia* (Papers and Monographs of the American Academy in Rome, 12; New Haven, 1950)

Baron, "Hugues de Saint Victor"
R. Baron, "Hugues de Saint Victor: contribution à un nouvel examen de son oeuvre," *Traditio* 15 (1959): 223–97

Baron, *Leonardo Bruni Aretino*
H. Baron, *Leonardo Bruni Aretino: humanistisch-philosophische Schriften* (Leipzig, 1928)

Barré, *Prières anciennes*
H. Barré, *Prières anciennes de l'occident à la mère du sauveur des origines à Saint Anselme* (Paris, 1963)

Bertalot, "Forschungen über Leonardo Bruni Aretino"
Ludwig Bertalot, "Forschungen über Leonardo Bruni Aretino," *Archivum romanicum* 15 (1931): 284–323

Bertalot, *Studien*
L. Bertalot, *Studien zum italianischen und deutschen Humanismus,* ed. P. O. Kristeller (Rome, 1975)

Beer, "Handschriftenschätze"
R. Beer, "Handschriftenschätze Spaniens," *Sitzungsberichte der Philosophisch-Historische Classe der Kaiserlichen Akademie der Wissenschaften* [Vienna], vol. 125 (1891), part 3

Belcari, *Laude spirituali*
Feo Belcari, *Laude spirituali* (Florence, 1863)

Bibliotheca Heberiana
Bibliotheca Heberiana. Catalogue of the Library of the Late Richard Heber (London, 1834–37)

Blayney, *Fifteenth-Century English Translations*
M. S. Blayney, *Fifteenth-Century English Translations of Alain Chartier's "Le Traité de l'Espérance" and "Le Quadrilogue Invectif"* (EETS, o.s., 270 and 281; Oxford, 1974)

Bloomfield, *Incipits*
M. W. Bloomfield et al., *Incipits of Latin Works on the Virtues and Vices, Including a Section of Incipits of Works on the Pater Noster* (Cambridge, Mass., 1979)

Boll. Mus. Civ. Padova
Bollettino del Museo civico di Padova (Padua, 1898–)

Branner, *Manuscript Painting in Paris*
R. Branner, *Manuscript Painting in Paris during the Reign of Saint Louis* (Berkeley, 1977)

Briquet
C. M. Briquet, *Les Filigranes,* ed. A. Stevenson (Amsterdam, 1968)

Brown and Robbins, *Index of Middle English Verse*
C. Brown and R. H. Robbins, *The Index of Middle English Verse* (New York, 1945)

Bruyne, *Préfaces de la Bible latine*
D. de Bruyne, *Préfaces de la Bible latine* (Namur, 1920)

Burn, *An Introduction to the Creeds*
A. E. Burn, *An Introduction to the Creeds and to the "Te Deum"* (London, 1899)

Butler, *Check List*
R. L. Butler, *A Check List of Manuscripts in the Edward E. Ayer Collection* (Chicago,1937)

CC
Corpus christianorum: series latina (Turnhout, 1954–)

CPL
E. Dekkers, *Clavis patrum latinorum,* 2d ed. (Steenbergen, 1961)

CSEL
Corpus scriptorum ecclesiasticorum latinorum (Vienna, 1866–)

CSM
Corpus scriptorum de musica

Carile, *Cronachistica veneziana*
Antonio Carile, *La Cronachistica veneziana (secoli xiii–xvi) di fronte alla spartizione della Romania nel 1204* (Florence, 1969)

Catalogo dei libri
Catalogo dei libri provenienti della biblioteca del Marchese Girolamo d'Adda (London, 1902)

Catalogue général des départements
Catalogue général des manuscrits des bibliothèques publiques des départements; later *Catalogue général des manuscrits des bibliothèques publiques de France: Départements*

Catalogue of Manuscripts in Stift Lambach
Katalog der Handschriften im Stift Lambach (University Microfilms for the Monastic Microfilm Library, St. John's University, Collegeville, Minn.)

Catalogus codicum manu scriptorum qui in bibliotheca Monasterii Mellicensis O.S.B. asservantur (University Microfilms for the Monastic Microfilm Library, St. John's University, Collegeville, Minn.)

Catalogue of the Manuscripts at Ashburnham Place (London, 1862)

Cazzaniga
I. Cazzaniga, *Incerti auctoris de lapsu Susannae (de lapsu virginis consecratae)* (Turin, 1948)

Checklist of the C. L. Ricketts Collection
Checklist of the C. L. Ricketts Calligraphy Collection Acquired by the Newberry Library June 1941. Mimeographed by the Newberry Library, s.d.

Chevalier, *Bio-Bibliographie*
C. U. Chevalier, *Répertoire des sources historiques du Moyen Age,* part 1, *Bio-bibliographie,* rev. ed. (Paris, 1905–7)

Cipolla, *Ricerche*
C. Cipolla, *Ricerche sull'antica biblioteca del monastero della Novalese* (Turin, 1894)

Collins, *Anglo-Saxon Manuscripts*
R. L. Collins, *Anglo-Saxon Vernacular Manuscripts in America* (Exhibition Catalogue, Pierpont Morgan Library, New York, 1976)

Colophons de manuscrits occidentaux
Bénédictins du Bouveret, *Colophons de manuscrits occidentaux des origines au xvi*[e] *siècle* (Fribourg, 1965–82)

Copinger
W. A. Copinger, *Supplement to Hain's "Repertorium Bibliographicum"* (London, 1895–1902)

Cottineau
L. H. Cottineau, *Répertoire topo-bibliographique des abbayes et prieurés* (Mâcon, 1936–37)

Coussemaker, *Scriptorum*
E. C. H. de Coussemaker, *Scriptorum de musica medii aevi novam seriem . . .* (Paris, 1864–76)

Cranz, *Bibliography of Aristotle Editions*
F. E. Cranz, *A Bibliography of Aristotle Editions 1501–1600* (Bibliotheca bibliographica aureliana, 38; Baden-Baden, 1971)

DBI
Dizionario biografico degli italiani (Rome, 1960–)

DHGE
Dictionnaire de géographie et d'histoire ecclésiastique (Paris, 1912–)

DNB
Dictionary of National Biography (London, 1908–9)

DTC
Dictionnaire de théologie catholique (Paris, 1909–50)

Da Schio, *Carmina*
Giovanni da Schio, *Antonii de Luschis carmina quae supersunt fere omnia* (Padua, 1858)

de Lettenhove, *Oeuvres de Froissart*
Baron J. Kervyn de Lettenhove, *Oeuvres de Froissart* (Brussels, 1867–77)

Delisle, *Le Cabinet des manuscrits*
L. Delisle, *Le Cabinet des manuscrits de la bibliothèque nationale* (Paris, 1868–81)

Delucchi, *Alcune laudi inedite*
Luisa Delucchi, *Alcune laudi inedite di Feo Belcari* (Genova, 1930)

de Marinis, *La Biblioteca napoletana dei re d'Aragona*
T. de Marinis, *La Biblioteca napoletana dei re d'Aragona* (Milan, 1947–52)

De Ricci
S. De Ricci with the assistance of W. J. Wilson, *Census of Medieval and Renaissance Manuscripts in the United States and Canada* (New York, 1935–40)

De Ricci, *English Collectors*
S. De Ricci, *English Collectors of Books and Manuscripts (1530–1930) and Their Marks of Ownership* (Cambridge, 1930)

Dictionnaire de spiritualité
Dictionnaire de spiritualité ascétique et mystique, doctrine et histoire (Paris, 1932–)

Dictionnaires des lettres françaises (Paris, 1951–64)

Doyle, "Prayer Attributed to Saint Thomas"
A. I. Doyle, "A Prayer Attributed to Saint Thomas Aquinas," *Dominican Studies* 1 (1978): 229–38

du Fresne de Beaucourt, *Charles VII*
G. du Fresne de Beaucourt, *Histoire de Charles VII* (Paris, 1881–91)

EETS, e.s.
Early English Text Society, extra series

EETS, o.s.
Early English Text Society, original series

Emden, *Biographical Register: Cambridge*
A. B. Emden, *A Biographical Register of the University of Cambridge to 1500* (Cambridge, 1963)

Emden, *Biographical Register: Oxford*
A. B. Emden, *A Biographical Register of the University of Oxford to A.D. 1500* (Oxford, 1957–59).

Epistolae regum principum
Epistolae regum, principum, rerumpublicarum ac sapientum virorum ex antiquis et recentioribus, tam graecis quam latinis historiis et annalibus collectae (Strasbourg, 1553)

Faye-Bond
C. U. Faye and W. H. Bond, *Supplement to the Census of Medieval and Renaissance Manuscripts in the United States and Canada* (New York, 1962)

Fisher, *Geographiae codex*
J. Fisher, *Claudii Ptolemaei Geographiae codex Urbinas Graecus 82 photographice depictus* (Leiden, 1932)

Flor. cas.
Florilegium Casinense. Bibliotheca Casinensis seu codicum manuscriptorum . . . cura et studio monachorum O.S.B. abbatiae Montis Casini (Monte Cassino, 1873–94)

Franks Collection of Book Plates
E. R. J. Gambier Howe, *Catalogue of British and American Book Plates Bequeathed to the Trustees of the British Museum by Sir Augustus Wollaston Franks* (London, 1903–4)

Friedberg, *Corpus iuris canonici*
A. Friedberg, *Corpus iuris canonici* (Leipzig, 1879–81)

GW
Gesamtkatalog der Wiegendrucke (Leipzig and New York, 1925–)

Gamber, *De lapsu virginis*
K. Gamber, *Niceta von Remesiana De lapsu Susannae* (Regensburg, 1969)

Garin, *Prosatori latini*
Eugenio Garin, *Prosatori latini del Quattrocento* (Milan, 1952)

Gelli, *3500 Ex Libris*
Jacobo Gelli, *3500 Ex Libris italiani* (Milan, 1908)

Gerbert, *Scriptores*
M. Gerbert, *Scriptores ecclesiastici de musica sacra potissimum* (Sankt Blasien, 1784)

Gjerlow, *Adoratio crucis*
L. Gjerlow, *Adoratio crucis, the Regularis concordia and the Decreta Lanfranci* (Oslo, 1961)

Glorieux
P. Glorieux, *Répertoire des maîtres en théologie de Paris au xiiie siècle* (Paris, 1933–34)

Glorieux, *La Littérature quodlibétique*
P. Glorieux, *La Littérature quodlibétique de 1260 à 1320* (Paris, 1925–35)

Goldschmidt, *Medieval Texts*
E. P. Goldschmidt, *Medieval Texts and Their First Appearance in Print* (London, 1943)

Goy, *Die Überlieferung*
Rudolf Goy, *Die Überlieferung der Werke Hugos von St. Victor* (Stuttgart, 1976)

Grabmann, *Guglielmo di Moerbeke*
M. Grabmann, *Guglielmo di Moerbeke, O.P.: il traduttore delle opere di Aristotle* (Miscellanea historiae pontificae, 2; Rome, 1946)

Grabmann, *Die Werke*
M. Grabmann, *Die Werke des heiligen Thomas von Aquin*, 2d ed. (*BGPTM*, vol. 22, pts. 1–2; Münster, 1949)

Grégoire
R. Grégoire, *Homiliaires liturgiques médiévaux: analyse de manuscrits* (Spoleto, 1980)

HLF
Histoire littéraire de la France (Paris 1733–)

HUWHA
Die handschriftliche Überlieferung der Werke des heiligen Augustinus (Vienna, 1969–)

Hain
L. F. T. Hain, *Repertorium bibliographicum* (Stuttgart, 1826–38)

Hauréau, *Initia*
B. Hauréau, *Initia operum scriptorum latinorum medii potissimum aevi ex codicibus manuscriptis et libris impressis alphabetice digessit* (Turnhout, 1973)

Hauréau, *Notices et extraits*
B. Hauréau, *Notices et extraits de quelques manuscrits latins de la Bibliothèque Nationale* (Paris, 1890–93; reprinted, Farnborough, Hants, 1969)

Hauréau, *Sur les poèmes latins*
B. Hauréau, *Sur les poèmes latins attribués à saint Bernard* (Paris, 1882)

Horae eboracenses
C. Wordsworth, ed., *Horae eboracenses: The Prymer of Hours of the Blessed Virgin Mary according to the Use of . . . York* (The Publications of the Surtees Society, 122; London, 1920)

Hughes, *Mass and Office*
A. Hughes, *Medieval Manuscripts for Mass and Office: A Guide to Organization and Terminology* (Toronto, 1982)

IMU
Italia medioevale e umanistica (Padua, 1958–)

Isambert, *Recueil des anciennes lois*
F. A. Isambert et al., *Recueil général des anciennes lois françaises* (Paris, 1821–33)

Ives and Lehmann-Haupt, *An English Thirteenth-Century Bestiary*
S. A. Ives and H. Lehmann-Haupt, *An English Thirteenth-Century Bestiary* (New York, 1942)

James, *Catalogue of Corpus Christi College*
M. R. James, *A Descriptive Catalogue of the Library of Corpus Christi College* (Cambridge, 1912)

Janauschek, *Bibliographia bernardina*
L. Janauschek, *Bibliographia bernardina* (Vienna, 1891; reprinted, Hildesheim, 1959)

Johannes von Neumarkt, *Schriften*
Joseph Klapper, ed., *Schriften Johanns von Neumarkt*, part 2 (Berlin, 1932)

Kaeppeli
T. Kaeppeli, *Scriptores ordinis praedictatorum medii aevi* (Rome, 1970–)

Kapsner, *Benedictine Bibliography*
O. L. Kapsner, *A Benedictine Bibliography* (Collegeville, Minn., 1962)

Ker, *English Manuscripts*
N. R. Ker, *English Manuscripts in the Century after the Norman Conquest* (Oxford, 1960)

Ker, *Medieval Libraries*
N. R. Ker, *Medieval Libraries of Great Britain: A List of Surviving Books*, 2d ed. (London, 1964)

Ker, *Medieval Manuscripts*
N. R. Ker, *Medieval Manuscripts in British Libraries* (Oxford, 1969–)

Kessler, *French and Flemish Illuminated Manuscripts*
H. Kessler, *French and Flemish Illuminated Manuscripts from Chicago Collections* (Exhibition Catalogue, The Newberry Library, Chicago, 1969)

Klapper, *Johannes Hagen*
J. Klapper, *Der Erfurter Kartäuser Johannes Hagen: Ein Reformtheologe des 15. Jahrhunderts* (Leipzig, 1960–61)

Kristeller, *Iter Italicum*
P. O. Kristeller, *Iter Italicum* (London, 1963–)

Kristeller, *Lauro Quirini*
P. O. Kristeller, Konrad Krautter, et al., *Lauro Quirini Umanista* (Florence, 1977)

Lacombe, "Medieval Latin Versions of the *Parva naturalia*"
George Lacombe, "Medieval Latin Versions of the *Parva naturalia*," *New Scholasticism* 5 (1931): 289–311

Långfors
A. I. E. Långfors, *Les Incipit des poèmes français antérieurs au xvi*[e] siècle (Paris, 1917)

Lanza, *Lirici*
Antonio Lanza, *Lirici toscani del quattrocento* (Rome, 1973)

Lebreton, "Sermons de Pierre le Mangeur"
M.-M. Lebreton, "Recherches sur les manuscrits contenant des sermons de Pierre le Mangeur," *Bulletin d'information de l'Institut de Recherche et d'Histoire des Textes* 2 (1953): 24–44

Leclercq and Rochais, *Sancti Bernardi opera*
J. Leclercq and H. Rochais, *Sancti Bernardi opera* (Rome, 1957–74)

Leroquais, *Bréviaires*
V. Leroquais, *Les Bréviaires manuscrits des bibliothèques publiques de France* (Paris, 1934)

Leroquais, *Heures*
V. Leroquais, *Les Livres d'heures manuscrits de la Bibliothèque Nationale* (Paris, 1927)

Leroquais, *Missels*
V. Leroquais, *Les Sacramentaires et les missels manuscrits des bibliothèques publiques de France* (Paris, 1924)

Leroquais, *Psautiers*
V. Leroquais, *Les Psautiers manuscrits latins des bibliothèques publiques de France* (Paris, 1940–41)

Lewis and McIntosh, *Descriptive Guide*
R. E. Lewis and A. McIntosh, *A Descriptive Guide to the Manuscripts of the Prick of Conscience* (Oxford, 1982)

Lexikon für Theologie und Kirche, 2d ed. (Freiburg im Breisgau, 1957–67)

Lockwood, "De Rinucio Aretino"
Dean P. Lockwood, "De Rinucio Aretino graecarum litterarum interprete," *Harvard Studies in Classical Philology* 24 (1913): 51–109

Lohr, "Medieval Commentaries"
C. H. Lohr, "Medieval Latin Aristotle Commentaries: Authors," *Traditio* 23 (1967), 24 (1968), 26 (1970), 27 (1971), 29 (1973), 30 (1974)

Lyell Catalogue
A. de la Mare, *Catalogue of the Collection of Medieval Manuscripts Bequeathed to the Bodleian Library, Oxford, by James P. R. Lyell* (Oxford, 1971)

MGH
Monumenta Germaniae historica

MGH, AA
Monumenta Germaniae historica . . . Auctores antiquissimi (Berlin, 1877–1919)

MGH, Epistolae
Monumenta Germaniae historica: Epistolae (Hanover, 1891–)

MGH, Poetae
Monumenta Germaniae historica . . . Poetae latini medii aevi (Berlin, 1880–)

MGH, SRM
Monumenta Germaniae historica: Scriptores rerum Merovingicarum (Hanover, 1885–)

Mandonnet, *Opuscula omnia*
P. F. Mandonnet, *S. Thomas Aquinatis opuscula omnia* (Paris, 1927)

Mann, *Petrarch Manuscripts*
N. Mann, *Petrarch Manuscripts in the British Isles* (Padua, 1975)

Manuscrits classiques latins
E. Pellegrin, C. Jeudy, Y.-F. Riou, and A. Marucchi, *Les Manuscrits classiques latins de la Bibliothèque Vaticane* (Paris, 1975–)

Manuscrits datés (Belgique)
F. Masai and M. Wittek, *Manuscrits datés conservés en Belgique* (Brussels, 1968–)

Martène and Durand, *Thesaurus novus anecdotorum*
E. Martène and U. Durand, *Thesaurus novus anecdotorum* (Paris, 1717–26; reprinted, Farnborough Hants, 1968–69)

Martène and Durand, *Veterum scriptorum . . . amplissima collectio*
E. Martène and U. Durand, *Veterum scriptorum*

et monumentorum historicorum, dogmaticorum, moralium amplissima collectio (Paris, 1724–33)

Masi, "A Newberry Diagram"
Michael Masi, "A Newberry Diagram of the Liberal Arts," *Gesta* 12 (1973): 52–56

Massera, "Iacopo Allegretti da Forlì"
A. Massera, "Iacopo Allegretti da Forlì," *Atti e memorie della regia deputazione di storia patria per le province di Romagna,* ser. 5, vol. 16 (1926)

McCulloch, *Medieval Latin and French Bestiaries*
F. McCulloch, *Medieval Latin and French Bestiaries* (University of North Carolina Studies in the Romance Languages and Literatures, 33; Chapel Hill, 1960)

McGinn, *Tradition of Aquinas and Bonaventure*
B. McGinn, *Tradition of Aquinas and Bonaventure* (Exhibition Catalogue, The University of Chicago Library, 1974)

Meertens, *De Godsvrucht*
M. Meertens, *De Godsvrucht in de Nederlanden; naar Handschriften van Gebedenboeken der XV*[e] *eeuw* (Antwerp, 1930–34)

Mémoires pour servir à l'histoire
Mémoires pour servir à l'histoire de France et de Bourgogne (Paris, 1729)

Méon, *Le Roman de la Rose*
D. M. Méon, *Le Roman de la Rose* (Paris, 1813)

Michels, *Corpus*
U. Michels, *Johannis de Muris: Noticia artis* etc. (*CSM* 17; s.l., 1972)

Michels, *Die Musiktraktate*
U. Michels, *Die Musiktraktate des Johannes de Muris* (Beihefte zum Archiv für Musikwissenschaft, 8; Wiesbaden, 1970)

Mittelalterliche Bibliothekskataloge Deutschlands
Mittelalterliche Bibliothekskataloge Deutschlands und der Schweiz, ed. P. Lehmann et al. (Munich, Bayerische Akademie der Wissenschaften, 1918–)

Mittelalterliche Bibliothekskataloge Österreichs,
ed. T. Gottlieb et al. (Vienna, Österreichische Akademie der Wissenschaften, 1915–)

Mohan, "Incipits of Logical Writings"
G. E. Mohan, "Incipits of Logical Writings of the XIIIth–XVth Centuries," *Franciscan Studies* 12 (1952): 349–489

Mone
F. J. Mone, *Lateinische Hymnen des Mittelalters* (Freiburg im Breisgau, 1853–55)

Monfasani, *Collectanea Trapezuntiana*
J. Monfasani, *Collectanea Trapezuntiana: Texts, Documents, and Bibliographies of George of Trebizond* (Binghamton, New York, 1984)

Monfasani, *George of Trebizond*
J. Monfasani, *George of Trebizond: A Biography and Study of His Rhetoric and Logic* (Leiden, 1976)

Munby, *Phillipps Studies*
A. N. L. Munby, *Phillipps Studies* (London, 1951–60)

Muratori, *Scriptores*
L. A. Muratori, *Rerum italicarum scriptores* (Milan, 1723–51)

Mynors, *Opera*
R. A. B. Mynors, *P. Virgilii Maronis opera* (Oxford, 1969)

Mynors, *Manuscripts of Balliol College*
R. A. B. Mynors, *Catalogue of the Manuscripts of Balliol College, Oxford* (Oxford, 1963)

Naz, *Dictionnaire de droit canonique*
R. Naz, *Dictionnaire de droit canonique* (Paris, 1935–65)

Notices et extraits des manuscrits
Notices et extraits des manuscrits de la Bibliothèque Nationale et autres bibliothèques (Paris, 1787–)

ÖN
Österreichische Nationalbibliothek

ORF
Ordonnances des roys de France de la troisième race (Paris, 1724–1849)

Oldfather, *Studies*
W. A. Oldfather et al., *Studies in the Text Tradition of Saint Jerome's Vitae patrum* (Urbana, Ill., 1943)

Oldham, *Blind Panels of English Binders*
J. B. Oldham, *Blind Panels of English Binders* (Cambridge, 1958)

Oldham, *English Blind-Stamped Bindings*
J. B. Oldham, *English Blind-Stamped Bindings* (*The Sandars Lecture, 1949*); Cambridge, 1952)

Orlandi, *Bib. Ant.*
S. Orlandi, *Bibliografia antoniniana* (Vatican City, 1961)

PG
J. P. Migne, *Patrologiae cursus completus . . . series graeca* (Paris, 1857–66)

PL
J. P. Migne, *Patrologiae cursus completus . . . series latina* (Paris, 1844–64)

PLS
A. Hamman, *Patrologiae latinae supplementum* (Paris, 1958–)

Pächt and Alexander, *Illuminated Manuscripts*
O. Pächt and J. J. G. Alexander, *Illuminated*

Manuscripts in the Bodleian Library (London, 1966–74)

Panofsky, *Early Netherlandish Painting*
E. Panofsky, *Early Netherlandish Painting* (Cambridge, Mass., 1953)

Pastor, *History of the Popes*
L. Pastor, *The History of the Popes* (St. Louis, 1898–1953)

Perdrizet, *Calendrier parisien*
P. Perdrizet, *Le Calendrier parisien à la fin du moyen âge d'après le bréviaire et les livres d'heures* (Paris, 1933)

Perrier, *Opuscula omnia*
J. Perrier, *S. Thomae Aquinatis . . . opuscula omnia necnon opera minora* (Paris, 1949)

The Phillipps Manuscripts
The Phillipps Manuscripts; catalogus librorum manuscriptorum in bibliotheca D. Thomae Phillipps, with an introduction by A. N. L. Munby (London, 1968)

Prete, *Codices barberiniani latini*
S. Prete, *Codices barberiniani latini, codices 1–150* (Vatican City, 1968)

Prete, *Comoediae*
S. Prete, *Publii Terenti Afri Comoediae* (Heidelberg, 1954)

Prete, *Two Humanistic Anthologies*
S. Prete, *Two Humanistic Anthologies* (Vatican City, 1964)

Pronay and Taylor, *Parliamentary Texts*
Nicholas Pronay and John Taylor, *Parliamentary Texts of the Later Middle Ages* (Oxford, 1980)

RH
C. U. Chevalier, *Repertorium hymnologicum* (Louvain, 1892–1920)

RTAM
Recherches de théologie ancienne et médiévale (Louvain, 1929–)

Raffaele, *Maffeo Vegio*
L. Raffaele, *Maffeo Vegio: Elenco delle opere, scritti inediti* (Bologna, 1909)

Resta, "Antonio Cassarino"
G. Resta, "Antonio Cassarino e le sue traduzioni da Plutarco e Platone," *IMU* 2 (1959): 207–83

Rézeau, "La Tradition des prières"
P. Rézeau, "La Tradition des prières françaises médiévales à propos d'un livre d'heures et de prières des Célestins de Metz (Metz, Bib. Mun., MS 600)," *Revue d'histoire des textes* 7 (1978): 153–84

Riese, *Anthologia latina*
A. Riese, *Anthologia latina* (Leipzig, 1894–1926)

Risse, *Bibliographia logica*
W. Risse, *Bibliographia logica* (Hildesheim, 1965–79)

Robbins, "Two Fourteenth-Century Mystical Poems"
R. H. Robbins, "Two Fourteenth-Century Mystical Poems," *Modern Language Review* 35 (1940): 320–329.

Robbins and Cutler, *Supplement to the Index of Middle English Verse*
R. H. Robbins and J. L. Cutler, *Supplement to the Index of Middle English Verse* (Lexington, Ky., 1965)

Rosweyde, *Vitae patrum*
H. Rosweyde, *Vitae patrum* (Antwerp, 1615)

Ruysschaert, *Codices vaticani latini*
J. Ruysschaert, *Codices vaticani latini: 11414–11709* (Vatican City, 1959)

SFRMP
Bulletin de la Société française de reproduction de manuscrits à peintures (Paris, 1911–38).

SHF
Société de l'histoire de France

SMRL
S. J. P. Van Dijk, *Sources of the Modern Roman Liturgy* (Leiden, 1963)

SR
Statutes of the Realm, printed by Command of King George III (London, 1810–28)

Sabbadini, "Antonio da Romagno e Pietro Marcello"
R. Sabbadini, "Antonio da Romagno e Pietro Marcello," *Nuovo archivio veneto,* n.s. 30 (1915): 207–46

Sabbadini, *Biografia documentata*
R. Sabbadini, *Biografia documentata di Giovanni Aurispa* (Noto, 1890)

Sabbadini, *Scoperte dei codici latini*
R. Sabbadini, *Le Scoperte dei codici latini e greci ne' secoli XIV e XV* (reprint edition with notes of the author edited by E. Garin; Florence, 1967)

Saenger, "A Lost Manuscript Refound"
P. Saenger, "A Lost Manuscript of Froissart Refound," *Manuscripta* 19 (1975): 15–26

Samaran and Marichal, *Catalogue des manuscrits*
C. Samaran and R. Marichal, *Catalogue des manuscrits en écriture latine portant des indications de date, de lieu ou de copiste* (Paris, 1959–)

Schaller and Könsgen, *Initia carminum*
D. Schaller and E. Könsgen, *Initia carminum la-*

tinorum saeculo undecimo antiquiorum (Göttingen, 1977)

Schenkl, *Bibliotheca*
H. Schenkl, *Bibliotheca patrum latinorum britannica* in *Sitzungsberichte der Philosophisch-Historische Classe der Kaiserlichen Akademie der Wissenschaften* [Vienna], vol. 126 (1892)

Schneider, *Die Deutschen Handschriften*
K. Schneider, *Die Deutschen Handschriften der Bayerischen Staatsbibliothek München,* vol. 5, part 2 (Wiesbaden, 1970)

Schneyer, *Repertorium*
J. B. Schneyer, *Repertorium der lateinischen Sermones des Mittelalters, für die Zeit von 1150–1350* (*BGPMT* 43; Münster, 1969–)

Schooner, *Codices manuscripti*
H. V. Schooner and H. V. Dondaine, *Codices manuscripti operum Thomae de Aquino* 1 (Rome 1967)

Schucan, *Das Nachleben*
L. Schucan, *Das Nachleben von Basilius Magnus "Ad adolescentes"* (Geneva, 1973)

Sinclair
K. V. Sinclair, *Prìeres en ancien français; nouvelles références* (Hamden, Conn., 1978)

Sonet
J. Sonet, *Répertoire d'incipit de prières en ancien français* (Geneva, 1956)

Stegmüller, *Repertorium biblicum*
F. Stegmüller, *Repertorium biblicum medii aevi* (Madrid, 1959–)

Stegmüller, *Rep. in sent. Petr. Lomb.*
F. Stegmüller, *Repertorium commentariorum in sententias Petri Lombardi* (Würzburg, 1947)

Taylor, *Universal Chronicle*
J. Taylor, *Universal Chronicle of Ranulf Higden* (Oxford, 1968)

Tenneroni, *Inizii*
A. Tenneroni, *Inizii di antiche poesie italiane religiose e morali* (Florence, 1909)

Thorndike, *History of Magic and Experimental Science*
L. Thorndike, *A History of Magic and Experimental Science* (New York, 1923–43)

Thorndike and Kibre
L. Thorndike and P. Kibre, *A Catalogue of Incipits of Mediaeval Scientific Manuscripts in Latin,* rev. ed. (Cambridge, Mass., 1963)

Tischendorf, *Evangelia apocrypha*
C. Tischendorf, *Evangelia apocrypha* (Leipzig, 1876)

Tractatus universi iuris (Venice, 1584–86).

Turner, *Monumenta iuris antiquissima*
C. Turner, *Ecclesiae occidentalis monumenta iuris antiquissima,* I, ii, 1 (Oxford, 1913)

Ullman, "Petrarch Manuscripts"
B. L. Ullman, "Petrarch Manuscripts in the United States," *Italia medioevale e umanistica* 5 (1962): 443–75

Ullman, *Sicconis Polentoni scriptorum*
B. L. Ullman, *Sicconis Polentoni scriptorum illustrium latinae linguae* (Papers and Monographs of the American Academy in Rome, 6; Rome, 1928)

Van den Gheyn, *Catalogue des manuscrits*
J. Van den Gheyn, *Catalogue des manuscrits de la Bibliothèque Royale de Belgique* (Brussels, 1919–48)

Van Dijk, *Ordinal*
S. J. P. Van Dijk, *The Ordinal of the Papal Court from Innocent III to Boniface VIII and Related Documents* (Spicilegium Friburgense, 22; Fribourg, 1975)

Van Dijk, *Origins*
S. J. P. Van Dijk and J. H. Walker, *The Origins of the Modern Roman Liturgy* (Westminster, Md., 1960)

Van Dijk, "Some Manuscripts"
S. J. P. Van Dijk, "Some Manuscripts of the Earliest Franciscan Liturgy," *Franciscan Studies* 16 (1956): 60–101

Van Dijk and Walker, *Myth of the Aumbry*
S. J. P. Van Dijk and J. H. Walker, *The Myth of the Aumbry* (London, 1957)

Van Wijk, *Het Getijdenboek*
N. van Wijk, *Het Getijdenboek van Geert Grote naar het Haagse Handschrift 133 E. 21* (Leiden, 1940)

Vega, *España sagrada*
A. C. Vega, *España sagrada* 56 (Madrid, 1957)

Volger, "Plato's Republik"
E. Volger, "Plato's Republik, Lateinisch von Antonio Cassarini aus Sicilien," *Philologus* 13 (1858): 195–204

Von Fischer, "Theoretikerhandschrift"
K. von Fischer, "Eine wiederaufgefundene Theoretikerhandschrift des späten 14 Jahrhunderts," *Schweizer Beiträge zur Musikwissenschaft* 1 (1972): 23–33

Von Hartel, *Sitzungsberichte*
W. von Hartel, *Sitzungsberichte der Philosophisch-Historische Classe der Kaiserlichen Akademie der Wissenschaften* [Vienna], vol. 112 (1886)

Voulliéme
E. Voulliéme, *Der Buchdruck Kölns bis zum Ende des fünfzehnten Jahrhunderts* (Bonn, 1903)

Wadding, *Annales minorum*
L. Wadding, *Annales minorum seu trium ordinum a S. Francisco institutorum,* 3d ed. (Quaracchi, 1931–56)

Walther, *Initia*
H. Walther, *Initia carminum ac versuum medii aevi posterioris latinorum* (Göttingen, 1959)

Walther, *Prov.*
H. Walther, *Proverbia sententiaeque latinitatis medii aevi* (Göttingen, 1963–64)

Warner, *Catalogue of Royal Manuscripts*
G. Warner and J. P. Gilson, *Catalogue of Western Manuscripts in the Old Royal and King's Collections* (London, 1921), 4 vols.

Warner, *Descriptive Catalogue*
G. Warner, *Descriptive Catalogue of Illuminated Manuscripts in the Library of C. W. Dyson Perrins* (Oxford, 1920), 2 vols.

Wattenbach-Levison, *Deutschlands Geschichtsquellen*
W. Wattenbach and W. Levison, *Deutschlands Geschichtsquellen im Mittelalter* (Weimar, 1952–)

Weale, *Early Stamped Bookbindings*
J. Weale, *Early Stamped Bookbindings in the British Museum: Description of 385 Blind-stamped Bindings of the XIIth–XVth Centuries* (London, 1922)

Wichner, *Catalogus Admontensis*
J. Wichner, *Catalogus codicum manuscriptorum Admontensis* (University Microfilms for the Monastic Manuscript Microfilm Library, St. John's University, Collegeville, Minn.)

Wilmart
A. Wilmart, *Auteurs spirituels et textes dévots du moyen âge latin* (Paris, 1932; reprinted Paris, 1971)

Wilmart, *Codices reg. lat.*
A. Wilmart, *Codices reginenses latini* (Vatican City, 1937–45)

Wilmart, *Precum libelli*
A. Wilmart, *Precum libelli quattuor aevi Karolini* (Rome, 1940)

Wilmart, "Prières médiévales"
A. Wilmart, "Prières médiévales pour l'adoration de la croix," *Ephemerides liturgicae* 46 (1932)

Winkler, *Die Flämische Buchmaleri*
F. Winkler, *Die Flämische Buchmalerei des XV. und XVI. Jahrhunderts* (Leipzig, 1925)

Wolkan, *Der Briefwechsel*
R. Wolkan, *Der Briefwechsel des Eneas Silvius Piccolomini* 1 (Fontes rerum austriacarum, 61; Vienna, 1909)

Zaccaria, "Le Epistole"
V. Zaccaria, "Le Epistole e i carmi di Antonio Loschi durante il cancellierato visconteo (con tredici inediti)," *Atti della Accademia Nazionale dei Lincei: classe di scienze morali, storiche e filologiche,* ser. 8, vol. 18, fasc. 5 (Rome, 1975)

Zaccaria, "Quattro epistole"
V. Zaccaria, "Quattro epistole metriche di Antonio Loschi," *Boll. Mus. Civ. Padova* 53 (1964): 24–26

Zambrini, *Le Opere volgari*
F. S. Zambrini, *Le Opere volgari a stampa dei secoli xiii e xiv,* 4th ed. (Bologna, 1884)

Zathey, *Catalogus*
J. Zathey, *Catalogus codicum manuscriptorum medii aevi Bibliothecae Cornicensis* (Wrocław, 1963)

Zumkeller, *Manuskripte*
A. Zumkeller, *Manuskripte von Werken der Autoren des Augustiner-Eremitenordens in mitteleuropäischen Bibliotheken* (Würzburg, 1966)

A CATALOGUE OF THE PRE-1500 WESTERN MANUSCRIPT BOOKS AT THE NEWBERRY LIBRARY

These scripts have been selected to complement those illustrated in the plates at the end of the volume.

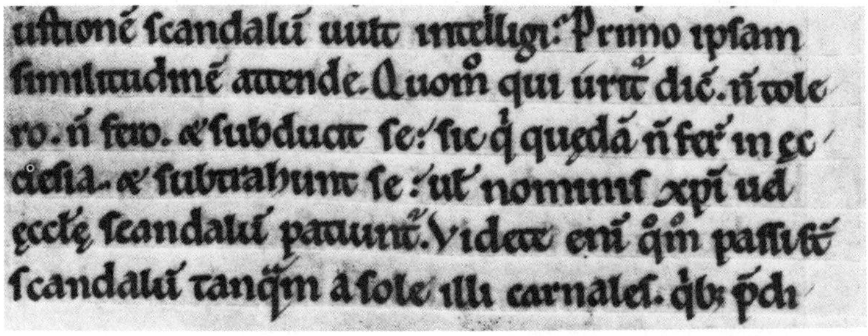

Anglo-Norman caroline textualis formata. MS 12.5, fol. 6

Proto-gothic textualis media. MS −14.1, fol. 109

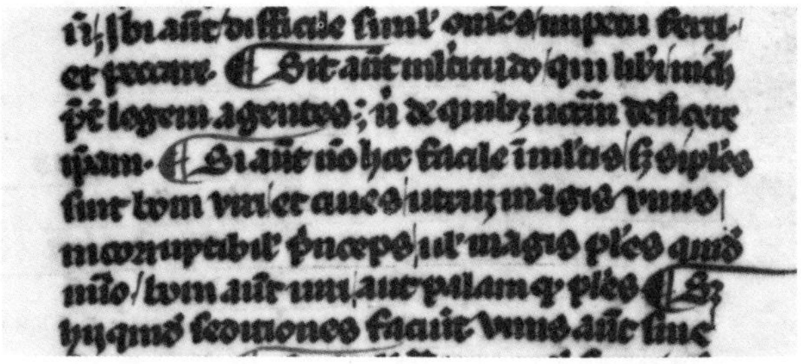

Italian gothic textualis media. MS 23.1, fol. 81

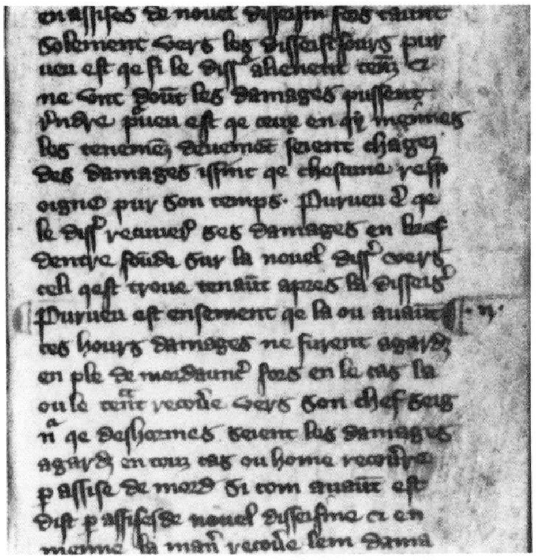

Cursiva anglicana media. MS 30, fol. 57v

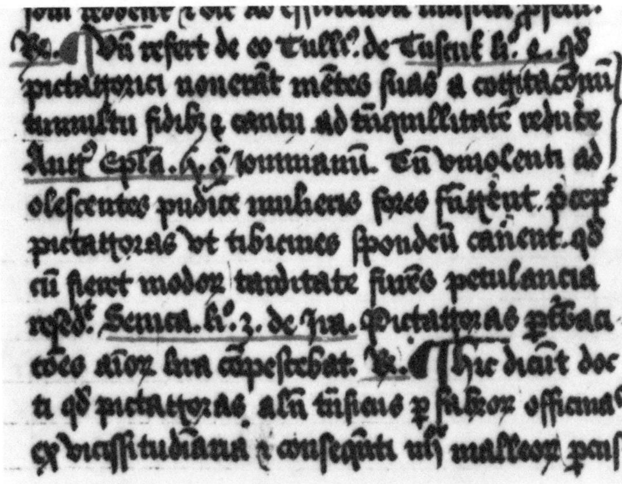

Bastard anglicana media. MS +33.1, fol. 57

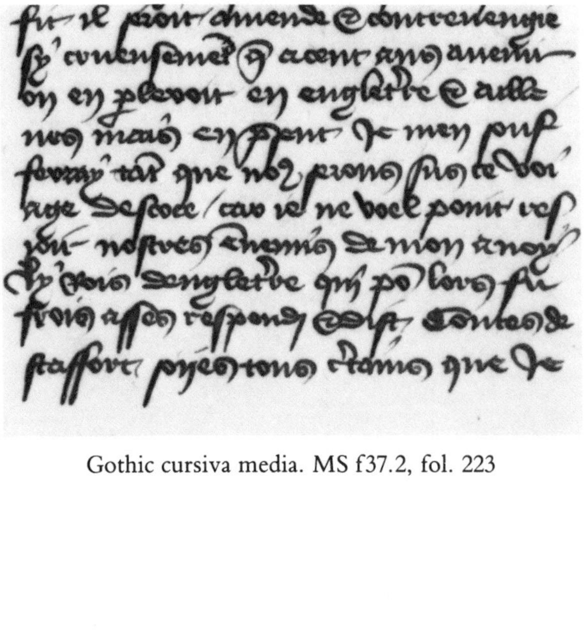

Gothic cursiva media. MS f37.2, fol. 223

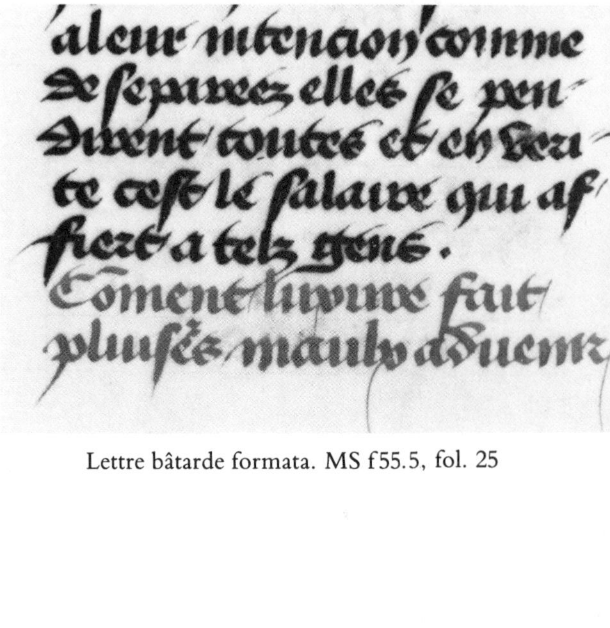

Lettre bâtarde formata. MS f55.5, fol. 25

f1

(54-1783)

Book of Homilies

Southern France [*Illustrated*] s. XI[1]

1. ff. 1–3 Homelias de aduentum (*sic*) domini (in red). Propiciante diuinitate, fratres dilectissimi . . . premia mereantur, prestante domino nostro . . .

f. 1 in margin (addition s. xii) Sermo sancti Augustini episcopi (in red).

Caesarius of Arles, *Sermo 187,* ed. G. Morin, *CC* 104 (1953): 763–66. *CPL* 1008. Grégoire, p. 509.

2. ff. 3–5 Alia. Sanctam et desiderabilem gloriosam ac singularem sollennitatem (*sic*) . . . ad aeternam beatitudinem feliciter peruenire.

f. 3 in margin (addition s. xii) Sermo sancti Leonis.

Caesarius of Arles, *Sermo 188,* ed. G. Morin, *CC* 104 (1953): 767–70. *CPL* 1008. Grégoire, p. 513.

3. ff. 5–6v Ad aduentum domini. Satis habundeque dixisse me credo superiori tractatu . . . corda mundamus, prestante domino nostro . . .

f. 5 in margin (addition s. xii) Sermo sancti Ambros[ii] episcopi (partially trimmed).

Maximus of Turin, *Sermo 61,* ending with a fragment from *Sermo 61a,* ed. A. Mutzenbecher, *CC* 23 (1962): 244–45, 250–51. *PL* 57:531–34 (*Sermo 1*) and 234–36 (*Hom. 4*). Grégoire, p. 513.

4. ff. 7–9 Ecce ex qua tribu nasciturus esset Christus . . . id est in uirtutum sublimitate collocatam.

f. 7 in margin (addition s. xii) Sermo sancti Ieronimi presbityri in aduentu domini (partially trimmed). Recopied s. xiv closer to the text.

Ps. Maximus of Turin, *Sermo 2. PL* 57: 845–48. Grégoire, p. 498. This text attributed to Jerome in Vienna, ÖN, lat. 618 (s. xv). *BHL* 990.

5. ff. 9–16 In illo tempore missus est angelus (Lc 1:26) . . . Latent quidem diuina misteria . . . inanes autem sunt dies impiorum.

f. 9 in margin (addition s. xii) Et reliqua omelia Amb[ro]sii episcopi (partially trimmed).

Incipit rewritten in s. xii.

Ambrose, *Expositio evangelii secundum Lucam,* II, 1–29, ed. M. Adrien, *CC* 14 (1957): 30–43. *CPL* 143. *PL* 15:1633–43. Grégoire, p. 504.

6. ff. 16–18v Homelia de aduentum (*sic*) domini. Legimus sanctum Moysen populo dei precepta dantem . . . et quę in terris (Col 1:20)

Ps. Augustine, *Sermo 245. PL* 39:2196–98. *CPL* 368. Grégoire, p. 505.

7. ff. 18v–21v Homelia sancti Iohannis (one word struck out by the scribe) Leonis pape de ieiunio. Si fideliter dilectissimi atque sapienter creationis nostre intelligimus exordium . . . et elemosinas nostras precibus suis dignabitur adiuuare, per . . .

Leo I, *Sermo 12. PL* 54:168–72. *CPL* 1657. Grégoire, p. 514.

8. ff. 21v–23 Alia homelia. Presidia dilectissimi sanctificandis mentibus nostris atque corporibus instituta . . . apostolum uigilias celebremus qui cum . . .

Leo I, *Sermo 18. PL* 54:182–85. *CPL* 1657. Grégoire, p. 509.

9. ff. 23v–24v Omelia alia. Cum de aduentu regni dei . . . umquam resultet affectus, prestante domino nostro.

Leo I, *Sermo 19,* abbreviated text (1–3 inc.). *PL* 54:185–87. *CPL* 1657. Grégoire, p. 494.

10. ff. 25–26 Agustinus de incarnationem (*sic*) domini. Gaudeamus, fratres, letentur et exultent gentes . . . cui creatura congrueret (*sic*) temporalis.

Augustine, *Sermo 186. PL* 38:999–1000. *CPL* 284. Grégoire, p. 500.

11. ff. 26–27 Item alia. Angelorum uocem postquam dominus Ihesus Christus natus uirginis partus . . . diffunditur in cordibus nostris non per nos ipsos sed per spiritum sanctum qui datus est nobis (Rom 5:5).

Augustine, *Sermo 193. PL* 38:1013–15. *CPL* 284. Grégoire, p. 491.

12. f. 27–27v Item alia. Misericors deus post lapsum generis humani, Christum filium suum carne uestiens . . . et pepperit Christum omnium saluatorem qui passionem (*sic*) et resurrectione sua nos liberauit.

Unidentified homily.

13. ff. 27v–30v Alia. Odie puer natus est nobis (Is 9:6) . . . Puer, inquam licet teneritudine membrorum inualidus . . . ut mereamini premium libertatis.

Ps. Augustine, *Sermo 120. PL* 39:1984–87. *CPL* 368.

14. ff. 30v–31v Leccio nobis alia. Natiuitatem domini dei filium confitemur, uirginis natum . . . nullus se illic dubite introire per Christum ubi credentem Christus etiam latronem introduxit, qui cum . . .

Unidentified homily.

15. ff. 31v–33v Alia leccio nobis. Saluator noster natus de patre sine die . . . etiam carne processit qui est benedictus cum patre et spiritu sancto in secula seculorum.

Dubious Augustine, *Sermo 369,* edition in C. Lambot, "L'Authenticité du sermon 369 de S. Augustin pour la fête de Noël," *Colligere fragmenta: Festschrift Alban Dold* (Beuron, 1952), pp. 103–12. *CPL* 285. Grégoire, p. 513.

16. ff. 33v–35 Item alia. Dominus noster Ihesus Christus qui erat aput patrem . . . in domino nostro miremur humilitatem ut edifficamur charitatem.

Augustine, *Sermo 190* (abbreviated recension). *PL* 38:1007–9. *CPL* 284. Cf. Grégoire, p. 247, no. 9.

17. f. 35–35v Item alia. Christus filius dei ante secula et etates de corpore paterno processit . . . uitam perpetuam recuperarat (*sic*), aduocante nos in omnibus aduocato nostro Christo deo et filio cui onor et gloria in secula seculorum. Amen.

Sermon attributed to Augustine in Madrid, Academia de la historia, 47 (F211; s. ix); *HUWHA* 4:215, 322; cf. *Flor. Cas.* 1:142.

18. ff. 35v–38 Item alia. Legimus sanctum Moysen populo dei precepta dantem . . . et que in terris.

Same text as no. 6 above.

19. f. 38–38v Item alia. Dubium non est, fratres dilectissimi, carnalem domini nostri aduentum in ac parte . . . gaudia in celis et terra suscipiat.

Ps. Augustine, *Sermo. PLS* 2:1036–37. Also attributed to Augustine in Madrid, Academia de la historia, 47 (F211; s. ix); *HUWHA* 4:215, 327.

20. ff. 38v–39 Item alia. Plurimum mirabilibus suis munera diuina respondetur in is uirtutum . . . et salutem humano generi dei filium, ędoceret qui regnat cum patre et filio et spiritu sancto . . .

Sermon attributed to Augustine in Madrid, Academia de la historia, 47 (F211; s. ix); *HUWHA* 4:215.

21. ff. 39–40v Item alia. Gaudeamus, fratres, latemur (*sic*) et exultent huniuerse gentes cunctique nationes quia sol iustitie hodie terris apparuit . . . ut eternum diem per eum qui nobis et nos eternos in tempore natus est percipere mereamur, ipso prestante . . .

Unidentified homily. Cf. Augustine, *Sermo 186,* text no. 10 above.

22. ff. 41–45v Homelia post natalem domini. Audistis, fratres karissimi, quem ad modum nobis beatus euangelista . . . non formationis sed reformationis domini nostri Ihesu Christi qui . . .

Ps. Augustine, *Sermo 128. PL* 39:1997–2001 with incipit of note b. *CPL* 368. Grégoire, p. 492.

23. ff. 45–48 Omelia Agustini in natale sancti Stephani. Hiesus filius Naue in heremo pugnabat . . . nisi pro tuis inimicis oraueris conuersus ad dominum Ihesum Christum qui . . .

Dubious Augustine, *Sermo 382. PL* 39:1684–86. *CPL* 285. Grégoire, p. 502.

24. ff. 48–51 Homelia alia. Fratres karissimi, hesterna die celebrauimus temporalem regis nostri natalem . . . regnum meruit possidere celorum cooperante domino qui . . .

f. 48 in margin (addition s. xii) Sermo sancti Fulgentii episcopi (partially trimmed).

Fulgentius, *Sermo 3. PL* 65:729–32. *CPL* 830. Grégoire, p. 500.

25. ff. 51–56 Dixit Ihesus Petro, sequere me (Io 21:19–20), et reliqua. In exordio huius lectionis beatus Iohannes euangelista tria nobis commendat . . . quia uerum est testimonium Iohannis ut credentes quod dixit, perueniamus ad eum quem predixit.

Incipit rewritten over original in s. xii.

Haymon d'Auxerre, *Sermo* printed in a different recension as Haymo of Halberstat, *Sermo 2. PL* 118:70–75.

26. f. 56–56v Xxx viii Homelia. O fratres karissimi quantam necem paruulorum . . . sub sua protectione perducat, cui est honor et gloria in secula seculorum. Amen.

Caesarius of Arles, *Sermo 222* with a variant incipit, ed. G. Morin, *CC* 104 (1953): 877–81. *CPL* 1008. Grégoire, p. 507.

27. ff. 57–60v Postquam consummati sunt dies octo . . . conciperetur (Lc 2:21) et reliqua. Circumciditur puer, ille puer qui erat uerbum in principio . . . (Io 1:1–5) Quid est hoc . . . in quo numero inueniri atque deputari optamus et obsecramus. Prestante domino nostro Ihesu Christo qui uiuit et regnat . . .

Augustinian cento. *PLS* 2:1213–18. Grégoire, p. 149, no. 31.

28. ff. 60v–63 Item alia. Propter quod memor (*sic*) estote (Eph 2: 11–12) . . . Idem gentes efesios in carne . . . et signum pacis unus est Christus.

Paraphrase with extracts of Jerome, *Commentarium in epistolam ad Ephesios*. *PL* 26:471–74. *BHM* 219. Grégoire, p. 509.

29. ff. 63–64v Omelia epiphania. Nuper celebrauimus diem quo ex iudeis dominus natus est . . . etiam ex gentibus peccatores perducere nos dignetur ad uitam eternam. Amen.

Augustine, *Sermo 199*. *PL* 38:1026–28. *CPL* 284. Grégoire, p. 507.

30. ff. 64v–66v Hodierni diei per uniuersum mundum nota sollennitas . . . Superest ut eum euangelizantes nouam uiam carpamus, non qua uenimus redeamus.

f. 64v in margin (addition s. xii) Sermo sancti Augustini episcopi, rewritten close to the text in s. xiv.

Augustine, *Sermo 202*. *PL* 38:1033–35. *CPL* 284. Grégoire, p. 502.

31. ff. 66v–68v Ad partum uirginis adorandum magi ab oriente . . . habeamus infatigabilem caritatem, qui . . .

f. 66v in margin (addition s. xii) Sermo sancti Augustini episcopi.

Augustine, *Sermo 200*. *PL* 38:1028–31. Grégoire, p. 490.

32. ff. 68v–70v Ante paucissimos dies natalem domini celebrauimus . . . nobis prebeant testimonium.

Augustine, *Sermo 201*. *PL* 38:1031–3. *CPL* 284. Grégoire, p. 250.

33. ff. 70v–75v In purificacione sancta Marie (in red). Si subtiliter a fidelibus quę sit huius diei festiuitas perpendatur . . . et ut uerum fatear, materno affectu et ipsum piissima facit.

Ps. Fulgentius, *In purificatione beatae virginis Mariae*. Text here as printed in *PL* 89:1291–97C. *CPL* 842. *BHM* 713; this manuscript recorded.

34. ff. 75v–77v Sic namque fratres olim per prophetam praedictum est . . . non formacionis set reformacionis domini . . .

Ps. Augustine, *Sermo 128* (excerpts). *PL* 39:1998–2001; cf. Grégoire, p. 514. *CPL* 368.

35. ff. 77v–78v Ait igitur, fratres karissimi, sancta et magna sinodus . . . ut duos filios esse dicemus.

Part of a cento formed from the writings of Cyrillus of Alexandria and others, edited in *Flor. cas.* 1:155 sqq.; cf. Grégoire, p. 491.

36. ff. 79–81v Rogo uos et admoneo, fratres karissimi, ut in isto legitimo . . . sub sua protectione perducat, qui . . .

f. 79 (addition s. xii) De quad[ra]gesima (partially trimmed). Rewritten in a hand of s. xiv closer to text.

Caesarius of Arles, *Sermo 199,* ed. G. Morin, *CC* 104 (1953): 803–7. *CPL* 1008. Grégoire, p. 512.

37. ff. 81v–86v Incipit omelia sancti Agustini de decem plagis (in red). Dominus et saluator noster, fratres karissimi, remedia nobis animarum prouidens . . . ad terram repromissionis poteritis feliciter peruenire, cui est honor et gloria in secula seculorum. Amen.

Caesarius of Arles, *Sermo 100,* ed. G. Morin, *CC* 103 (1953): 407–13; this manuscript collated for the edition. *CPL* 1008.

38. ff. 86v–88v Incipit omelia de quo scriptum est indurauit dominus cor pharaonis (in red). Quocies lectio illa legitur, fratres dilectissimi, in qua frequenter audiuimus quor (*sic*) pharaonis . . . (ends imperfectly at the end of the quire) sic enim ipse cum castigaretur, iustitia //

Caesarius of Arles, *Sermo 101* (1–5 inc.), ed. G. Morin, *CC* 103 (1953): 416–19. *CPL* 1008. Grégoire, p. 331.

39. ff. 89–90 Incipit omelia de resurrectione domini nostri Ihesu Christi (in red). Domini nostri Ihesu Christi saluatoris onorabilem solempnitatem, sua fauente clementia, fratres charissimi . . . cum suis congregemur ad celum ipso donante qui . . .

Ps. Augustine, *Sermo*. *PLS* 2:1251–53. Grégoire, p. 497.

40. ff. 90–91v Item alia de resurrectione (in red). Passionem uel resurrectionem domini et saluatoris nostri Ihesu Christi, fratres dilectissimi . . . et hominem quem fecerat liberauit, cui est . . .

Ps. Augustine, *Sermo 160*. *PL* 39:2059–61. *CPL* 368. Grégoire, p. 508.

41. ff. 91v–93 Item alia ut supra (in red). Lux hodie clara refulsit . . . exultemus et letemur in ea.

Ps. Augustine, *Sermo*. *PLS* 2:866. Grégoire, p. 505.

42. ff. 93–94 Item alia (in red). Gaudete, fratres karissimi, quia redemptionis nostre precium persolutum est . . . ut stolam inmortalitatis haccipere mereamur ut ad eterni sponsi thalami (*sic*) peruenire mereamur, prestante domino nostro.

Caesarius of Arles, *Sermo 203,* ed. G. Morin, *CC* 104 (1953): 817–19. *CPL* 1008; cf. Grégoire, p. 500.

43. ff. 94v–96 Item de resurreccione (in

red). Pascha Christi, fratres dilectissimi, regnum est cęlorum . . . quam custodire protegereque dignetur, per Ihesum Christum filium suum dominum nostrum qui cum eo uiuit et regnat in secula seculorum. Amen.

Two fragments: Caesarius of Arles, *Sermo 204,* ed. G. Morin, *CC* 104 (1953): 819–20, and Anonymous of Africa, *PLS* 2:1289–90. Grégoire, p. 508.

44. f. 96–96v Item alia (in red). Non minus etiam letare . . . (ends imperfectly at the end of the quire) sicut nobis in futurum uitam et gloriam pollicentur ita etiam //

Ps. Maximus of Turin, *Sermo 36a. PL* 57:606–7c, without the passage Laetemur ergo . . . prodit auctorem. Grégoire, p. 507.

45. ff. 97–98v In natale sancti Iohannis Baptiste Augustinus etiam (?) dixit (in red). Hodie natalem sancti Iohannis, fratres karissimi, celebramus quod nulli humquam sanctorum legimus . . . concedat uobis felicem perseuerancia (*sic*) custodire, qui cum . . .

Caesarius of Arles, *Sermo 216,* ed. G. Morin, *CC* 104 (1953): 858–61. *CPL* 1008. Grégoire, p. 501.

46. ff. 98v–100 Item ubi supra (in red). Sancti Iohannis Babtistę natalicie hodie prosecuturus . . . uideretur esse condicionis humanae.

Maximus of Turin, *Sermo 6,* ed. A. Mutzenbecher, *CC* 23 (1962): 21–22. Grégoire, p. 513.

47. ff. 100–101 In natale ubi supra homelia. Sancti Iohannis iudiciis nostris (*sic*) mox uerbi diuini . . . locutus est uerbum.

Ps. Augustine, *Sermo. PLS* 2:1257–58. Grégoire, p. 174.

48. ff. 101–102 Cui supra. Imperator celi et terrae ut nos (*sic*) fuisset uisitaret dignatur (*sic*) . . . praestet etiam et prosperam uitam nobis qui uiuit et regna (*sic*) . . .

Ps. Augustine, *Sermo 200. PL* 39:2118–19. *CPL* 368. Grégoire, p. 502.

49. ff. 102–103 Homelia Petri et Pauli. Filioli mei, audite nos et liberate uos. Currite pro uobis et nobis . . . gencium multitudo credencium, per dominum nostrum Ihesum Christum qui cum patrem (*sic*) et spiritu sancto uiuit et regnat in secula seculorum. Amen.

Ps. Augustine, *Sermo 204. PL* 39:2124–25. *CPL* 368. Grégoire, p. 499.

50. ff. 103–104 In natale eorum supra. Natalem hodie iuuante domino apostolorum celebramus . . . ut celum interemptus posideas (*sic*) per omnia secula.

Ps. Augustine, *Sermo. PLS* 2:1001–10. Grégoire, p. 506.

51. ff. 104–105 Hunde supra. Cum omnes beati apostoli parem graciam apud dominum sanctitatis obtineant . . . sed sancta horacio humilia superbia huniuersa deicit uannitate (*sic*).

Maximus of Turin, *Sermo 1,* ed. A. Mutzenbecher, *CC* 23 (1962): 1–4. *PL* 57:401–6 (*Hom. 72*). Grégoire, p. 495.

52. ff. 105v–106v De sancti Petri propria. Tempus amonet (*sic*), fratres, ut euangelicum capitulum quod nuper lectum est . . . dies autem adpropinquauit Ihesus Christus dominus noster qui uiuit . . .

Maximus of Turin, *Sermo 110* (extracts), cf. edition of A. Mutzenbecher, *CC* 23 (1962): 427–28. *PL* 57:723–24 (*Hom. 54*). Grégoire, p. 516.

53. ff. 106v–107v Item alia. Didicimus fratres quod ad similitudinem Euę beatum Petrum hostiaria quoque mulier . . . et qui prius se ipsum non rexit a domino directus est, ipso domino adiuuante qui uiuit . . .

Maximus of Turin, *Sermo 76,* ed. A. Mutzenbecher, *CC* 23 (1962): 317–18. *PL* 57:349–52 (*Hom. 53*). Grégoire, p. 496.

54. ff. 107v–108v Item ubi supra. Petrus enim primus apostolorum . . . misericordiam consecuntur (*sic*).

Elaboration of John Chrysostom, *Homilia in Petrum et Eliam* (*PG* 50:725–36). Grégoire, p. 509.

55. ff. 108v–111 In natale plurorum martirum. Dixit dominus Ihesus discipulis suis, Ecce ego mitto uos (Mt 10:16) . . . et diuersis temporibus facta inuenimus, prestante domino nostro Ihesu Christo qui nos redemit sanguine suo, ipse qui uiuit . . .

Ps. Augustine, *Sermo. PLS* 2:885. A cento formed from the writings of Augustine; contents listed by Grégoire, p. 496.

56. ff. 111–113v In natale sancte Marie. Scimus, fratres karissimi, auctori nostro multum nos debere conditos (written over an erasure) . . . qui suam matris fecunditatem atulit et uirginitatem pudoris non amisit, ipsum adhoremus regem angelorum qui uiuit et regnat . . .

Ps. Jerome, *Sermo de natiuitate beate Mariae. BHM* 310; this manuscript recorded. Grégoire, p. 512.

57. ff. 113v–118v Incipit omelia sancti Gregorii in sancti angeli Michahel (*sic*). Angelorum quippe et hominum . . . quia per charitatem spiritus ab alio in aliis habentur.

Gregory the Great, *Homiliae in evangelia*, II, 34, vi–xiv. *PL* 76:1249–55. *CPL* 1711. Grégoire, p. 491. This recension also in Paris, BN, lat. 17002 and 3783, both from the abbey of Saint Pierre de Moissac.

58. ff. 118v–120v Homelias (*sic*) de ieiunio. Sacramentum dilectissimi in septimo mense ieiunium . . . apud beatissimum apostolum Petrum ut piarum houium deprecacionibus gloriosissimi pastoris patrocinetur horacio, per dominum nostrum Ihesum Christum regnantem, qui cum patre et spiritu sancto in secula seculorum. Amen.

Leo I, *Sermo 90*. *PL* 54:447–50. *CPL* 1657. Grégoire, p. 513.

59. f. 120v De ieunio. Omnis dilectissimi diuinorum erudicio . . . (ends imperfectly in the middle of the ultimate line at the end of the quire) post concupiscentias tuas non eas //

Leo I, *Sermo 93* (1, inc.). *PL* 54:456. *CPL* 1657. Grégoire, p. 508.

60. ff. 121–135 Incipit omelia sancti Agustini episcopi. Fratres karissimi, spiritus sanctus per prophetas, sacerdotes et leuitas et omnes fidei catholice doctores ęcclesię admonet dicens . . . (ends imperfectly on a small inserted leaf of s. xiv at the end of the quire) aut argentum aliquis porrigere. Insensum.

f. 135v blank.

Pirmin, *De singulis libris canonicis scarapsus*, ed. G. Jecker in *Die Heimat des hl. Pirmin des Apostels der Alamannen* (Beiträge zur Geschichte des alten Mönchtums und des Benediktinerordens, 13; Münster, 1927), pp. 34–69 (line 14).

61. f. 136–136v In natale martirum omelia. Cum omnium sanctorum martirum, fratres karissimi, natalem deuotissime celebramus . . . si sociemus illis tam religione quam corpore, adiuuante domino nostro Ihesu Christo qui nos redemit sanguine suo, qui uiuit . . .

Maximus of Turin, *Sermo 12*, ed. A. Mutzenbecher, *CC* 23 (1962): 41–42. *PL* 57:427–30 (*Hom. 8*). Grégoire, p. 495.

62. ff. 136v–138 Item de commune supra. Quociescumque, fratres karissimi, sanctorum martirum sollempnia celebramus . . . aut si forte subrepserint, cito per caritatem quę est in Christo Ihesu qui nos reduxit de morte ad uitam reuocati fuisti per omnia secula seculorum. Amen.

Caesarius of Arles, *Sermo 223*, ed. G. Morin, *CC* 104 (1953): 882–85. *CPL* 1008. Grégoire, p. 511.

63. ff. 138v–139v Homelia de quo supra. Quoniam dies martirum sanctorum est . . . si uultis peruenire ad martiru (*sic*) palmam, per dominum nostrum Ihesum Christum cui est honor et gloria in secula seculorum. Amen.

Ps. Maximus of Turin, *Sermo 89*. *PL* 57:711–12. Grégoire, p. 511.

64. ff. 139v–141v De confessorum (*sic*) incipit homelia. Scriptum enim in lectione euangelica . . . et post et apud dominum coronam confessionis accepit, ipso adiuuante qui uiuit . . .

Ps. Maximus of Turin, *Sermo 24*. *PL* 57:893–96. *CPL* 222. Grégoire, p. 514.

65. ff. 141v–143v Item unde supra omelia. Ad sancti ac beatissimi istius patris nostri illi cuius hodie festa celebramus laudes addisse (*sic*, but corrected by a later hand) aliquid . . . et in illa die incolumes oues suas pastor bonus Ihesus Christus agnoscat qui nos redemit proprio suo cruore cum sanctis et fidelibus suis ad dextera sua (*sic*) dignetur nos collocare per . . .

Ps. Maximus of Turin, *Homilia 78*. *PL* 57:417–22; cf. *CPL* 220. Grégoire, p. 490.

66. ff. 144–148 Audistis, fratres karissimi, dum euangelica lectio legeretur ubi dominus in parabolis decem uirginibus asseruit, quinque esse fatuae et quinque prudentes dicuntur. Non michi facile indagare uidetur hec parabola. Uerumptamen secundum . . . ut uentus temptationis augeat ignem potius quam extinguat, prestante domino nostro . . .

Augustine, *Sermo 93*. *PL* 38:573–80. *CPL* 284. Grégoire, p. 492.

67. ff. 148–150 In dedicatione ęcclesie omelia. Quotiescumque, fratres karissimi, altaris uel templi festiuitatem colimus . . . audiri mereamur domino nostro Ihesu Christo. Uenite benedicti ad dextra mei patri (*sic*) accipite regnum quod uobis est preparatum ab origine mundi et nunc et in infinita secula per omnia secula seculorum. Amen.

Caesarius of Arles, *Sermo 227*, ed. G. Morin, *CC* 104 (1953): 897–900. *CPL* 1008. Grégoire, p. 511.

68. ff. 150–151v Incipit alia. Recte festa

ęcclesię colunt . . . non abebit de satietate fastidium, ad quem (*sic*) bona ipse nos perducat rex angelorum qui uiuit et regnat . . .

Eusebius Gallicanus, *Homilia 47,* ed. J. Leroy and F. Glorie, *CC* 101A (1971): 555–63; this codex collated. *PL* 39:2171–72. *CPL* 966. Grégoire, p. 512.

69. ff. 151v–153 Unde supra. Unusquisque propriam mercedem accipiet. Ait sermo diuinus, fratres karissimi, sic nuper audiuimus. Unusquisque propriam mercedem accipiet secundum suum laborem . . . nos inflamemus quod ille in oculto mentis igniuerit, quod ipse prestare dignetur qui cum eterno patre et spiritu sancto uiuit et regnat, deus per omnia secula seculorum. Amen.

Eusebius Gallicanus, *Sermo 3,* ed. J. Leroy and F. Glorie, *CC* 101B (1970): 837–41. Dubious Caesarius of Arles, *Sermo in dedicatione ecclesiae,* ed. G. Morin in *Revue benedictine* 23 (1906): 368–70; this manuscript collated. Attributed to Augustine in Épinal, BM, 3 (s. xii), f. 216. *CPL* 1017a.

70. ff. 153–157 Sermo quod est octauo idus augusti de transfiguratione domini nostri Ihesu Christi. De regionibus messis gaudii de uinea fructus suauitatis . . . in eos adorat sine errore per quem et cum quo patri et filio et spiritu sancto honor et gloria, magnitudo et magnificentia, uirtus et potentia, regnum et imperium, nunc et semper et in infinita secula seculorum. Amen.

Dubious Ephrem, *Sermo in transfigurationem domini. Flor. Cas.* 3:28–31. *CPL* 1150. *Dictionnaire de spiritualité* 4 (1960): 817.

71. ff. 157–159 De trinitate. Omnes qui christiani nomine dignitate censemuri (*sic*), fratres karissimi, inquirere et scire tactus nostrę (*sic*) substanciam ipsam quam a deo inluminati sumus racionem constringimur . . . ad quam nos perducat trina maiestas, pater et filius et spiritus sanctus qui est huna deitas. Amen.

Ps. Eusebius Gallicanus, *Sermo 9,* edited from this codex by J. Leroy and F. Glorie, *CC* 101B (1971): 889–94.

72. ff. 159–160v Agustinus de caritate. Diuinarum scripturarum multiplicem abundanciam . . . sermo non solum sit grauis, set etiam breuis per dominum nostrum Ihesum Christum cui est honor et gloria, uirtus et imperium, in secula seculorum.

Augustine, *Sermo 350. PL* 39:1533–35. *CPL* 284.

73. ff. 160v–162v Iterum de caritati. Si caritate uestre non possumus frequencius presentare . . . Ad quod gaudium nos dominus pro sua pietate perducat, cuius regnum et imperium sine fine permanet in secula seculorum.

Caesarius of Arles, *Sermo 22,* ed. G. Morin, *CC* 103 (1953): 99–103; this manuscript collated. *CPL* 1008.

74. ff. 162v–164v De elemosina omelia. Remedia peccatorum, fratres, medecina est helemosinarum . . . et bene intelligite, faciamus misericordiam et dominus Ihesus Christus faciat nobis in uitam eternam. Amen.

Ps. Augustine, *Sermo 310. PL* 39:2340–42. *CPL* 368. Grégoire, p. 318, no. 20.

75. ff. 164v–166v Sancti Agustini ubi pulsat nuper ad ianuam. Suauis dominus et mitis, fratres karissimi . . . et in omnibus Christo donante eius mandata seruemus.

Ps. Augustine, *Sermo 85. PL* 39:1909–11. *CPL* 368.

76. ff. 166v–167v Incipit dogmatum sancti Agustini. Credimus hunum deum esse patrem et filium et spiritum sanctum . . . (ends imperfectly at the end of the quire) et Tertullianus, nihil corporaliter effigiatum ut Anthropomorphus // (addition in the margin) qui uiuit et re[gnat].

Gennadius of Marseille, *De ecclesiasticis dogmatibus,* 1–4 inc. *PL* 42:1213–14. *CPL* 958a.

77. ff. 168–172 (Begins imperfectly in lectio ii at the beginning of the quire) // qui superna celorum regna spiritibus angelicis ad laudem et gloriam atque honorem sui nominis et maiestatis . . . etsi adhuc hic tenemur in infirmitate corporis, tamen ad eos de quibus loquitur toto corde tendamus ut cum ipsis postmodum in eterna secula gaudere mereamur. Per infinita secula seculorum. Amen.

Ps. Bede, *Sermo,* ed. J. E. Cross, "'Legimus in ecclesiasticis historiis': A Sermon for All Saints and Its Use in Old English," *Traditio* 33 (1977): 107–21. *PL* 94:452–55. Grégoire, pp. 67–68, 102.

78. ff. 172–175 Hodie, dilectissimi, hominium sanctorum sub una sollempnitate . . . cito ad Christum uenire contingat eum quem huius hitineris ducem habeamus, salutis auctorem dominum nostrum qui uiuit et regnat in secula.

f. 175v blank.

Augustine, *Sermo 209. PL* 39:2135–37. *CPL* 1369.

Parchment (yellow and stiff with clear distinction between hair and flesh sides). ff. 175. 293 × 161 mm (230–38 × 117–23 mm). Troparium shaped. 1–16[8], 17[6+1], 18–22[8]. Quires 1–3 numbered by the scribe "vi q"–"viii q"; quire 6 numbered "viiii q"; quires 13–15 numbered "iii q"–"v q" within red and black rectangular frames, in the lower left margin of the verso of the last leaf. A later medieval hand has numbered quires 1–21, except 17, in hard point i–xxi. Prickings occasionally visible on outer margins. Ruled in hard point with single boundary lines except for quire 17 which is ruled in pen; f. 135 ruled in pen in two columns but ruling ignored by the scribe. Quires 1–16 and 18–22 written in caroline textualis media with incipient word separation with syllables often written as separate words, in 31 long lines, by at least five hands: Hand A appears to have written quires 1–3, 6–7, 13–15, 20 (beginning on f. 157), and 21; Hand B has written quires 4–5, 16, and 22; Hand C has written quires 8, 9, 10, and 11 (to the top of f. 81v); Hand D has written quire 11 (ff. 81v–88v only). Hand E has written quires 18, 19, and 20 (ff. 152–57 only). Occasional portions of text erased and rewritten in s. xii. Quire 17 written in gothic textualis media, in 31 long lines, with writing beginning on the first ruled line except on f. 129, with long terminal s, and with generous spacing between letters in order to match the rest. Headings and incipits in mixed rustic capitals, uncials, and minuscules in orange-red (especially ff. 81v–98v) and, more often, touched with orange and red, sometimes appearing to be written in orange-red but always a trace of the ink of the text visible. Titles rewritten in margin in s. xi, xii, and xiv, apparently to serve as finding aids. Many corrections in the text and in the margins, s. xi and s. xii. Marginal numbering of lessons, mostly contemporary but occasionally dating from s. xii. ff. 1–57, pen initials, some with incipient floral decoration and touched with orange at the beginning of each text, 2–8 lines high. f. 27v, an initial decorated with a human face, touched with orange, 2 lines high. ff. 81v–96, initials within the text touched with orange.

Bound in French gold-stamped blue morocco over pasteboard, s. xix.

Written in southwestern France probably at the abbey of Saint Pierre de Moissac in the first half of the eleventh century. The script shape and prominence given to Saint Peter suggest the identity of the abbey. See also notes to text 57. Quire 17 written in s. xiv. f. 91v, a gothic letter a (s. xv?) written in the outer margin. Purchased by Sir Thomas Phillipps in Paris, c. 1835, Munby, *Phillipps Studies;* "Phillipps MS 1326" written on f. 1, lower margin. The same number written on verso of the first front flyleaf by the same hand and beneath the Phillipps stamp on the second front flyleaf by another hand. Recorded by Schenkl, *Bibliotheca* 4, ii, 38–42. In the library of Jacques Rosenthal, Munich, recorded in his catalogue no. 83 (s.d.), pp. 53–56 and plates xi and xii. Inherited by Bernard Rosenthal; acquired by the Newberry in 1954 from his catalogue no. 1, p. 34 and plate on pp. 32 and 33. Acquisition announced by M. P. Cunningham, *Newberry Library Bulletin* 3 (1955): pp. 242–43 and plate facing p. 248.

Second folio: precepit exibere.

Faye-Bond, p. 151. M. P. Cunningham in *Sacris erudiri* 7 (1955): 267–301. J. Leroy and F. Glorie, *CC* 101 (1970): xxvii.

f2

(Ry 6)

Julian of Toledo, *Prognosticon;* Ephrem the Syrian, *Sermones,* etc.

Southern France [*Illustrated in Color*] s. XI

1. f. 1–1v Homo quilibet de domo Israhel at de aduenis qui peregrinantur inter eos (Lev 17:10–12) . . . Omnem autem sanguinem omne fraternum odium intellegamus . . . et alternum odium coartat uitam nostram.

"Rabanum" written twice in right margin, largely rubbed out.

Extracts from Rabanus Maurus, *Expositiones in Leviticum,* V, 8; cf. *PL* 108:431–34. Stegmüller, *Repertorium biblicum,* 7024.

2. ff. 1v–2 De libro beati Augustini contra Faustum manicheum de quescione ciborum. Morticinum autem puto quod ad escam usus hominum non admisit . . . sed quę iniquitas committat peccata condemnans.

Augustine, *Contra Faustum,* XXXII, 13, incomplete at the beginning; ed. J. Zycha, *CSEL* 25, pt. 1 (1891): 771–73. *CPL* 321.

3. ff. 2–53 Sanctissimo ac prę cęteris familiarissimo michi domino Idalio barcinonenis sedis episcopus (*sic*). Diem illum redemptorum omnium receptione conspicuum . . . (f. 5) In nomine domini incipit prognosticorum futuri seculi. Incipiunt capitula de origine mortis humane . . . Peccatum primi hominis actum esse . . . nisi peruenire ad regnum cuius nullus est finis. Explicit liber [tertius].

Table of *capitula* not present.

Julian of Toledo, *Prognosticon futuri saeculi.* The text of the response of Idalius to the epistolary preface of Julian is wanting. *PL* 96:453–524. *CPL* 1258.

4. ff. 53–59 Incipit de psalmo quinquagesimo sancti Iohannis episcopi. Ad hesternę

cęne uos reliquias aduocamus, fratres karissimi, sicut mensam et reliquias dilectissime audis, nihil corporaliter sentire debeas suspiceris, non enim carnes concidemur si uerbum dei insinuamur uestre menti . . . et humanitate donabo ideoque Dauid.

Ps. John Chrysostom, homily on Psalm 50, a version differing from that recorded by A. Wilmart, "La Collection des 38 homélies latines de saint Jean Chrysostome," *Journal of Theological Studies* 19 (1918): 309. J. A. De Aldama, *Repertorium pseudochrysostomicum* (Paris, 1965), no. 474; cf. *PG* 55:575–88.

5. f. 59–59v Incipit ordo ad penitenciam dandam sicut uenerabilis Bedae presbyter conposuit. In primis interrogat eum episcopus de credulitate sua sic. Credis in patrem . . . Et firmiter annunciat ei si se ipsum saluare desiderat de octo uiciis principalibus . . . ut quos consciencia reatus acusat.

A short instruction in giving confession and penance corresponding in part to the *Ordo ad dandam poenitentiam* attributed to Bede and Egbert, ed. H. J. Schmitz, *Die Bussbücher und das kanonische Bussverfahren,* vol. 2 (Düsseldorf, 1898; reprinted Graz, 1958), pp. 680, 683. Another copy of this text is in Troyes, BM, 2437 (s. x).

6. ff. 60–66v Incipit liber sancti Efrem diaconi, xxx (*sic*). Gloria omnipotenti deo qui hos nostrum superno nutu aperuit . . . proin spiritu infirmabuntur in eis. Gloria patri . . .

Ephrem, *De die iudicii et de resurrectione,* ed. Assemanus, *Ephraemi Syri opera omnia* 3:553–57. *CPL* 1143, i. *Dictionnaire de spiritualité* 4:816. For additional manuscripts, see Hauréau, *Initia* 7:76, 230.

7. ff. 66v–72v Incipit liber sancti Effrem diaconi. Liber ii. Beatus qui odio habuerit unę (*sic*) mundum . . . ad patriam luminum peruenire.

Ephrem, *De beatitudine anime,* ed. Assemanus, *Ephraemi Syri opera omnia* 1:148. *CPL* 1143, ii.

8. f. 72v Incipit liber sancti Effrem. Liber iii. Dominus Iesus Christus qui descendit de sinu patris et effectus est nobis uiam salutis prę poenitent // (codex ends imperfectly).

Ephrem, *De poenitentia,* ed. Assemanus, *Ephraemi Syri opera omnia* 1:148. *CPL* 1143, iii.

Parchment, many leaves very defective. ff. 72. 277 × 190 mm (215–220 × 125 mm). $1–9^8$. Ruled in dry point. Quires 1–7 written in caroline textualis media, in 28 long lines; quire 9 written in caroline textualis media tending to currens, in 21 long lines, by a second hand. Imperfect word separation throughout; syllables frequently written as separate words. Headings in rustic capitals with occasional uncial and minuscule forms. Quires 1–8, hollow initials filled with green, orange, and yellow, some decorated with scrolls, human heads, fanciful birds or beasts, 3–5 lines high. First lines of sections of text often washed with green, orange, and yellow. Quire 9, two hollow initials on ff. 66v and 72v with interlaced leaf design, 4 lines high.

Bound in brown calf, s. xviii.

Written in France, probably southern France in the first two-thirds of the eleventh century. f. 1, "liber de origine mortis humane" written by a contemporary hand, rubbed out and written again by an eighteenth-century hand which also wrote a summary table of contents on the first front flyleaf. A more detailed table of contents by another modern hand on the second front flyleaf. Acquired by the Newberry from E. P. Goldschmidt, January 1932, catalogue no. 23, item no. 2.

Second folio: -tur pro tempore.

De Ricci, 1:542.

f3
(Ry 15)
Miscellany

Italy s. XI^2

1. ff. 1–7v (begins imperfectly on the first leaf of the quire) // eius sanctissima protinus uerba legi . . . quam in his etiam uerbis ultimam commendauit apostolus.

Anonymous, *Expositio super missam. PL* 138:1174D–86. See Cipolla, *Ricerche,* p. 64, also published as "Notizie di alcuni codici dell' antica biblioteca novaliciense," *Memorie della Reale Accademia delle Scienze di Torino,* ser. 2, vol. 44 (1844).

2. f. 8 Editio sancti Bonifatii episcopi quomodo possit poenitentia septem annorum uno anno compleri (in red). Triduana pro triginta diebus et noctibus . . . xii menses possunt redimere. Pro ebdomada ccc psalmos flectendo genua in ęcclesia aut in uno loco per ordinem.

Boniface, *De poenitentia. PL* 89:887–88. Manuscripts listed by A. Nürnberger, "Zur Handschriftlichen Ueberlieferung der Werke des hl. Bonifatius," *Neues Archiv der Gesellschaft für ältere Deutsche Geschichtskunde* 8 (1883): 319. This manuscript unrecorded.

3. ff. 8–9 Cur LXX^{ma} LX^{ma} et XL^{ma} dicantur. Si diligenter his quę ex aeuangelica uel apostolica lectione . . . ad huc si posset eam retinere cupientes.

Anonymous text on liturgy. Cipolla, *Ricerche,* p. 65, no. 3.

4. ff. 9–12 Domino beatissimo et uere apostolico, uerę et aeternę sapientię, amatori D. [sancte] uirdunensis aecclesie ierarchio (*sic*) . . . in caelesti gloria uos summum sacerdotem consociet, domine beatissime praesul.

Remigius of Auxerre, *Letter on the Hungarians to the Bishop of Verdun,* edited from this codex by R. B. C. Huygens, "Un Témoin de la crainte de l'an 1000 . . . ," *Latomus* 15 (1956): 225–38. *PL* 131:963–68.

5. f. 12 Quidam putant lege dei prohibitum ne uel hominum uel quorumlibet animalium sine rerum similtudines (*sic*) sculpamus . . . Unde et pictura grecę zoographia uocatur.

An anonymous brief treatise in defense of the cult of images. Cipolla, *Ricerche,* p. 65, no. 5.

6. f. 12–12v

Prima dies Phoebi sacrato nomine fulget . . .
Emicat alma dies Saturno septima compta.

Nomina feriarum. Riese, *Anthologia latina,* vol. 1, pt. 2, p. 43, no. 488. Schaller and Könsgen, *Initia carminum,* 12491. This manuscript recorded as Cheltenham no. 8642.

7. f. 12v De ambigenis animantibus (in red).

Haec sunt ambigenę (*sic*) quę nuptu dispare constant . . .
At lupus et catula formant coeundo liciscam.

Eugenius of Toledo, *De animantibus ambigenis,* "six"-line recension, ed. F. Vollmer, *MGH, AA* 14:258. Schaller and Könsgen, *Initia carminum,* 6000. Y. Riou, "Quelques aspects de la tradition manuscrite des *Carmina* d'Eugène de Tolède," *Revue d'histoire des textes* 2 (1972): 18–22. This manuscript recorded.

8. f. 12v Cum unus sit aer in duo diuiditur . . . quoque in aere fiunt.

On the nature of air.

9. ff. 12v–13v De ceroma (in red). Quęstiunculam mihi datam . . . in his, quę efferenda sunt, iuste dampnari. Explicit.

Lupus Ferrariensis, *Quid sit ceroma,* ed. E. Dümmler, *MGH, Epistolae* 6:114–17. *PL* 96:1385–88.

10. ff. 13v–14 Olympias est apud grecos annus . . . deflorare ad beuiare id est quasi flores colligere. Addiar dampner. Lichinum, lucerna.

Greek-Latin glossary, cf. Isidore, *De natura rerum,* V, 37; Cambridge, Corpus Christi 30, f. 87, and Vat. lat. 1053, f. 79.

11. f. 14v

Ambrosius fueram sed nunc sum uile cadauer . . .
Tu modo qui uiuis nunc mihi redde uicem.

Epigram in Memory of Ambrose, edited from this manuscript by E. de Levis, *Anecdota sacra* (Turin, 1789), pp. xxxiv–xxxv. Schaller and Könsgen, *Initia carminum,* 700.

12. ff. 14v–19v Incipit uita beati Gregorii papae a uenerabili Beda presbytero conscripta (in red). Gregorius urbe romulaeae patre Gordiano aeditus . . . facilius poterat haec etiam ipse promereri. Haec breuiter de uita uel actibus . . . Sepultus uero est in aecclesia beati Petri . . . quandoque in ipso cum ceteris sanctae aecclesię pastoribus resurrecturus in gloria.

Paul the Deacon, *Vita Gregorii,* ed. H. Grisar, *Zeitschrift für Katholische Theologie* 11 (1887): 162–72. Wattenbach-Levison, *Deutchlands Geschichtsquellen* 2 (1953): 219, n. 172. *BHL* 3639.

12 bis. ff. 19v–20 Scriptum que in tumba ipsius epitaphium huius modi. Suscipe, terra, tuo corpus de corpore sumptum . . . iam sine fine tenes.

Epitaph of Gregory as in the Basilica of Saint Peter (follows without separation *Vita Gregorii* supra). I. de Rossi, *Inscriptiones Christianae urbis Romae* (Rome, 1861–88) II, i, 52, 78, 112, 166, 209, and 253. Schaller and Könsgen, *Initia carminum,* 15938.

13. f. 20

Fundite, corda, preces, lacrimosas mittite uoces . . .
Uite concessit, spes comes alma fuit.

Eulogy of Bruno of Cologne, ed. K. Strecker, *MGH, Poetae* 5:302–3. Schaller and Könsgen, *Initia carminum,* 5437.

14. ff. 20–26 Pauendum de Theophilo diacono ac uicedomino (in red). Factum est priusquam incursio fieret in romanam rempublicam . . . talique confessione glorificans dominum, migrauit ad dominum, cui est gloria . . . Amen.

Vita Theophili, ed. *Acta sanctorum,* Febr. 1:483–87. *Flor. cas.* 3:300–305. *BHL* 8121. See C. Neuhaus, *Die Quellen zu Adgars Marienlegenden* (Aschersleben, 1882), pp. 56–57.

15. ff. 26–28 Incipit sermo sancti Augustini de originali peccato (in red). Unde, fratres karissimi, qualiter trahatur originale peccatum

. . . ante conspectum aeterni iudicis apparebimus.

Caesarius of Arles, *Sermo 157,* ed. G. Morin, *CC* 104 (1953): 717–21. This manuscript = text II, 41; consult *CC* 103 (1953): cx. For attribution, see G. Morin, *Revue Benedictine* 16 (1899): 241–48. *CPL* 1008.

16. ff. 28–37v Conuersio uel penitentia sacrae Mariae aegyptiacae (in red). Secretum regis cęlare bonum est, opera autem domini reuelare . . . honorificum est . . . Zosimas autem in eodem degens monasterio impleuit annos centum . . . nunc et semper et in secula seculorum. Amen.

Translation of Paul the Deacon. *PL* 73:671–90. *BHL* 5415.

17. ff. 38–42 Conuersio uel penitentia sanctae Pelagiae (in red). Uerba sacerdotis tanti . . . Sacratissimus episcopus Antiochie ciuitatis conuocauit ad se omnes prope se consistentes episcopis (*sic*), pro certa quadam causa . . . Haec uita meretricis, hęc conuersio desperatę, cum qua et nos faciat deus inuenire misericordiam suam in die iudicii quoniam ipsius est honor et gloria in secula seculorum. Amen.

Ed. F. Dolbeau in *Pélagie la Pénitente, métamorphoses d'une légende,* vol. 1 (Paris, 1981), pp. 181–216; this manuscript collated. *BHL* 6605. *PL* 73:663–72. *Acta sanctorum,* Oct. 4:261–66.

18. ff. 42–43v Passio sanctae Marinę martir[is] Christi (in red). Erat quidam secularis habens unicam filiam . . . orationibus sanctę uirginis multa fecit mirabilia per uirtutem domini nostri Ihesu Christi qui uiuit et regnat in secula seculorum. Amen.

PL 73:691–94. *Acta sanctorum,* Iul. 4:286–88. *BHL* 5528.

19. ff. 43v–48v Incipit uita sanctae Eufrosine uirginis (in red). Fuit uir in Alexandria nomine Paphnutius, honorabilis in omnibus et custodiens mandata dei . . . die autem migrationis eorum ad deum celebrant in eodem monasterio usque in presentem diem, glorificantes deum patrem et filium . . . Amen.

PL 73:643–52. *Acta sanctorum,* Febr. 2:537–41. *BHL* 2723.

20. ff. 48v–55v VII kalendas decembris passio sanctae Caterine martyris (in red). Regnante igitur Maxentio Cesare, Maximiani augusti filio . . . decollauerat eam uigesimo quinto die mensis nouembris. Finito namque illius sanctissimo certamine . . . et ad posterorum fidelium memoriam profuturam. Hęc namque passio . . . ego Petrus . . . de inepto famine eleuans . . . Per omnia secula seculorum. Amen.

Cf. Ps. Athanasius, *Passio sanctae Catherinae Alexandriae,* ed. H. Varnhagen, *Zur Geschichte der Legende der Katharina von Alexandrien* (Erlangen, 1891), pp. 10–18. *BHL* 1659. Followed by the Epilogue as published by A. Mai, *Spicilegium romanum* (Rome, 1839), 4:283. *BHL* 1661.

21. ff. 55v–57v Reuersio sanctae Crucis (in red). Tempore illo postquam Constantino augusto contra Maxentium tyrannum properanti . . . tunc imperator, oratione peracta, offerens multa donaria . . . Explicit reuersio sanctae crucis. Amen.

Exaltatio sanctae crucis. BHL 4178.

22. ff. 57v–61v De translatione sancti Benedicti abbatis (in red). Cum diu gens langobardorum . . . utsi scriberentur proprio indigerent libro, *praestante domino nostro Iesu Christo. Amen.* Words in italics in script of s. xvii.

Adrevald, *Historia translationis sancti Benedicti. PL* 124:901–10. E. de Certain, *Les Miracles de Saint Benoît* (SHF, Paris, 1858), pp. 1–14. *BHL* 1117.

23. ff. 62–73 Sermo beati Hieronimi ad Paulam et ad uirgines sub ea degentes de assumptione sanctae Mariae (in red). Cogitis me, o Paula . . . ut cum Christus uirginis filius apparuerit in fine saeculi, cum ipso et uos appareatis in gloria. Amen.

Paschasius Radbertus, *Ad Paulam et Eustochium de assumptione Mariae uirginis,* ed. A. Ripberger, *Der Pseudo-Hieronymus-Brief IX "Cogitis me": ein erster Marianischer Traktat des Mittelalters von Paschasius Radbert* (Spicilegium Friburgense 9; Fribourg, 1962), pp. 57–113. Ps. Jerome, *Epistola IX, PL* 30:126–47. See G. Quadrio, "Il trattato de assumptione B.M.V. dello Ps-Agostino, e il suo influsso nella teologia assunzionistica latina," *Analecta gregoriana* 52 (1951): 177–80. *CPL* 633. *BHM* 309. This manuscript unrecorded.

24. ff. 73v–74 Unde supra (in red). Creator omnium et auctor uitę . . . cum eterno patre una cum spiritu sancto in secula seculorum. Amen.

Ps. Ildefonsus, Bishop of Toledo, *Sermo XII, De sancta Maria.* Barré, *Prières anciennes,* p. 110, n. 47. *CPL* 1257. *BHM* 714. *PL* 96:279–80.

25. ff. 74–87 Amphilochii episcopi in uita et miraculis sancti patris nostri Basilii archiepiscopi Capadociae (in red). Dilectissimi, non erat indecorum fideles filios patris contristari defunctione . . . cum cęteris dormiuit. Requieuit autem angelicam uitam in terra agens magnus Basilius . . . nunc et semper in secula seculorum. Amen.

Ps. Amphilochius, *Vita Basilii,* trans. Euphemius, edited in the pre-Rosweydus editions of the *Vitae patrum. BHL* 1023.

26. ff. 87–90v Incipit uita sancti Hieronimi presbyteri (in red). Hieronimus noster in oppido Stridonis . . . Omne uitę suę tempus impleuit annis lxxxviiii et mensibus sex.

Vita Hieronymi, PL 22:175–84. *BHL* 3869. *BHM* 901; this manuscript recorded.

27. ff. 90v–103v Passio beatissimorum martyrum Dionisii episcopi, Rustici archipresbiteri et Eleutherii archidiaconi (in red). Post beatam ac salutifferam (*sic*) domini nostri Ihesu Christi passionem et adorandam eius ab inferis . . . uitam cum tyrannico principatu miserabiliter, ut par erat, amisit, regnante domino nostro Iesu Christo, cui est honor et gloria in secula seculorum. Amen.

Hilduin, *Passio Dionysii. PL* 106:23–50. *BHL* 2175.

28. ff. 103v–107v Incipit uita beatissimi Dionisii mediolanensis episcopi (in red). Tanta prerogatiua gratię . . . Quęso etiam, Christi inclite, sacer[dos], ut mihi tuo famulo . . . qui cum patre et spiritu sancto uiuit et regnat in secula seculorum. Amen.

Acta sanctorum, Mai 6:44–48. Muratori, *Scriptores,* vol. 1, pt. 2, pp. 223–27. *BHL* 2168.

29. f. 107v Contemporary record of donation of wine to the Benedictine Abbey of Saint Peter's at Novalesa.

30. ff. 108–123v Incipiunt gesta langobardorum eorumque originem (*sic*). Incipiunt capitula libri primi. Quod septemtrionalis plaga quanto magis . . . (ends imperfectly at the end of the quire) sunt posite ciuitates Cap. xviii //

Paul the Deacon, *Historia langobardorum,* Books I and II to chapter 17, ed. L. Bethmann and G. Waitz, *MGH, Scriptores rerum langobardicarum et italicarum* (Hanover, 1878), pp. 12–187. Newberry manuscript listed as *Codex novaliciensis,* p. 42, note 3. See also G. Caltigoris, "Di un nuovo manoscritto delle *Historia langobardorum,*" *Bullettino dell' Istituto Storico Italiano* 10 (1891): 47 sqq. Cipolla, *Ricerche,* pp. 70–72. Table of contents of Newberry manuscript edited, K. Hampe, "Reise nach England vom Juli 1895 bis Februar 1896," *Neues Archiv der Gesellschaft für ältere Deutsche Geschichtskunde* 22 (1897): 234–39.

ff. 20 and 28, white vine stem initials decorated with yellow, green, and orange-red; f. 74, white vine stem initial, uncolored; f. 90v, white vine stem initial decorated with brown and yellow. f. 14v, similar initial historiated with fantastic animal; f. 48v, initial historiated with dog, bird, and fantastic animal; f. 62, orange-red initial decorated with green; f. 38, red initial washed with yellow; f. 62, red initial filled with green; ff. 42–103v, simple red initials; ff. 108–115, initials in ink of text, marked in red.

Parchment. ff. 123. 260 × 168 mm (204 × 120 mm). $1–4^8$, 5^6 (1 wanting), $6–13^8$, 14^6, $15–16^8$. An undetermined number of folios removed from the beginning of the manuscript. Two books bound together already in s. xviii. Quire 15 numbered 1 on f. 115v. Ruled in hard point, prickings visible. ff. 1–108 written in caroline textualis formata by several hands in 35 long lines. ff. 108–15 written in caroline textualis media in 30–31 long lines by several hands. Breaks include ff. 28 and 38. Separation of words and word-blocks with spaces falling frequently between syllables in ff. 1–107v; separation of words in the final quire only. *Traits d'union* present throughout but very rare in all but the final quire where they are common. f. 107v, notes confirm that ff. 1–107 was a separate book before being bound together with ff. 108–115. Notes and restoration of obliterated portions date from the eighteenth century. ff. 1–107v, headings; and ff. 108–115, headings in rustic capitals. ff. 1 and 8v, corrections by rubricator.

Bound in cardboard with parchment back, s. xviii. Old shelf number 20, summary contents, and "saec xii" written on spine. No. 8642 (Phillipps number) also on front pastedown and lower margin of f. 1.

Written in northern Italy in the middle of the eleventh century, at Novalesa [Cottineau 2:2103], as indicated by note on f. 107v confirming perpetual wine supply to Saint Peter's at Novalesa. f. 12, s. xviii marginal note confirms presence at Novalesa. The last quire written a little later. Given by the Abbot of Novalesa in the eighteenth century to Eugenio de Levis. See his *Anecdota sacra* (Turin, 1784), p. xxxiv sqq. Two of de Levis's copies are in Turin at the Archivio dell'Economato and the Biblioteca Nazionale (Miscell. LXXI). Sold in March 1821, by Thomas Thorpe to Richard Heber (1773–1833); see De Ricci, *English Collectors,* pp. 102–8. No. 8642 in the Phillipps collection, *The Phillipps Manuscripts,* p. 131. Schenkl, *Bibliotheca* 1:101–3. Sold at auction in 1935 to Seymour de Ricci; Munby, *Phillipps Studies* 5:88–89. Acquired by the Newberry from E. P. Goldschmidt in 1936, listed catalogue no. 100, item no. 71.

Second folio: id est filium paternam.

De Ricci, 2:2278. C. S. Montel, "Antiche biblioteche e codici miniati in Valle di Susa," in G. Romano, *Valle di Susa: arte e storia dall' XI al XVIII secolo* (Turin, 1977), p. 225.

f4

(Ry 193)

Evangelistary

South Germany s. XI²

1. f. 1 (addition s. xii) List of feasts, by several hands, including Taciani martiris Christi, Petri apostoli, Laurentii martiris, Bartholomei apostoli et martiris, Dedicatio . . . ecclesiae beati Michaelis archangeli domini, Decollatio . . . beati Iohannis Baptiste, Deposicio beati Galli confessoris.

f. 1v Ruled for a four-paneled illumination of the Evangelists but left blank.

2. ff. 2–101 Secundum Matheum. Cum Esset Desponsata . . . Gospel lessons beginning at Christmas and ending "Feria VI^a" before Christmas.

3. ff. 101–102v Gospel lessons (headings in red): De sancta trinitate, De sancta Maria, In natiuitate sancti Stephani, In natiuitate sancti Iohannis, In natiuitate sanctorum innocentum (*sic*).

4. ff. 102v–114v Incipit breuiarium de sanctis (in red). List of about 160 feasts divided into groups with proper Gospel lessons. Feasts in red and black in order of the liturgical year beginning with Silvester and ending with Thomas the Apostle. Feasts include: In natiuitate Philippi et Iacobi (in red), Iacobi apostoli (in red), Uigilia Bartholomei apostoli, natiuitate Bartholomei (in red), In festo sancti Michaelis (in red), Galli episcopi, Martini episcopi, Othmari.

5. ff. 114v–123 In uigilia apostolorum et unius [secundum] Iohannem . . . In natiuitate unius martiris . . . De uno confessore qui fuit episcopus . . . In natiuitate uirginum . . . Gospel lessons for the Common of Saints.

6. f. 123 In dedicatione ecclesię secundum Lucam (in red). Gospel lesson for the Mass.

7. f. 123v In dedicatione altaris (in red). Gospel lesson for the Mass.

8. f. 123v Pro omni gradu ecclesię (in red). Gospel lesson for the Mass.

9. ff. 123v–128 Gospel lessons for Votive Masses (headings in red): Pro rege, Pro omni gradu ecclesię, Pro concordia, Pro temptatione carnum, Pro petitione lacrimarum, Pro peccatis, Pro salute unius, Pro salute uiuorum, Pro exercitu uel principibus uel pro cuncto populo Christiano uel pro quacumque tribulatione, Pro pace, Contra aduersitates, Pro inimicis . . . , In tempore belli, Pro elemosinas facientibus, Pro iter agentibus, Pro infirmis, Ad pluuiam postulandam, Ad serenitatem. Five additional lessons without specification of use; a sixth reading from Matthew added s. xii.

10. f. 128v (addition s. xii) Scrutinii diem, diletissimi fratres . . . inculpabile deo adiuuante ministerium peragere ualeamus.

Formula of the *Denunciatio scrutinii*. *PL* 78:993–95. For a list of editions and manuscripts, see Andrieu, *Ordines romani,* 1:8.

Parchment. ff. 128. 245 × 180 mm (170 × 138 mm). 1–12⁸, 13¹⁰, 14–15⁸, 16⁶. Ruled in hard point. Written in late caroline textualis in 23 long lines. The double ii accented in text 1 only. Headings in orange-red script of text. Incipits in rustic capitals. Gold-filled initials outlined in red with ottonian-style vine stem decoration, gold turning to green with age. Some initials left unfilled. Minor red initials.

Bound in geometrically ruled calf over original boards. Two late medieval rear-to-front-edge clasps and ten front and rear bosses missing.

Written in south Germany in the late eleventh century, probably in a monastery linked to Saint Gall, note inclusion of saints venerated at Saint Gall, above ff. 1 and 102–114v, and presence of Saint Gall neumes on f. 49. Sparse marginalia of s. xii and s. xiii. Acquired by the Newberry as a missal for the use of Würzburg from International Antiquariat (Menno Hertzberger), 1951.

Second folio: Secundum Matheum

Faye-Bond, p. 151.

f6

(Ry 3; C19163)

Isidore of Seville, *Sententiae;*

Saints' Lives and Other Devotional Treatises

Austria or South Germany s. XII¹

1. ff. 1–50v Quod deus summus et incommutabilis sit (in red). Summum bonum deus est . . . (ends imperfectly in mid folio) Ideo interdum oratio electorum in pressuris eorum differtur, ut impiorum.

f. 1, marginal notes with pointing hands and rudimentary table of contents, s. xiv, which includes four books.

Isidore of Seville, *Sententiae,* I–III, 7 inc. *PL* 83:538–676. *CPL* 1199.

2. ff. 51–118v Prologus libelli huius (in red). Appetis, Heinricę, mihimet specialis amicę . . . (f. 53) Incipit dialogus de tribus questionibus idem de diuinę pietatis agnitionę iudiciorumque diuinorum diuersitatę nec non de uaria bene agendi facultatę (in red) . . . Cur non, Othlohę, quoniam conuenimus, aptę de salute nostra . . . satis me fecisse spero.

Othlo, Monk of Saint Emmeram, *Dialogus de tribus questionibus,* ed. B. Pez, *Thesaurus anecdotorum* (Augsburg, 1721–23), vol. 3, bk. 2, cols. 143–250. *PL* 131:59–135.

3. ff. 119–121 Incipit de quodam penitentiam agentę ex uisionę (in red). His temporibus monasterium uirginum . . . uel ad perpetuam perdicionem disticti[u]s examinans tollat.

Vision of Adamnain of Coldingham, Bede, *Historia ecclesiastica,* IV, 25 (23), ed. B. Colgrave and R. A. B. Mynors (Oxford, 1969), pp. 420–26. *Acta sanctorum,* Jan. 2:1120–21. *BHL* 1:12. *CPL* 1375.

4. ff. 121v–122v Incipit uisio cuiusdam pauperculę mulieris (in red). Fuit namque in Laudonico pago quedam mulier paupercula . . . cuncta tradidit, lumenque recepit.

Wattenbach-Levison, *Deutschlands Geschichtsquellen* 3 (1957): 317–18. This edition lists six manuscripts of this text including this one as Lambach codex 77.

5. ff. 122v–132 Prefessio (*sic*) in uisionem Wettini (in red). In prouincia alamannorum uel sueborum . . . sumpto uiatico, ultima[m] uitę huius instabilis clausit horam. Explicit uisio Wettini (in red).

Heito, Abbot of Reichenau, *Visio Wettini,* ed. E. Dümmler, *MGH, Poetae* 2:267–75.

5 bis. f. 132–132v Uenerabillimo in Christo patri illi Wettinus iam deuotus uester eternam in domino salutem. Scripsi uobis in mortis periculo . . . Nescius hoc scripsi, penitusque stupore mouebar.

Extract from Walahfridus Strabus, *Visio Wettini,* ed. E. Dümmler, *MGH, Poetae* 2:332.

6. ff. 132v–146 Incipit uisio Fursei abbatis (in red). Fuit uir uitę uenerabilis Furseus nomine . . . ubi praestantur beneficia orationum, adiuuante domino nostro Ihesu Christo . . . Amen.

Vita S. Fursei with appendix. *BHL* 3209 followed by 3211. *Vita* edited by L. Surius, *De probatis sanctorum historiis* (Cologne, 1576–81), 1:365–72. J. Mabillon, *Annales sanctorum ordinis S. Benedicti* (Paris, 1703–39), 2:300–309. B. Krush, *Passiones vitaeque sanctorum aevi merovingici, MGH, SRM* 4:434–49. This manuscript unrecorded.

7. ff. 146–165 Huius mutabilis conuersionis actuumque et morum uitam et penitentię magnum uirileque certamen uenerabilis Marię egyptiacę . . . de greco transtulit in latinum Paulus uenerabilis diaconus sanctę Neapolis ęcclesię (in red). Secretum regis celare bonum est, opera autem dei revelare . . . honorificum est . . . Zosimas in eodem degens monasterio, impleuit annos centum . . . Amen. Explicit uita Marie egiptiace.

PL 73:671–90. *BHL* 5415.

8. ff. 165v–176 Incipit confessio sancti Cypriani martyris et episcopi (in red). Quicumque in Christi mysteriis proficitis . . . et merces aput deum qui liberauit me de morte eterna et deduxit me ad Iesum Christum dominum nostrum, cui sit gloria et honor in secula seculorum. Amen.

Caecilli Cypriani opera (Oxford, 1682), part 2, 54–60. Martène and Durand, *Thesaurus novus anecdotorum* 3:1629–46. *BHL* 2049.

9. ff. 176–178 Incipit passio sancti Cypriani (in red). Dum completi fuissent prophetici sermones, et quę uerę dicta de Christo ex eo qui exiit . . . In quo loco nunc omnes qui demonia habent et uarias infirmitates accipiunt sanitatem a domino per orationes beatissimorum martyrum, glorificantes patrem et filium . . . Amen.

Martène and Durand, *Thesaurus novus anecdotorum* 3:1645–50. *BHL* 2051.

10. ff. 178–182v Uita sancti Alexii (in red). Fuit uir Rome magnus et nobilis Euphemianus nomine . . . per quod omnes quicumque sincera mentis intentione deprecatus fuerit peticionis effectum sine dubio consequi ualet . . . Amen.

Acta sanctorum, Iul. 4:251–53. H. F. Massmann, *Sanct Alexius Leben* (Bibliothek der Gesammten Deutschen National-Literatur, 9; Leipzig, 1843), pp. 167–71. *BHL* 286.

11. ff. 182v–190v Incipit de quodam uicedomino (in red). Factum est priusquam incursio fieret in romanam rempublicam . . . talique confessione glorificans deum migrauit ad dominum, cui est gloria . . . Amen.

Vita Theophili de Adana, trans. Paul the Deacon, *Acta sanctorum,* Febr. 1:483–87. "*Flor. cas.*" 3:300–305. *BHL* 8121.

12. ff. 191–198 Vita Symeonis sancti (in red). Sanctus Symeon ex utero matris sue a domino electus est . . . sed propter ius iurandum nemini dedit. Ego humilis et peccator Antoninus nomine in quanto potui, lectionem hanc breuiter exposui . . . et commemorationem eius fecerit, mercedem ab altissimo recipiet, cui est honor . . . Amen.

PL 73:325–34. *BHL* 7957.

13. ff. 198–202v Ab Adam usque ad diluuium anni sunt ccxlii . . . et erit pax in his temporibus qualis umquam non fuit.

The Tiburtine Sibyl. See D. Flusser, "An Early Jewish-Christian Document in the *Tiburtine Sibyl,*" *Mélanges offerts à Marcel Simon: paganisme, judaisme, christianisme, influences et affrontements dans le monde antique* (Paris, 1978), pp. 153–83; P. J. Alexander, *The Oracle of Baalbek: The Tiburtine Sibyl in Greek Dress* (Washington, D.C., 1967), pp. 3–4 and 48–65, passim. Same text infra, ff. 220–224.

14. f. 202v In diebus Georii (*sic*) patris sanctissimi fuit plaga facta in Hierusalem super christianos et sarracenos et iudeos . . . (ends imperfectly, two folios removed after f. 202) et uenit grando et tempestas. Tercia autem uice fecerunt //

Fragment on plagues apparently added subsequent to the copying of ff. 1–202. This text also in Darmstadt, Hessische Landes- und Hochschulbibliothek, 768 (s. xv), ff. 128v–129.

15. ff. 203–219v Sanctus Brandanus Finlocha nepos Althi . . . cum suis monachis reuersus est ad locum suum. Explicit.

Navigatio S. Brandani, ed. C. Selmer (Notre Dame, 1959); this manuscript described, pp. xxxiv–xxxv.

16. ff. 220–224 Ab Adam usque ad diluuium anni sunt ccxlii . . . et erit pax in his temporibus qualis umquam non fuit.

Same as text 13, above.

17. ff. 224–228v [Q]uando expulsi sunt Adam et Eua de paradyso . . . (ends imperfectly, missing leaf) sepelierunt eam filii eius. Cum essent //

Vita Adae et Evae, ed. W. Meyer, *Abhandlungen der Königlich-Bayerischen Akademie der Wissenschaften: Philosophisch-Philologische Classe,* vol. 14, pt. 3 (Munich, 1878), pp. 185–250. This manuscript not recorded. See also, Stegmüller, *Repertorium biblicum,* 74,10. To those listed add Paris, BN, lat. 3768, f.1.

Offset traces of unidentified caroline minuscule manuscript fragments contemporary with or slightly earlier than this manuscript on the inside wooden boards of the binding.

Parchment. Many leaves defective. ff. 228. 240 × 195 mm (200 × 145 mm). 1–3^{8}, 4^{8} (1 wanting), 5–6^{8}, 7^{4} (1 wanting), 8^{2}, 9^{6}, 10^{8} (7–8 wanting), 11^{1+8}, 12–18^{8}, 19^{8} (8 wanting), 20–22^{8}, 23^{8} (1 leaf wanting, binding too tight to specify), 24–27^{8}, 28^{6} (4–6 stubs only), 29–30^{8}, 31^{8} (8 wanting), 32^{4} (4 wanting with loss of text). ff. 1–183, quires numbered by rubricator I–XXV: I–III on lower margin of recto of first folio, IIII–XXV on verso of last folio. Two quires numbered VIII, quire 10 is unnumbered. ff. 184v–228, numbered in black I^{us}–V^{us} on the verso of the last folio. ff. 203–228 appears to be a contemporary or, more likely, slightly later manuscript separate from the original codex formed by ff. 1–202v (this would explain repetition of text 13). Prickings in outer margin throughout. Ruled in hard point and pencil. Written by several scribes in late caroline and protogothic textualis, in 22–26 long lines on ff. 1–203; 24 long lines on ff. 202–228. Hyphens used to indicate divided words at the ends of lines in the prior portion of the manuscript. ff. 51, 165v, 202v–203, changes in hand visible. Cedilla frequently used for ae diphthong and for terminal e. Headings in rustic capitals mixed with uncials and in script of text written in orange-red. Some incipits in rustic capitals mixed with uncials often touched with orange-red. ff. 1–202, minor red initials by the rubricator.

Bound in alum-tawed skin over twelfth-century boards, possibly beech, central fore-edge clasp, back-to-front, wanting. Trace of label on spine and front cover. Traces of text visible on boards from removed pastedowns; see K. Holter, "Zum Gotischen Bucheinband im Österreich: die Buchbinderwerkstatt des Stiftes Lambach," *Gutenberg Jahrbuch,* 1954, pp. 280–89.

Written in Austria or south Germany in the first half of the twelfth century. Belonged to Lambach Benedictine Abbey Library, formerly Manuscript 77. Acquired by the Newberry from E. P. Goldschmidt (cat. no. 23, lot no. 70), in 1931.

Second folio: -at iedeo

De Ricci, 1:540. R. J. Hayes, *Manuscript Sources for the History of Irish Civilization* (Boston, 1965), 1:8.

+7

(Ry 194; 51-1754)
Cistercian Missal

Germany [*Illustrated in Color*] c. 1173

1. f. 1 Angelicum carmen (in red). Gloria in excelsis deo . . .

2. f. 1 Credo in unum deum patrem omnipotentem factorem celi et terre . . .

3. f. 1v (addition s. xii[2] by two hands) Mass of Bernard of Clairvaux followed by a prayer and hymn to Elizabeth of Hungary (addition s. xiii[1] by two hands): De sancta Elyzabet. Tuorum corda fidelium . . . *SMRL* 2:304; Ymnus de sancta Elisabet. Deus tuorum militum pauperum atque diuitium . . . *RH* 4531.

4. ff. 2–3v Oratio ante missam dicenda edita a beato Ambrosio mediolanensi archiepiscopo summe sacerdos (in red) et uere pontifex . . . Leroquais, *Missels* 3:46.

5. ff. 3v–95v Proper of Time from the first Sunday of Advent to the twenty-fifth Sunday after Pentecost; includes lessons, offertories, and communions.

6. f. 95v (addition s. xii[2]) De sancto Bernhardo (in red). Mass of Bernard of Clairvaux (canonized 1174), same text as f. 1v above.

7. ff. 96–133v Proper of Saints containing lessons, offertories, and communions, beginning with Stephen and ending with the Eleven Thousand Martyrs, partly an addition of s. xiii written on a separate sheet to replace a removed portion of f. 133; further additions (f. 133v), s. xv. f. 106 (marginal addition s. xiii) A[da]lberti episcopi et martyris. f. 124v (addition s . xiv, over an erasure) Wenzelai martiris, with cross-reference ("Quere in fine libri") to entry on f. 205v, infra.

8. ff. 134–144 Noted prefaces followed (f. 140v) by the Canon of the Mass with the textual variants of Cistercians listed by Leroquais, *Missels* 1:337. Folios 137–144 postdate the body of the text and are an addition or substitution, s. xiv.

9. f. 144v (addition s. xiv) Mass for Christmas Eve.

10. ff. 145–169 Proper of Time containing collects, secrets, and postcommunions, first Sunday in Advent to twenty-fifth Sunday after Pentecost.

11. ff. 169v–186 Proper of Saints containing collects, secrets, and postcommunions, Stephen through Thomas the Apostle. f. 170 (addition in margin), Thome episcopi cantuarienis (canonized 1173). ff. 181v–182v, In dedicatione ęcclesię. ff. 182v–183, In dedicatione altaris (7, 8, or 9 October). f. 184, Cesarii et Benigni. f. 184v (addition in margin), Malachie episcopi (canonized 1199). Thirteenth-century marginal additions also include Dominic (f. 177) and Francis (f. 181). f. 176, "Sanctorum Kyliani et sociorum eius," entry struck out by an early hand.

12. ff. 186–189v Common of Saints.

13. ff. 189v–195v Votive Masses (titles in red): De santa trinitate commemoratio (two Masses), De sacra cruce, In aduentu de sancta Maria, Commemoratio per annum de sancta Maria, Ad suffragia omnium sanctorum, Pro pontifico uiuo, Pro episcopis et abbatis, Pro pace, Pro peccatis, Pro familiaribus, Pro quacumque tribulatione, Pro quacumque necessitate, De aduersitate ęcclesie, Ad pluuiam postulandam, Pro serenitate, Ad repellandam (*sic*) tempestatem, De iter agentibus, two Masses titled "missa uotiua," Pro salute uiuorum, Pro infirmis.

14. ff. 196–197v Masses for the Dead.

15. ff. 198–199 Officium defunctorum (in red). Marginal additions, s. xiv.

16. f. 199–199v Missa de sapientia; Iste missę non solent cantari in conuentu (in red).

17. ff. 199v–203 Votive masses (titles in red): Missa de spiritu sancto, De patronis loci, De karitate, Pro se ipso, Pro immundis cogitationibus, Pro petitione lacrimarum, Pro humilitate, Pro abbate uiuo, Pro congregatione, Pro imperatore et pro rege, Pro abbate defuncto, Pro patre et matre.

18. f. 203–203v Missa sacerdotis (in red).

19. ff. 204–207v Additional Masses, s. xiv (titles in red): Decem milium martyrum officium, Margarite uirginis, Missa de sancta Anna, Wencesslau martiris (ff. 205v–206v), De corpore Christi, Francisci confessoris, Cythmundi episcopi et confessoris, Pro quacumque tribulatione, Remigii episcopi et confessoris.

20. flyleaf (addition s. xiii) Augustinus. Si tantum reatum, domine, nostre delinquentie cogitemus . . . qui uisitas in dolore gementem. Per redemptionem mundi dominum nostrum Ihesum Christum.

Anselm, *Oratio 33. PL* 158:926.

f. 140v Historiated initial, Christ on the Cross in green, red, brown, and magenta. ff. 3v, 136, 145, 181v, three large white vine stem initials in red, blue, orange, purple, and green. Twenty-two smaller vine stem initials, 4–10 lines high, and numerous simple initials in the same colors throughout, 1–7 lines high. The vine stem initials at the end of the codex are of inferior quality. ff. 137–144v, 204–207v, German style red initials in three different inks and hands dating from s. xii–xiv. f. 144v, flourished initial of s. xiv.

Parchment. Contemporary sewing visible on some leaves. ff. i + 208. Modern foliation 1–45, 45a, 46–207. The flyleaf is an old pastedown. f. 133, large portion removed and replaced s. xiii. 316 × 218 mm (225 × 150 mm); ff. 140v–144 (220 × 135 mm); ff. 204–207v (230 × 148 mm). 1^8, 2^8 (1 wanting), 3–5^8, 6^{10} (1 wanting), 7^6, 8^{10}, 9^8 (1 wanting), 10–16^8, 17^8 (1 wanting), 18^4, 19–25^8, 26^4. Prickings visible occasionally on outer margins. Ruled in pencil, columns reserved for long initials on either side. ff. 204–207v in brown ink. Written in proto-gothic textualis in 32 long lines beginning on first ruled line. ff. 140–144 in gothic textualis formata clearly modeled on a proto-gothic exemplar, note especially use of half-uncial d, in 19 long lines. ff. 204–207v in gothic textualis in 30 long lines with writing beginning on the second ruled line. Additions in various proto-gothic scripts.

Bound in blind tooled white pigskin, s. xvii, two rear-to-front clasps. Spine title, "Missale antiquum manuscriptum in membrana."

Written probably in southern Germany in the second half of the twelfth century before c. 1173, date of canonization of Thomas à Becket added in the Proper of Saints (f. 170). Presence of Kilian (f. 176) in the Proper of Saints indicates diocese of Würzburg. ff. 1v and 95v, addition of Masses for Bernard and rubric on f. 199 indicate a Cistercian abbey. Date of Mass for the foundation of the church inserted in the Proper of Saints suggests that this missal was prepared for use in the Abbey of Erbach (founded 1135). Leaves 4–11 of quire 14 (conclusion of noted prefaces and Canon of the Mass) written late s. xiv and perhaps substituted as part of a liturgical updating of the book. Belonged to Cistercian Abbey of Hohenfurt in Bohemia (founded in 1259, daughter of Erbach) in 1282 or shortly thereafter; see dated note verso of flyleaf containing numerous Bohemian names: "Poizlaus seruus domini, Wokkonis de Crumwenaw homicidium Hainrico iudici in Altouado a prefato Poizla eidem impositum in presencia domini Wokkonis et domini Adam abbatis . . . in Altouado ob remedium domini Witigonis de Crumwenaw . . . misericorditer relaxauit . . . Acta sunt hec anno domini 1282." An excerpt follows in which Peter Woks I of Rosenberg grants privilege to the abbey "quod nulli liceat gladium . . . super aliquam personam nudam extrahere." Kilian struck out (f. 176) at this time as no longer relevant. Additions: Elizabeth (f. 1v, s. xiii), Adalbert (f. 106, s. xiii), and Wenzelaus (f. 124v and 205, s. xiv) indicate presence in Bohemia. Recto of flyleaf, pen trails "domine et michi," etc., largely effaced even under ultraviolet lamp, may be partially in Czech. ff. 141–142, headings and marginal notes added in formal humanistic cursive in violet ink, s. xvi. f. 39, in lower margin, "C + M + B +, 1556." This codex still in Hohenfurt in 1891, recorded *Xenia Bernardina,* vol. 2, pt. 2 (Vienna, 1891), pp. 192–93, codex LXXV = old shelf-mark on spine of this manuscript. Emile Hirsch Sales Catalogue, *Valuable Manuscripts of the Middle Ages Mostly Illuminated,* no. 16 (undated, c. 1935), plate 14. Acquired by the Newberry from Otto Ranschburg (New York), 1951.

Second folio: Oratio ante.

Faye-Bond, p. 151.

8

(Ry 16; H5435)
Collection of Patristic Texts

Austria s. XII^2

1. ff. 1v–24 Capitula huius libri, epistola Hieronimi ad Algasiam (in red) . . . (table of contents of entire codex). (f. 2) Incipit prefatio epistole Hieronimi presbyteri ad Dalagasiam (in red). Filius meus Apodemius . . . id est antichristum, suscepturi sunt.

f. 1 blank.

Jerome, *Epistola ad Algasiam. BHM* 121; this manuscript recorded.

2. ff. 24–41v Item liber ad Edibiam de questionibus xii . . . (in red). Quomodo perfectus esse . . . (table of chapter headings). Incipit prefatio (in red). (f. 25) Ignota uultu fidei michi ardore notissima es . . . et accenduntur et extinguntur in nobis.

Jerome, *Epistola ad Hedybiam. BHM* 120; this manuscript recorded.

3. ff. 41v–43 Magnis nos prouocas questionibus et torpens otio ingenium . . . sed eorum merita describuntur, apud quos esse uel non esse dignatur.

Jerome, *Epistola ad Marcellam*. *BHM* 59. This text not listed on table f. 1v and unrecorded by Lambert in *BHM*.

4. ff. 43–64v Incipit epistola Hieronimi presbyteri ad Demetriadem uirginem (in red). Si summo ingenio parique fretus scientia . . . quo gloria ęternitatis acquiritur.

f. 65–65v blank.

Pelagius, *Ad Demetriadem de virginitate et vitae perfectione*. *CPL* 633, 737. *BHM* 301. *PL* 30:15–45, 33:1099–1120. This manuscript unrecorded.

5. ff. 66–101v Prologus Cassiodori senatoris (in red). Cum studia secularium litterarum magno desiderio feruere cognoscerem . . . si pro nobis inuicem pio domino supplicemus. Finit liber Cassiodori (in red).

Cassiodorus, *Institutiones,* part 1, ed. R. A. B. Mynors (Oxford, 1937), pp. 1–85. *CPL* 906.

6. ff. 101v–103 Incipit breuis editio de grammatica (in red). Grammatica a litteris nomen accepit . . . ita multis et claris scriptoribus tractata dilatatur.

Cassiodorus, *De grammatica* = *Institutiones,* II, ed. cit., pp. 93–97.

7. ff. 103–105v Incipit de arbore in paradyso posita (in red). In ueteri testamento, id est genesis, legimus dominum dixisse ad Adam . . . et auditor absentiam procuret.

Ps. Augustine, *Sermo 1 in Genesim 2, 16–17,* chapters 1–5 inc. *CPL* 368. *PL* 39:1735–39.

8. ff. 105v–107v Tractatus unde supra (in red). Debitum de quo supra curo soluere sermone sicut . . . non est iudicandus . . . Adam pro Cain, sic nec deo quod Adam peccauit imputamus.

Ps. Augustine, *Sermo 1 in Genesim 2, 16–17,* chapters 5–9. *PL* 39:1739–41. This portion separated in other manuscripts, e.g., Rome, Biblioteca Vallicelliana, T. 19 (s. xi), ff. 104v–105v, and Verdun, BM, 53 (s. xi). See *PL* 39:1739, n. 2.

9. ff. 107v–112 Annotatio interrogationum scelesti Pelagiani et responsionum sancti Augustini pari numero digestorum, ita ut unicuique interrogationi eiusdem ordinis conueniat, id est prima prime, secunda secunde et sic usque ad ultimum interrogationes (*sic*) Pelagianorum; Pelagianus inquit (in red). Ante omnia inquit interrogandus qui negat . . . sine dei gratia non posse sanari. Explicit conflictus Augustini cum Pelagiano (in red).

Numbered reference points in margins in red.

Caelestius, *Definitiones*. *CPL* 767 = excerpts from Augustine, *De perfectione iustitiae hominis,* chapters 2–6. *CSEL* 42 (1902): 4–12. *PL* 44:293–97. *CPL* 347.

10. ff. 112–114v Prologus Hieronimi in epistola quam ad Eustochium de uirginitate seruanda conscripsit, testatur quod ante tribunal Christi uerbera sustinuit eo quod libros Ciceronis legere solitus erat; Unde ad prefatam ait uirginem: Ne tibi (in red) diserta . . . Paulo post in eadem epistola subiungitur (in red). Infinita de scripturis exempla . . . per ora lacrime. Finit epistola Hieronimi ad Eustochium (in red).

Jerome, *Two Excerpts from Epistle 22* (29, vi–30 and 32, v–35, iii). *CSEL* 54 (1910): 188–91 and 195–98. Same excerpts with identical rubrics recorded by H. Butzmann, *Die Weissenburger Handschriften, Kataloge der Herzog-August-Bibliothek Wolfenbüttel* (Frankfurt am Main, 1964), Weissenburg 73 (s. ix), f. 93 (also follows excerpts of Caelestius, *Definitiones*). *BHM* 22; this text recorded.

11. ff. 114v–140 Incipit liber sancti Augustini de magisterio (in red). Quid tibi uidemur efficere uelle cum loquimur . . . ut tuis uerbis asserebatur. Finit liber sancti Augustini de magisterio (in red).

Augustine, *De magistro*. *CPL* 259. *PL* 32:1193–1220.

12. ff. 140–167v Incipiunt capitula (in red). [table of chapters] . . . Incipit liber Magni Aurelii Cassiodori de anima . . . ; Cum iam suseepti (*sic,* in red) operis optato fine gauderem . . . probabili se meruerunt conuersatione tractare. Finit liber Cassiodori (in red).

Cassiodorus, *De anima*, ed. J. W. Halporn, *Traditio* 16 (1960): 39–109. List of editions given by Halporn, ibid., pp. 59–62, and "The Manuscripts of Cassiodorus's *De anima*," *Traditio* 15 (1959): 385–87. *PL* 70:1279–1308. *CPL* 897.

13. ff. 167v–174v Incipit notatio Notkeri cenobite Sancti Galli de illustribus uiris . . . ; Cum prudens sis (in red) et prudentis nomen heredites . . . et libello finem impono. Uale. Finit liber Notkeri de illustribus uiris (in red).

Notker Balbulus, *Notatio de illustribus uiris,* ed. E. Dümmler, *Das Formelbuch des Bischofs Salomo III von Konstanz* (Leipzig, 1857), pp. 64–78. *PL* 131:993–1004. Stegmüller, *Repertorium biblicum,* 6044.

14. ff. 175–182v Incipit de rationali et ratione uti a sapientissimo uiro Gerberto et apostolice sedis summo pontifice excussum, exigente Ottone Augusto tercio; Domino et

glorioso (in red) Ottoni Cesari . . . Cum in Germania feruentioris anni tempore demoraremur . . . quod sacris auribus potuerit placuisse.

Gerbert d'Aurillac, *De rationali et ratione uti,* in *Oeuvres,* ed. A. Olleris (Clermont-Ferrand, 1867), pp. 297–310. Preface ed. J. Havet, *Lettres de Gerbert* (Paris, 1889), pp. 234–37. This manuscript unrecorded. *PL* 139:157–68.

15. ff. 182v–184v Oratio Gerberti archyepiscopi habita in concilio mosomensi (in red). Semper, quidem, reuerentissimi patres . . . omnes in commune oramus.

Gerbert d'Aurillac, *Concilium Mosomense,* in *Oeuvres,* ed. A. Olleris, pp. 245–49. *PL* 139:343–46; 138:166C–68B. This manuscript unrecorded.

f. 2, historiated initial of Jerome in orange-red and black. f. 66, historiated initial of Cassiodorus in same colors with yellow wash. f. 68v, white vine stem initial in same colors. f. 108, initial historiated with naked figure (Adam?), same colors. f. 114v, initial historiated with Augustine and Adeodatus, same colors. All initials 7–11 lines high. f. 177v, diagram in orange-red and yellow. ff. 140v, 167v, and 175, decorated initials in orange-red and yellow. Minor orange-red initials throughout. f. 165, sketch for a white vine stem initial.

Parchment. ff. 184. 267 × 176 mm (196 × 129 mm). 1^{1+8}, $2–22^{8}$, 23^{8} (8 wanting). Modern foliation erroneous. ff. 182–183, bottom margins removed. Prickings visible in outer margins. Ruled in hard point. ff. 1–64, quires numbered I–VIII; ff. 65–183, quires I–XV within red and black square frames, often double with outer square red and inner square black. Written in protogothic textualis in 29–30 long lines by several hands; a major break follows f. 64v. Headings and incipits in orange-red in rustic capitals and in script of text; points frequently used to separate words. Scribe's instructions for incipits visible on ff. 139 and 166v. Contemporary corrections on ff. 66–183 and passim.

Bound in alum-tawed skin over original boards, s. xii^2. Brass studs, two clasps missing. Cover label in gothic textualis, s. xv, "Ieronimus ad Algasiam et ad quasdam alias matronas, Cassiodorus de expositoribus sacre scripture, idem de anima, Augustinus contra Pelagium, Idem de magisterio, et pluria alia." On spine, modern labels, "XI opera" and "264." An older title effaced on the spine.

Written in Austria at Admont in the second half of the twelfth century. Sparse marginal notes and nota marks of s. xiv–xv. Inscription of s. xiv on inner side of rear binding. "Iste liber pertinet ad sanctum Blasium in Adnund. Si quis abstulerit anathema sit." Listed in c. 1376 and 1380 inventories of the abbey library, *Mittelalterliche Bibliothekskataloge Österreichs* 3:20, line 42; cf. 21, line 18, and 43, line 20. Number 264 on spine is the shelf-mark of this codex recorded in the nineteenth-century manuscript catalogue of the Admont Library: Wichner, *Catalogus Admontensis,* p. 135. Acquired by the Newberry from E. P. Goldschmidt, 1936, listed catalogue no. 100, item no. 25.

Second folio: Incipit prefatio; second folio of text: ne omnino.

De Ricci, 2:2280. F. Wickhoff, *Beschreibendes Verzeichnis der illuminierten Handschriften in Österreich* (Leipzig, 1905–38), vol. 4, part 2, p. 54 and fig. 53 (f. 114v).

f9

(Ry 27; E39033)
Boethius, *De Musica,* etc.

Austria s. XI^2 or XII^1

1. ff. 1–62v Incipit armonice institutionis liber I; Proemium . . . (in red) . . . Omnium quidem perceptio sensuum ita sponte . . . Non spissis uero ut in diatonicis generibus nusquam una.

Eleventh-century glosses and thirteenth-century marginal notes becoming sparse after initial portion of text.

Boethius, *De musica,* ed. G. Friedlein (Leipzig, 1867; reprinted 1966), pp. 177–371. *CPL* 880. Manuscript listed, M. Masi, "Manuscripts containing the *De musica* of Boethius," *Manuscripta* 15 (1971): 89–95; supplemented by Masi, "A Newberry Diagram," pp. 52–56, n. 4. Text accompanied by two contemporary glosses: Gloss A begins on f. 1, Calcidios. Diffinito sensus. Sensus est passio corporis . . . ; Gloss B begins on f. 1, Notandum quod cum omnis ars in ratione contineatur . . . ; cf. Ps. Bede, *De musica. PL* 90:909–29.

2. ff. 62v–63v Differentie et varietates octo modorum siue troporum (in red).

A tonarius with incipits from various hymns and parts of the Mass.

3. ff. 63v–65 De nomine musice. [M]usica est peritia modulationis sonu cantuque consistens . . . (ends imperfectly in mid folio) fuit enim apud gentiles deus.

Isidore of Seville, *Sententiae de musica,* ed. Gerbert, *Scriptores,* 1:20–23 = *Etymologiae,* III, 15–21, viii, ed. W. M. Lindsay (Oxford, 1911). This extract copied separately in many manuscripts including Valenciennes, BM, 384–385 (s. ix) and Brussels, BR, 2753 (s. x). *CPL* 1186.

4. f. 65v (addition, s. xii) Diagram of the

liberal arts, ed. Masi, "A Newberry Diagram," pp. 55–56 and fig. 3.

Flyleaves from an unidentified thirteenth-century commentary on the Gregorian Decretals almost certainly from the same codex as the pastedowns of MS 11.

Parchment well prepared, velvety and rather thick. ff. 58 + ii. Second flyleaf loose, very likely once preceded the text. Seven diagrams on irregular inserts contained in first text. Modern foliation 1–66 includes diagrams and one flyleaf. 275 × 210 mm (207 × 135 mm). $1–6^{8}$, 7^{10}. Quires numbered in lower margin on recto of first leaf with late medieval arabic numerals. Prickings in outer margins. Ruled in hard point. Written in caroline textualis media in 32 long lines; ff. 62v–63v, in two columns. Orange-red headings in mixed uncials and rustic capitals. Flyleaves written in gothic textualis media in 55 lines in two columns. *Traits d'union* present in text 4 only. Gloss joined to text by complex emblematic tie notes. f. 6, St. Gall neumes present in the gloss. White ivy stem initials drawn in orange, 4–8 lines high, on grounds of blue and green at beginning of each of the five books of the *De musica*. Orange-red diagrams forming part of the original codex; f. 65v, diagram in red.

Bound in wooden boards with half leather back removed, s. xii. Parchment label "Musica," s. xv, pasted on front cover. "491" Admont shelf-mark pasted on spine. Pierpont Morgan Library MSS 857 and 858 (also from Admont) have almost identical bindings.

Written in Austria in the late eleventh or early twelfth century. Bears stamps on both flyleaves of Admont Benedictine monastery. Flyleaf ii, in modern black ink, "Bibliothecae Admontis." Cited in the catalogue of 1380, *Mittelalterliche Bibliothekskataloge Österreichs* 4:62, line 1. Recorded in the nineteenth-century manuscript catalogue of Admont Library, Wichner, *Catalogus Admontensis,* p. 207, no. 409. Sold in 1937 to L. and A. Brecher (Brünn). Sold by E. P. Goldschmidt, recorded catalogue no. 265, item no. 3, plates II and III and plate facing verso of front cover. Acquired by the Newberry from Gilhofer and Ranschburg (Vienna) in 1939.

Second folio: ΔΙΑ ΤΕ ΤΑΡ

Faye-Bond, p. 150.

– 10

(Ry 18)

Boethius, *De Consolatione Philosophiae*

Germany s. XI

ff. 1–136 Anicii Manlii Seuerini Boetii uiri illustris et consularis ordinarii patricii liber de consolatione philosophię incipit (in red). Carmina qui quondam studio florente peregi . . . cum ante oculos agitis iudicis cuncta cernentis.

Contemporary interlinear and marginal notes and corrections.

ff. 136v–138v blank.

Ed. L. Bieler, *CC* 94 (1958). *PL* 63:579–862. *CPL* 878.

Parchment. ff. ii + 138 + i. Modern foliation, ff. 8–145; front flyleaf is f. 1; refoliated ff. 1–138. Six folios of the first quire have been removed. Palimpsest formed from an unidentified text of s. x. 118 × 75 mm (94 × 56 mm). 1^{6} (entirely wanting), $2–17^{8}$, 18^{10}. Ruled in green ink. Written in caroline textualis in 15 long lines. Script is "slightly cursive" with s and f frequently descending somewhat below the line. Ct ligature and cedilla for ae diphthong present. Words not always separated. Alphabetical construction notes copied by the scribe. *Traits d'union* and diastoles added in the twelfth century. Occasional Greek phrases. Headings in red in script of text. Lower marginal decoration in red and green: f. 9, vine tendril; f. 11, a dog; f. 20, floral motif. ff. 16, 20v, 43v, 56v, 114, and 130, decorated initials in red and green, some filled with human faces.

Bound in untanned stamped leather, s. xv. Stamps decorating front and back panel include three lilies within a lozenge and small rosettes, both repeated several times. Old shelf-mark 20 on spine. Pastedowns are Gregorian chant fragments, s. xii, rear pastedown with neumes on staffs ruled in green and red ink. Front flyleaf served as title page in the fifteenth century.

Written in Germany in the eleventh century. Decoration and *prosodiae* added in the twelfth century. Belonged to the Augustinian canons of Hammersleve near Magdeburg. [Cottineau, 1:1375.] Front flyleaf bears inscription, s. xii "Liber sancti Pancratii monasterii in Hamersleue" and in a fifteenth-century hand "Liber sancti Panacracii martiris Hamersleue ordinis canonicorum regularium, Boecius de consolatione philosophia." Acquired by the Newberry from H. P. Kraus (Vienna, cat. 10, lot no. 3), in 1936.

Second folio: reuerendi admodum.

Faye-Bond, p. 148.

f11

(Ry 22; I 8100)

Aenigmata Hexasticha;

Isidore of Seville, *Etymologiae* (Part I)

Austria s. XII^{1}

1. ff. 1–7 Incipiunt questiones enigmatum rethoricę artis claro ordine dictante; De olla (in red).

Ego nata duos patres habere dinoscor . . .

Odiuntque lucem, noctis secreta mirantur.

Aenigmata hexasticha 1, 3, 2, 4–28, 30, 29, 31–62, ed. K. Strecker, *MGH, Poetae,* vol. 4 pt. 2, pp. 732–59. Strecker lists eight manuscripts of which this is no. 6. Revised edition, F. Glorie, *CC* 133A (1968): 541–610. On this manuscript, see C. E. Finch, "The Riddles in Cod. Barb. Lat. 1717 and Newberry Case MS f. 11," *Manuscripta* 17 (1973): 3–11. *CPL* 1561.

1 bis. f. 7–7[v] De oue lxi (in red). Unum nomen nuncupatur . . . atque exerciatus capiat quam non potest ociosus.

A riddle in prose, ed. Finch, loc. cit., pp. 6–7.

2. ff. 7v–168v Ut ualeas quę requiris cito . . . (f. 12) Incipiunt libri Isydori iunioris spalensis episcopi ad Braulionem Cesaraugustanum episcopum uel ad Sisebuttum suum scilicet dominum et filium scripti (in red). Domino meo et dei seruo Braulioni episcopo Isydorus salutem in domino . . . Disciplina a discendo nomen accepit . . . (ends imperfectly at the end of the quire) multa generis turba diffunditur et in genesi dixit Abraham //

f. 168v, in a cursive hand of s. xiv is written "Hic est defectus cum dicitur: Dixit Abraham ad Loth, Queso non sit rixa et cetera ad tria folia."

Isidore of Seville, *Etymologiae,* Books I–IX, 6, ix, prefaced by the "Index librorum" and epistles 1–6, ed. W. M. Lindsay (Oxford, 1911). *PL* 82:73–357c. *CPL* 1186. For a listing of 1,098 manuscripts of Isidore in European libraries, see J. M. Fernandez Caton, *Las Etimológias en la tradición manuscrita medieval estudiada por el Prof. Dr. Anspach* (Léon, 1966).

Pastedowns are formed from an unidentified thirteenth-century commentary on the Gregorian *Decretals,* almost certainly from the same codex as the flyleaves of MS f9.

Parchment. ff. 168. 270 × 195 mm (180 × 133 mm). 1–21[8]. Quires numbered in roman numerals on verso of last folio in lower margin. Prickings in outer margins. Ruled in hard point. Written in proto-gothic textualis formata in 29 long lines. Headings and incipits in rustic capitals and in script of text in orange-red ink. Guides to the rubricator written on the fore edges, possibly as a reference aid. f. 12v, orange-red initial 9 lines high historiated with a winged dog.

Bound in deerskin with rules over boards, s. xiii, three bands, single rear-to-front clasp missing. Front label, s. xv, "Prima pars ethimoloiarum (*sic*) Ysidori" written in hybrida; older title in textualis beneath.

Written in Austria in the first half of the twelfth century. ff. 1 and 168v bear stamp of the Benedictine monastery library of Admont in Austria. Listed in the catalogues of that library prepared in c. 1376 and 1380, *Mittelalterliche Bibliothekskataloge Österreichs* 3:21, line 39, and 3:45, line 33. No. 277 on spine is former number of this manuscript in the Admont Library, Wichner, *Catalogus Admontensis* p. 142. Acquired by the Newberry in 1937 from E. P. Goldschmidt.

Second folio: Gemina sed soror.

Faye-Bond, p. 149.

12.1

(Ry 24)

Augustine, *De Vera Religione, De Doctrina Christiana;* Dubious Vigilius Thapsensis, *Contra Felicianum Arianum de Unitate Trinitatis;* etc.

England s. XII med.

1. ff. 1–34 Aurelii Augustini de uera religione liber incipit (in red). Cum omnis uitę bonę ac beatę uia in uera religione sit constituta . . . Ipsi gloria in secula seculorum. Amen. Explicit.

Chapter divisions marked in outer margins with arabic numbers, some chapter headings, all of s. xiv.

Augustine, *De vera religione,* ed. K. D. Daur, *CC* 31 (1961). *PL* 34:121–72. Manuscripts listed by K. D. Daur, "Prolegomena zu einer Ausgabe von Augustins *De vera religione,*" *Sacris erudiri* 12 (1961): 65; this manuscript recorded as Cheltenhamensis 241. *CPL* 264.

2. f. 34–34v Sententia beati Augustini de libro retractationum (in red). Libros de doctrina christiana . . . in libro eius legitur, quem de sacramentis siue de philosophia scripsit.

Augustine, *Retractationes,* II, xxx, ed. P. Knöll, *CSEL,* 36, i, 2 (1902): 135–37. *PL* 32:631–32. *CPL* 250. On use of excerpts of the *Retractationes* in twelfth-century Augustine manuscripts see J. de Ghellinck, "Une edition ou une collection médiévale des opera omnia de Saint Augustin," *Liber Floridus, Mittellateinische Studien: Paul Lehmann zum 65. Geburtstag* . . . (St. Ottilien, 1950), pp. 63–82.

3. ff. 34v–104v Hoc opus sic incipit. Incipit prologus beati Augustini in librum de doctrina christianorum (in red). Sunt pręcepta quędam tractandarum scripturarum . . . quantulacunque potui facultate disserui. Aurelii Augustini doctoris ypponiensis episcopi de doctrina christiana, liber quartus explicit (in red).

Chapter divisions marked with arabic numbers in outer margins, s. xiv, reworked, possibly in the first half of the seventeenth century.

Augustine, *De doctrina christiana,* ed. B. M. Green, *CSEL* 80 (1963). *CC* 31 (1961). *PL* 34:15–122. *CPL* 263.

4. ff. 104v–118 Incipit disputatio beati Augustini episcopi contra Felicianum hereticum de trinitate (in red). Extorsisti mihi, karissime fili, optate . . . cum iustis ceperit retribuere mercedem. Explicit.

Dubious Vigilius Episcopus Thapsensis, *Contra Felicianum arianum de unitate trinitatis. PL* 42:1157–72. *CPL* 808.

5. f. 118–118v Simbolum dictatum a beato Augustino (in red). Credimus in unum deum . . . a Christo domino premia consecuturi regni celorum. Amen. Explicit.

f. 119 blank.

Dubious Gregorius Episcopus Illiberitanus, *De fide catholica* or *De fide apud Bethleem* = Ps. Jerome, *Epistola 15* and Ps. Augustine, *Sermo 235,* ed. Burn, *An Introduction to the Creeds,* pp. 245–46. *BHM* 315.

6. f. 119v Sciendum est quod (?) qui totus in obediencia positus est . . . et ad uitam beatam diuina potentia introducit.

Unidentified fragment (addition s. xiii?).

f. 120, fourteenth-century Latin notes on contents of the volume with reference to arabic chapter numbers; a fourteenth-century pen trial; f. 120v, three caution notes: [1.] Caucio. Caucio domini Willelmi de Burghildbyri exposita in cista de Rothbiri exposita in in (*sic*) crastino sancte Frideswyde post festum sancti [illegible] anno domini m° ccc° xxv pro duobus marcis et habet supplementum uidelicit (?) bibliam. [2.] Caucio domini Willelmi de Burghildbiri exposita in cista de Routhbir[i] pro duobus marcis die sancti Martini anno domini m° ccc° xxvi et habet suplementum. [3.] Caucio domini Willelmi de Burghildbiri exposita in cista de Rothburi pro duobus marcis die sabati proxima ante festum sancti Thome apostoli anno domini m° ccc xxvii° et habet suplementum. See provenance section below.

Parchment. ff. 120. Front and rear paper flyleaves added in s. xviii. The original table of contents cut out and removed from original position in s. xviii in rebinding, pasted on rear flyleaf. Transcriptions of this and ownership inscription cut out and removed in rebinding now on front flyleaf. Trimmed to 260 × 190 mm (180 × 112 mm). $1–15^8$. Catchwords (s. xiii?) visible at the end of some quires. Prickings occasionally visible in outer margins. Ruled in hard point with double boundary lines, the first two horizontal lines above and the last below extend into margins. Written in proto-gothic textualis media formata in 31 long lines. Text 6 written in a more documentary script beginning on the second ruled line. Cedilla used for ae diphthong; ampersand present. Initial and final words of each text in mixed rustic capitals and uncials. Headings in the script of the text in dark red ink. Patterned blue, green, and dark red initials 4–7 lines high, similar to those described by J. J. G. Alexander, "Scribes as Artists: the Arabesque Initial in Twelfth Century English Manuscripts," *Medieval Scribes, Manuscripts, and Libraries: Essays Presented to N. R. Ker* (Oxford, 1978), pp. 103–04 and pl. 13. Marginalia, s. xiii, by the same hand which added Latin notes on f. 120. Anglicana marginalia, early s. xiv, throughout.

Bound in modern boards by the Newberry.

Written in England in the middle of the twelfth century, at Saint Mary's Reading, to which it belonged [Cottineau 2:2417]. f. 1, "Liber sancte Marie Radyings quem qui alienaverit anathema sit" written in gothic cursiva, s. xiii; cf. Warner, *Catalogue of Royal Manuscripts* 1:325 and C. R. Borland, *A Descriptive Catalogue of the Western Medieval Manuscripts in Edinburgh University Library* (Edinburgh, 1916), pl. xxiv. Item 1 recorded in the Franciscan *Registrum* 1:13 as being at St. Mary's Reading. Recorded in the late twelfth-century inventory of this library, Barfield, "Lord Fingall's Cartulary," p. 119; now BL, Egerton 3031, see *Catalogue of the Additions to the Manuscripts 1921–25* (London, 1950), pp. 302–3. Ker, *Medieval Libraries,* p. 155. Used three times as collateral for a loan by Willelmus de Borghildbiri from the Robery chest at Oxford University in 1325, 1326, and 1327; see three caution notes, the first two crossed out, on f. 120; cf. Mynors, *Manuscripts of Balliol College,* pp. 5, 24, 74, 84, and 319; G. Pollard, "Medieval Loan Chests at Cambridge," *Bulletin of the Institute of Historical Research* 17 (1940): 120; Warner, *Catalogue of Royal Manuscripts* 2:47; G. Pollard, "Epilogue to the Printing of the Medieval Archives of the University," in W. A. Pantin and W. T. Mitchell, *The Register of Congregation, 1448–1463* (Oxford, 1972), pp. 418–20. Belonged to J. Reynoldes, 1577, "Some Notes on the Library of Reading Abbey," *The Bodleian Quarterly Record* 8 (1935): 53–54. See also Warner, *Catalogue of Royal Manuscripts* 2:142. Flyleaf ii, "James Bowen Salop anno 1748." This codex and MSS 12.2–12.7 rebound by him. Signature T. Fownes. For another Bowen-Fownes manuscript from Reading and related references, see De Ricci 2:1670–71. Twelfth-century ex libris "copied from the old cover" and table of contents both copied in a pseudo-gothic script by the same hand on verso of front flyleaf. Formerly no. 241 in the library of Sir Thomas Phillipps. Acquired by the Newberry from William H. Robinson (cat. 50, 1934, lot no. 3) in 1937.

Second folio: fabricata constare.

Faye-Bond, p. 149.

12.2

(Ry 24)

Augustine, *De Quantitate Animae,* etc.; Isidore of Seville, *De Fide Catholica contra Iudaeos;* Hugh of Amiens, *Dialogi*

England s. XII med.

1. f. 1–1v Sententia beati Augustini doctoris de libro retractationum (in red). In eadem urbe scripsi dialogum in quo de anima multa quęruntur . . . Quoniam uideo te abundare otio.

Augustine, *Retractationes,* I, viii, ed. P. Knöll, *CSEL* 36 (1902): 34–36. *PL* 32:594. *CPL* 250.

2. ff. 1v–50v Aurelii Augustini doctoris eximii de quantitate animę liber incipit (in red) . . . (text begins imperfectly on f. 2) // [sim]plex animę natura dici potest, quia ex aliis naturis non est . . . sed etiam me ipsum opportuniorem reseruabo. Aurelii Augustini doctoris eximii de quantitate animę liber explicit (in red).

Augustine, *De quantitate animae,* beginning in chapter 2. *PL* 32:1036–80. *CPL* 257.

3. ff. 50v–55 Sermo sancti Augustini episcopi de uerbis apostoli. Fundamentum aliud nemo potest ponere preter id quod positum est, qui est Christus Ihesus (1 Cor 3:11–15; in red). In lectione apostolica . . . et elemosinarum largitate redimamus, prestante domino nostro Ihesu Christo qui cum patre et spiritu sancto uiuit et regnat in secula seculorum. Amen.

f. 55v blank.

Ps. Augustine, *Sermo 115. PL* 39:1946–49. *CPL* 368.

4. ff. 56–102v Incipiunt capitula in libro Ysidori contra Iudaeos (in red) . . . (f. 57) Dominę et sanctę sorori florentinę Isydorus. Quędam quę diuersis temporibus in ueteris testamenti libris . . . in quibus habitat in eternum. Amen.

Isidore of Seville, *De fide catholica contra Iudaeos. PL* 83:449–538. *CPL* 1198.

5. ff. 103–113 Mater uirtutum caritas, ubique magnifica, nusquam est solitaria, nunquam ociosa . . . semper ad summa referendo quiescas. Per seculorum secula. Amen.

Hugh of Amiens (Abbot of Reading, 1123–30), *Quaestiones theologicae,* book 7 only. *PL* 192:1229–48. See F. Bliemetzrieder, "L'Oeuvre d'Anselme de Laon et la littérature théologique contemporaine: Hugues de Rouen," *RTAM* 6 (1934): 263 sqq.; D. van den Eynde, "Nouvelles précisions chronologiques sur quelques oeuvres théologiques du XIIe siècle," *Franciscan Studies* 13 (1953): 74–77. Stegmüller, *Repertorium biblicum,* 371.

6. f. 113v–114 (addition s. xvi) Excerpt of an English translation of text 3, above. Signed J. Reynoldes. Also his pen trials.

f. 114v blank.

Parchment with front paper flyleaf, s. xviii. ff. 114. One folio removed following f. 1, apparently subsequent to modern foliation of every tenth leaf. ff. 50 and 103, lower outer portion of margin removed. Trimmed to 240 × 180 mm (175 × 110 mm, texts 1–4 only). Flyleaf has pasted on it ownership inscription and original table of contents, written on parchment, cut out and removed from original position in rebinding, s. xviii. Table lists texts 1–4 only; bound together with text 5 before the late twelfth century, cf. Barfield, "Lord Fingall's Cartulary," pp. 118–19. 1^8 (2 removed), $2–12^8$, 13^8 (8 wanting), 14^4, 15^8. ff. 1–102, ruled in hard point with single boundary lines. ff. 103–113, ruled in pencil. The first two and the last two horizontal lines extended into margin, throughout. ff. 1–102, written in Anglo-Norman caroline textualis media in 24 long lines; texts 1–3 by one scribe, text 4 by another. ff. 103–113, written in caroline textualis media, with closer affinities to documentary script, in 33–36 long lines. Beginning and concluding words in mixed rustic capitals and script of text throughout. Headings in script of text in dark orange-red ink. ff. 1–102, red, purple, green, and yellow initials 1–7 lines high. f. 103, flourished initial in green and red decorative pattern. ff. 1–102v, scribal marginal corrections. Anglicana marginalia, early s. xiv, throughout.

Bound in modern boards by the Newberry identical to MS 12.1.

Written in England, at Saint Mary's Reading, in the middle of the twelfth century, see MS 12.1. Flyleaf i^v, "Hic est liber sancte Marie de Radings quem qui celauerit uel fraudem de eo fecerit, anathema sit," written by a twelfth-century hand; "Marie de Radings" written over an erasure. Item 1 is recorded in the Franciscan *Registrum* 1:8 as being at St. Mary's Reading. In late twelfth-century inventory, Barfield, "Lord Fingall's Cartulary," p. 118. Ker, *Medieval Libraries,* p. 155. f. 1, signature of J. Reynoldes, followed by a roman numeral, partly trimmed; ff. 113v–114, his miscellaneous notes. f. 1^v bears signature T. Fownes and Phillipps stamp, 241. See provenance of MS 12.1. Acquired by the Newberry in 1937 from William H. Robinson.

Second folio: -plex anime.

Faye-Bond, p. 149.

12.3
(Ry 24)
Augustine, *De Sermone Domini in Monte, In Iohannis Epistulam ad Parthos Tractatus X;* Ambrose, *De Officiis Ministrorum*

England s. XII med.

1. ff. 1–44v Aurelii Augustini doctoris de sermone domini in monte liber [I] incipit (in red). Sermonem quem locutus est dominus noster Ihesus Christus in monte . . . si uolumus edificari super petram.

Headings rewritten and divisions marked for use as a book of homilies.

Augustine, *De sermone domini in monte,* ed. A. Mutzenbecher, *CC* 35 (1967). *PL* 34:1229–1308; cf. *PL* 47:1199–1200. *CPL* 274.

2. ff. 45–84v Incipit tractatus primus sancti Augustini in epistolam sancti Iohannis apostoli ab eo, Quod erat ab inicio, usque ad id quod ait, Quam (*sic*) tenebrę, excecauerunt oculos eius (Io 2:11; in red). Meminit sanctitas uestra euuangelium secundum Iohannem . . . quam tu credas Christo prędicanti. Explicit expositio sancti Augustini super epistolam sancti Iohannis (in red).

Augustine, *In Iohannis epistulam ad Parthos tractatus x. PL* 35:1977–2062. *CPL* 279.

3. ff. 85–146 Incipit liber I[us] sancti Ambrosii episcopi de officiis ministrorum (in red). Non arrogans uideri arbitror . . . series tamen uestustatis (*sic*) quodam conpendio expressa plurimum instructionis conferat. Explicit liber tercius beati Ambrosii de officiis ministrorum.

f. 146v blank.

Ambrose, *De officiis ministrorum,* ed. J. G. Krabinger (Tübingen, 1857). *PL* 16:25–184. *CPL* 144.

Parchment with paper flyleaves of s. xviii. ff. iii + 146 + i. Rear flyleaf has pasted on it original table of contents cut out and removed from original position in rebinding in s. xviii. Trimmed to 258 × 190 mm (213 × 140 mm). f. 48, portion of outer margin removed to form a tab, now wanting. $1–13^8$, 14^6, $15–17^8$, 18^{12}. Quires 7–18, first and third and penultimate and last lines extending into margin. Ruled in pencil and hard point with single boundary lines. Written in protogothic textualis and caroline textualis by several hands. On change to two-column format and pencil ruling, see Ker, *English Manuscripts,* p. 41. Incipits and explicits in mixed rustic capitals and uncials. Headings in script of text in orange-red ink. f. 31, correction by rubricator. Ink varies from brown to very black. Written in 35 lines in two columns. Quire 17 written in 34 lines; quire 18 written in 31 lines. Red and green patterned initials 7–10 lines high.

Bound in modern boards by the Newberry identical to MS 12.1.

Written in England in the middle of the twelfth century, at Saint Mary's Reading; see MS 12.1. The first item appears in the Franciscan *Registrum* 1:19 as being at St. Mary's Reading. Listed in the late twelfth-century inventory, Barfield, "Lord Fingall's Cartulary," p. 119. Ker, *Medieval Libraries,* p. 155. Flyleaf iii, copy of ownership inscription of Reading Abbey. f. 1, signature of J. Reynoldes, followed by a roman numeral. Flyleaf iii, "James Bowen Salop anno 1748." Twelfth-century Saint Mary's Reading ex libris "copied from the old cover" and table of contents all in a pseudo-gothic script by the same hand. Flyleaf iv bears signature T. Fownes and Phillipps stamp, no. 241. See provenance of MS 12.1. Acquired by the Newberry in 1937 from William H. Robinson.

Second folio: -bantur amittunt.

Faye-Bond, p. 149.

12.4
(Ry 24)
Augustine, *De Genesi ad Litteram*

England s. XII^2

1. f. 1v Sententia de libro retractationum (in red). [P]er idem tempus de genesi libros duodecim scripsi ab exordio . . . Omnis diuina scriptura bipartita est.

Added in the late twelfth century to the verso of the flyleaf.

f. 1 blank.

Augustine, *Retractationes,* II, i, ed. P. Knöll, *CSEL* 36 (1902): 159–60. *PL* 32:640. *CPL* 250.

2. ff. 1v–120 Incipit liber sancti Augustini qui grece dicitur examerон super genesim ad litteram, libri xii[ci] (in red). (Begins imperfectly in chapter 17 of Book I on f. 2) // nox que nobis notissima est . . . quod duodecim uoluminibus continetur, isto tandem fine concludimus. Explicit liber xii[us] (in red).

Number of chapter divisions marked in outer margins in s. xiv reworked by a post-medieval hand possibly in the first half of the seventeenth century, as in MS 12.1.

f. 120v blank.

Augustine, *De genesi ad litteram liber,* ed. J. Zycha, *CSEL* 28, pt. 1 (1894): 26 (line 9)–435. *PL* 34:259–486. One quire of text missing after f. 97v = *PL* 34:427, line 2–441, line 34. *CPL* 266. Partial list of manuscripts,

J. H. Taylor, "The Text of Augustine's *De genesi ad litteram,*" *Speculum* 25 (1950): 87–93.

Parchment with paper flyleaves of s. xviii. ff. i + 119. Modern foliation begins on the flyleaf. Break in text indicates at least one quire missing before f. 2; another quire removed after f. 97. 260 × 193 mm (214 × 139 mm). 1–14⁸, 15⁸ (8 wanting). Prickings in inner margins. Ruled in hard point and pencil with double boundary lines and numerous horizontal lines extending into margins. ff. 2–120, written in proto-gothic textualis formata in 30 long lines. Ampersand and cedilla present. f. 1v, an addition in proto-gothic textualis media, ae diphthong written out. Headings in red in script of text. f. 120, instruction to rubricator present. Red initials patterned 4–6 lines high.

Bound in modern boards by the Newberry identical to MS 12.1.

Written in England in the third quarter of the twelfth century, at Saint Mary's Reading. Appears in the Franciscan *Registrum* 1:51 as being at St. Mary's Reading. Listed in the late twelfth-century inventory, Barfield, "Lord Fingall's Cartulary," p. 119. Ker, *Medieval Libraries,* p. 155. f. 1, signature of J. Reynoldes (?) rubbed out. Flyleaf ii bears signature of T. Fownes; flyleaf iv, stamp of Sir Thomas Phillipps, no. 241. f. 1, "Phillipps MSS 241" written in black ink. See provenance of MS 12.1. Acquired by the Newberry from William H. Robinson, 1937.

Second folio: -tis dici non potest.

Faye-Bond, p. 149.

12.5

(Ry 24)

Augustine, *In Iohannis Epistolam ad Parthos Tractatus X;* Martin of Braga, *Formulae Vitae Honestae*

England s. XII med.

1. ff. 1–68v (begins imperfectly) // gaudium dicit, in ipsa societate . . . quam tu credas Christo predicanti. Explicit expositio sancti Augustini super epistolam sancti Johannis euangeliste.

Marginal corrections by the scribe. Headings reworked and expanded, s. xii. f. 3, index notes, s. xv. Occasional notes, s. xvi throughout. f. 40, index tab, s. xvi.

ff. 69–70v blank.

Augustine, *In Iohannis epistolam ad Parthos tractatus x. PL* 35:1980–2062; see MS 12.3, text 2.

2. ff. 71–74 Incipit libellus Martini episcopi ad Mi[ronem] [r]egem galliciȩ (in red). Gloriosissimo et tranquillissimo et insigni catholicȩ fidei prȩdito pietate Mironi regi . . . contemnat ignauiam.

f. 74v blank.

Martin, Bishop of Braga, *Formulae vitae honestae,* ed. Barlow, *Opera omnia,* pp. 204–50. Bloomfield, *Incipits,* 2233; this manuscript unrecorded. *CPL* 1080.

Parchment with front paper flyleaf of s. xviii. ff. 74. Two folios wanting preceding f. 1. ff. 59–74 damaged by holes which have destroyed small portions of the text. Paper flyleaf of s. xviii bearing old title "Augustinus Super Epistolam Iohannis apostoli," s. xiii (?), removed from original position in rebinding. Trimmed to 240 × 180 mm (180 × 100 mm for text 1 only). 1⁸ (1 and 2 wanting with loss of text), 2–9⁸, 10⁴. Prickings visible throughout in outer margins. ff. 1–70, ruled in hard point with double boundary lines, first two horizontal lines above and last three below extending into margins. ff. 71–74, ruled in pencil with double boundary lines, first and third and antepenultimate and last extending into margin. ff. 1–68, written in Anglo-Norman caroline textualis formata in 30 long lines (see Examples of Selected Scripts); ff. 71–74, in proto-gothic textualis media in 32 long lines. Ampersand and cedilla in both scripts. Headings in red in script of text. f. 71, title of text 2 added in a sixteenth-century hand to restore damage to f. 70. f. 72v, guide to rubricator written horizontally in outer margin in proto-gothic textualis. ff. 1–68v red or green initials; ff. 71–74 orange, red, or green initials.

Bound in modern boards by the Newberry identical to MS 12.1.

ff. 1–68v written in England in the second quarter of the twelfth century, ff. 71–74 in third quarter of the twelfth century, at Saint Mary's Reading. Listed in inventory of the late twelfth century, Barfield, "Lord Fingall's Cartulary," p. 119. Ker, *Medieval Libraries,* p. 155. f. 1, "No. 5" written by an eighteenth-century hand. Flyleaf iᵛ bears signature T. Fownes and Phillipps stamp no. 241, see provenance of MS 12.1. Acquired by the Newberry from William H. Robinson, 1937.

Second folio: salus nulla.

Faye-Bond, p. 149.

12.6

(Ry 24)

Augustine, *De Libero Arbitrio, De Natura Boni;* Quodvultdeus, *Sermo 10;* etc.

England s. XII med.

1. ff. 1–52 (begins imperfectly on the second leaf of the quire) // non paruo interuallo

peccata referentur in deum . . . et ab hac disputatione requiescere aliquando compellit. Explicit liber II (*sic*) de libero arbitrio (in red).

Rubrics as if for two books only. Correct numbers in arabic numerals in upper margins, s. xiv. Index notes of s. xii². Numbered chapter divisions, s. xiv in margins as in MSS 12.1 and 12.4. An undetermined number of folios missing before f. 1 included the beginning of this text and Augustine's *Unum malum*, see physical description below.

Augustine, *De libero arbitrio,* beginning in chapter 2, ed. G. M. Green, *CSEL* 74 (1956). *PL* 32:1224–1310. *CPL* 260.

2. ff. 52–63 Aurelii Augustini, De natura boni prologus (in red). Liber de natura boni aduersum manicheos est . . . Summum bonum, quo superius non est . . . uitam ęternamque preponant. Amen.

Augustine, *De natura boni,* ed. J. Zychia, *CSEL* 25, pt. 2 (1892): 855–89. *PL* 42:551–71, cf. 47:1223–24. *CPL* 323. Prologue formed from *Retractiones,* II, ix.

3. ff. 63–73v Incipit liber Aurelii Augustini contra quinque hereses. Debitor sum, fratres, fateor . . . qui credentes in se custodit. In secula seculorum. Amen.

Quodvultdeus Episcopus Carthaginensis, *Sermo adversus quinque haereses,* ed. R. Braun, *CC* 60 (1976): 259–301. *PL* 42:1101–06. *CPL* 410.

4. f. 73v (addition s. xiv) Music for the feast of James the Apostle. Continues in the lower margin on f. 74.

5. ff. 74–76v In natali sancti Jacobi apostoli . . . (in red).

Noted office for the service of James the Apostle. Rectangular notation on four-line staff drawn in red ink.

The presentation of the music is similar to London, BL, Harley 978, commented on by E. J. Dobson and F. L. Harrison, *Medieval English Songs* (London, 1979), pp. 143–44.

6. f. 76v (addition c. 1200) Office for the Octave of James the Apostle.

Parchment with paper flyleaves of s. xviii. ff. 76. Flyleaf iᵛ has pasted on it the original table of contents and ownership inscription, written on parchment, cut out and removed from the original position in rebinding in s. xviii. Table and the late twelfth-century Reading catalogue indicate that Augustine's *Unum malum* preceded the *De libero arbitrio* in this codex. Trimmed to 260 × 190 mm (195 × 133 mm). The lower margin of ff. 73 and 74 folded and untrimmed. 1^{8} (1 wanting), $2–5^{8}$, 6^{7} (5 inserted), $7–9^{8}$, 10^{8} (6 and 8 wanting). Ruled in hard point save for lower portion of f. 73v which was ruled in pen in s. xiv. Some prickings visible in inner margins in quires 6 and 8. Single boundary lines with various horizontal lines above and below extending into margins, some leaves three lines below. Written in Anglo-Norman caroline textualis media in 32 long lines by two principal scribes; break follows f. 14v, line 14. Ampersand and cedilla present. Opening and concluding words in mixed roman capitals and uncial letters. Headings in script of text in red. Red and green initials, some decorated with green foliage. Marginal corrections by the scribe.

Bound in modern boards by the Newberry identical to MS 12.1.

Written in England in the middle of the twelfth century, probably at Saint Mary's Reading. Flyleaf iᵛ, "Hic est liber sancte Marie Radings quem qui celauerit uel fraudem de eo fecerit, anathema sit," inscription s. xii (?). Item 1 recorded in the Franciscan *Registrum* 1:9 as being at St. Mary's Reading. Listed in late twelfth-century inventory, Barfield, "Lord Fingall's Cartulary," p. 118. Ker, *Medieval Libraries,* p. 145. *Nota* marks, pointing hands, s. xv. "No. 6" written by an eighteenth-century hand in upper margin. Flyleaf ii bears signature of T. Fownes. Flyleaf iᵛ, stamp no. 241 of Sir Thomas Phillipps. See provenance of MS 12.1. Acquired by the Newberry from William H. Robinson, 1937.

Second folio: uidetur sine metu.

Faye-Bond, p. 149.

12.7
(Ry 24)
Augustine, *Confessiones*

England s. XII²

1. f. 1 [I]ncipit retractatio sequentis operis (in red). [C]onfessionum mearum libri tredecim . . . Res autem in abdito est ualde.

First folio mutilated by removal of initials.

Augustine, *Retractationes,* II, xxxii, ed. P. Knöll, *CSEL* 36 (1902): 137–38. *PL* 32:632.

2. ff. 1–115v Aurelii Augustini eximii doctoris confessionum liber primus incipit (in red). [M]agnus es, domine . . . sic inuenietur, sic aperietur. Amen.

ff. 116–117 blank. Occasional marginal notes, s. xiii and xvi.

f. 117v, brief excerpt from book 13.

Augustine, *Confessiones,* ed. M. Skutella (Leipzig, 1934). *PL* 32:659–868. *CPL* 251.

Parchment with paper flyleaf of s. xviii bearing original parchment ownership mark on verso, removed from original position in s. xviii. ff. i + 117. A leaf removed after f. 32. Initials removed on ff. 1 and 67; f. 9, initial partly cut. Trimmed to 258 × 190 mm (205 × 120 mm). 1–4[8], 5[8] (1 wanting with loss of text), 6–14[8], 15[6]. Ruled in pencil with single boundary lines, the first two horizontal lines above and the last two below extending into margin. Written in Anglo-Norman caroline textualis formata in 34 long lines. Headings in dark red in script of text. Heading on f. 1 and initial and concluding words of each text in rustic capital and uncial letters. Decorated initials in red and green 6–8 lines high.

Bound in modern boards by the Newberry identical to MS 12.1.

Written in England in the third quarter of the twelfth century, at Saint Mary's Reading. Flyleaf i[v], "Hic est liber sancte Marie de Radings quem qui celauerit uel fraudem de eo fecerit, anathema sit," of s. xii, "Marie de Radings" written over an erasure. Listed in the late twelfth-century inventory, Barfield, "Lord Fingall's Cartulary," p. 119. Ker, *Medieval Libraries*, p. 145. f. 1, signature of J. Reynoldes followed by a roman numeral partially trimmed. "No 7" written by an eighteenth-century hand in the upper right margin. Flyleaf i[v], signed T. Fownes and bears Phillipps stamp, no. 241. See provenance of MS 12.1. Acquired by the Newberry from William H. Robinson, 1937.

Second folio: et iustissime.

Faye-Bond, p. 149.

+13

(344984)

Augustine, *Enarrationes in Psalmos* (Part I)

England s. XII med.

ff. 1–160v Aurelii Augustini doctoris expositiones super psalmos prima pars incipit. Beatus uir qui non abiit in consilio impiorum (in red) de domino nostro Ihesu Christo, hoc est homine dominico, accipiendum est . . . deus de illo exiget suam. Aurelii Augustini doctoris expositionis super psalmos prima pars explicit (in red). Hic est liber ecclesie sancte Marie de Fforda quicum alienauerit, anathema sit.

Alternative readings and corrections in red boxes in margins, linked to text by tie marks. Pointing hands in pencil and marginalia in gothic cursiva in ink, s. xv.

Commentary on Psalms 1–50, ed. E. Dekkers and J. Fraipont, *CC* 38 (1956). *PL* 36:67–599. *CPL* 283.

Parchment. ff. 160 + i. Modern foliation, 1–161; initial folios damaged by water and repaired. Trimmed to 381 × 256 mm (295 × 196 mm). 1–20[8], catchwords partially trimmed. ff. 1–159v, ruled in hard point with double boundary lines, two horizontal lines above and below extending into margin. f. 160–160v, ruled in ink (s. xiv). Prickings visible in some outer and lower margins. Quire 9 pricked in inner margins. ff. 1–159, written in caroline textualis formata of the Norman variety, see Ker, *English Manuscripts*. f. 160, in gothic textualis of s. xiv, written with an unusual gothic ampersand, minimal fusion, and long terminal s to complement the already existing codex. Headings and incipits in orange-red. Plain initials in blue, green, or orange-red up to 13 lines high, throughout.

Bound in English stamped calf, c. 1750.

Main codex (ff. 1–160v) written in England in the second third of the twelfth century, certainly before c. 1170 when dry point ruling disappeared; cf. Ker, *English Manuscripts*, p. 42. f. 160 written in s. xiv at Cistercian Monastery of Ford [Cottineau 1:1191–94], to whose library the codex then belonged; Ker, *Medieval Libraries*, p. 88. f. 161, note of s. xv by the same hand responsible for the marginalia, "Edward Schepherde promysyd to pay xv[s] furtnyght after seynt James day nex ensuing. Item, a bargayn mayd for v pense a wek on seynt Mary Maudelyns eve with Elizabeth Whawen. Of þis Shep-er[de] is recuyed vi s. viii[d] parte of þis xv[s] above wretyn. On sent Johanne a baptist day Rychard Gye have recuyd iii score of rede shevys." f. 1, signature of W. Smethwik, s. xvi. f. 160v, "Sept. 1, 1748 by the hands of Mr. Denisham of Tiverton. Mr. Richards [of] Exeter returned this manuscript to the Abbey of Ford [signed] Francis Gwyn." f. 73, "Richarde Cabel"; f. 72, "Ry Cabil"; inscription in cipher by Cabel on f. 125. Typed dealer description, suggesting that this codex may have been written at St. Alban's, pasted to front endpaper. Acquired by the Newberry in 1925 from G. D. Smith (New York), list no. 30.

Second folio: loquitur, dixit.

De Ricci, 1:539.

−14.1

(57-1141)

Peter Comestor and Others, Sermons.

France s. XII[2]

1. pp. 1–5 (begins imperfectly) // de (?) eo in lege psalmis et prophetis, spiritus sancti sunt organum per eos enim spiritus sanctus quedam secreta loquitur . . . Ad hoc tam dignum sacramentum ut digne accedamus adiuuet ipse qui fecit nos iudex, noster dominus Ihesus Christus qui uenturus est et cetera.

Unidentified sermon.

2. pp. 6–12 [P]ortio mea domine dixi custodire legem tuam (Ps 118:57). Satis accurate,

nec sine breuitate morosa formam sacre religionis, propheta nobis expressit . . . de agone ad palmam, de labore ad quietem, Ihesus Christus dominus noster.

Peter Comestor, *Sermo ad monachos*. Schneyer, *Repertorium* 4:643, no. 108. *PL* 198:1841–44.

3. pp. 12–16 [O]mni custodia custodi cor tuum (Prov 4:23) . . . In superficie litere apparet quia pater loquitur ad filium, sed quis pater . . . et de puluere suscitabit uos Ihesus Christus et cetera.

Peter Comestor, *Sermo in electione prelati*. Schneyer, *Repertorium* 4:643, no. 100. *PL* 198:1839–41.

4. pp. 16–20 [U]t intinguatur (*sic*) pes tuus in sanguine (Ps 67:24–25) . . . Uiderunt apostoli ingressum domini in celum . . . ad quam nos perducat dominus noster, iudex noster, cum uenerit iudicare uiuos et mortuos et seculum per ignem. Amen.

Peter Comestor, *Sermo de Petro et Paulo apud sanctam Genovefam*. Schneyer, *Repertorium* 4:646, no. 139.

5. pp. 21–27 [E]mitte agnum domine (Is 16:1) . . . Uerbum hoc propheticum est et prophete uerbum. Semel locutus est deus per Isaiam, sed triplicem habet hoc uerbum intelligentiam . . . agnus dei saluator mundi, qui uenturus est iudicare mundum.

Geoffroy de Saint Thierry, "De adventu" (title written by the scribe in lower margin). Schneyer, *Repertorium* 2:162, no. 34. Also in Paris, BN, lat. 3563 (s. xiii), f. 32.

6. pp. 27–35 [U]incenti dabo edere de ligno uite quod est in paradiso dei mei (Apoc 2:7). Audistis promisio (*sic*) facta est. Esus enim ligni uite promittitur uincenti . . . ut det nobis cum uincentio edere lignum uite in paradiso, quod est Christus dominus noster, qui uenturus est iudicare uiuos et mortuos et seculum per ignem. Amen.

Peter Comestor, *Sermo de vincentio ad claustrales*. Schneyer, *Repertorium* 4:646, no. 152. Text differs from *PL* 198:1741–44.

7. pp. 35–42 [D]icite pusillanimes, confortamini, ecce deus noster ueniet (Is 35:4–6) . . . Ante aduentum domini, fratres karissimi, in tanta caligine totum genus humanum uoluebatur . . . et perducere dignetur nos ad celeste regnum, ubi gaudium et pax et iubilatio Ihesus Christus dominus noster qui cum patre et spiritu sancto uiuit et regnat deus per omnia secula seculorum. Amen.

Geoffroy Babion, *Sermo in adventu dominica prima*. Schneyer, *Repertorium* 2:150, no. 1. Text differs from *PL* 171:343–47.

8. pp. 42–49 [O]ritur sol et occidit (Eccl 1:5) . . . Si simplicatem (*sic*) horum uerborum . . . dominus noster, iudex noster, qui uenturus est iudicare uiuos et mortuos et seculum per ignem. Amen.

Peter Comestor, "De assensione" (title written by the scribe in lower margin). Schneyer, *Repertorium* 4:643, no. 103.

9. pp. 49–59 [P]rimo tempore alleuiata est terra Zabulon (Is 9:1) . . . Isaias uir nobilis et urbane eloquencie decem tribuum captiuitatem . . . nolite moneri donec ueniat qui soluat nos dominus noster Ihesus Christus qui uenturus est iudicare uiuos et mortuos et seculum per ignem. Amen.

Peter Comestor, *Sermo*. Schneyer, *Repertorium* 4:644, n. 109; cf. Lebreton, "Sermons de Pierre le Mangeur," p. 39. See also Hauréau, *Notices et extraits* 5:156.

10. pp. 59–64 [U]erbum abreuiatum (*sic*) faciet dominus super terram (Rom 9:28). Uerbum breue de uerbo abreuianda dixit scriptura, sed licet fuerit breue uerbum scripture . . . ne aut de breuiatione uerbi locuti faciamus contra hoc de quo egimus.

Peter Comestor, *Sermo*. Schneyer, *Repertorium* 4:646, no. 144. Also in Paris, BN, lat. 3301 C (s. xii), f. 6.

11. pp. 64–69 [S]i fornicatus est Israel (Os 4:15) . . . Uerba hec, fratres mei, Osee sunt prophete . . . qui in presenti nos carnis sue edulio nos reficit et in futuro uisionis sue satiabit dominus noster Ihesus Christus qui cum patre et spiritu sancto uiuit et regnat dominus per omnia secula.

Sermo in Synodo, attributed to "Mauricii episcopi," in Oxford, BL, Laud lat. 105, to Peter Comestor in Paris, BN, lat. 3705; see Lebreton, "Sermons de Pierre le Mangeur," p. 40; Schneyer, *Repertorium* 4:644, no. 122.

12. pp. 70–74 [N]ascetur nobis paruulus (Is 9:6). Tria quidem in serie ista concurrunt, festiua de Christi incarnatione gratulatio . . . Ipse primus surrexit a mortuis de cetero non moriturus et omnino reuixit.

Geoffroy de Saint Thierry, *Sermo in nativitate domini*. Schneyer, *Repertorium* 2:160, no. 10.

13. pp. 74–79 [F]ecit deus duo magna luminaria (Gen 1:16–20) . . . Sic uoluit deus, fratres karissimi, facere creaturas mundi, ut in initio creationis aliquid nobis significaret mis-

terii . . . Nunc autem qui dixit, Ego sum pastor bonus (Io 10:11), uos pastores suos idoneos faciat, gregesque suos uobis commissos conseruet et eos uobiscum in celestem Iherusalem, ubi pax et gaudium et uita sunt, perducat qui uiuit et regnat deus per omnia secula seculorum. Amen.

Geoffroy Babion, *Sermo ad sacerdotes*. Schneyer, *Repertorium* 2:155, no. 63. *PL* 147:233–36, 171:924–26.

14. pp. 79–88 [F]aciant filii in tempore suo quartadecima die primi mensis ad uesperam iuxta omnes cerimonias et iustificationes eius (Num 9:2). Qui (*sic*) domini et redemptoris nostri passionem, fratres, in his diebus maxime frequentamus, attendere nos oportet sollicite, qualiter eam imitari debeamus . . . ne in patria locum perdat cum ipso opitulante, qui uenturus iudicare uiuos et mortuos et seculum per ignem. Amen.

Maurice de Sully, "De passione" (title written by the scribe in lower margin). Schneyer, *Repertorium* 4:176, no. 90. Other manuscripts: Paris, BN, 3570 (s. xiii[1]), f. 74v. Hauréau, *Notices et extraits* 2:256; *Initia* 2:260.

15. pp. 88–93 [U]erbum crucis pereuntibus stultitia est (1 Cor 1:18) . . . Fratres karissimi, quia fidelibus locuturi de misterio crucis sumus, ideo non credimus . . . ut nobis communiter sit salus, ipso adiuuante qui uiuit et regnat.

Geoffroy Babion, *Sermo de cruce domini*. Schneyer, *Repertorium* 2:152, no. 28. *PL* 71:683–85.

16. pp. 94–102 [H]ec dies, quam fecit dominus (Ps 117:24). David plenus gratia et benedictione celesti pregustans odoratu delicatissimo illum diu et multum et a multis desid[er]aturum (*sic*) solempnitatis hodierne triumphum . . . ut semetipsum nobis ostendat, qui est semper deus benedictus in secula seculorum. Amen.

Geoffroy de Saint Thierry, "De resurrectione" (title written by the scribe in lower margin). Schneyer, *Repertorium* 2:160, no. 11. Partial ed. L. Bourgain, *La Chaire française au XIIe siècle* (Paris, 1879; reprinted Geneva, 1973), pp. 53–54.

17. pp. 102–108 [S]ecundum dies ligni erunt dies populi mei (Is 65:22–24) . . . His uerbis spiritus sanctus per Isaiam humilia erigit corda, et superborum obstruit ora, pauperibus spiritu magnam spem tribuit . . . Bonus iste Christus est qui et lignum uite intelligitur, ad cuius comparationem nemo bonus, cuius regni mereamur coheredes fieri, ipso nobis prestante domino nostro Ihesu Christo qui uiuit et regnat deus per omnia secula seculorum. Amen.

Peter Lombard, *Sermo in Johanne apostolo* (original title in lower margin rendered illegible by trimming). Abbreviated version, conclusion wanting; cf. *PL* 171:723–26. Schneyer, *Repertorium,* 4:701, no. 5. Peter Lombard, *Sententiae,* ed. I. Brady, vol. 1 (Rome, 1971), p. 100. This manuscript unrecorded.

18. pp. 108–111 [U]eni sancte spiritus reple tuorum corda fidelium (Antiphon, *RH* 21252) . . . Spiritus deus est et ideo deus in spiritu adorandus est et deus spiritus est, et ideo deus per spiritum adorandus est . . . accende caritate, quem nobis prestret (*sic*) pius et misericors dominus.

Dubious Peter Comestor, *Sermo*. Schneyer, *Repertorium* 4:646, no. 141. Incipit and explicit differ from Paris, BN, lat. 3537 (s. xii), f. lv. Lebreton, "Sermons de Pierre le Mangeur," p. 42. Another copy, Paris, Maz. 841, f. 54.

19. pp. 111–117 [A]udi, Israel, precepta uite et scribe ea in corde tuo (cf. Deut 4:1) . . . Diligenter, fratres, debetis attendere, que diximus, non enim mea sed ipsius proposuimus uerba ueritatis . . . Dabo tibi plenitudinem beatitudinis, quo ad corpus et quo ad animam preualet hec terra cuius incolas nos faciat, qui uiuit et regnat deus per omnia secula seculorum. Amen.

Peter Comestor, *Sermo de libro vitae*. Schneyer, *Repertorium,* 4:637, no. 14. Text differs from *PL* 171:814–18.

20. pp. 117–119 [D]e penitentia docetur in euangelio. Si frater tuus habet aliquid aduersum te (cf. Mt 18:15) . . . Peccasti per auaritiam . . . ergo ipso duce, qui est uia ueritas et uita cuius regnum et imperium in secula seculorum. Amen.

Unidentified sermon on penitence.

21. pp. 119–125 [F]ac tibi duas tubas ductiles argenteas ad conuocandum populum (Num 10:2). Magna est, fratres mei, huius diei sollempnitas, magna est hodierna celebritas in qua Petri et Pauli passionem recolit ecclesia . . . ut eterne sollempnitati sanctorum angelorum mereamur adesse. Ad quam nos perducat Ihesus Christus dominus qui uiuit et regnat deus per omnia secula seculorum. Amen.

Peter Comestor, *Sermo de sanctis Petro et Paulo*. Schneyer, *Repertorium* 4:640, no. 60. Cf. *PL* 171:662–64.

22. pp. 125–132 [U]eritatem dico uobis

. . . Mirabilis ista conditio si non abiero inquit Paraclitus non ueniet. Si autem abiero mitam (*sic*) eum ad uos (Io 16:7). Ex ipso pendere uidebantur solatia suorum hunc autem nisi eo abeunte Paraclitum consolatorum . . . patris suscipiamur, qui est deus benedictus in secula. Amen.

Unidentified sermon.

23. pp. 132–140 [I]ntrauit Ihesus in quoddam castellum et cetera (Lc 10:38). Oportune (*sic*) satis hoc mihi in loco prophetica exclamatio assumenda uidetur, O Israel . . . quam repleuerat oleo gratie pre participibus suis Christus Ihesus filius eius dominus noster.

Bernard of Clairvaux, *Sermo in assumptione virginis*. Schneyer, *Repertorium* 1:448, no. 106. Leclercq and Rochais, *Sancti Bernardi opera* 5:231–38. *PL* 183:417–21.

24. pp. 140–145. [T]ulit Moises uirgam Aaron (cf. Num 20:9) . . . Murmurauerunt filii Israel quod Aaron pre ceteris sacerdotio fungeretur, sed ad indicium uirge que in spatio unius noctis inter alias uirgas floruit . . . ora pro nobis benedictum inter homines dominum nostrum Ihesum Christum, qui uenturus est iudicare uiuos et mortuos et seculum per ignem. Amen.

Hilduin, *Sermo in assumptione beatae virginis Mariae*. Schneyer, *Repertorium* 2:718, no. 30.

25. pp. 145–148 [U]ie Sion lugent (Lam 1:4) . . . Fratres, hodie ad sanctam ecclesiam conuenistis, sed quia multi sunt qui ad ecclesiam uadunt . . . Cauete uobis ne de talibus sitis, sed de illis de quibus non flent uie Sion de quibus uelit uos esse Christus Ihesus qui uiuit et regnat deus.

Unidentified sermon.

26. pp. 149–153 [S]uper flumina Babilonis (Ps 136:1) . . . Fratres, estote attenti qui simul hodie conuenistis et congregati estis . . . ut per hanc scalam dilectionis et misericordie conscendere ualeamus ad habitaculum superne ciuitatis, ipso prestante domino nostro Ihesu Christo qui cum patre et spiritu sancto uiuit et regnat deus per omnia secula seculorum.

Extracts from the copy of this sermon in Bruges, Bibliothèque Publique 507 (s. xiii), ed. A. de Poorter, "Catalogue des manuscrits de prédication médiévale de la bibliothèque de Bruges," *Revue d'histoire ecclésiastique* 24 (1928): 116–17. This sermon also in Vat. lat. 700 (s. xiii), f. 147.

27. pp. 153–157 [L]auda Iherusalem dominum (Ps 147:12) Iherusalem ciuitas sancta et ciuitas sancti, sancta ecclesia est . . . offerentes illi uitulos labiorum nostrorum qui uenturus est iudicare uiuos et mortuos et seculum per ignem. Amen.

Richard of Saint Victor, *Sermo in dedicatione ecclesiae*. Schneyer, *Repertorium* 5:162, no. 3. *PL* 177:905–7. See also Hauréau, *Initia* 4:7v.

28. pp. 157–165 [S]i quis diligit me (Io 14:23–24) . . . Unde psalmista, Furor illis . . . Ecce sermones, fratres karissimi . . . ut digne possitis eum suscipere, eo adiuuante qui uiuit et regnat deus per omnia secula.

Geoffroy Babion, *Sermo dominica in quadragesima*. Schneyer, *Repertorium* 2:151, no. 10. *PL* 171:471–76.

29. pp. 165–185 [I]n primo ordine canonis tria apponimus, pro tribus rogamus, et ideo tres cruces facimus . . . Properia quando dicitur agnus dei, in duobus primis est conuenientia, in tertio differentia.

Dubious Richard of Wedinghausen, *Libellus de canone mystici libaminis* (chaps. 2–10). *PL* 177:459–69. B. Hauréau, "Notice sur une Exposition de la Messe," *Notices et extraits des manuscrits*, vol. 24, pt. 2 (1876), pp. 145 sqq. Another copy, London, BL, Royal 8 A XXI (s. xiii), f. 157.

30. p. 186 Serena uirginum, lux luminum plena, templum trinitatis . . . plausu leti tribus (?) benedicamus domino.

RH 18828, cf. 5:367.

Parchment. ff. 92. Modern pagination 1–186 omits pp. 86–87. Three quires containing an undetermined number of folios missing from the beginning. Two modern flyleaves. Trimmed to 144 × 110 mm (115 × 85 mm). Many folios irregular with holes present prior to writing. 1–3 wanting, 4^8 (1–2 wanting with loss of text), 5–14^8, 15^6. Quires numbered IIII^{us}–XV^{us} on lower margin center of verso of last leaf and 1–12 by a modern hand in lower margin center of recto of the first leaf, removed by trimming on some folios. Ruled in pencil. Written in proto-gothic textualis media in 21–25 long lines, centered on every other ruled line beginning on the first ruled line (see Examples of Selected Scripts). Space for minor initials and line fillers left blank at beginning of texts 1–28 and at the beginning and within text 29.

Bound in worn red velvet over boards, probably s. xvii.

Written in France in the second half of the twelfth century. p. 186, "Rainauldus me scripsit. Amen dico uobis"; cf. *Colophons de manuscrits occidentaux*, 16403–05. p. 185, "Amen dico uobis. Amen EABO[or D]M" written by the scribe. p. 1, early modern italic inscription, "Communitatis dompmartinensis 1682," i.e., Premonstratensian congregation of Saint-Josse-au-Bois [Cottineau 1:983]. On first flyleaf, modern inscription describes contents as "Manuscrit fin du XIIIe, début du XIVe s. provenant de la communauté de Dampmartin. C'est un commentaire sur les Evangiles, etc. A la fin un trope sur le benedicamus domino. Apparemment complet." Acquired by the Newberry from Ifan Kyrle Fletcher (London), 1957.

Second folio: debent inueniri.

+15
(13185)
Missal (Part I only)

Germany c. 1250

1. ff. 1–106 Proper of Time, first Sunday in Advent through Holy Saturday. Noted hymns: ff. 97v–98, Popule meus, quid feci tibi . . . *SMRL* 2:513; ff. 99–101v, Exultet iam angelica turba celorum . . . *RH* 5868.

2. f. 106 Prefacio cottidiana (in red). f. 106v, full-page illumination.

3. ff. 107–109 Canon of the Mass.

4. ff. 109–110v Nine prefaces for special feasts.

5. ff. 111–137v Proper of Saints, Andrew through Ambrose. f. 119, Wilhelmi episcopi et confessoris; f. 125, Emerenciane uirginis; f. 128v, Brigite uirginis, in purificatione sancte Marie; f. 134, Albini episcopi et confessoris; f. 135, Gutberti.

6. ff. 137v–144 Common of Saints.

7. ff. 144–145v In dedicatione ecclesie (in red).

8. ff. 145v–146 In noua dedicatione (in red).

9. f. 146–146v Dedicatio altaris (in red).

10. ff. 146v–162 Votive Masses (titles all written in red): Missa de sancta trinitate, De spiritu sancto, De sancta cruce, De sancta Maria in aduentu domini, Sabbato per totum annum de sancta Maria, Ad poscenda suffragia sanctorum, Pro peccatis, Pro familiaribus, Pro pace, Pro tribulatione, Pro congregacione, Missa propria sacerdotis, Pro intimo amico, Ad postulandam pluuiam, Pro serenitate, Pro iter agentibus, Pro infirmis, Collecta pro episcopo, Pro episcopis et abbatibus, Pro aduersitate ecclesie. Ad repellendam tempestatem, Missa uotiua, Item unde supra, Pro salute uiuorum, Pro captiuis, Pro rege (two Masses), Pro humilitate, Pro temptacione, Pro temptacione uel cogitatione (in margin in a different shade of red), Pro peticione lacrimarum, Pro karitate, Pro concordia, Pro pestilencia et fame.

11. ff. 162–66 Masses for the Dead (all titles written in red): Missa pro defunctis, Pro episcopo defuncto, In anniuersario defuncti (three Masses), Pro femina defuncta, Pro defunctis, Pro fratribus et familiaribus, Pro patre et matre, Pro hiis qui in cymiterio iacent, Pro fidelibus defunctis, Generalis (three Masses, manuscript ending imperfectly in the third).

f. 106v Full-page illumination of the Crucifixion on a tree with a pelican in her piety, a lion breathing on her cubs, and Mary and John the Evangelist, in gold, red, violet, blue, and green. Historiated initials in same colors except violet: f. 1, King David elevates his soul, 17 lines high (Advent); f. 9, the Nativity, 10 lines high (In primo Galli cantu); f. 11, Virgin and Child, 15 lines high (In sanctissimo die); f. 128v, Infant Jesus between Mary and Joseph with an altar below, the letter S as a green dragon, 8 lines high (In purificatione sancte Marie); f. 136, Christ at the Resurrection, 8 lines high, very deteriorated (In annunciacione beate uirginis); f. 73, 8-line-high illuminated initial D as a blue dragon, decorated in the same colors; f. 107, 12-line-high illuminated initial T historiated with two gold dragons. f. 14, 9-line-high illuminated initial E. Alternating red and blue initials, flourished in red throughout, 2–3 lines high. Minor initials in red, characteristically German.

Parchment. ff. 166. Trimmed to 348 × 265 mm (240 × 180 mm). 1^8 (1 wanting), $2–11^8$, 12^{10} (1 leaf wanting, binding too tight to specify), $13–14^8$, 15^{14}, $16–20^8$. Ruled in brown ink with double column reserved on outer margins for larger initials. Written in gothic textualis formata in 25 long lines, all below the first ruled line. Only a trace of the vertical stroke of t goes above the horizontal stroke. Headings in red in script of text.

Bound in gold-stamped calf, s. xvi, framed image of Christ on verso and recto with legend, "Ihesus Christus filius dei uiui, saluator mundi, rex regum et dominus dominante." One of two rear-to-front fore-edge clasps wanting. Spine title: "Missalis Antiqs. MSS. Pars I."

Written in Germany c. 1250. Saints of Proper and illuminations suggest Rhine valley, possibly Cologne. f. 106, marginal suffrage to the Virgin added s. xv. ff. 152v–153, collects added in German script, s. xvii. Gift of B. F. Stevens to the Newberry, 1889.

Second folio: Excita domine corda.

De Ricci, 1:523.

16
(23815)
Latin Bible

France s. XIII²

1. Front pastedown (addition c. 1400) Ab Adam usque ad Christum . . . Brief biblical chronology from the creation to the destruction of the temple.

2. Flyleaf, brief theological distinction beginning, Circa dilectionem nota quod . . .

3. Flyleaf verso (addition s. xv) [T]ota biblia diuiditur in duas partes, scilicet in uetus et nouum testamentum . . . et dictum est regnum Iuda.

Biblia abbreviata. For another copy, see Metz, BM, 562.

4. ff. 1–478 Bible in the usual order with the customary set of 64 prologues as listed by Ker, *Medieval Manuscripts* 1:96–97. Ecclesiasticus, Multum nobis . . . uitam agere, and Luke 1:1–4 treated as prologues.

Text accompanied by sparse marginal notes, s. xiii–xv, some liturgical, some with pointing hands.

f. 478v blank.

5. ff. 479–522v Aaz apprehendens . . . consiliatores eorum.

Usual dictionary of Hebrew names accompanied by instructions to the rubricator in lower margin, partially trimmed. Stegmüller, *Repertorium biblicam,* 7709.

6. ff. 523–525 (addition s. xvi). Capitula biblie metrificata per fratrem Barthelomeum Trudentini ordinis predicatorum. Capitula genesis. Sex opera dierum, prohibet deus fructum . . . librum sume (?) tibi.

ff. 525v–526v blank.

Mnemonic resume of the Bible, Genesis through Isaiah. This text unrecorded among the works of Bartholomeus Trudentini; Kaeppeli, 1:172–73. Anonymous in Oxford, BL, Marshall 86, and Klosterneuburg Stiftsbibliothek, 428.

7. f. 527 (addition c. 1400) Table of the books of the Old and New Testaments with the number of chapters in roman numerals.

8. f. 527v (addition s. xvi¹) Ad sciendum quo tempore sit legendum . . .

Sixteen verses on seasonal readings of the Bible.

9. Rear pastedown (addition s. xv) Table of the books of the Old Testament with note, "Tabula capitule incepta fuit 20 iulii sex, prohibet (*sic*)." Below, a table of multiples of seven written by a different hand.

Parchment unusually yellowed. ff. ii + 526 + ii. Modern foliation beginning on the first flyleaf, 1–527. 232 × 150 mm (157 × 99 mm). 1–29¹⁶, 30¹⁴, 31¹², 32–33¹⁶, 34⁴. Catchwords partially trimmed. Quires numbered by a modern hand in lower right corner on recto of first leaf. Ruled in pencil with separate column for a gloss. Prickings visible at top and bottom. Written in gothic textualis media in 46 lines in two columns; ff. 479–52 in three columns. Chapter headings in red in script of text. Text 5 written in *lettre bâtarde* media in 24 long lines. Headings in red and blue in rustic capitals and uncials. Chapter numbers in red and blue roman numerals in margins. Red initials with blue flourishes alternating with blue initials with red flourishes throughout.

Bound in gold-stamped French brown calf over pasteboard, c. 1680. Front pastedown formed from a palimpsest of a fragment of an unidentified text, s. xiii.

Written in France in the second half of the thirteenth century. f. 522v, inscription, s. xv; partially retraced in s. xvii or xviii "Ego Thomas Troteti presbyter ac baccalaureus in decretis et rector [illegible] nunc Fontinaci Comitis malleatensis diocesis emi presentem bibliam a magistro Iohanne Terrerii, baccalaureo in legibus genuenensis diocesis per medium Moysi de portas iudei et librarii de Auiniona precio xlv florini auri et hoc in Auiniona et in presentia dominorum Iacobi Rosseti et Guilelmi de Uiridario gronopolitanenis (?) et tarentasenis diocesis, Iohannis Clauelli clerici pictauensis diocesis et dicti iudei. Factum die xv mensis ianuarius anno a natiuitate domini mcccc xxi. [Signed] Thomas Troteti, manu propria." From the fifteenth to the eighteenth centuries, in the library of the Celestine convent of Avignon [Cottineau 1:229–30]. f. 1, lower margin, inscription, s. xv, in brown ink: "Fratrum celestinorum de Auinione" crossed out; below, a pressmark by another hand, s. xv or xvi, "Sig A. 26." f. 362, "Celestinorum Auiniones" by a different hand, s. xv² or xvi¹ in black ink. f. 522v, below the colophon, "Ista biblia *est fratrum celestinorum de Auinione,*" written by the same hand as f. 1, words in italics struck out. Above, a pressmark "A E 2°." f. 523, another ex libris, possibly of the Celestines of Avignon, struck out and now illegible. Recorded in the 1765 catalogue of the Celestine library as "4 A 112." *Catalogue général des départements,* series in 8°, vol. 27, p. xxix. f. 526, unidentified modern ex libris. Handwritten description of this codex written in French on blue square ruled paper in s. xix, tipped into the front flyleaf. ff. 1–12, embossed with a cross within a small circle, two or three times on each leaf. No. 6 from the collection of

Henry Probasco, acquired by the Newberry 1 December 1890.

Second folio: cogitacione conciperet.

De Ricci, 1:524.

– 17
(23813)
Latin Bible

France s. XIII²

1. ff. 1–381v Latin Bible in the usual order with the 64 prologues as in Ker, *Medieval Manuscripts* 1:96–97. Luke 1:1–4, treated as the first prologue to Luke.

f. 382–382v blank.

2. ff. 383–414v Aaz apprehendens . . . consiliatores eorum. Expliciunt interpretaciones hebraicorum nominum (in red).

Stegmüller, *Repertorium biblicum,* 7709.

3. f. 414v (addition, s. xiii²). Customary prefaces for the Mass for major feasts, unrubricated, ending imperfectly.

Parchment. ff. 414. Trimmed to 168 × 100 mm (116 × 74 mm). 1–23[16], 24[14], 25–26[16]. Quire no. 2 numbered "ii[us]" in lower margin center of the verso of the last leaf. Ruled in pencil. Written in gothic textualis media with pointed a and long terminal s in 50–53 lines in two columns. ff. 414v in a similar script by another hand. Headings of books in red in script of text. Running headings in upper margin in red and blue rustic capitals and uncials; chapters numbered in red and blue roman numerals. f. 1, gold Genesis initial (badly torn) decorated with blue and red 26 lines high extended to form an inner bracket border with leaf decoration. Each book begins with a large red and blue flourished initial. Minor red initials with blue flourishes alternating with blue initials with red flourishes throughout. Simple alternating red and blue initials within books written in verse. ff. 1–20, 178–186, and 205v–381v, red touches used for punctuation. Psalms numbered in roman numerals in outer margins, ff. 186v–205v.

Bound in English stamped brown morocco, c. 1870, by Robert Riviere.

Written in France in the second half of the thirteenth century. No. 4 from the collection of Henry Probasco, acquired by the Newberry 1 December 1890.

Second folio: -nores artes ueniam.

De Ricci, 1:523.

– 18
(23812)
Latin Bible

France s. XIII²

1. ff. 1–451v Latin Bible in the usual order with 55 of the 64 prologues as in Ker, *Medieval Manuscripts,* 1:96–97. Wanting: Stegmüller, *Repertorium biblicum,* 327, 343, 357, 468, 513, 526, 551, 589, and 590. Additions: 430, 506, 509, 514, 593, and 595; the third prologue to Obadiah (f. 331v), "Abdias quanto breuior . . . quibusdam urbis"; prologues 3–5 to Jonah (f. 332), "Nullus typi sui . . . incredulus perit," "Cum Ionas secundum interpretationem Christi et figuram Christi . . . in hac uerba precipit," "Sic ait Herodatus . . . subuersum fuisse"; both prologues to Micah (f. 333), "Sermo dei qui super ad prophetas descendit . . . apparentibus suum imposita," and "Sub Ozia ceperunt prophetare Ozee, Amos, Ysayas . . . primum de Samaria, secundo de Iherusalem"; second prologue to Nahum (f. 334v), "Cum Ionas et Naum de eadem Niniue . . . per chaldeos futuram pronunciauit." Psalms written on quires 14 and 15 (= ff. 200–222). Prefaces to the Mass for major feasts and *infra actiones* on f. 222–222v fill out end of quire 15.

2. ff. 452–459v Apocrypha. 4 Ezra written as three books, divided at the end of 4 Ezra 3 and 4 Ezra 14, followed by the *Oratio Manassae.*

Stegmüller, *Repertorium biblicum,* 93,2.

3. ff. 460–488v Incipiunt interpretationes hebraicorum nominum . . . (in red). (Begins imperfectly in the second line of the text) Aad testificans . . . consiliantes eorum.

Stegmüller, *Repertorium biblicum,* 7709.

4. f. 488v (addition s. xiv) Table of books of Old and New Testaments with numbers of chapters in arabic numerals.

5. ff. 489–490v (addition s. xv med.) Table of books of the Bible with numbers of chapters and indication of folio in arabic numerals. Titles underlined. f. 489, incipits given for seven nocturnal divisions of the liturgical psalter and for vespers.

Blue initials on magenta grounds alternating with magenta initials on blue grounds at beginnings of books, some decorated with flora and occasionally with dogs and animal-headed birds which form tails to initials. Some initials extended to form left borders; the Genesis initial on f. 4 reproduced by Branner, *Manuscript Painting in Paris,* fig. 151. Minor red initials with pale blue flourishes and pale blue initials with red flourishes at beginning of chapters. Alternating simple red and pale blue initials.

Parchment. ff. 490. Arabic foliation of s. xv by a contemporary hand to text 5, 1–490, two folios numbered 20 (the second by the same hand in roman numerals) and two folios 191; no folios 144 and 328. f. 22 follows f. 26, text not disordered but erasure of chapter numerals on f. 22–22v indicates that this was formerly bound out of order following f. 21. Trimmed to 150 × 105 mm (116 × 74 mm). 1–12^{16}, 13^{8}, 14^{16}, 15^{8} (8 wanting), 16–29^{16}, 30^{12}, 31^{16+1}, 32^{14} (a leaf wanting, binding too tight to specify), 33^{2}. Quires numbered in roman numerals 1–26 in lower margin center of the verso of the last leaf omitting the book of psalms and dictionary of names. Catchword visible on f. 351v. Modern arabic numbering of quires in lower left margin of the recto of the first leaf. Ruled in pencil. ff. 1–222 and 223–459v, written in gothic textualis media in 50 lines in two columns. f. 222–222v (prefaces of the Mass), written in gothic textualis formata in 50 lines in two columns. Text 3, written in gothic textualis media in 56 lines in three columns. Text 5, written in gothic cursiva media with unlooped d's in 32 long lines. Book headings in red in script of text. Running headings in upper margin in red and blue in rustic capitals and uncials. Chapter divisions in red and blue roman numerals.

Bound in brown morocco with gold-etched black mosaic strapwork incorporating the monogram of Henry Probasco, red morocco doublure by Hardy-Mennil; modern gilt edges, s. xix^{2}.

Written in France in the second half of the thirteenth century. Branner, *Manuscript Painting in Paris,* p. 213, attributes this manuscript to the Parisian atelier of Gautier Lebaube. ff. 320–322, possibly anglicana notes, s. xiv, partially trimmed. No. 3 from the collection of Henry Probasco, acquired by the Newberry 1 December 1890.

Second folio: eunucho nec.

De Ricci, 1:523.

–19
(324355)
Franciscan Bible

France c. 1250

1. ff. 1–535v Bible in the usual order with the 64 prologues as in Ker, *Medieval Manuscripts,* 1:96–97. Additions: 414, 430, 480, 504, 529, 530, 535, 540, 631, 812, 817, 822, 823, 824, 825, and second prologue to Micah (f. 369v), "Micheas secundum hebraicam ueritatem . . . libris apparentibus, sunt imposita."

2. ff. 536–579v Incipiunt interpretationes hebraicorum nominum . . . (in red). Aaz apprehendens . . . consiliatores eorum.

Stegmüller, *Repertorium biblicum,* 7709.

3. ff. 579v–582v Table of biblical lessons for the Proper of Saints in calendrical order followed by lessons for the Common of Saints with reference to book, chapter, alphabetical subdivision of chapter a–e, and incipit of verse. f. 581, Sancti Francisci patris nostri; f. 581v, Sancti Edmundi regis et martiris; f. 582v, Ad magistros et scolares.

4. ff. 583–584 3 Ezra of the Apocrypha titled "Esdre I^{us}."

5. ff. 584–585v Calendrical table of incipits for lessons for the Temporal of the Mass with additions of the fifteenth century on f. 585v.

17 blue initials on magenta grounds alternating with magenta initials on blue grounds, historiated miniatures in red, blue, orange, gray, white, and gold, 8–10 lines high frequently extended to form partial borders: f. 1, Jerome; f. 4v, the Creation in five panels, the Expulsion from the Garden, Christ seated, the Crucifixion between Mary and John the Evangelist with a Franciscan friar kneeling below, in all 47 lines high; f. 71v, Moses watching Aaron placing tablets in the Ark; f. 109, Elkanah and wives at the altar; f. 123, David ordering the execution of Amalekite; f. 161v, pedigree register; f. 205, Tobit and swallow; f. 209, Judith assassinating Holofernes; f. 220v, God observing Job on the dung heap and the Devil, reproduced by Branner, *Manuscript Painting in Paris,* fig. 316 and p. 18; f. 231, King David with his harp, reproduced by Branner, ibid., fig. 306; f. 258, Solomon instructing Rehoboam; f. 300, two men sawing Isaiah's head with a two-man saw; f. 387, Hosea and Gomer; f. 409v, beheading of an idolatrous Jew; f. 433v, the Tree of Jesse, 23 lines high; f. 480v, Paul bearing a sword; f. 510v, the Ascension. Many other initials of the same size and color decorated with dogs, centaurs, a merman, hybrid dragon monsters (some with human heads), birds with human heads, and other hybrids. These initials attributed by Branner, *Manuscript Painting in Paris,* p. 231, to the early Aurifaber atelier in Paris. Red and blue flourished initials frequently extended to form borders to the left of one or the other written columns.

Parchment. Rear pastedown parchment of southern preparation. ff. 585 + i. 139 × 93 mm (91 × 64 mm). $1–9^{24}$, 10^{14}, $11–19^{24}$, 20^{22}, 21^{26}, 22^{22}, 23^{22} (20–22 wanting), 24^{24}, 26^{26}. Catchwords mostly trimmed, but visible on ff. 24v, 254v, 278v, 374v, and 398v. Ruled in pencil. Special column prepared for gloss. ff. 580–582v, 3 columns prepared for points of reference. Written in gothic textualis media in 47 lines in two columns. Headings of books in red in script of text. Chapters numbered in roman numerals in red and blue. Running headings in upper margins in rustic capitals and uncials in red and blue. Red touches used as punctuation.

Bound in Italian or, more likely, in Spanish black calf, s. xv. Interior of panel decorated by two rope-motif stamps and small circular stamps, repeated numerous times. An inner panel in the center with ten double circular stamps in the interior. Same pattern front and back. Two fore-edge clasps wanting; rebacked, s. xix.

Written in Paris in the second half of the thirteenth century. Reference to Francis on f. 581 and to masters and scholars on f. 582 indicates that this Bible was made for Franciscan use. Note Clare not mentioned. A Franciscan provenance is confirmed by the rubric to the prologue of Psalms (f. 231, Stegmüller, *Repertorium biblicum,* 414), "Origo prophetie Dauid regis Ierusalem psalmorum numero cl lege in pace, frater karissime atque soror." Mention of King Edmund on f. 581v indicates a possible link to England or to friars of English origin; cf. Perdrizet, *Calendrier parisien,* p. 56. Rear pastedown, an inscription, possibly a partially erased shelf-mark. Acquired by the Newberry from Edward E. Ayer, December 1920.

Second folio: in lege.

De Ricci, 1:537.

20

(23866)

Peter Lombard, *Sententiae*

Southern France s. XIII med.

ff. 1–206v Cupientes (in blue) aliquid de peniuria ac tenuitate nostra cum paupercula . . . per media ad pedes usquę uia ducente peruenit. Amen.

Peter Lombard, *Liber sententiarum,* ed. I. Brady (Rome, 1971–81) and Jean Aleaume (Paris, 1535), reprinted *PL* 192:519–962. For other manuscripts and editions, see J. de Ghellinck, "Pierre Lombard," *DTC,* vol. 12, pt. 2, pp. 1971–74. Text accompanied by substantial glosses, portions rubricated, beginning, "Cupientes aliquid. Nota quod duplex prohemium . . ." This is not a continuous gloss and does not correspond to any text listed by Stegmüller, *Repertorium commentariorum.* It is written by at least three different thirteenth-century southern hands, supplemented by *distinctiones,* s. xiii, and by brief notes, s. xiii–xiv. Flyleaf contains a table of *distinctiones* with reference to the text by two southern hands, the smaller of which is quite possibly one of the hands of the gloss, e.g., "opiniones magistri sentenciarum non sustinentur a modernis. In primo libro quod numeralia non ponunt in diuinis, sed priuant, di. xxiiii; quod non est caritas creata, di xvii," etc. Questions broached include matters of heresy, e.g., "Uersus: Est heresis crimen quod nec confessio celat."

Four magenta initials on gold grounds 10 lines high historiated in magenta, blue, and white at the beginning of each book: Prologue (f. 1), Peter Lombard as bishop, teaching; Book I (f. 3), Ecclesia et synogoga; Book II (f. 59v), creation of Eve; Book III (f. 112v), the Nativity; Book IV (f. 153), Holy Communion. Iconography in the tradition of Paris and northern France; cf. Branner, *Manuscript Painting in Paris,* pp. 222–23, figs. 215 and 226; and L. Morel-Payen, *Les plus beaux manuscrits et les plus belles reliures de la bibliothèque de Troyes* (Troyes, 1935), plate 4, fig. 2. Brady, ed. cit., 1:131.

Parchment of southern preparation. ff. 206 + i. 210 × 157 mm (125 × 80 mm). Medieval roman numeral numbering of *distinctiones* partly visible in upper left and right. $1–2^{12}$, $3–19^{10}$, 20^{12}. Leaves signed a–e, a–d, and i–iiii in red and blue ink. First leaf after the midsection of the quire marked with a plus sign.

Ruled in pen. Written in southern gothic textualis media in 36–38 lines in two columns, beginning below the first ruled line. Incipits in red and blue gothic capitals. *Distinctiones* marked in red and blue roman numerals in outer margins, see J. de Ghellinck, "Pierre Lombard," *DTC,* vol. 12, pt. 2, pp. 1967–69.

Bound in modern red velvet over boards.

Written in southern France in the middle of the thirteenth century. In Italy in the fifteenth century. Verso of flyleaf, inscription written in an Italian humanistic cursiva: "Hęc linea bis sex ducta indicat mensuram domini nostri Iesu Christi, sumpta est autem Constantinopoli ex aurea cruce ad formam corporis Christi. Pro lv f." Cf. Leroquais, *Heures,* 1:170. A similar inscription is to be found in Cambrai, BM, 508 (s. xii), f. 1; see also MS 105, text 25. ff. 109v–110, notes by another Italian hand, showing humanistic influence. No. 41 in the collection of Henry Probasco, acquired by the Newberry 1 December 1890.

Second folio: An filius cum sit.

De Ricci, 1:529.

f21
(Ry 34; 12261)
Lancelot du Lac (in prose)

France c. 1300

ff. 1–354 En la marche de Gaule et de la petite Bretengne avoit .ii. rois anciennement qui avoient ii sereurs germiennes . . . mes atant se test ore li contes de lui et retorne a parler d'Agrauain son frere.

f. 354v blank.

Sections one and two of the prose Lancelot. Editions: A. Micha, *Lancelot: Roman en prose du XIIIe siècle* (Paris, 1978–83), vols. 7, 1, and 2; H. O. Sommer, *The Vulgate Version of the Arthurian Romances* (Washington, 1909–16), vol. 3, and vol. 4 to p. 362. Partial edition, G. Hutchings, *Le Roman en prose de Lancelot du Lac: le conte de la Charrette* (Paris, 1938). B. Woledge, *Bibliographie des romans et nouvelles en prose française antérieurs à 1500* (Geneva, 1954), no. 96; *Supplement 1954–73* (Geneva, 1975); this manuscript recorded on p. 53. For additional manuscripts, see A. Micha, "Les Manuscrits du *Lancelot en prose*," *Romania* 81 (1960): 145–87 and 84 (1963): 28–60, 478–99.

Three miniatures in the style of Paris, 11 lines high all on folios copied by the first hand. f. 1, the two kings and their sisters (severely damaged). f. 200, Galahad and a companion behind him in armor on horseback riding through trees on a gold background. f. 292, Méléagant's sister in a boat approaches Lancelot, watching from a tower. Alternate blue and red flourished initials throughout; those on ff. 49–127 frequently have penned representations of human faces and foliage. This manuscript noted by Branner, *Manuscript Painting in Paris*, p. 225.

Parchment. ff. 354. Modern paper flyleaves. Some folios repaired. Trimmed to 200 × 280 mm (211–25 × 148–50 mm). $1–15^8$, 16^8 (8 wanting), $17–30^8$, 31^6, $32–36^8$, 37^6, $38–43^8$, 44^{10}, 45^6. Quires numbered in upper left corner of first folio. Ruled in pencil. ff. 1–48 and 128–354, in 40 lines in two columns. ff. 49–126, in 34 lines in two columns. f. 127, irregularly ruled indicating that ff. 49–127 were written to fill in for folios lost from a preexisting manuscript. Prickings visible on inner margins of ff. 49–127 only. Written by two scribes: ff. 1–48 and 128–354, in an early gothic textualis media, irregular word separation; ff. 49–127, in a later and more angular gothic textualis with increased fusion. Guides to rubricator present in the earlier portion only.

Bound in red morocco for the duc de la Vallière (1708–80).

Written in France, probably in Paris, c. 1300, the segments ff. 1–48 and 128–354 perhaps somewhat earlier. f. 354, an ex libris, probably medieval, erased; f. 1, chain mark still visible. Formerly in the library of Anne de Graville, see A. Vernet, "Les Manuscrits de Claude d'Urfé (1501–1558) au château de la Bastie," *Académie des inscriptions et belles-lettres: comptes rendus*, 1976, p. 84, especially n. 20. f. 1, "A mademoiselle Anne de Graville de la succession de feu monseigneur l'amiral V^c XVIII." Partially retraced in s. xviii; cf. Delisle, *Le Cabinet des manuscrits* 2:381. Inherited by Claude d'Urfé = Catalogue of Amsterdam, no. 37. Vernet, op. cit., p. 95. f. 1, in an early modern cursive hand, "Chronique de Bretagne"; in the upper right margin, an eighteenth-century hand has written the number 27. In the library of La Vallière. "v4004" inscribed on rear flyleaf iv refers to entry in G. de Bure, *Catalogue des livres de la bibliothèque de feu M. le Duc de la Vallière, première partie* (Paris, 1783), p. 611. Old library shelf-mark "c. v. 29" on rear flyleaf iv. Purchased for 31 francs, 10 sous by Tilliard for Pierre-Antoine Bolongaro-Crevenna. The number 5136 on a rectangular label affixed to the front pastedown is the entry of this manuscript in the *Catalogue des livres de la bibliothèque de M. Pierre-Antoine Bolongaro-Crevenna*, vol. 3, part 2 (Amsterdam, 1789), pp. 90–91; the catalogue description includes the present binding. The same pastedown also bears the armorial bookplate of George Folliott. At his death, sold by Sotheby's 12 May 1930, lot no. 81. Purchased by Bernard Quaritch for 300 pounds and resold to the Newberry in 1939.

Second folio: -nit premierement de poincon.

Faye-Bond, pp. 150–51. E. Kennedy, *Lancelot do Lac: The Non-Cyclic Romance* (Oxford, 1980), 2:8. F. Sweetzer, "La Réincarnation de Lancelot dans la roman en prose," *Oeuvres et critiques* 2 (1980–81): 139. P. Saenger, "Un manuscrit de Claude d'Urfé retrouvé à la Newberry Library de Chicago," *Bibliothèque de l'École des Chartes* 139 (1981): 250–52.

21.1
(55-2568)
Alain de Lille, *Anticlaudianus*

England s. XII ex.

1. ff. 1–39 Incipit anticlaudianus Alani de Antiruffino (in red). Auctoris mendico stilum phalerasque poete . . . supplantare nouas, tandem post fata silebit. Explicit anticlaudianus Alani de Antiruffino (in red).

Alain de Lille, *Anticlaudianus* in an abbreviated recension; cf. R. Bossuat, *Anticlaudianus texte critique* (Paris, 1955), pp. 57–98. Portion of text omitted on f. 15 added with a tie mark on f. 12, a tipped-in leaf. Other omissions added in margins.

2. ff. 39v–40v Incipit prologus Alani de sequenti opere (in red). Hoc opus fastidire non audeant qui adhuc nutricium uagientes in cuius inferioris discipline lactantur . . . In hoc itaque opere agitur de iiii artificibus . . . et auctor operis exprimitur contradicitur Alani et opus auctoris contradicitur anticlaudiani. Auctoris mendico stilum et cetera (in red).

Summarium of the *Anticlaudianus* preceded by twelve lines not in the printed text, cf. ed. cit., pp. 199–201.

3. ff. 40v–42 Equorum descriptio quos monitu nature ratio presentauit (in red).

Primus equus cultu, forma cursuque sodales . . .
Firmior effetus illarum uota linguauit.
Predictos ratio et cetera qui subsequntur (*sic*).

f. 42v blank.

Anticlaudianus, IV, 95–213, a portion omitted from the abbreviated recension above.

Parchment. ff. 42. 207 × 122 mm (155 × 60 mm). 1^8, 2^9 (f. 12 tipped in), $3–4^8$, 5^9 (8 inserted). Quires 1, 2, and 4 numbered in roman numerals, visible on the lower margin verso of the last leaf. f. 12, smaller added leaf written on one side only.

Prickings visible in outer margins. Ruled in pencil. Written in proto-gothic textualis with caroline ct ligature and tyronian *et* symbol in 37 long lines, beginning on the first ruled line. All headings, including running marginal headings, in red in script of text. Initial letters on each verse form a separate column, balanced by a column of points and commas on the right. f. 1, blue and red flourished initial 6 lines high. Alternating red and blue initials with contrasting flourishes throughout.

Bound in parchment over paper boards, s. xix–xx.

Written in England in the last quarter of the twelfth century; note writing on the first ruled line; a and r in script are characteristically English; pencil note on modern flyleaf suggesting Winchester is without validity. In 1907, in the library of Lord Mostyn, Mostyn Hall, Cheshire, see De Ricci, *English Collectors,* pp. 180–181. f. 1, inscription "Mostyn no. 87" in lower margin. "MS 101" and "(126)" written in upper margin in ink by two other hands. Acquired by the Newberry from H. P. Kraus, 1955.

Second folio: Nomine censeri fas.

Faye-Bond, p. 151. H. Baron, *Newberry Library Bulletin* 4 (1958): 78. J. Leclercq, "Texts et manuscrits cistercien dans diverses bibliothèques," *Analecta sacri ordinis cisterciensis* 18 (1962): 121–34.

22
(23814)
Latin Bible

Spain c. 1300

1. ff. 1–281v Bible in the usual order except for Colossians which follows 2 Thessalonians, with 45 of the prologues as in Ker, *Medieval Manuscripts* 1:96–97. Many of the additions drawn from Isidore, *De ortu et obitu patrum* and *In libros veteris et novi testamenti proemia, CPL* 1191 and 1192. Wanting: Stegmüller, *Repertorium biblicum,* 327, 341, 343, 468, 491, 507, 510, 511, 512, 513, 521, 528, 543, 547, 553, 589, 685, 699, 839. Additions: 337, 350, 456, 481, 5199, 476, 5202, 5203, 495, 5204, 5206, 5207 (end varies from *PL* 83:144), 199, 5208, 5209, 5210, 5211, 5212, 5213, 5214, 5215, 5216, 5217, 5218, 545, 544, 670, 669, 664, 699, 636, 638, 834, 829, and first prologue to 1 Kings, "Incipit prologus Iheronymi presbyteri. Plenitudo noui ac ueteris testamenti . . . nullatenus sunt recipienda. Regum liber . . . urbem et templum," = the general prologue to Isidore, *Liber proemiorum, PL* 83:158–60 followed by Stegmüller, *Repertorium biblicum,* 5185; third prologue to Amos = Isidore, *De ortu et obitu patrum,* 81–82, *PL* 83: 144; second prologue to Obadiah = Isidore, *De ortu et obitu patrum,* 83, *PL* 83:144; third prologue to Jonah = Isidore, *De ortu et obitu patrum,* 84–85, *PL* 83:144–145; second prologue to Micah, "Item de ortu uel obitu eiusdem Micheas de Morastim . . . iudicis Israel" = Stegmüller, *Repertorium biblicum,* 525. Luke 1:1–4 used as second prologue to Luke; second prologue to Acts, "Petrus et Iohannes, Yacobo (*sic*) et Andreas . . . filius consolationis qui uendidit agrum," = Stegmüller, *Repertorium biblicum,* 636, first sentence only; second prologue to Apocalypse, "Hic est Iohannes euangelista unus ex discipulis domini . . . in principio canonis incoruptibile principium = Stegmüller, *Repertorium biblicum,* 624, halfway through.

Alphabetically keyed index notes ap, b, c, dg, e, etc., written in sequence in outer margin, s. xv. Occasional notes, s. xiv–xv, added by several hands.

f. 282 blank.

2. ff. 282v–305 Incipiunt interpretationes hebraicorum nominum secundum ordinem al-

phabeti (in red). Aac (*sic* without a cedilla) apprehendens uel apprehensio . . . (f. 283) aad testificans . . . consiliatores eorum.

Stegmüller, *Repertorium biblicum,* 7709.

3. f. 305v Prologus Ambrosii fratris genesi . . .

Tables of incipits of the chapters of the general prologue with references to folios, followed by a commentary.

f. 306 blank.

4. ff. 306v–308v Table of chapters for the Pentateuch. Ends: Hic sunt cccvi folia et iiia conscripta.

f. 309–309v blank.

Rear pastedown (addition s. xv), list of the generations from Adam to Noah.

Parchment of southern preparation. Only a fragment of the front pastedown remains. ff. i + 309 + i. 186 × 130 mm (130 × 84 mm). 1^{16} (1 wanting), $2–4^{16}$, 5^{18}, $6–13^{16}$, 14^{12}, $15–17^{16}$, 18^{16} (13 and 14 removed, 16 wanting), 19^{16}, 20^{14} (12–14 wanting). Ruled in pencil. Prickings visible in outer margins. Written in Spanish gothic textualis media with pointed a and trailing terminal s in 59 lines in two columns; ff. 283–305 in 63 lines in three columns. Ink of uneven color, light brown to black. Chapter headings in red in script of text. Guides to rubricator present. Two sets of running headings: above, in script of text in red and ink of text; below, in red and blue rustic capitals and uncials. Red initials with very bright blue flourishes alternating with dark blue initials with red flourishes up to 24 lines high. Free-floating pieces of red and dark blue feather-like and other decorative flourishing in margins.

Bound in Spanish red-brown morocco over boards, s. xv. Ruled panels decorated by an interlaced rope motif stamp, repeated numerous times; an eight-pointed star formed by two superimposed ruled squares in the center. Same pattern front and back. Two fore-edge clasps with latches decorated with a "c" and a lozenge with three horizontal bands, possibly a heraldic element. A fragment of a table of contents, s. xv, beginning with the general prologue remains on the verso of the front cover.

Written c. 1300, probably in Spain as suggested by the choice of prologues and presence of characteristically Spanish line endings in the script. Belonged to the Carthusian monastery of Paular in the fifteenth century [Cottineau 2:2231]. Rear pastedown, erased inscription visible under ultraviolet light, "Este libro es del monastiro (?) de Santa Maria al Paular." Above, a brief reckoning of generations, Adam to Noah. Below, numbers, possibly a shelf-mark, s. xv; "clxxx," written three times, followed by "69 xl." ff. 305v, 306, and 309–309v, sixteenth-century pen trials of Latin phrases and alphabets, erased on f. 305v. Some marginal notes erased. f. 281v, cross with three nails, drawn in pen probably dating from early modern period. No. 5 from the collection of Henry Probasco, acquired by the Newberry 1 December 1890.

Second folio: filio Nabath usque.

De Ricci, 1:523.

+22.1

(61-1745)

Peter of Poitiers,

Compendium Historiae in Genealogia Christi

Southern France s. XIII in.

Considerans sacre historie prolixitatem . . . [explicit effaced and illegible].

Cf. editions of U. Zwingli the Younger, *Genealogia et chronologia sanctorum patrum* . . . (Basel, 1592), and H. Vollmer, *Deutsche Bibelauszüge des Mittelalters zum Stammbaum Christi* (Potsdam, 1931), p. 127 sqq. See P. S. Moore, *The Works of Peter of Poitiers: Master in Theology and Chancellor of Paris (1193–1205)* (Publications in Medieval Studies, the University of Notre Dame, Notre Dame, 1936), pp. 101–6, for manuscripts and editions. Moore's list of manuscripts is supplemented by Stegmüller, *Repertorium biblicum,* 6778 sqq.; cf. Glorieux, 100f. This manuscript unrecorded.

Parchment roll of six sewn segments. 211 × 36 cm. Genealogical table drawn in black and red ink with double roundels, front portion filled with green; Romanesque arch motifs used for table, columns partially filled with green and red. Green ink has eaten into parchment; one circular portion of manuscript 160 mm in diameter missing with loss of a diagram. Written in gothic textualis with southern features.

Written in southern France in the early thirteenth century. Acquired by the Newberry from Bernard Rosenthal (cat. 12, item no. 33), in 1961.

+23

(Ry 30; J280)

Aristotle, *Physica, De Coelo et Mundo, Metaphysica, Parva Naturalia,* etc.

Germany or Austria s. XIV[1]

1. ff. 1–29 Quoniam (in red and blue) quidem intelligere et scire conuenit circa omnes . . . et nullam habens magnitudinem. Explicit liber phisicorum Aristotilis. Amen.

Aristotle, *Physica.* Old translation; see *AL* 1:52, no. 16; Grabmann, *Guglielmo di Moerbeke,* p. 90.

2. ff. 29v–47 De natura (in red and blue)

scientia fere plurima uidetur circa corpora . . . determinatum sit nobis hoc modo. Explicit liber Aristotilis de celo et mundo. Amen. Amen. Et cetera lator (*sic*). Amen. Explicit et cetera (in red).

Aristotle, *De coelo et mundo*. Translation attributed to William of Moerbeke; see *AL* 1:54, no. 19; Grabmann, *Guglielmo di Moerbeke*, pp. 91–92. *GW* 2337, 2340, and 2342. See also Cranz, *Bibliography of Aristotle Editions*. Partial list of manuscripts, Thorndike and Kibre, 382.

3. ff. 47v–58 De generatione (in red and blue) autem et corruptione et natura generatorum . . . (f. 57v) quale contingit non esse et cetera . . . (f. 58) Explicit, amen et cetera (in blue). Explicit liber Aristotilis de generatione et corruptione. Amen.

f. 57d, line 9 to end of folio blank; f. 58 begins with repetition of portion of text as it begins on f. 57, crossed out by the rubricator.

Aristotle, *De generatione et corruptione*. New translation; see *AL* 1:55, no. 22; Grabmann, *Guglielmo di Moerbeke*, p. 92. *GW* 2337 and 2387. See also Cranz, *Bibliography of Aristotle Editions*, p. 125. Partial list of manuscripts, Thorndike and Kibre, 374.

4. ff. 58–70v Bonorum (in red and blue) honorabilium notitiam opinantes . . . aut secundum . . . linguam autem habet ut significet aliquid alteri. Explicit de anima liber Aristotilis et cetera.

Aristotle, *De anima*. Translation revised by William of Moerbeke; see *AL* 1:58, no. 27; Grabmann, *Guglielmo di Moerbeke*, pp. 95–96. *GW* 2337, 2339, and 2349. See also Cranz, *Bibliography of Aristotle Editions*, p. 116. Partial list of manuscripts, Thorndike and Kibre, 179.

5. ff. 71–92 De primis (in red and blue) quidem igitur causis nature . . . plantam et alia talia. Explicit liber metheororum Aristotilis. Amen.

Aristotle, *Meteora*. New translation; see *AL* 1:57, no. 25. Partial list of manuscripts, Thorndike and Kibre, 385.

6. ff. 92–130. Omnes (in red and blue) homines natura scire desiderant. Signum autem est sensuum dilectio. Preter enim . . . agere debentes . . . encia uero non uolunt disponi male, nec bonum pluralitas principatum, unus ergo princeps. Expliciunt duodecim libri methaphisice Aristotilis.

Aristotle, *Metaphysica*. Translation of William of Moerbeke; see *AL* 1:65, no. 42; Grabmann, *Guglielmo di Moerbeke*, p. 98 sqq.; cf. *GW* 2419, etc. Cranz, *Bibliography of Aristotle Editions*, p. 129. Partial list of manuscripts, Thorndike and Kibre, 986.

7. ff. 130–135 In hoc tractatu intendimus perscrutari de rebus ex quibus componitur corpus celeste . . . hec questio est ualde bona. Explicit expliceat ludere scriptor eat (in red). Explicit libellus Auerroys de substantia orbis.

Averroes, *De substantia orbis*. *GW* 2336–39 and 2427. Cranz, *Bibliography of Aristotle Editions*, p. 183. Partial list of manuscripts, Thorndike and Kibre, 681.

8. ff. 135v–140v Omnis causa primaria plus est influens . . . sicut ostendimus. Explicit liber de causis causarum.

Ps. Aristotle, *Liber de causis* (composed of extracts of Proclus, *Elementa theologica*). Translated from the Arabic by Gerard of Cremona. See *AL* 1:94. Editions: A. C. Klebs, *Incunabula scientifica et medica* (*Osiris*, vol. 4; 1938), nos. 82.7 and 92.3; Cranz, *Bibliography of Aristotle Editions*, p. 120. Partial list of manuscripts, Thorndike and Kibre, 996.

9. ff. 140v–145v Quia paruus error in principio magnus est in fine . . . in quo est finis et consummatio sermonis. Explicit liber de ente et essentia fratris Thome de Aquino. Amen.

Thomas Aquinas, *De ente et essentia*. Grabmann, *Die Werke*, pp. 342–43. Editions: Mandonnet, *Opuscula Omnia*, 1:145–64; Perrier, *Opuscula omnia* (Paris, 1949), 1:24–50 (this manuscript recorded). For other manuscripts see also Thorndike and Kibre, 1227.

10. ff. 145v–150 Postquam premissus est a nobis sermo . . . cuius uolumus declarationem. Explicit liber de proprietatibus elementorum Aristotilis.

Ps. Aristotle, *De proprietatibus elementorum*. Translation from the Arabic by Gerard of Cremona. *AL* 1:91–92, no. 85. *GW* 2341.

11. ff. 150–155v Quoniam autem de anima secundum se determinatum est . . . de memoranda et reminisscentia (*sic*) et de sompno et de uigilia. Explicit liber de sensu et sensato Aristotilis.

Aristotle, *De sensu*. New translation; see Lacombe, "Medieval Latin Versions of the *Parva naturalia*," p. 302. *AL* 1:60, no. 33. For editions of the *Parva naturalia*, see *GW* 2425, etc. Cranz, *Bibliography of Aristotle Editions*, pp. 146–54. Partial list of manuscripts, Thorndike and Kibre, 1262.

12. ff. 155v–160 De sompno autem et de uigilia considerandum est quid sint . . . et utrum agenda ab homine . . . de diuinatione dictum est. Explicit liber de sompno et uigilia.

Aristotle, *De somno.* New translation; see Lacombe, "Medieval Latin Versions of the *Parva Naturalia,*" p. 303. *AL* 1:60, no. 35.

13. ff. 160–161v Reliquorum autem primum considerandum de memoria et memorari quid sit et propter quam causam causam (*sic*) sit . . . per quam causam dictum est. Explicit liber de memoria et reminiscentia Aristotilis.

Aristotle, *De memoria.* New translation; see Lacombe, "Medieval Latin Versions of the *Parva Naturalia,*" p. 301. *AL* 1:60, no. 34.

14. ff. 161v–163 Ab eo autem quod est hoc quidem longe uite animalium (?) autem breuis uitc ct de uite totaliter longitudine et breuitate considerandum autem causas . . . Hiis enim determinatis finem utique habebit que de animalibus methodus. Explicit liber de longitate et breuitate uite.

Aristotle, *De longitudine.* New translation; see Lacombe, "Medieval Latin Versions of the *Parva Naturalia,*" pp. 303–4. *AL* 1:60, no. 36.

15. ff. 163–164 De iuuentute et senectute et uita et morte . . . quo autem modo et qualiter dicendum sencientibus (*sic*) rationem magis. Explicit liber de iuuentute et senectute.

Aristotle, *De iuventute.* See Lacombe, "Medieval Latin Versions of the *Parva Naturalia,*" p. 305 sqq. *AL* 1:60, no. 37. Partial list of manuscripts, Thorndike and Kibre, 377.

16. ff. 164–165v De respiratione enim aliquid pauci phisicorum dixerunt . . . et tantas habent difficultates. Explicit liber de respiratione Aristotilis.

Aristotle, *De respiratione.* See Lacombe, "Medieval Latin Versions of the *Parva Naturalia,*" p. 305 sqq. *AL* 1:60, no. 37a.

17. ff. 165v–168 Quoniam autem dictum est prius quod uiuere . . . quia in speculationis (*sic*) fere de omnibus dictum est. Explicit liber Aristotilis de morte et uita. Amen.

Aristotle, *De morte.* New translation; see Lacombe, "Medieval Latin Versions of the *Parva Naturalia,*" p. 305 sqq. *AL* 1:60, no. 37b. Partial list of manuscripts, Thorndike and Kibre, 1263.

18. ff. 168–169v Habitum querit autem erit utique . . . quam uocamus kalok agiam (*sic*) et cetera. Explicit liber de bona fortuna Aristotilis. Amen.

Aristotle, *De bona fortuna* (= Book II of the *Magna moralia*). Translation of Bartholomew of Messina. See M. Grabmann, *Forschungen über die lateinischen Aristotelesübersetzungen des XIII. Jahrhunderts* (*BGPTM,* vol. 17, pts. 5–6; Münster, 1916), pp. 237–38. *AL* 1:72, no. 50.

19. ff. 169v–172 De motu autem eo qui est animalium . . . et communi motu diximus causas. Explicit liber de motu animalium.

Aristotle, *De motu animalium.* Translation of William of Moerbeke; see *AL* 1:82, no. 68; Grabmann, *Guglielmo di Moerbeke,* p. 125; *GW* 2340 and 2341; Cranz, *Bibliography of Aristotle Editions,* p. 118. Partial list of manuscripts, Thorndike and Kibre, 381.

20. ff. 172–173v Sicut scribitur a philosopho in de motibus animalium . . . in presenti disputatione relinquimus inquirendum. Quia omne quod mouetur . . . calefit et infrigidatur. Explicit liber de motu cordis. De motu (in red).

Thomas Aquinas, *De motu cordis.* Grabmann, *Die Werke,* pp. 347–48. Edition of prologue, G. Morin, "A Travers les Manuscrits de Bâle," *Basler Zeitschrift für Geschichte und Altertumskunde* 26 (1927): 216–17; edition of text, Mandonnet, *Opuscula omnia* 1:28–32; Perrier, *Opuscula omnia* 1:62 sqq. Partial list of manuscripts, Thorndike and Kibre, 1226.

21. ff. 173v–175 Cum in omni specie entis sit aliquod summum bonum possibile . . . gloriosus et sublimis, qui regnat in secula seculorum. Amen. Explicit Boecius de summo bono. Amen; Amen (in red).

Boethius de Dacia, *De summo bono,* ed. M. Grabmann, *AHDLM* 6 (1931): 297–307; rev. *Corpus philosophorum danicorum medii aevi,* vol. 6, pt. 2 (1976), xxiv–xlv and 369–91; this manuscript collated as codex C.

22. ff. 175–176 Unitas est qua unaquaque res una dicitur . . . est id quod est esse. Explicit de unitate et uno.

Ps. Boethius, *De unitate. PL* 63:1075–78; critical ed. P. Correns, *Die dem Boethius fälschlich zugeschriebene Abhandlung des Dominicus Gundisalvi De Unitate* (*BGPM,* vol. 1, pt. 1; Münster, 1891). Partial list of manuscripts, Thorndike and Kibre, 1601.

23. ff. 176–177 Ex pura terra lapis non fit quia continuationem non facit . . . accidunt res quedam extranee. Expliciunt mineralia Auicenne.

Avicenna, *De congelatione* or *De mineralibus* (translation of Alfredus Anglicus), ed. E. J. Holmyard and D. C. Mandeville, *Avicennae "De congelatione et conglutinatione lapidum," Being Selections of the "Kitab Al-Shifa"* (Paris, 1927). Partial list of manuscripts, Thorndike and Kibre, 1565.

24. ff. 177–180 Interrogasti me de differentia spirito (*sic*) et anime, honoret te deus . . . quia iam elongatum tempus est et cetera. Explicit liber de differentia spiritus et anime.

Costa Ben Luca, *De differentia spiritus et animae*. Anonymous translation; *AL* 1:94, no. 6. Partial list of manuscripts, Thorndike and Kibre, 771.

25. ff. 180–181 Dubium autem apud multos esse solet quomodo elementa sunt uel manent in mixto . . . nec ambo saluatur n. (*sic* for virtus) eorum. Explicit libellus de miscibilibus et mixtis et cetera.

Thomas Aquinas, *De mixtione elementorum*. Grabmann, *Die Werke*, p. 346. Mandonnet, *Opuscula omnia* 1:19–21. Perrier, *Opuscula omnia* 1:19–22; cf. Thorndike and Kibre, 189.

26. f. 181 Forma multiplex habet esse, quia primus per naturam . . . et hoc per prima et uera et notiora principia. Explicit tractatus de forma.

Grabmann, *Die Werke*, p. 208. Thorndike and Kibre, 567.

27. f. 181–182 Capitulum de diluuiis dictis in thimeo Platonis . . . putabantur a quibusdam fieri sine gingnitione (*sic*). Explicit capitulum de diluuiis. Amen.

ff. 182v–183v blank.

Avicenna, *Libellus de diluviis* (= last chapter of the *Metheora*), ed. M. Alonso, *Andalus* 14 (1949): 306–8. Partial list of manuscripts, Thorndike and Kibre, 188, 421, and 517.

Parchment. ff. 188. Modern foliation 1–183, unnumbered folios after ff. 7, 14, 32, 112, and 116. 331 × 252 mm (210 × 143 mm). $1–7^8$, 8^{10} (5 stub only), $9–22^8$, 23^{12} (12 wanting). Quires numbered I–XXII on lower margin of verso of last folio. Catchwords. First 10 leaves of last quire signed 1–10. Prickings visible in outer margins. Written in Northern European gothic textualis media in 40 lines in two columns. Headings in gothic textualis media formata by same hand as text in ink of text; at beginning of texts 1–6 initial word or words written alternately in red and blue. f. 1, flourished initial 8 lines high extended to form partial margins. Alternating blue and red flourished initials and paragraph marks throughout.

Bound in brown morocco, s. xviii.

Written in Germany or Austria in the first half of the fourteenth century. f. 1, in a seventeenth-century hand, "Monasterii Mellicensis L. 35 (or 31)." For other examples of this inscription, see *Lyell Catalogue*, pp. 179, 185, 190, and 200. Bears modern stamps, "Bibliothek zu Melk" and "Bibliothek des Stiftes Melk." Recorded in 1483 catalogue of Melk library as "F 1," *Mittelalterlicher Bibliothekskataloge Österreichs* 1:234, line 1. Formerly Melk no. 529 (J47). Recorded in the nineteenth-century manuscript catalogue of the Melk library, *Catalogus codicum manuscriptorum qui in bibliotheca monasterii Mellicensis O.S.B. asservantor,* reel II, 763. *AL* 2:266–67. Acquired by the Newberry from E. P. Goldschmidt, catalogue no. 47 (1938).

Second folio: uere est.

Faye-Bond, p. 150, no. 15. L. Battalon, "Aristoteles latinus: complements," *Bulletin de la société internationale de la philosophie médiévale* 1 (1959): 115. *AL* 2, *Supplementum,* pp. 48 and 54. H. F. Dondaine and H. V. Schooner, *Codices Manuscripti operum Thomae de Aquino,* vol. 1 (Rome, 1967), p. 224. M. T. d'Alverny, "Avicenna latinus IX," *AHDLM* 37 (1970): 327–31. McGinn, *Tradition of Aquinas and Bonaventure,* p. 6.

23.1

(54-819)

Aristotle, *Politica* and *Rhetorica*

Italy s. XIV²

1. ff. 67–104 Politicorum Aristotilis liber primus incipit rubrica (in red). Quoniam omnem ciuitatem . . . manifestum quod omnes . . . et quod decens. Explicit liber politicorum deo gracias.

Marginal index notes in a contemporary Italian hand, occasional extended comments, pointing hands.

Aristotle, *Politica*. Translation of William of Moerbeke; see *AL* 1:74–75, no. 54; ed. F. Susemihl, *Aristotilis politicorum libri octo cum translatione Guilelmi de Moerbeka* (Leipzig, 1872); cf. W. L. Newman, *The Politics of Aristotle* (Oxford, 1887–1902), 2:xliii–lxvii. Grabmann, *Guglielmo di Moerbeke*, pp. 111–13.

2. ff. 104v–129v Aristotilis Stagerite primus liber rethorice incipit rubrica (in red). Rethorica est conuertibilis dyaletice . . . (f. 113) Incipit liber secundus rethorice Aristotelis (in red). Ex quibus quidem oportet et exhortari et dehortari . . . Dixi, audite, habete, iudicate. Explicit rethorica Aristotilis.

Marginal notes as in text 1.

Aristotle, *Rhetorica*. Book I, old translation; Books II–III, translation of William of Moerbeke; see *AL* 1:77, nos. 58 and 59; Books II–III, ed. L. Spengel, *Aristotelis ars rhetorica*, vol. 1 (Leipzig, 1867), pp. 339–42. Grabmann, *Guglielmo di Moerbeke*, pp. 115–16.

f. 130–130v blank.

Parchment prepared in southern fashion. ff. 64. Old foliation 67–130. 366 × 245 mm (232 × 152 mm). Part of a larger codex. 1–5[12], 6[4]. Catchwords present on bottom right framed in four groups of three dots each. Leaves signed differently in each quire beginning a followed by a horizontal stroke; a second series of signatures particular to each quire visible on some leaves. Written in Italian gothic textualis media in 54 lines in two columns (see Examples of Selected Scripts). Headings by the same hand in orange-red. Running headings in upper and outer margins in orange-red and blue in semi-gothic textualis. Guides to rubricator present. ff. 69, 104, 113, and 122 (i.e., at the beginning of the *Politica* and of each book of the *Rhetorica*), illuminated acanthus-leaf initials in blue, gray, lilac, orange-red, and gold, 4–13 lines high. Alternating orange-red and blue minor initials and paragraph marks throughout.

Bound in modern limp parchment.

Written in Italy, possibly in Bologna as suggested by script and decoration, in the second half of the fourteenth century. Sparse contemporary marginal notes throughout. Acquired by the Newberry from the library of the Illinois Institute of Technology, 1954.

Second folio: principatum et politicum.

Faye-Bond, p. 151. *AL* 1:241.

24
(23817)
Noted Franciscan Breviary

Italy c. 1230/s. XIV

1. f. 1 (addition s. xiv) Benedictione perpetua . . . Unigenitus dei filius . . . Spiritus sancti gratia . . . Deus pater omnipotens . . . Christus perpetue . . . Ingnem sui amoris . . . Euangelica lectio . . . Cuius festum . . . Ad societatem ciuium . . . Ille nos benedicat . . . Diuinum auxilium . . . Per euangelica dicta . . . Uerba sancti euangelii . . . Benedictions for the lessons of the Divine Office, *SMRL* 2:340.

1 bis. f. 1 in upper margin, a very brief excerpt from Martin, Bishop of Braga, *Formulae vitae honestae,* s. xiii, Si prudens esse cupis in futurum prospectum intende . . . Hec Bernardus de quatuor uirtutibus; ed. Barlow, *Opera omnia,* p. 239.

2. f. 1v (addition s. xiii) Infrascripte indulgentie date sunt a diuersis summis pontificibus in locis fratrum minorum . . . Obituary notes and a recipe added by later hands, c. 1300.

3. f. 2 (addition s. xiii) Hec sunt festa que secundum decretales et decreta debent obseruari . . . Et illa festa que singuli episcopi in suis episcopatibus cum clero et populo collaudauerint celebranda, sicut Perusii festum sancti Erculani et Constantii.

4. f. 2 (additions s. xiii) Nota quod secundum Augustinum est uisio triplex quarum quelibet dicitur celum scilicet corporalis, ymaginaria et intellecualis . . . tertio modo Paulus. Unidentified extract of scholastic distinctions.

5. f. 2–2v (addition s. xiii[2]) Mclxxxxiiii foro scarepate (?) le rocche da Sese [= Assisi] . . . A brief chronicle of Perugia in Italian and Latin with entries by at least two hands; last entry 1289, records entry of Friar Bartholus Blancellus to the order of friars (autograph).

6. f. 2v (addition after 1266) Viii° kalendas ianuarii luna. Anno Cesaris Augusti quadragesimo secundo, ebdomada iuxta Danielis prophetiam sexagesima sexta olympiade autem centesima et nonagesima tertia, sextam mundi etatem, suo piissimo consecrans aduentu Ihesus Christus filius dei uiui in Bethleem nascitur, hic subsiste et genuflecte. Eodem die natale sancte Anastasie . . . Et alibi aliorum plurimorum sanctorum martirum confessorum atque uirginum. Martyrology entry for Christmas Eve in accordance with the statutes of the chapter of Paris (1266); cf. *SMRL* 2:439. See Van Dijk, "Some Manuscripts," p. 62, n. 6a.

7. f. 3 (addition s. xiii[2]) Gaude uirgo prophetata patriarchis figurata supernali radio . . . Ten joys of the Virgin, version unrecorded *RH*. Incipit of this text also written on f. 257v by the same hand.

f. 3v blank.

8. ff. 4–29v Liturgical Psalter. This section without musical notation. Numerous marginal corrections, s. xiii ex.–xiv.

9. ff. 29v–30v Daily canticles, Te Deum, Pater noster. Credo in deum, patrem omnipotentem, creatorem celi et terre . . . , Gloria in excelsis deo . . . , Credo in unum deum, patrem omnipotentem, factorem celi et terre . . . , Quicumque uult saluus esse . . . Leroquais, *Psautiers* 1:lv.

10. ff. 30v–31v Haymonian litany and collects, ed. Van Dijk, *Origins,* pp. 520–23. f. 30v, Erculanus and Constantius added in lower margin.

11. ff. 31v–33v Calendar of the Roman court, c. 1230, all entries in black ink; ed. Van Dijk, *Ordinal,* pp. 33–57. Among the additional feasts added by various hands are: Apud Spoletum sancti Pontiani martiris (21 January), Fulginei sancti Feliciani episcopi et martiris (24 January), Sancti Constantii episcopi et martiris (29 January), Translatio corporis sancti Erculani episcopi et martiris (1 March), Decollatio sancti Erculani episcopi et martiris (7 November). Other corrections make calendar conform to Franciscan calendars of c. 1260. f. 33v, note on the difference between Jewish and Gentile reckoning of days, s. xiv.

12. ff. 34–164 [I]n nomine domini. Incipit ordo breuiarii fratrum minorum secundum consuetudinem romane curie . . . (in red). Proper of Time, in part corrected to agree with Haymo of Faversham's *Ordo breviarii;* cf. Van Dijk, *Ordinal,* p. 90 sqq.; *SMRL* 2:17–114. f. 87, in pre-Haymonian Lenten litany, names of Dominic and Catherine written over erased entries.

13. f. 164 In omnibus festiuitatibus que in sabbatis . . . et tertio nonas eiusdem mensis (entirely in red). General rubric of the breviary, before 1227, partly erased and corrected to agree with Haymo of Faversham's *Ordo breviarii;* cf. Van Dijk, *Ordinal,* pp. 352–54; *SMRL* 2:114–21.

14. ff. 164–215v Incipiunt festiuitates sanctorum per totum annum. In festo sancti Saturnini . . . (in red). Proper of Saints, Saturninus through Francis. Ends with nine lessons for the feast of Francis drawn from Thomas of Celano's *Legenda choralis,* ed. *Analecta franciscana* 10 (1944): 118–26; cf. *SMRL* 2:120–67. Text accompanied by numerous marginal corrections, s. xiii ex.–xiv. See Van Dijk, "Some Manuscripts," pp. 63–64.

15. f. 216–216v (addition s. xiv) In festo sancte Helisabet . . . (in red). Office taken from the *Commune sanctorum,* cf. *SMRL* 2:183. Nine proper lessons for Elizabeth from an unidentified source. First lesson begins: Beata Helysabet tam progenie quam moribus nobilissima. . . . See Van Dijk, "Some Manuscripts," p. 64.

16. ff. 216v–217 (addition s. xiv) In sancte Caterine uirginis et martiris oratio (in red). Collect and nine lessons for the feast of Catherine of Alexandria, cf. *SMRL* 2:173. Lessons drawn from James of Voragine, *Legenda aurea,* ed. J. G. T. Graesse (Dresden, 1846), pp. 789–92. See Van Dijk, *Origins,* pp. 387–89, and "Some Manuscripts," p. 64.

17. ff. 217–218v (addition s. xiv) In festo sancte Clare uirginis . . . (in red). Rhythmical office and nine lessons for Clare = Besançon, BM, 58, ff. 562 and 605v. Lessons drawn from "Tres legendae minores sanctae Clarae assisiensis s. xiii," ed. M. Bihl, *Archivum franciscanum historicum* 7 (1914): 39 sqq. See Van Dijk, *Origins,* pp. 387–89, and "Some Manuscripts," pp. 64, 260, and 262.

18. ff. 218v–219v (addition s. xiv) In festo niuis sancte Marie . . . (in red), cf. Besançon, BM, 58, f. 604; Van Dijk, "Some Manuscripts," pp. 64 and 262, n. 104. Lessons from *Flor. cas.* 1:254.

19. ff. 219v–226v (addition s. xiv) Franciscus primus dictus est Iohannes . . . omnis sit laus honor et gloria in secula seculorum. Amen. Explicit. = Bonaventure, *Legenda minor, BHL* 3110, ed. *Analecta franciscana* 10 (1944): 653–58. Division of lessons, content notes, and corrections noted in outer margins.

20. ff.226v–227v (addition s. xiv) In festo translationis (in margin). [F]ranciscus igitur seruus et amicus . . . mirificans sanctum suum magnificentia uirtutis altissimi, cui est honor et gloria per infinita secula seculorum. Amen. Finis. = Bonaventure, *Legenda maior,* ch. 15, ed. *Analecta franciscana* 10 (1944): 623–26. *BHL* 3107. Division of lessons written in margin.

21. ff. 228–236 In festo sanctorum martirum Sergi et Bachi . . . Proper of Saints, conclusion.

22. ff. 236–249v Common of Saints.

23. ff. 249v–250 [I]ncipit officium beate Marie uirginis secundum consuetudinem romane curie . . . (in red).

24. f. 250 Duplex officium agitur in natiuitate domini . . . et basilicarum Petri et Pauli (entirely in red). Pre-Haymonian list of double feasts; Van Dijk, *Ordinal,* p. 475.

25. ff. 250–251v Regem cui omnia uiunt . . . Pre-Haymonian Office of the Dead; cf. Van Dijk, *Ordinal,* p. 476.

26. ff. 251v–252 Ordo minorum secundum consuetudinem romane ecclesie ad uisitandum infirmum . . . (in red).

27. f. 252 Ordo ad communicandum infirmum . . . (in red).

28. ff. 252–253v Ordo commendationis anime . . . (in red). Pre-Haymonian ritual = Assisi Bibl. Com. 611, f. 305v sqq.; Besançon, BM, 58, f. 554 sqq. Vat. lat. reg. 1742, f. 186v. See Van Dijk, "Some Manuscripts," p. 65.

29. ff. 253v–256v Ten different settings for Psalm 94, Uenite exultemus . . .

30. ff. 257 (addition s. xiii) Notes for or extracts from a biblical concordance.

31. f. 257v (addition s. xiii) Isti sunt modi dilatandi sermones qui sunt viii. Primus modus, ponendo . . . contemplatiua et actiua, fides et spes. Extensive marginal commentary.

32. f. 258 (addition s. xiv) Aue uerum corpus natum de Maria uirgine . . . *RH* 2175, Salutation to the Virgin for two voices, edited with transcription of the music, Van Dijk and Walker, *Myth of the Aumbry,* pp. 90–96; A. Hughes, "New Italian and English Sources of the Fourteenth to Sixteenth Centuries," *Acta musicologia* 39 (1967): 175–78 and plate following p. 182.

33. f. 258v (addition s. xiv) In festo beati Antonii . . . The three hymns for the Office of the Feast of Anthony of Padua, *SMRL* 2:142–43; *RH* 5408, 10530, and 9561. See below, ff. 264v–265.

34. f. 259 (addition s. xiv) Reminiscens beati sanguinis quem profudit amator hominis profundo lacrimas . . . *RH* 17302.

35. f. 259 (addition s. xiv) Aue uiuens hostia ueritas et uita in quo sacrificia . . . John Peckham, *De corpore Christi,* verses 1–4. Van Dijk and Walker, *Myth of the Aumbrey,* p. 67, n. 5; C. T. Martin, *Registrum epistolarum fratris Johannis Peckham* (Rolls Series, 77; London, 1882–85), 3:cxiv sqq.

35 bis. (addition s. xiv) Prosa in resurrectione domini. Qui se ipsum immolauit pro delictis omnium . . . ut perducat et inducat ad suam celi gloriam. Amen.

36. ff. 259v–260 (addition s. xiv) De sermone sancti Augustini in festo natiuitatis domine (in margin). Denique post illius benedicibilis presagium . . . sit tibi assidue exorare pro populo dei que meruisti benedicta pretium offerre mundi, qui uiuit et regnat in secula seculorum. Amen. A cento beginning in Ps. Augustine, *Sermo 120,* 6, and including material from Ps. Augustine, *Sermo 119;* cf. *PL* 39: 1983–84 and 1986.

37. f. 260 (addition s. xiv) De officio misse (in margin). Nota quod beatus Iacobus frater domini et Basilius cesariensis uidentur tradidisse ordinem dicendi missam . . . sine stola et manipulo di. 21 ecclesiastica. Short note on the Mass, based on the Decretals.

38. ff. 260v–264 (addition s. xiv) Incipit officium sacratissimi corporis Ihesu Christi (in margin). Sacerdos in eternum . . . (f. 261) Lectio I. Immensa diuine largitatis beneficia . . . (f. 263) Infra ebdomadam de sermone Ambrosii de sanctitate [et] de consecratione. Huius sacramenti figura precessit . . . Office of Corpus Christi established by the General Chapter of Marseille (1319) as modified by the General Chapter of Cahors (1338) cited in note in lower margin, f. 260v, reproduced in Van Dijk, "Some Manuscripts," p. 67. Many marginal additions.

39. ff. 264v–265 (addition s. xiv) In festo beati Antonii . . . Office for the Feast of Anthony of Padua as established by the General Chapter of Toulouse, 1307; *SMRL* 2:284 and 451. Van Dijk, *Origins,* pp. 382–85.

40. ff. 265v–266 (addition s. xiv) Tabula aduentus (in red in margin). In anno illo in quo natiuitas domini uenerit in dominica . . . Explicit tabula. *Parisian Table of Anthems before Christmas, SMRL* 2:399–408.

41. f. 266v (addition s. xiv) Legenda beati Ludouici episcopi (in margin). Iohannes episcopus . . . (ends imperfectly at the end of the leaf) deseruit totaliter et contempsit. Nam // Bull of canonization of Louis, Bishop of Toulouse, divided by marginal index notes into lessons.

42. f. 266v (addition s. xiv in lower margin) Totius uite ipsius beati Ludouici decursus fuit . . . Anno incarnationis dominice m° ccc° xvi° septimo idus aprilis papa Johannes XXII[us] . . . sanctorum cathalogo cum maximis sollempniis in ciuitate Auinionis ubi tunc romana curia residebat, ascribi fecit. Martyrology entry for Louis of Toulouse.

Parchment of Italian preparation. ff. 266. Modern foliation 1–265: ff. 260–265, every leaf, elsewhere every fifth leaf. Error in foliation: f. 175 should be f. 176, all subsequent foliation deficient by one. 197 × 140 mm (135 × 100 mm, quire 27: 143 × 96 mm). 1^{4} (1 wanting), 2^{12}, 3^{6}, 4^{12}, $5–6^{10}$, 7^{12}, $8–22^{10}$, 23^{12}, $24–26^{10}$, 27^{10} (10 wanting with loss of text). Catchwords occasionally enclosed in rectangles present for the original book only beginning with quire 5. Quires 2–4, prickings visible in outer margins; quires 5–22 and 24–26, prickings visible in lower margins. Ruled in pencil. Written in Italian gothic textualis media by at least two hands, beginning below the first ruled line. Script characterized by a trailing terminal s. Psalter written in 47 lines in two columns. Remainder of the original book in 63 lines in two columns, some portions in very black Italian ink. Additions in quire 23 in Italian gothic textualis media with one-story a, long s slightly below the line in 48 lines. Quire 27 written in a similar script characterized by regular use of long terminal s, in 37 lines in two columns. Headings in red in scripts of text. Quires 5–22 and 26 have alternating red and blue initials with an occasional black initial. Capitals touched in red. Quires 2–4 and 23 have red and blue flourished and alternating minor red and blue simple initials. Quire 27 has red initials only with black paragraph marks.

Bound in geometrically ruled olive morocco binding, Italian, possibly Venetian, c. 1700.

Written in Italy before or about 1230; inclusion of Dominic (canonized 1232) on f. 86v is a correction. Quires 2–4 written c. 1260. In Franciscan convent of Perugia in s. xiii². Quire 1 added at this time with texts and notes written by Friar Bartholus Blancellus on ff. 1v–2v; additions to litany and calendar of Perugian saints. Quires 23 and 26 added in s. xiv. f. 257v, an erased ex libris illegible under ultraviolet light. f. 226v, an erased number (s. xvi?), possibly a shelf-mark. No. 8 in the collection of Henry Probasco, acquired by the Newberry December 1890.

Second folio: eius omnium.

De Ricci, 1:524. Hughes, *Mass and Office,* p. 402.

24.1
(53-1025)
Rolandino Passageri, *Summa Artis Notariae; Tractatus Notularum*

Verona [*Illustrated*] 1294

1. ff. 2–71
Ihesus sacri uentris fructus
Pie matris prece ductus
Sit uia dux et conductus
Liber in hoc opere. Amen.

Antiquis temporibus super contractuum et instrumentorum formas . . . In nomine domini, amen; Anno eiusdem millesimo duccentesimo quinquagesimo quinto indictione terciadecima, die sextodecimo intrante decembri . . . (in red). Antonius filius quondam Boetii . . . bonorum omnium tributatur auctori, cui laus et gratiarum actio, honor, et gloria in secula secullorum. Amen.

Explicit liber summe deo gratias. Amen.
Finito libro refferamus gratiam Christo
Qui scripxit scribat simpliciter cum
domino uiuat
Uiuat in celis Tomaxinus homo fidelis
Scriptor sum talis mea monstrat littera
qualis (in red).

Rolandino Passageri, *Summa artis notariae.* Hain, 1848–55 and 12084–93. Copinger, 4535–36. Editions and manuscripts, see F. K. von Savigny, *Geschichte des Römischen Rechts im Mittelalter,* vol. 5 (Heidelberg, 1850), pp. 543–44; R. Stintzing, *Geschichte der populären Literatur des Römisch-Kanonischen Rechts in Deutschland* (Leipzig, 1867), pp. 296–99; *Catalogue général des départements,* vol. 37, pt. 1, pp. 527–28. See also H. Bresslau, *Handbuch der Urkundenlehre für Deutschland und Italien* (Berlin, 1912–31), 2:255–56; Naz, *Dictionnaire de droit canonique* 4:1251–53; Walther, *Initia,* 9856; *RH* 28690. The date of composition given in the rubric agrees with that in Tours 662 (s. xiv).

2. ff. 71v–83v Incipit tractatus de notulis (in red). Tractaturi de arte notarie. Primo uidamus (*sic*) quid sit notaria . . . nichil plus quam dictum est in summa requiras. Expletus liber iste die mercurii xxiiii, intrante nouembre Uerone, in domibus ecclesie sancti Marchi ad carcerem Uerone, anno domini millesimo duccentesimo nonagesimo quarto indictione septima. Scriptor sum talis mea mea (*sic*) monstrat littera qualis (in red).

Rolandino Passageri, *Tractatus notularum.* This text follows the *Summa artis notarie* in most editions and in some manuscripts, e.g., Tours, BM, 660 (s. xiv), 661 (s. xiv), and 662; Paris, BN, lat. 4592.

Front flyleaf is a fragment of an unidentified grammatical text, Italy s. xiv, with red and blue alternating initials.

Parchment prepared in southern fashion. ff. i + 82. Modern foliation includes flyleaf. Trimmed to 245 × 179 mm (186–92 × 125–39 mm). $1–9^{8}$, 10^{10}. Quires 2–5, catchwords within rectangles and quires numbered *primus, secundus,* etc., within similar rectangles to the left of the catchwords; quire 3, rectangle in red. Ruled in pencil. Prickings visible in outer margins. Written in Italian gothic textualis media with one-story often pointed a in 31 long lines. Headings in similar but larger script. Headings and colophons in red in script of text. f. 1, red and blue flourished initial 8 lines high extended to form border in upper margin. Alternating minor red and blue initials with contrasting flourishes. Alternating red and blue paragraph marks. Notes and nota marks with pointing hands, s. xiv in Italian gothic cursiva. Running indication of chapters in arabic and roman numerals visible on the rectos and versos of some leaves, s. xiv. Remnants of a wax drop seal on flyleaf.

Bound in heavy wooden boards on three bands with remains of two fore-edge clasps and four of five bosses, restored to half leather; rear board replaced. Chain mark on bottom center margin on final folios.

Written in the Augustinian priory of San Marco, Verona [Cottineau, 2:3344] in 1294 by Tomaxinus, see f. 83v. Recorded *Colophons de manuscrits occidentaux,* 17818. f. 83, lower margin, a later note: "Et ego Antonius quondam magistri Andree Fabri habitator quadruuii publica imperiali auctoritate notarius et iudex ordinarius suprascriptis omnibus et singulis presens fui et ea rogatus fideliter scripsi et publicaui," cf. transcription note of s. xviii attached to verso of front cover. f. 83v, "Ista summa est Iacobi de Rudubrio(?)," visible only under ultraviolet light, traces of four heraldic devices and a notarial seal; many notes by various hands greatly effaced, one dated 1420; another is a Hebrew inscription, possibly recording the use of this book as collateral for a loan. Old number 21 written on front flyleaf. Acquired by the Newberry from Nichola Rauch (Geneva), catalogue new series, no. 3 (March 2–4, 1953), lot no. 10.

Second folio: per se et.

Faye-Bond, p. 152.

24.5
(69-109)
Simon de Lenis, *Commentarii in Secundum Sententiarum Petri Lombardi*

Italy s. XIV[1]

ff. 1–114v Creationem rerum insinuans scriptura hic queruntur 3. Primum est de rerum principio . . . ad rationem obedientie ipsius exequentis ipsius exequentis (*sic*). Explicit.

ff. 114v–116v, table of distinctions. Ends on f. 116v, "Explicit tabula per fratrem Hugonem de Brunforte facta, Amen." Occasional marginal notes in lead (by the same hand that provided the guides to the rubricator).

Glorieux, 331a. Stegmüller, *Rep. in sent. Petr. Lomb.,* 817; one manuscript, Todi 120, recorded; this manuscript unrecorded. On Simon de Lenis, see P. Glorieux, "Notices sur quelques théologiens de Paris de la fin du XIIIe siècle," *AHDLM* 3 (1928): 229–31.

Pastedowns, s. xv ex.–xvi form a continuous fragment from matins of the Office of the Dead, as in a Roman breviary; cf. *SMRL* 2:192–93. Note, at the foot of the front pastedown, "Require residuum a parte posteriori in fine libri."

Parchment of Italian preparation. ff. 116. 231 × 160 mm (167 × 118 mm). $1–9^{12}$, 10^{8}. A medieval front flyleaf cut out with damage to f.1. Catchwords in orange rectangular frames. Traces of lead leaf signatures. Ruling not visible. Written in Italian gothic textualis media in 43 lines in two columns. *Distinctiones* marked in red and blue in upper margins. Guides for the rubricator present in lead. f. 1, red and blue flourished initial 4 lines high. Red and blue alternating initials with contrasting flourishes throughout. Alternating red and blue paragraph marks. Marginal corrections within orange rectangles.

Bound in pink geometrically ruled leather, s. xv. Two cloth fore-edge clasps wanting. Cover bears modern title: "Questiones theologice" and pressmark "H 21."

Written in Italy in the first half of the fourteenth century. f. 114v, partially erased ex libris "Hic liber est conuentus concessus ad usum fratris sancti [illegible] ordinis. H[?][?]." Rear pastedown, "Manoscritto autografo dell'Utimo comprato da me Georgio Garisi il 5 gennaio 1882 per lire 800." Acquired by the Newberry from Hamill and Barker (Chicago), 1968.

Second folio: Si facta aut.

25
(Ry 198; 45-340)
Libellus Multorum Naturalium

Italy s. XV[1]

ff 1–12 Libellus multorum naturalium et rerum probatarum ualde bonum (*sic*) et utilissimum (*sic*) et primo ad faciendum aquam in finissimo colorre (*sic*) azuri tinta (in red). Recipe salis armoniaci, calcine albe partes equales . . . comedat de dicto medicamine quantum est nux et continuando hoc diebus xxxv liberabitur.

"Ihesus" written in red in the upper margin of f.1 by the scribe.

f. 12v blank.

A book of 89 recipes including instructions on how to prepare inks, glue, erasure fluid, and other materials pertaining to book-making. Edited with plates of f. 2v and f. 4, D. Bommarito, "Il ms. 25 della Newberry Library: la tradizione dei ricetti e trattati sui colori nel Medioevo e Rinascimento veneto e toscano," *La Bibliofilia* 87 (1985): 1–38.

Paper with *monts* watermark; cf. Briquet 11666 sqq. ff. 12. 220 × 140 mm (145 × 70 mm). One quire of 6 bifolia. Frame ruled in pencil with two upper lines. Written in Italian mercantesca formata with occasional long terminal s in 30–32 long lines beginning on the second upper ruled line.

Bound in parchment over paper boards, s. xix.

Written in northeast Italy, probably in the Veneto as indicated by the dialect of the Latin text, in the first half of the fifteenth century. Acquired by the Newberry from H. P. Kraus, 1945.

Second folio: usque sed.

26
(23815)
Franciscan Breviary

Italy s. XIV med.

1. ff. 1–80v Liturgical psalter followed by the Te deum, Gloria in excelsis deo . . . , Pater noster, Credo in deum patrem omnipotentem creatorem celi et terre . . . , Credo in unum deum patrem omnipotentem factorem celi et terre . . . Quicumque uult saluus esse . . . Cf. Leroquais, *Psautiers,* 1:1v.

2. ff. 80v–83 Litany followed by six prayers: Deus cui proprium est misereri . . . , Omnipotens sempiterne deus qui facis mirabilia . . . , Pretende domina tua . . . , Actiones nostras quos de aspirande . . . , Omnipotens sempiterne deus, misereris famulis et famulabus tuis . . . , Ure igne sancti spiritus . . .

3. ff. 83v–100v Hymnal. f. 99, In festo beati Francisci.

4. ff. 101–316 Incipit breuiarium ordinis fratrum minorum secundum consuetudinem Romane ecclesie. In primo sabbato de auento (*sic*) . . . (in red). Proper of Time.

5. ff. 316–319 Aduentus domini celebratur . . . (entirely in red). *Rubricae generales,* ed. *SMRL* 2:114–21.

6. ff. 319–321v In anno illo in quo natiuitas domini in dominica uenerit secundum subsequentem tabulam procedatur (in red). *Parisian Table of Anthems before Christmas,* ed. *SMRL* 2:401–8.

7. ff. 322–445v Proper of Saints beginning imperfectly in feast of Andrew, ending in feast of Catherine. f. 362, In translatione sancti Francisci (in red); f. 426, Octave of Francis. Fourteenth-century Franciscan feasts not included.

8. ff. 445v–468 Incipit commune sanctorum (in red).

9. ff. 468–471 In dedicatione uel in aniuersario dedicationis ecclesie (in red).

10. ff. 471–476v Incipit ordo officii beate uirginis (in red).

11. ff. 476v–477v Ordo ad communicandum infirmum (in red).

12. ff. 477v–479v Ordo ad ungendum infirmum (*sic,* in red).

13. ff. 479v–490 Ordo commendationis anime (in red).

14. f. 490–490v Incipit officium in agenda defunctorum (in red).

15. ff. 490v–493 Incipit ordo ad benedicendam mensam per totum annum (in red).

16. f. 493–493v In anno in quo kalende septembris uenerint die dominico ystorie dicti mensis sic ordinantur. Dominica prima mensis septembris ponitur liber Job . . . (entirely in red). *Parisian Table for the Scripture Reading of September,* often attributed to Boniface VIII, *SMRL* 1:168, 181, 240, and 242–44. Van Dijk, *Ordinal,* pp. 342–46.

17. f. 494 Petrus apostolus Ihesu Christi electis aduenis dispersionis Ponti, Galatie, Capadotie, Asie et Bitinie secundum prescientiam . . . Benedictus deus et pater domini nostri Ihesu Christi. Amen. 1 Petr 1:1–3, epistle for the feast of the Chair of Peter, *SMRL* 2:277.

18. f. 494–494v Quando natale dei uenerit die lune secundum istam rubricam procedatur die Ueneris festum sancti Thome episcopi et martiris . . . per horas [illegible] sicut in natiuitate (text in red, cues in black). . . . Unrecorded *SMRL.*

Eighteen historiated initials (2–5 lines high) in pink and gold on blue grounds with heads and busts only of human figures. f. 1, Jesus blessing King David; f. 11, King David pointing to his head; f. 18, King David covering his mouth; f. 25, head of a male figure (Dixit insipiens); f. 32, King David on the waters; f. 40v, King David ringing bells; f. 48, friars (in gray with nimbi) singing; f. 56v, Christ; f. 83v, a bishop; f. 101, a male head; f. 176, Paul; f. 242v, Three Marys at the tomb; f. 265v, Ascension; f. 271v, Descent of the Holy Spirit; ff.

339, 403, 411, the Virgin as a Franciscan sister in gray habit; f. 445v, a male head with nimbus. Floral decoration of initials extends to form partial borders. Alternating red initials with violet flourishes and blue initials with red flourishes throughout. Psalter has alternating simple red and blue initials. Blue paragraph marks throughout. Red touches used as punctuation.

Parchment of Italian preparation. ff. 494. Modern foliation erroneous. 147 × 110 mm (90 × 68 mm). 1–4^{12}, 5^{16}, 6–26^{12}, 27^{12} (6–7 wanting), 28–41^{12}. Catchwords. Ruled in pencil. Written in Italian gothic textualis rotunda media in 27 lines in two columns. Running headings in upper margin by an Italian hand of the late sixteenth century.

Bound in parchment over pasteboard, s. xviii (?).

Written in Italy, perhaps central Italy, in the middle of the fourteenth century. f. 494v, notes of a recipe, s. xvi. No. 9 from the collection of Henry Probasco, acquired by the Newberry 1 December 1890.

Second folio: in idipsum.

De Ricci, 1:524.

+27

(Ry 145; 52-2267)

Albizzi Register

Florence [*Illustrated*] 1339–60

ff. 1–48v Register and memorial book of Pepo d'Antonio di Lando degli Albizzi, 1339–60. f. 1, "In nome di dio e de la beata vergine madre madonna santa Maria e di tutti i santi e sante di paradiso che mi deano bene a fare e bene a dire e che mi deano guadagnio chon salvamento de l'anima e del chorpo. Amen / M ccc xxx uiiii / Questo libro e di Pepo d'Antonio di Lando degli Albizi prop[r]io. In prima mente scriveremo in sino alle xxii charte tuti miei fatti prop[r]i e di merchatantia e d'ogni altra chosa fuori di merchatantia, e chi mi dovese dare. / E dalle xxii charte insino alle xxxii scriveremo chi dovra avere da me. E dalle xxxii charte inanzi scriveremo tute altre mie memorie." This Pepo was the son of Antonio degli Albizzi, *DBI* 2:20–21. Marginal and interlined additions with references to folios in other colored registers and to the family archives. For a similar book, see A. Petrucci, *Il Libro di recordanze dei Corsini, 1362–1457* (Fonti per la storia d'Italia pubblicate dell'Istituto Storico Italiano per il Medio Evo, no. 100; Rome, 1965).

Parchment. ff. i + 40 + i. Original foliation in roman numerals 1–24, 33–48. f. 5, loose, worn, and cropped; it appears to have been used as a pastedown in another book. ff. 25–32 wanting. 292 × 202 mm. Written space very irregular. 1^8 (5 cut out and now loose), 2–3^8, 4^8 (entire quire wanting), 5–6^8. Written in Italian "mercantesca" gothic cursiva in a highly variable number of long lines.

Bound in original limp pink stained leather case with buckle; flyleaves are limp parchment wrappers. Monogram of "Pax" formed from the initials P. A. and a star on front cover. 1339 and 1396 written in black ink on the spine.

Written in Florence by Pepo degli Albizzi, 1339–60. "Pepo" written within a rectangular frame on the rear cover. "458" and "27" written in black ink on front cover and struck out in black. "210" written in black and not struck out. On the verso of the front cover, "No. 485 (*sic*) in Catalogue Albizzi" written in pencil, "Cabinet i. d." written in pencil by another hand, and the bookplate of the Fifth Lord Vernon (1803–66); see De Ricci, *English Collectors,* pp. 115–16. Acquired by the Newberry from H. P. Kraus, 1952.

Faye-Bond, p. 152.

27.1

(52-15)

Matteo de' Libri, *Arringhe* (in Tuscan dialect)

Tuscany c. 1350

1. f. 1. (Contemporary additions) Four fragments of Italian love songs by four hands. The first begins, "Piagniendo e [illegible] uando [illegible] no . . ." The second and the fourth are the same text beginning, "Madonna si uo poso tuto dire a compimento tuto quelo che score . . ." The fourth ends, ". . . e sire auendo di lei la uolensa [illegible]." The third is the incipit only, "Io chiaruo merce a su."

f. 1v blank.

2. ff. 2–16 Come deue dire nel consillio quando si tratta di chiamare podesta (in red). Io chiamo merçe a dio nostro signore e a la sua madre madonna santa Maria e a messer santo Giouanni . . . Piaccia ad dio che possiate prendere la millior parte. Finito libro referamus gratiam Christo. Qui scripsit scribat semper cum domino uiuat, uiuat in celis Çucherus cum Christo fidelis. Amen. Manus scriptoris saluetur omnibus horis. Amen.

f. 16v blank.

Matteo de' Libri, two quires containing *arringhe* in Tuscan dialect in an order differing from other manuscripts, ed. P. Cherchi, "Una nuova versione toscana delle *Arringhe* di Matteo dei Libri," in *Andrea Cappellano, i trovatori e altri temi romanzi* (Rome, 1979), pp. 176–93. Oration 11 ends imperfectly at the end of quire 1; oration 12 begins imperfectly at the beginning of quire 2. See also L. Chiappelli, *Le Dicerie volgari de Ser Natteo de' Libri da Bologna secunda una redazione pistoiese* (Pistoia, 1900), and P. O. Kristeller, "Matteo de' Libri, Bolognese Notary of the Thirteenth Century, and His *Artes Dictaminis,*" in *Miscellanea Giovanni Galbiati* (Milan, 1951), 2:283–320.

Parchment of southern preparation. ff. i + 15. Formerly part of a larger codex. Foliated in modern pencil 1–16, flyleaf foliated as f. 1; quire 2 foliated 1–7 in red arabic numerals in lower right of each recto. Early modern pen foliation 203–217 corrected to 213–227 excludes the flyleaf. 200 × 152 mm (134 × 105 mm). 1^8, 2^8 (8 wanting). Catchwords on f. 9v surrounded by red and black decorative rectangles do not match initial line on f. 10. Ruled in pencil. Written in Italian gothic rotunda media with a one-story a in 27 long lines. Decorative flourishes from descenders extended into the lower margin. Heading for each speech (except no. 12, which is wanting) written in red in script of text. f. 2, red flourished initial 6 lines high. Each subsequent oration (except no. 12) begins with a simple red initial.

Quarter bound in calf back over pasteboard, s. xix.

Written c. 1350 by the scribe Çucherus in Tuscany but not in Florence as indicated by the dialect. Cover embossed with arms of the Strozzi family; f. 1, gold armorial library stamp with the Strozzi motto "Expecto." Acquired by the Newberry from H. P. Kraus, 1951.

Second folio: che ui piaccia.

Faye-Bond, p. 152.

f28

(Ry 23; 17602)
Jean de Meun, *Le Testament;*
Jean Chapuis, *Le Trésor*

France s. XV[1]

1. ff. 1–31

Li peres et filz et li sains esperiz
Ung dieu en troiz personnes aourez et cheriz . . .
Et lui prit humblement que nous soions escript
Ou sainct livre de vie que il meismes escrist.
Explicit testamentum magistri Johannis de Meduno (the last 4 letters written over an erasure). Deo gracias.

f. 1, "Le Testament" written in upper margin by another hand.

f. 31v blank.

Jean de Meun, *Le Testament,* ed. Méon, *Le Roman de la Rose,* 4:1–116. For a list of 116 manuscripts, including this one (as MS 10), see S. Buzzetti Gallarati, "Nota bibliografica sulla tradizione manoscritta del *Testament* di Jean de Meun," *Revue Romane* 13 (1978): 2–35, and esp. p. 28.

2. ff. 32–43v

O glorieuse trinite
Une essence en vraie unite . . .
Prendras en gre que je chapuiz
Car ce te plaist qu'on en peut faire
Explicit le codicille maistre Jehan de Meun. Deo gracias.

f. 32, "Codicille" written in upper margin by another hand.

f. 44–44v blank.

Jean Chapuis, *Les Sept articles de la foi* or *Le Trésor,* ed. Méon, *Le Roman de la Rose* 3:331–95. For attribution, see P. Paris, "Jean de Meun," *HLF* 28 (1881): 428. Långfors, *Les Incipit,* pp. 239–40. This manuscript unrecorded.

Paper. ff. iii + 44 + ii. 290 × 220 mm. Written space: ff. 1–31, 200 × 105 mm; ff. 32–43v, 200 × c. 135 mm. $1–5^8$, 6^4. Catchwords. Prickings visible on some folios. Ruled in pencil; ff. 32–44v, ruled for two columns. Written in *lettre bâtarde* media: ff. 1–31 in 35 long lines; ff. 32–43v in 35 lines in two columns. f. 1, gold dentelle initial decorated with white patterning on a ground of red-brown and blue 4 lines high. In first text, every fourth initial in red; in second text, every twelfth initial in red; others washed in yellow. ff. 1 and 32, place for miniatures left blank.

Bound in modern, imitation Renaissance, tooled leather over boards. Pastedowns formed from fragments of vernacular agreement concerning an inheritance, s. xv.

Written in France, in the first half of the fifteenth century. Inscription "Bonchart" s. xvi on verso of last flyleaf. Sold by Thomas Thorpe to Sir Thomas Phillipps, his stamp on front flyleaf, 2528, same number written in ink on verso of second flyleaf. Munby, *Phillipps Studies* 3:149. Acquired by the Newberry from Paul Gottschalk (New York), 1937.

Second folio: Se je vail.

Faye-Bond, p. 149.

29

(66-1827)

Peter of Poitiers, *Compendium Historiae in Genealogia Christi*

Italy s. XIV²

ff. 2–8 Considerans hystorie sacre prolixitatem . . . regressus unde uenerat uisa sua manifestans et audita.

ff. 1–1v and 8v blank.

Cf. editions of U. Zwingli, *Genealogia et chronologia sanctorum patrum* . . . (Basel, 1592), and H. Vollmer, *Deutsche Bibelauszuge des Mittelalters zum Stammbaum Christi* (Potsdam, 1931), p. 127 sqq. See P. S. Moore, *The Works of Peter of Poitiers: Master in Theology and Chancellor of Paris (1193–1205)* (Publications in Medieval Studies, the University of Notre Dame; Notre Dame, 1936), pp. 101–6, for a description of manuscripts and editions. His list of manuscripts supplemented by Stegmüller, *Repertorium biblicum,* 6778 sqq. Glorieux, 100f. This manuscript unrecorded.

f. 1v, drawing of a menorah, s. xvii or xviii. Rear paper flyleaf, a woodcut of Noah's ark from an unidentified incunable printing of H. Schedel, *Nuremberg Chronicle,* tipped in.

Parchment. ff. 8. 428 × 328 mm (258 × 195 mm). One quire of 8 leaves. Portions of text obliterated by water staining. Ruled in ink. Written in Italian gothic textualis rotunda formata in 77–79 lines in two columns. Headings in red in script of text. Alternating red and blue initials. Genealogical diagrams with roundels drawn in red ink, filled with yellow, blue, and red. Minor initials touched with yellow.

Bound in modern limp parchment embossed with gold. Title in pen: "Genealogia ab Adam usque ad Christum."

Written in Italy, possibly central Italy as suggested by the minor initials, in the second half of the fourteenth century. Outer leaves formerly served as a limp binding and are covered with numerous jottings. f. 1 includes fragments of Italian verse and musical notation. f. 8v, names s. xvi: Giuseppe Lupi (several times), Augustinus Justinianus episcopus (at least twice), Nicolaus Justinianus (twice), and numerous pen trials in Latin and Italian including prayers and epistolary salutations. Verso of front cover, bookplates of the Fifth Lord Vernon (1803–66), see De Ricci, *English Collectors,* pp. 115–16, and of R. P. Holgrave-Graham. Acquired by the Newberry from Bernard Rosenthal, 1966.

Second folio: Isti dathan.

30

(54-757)

English Statutes

England s. XIV¹

1. f.1 (Magna Carta as confirmed by Edward I in 1297.) Edwardus dei gratia rex anglie . . . XI° die februarii anno regni nostri nono; cf. *SR* 1:114–19. 2. f. 9, Incipit carta de foresta (confirmation of Edward I). *SR* 1:20–22. 3. f. 13, Incipit sententia lata anno domini mccliii (the sentence of curse given by the bishops on the breakers of charters). *SR* 1:6. 4. f. 14v, Incipiunt capitula prouisionis de Merton ultime . . . *SR* 1:1–41. 5. f. 19v, Incipiunt de Marleberge . . . *SR* 1:19–25. 6. f. 31v, Incipiunt capitula Westmonasterii primi . . . (in French). *SR* 1:26–39. 7. f. 57, Incipiunt capitula Gloucestre . . . (in French). *SR* 1:45–50. 8. f. 63v, Incipiunt explanaciones eorundem . . . *SR* 1:50. 9. f. 64v, Incipiunt capituli (*sic*) Westmonasterii secundi . . . *SR* 1:71–95. 10. f. 112, Incipit statutum de emptoribus terrarum . . . *SR* 1:106–7. 11. f. 113, Incipit statutum religiosorum . . . *SR* 1:51. 12. f. 114v, Incipit statutum de mercatoribus . . . (in French). *SR* 1:98. 13. f. 119v, Incipiunt districciones scattarii (*sic*) . . . (in French). *SR* 1:197–98. 14. f. 121, Incipiunt statuta eiusdem . . . (in French). *SR* 1:196–97. 15. f. 127v, Incipiunt statuta de rageman . . . (in French). *SR* 1:44. 16. f. 128v, Incipiunt circumspecte agatis . . . *SR* 1:101–2. 17. f. 130v, Incipit statutum de conspiritoribus . . . (in French). *SR* 1:216, first section only, ending imperfectly. 18. f. 131, Statute of Winchester, beginning imperfectly. *SR* 1:96–98. 19. f. 135, Incipit statutum de bigamis . . . *SR* 1:42–43. 20. f. 136v, Incipit modus faciendi homagium . . . *SR* 1:227–28. 21. f. 138v, Incipit modus columniandi (*sic*) essonium . . . *SR* 1:217–18. Codex ends imperfectly, episcopo quod factum // = *SR* 1:218.

Parchment. ff. 138. Modern indication of foliation partially inaccurate. Two folios missing after f. 130; an undetermined number of leaves missing at end. Trimmed to 90 × 65 mm (68 × 50 mm). $1–10^{12}$, 11^{12} (11–12 wanting), 12^{10} (9–10 wanting). Quires numbered 1–12 in arabic numerals on upper left corner of the first leaf. Ruled in crayon, double boundary lines. Prickings visible in outer margins of some folios. Written in cursiva anglicana media in 22 long lines (see Examples of Selected Scripts). Running marginal headings added by a later hand, partially trimmed. Blue initials with red flourishes at the beginning of each statute. f. 1, flourished initial extends into a full border. Alternating red and blue paragraph marks throughout.

Bound in red morocco, s. xviii. Spine title: Magna Charter.

Written in England, certainly after 1297, date of the confirmation of Magna Carta by Edward I, probably in the early fourteenth century, possibly for a lawyer as a pocket reference copy. f. 118v, signature, Thomas Bruere, s. xv, in upper margin; cf. Emden, *Biographical Register: Oxford* 1:262. Second front flyleaf of s. xviii bears unidentified armorial bookplate, partially removed. Armorial bookplate of John Towneley (1740–1813) on front pastedown; see De Ricci, *English Collectors,* pp. 88–89. Verso of front flyleaf bears old shelfmark (?) "Dfm No. 1" in black ink, "1684" in purple pencil circled in black pencil, old price "£5.50" and note "circa 1400." Acquired by the Newberry from the Illinois Institute of Technology, 1954.

Second folio: Custos autem.

Faye-Bond, p. 152.

31
(Ry 8)
Spiritual Texts

England s. XIV med.

f. 1 Liber sancti Bernardi de conscientia . . . Table of contents of entire codex.

The first unnumbered folio, recto and verso, and f. 1v blank.

1. ff. 2–25v Liber sancti Bernardi de conscientia (in red). Domus hec, in qua habitamus, ex omni parte sua ruinam minatur . . . (ends imperfectly, word in italics is a catchword) quid facturus es in die iudicii, ubi omnibus exposata erit tua *conscientia* //

Ps. Bernard of Clairvaux (Ps. Hugh of Saint Victor), *De interiore domo* (chapters 1–21 inc.). *PL* 184:507–30C. Bloomfield, *Incipits,* 1787. This manuscript recorded. According to the table of contents, three texts now missing followed here: *Disputacio bona inter corpus et animam, Ritmus de quadragesima,* and *Oratio sancti Bernardi.*

2. ff. 26–38v Incipit tractatus de arra anime (in red). Considera queso, anima mea, quid est quod super omnia diligis. Ecce scio quod uita tua . . . hoc totis precordiis concupisco scilicit dominum meum Ihesum Christum qui uiuit et regnat et cetera. Amen. Explicit tractatus utilis de arra anime.

Hugh of Saint Victor, *Soliloquium de arrha animae,* ed. K. Müller (Bonn, 1913). *PL* 176:951–70 and 40:851–56 (partial). Begins with the second paragraph of the printed text. For manuscripts, see Goy, *Die Überlieferung,* pp. 277–329; this manuscript recorded, p. 287, no. 63.

3. ff. 38v–66v Hic libellus de emendacione uite siue de regula uiuendi, et distinguitur in duodecim capitula; primo de conuersione, secundo de contemptu mundi . . . (in red). Ne tardes conuerti ad dominum (Eccl 5:8) . . . Nam subito rapit miseros . . . et melodia ipsum eternaliter laudare. Amen. Expliciunt duodecim capitula.

Richard Rolle, *De emendatione vitae,* ed. M. de la Bigne, *Maxima bibliotheca veterum patrum* (Lyon, 1677), 36:609–18; *Speculum spiritualium* (Paris, 1510), f. 209; *De emendatione* . . . (Antwerp, 1553). For manuscripts, see Bloomfield, *Incipits,* 3191, and Allen, *Writings Ascribed to Richard Rolle,* pp. 230–40. This manuscript unrecorded.

4. ff. 67–73v Titulus sancti Martini de Formula honeste uite (in red). Gloriosissimo ac tranquillissimo et insigni catholice fidei . . . contempnet ignauiam. Explicit.

Martin of Braga, *Formulae vitae honestae,* ed. Barlow, *Opera omnia,* pp. 204–50. Bloomfield, *Incipits,* 2233. This manuscript unrecorded. *CPL* 1080.

5. f. 74

Te celi chorus [largely effaced] predicat
Et tuas sanctitas [illegible] . . .
Cum Christo fui sedibus. Amen.

Dubious Bernard of Clairvaux, *Jubilius,* last stanza only, ed. A. Wilmart, *Le Jubilius dit de St. Bernard* (Rome, 1943). *PL* 184:1320. "Te celi," a catchword on f. 73v.

6. f. 74

Uos qui transsitis, si crimina flere uelitis . . .
Nec uelet eius amor per quem me diminuuntur.

Unidentified poem.

7. ff. 74v–112v Hic incipit meditatio de passione domini nostri Ihesu Christi et primo ponitur meditatio de cena domini in speciali, secundo de passione in generali (in red). Adueniente iam et imminente tempore miseracionum et misericordiarum domini . . . atque dicentes, Benedictus qui uenit rex glorie. Amen (in red).

Ps. Bonaventure, *Meditationes de passione Christi,* ed. M. J. Stallings (Washington, D.C., 1965), pp. 87–130. Eight lines of the printed text wanting at the end.

8. ff. 112v–115v
A Ihesu þow sched þi blode . . .
Swet Ihesu þou swete þi blode.
Amen (in red).

A devotion on the events of the Passion, ed. Robbins, "Two Fourteenth-Century Mystical Poems," pp. 323–25. In table on f. 1, this text listed as "Item littera fratris Uttoni (?) ordinis predicatorum."

9. ff. 116–134v (begins imperfectly, a quire wanting after f. 115) // fili Dauid, miserere mei, dum tempus est miserendi, ne dampnes in tempore iudicandi . . . et sic memento mei deus quia tuo amore langueo. Explicit:
Hec quicumque legis
Summi pete munera regis
Exili scripta labore
Pro peccatore
Ut michi gratia ueraque gloria celitus
assint; Amen (in red).

William of Rymington, *Stimulus peccatoris,* ed. R. O'Brien, *Citeaux* 16 (1965): 288–301. Chapters 2 and 3 of the final section omitted. Identified in table on f. 1, "Item meditationes plurimorum sanctorum sacre scripture." Text on ff. 118v–122v, only, attributed in heading to Anselm. This manuscript unrecorded.

10. ff. 135–136v
Ihesu swete his þo loue of þe . . .
þere I ne þe may wyt hevn se.

Dubious Bernard of Clairvaux, *Jubilius* (see above, text 5), in English translation, ed. Robbins, "Two Fourteenth-Century Mystical Poems," pp. 325–27.

Parchment. Paper pastedowns and rear flyleaf. ff. i + 137 + i. Modern foliation begins with f. 2. 152 × 114 mm (120–30 × 85–90 mm). Upper portion of f. 1 wanting. 1^{2}, $2–14^{8}$, $15–16^{10}$, 17^{12} (1 wanting). Quires 2–11, catchwords in plain rectangles; quires 12–17, in crinkled rectangles. Quires missing after f. 25 where catchwords do not match f. 26; and after f. 115 where catchwords *sic est tradita* do not match f. 116. ff. 2–73, prickings visible on inner and outer margins. ff. 1–73, ruled in very light pencil and frame ruled in brown crayon; ff. 74–136, ruled in pencil and hard point. ff. 2–74, written in anglicana formata media in 21–23 long lines; ff. 74v–136, written in gothic textualis precisa media in 20 long lines. This latter script appears to be a conscious imitation of proto-gothic script of the twelfth century, consistent with the occasional presence of hard-point ruling in this portion. Headings in red in script of the respective texts. Minor red initials. Red touches used as punctuation.

Bound in deerskin over boards, s. xv, two fore-edge clasps, one wanting. Pastedowns and rear flyleaf, vernacular writing exercises of late s. xv.

Written in England in the middle of the fourteenth century, possibly during the lifetime of Richard Rolle. On spine, "211" written in large red numerals, former shelf-mark in the library at Whitchurch, Hants; see N. Ker, *Parochial Libraries of Great Britain* (London, 1959), pp. 104–5. Sold at Sotheby's 7 November 1927, lot no. 4. Acquired by the Newberry from James Tregaskis (London), April 1932.

Second folio: Domus hec. Incipit of f. 3: derelinquere illatam.

De Ricci, 1:542.

31.1
(54-1796)
Collection of Moralized Texts

Bohemia s. XIV[2]

1. ff. 1–13v Incipit exposicio Fulgencii de ymaginibus deorum (in red). Cum antiqui plures deos posuerunt et quasdam rerum uirtutes deos crediderunt . . . Saturnus pingebatur homo senex curuus tristis et pallidus in una manu falcem tenebat . . . Istis igitur premissis uelud quibusdam preambulat, incipiendum est a primo libro Ouidii.

Marginal index notes of texts cited in hand of scribe.

Pierre Bersuire, *De formis figurisque deorum,* ed. J. Engels, *Petrus Berchorius. Reductorium morale liber XV; Ovidus moralizatus Cap. 1, De formis figurisque deorum. Textus e codice Brux. bibl. reg. 863–9 critice editus* (Wekmatial uitgegeven door het Instituut voor laat Latijn der Rijksuniversiteit Utrecht, 3; Utrecht, 1966). Printed under the name of Thomas Waleys, *Metamorphosis ovidiana moraliter explanata* (Paris, 1515), ff. 2–19. Other editions and manuscripts, see J. Monfrin, "Manuscrits et éditions de Pierre Bersuire," *HLF* 39 (1962): 437–40 and 444–45.

2. ff. 13v–15v [U]alerius libro iii° ponit enigmata Aristotilis septem. Primum est stateram ne transilias. Ista statera est uita humana . . . subito enim uenit ira illius et in tempore uindicte disperdet te et cetera. Igitur patent vii enigmata satis declarata. Deo gracias.

Dubious Robert Holcot, *Ps. Aristotelis Aenigmata moralisata.* Bloomfield, *Incipits,* 1421. This text attributed to Holcot in Bordeaux, BM, 2717 (s. xv), ff. 23–24v, and Paris, Maz., 986 (s. xiv), ff. 115–119. Anonymous in other manuscripts.

3. ff. 15v–25v In ciuitate atheniensi fuit constituta lex. Cecus de publico mille denarios recipiat. Spiritualiter, ciuitas paradisi legem statuit et a deo statutum est propter bonum . . . Abdicat eos deus et eternaliter punit qui ei nolunt obedire declamacione xxii[a]. Finiuntur declamationes moralizate Senece comparate per honorabilem uirum dominum Bizybiconem archdiaconum et uicarus (*sic*) in spiritualibus. Zdrawa bud Maria mylosti plna ctna knyezno.

Nicolaus Trevet, *Declamationes Senecae moralizatae.* Kaeppeli, 3145. See also E. Franceschini, *Studi e note di filologia latina medievale* (Milan, 1938), p. 23, n. 3; Th. Walter, *L'Exemplum dans la littérature religieuse et didactique du Moyen-Age* (Paris, 1927), p. 363. This manuscript unrecorded.

4. f. 26–26v Richardus in libro excepcionum suarum. Sermo. Diliges dominum deum tuum et cetera (Deut 6:5). Postquam homo creatorem per culpam primordialem deseruit . . . quem consortem habitur (*sic*) sumus in patria, quod nobis prestare dignetur qui uiuit et regnat in secula seculorum. Amen.

Richard of Saint Victor, *Liber exceptionum,* II, iii, 4, ed. J. Châtillon, *Textes philosophiques du moyen age* 5 (1958), 252 = Richard of Saint Victor, *Sermo de mandato dilectionis. PL* 177:1177–79. Schneyer, *Repertorium* 5:168, no. 88. Attributed in many manuscripts to Maurice de Sully.

5. f. 26v De X uirginibus. Simile est regnum celorum x uirginibus et cetera (Mt 25:1). Decem uirgines sunt uniuersi credentes bona opera exibentes . . . mala euadamus deserendo culpam, bona promereamur sectando iusticiam. Amen.

Richard of Saint Victor, *Liber exceptionum,* II, xiii, 1, ed. cit., p. 478.

6. ff. 27–43 Desiderii tui, karissime, peticionibus satisfacere cupiens columbam . . . Denique dum Moyses leuabat manus suas superabat Israel, cum remitteret manus suas conualescebat Amalech (cf. Ex 17:11).

Hugues de Fouilloy, *De avibus.* Fulcia and ibis in reverse order from *PL* 177:13–56 (Book I of *De bestiis*). See H. Peltzer, "Hugh de Fouilloy," *Revue du Moyen-Age latin* 2 (1946): 41–42. McCulloch, *Medieval Latin and French Bestiaries,* pp. 30–33. Goy, *Die Überlieferung,* p. 492.

7. ff. 43–44 Incipit tractatus Hugonis prioris de diuersis coloribus ac naturis columbarum; Sequitur capitulum (in red). Phisiologus dicit multis ac diuersis coloribus esse columbas . . . a dyabolo deuoratus est et periit. Explicit liber de auibus (in red).

Tractatus de diversis coloribus ac naturis columbarum = *Physiologus* (London, BM, Royal 2 C XII), chapters 22–24, ed. M. F. Mann, *Der Bestiaire Divin des Guillaume le Clerc* (Französische Studien, VI, 2; Heilbronn, 1888), pp. 64–67. McCulloch, *Medieval Latin and French Bestiaries,* pp. 28–30. On this recension, see Ives and Lehmann-Haupt, *An English Thirteenth-Century Bestiary,* pp. 8–9. Modern pencil notation "Oudin II, 1107" is an erroneous allusion to Hugh de Fouilloy's (spurious Hugh of Saint Victor) *De avibus,* as noted by Casimir Oudin's *Commentarius de scriptoribus ecclesiae antiquis* (Leipzig, 1722), 2:1107.

8. ff. 44–52v Incipiunt dicta Iohannis Crisostomi de naturalibus; In primis de leone (in red). Igitur Iacob benedicens filium suum Iudam dicebat, Catulus leonis Iuda . . . Draco est hostis casti animalis dyabolus inimicus filii uirginis et cetera. Amen.

Dicta Chrysostomi. Contents differ somewhat from other analyzed manuscripts: "De leone, [Panthera,] [Unicornis,] [Syrena,] [Ydrus,] [Hyena,] Onager, Simea, De elephante, [Aspis,] Lupus, De pluribus canibus, De lapidibus ignitis, [De adamante, two recensions,] Mermecolion lapis marinus, De belua marina, De secunda astutia, Ancula, De lacerta, Serra, Genus uipperarum, Ceruus, De capra, De uulpe, Asidi (*sic*) uel strucio, De castore, De formica, De herinacio, De salamandra, Mustela, De basilisco, De dracone." The greater portion edited by F. Wilhelm in *Münchener Texte,* Heft 8B, part 1 (1916), pp. 17–44. This version corresponds more closely to that of the Hoefer bestiary described by Ives and Lehmann-Haupt, *An English Thirteenth-Century Bestiary,* pp. 10–13, and McCulloch, *Medieval Latin and French Bestiaries,* pp. 41–44. In the Hoefer bestiary, the *Dicta Chrysostomi* also follows the *Tractatus de diversis coloribus ac naturis columbarum.* The Newberry text, however, lacks some of the Hoefer material and has additional entries of its own.

Parchment, furry, with paper pastedowns (*cloche* watermark partly visible). ff. i + 52 + i. Contemporary arabic foliation (top center recto) by scribe begins with the second leaf. 255 × 172 mm (187 × 121 mm). $1\text{–}2^{10}$, 3^{6}, $4\text{–}5^{10}$, 6^{6}. Catchwords on ff. 10v, 20v, and 26v. Quires numbered on bottom verso of last folio, primus, II–VI. Ruled in ink. ff. 1–25v, 27–52v, written in gothic textualis rotunda media in 41 long lines. Headings in orange-red in script of text. f. 26 recto and verso written by the same hand entirely in gothic cursiva media. Heart-shaped symbol of scribe at the end of each text; f.

27, with inscription: "In nomine Ihesu Christi, amen." Symbol also written across bottom leaf ends with illegible word (name?). f. 1, flourished initial in red; Germanic minor red initials throughout. Diagrams on ff. 27v and 30. ff. 1–13v, 27v–52, places for illustrations left blank. Frequent index notes, by the scribe, in margins throughout.

Bound in deerskin over boards, s. xv, two back and front clasps and bosses wanting. Label on front cover, s. xv: "Fulgencius de ymaginibus deorum." Modern spine label "Fulgentius" and shelf-mark "48[3]." Title (?) across lower edge.

Written in the second half of the fourteenth century in Bohemia (see explicit, f. 25v), as were many Admont texts. On f. 52v, "Benedicite domino Ihesu Christo Amen." Verso of front cover, gothic cursiva inscription struck out, old shelf-mark no. 46us (?). ff. 1 and 42v, modern stamp "Bibliotheca Admontensis." Front pastedown, old inscription obliterated by green sticker "Admonter Bibliothek, Schrank 71, No. 483." This manuscript no. 483 in Wichner, *Catalogus Admontensis*, p. 205. Wichner notes this manuscript sold to L. and A. Brecher (Brünn); cf. *Mittelaltiche Bibliothekskataloge Österreichs* 3:9, line 20. Acquired by the Newberry from Lathrop C. Harper, 1954.

Second folio: secum habent ut ipsis.

Faye-Bond, p. 152.

31.2
(Ry 199; 45-560)
Patristic Miscellany

Italy s. XIV^{2}–XV^{1}

1. ff. 1–8 Quadam die nimiis quorumdam secularium tumultibus depressus, quibus in suis negotiis plerumque cogimur soluere . . . (ends imperfectly in mid folio) et ille cum simia ueniens cimbala percussit. Subiunsit tamen atque ait.

Gregory the Great, *Dialogorum libri,* I, 1–9 (inc.). *PL* 77:149–93A. *CPL* 1713.

2. f. 8v (written vertically) Adhuc in monasterio meo positus cuiusdam ualde uenerabilis uiri relatione cognoui quod dico . . . ostenderet ei uir ille sinplici corde seruisse (*sic*).

Gregory the Great, *Dialogorum libri,* IV, 10. *PL* 77:333–36.

3. f. 8v (written vertically in lighter ink) In eisdem quoque omeliis rem narrasse me recolo . . . (ends imperfectly at the end of the quire) morum quidem diuitiis plene sed //

Gregory the Great, *Dialogorum libri,* IV, 15 (inc.). *PL* 77:344B–C.

4. ff. 9–19v Ego sum occecata et obtenebrata et sine ueritate ideo filioli mei omnia uerba mea que a me habetis, sicut a persona maligna suspecta habeatis et omnia bene notetis et nullis uerbis credatis . . . sed debet appetere perfectam Christi crucifixionem, dolorosam pauperem et desperatam. Deo gratias.

Unidentified text.

5. ff. 20–22v Beati mundo corde, quoniam ipsi deum uidebunt (Mt 5:8). Ecce breue secundum suaui et multiplici sensu refertur et ad pastum . . . gaudium quod nemo tollet et pacem inmutabilem, pacem in idipsum dormiens . . .

Unidentified text.

6. ff. 22v–23 De collationibus (in margin). Finis quidem nostre professionis est regnum dei siue regnum celorum . . . (ends imperfectly in mid folio) Que si pre oculis nostris iugiter statuta.

John Cassian, excerpts from *Conlationes,* I, 4, iii, and I, 5, iii–iv, ed. M. Petschenig, *CSEL* 13 (1886), p. 10, lines 5–10, and p. 11, lines 20–27. *CPL* 512.

7. f. 23v (addition s. xv^{1}) Uniuersis ad quos presentes aduenerint, magister David phylosophorum maximus et omnes alii phylosophi sibi concordantes, salutem. Nouerint quod anno a natiuitate millesimo iii^{c} lxxxxv^{o} . . . conuenerunt et concordati sunt super hiis phylosophis Grecie et Arabie, Yspanie et Francie. Datum Parisius xx^{a} ianuarii.

"Toledo Letter," ed. H. Grauert, "Meister Johann von Toledo," *Sitzungberichte der Philosophisch-Philologischen und der Historischen Classe der Königlichen Bayerischen Akademie der Wissenschaften,* 1901, pp. 283–85.

8. f. 24 (addition s. xv) Three lines beginning, "Omnipotens diabolica percusio . . ."

Paper. ff. 24. Two separate quires, once part of a larger codex. Quire 1, watermark of a bird or griffin partly visible, 147 × 111 mm (117–20 × 95 mm). Quire 2, watermark of a *tête de boeuf* partly visible on the outer bifolium; an unidentified watermark, possibly two keys, partly visible on the inner bifolium, 149 × 113 mm (112–15 × 92 mm). 1^{8}, 2^{16}. Quire 1, frame ruled in pen on three sides, omitting the lower margin, except ff. 1–1v and 2v–4 which are unruled. Quire 2, frame ruled in pen on three sides, lower line omitted. Quire 1, written in Italian gothic cursiva media in 32–35 long lines. Quire

2, written in Italian gothic textualis media to currens in 36–43 long lines. Text 7 added in Italian gothic cursiva media. Entire codex written in black Italian ink. Penned initials 1–2 lines high filled and touched with red ink throughout.

Unbound, strips of a parchment document used to anchor sewings.

Written in Italy in the second half of the fourteenth century or the first half of the fifteenth century. f. 24v, fifteenth-century pen trials. Acquired by the Newberry in 1945 from Louis C. Karpinski (Ann Arbor, Michigan).

–32

(Ry 25)

Stations of Rome

England c. 1400

Quicumque intuetur hei (*sic*) arma domini nostri Ihesu Christi, de peccatis suis confessus et contritus, habet tres annos indulgencie ex concessione sancti Petri primi. Item trigintas [illegible] [Ponti]fices dederunt quilibe[t] [illegible] -dit centum dies indulgencie . . . (in red).

He þat wil his soule leche (in red) . . .
Graant us parte of þis pardon
And þere to his holy benisonne. Amen.

Ed. F. J. Furnivall, *Political, Religious, and Love Poems, EETS,* o.s., 15 (London, 1866), pp. 113–44; rev. ed. (1903), pp. 143–73; *Stations of Rome, EETS,* o.s., 25 (London, 1867), pp. 1–24. This manuscript not collated. Brown and Robbins, *Index of Middle English Verse,* 1172; additional manuscripts 1962. Robbins and Cutler, *Supplement to the Index of Middle English Verse,* p. 1168.

Roll begins with a miniature of Christ on the Cross with the instruments of torture, accompanied by Mary and John the Evangelist. On the left, the mocking Jew; on the right, an unidentified seminude figure. Above, Christ or God the Father seated, accompanied by two standing figures with nimbi, the right one female, all deteriorated, upper right corner entirely missing. Rubric begins with magenta initial 6 lines high on a ground of blue and pink, accompanied by a piece of marginal floral decoration in the same colors and green. Text begins with a red and black initial 12 lines high, the interior decorated with patterned oak leaves. Minor red initials with flourishes in red and, after the first, in the ink of the text throughout. First letter of each line touched in red.

Roll of five membranes. On the use of rolls for literary texts in England, see R. H. Robbins, "The Arma Christi Rolls," *Modern Language Review* 34 (1939): 415–21. Erased writing on verso of first two sheets, text not identifiable. 461 × 10 cm. Ruled in brown pen. Written in cursiva anglicana formata in 167 long lines per sheet. Headings in red in script of text.

Written in England in a provincial scriptorium, c. 1400. Formerly in the library of Reginald Cholmondeley, Condover Hall, Shropshire. See *Fifth Report of the Royal Commission on Historical Manuscripts* (London, 1876), p. 334. Acquired by the Newberry from William H. Robinson, Catalogue 63 (1938), lot no. 71.

Faye-Bond, p. 149.

32.1

(Ry 224; 60-2515)

Modus Tenendi Parliamentum; Tractatus de Senescalcia Anglie

England s. XV^2

1. ff. 2–5v Hic discribitur modus quomodo parliamentum regis Anglie et anglorum suorum tenebatur . . . nihilominus sentietur esse plenum. Explicit modus parliamenti.

f. 1–1v blank.

Modus tenendi parliamentum ("A" recension), eds. Pronay and Taylor, *Parliamentary Texts,* pp. 67–79. This manuscript cited *ibid,* p. 14, n. 4; p. 30, n. 37; p. 203, n. 8.

2. ff. 5v–6v Hic annotatur quis sit senescallus Anglie et quid eius officium. Senescalcia Anglie pertinet ad comitiuam leicestriensem . . . decollatus apud le Blakelowe in comitatu Warrwici.

Ed. L. W. Vernon-Harcourt, *His Grace the Steward and Trial of Peers* (London, 1907), pp. 164–67. This manuscript unrecorded.

Parchment. ff. 6. One quire of six leaves. 345 × 240 mm (230 × 170 mm). Formerly part of Oxford, BL, Hatton 10; see K. L. Scott, "A Late Fifteenth-Century Group of Nova Statuta Manuscripts," *Manuscripts at Oxford: An Exhibition in Memory of Richard William Hunt (1908–1979),* ed. A. C. De la Mare and B. C. Barker-Benfield (Oxford, 1980), p. 104. Ruled in hard point. Written in legal cursiva anglicana formata, showing infusion of secretary traits, in 40 long lines. Headings in gothic textualis quadrata formata. ff. 2 and 5v, partial floral marginal decoration in green, blue, red-brown, and gold. Three illuminated gold initials 4 lines high decorated with white floral patterns on grounds of red-brown and blue. Alternating red and blue paragraph marks. Some water staining.

Unbound.

Written in England in the fifteenth century, certainly before 1495, date of the last statute added to Hatton 10. f. 1, bears inscription "Modus tenendi parliamenti" in hand of c. 1500 (cf. Pronay and Taylor, *Parliamentary Texts,* p. 63), recopied on the same folio in a seventeenth-century hand. Acquired by the Newberry from Bernard Rosenthal, 1960.

Second folio: excusationes.

32.5

Treatises on Logic

Rimini [*Illustrated*] 1454–56

1. ff. 1–3v Arguendo a sensu composito ad sensum diuisum . . . consequentia est bona et formalis et sic de aliis et cetera. Amen. Explicit tractatus de sensu composito et diuiso editus a magistro Entisbero doctore anglico feliciter et cetera, A. D. W. (= Adam de Wesalia) sub anno domini 1456 in uigilia Luce euangeliste. Amen.

f. 4 blank; f. 4v, diagram for the following text (words in capitals added, s. xv).

William of Heytesbury, *De sensu composito et diviso.* Editions listed, Risse, *Bibliographia logica,* vol. 1, passim. This manuscript not recorded by J. A. Weisheipl, "Repertorium mertonense," *Mediaeval Studies* 31 (1969): 214. Mohan, "Incipits of Logical Writings," p. 359. To these lists add Vat. lat. 2138.

2. ff. 5–53v Conspiciens in circuitu librorum magnitudinem . . . at secundum quod in mei exordio primitus in asserendo promisi. Ihesus Christus; Amen Maria (in red) completum in Stephani prothomartyris et sic est finis tocius loyce magistri Pauli de Ueneciis, scriptum per me fratrem Adam de Wesalia de prouincia Colonie dum esset studens Arimini anno domini 1454.

Diagrams on ff. 6 and 8. ff. 5 and 53v, extensive marginal notes by a contemporary Italian hand.

Paulus Venetus, *Logica parva.* For editions, see Risse, *Bibliographia logica,* vol. 1, passim. This manuscript not recorded by C. H. Lohr, "A Note on Manuscripts of Paulus Venetus, *Logica,*" *Manuscripta* 17 (1973): 35–36. Zumkeller, *Manuskripte,* no. 738.

3. ff. 54–65v Consequentia est illatio consequentis . . . per impossibilitatem copulatiue sibi opposite, et sic de aliis de quibus pro nunc amplius non dicatur. Amen. Expliciunt consequentia Strodi per me fratrem Adam scriptum de Wesalia anno domini 1456.

f. 66–66v blank.

Ralph Strode, *Consequentiarum formulae.* For editions, see Risse, *Bibliographia logica,* vol. 1, passim. This manuscript unrecorded in Mohan, "Incipits of Logical Writings," pp. 380–81.

4. ff. 67–72v Fallacię, sancti Thome de Aquino ordinis fratrum prędicatorum (added in margin by an Italian hand showing humanistic influence). Quia logica est rationalis scientia . . . (ends imperfectly in mid folio) Sequitur de fallacia secundum ignorantiam elenchi. Est autem elenchus.

Text accompanied by substantial unidentified notes in the hand of the scribe, continuing on to f. 73 (a smaller added leaf). f. 73v blank.

Thomas Aquinas, *De fallaciis,* ending imperfectly in the beginning of chapter 11, ed. Mandonnet, *Opuscula omnia* 4:508–27. Grabmann, *Die Werke,* pp. 348–52. Mohan, "Incipits of Logical Writings," p. 447.

5. f. 72v Notes, late s. xv, Italy, on the moderate consumption of wine, citing Ps. Boethius, *De disciplina scholarium.*

Paper of two types intermixed, some quite light and shiny, some yellowed and fuzzy, the latter having a simple Latin cross watermark, cf. Briquet 5590, visible on ff. 39 and 40. ff. ii + 73. Trimmed to 201 × 145 mm (150 × 103 mm). f. 73, a small leaf tipped in. Collation not practicable. Ruled in pen and hard point for two columns ff. 1–66v. Frame ruled without horizontal ruling after the first leaf for long lines ff. 67–72v. ff. 1–4 and 32–66, written in lower Rhine Valley hybrida media incorporating some Italian traits by Adam de Wesalia, O.P. His writing usually hung on the first ruled line. ff. 5–31v, in a similar script by another hand; all in 38–46 lines in two columns beginning, in this section only, on the first ruled line. ff. 67–72v, written in gothic cursiva media in c. 34–47 long lines. ff. 67–73, marginalia in gothic cursiva currens. Headings in humanistic rustic capitals on ff. 5–31v and in Italianate textualis rotunda on ff. 1–5 and 32–66. Red initials and paragraph marks. Text 5 added in humanistic textualis.

Bound in modern half morocco over pasteboard. Spine title gives date as 1476, an easy misreading for 1456 in the text.

Written in Rimini by Adam de Wesalia, O.P., a German scribe with Italian training (signed on ff. 3v, 53v, and 65v), dated 1454–56. Other portions of the text also reflect a mixture of Northern and Italian traits, with Italian traits particularly strong on ff. 5–31v. Possibly from the library of the Dominicans of Verona. Flyleaf ii[v], "Iste liber est conuentus ueronenisis (*sic*) ordinis fratrum praedicatorum in primo deposito a sinistris 19," written in

Italian humanistic cursiva, s. xv. This ex libris may be fraudulent by Guillaume Libri. For other manuscripts of this library, see T. Kaeppeli, "Antiche biblioteche domenicane in Italia," *Archivum fratrum praedicatorum* 36 (1966): 72–73. At the end of s. xviii, in the library of Marchese Paolino Gianfilippi (Verona), *Colophons de Manuscrits,* 241. Purchased in 1843 for the collection of Joseph Barrois, his number 426 written on green circular sticker on spine. Recorded by L. Delisle, "Notice sur des manuscrits du fonds Libri conservé à la Laurentienne," *Notices et extraits des manuscrits,* vol. 32, pt. 1 (1886), appendix 2, no. 20, p. 116; cf. De Ricci, 1:594 and 895. Sold to Lord Ashburnham, recorded in *Catalogue of the Manuscripts at Ashburnham Palace* (London, 1862); *Eighth Report of the Royal Commission on Historical Manuscripts,* appendix, part 3 (London, 1881), p. 89. Sold at Sotheby's, 10 June 1901, lot no. 582; "582" written in blue crayon within a circle on front pastedown. Clipping from the catalogue tipped to flyleaf ii^{v}, entry for this book partially visible on the verso. On the Barrois collection and Ashburnham sale, see De Ricci, *English Collectors,* p. 134. In s. xx, in the library of Sir Israel Gollancz. Gift of Louis H. Silver to the Newberry, c. 1964.

Second folio: ad terminum communem.

McGinn, *Tradition of Thomas Aquinas and Bonaventure,* p. 6.

32.9

Pricke of Conscience

England c. 1400

1. pp. 1–197

The migthe of þe fader almyȝty . . .
To the whiche ioyes that have noon ende
God bringe us thirdre when we hennes wende
And that it mote so be
With herte stedfaste amen say we.
Here then endes the tretice alle
Which that men prik of conscience kalle
Explicit expliceat sic benedictus eat.
Amen (colophon and five final lines of text in red).

Pricke of Conscience in Midlands dialect (possibly Northamptonshire), latter portion abbreviated, ed. R. Morris (Berlin, 1863). Allen, *Writings Ascribed to Richard Rolle,* pp. 372–97. This manuscript recorded by Brown and Robbins, *Index of Middle English Verse,* 3248 (no. 76).

2. pp. 1–29 For the loue of Philippe kynge of Ffraunce that god hath in his kepynge . . . shal nort be overcome in no bataile. Explicit Lapidarye. Ande in tyme beþ merye, quod Hull.

p. 1 in upper margin, s. xvii or xviii, "Philip le Bele, king of France – 1279."

pp. 30–31 blank.

Lapidary of Philip the Fair, translation into Midlands dialect; cf. edition of J. Evans and M. Serjeantson, *English Medieval Lapidaries,* EETS, o.s., vol. 190 (London, 1933), p. 17 sqq. See also, J. Evans, *Magical Jewels of the Middle Ages and the Renaissance* (Oxford, 1922), pp. 78–79. New edition based on this codex edited by G. R. Keiser, *The Middle English 'Boke of Stones,' the Southern Version* (Brussels, 1984).

[3.] Table of contents of s. xvii on verso of front cover lists a third text: "Rebianus (*sic*) concerning the beginning of the world." This entry obliterated and clearly visible only under ultraviolet lamp. Seventeenth-century glossary on rear pastedown.

Parchment, rather stiff. ff. 114. Paginated 1–197 and 1–29. The last leaf is not paginated. Trimmed to 195 × 132 mm (pp. 1–197: 153 × 94 mm; pp. 1–29: 133 × 95 mm). $1–9^{12}$, 10^{6}. Space in binding indicates missing quires confirmed by seventeenth-century table on verso of front cover which lists a third text. Catchwords in red rectangles. f. 173, trace of a leaf signature. Written in anglicana formata in 26–31 long lines. Headings in red in script of text. First folio approaches bastard anglicana. f. 1, illuminated initial extended to form full gold spike border with red, blue, and green foliage decoration. Letters P A (or F) S M in corners (clockwise, from upper left). Blue initials with red flourishes throughout, forming full borders on pages 14, 25, 73, 121, 139, and 142.

Bound in tooled calf over wooden boards, London, c. 1540. Two rolls used, one of which used for the margins contains medallion head similar to Oldham, *Blind Panels of English Binders,* H M. 6. The other contains a floral motif used to form a large lozenge in the center of the panel.

Written in England, the dialect suggests Northamptonshire, c. 1400. p. 30 of second pagination, brief invocation of God, s. xv, "Deus qui uiuorum dominaris simul mortuorum omniumque misereri mei," written in gothic cursiva in violet ink. Bound in London in s. xvi. Marginalia of s. xvi mostly in second text; marginal notes of s. xviii passim. Modern library shelf-marks on verso of front cover, "L.J.II.1," in pen; "L.H.II," in pencil. Formerly in the library of Lord Tollemache. On the catalogues of this library, see Robert Spencer's introduction to L. Hewitt ed., *The Sampson Lute Book Formerly Known as the Tollemache Lute Manuscript* (Leeds, 1974), and Sotheby's sales catalogue 14, 14 June 1965, pp. iii–

viii. Sold at Sotheby's, 6 June 1961. Catalogue includes plate of f. 1. Acquired by the Newberry from Louis H. Silver, 1964.

Second folio: In his.

Lewis and McIntosh, *Descriptive Guide,* p. 49.

33
(C19169)
Pricke of Conscience

England s. XIV²

ff. 1–99v (begins imperfectly) // and lacketþ ȝong men þat *now are seene* (italic portion visible only under ultraviolet light) . . . (ends imperfectly) þus may þis tretis with þe sentence //

Pricke of Conscience, edition: ed. R. Morris (Berlin, 1863), lines 797–9571, lines 8780–9256 wanting between p. 190 and p. 191. Text somewhat condensed. Dialect indicates southwest Lincolnshire. This manuscript recorded by Allen, *Writings Ascribed to Richard Rolle,* pp. 373–74. Brown and Robbins, *Index of Middle English Verse,* 3428. Robbins and Cutler, *Supplement to the Index of Middle English Verse,* p. 382.

Parchment, stiff and fuzzy. ff. 99. Modern pagination 1–198. Water damage on initial and concluding folios; folios removed both at beginning and end. Trimmed to 205 × 111 mm (185 × 80 mm). 1⁸ (stubs only), 2⁸ (1–2 removed with loss of text, 3–13⁸, 14⁸ (2–7 removed with loss of text), 15⁸ (4–8 removed), 16² (stubs only). Ruled in brown pen. Written in cursiva anglicana formata in 39 long lines. Headings and Latin prose sections in red in script of text. Initial letter of each line touched in red; alternating red and blue couplet marks. Occasional fifteenth-century marginalia including pointing hand nota marks. Book divisions marked in upper right hand corner by a contemporary hand.

Bound in calf over pasteboard, s. xviii. Old shelfmark 27 on label on spine.

Written in England in the second half of the fourteenth century. Belonged to Timothy Neve (1694–1757). *DNB* 14:241. Verso of front cover, inscription of s. xviii, "Mr. Neve secretary of the Gentlemen's society in Peterboro presents this ancient but imperfect manuscript to ye said society. It consists of seven books in English missing the greate part of ye first book lost and part of ye last . . ."; a brief description of the contents follows. Below, circular bookplate bearing interlaced "PS" (= Peterborough Society?), numbered 27. Verso of back cover bears bookplate of Peterborough Public Library reference department no. 1590, class no. 821.1. Note on bookplate: "198 pages," signed "N. J. W." Sold by Sotheby's 16 July 1928, lot no. 556 to James Tregaskis from whence to the Newberry in the same year.

Second folio: And gnawe on þat.

De Ricci 1:541. A. McIntosh, "Two Unnoticed Interpolations in Four Manuscripts of the *Pricke of Conscience,*" *Neuphilologische Mitteilungen* 77 (1976): 69. R. E. Lewis, "The Relationship of the Vernon and Simeon Texts of the *Pricke of Conscience,*" in *So meny Longoges and Tonges: Philological Essays in Scots and Mediaeval English Presented to Angus McIntosh,* ed. M. Benskin and M. L. Samuels (Edinburgh, 1981), pp. 257 and 259. Lewis and McIntosh, *Descriptive Guide,* p. 50.

+33.1
(Ry 11; 57-2403)
Ranulf Higden, *Polychronicon* and Related Texts

England s. XV¹

1. ff. 1–7 Alphabetical table to the *Polychronicon,* referring to book and chapter in arabic numerals.

f. 7v blank.

2. ff. 8–11v Incipit cronica bona et compendiosa de regibus Anglie tantum a Noe post diluuium usque in hunc diem. Noe fuerunt tres filii . . . in regnum successit Anglorum anno etatis sue undecimo.

Abbreuiationes chronicorum without name of author. Present in five other manuscripts, four of which contain the *Polychronicon.* See Taylor, *Universal Chronicle,* p. 184; T. Tanner, *Bibliotheca britannico-hibernica* (London, 1748), p. 403; Pronay and Taylor, *Parliamentary Texts,* p. 21.

3. ff. 11v–13v Ista littera sequens extracta fuit ab omnibus cronicalis omnium cathedralium ecclesiarum Anglie et composita per cancellarium et magistros Oxonii in parliamento apud Lincolnum, anno domini m°ccc ad respondenum pape pro quadam bulla missa regi ex falsa suggestione scottorum; Responsio regis Edwardi filii regis Henrici ad quamdam bullam per papam Bonifacium viii sibi directam ex falsa suggestione scottorum anno domini m° ccc° iubileo (in red). Sanctissimo in Christo patri domino Bonifatio . . . Infrascripta non in forma nec in figura iudicii . . . si placet, paternis affectibus commendata.

The reply of Edward I to the Bull *Scimus fili,* ed. E. L. G. Stones, *Anglo-Scottish Relations 1174–1328: Some Selected Documents* (Oxford, 1970), pp. 192–218.

For elucidation of the rubric, see E. L. G. Stones and G. G. Simpson, *Edward I and the Throne of Scotland, 1290–1296* (Oxford, 1978), 1:154–55.

4. ff. 13v–14 Littera comitum et baronum Anglie eidem domino pape directa responcioni regis concordantis (in red). Sanctissimo in Christo patri domino Bonifacio . . . Sui devoti filii . . . Datum Lincolnum duodecimo die ffebruariorum anno domini millesimo tricentesimo.

f. 14v blank.

T. Rymer, *Foedera* (2d ed., London, 1726–35), 2:873–75.

5. ff. 15–142 Prologus, capitulum primum (*sic* in red). Post preclaros artium scriptores . . . (ends imperfectly at the end of an imperfect quire) Johannes regis frater de capcione //

Index notes in outer margins with reference to historical personae and, beginning in Book II, to the year, displayed in two columns, relative to changing reference points as in the edition.

Ranulf Higden, *Polychronicon,* ed. J. R. Lumby, Rolls Series, 41 (London, 1865–86), to vol. 8, p. 102. Manuscripts listed by Taylor, *Universal Chronicle,* pp. 152–59. This manuscript unrecorded.

f. 15, historiated initial 6 lines high depicting Anthony, full acanthus borders decorated in blue, green, and gold. Initials with floral decoration 6 lines high at the beginning of books II–VII. Minor gold dentelle initials with white patterning on grounds of magenta and blue throughout. Guides to rubricator present. f. 15, right margin badly cut; f. 16, large initial removed; f. 47, small initial removed. Decorations similar to Cambridge, Saint John's College H 1.

Parchment. ff. 142. 380 × 260 mm (268 × 175 mm). 1^8 (8 wanting), 2^8 (8 wanting), $3–17^8$, 18^4, 19^4 (imperfect with loss of text). Leaves signed a^1–qiiii (all leaves of quire 18 signed, quire 19 unsigned). Catchwords present, written in scrolls in inner lower margin except for f. 138 where catchword has no scroll and is in outer lower margin. Ruled in pen, prickings visible. Table ruled with special columns. Written in bastard anglicana media in 54 lines in two columns (see Examples of Selected Scripts). Running headings and chapter headings in red in script of text. Marginalia, s. xv–xvii.

Bound in purple calf, s. xix.

Written in England in the first half of the fifteenth century. f. 15, arms of Bothe family of York. On f. 14v, in littera textualis quadrata is written: "Orate pro anima Magistri Roberti Bothe quondam decani ecclesie cathederalis eboracensis *qui dedit hunc librum cathenandum in aula regia* [italicized words visible only under ultraviolet light] universitatis Cantabrigie anno domini m° cccc^{mo} lxxxix cuius anime propicietur deus. Amen." On Bothe, see Emden, *Biographical Register, Cambridge,* pp. 79–80. On the library of King's Hall, see Ker, *Medieval Libraries,* p. 26; this manuscript not listed. Lower on f. 14v, in a sixteenth-century hand is written "Edwardus Aiscoughe [= ? Edward Ayscough (1549?–1617), *DNB* 1:770] hunc librum possidet." Formerly Phillipps MS 1049, number written under stamp on f. 1 and in ink on front pastedown. On front flyleaf is pasted a clipping from a nineteenth-century sales catalogue, printed in London by J. Barker, listing this manuscript as no. 6089 with pencil notation "Sir T. P." Clipping appears to include another Phillipps MS, no. 1052, acquired from Thomas Townley: this is no. 6091 in the clipping and is also noted "Sir T. P." On f. 1, in pencil, in the writing of Sir Thomas Phillipps, "From Mr. Yarnold's Library," i.e., the library of Charles Yarnold of Great Saint Helens, sold at auction 6 June 1825; see Munby, *Phillipps Studies* 3:147. Acquired by the Newberry from John F. Fleming (New York), 1957.

Second folio: De Botulphi.

+33.3

John Lydgate, *The Fall of Princes*

England c. 1470

ff. 1–201

He [illegible] -did somtyme his best diligence . . .

who wil encrese by uertu [illegible] must ascende

Explicit liber Bochacii.

f. 201v blank.

John Lydgate, *The Fall of Princes,* recension with the Rome stanza, lines 4481–87 of the edition of H. Bergen, EETS, e.s., nos. 121–23 (London, 1924–27). Brown and Robbins, *Index of Middle English Verse,* 1168. Robbins and Cutler, *Supplement to the Index of Middle English Verse,* p. 133. One bifolium of text (= Book IX, lines 1114–1449) missing after f. 189.

Parchment. ff. 201. Trimmed to c. 289 × 195 mm (230 × 150 mm). Some shrinkage due to water damage; portions of text at beginning and end rendered illegible; ink has eaten through the parchment at the end. 1^6, $2–18^8$, $19–20^6$, 21^8, 22^6, 23^{10}, 24^8 (4–5 removed with loss of text), 26^{8+1}. Error in binding: ff. 197–198 should follow f. 192. Catchwords in scrolls. f. 49, prickings visible. Written in 42 lines in two columns in secretary cursiva formata incorporating anglicana traits. Explicit of each book in gothic textualis quadrata formata. Headings in red in script of text. Book numbers written in large roman numerals on rectos and versos, partially trimmed. Blue, magenta, and green initials on gold grounds 6 lines high at the beginning of each book; on f. 1, accompanied by full acanthus spray border in the same colors; at the beginning of books II–VIII, accompanied by single column borders. These borders by an illuminator active in London c. 1455–75, who decorated books written by the scribe Ricardus Franciscus. A full list of this illuminator's work will appear in K. L. Scott, *Later Gothic Manuscripts,* vol. 9 of J. J. G. Alexander, *A Survey of Manuscripts in the British Isles*. Small gold dentelle initials with white patterning on grounds of blue and magenta accompanied by sprigs of floral decoration.

Bound in red morocco, s. xix.

Written in London c. 1470, as indicated by the decoration and the dialect. f. 45, "Forget nott" written in a hand of c. 1500 followed by a monogram of the letters F, E, N, R, G, E, T, and closed S. On the closed S see the descriptions of the bindings of MSS 52 and 83. On front pastedown, bookplates of George B. Leighton of Monadnock Farms and Geo[rge] E. Leighton, Saint Louis, with monogram shield titled "Wrenwood." Acquired by the Newberry from Louis H. Silver, 1964.

Second folio: And as thet.

+33.5

John Gower, *Confessio Amantis*

England s. XV med.

ff. 1–110 (begins imperfectly at the beginning of the third quire) // In middlerth I sey al so . . . oure joie may be endles. Amen. Explicit iste liber, qui transeat, obsecro liber . . . Perpetuis annis stet pagina grata Britannis. Epistula super huius operis complementum Iohannis Gower a quodam philosopho transmissa . . . Nomenque presentis opusculi confessio amantis specialiter intitulatur.

John Gower, *Confessio amantis,* beginning Book I, line 3305, ed. G. C. Macaulay, *The English Works of John Gower,* EETS, e.s., 81–82 (1900–1901) = *Complete Works of John Gower* (Oxford, 1899–1902), vols. 2 and 3. This manuscript listed p. cli. First version unrevised as classified by J. H. Fisher, *John Gower, Moral Philosopher and Friend of Chaucer* (New York, 1959), p. 305, appendix A, MS 25 (listed as Castle Howard Manuscript); Brown and Robbins, *Index of Middle English Verse,* 2662 (listed as text of Earl of Carlisle); Robbins and Cutler, *Supplement to the Index of Middle English Verse,* p. 305 (listed as text of Louis H. Silver).

Parchment. ff. 111. Foliated 1–92, 92b, 93–110. Water damage, especially on ff. 1–4 and 109–110. 17 folios wanting at beginning since s. xviii, see note on flyleaf transcribed below. 4 folios (= Book VI, lines 264–1306) missing after f. 73; ff. 71–72 should follow f. 66; f. 103 should follow f. 106. Six paper flyleaves, s. xviii. 340 × 280 mm (300 × 145 mm). 1–2 wanting, 3^8, $4–10^8$. The remainder of the codex disturbed in rebinding, collation impracticable. Frame ruled in pencil. Quires numbered IV–XV on lower margin recto of the first leaf. Written in secretary cursiva formata in 64–74 lines in two columns. Latin prose sections underlined in red. Alternating red and blue minor initials; red paragraph marks.

Bound in quarter parchment with marble paper over paperboards, s. xviii.

Written in England in the middle of the fifteenth century. f. 110, effaced notes and inscriptions s. xv, "Item of Thomas Flynn," "Per me Thomas Goldsmyth the Young," followed by a brief epigram and the signature of Thomas Goldsmyth, below. f. 110v, pen trials in Latin, French, and English. f. 109v, signature of John Willing, s. xviii, De Ricci, *English Collectors,* p. 65; *DNB* 12:1182–83, old number 38 in pen. Flyleaf i, inscription, s. xviii, "Johannes Gower De confessione amantis obiit 1404 . . . This book is imperfect till the latter end of the first book. It begins at *In midel erth et cetera* (italicized words in brackets in a script imitating that of the text) at the bottom of fol. xxvi, printed by Thomas Bertholette MDLIIII." See Pollard and Redgrave, 12144. Formerly in the library of the Earl of Carlisle at Castle Howard. Verso front cover, labels: "From Castle Howard January 1898," "From Castle Howard September 1899," "Sent to [illegible] office." These notes may refer to Macaulay's borrowing of this manuscript for his edition. Acquired by the Newberry from Louis H. Silver, 1964.

Second folio: Hic ponit confessor.

f33.7

Thomas Hoccleve, *The Regiment of Princes*

England s. XV med.

ff. 1–79
Musyng open þe restles bisynesse . . .
þat knoweth he whom þing is hyd fro.
C'est tout.

Latin index notes in outer margin.

ff. 79v–80v blank.

Ed. F. J. Furnivall, EETS, e.s., 72 (London, 1897). This manuscript recorded as no. 43 by M. C. Seymour, "The Manuscripts of Hoccleve's *Regiment of Princes,*" *Edinburgh Bibliographical Society Transactions,* vol. 4, pt. 7

(1974), pp. 253–93. Brown and Robbins, *Index of Middle English Verse,* 2229, no. 39.

Parchment and paper, *tête de boeuf* watermark; cf. Briquet 14938. Outer bifolio of each quire is parchment. ff. 80. 288 × 215 mm (200 × c. 105 mm). $1–10^8$. Catchwords present in large scrolls except f. 80v, no catchword, and f. 56v, catchwords not in scroll. Frame ruled in pencil. Written in secretary cursiva media in 29–35 long lines. Marginal index notes in script of text. f. 1, blue initial with red flourishes 8 lines high. Similar smaller flourished initials throughout.

Bound in levant morocco, s. xx.

Written in England in the middle of the fifteenth century. f. 80v, note of scribe, "Jhesu Maria / Helpe me / Amen." f. 80v, old shelf-mark "No. 4" in very black ink. Formerly in the library of William Constable, Esquire (d. 1888), his armorial bookplate on front pastedown, *Franks Collection of Book Plates,* 6646. Rear pastedown, label with signature of W. A. Andrews, dated June 1889; armorial bookplate, "Victoria concordia crescit," no name. In the library of Lord Amherst of Hackney (d. 1908), his bookplate removed in rebinding, see S. De Ricci, *A Hand-List of a Collection of Books and Manuscripts Belonging to the Right Honourable Lord Amherst of Hackney* (Cambridge, 1906), p. 4, and *English Collectors,* pp. 165–66. Offered for sale by Bernard Quaritch, catalogues 321 (December 1912), item no. 24, and 344 (June 1916), item no. 19. Bookplate of Wilfred Merton dated 1920 on front pastedown. Sold at Merton's death in 1957 to Martin Breslauer; his catalogue 90 (1958), item no. 24, plate 13 depicts f. 1. Purchased by John F. Fleming, his catalogue dated 1961; sold to Louis H. Silver; acquired by the Newberry from him, 1964.

Second folio: ffor when a weneth.

–34

(Ry 5; c 19170)

John of Hoveden, *Philomena*

Holland — s. XV med.

ff. 4–118v

Aue, uerbum, ens in principio . . .

Qui es uerbum ens in principio.

ff. 1v–3v and 119–120 blank.

John of Hoveden, *Philomena,* ed. C. Blume, *Johannes de Hovedene "Philomena"* (Hymnologische Beiträge, Quellen und Forschungen, 4; Leipzig, 1930). Manuscripts listed, F. J. E. Raby, *Poems of Hoveden* (Publications of the Surtees Society, 154; London, 1939), pp. xlvii–xlix. This manuscript unrecorded. See also, F. J. E. Raby, *Christian Latin Poetry from the Beginnings to the Middle Ages* (Oxford, 1953), pp. 390–91 and 487.

Parchment. ff. 120. 124 × 86 mm (75 × 50 mm). $1–15^8$. Quires signed a, i, etc. Pastedowns formed from first leaf of quire 1 and last leaf of quire 15. Ruled in pencil. Prickings visible in outer margins. Written in *lettre bâtarde* media in 20 long lines. f. 4, blue initial decorated with pink, green, and gold floral motifs; gold stem extended to form a bracket left acanthus border. Alternating red and blue initials and paragraph marks.

Bound in modern brown calf over paperboard.

Written in Holland or Germany in the lower Rhine Valley in the middle of the fifteenth century. Acquired by the Newberry in 1931 from E. P. Goldschmidt, catalogue 21, item no. 15; catalogue 23, item no. 193.

Second folio: Uber uber.

De Ricci, 1:541.

35

Book of Hours, Use of Salisbury

Bruges — c. 1455

1. ff. 1–6v Calendar in violet and black with major feasts in red encompassing a mixture of English and Flemish saints, all in the usual Bruges format of six folios. Feasts include Sancti Uulfranni episcopi (19 January, in red), Baltildis uirginis (30 January), Sancti Blasii episcopi (3 February), Cathedra Petri (21 February, in red), Sancti Edwardi regis (18 March), Sancti Dunstani archiepiscopi (19 May), Translatio Edmundi episcopi (9 June), Sancti Kenelmi martiris (17 July), Sancti Ozwaldi regis (5 August), Sancte Cutburge uirginis (31 August), Egidii abbatis (1 September), Sancti Cutberthi episcopi (4 September), Remigii et Bauonis (1 October, in red), Sancti Hugonis episcopi (17 November), Sancti Edmundi regis (20 November), Grisogonii martiris (24 November). Translation of Thomas à Becket on 7 July and his feast on 28 December erased. In upper lines of calendar, Latin month verses, Prima dies mensis et septima trucat (*sic*) ut ensis . . . Walther, *Initia,* 14563.

f. 7 blank and unruled; 7v, miniature for the following text.

2. ff. 8–13v Oratio deuota ad dominum nostrum Ihesum Christum (in violet). O domine Ihesu Christe, eterne dulcedo te amancium . . . te merear laudare cum omnibus sanctis tuis in eternum. Amen.

f. 14 blank and unruled; f. 14v, miniature for the following text.

Series of fifteen prayers to Jesus; Leroquais, *Heures,* 2:98–99. *Horae eboracenses,* pp. 76–80. This text often attributed to Bridget.

3. ff. 15–34v Suffrages of the Saints. Memoria de sancta trinitate . . . , Memoria de sancto Iohanne Baptista . . . , Memoria de sancto Georgio . . . , Memoria de sancto Christoforo martir (*sic*) . . . , Memoria de sancto Thoma cantuariensis (*sic*) (rubric and text scratched out, s. xvi) . . . , Memoria de sancta Anna . . . , Memoria de sancta Maria Magdalena . . . , Memoria de sancta Catherina . . . , Memoria de sancta Barbara . . . , Memoria de sancta Margareta. . . .

f. 35 blank and unruled; f. 35v, miniature for the following text.

4. ff. 36–74v Incipiunt hore beate Marie uirginis secundum consuetudinem Anglie (in violet). Hours of the Virgin, use of Salisbury. ff. 48v–53, after lauds, suffrages to Holy Spirit, Holy Trinity, the Holy Cross, Michael, John the Baptist, Peter and Paul, Andrew, Stephen, Lawrence, Thomas of Canterbury (crossed out, s. xvi), Nicholas, Mary Magdalene, Catherine, Margaret, All Saints, for peace, to the Holy Cross. Hours of the Cross worked in. Office of the Virgin followed by Salue regina and prayer, Omnipotens sempiterne deus qui gloriose uirginis . . .

5. ff. 74v–75 Oratio ad Mariam (in violet). Gaude, flore uirginali . . . sed durabunt et florescent in perhenni gloria.

Leroquais, *Heures* 1:xxvii, 2:409. *RH* 6810.

6. f. 75v Dulcissime domine Ihesu Christe qui beatissimam genitricem tuam . . . feliciter peruiamus (*sic*) eterna. Qui uiuis et regnas.

Leroquais, *Heures* 1:282.

7. ff. 75v–76 Oratio de domina nostra (in violet). Gaude uirgo mater Christi que per aurem concepisti, Gabriele nuntio . . . per te detur nobis frui in perhenni uirginem gaudio. Amen.

Leroquais, *Heures* 2:409. *RH* 7017.

8. f. 76 Oratio (in violet). Deus qui beatissimam uirginem Mariam in conceptu et partu uirginitate reseruata duplici gaudio letificasti . . . et precibus intercessione ualeamus peruenire. Per Christum dominum nostrum.

f. 76v blank; f. 77 blank and unruled; f. 77v, miniature for the following text.

Leroquais, *Heures* 1:54.

9. ff. 78–82 Eas uideas laudes qui sacra uirgine gaudes et uenerando piam studeas laudare Mariam uirginis uita eterne (*sic*) cum ueneris ante figuram pretereundo, caue ne taceatur aue inuenies ueniam sic salutando Mariam; Salue (in violet). Salue, uirgo uirginum, stella matutina, sordidorum . . . in gloria sua collocare in secula seculorum. Amen.

Attributed to Bonaventure, *Carmina super canticum "Salve regina,"* Bonaventure, *Opera omnia* (Rome, 1596), 6:489–90. *RH* 18318. Glorieux, 305, bs. See MS 56, text 74.

10. f. 82 Oratio (in violet). Deus qui de beate Marie uirginis utero uerbum tuum . . . apud te intercessionibus adiuuemur. Per eundem Christum dominum nostrum. Amen.

SMRL 2:472 usually follows the above text.

11. ff. 82–83v Oratio de sancta Maria (in violet). O intemerata et in eternum benedicta . . . O Iohannes . . . Uobis duobus ego miserrimus peccator . . . et post huius uite cursum ad gaudia me ducat electorum suorum benignissimus paraclitus.

Wilmart, pp. 488–90.

12. ff. 83v–85 Item alia oratio ad uirginem Mariam (in violet). Obsecro te domina sancta Maria . . . Et michi famulo tuo . . . Maria, mater dei et misericordie. Amen.

f. 86 blank and unruled; f. 86v, miniature for the following text.

Leroquais, *Heures* 2:346–47.

13. ff. 87–89 Quicumque hec septem gaudia in honore beate Marie uirginis semel in die dixerit [centum dies indulgenciam obtinebit a domino papa Clemente] qui hec septem gaudia proprio stilo, composuit (in violet, words in brackets crossed out, s. xvi). Uirgo templum trinitatis, deus summe bonitatis . . . ad eternum gaudium . . .

Philippe de Grève, *VII gaudia beatae Mariae.* Wilmart, p. 329, n. 1.

14. f. 89–89v Deprecor te sanctissima Maria mater dei pietate plenissima . . . intercedas pro me peccatore .N. famulo tuo . . . uitam et requiem sempiternam. Amen.

f. 90 blank; f. 90v, miniature for the following text.

Leroquais, *Heures* 2:395.

15. ff. 91–93v Ad ymaginem domini nostri Ihesu Christi (in violet). Omnibus consideratis . . . quem Christus eripuit.

Jean de Limoges, *De passione Christi,* often found in books of hours; Wilmart, p. 584 (note to p. 527). *Analecta hymnica* 31:87–89. Text followed by Kyrieleyson; cues for Pater noster and Et ne nos; Christus factus est pro nobis obediens . . . ; Ora pro nobis sancta dei genitrix . . . ; Ualde honorandus est . . .

15 bis. ff. 93v–94 Omnipotens sempiterne deus qui unigenitum filium tuum dominum nostrum Ihesum Christum crucem coronam spineam et quinque uulnera subire . . . a peccatorum nostrorum nexibus eorum precibus liberemur. Per . . .

16. ff. 94–95v Incipit oratio uenerabilis Bede presbiteri de qua fertur quod cotidie et deuote flexis genibus eam dicens nec dyabolus nec mali homines ei poterint nocere nec sine confessione morietur et per tringinta dies ante obitum suum uidebit gloriosam uirginem Mariam in auxilium sibi preparatam; Oratio septem uerborum domini nostri Ihesu Christi (in violet). Domine Ihesu Christe qui septem uerba die ultima uite tue in cruce pendens dixisti . . . in regno meo epulari, iocundari et commorari per infinita secula seculorum. Amen.

The rubric has been partly effaced by an incompletely removed paper masking sheet, s. xvi.

Leroquais, *Heures* 2:342 and 128, in the latter instance attributed to Bede. *Horae eboracenses,* pp. 141–42. See also MS 82, text 17.

17. ff. 95v–96 Oratio (in violet). Precor te, piissime domine Ihesu Christe, propter eximiam caritatem qua humanum genus dilexisti quando tu rex celestis pendebas in cruce . . . propter magnam misericordiam tuam michi tribuere digneris. Amen.

Leroquais, *Heures* 2:443. Wilmart, p. 378n (no. 12).

18. f. 96–96v Oratio (in violet). Gratias ago tibi domine Ihesu Christe qui uoluisti pro redemptione mundi a iudeis reprobari . . . quo perduxisti tecum crucifixum latronem et omnes sanctos et sancti (*sic*). Qui . . .

Leroquais, *Heures* 2:412. Cf. MS 56, text 37, and MS 82, text 26.

19. f. 97 Salutationes ad sacrosanctum sacramentum (in violet). Aue, domine Ihesu Christe, uerbum patris, filius uirginis . . . uera fons amoris pax dulcedo requies nostra uita perhennis. Amen.

Wilmart, pp. 412–13, no. 3.

20. f. 97–97v Oratio (in violet). Aue, principium nostre creationis, aue precium nostre redemptionis . . . et concede michi famulo tuo .N. . . . et fideliter accipere merear. Amen.

Wilmart, p. 587.

21. f. 97v Ad sacrosanctum sacramentum (in violet). Aue, uerum corpus natum de Maria uirgine . . . O pie, O Ihesu fili Marie, miserere nobis.

Leroquais, *Heures* 2:382. *RH* 2175.

22. ff. 97v–98 Oratio (in violet). Aue caro Christi cara, immolata crucis ara, redemptoris hostia . . . fac redemptos luce clara tecum frui gloria. Amen.

Wilmart, p. 379n.

23. f. 98 Oratio (in violet). Anima Christi, sanctifica me; corpus Christi, salua me . . . in secula seculorum. Amen.

Lexikon für Theologie und Kirche 1:563–64. Leroquais, *Heures* 2:340. *RH* 1090.

24. f. 98–98v Cuilibet dicenti hanc orationem inter eleuationem corporis Christi et tercium agnus dei dominus [papa Bonifacius sextus concessit dua milia annorum indulgenciarum] ad supplicationem Philippi regis Francie; Oratio (in violet, portion in brackets crossed out, s. xvi). Domine Ihesu Christe qui hanc sacratissimam carnem tuam et pretiosum sanguinem tuum de gloriose uirginis Marie utero . . . et ab uniuersis malis presentibus, preteritis et futuris nunc et in euum. Per . . .

f. 99 blank and unruled; f. 99v, miniature for the following text.

Wilmart, p. 378n (no. 10).

25. ff. 100–106v Incipiunt septem psalmi penitentiales (in violet).

26. ff. 106v–108 Incipiunt xv psalmi (in violet). Cues only for psalms 119–130, followed by psalms 131, 132, and 133.

27. ff. 108–114v Letania (in violet). Chad, Gildard, Cedd "Swichine" and "Burine" among the confessors; Praxedis, Petronilla, Edith, and Afra among the virgins; Thomas of Canterbury erased from among the confessors. Litany proper followed by six short prayers: Deus cui proprium est . . . ; Exaudi, quesumus, domine . . . ; Omnipotens sempiterne

deus qui facis mirabilia . . . ; Deus qui caritatis dona . . . ; Ineffabilem misericordiam tuam . . . ; Pietate tuo quesumus, domine. . . . Cue only for Deus a quo sancta desideria . . .

f. 115 blank and unruled; f. 115v, miniature for the following text.

28. ff. 116–135v Incipiunt uigilie mortuorum (in violet).

f. 136 blank and unruled; f. 136v, miniature for the following text.

29. ff. 137–147v Incipiunt commendationes animarum (in violet).

f. 148 blank; f. 148v, miniature for the following text.

Leroquais, *Heures* 2:391; cf. *Horae eboracenses,* pp. 111–14.

30. ff. 147v, 149–153 Incipit psalterium de passione domini (in violet). Psalms 21–29 and 30, 1–6 with cues only for 22–24, 26, and 29. Followed by the prayer, Respice, quesumus, domine super hanc familiam tuam . . . et crucis subire tormentorum (*sic*). Cf. *Horae eboracenses,* pp. 114–15.

31a. f. 153v Rubric for the *Psalter of Saint Jerome* almost exactly as printed in *Horae eboracenses,* pp. 116–23; cf. Leroquais, *Heures* 2:89 and 456. Traces of paper mask, s. xvi.

31b. f. 154 Oratio (in violet). Suscipere digneris, domine deus omnipotens, istos psalmos consecratos . . . per omnia secula seculorum. Amen.

ff. 154v–155 blank; f. 155v, miniature for the following text.

Leroquais, *Heures* 2:456. This prayer frequently precedes the *Psalter of Saint Jerome*.

31c. ff. 156–166 Incipit psalterium beati Iheronimi (in violet).

31d. f. 166 Oratio (in violet). Omnipotens sempiterne deus clemenciam tuam suppliciter deprecamur ut me famulum tuum .N. . . . atque defunctis proficiat ad gloriam sempiternam. Per . . .

f. 166v blank.

This prayer usually follows the *Psalter of Saint Jerome*.

Twenty-seven full-page miniatures on inserted leaves accompanied by two different border schemes. Border A: blue, green, orange acanthus spray with a gold ivy stem frame, English in appearance. Border B: blue, gold, violet acanthus spray with floral decoration including thistles, violets, and strawberries, very similar to the Bruges borders associated with Willem Vrelant. Each border accompanied by initials in matching colors 5 lines high. f. 7v, Christ with angels playing music on an instrument belonging to the lute family and a harp on either side, border A; f. 14v, Gnadenstuhl Trinity, border B; f. 17v, John the Baptist, border B; f. 19v, George, border B; f. 21v, Christopher, border B; f. 23v, Martyrdom of Thomas à Becket, border B; f. 25v, Anne, the Virgin and Child, border B; f. 27v, Mary Magdalene, border B; f. 29v, Catherine, border B; f. 31v, Barbara, border B; f. 33v, Margaret, border B; f. 35v, Jesus in the Garden of Gethsemane, border A; f. 42v, the Kiss of Judas, border B; f. 54v, Christ before Pilate, border B; f. 58v, the Flagellation, border B; f. 61v, Jesus carrying the Cross, border B; f. 64v, the Crucifixion, border B; f. 67v, Deposition from the Cross, border B; f. 70v, the Entombment, border B; f. 77v, the Coronation of the Virgin, border B; f. 86v, Mary ascending the steps at the Temple, border B; f. 90v, Adam and Eve in the Garden below the *Arbor Vitae,* the devil as a female-headed snake entwined around it, border B; f. 99v, Last Judgment, border A; f. 115v, funeral service by priests and black monks, border B; f. 136v, God the Father receiving two naked souls, border B; f. 148v, Man of Sorrows, behind him the instruments of torture, border B; f. 155v, Jerome at his desk, border B. Nine historiated initials 5 lines high. f. 91, the three crosses accompanied by a full border of type B. Probable change of artist. f. 91v, two initials, Jesus and the stigmatum on right hand accompanied by a bracket left type B border. f. 92, two initials, stigmatum on left hand and the wounds of Christ accompanied by a bracket left type B border. f. 92v, two initials, stigmatum on the left foot and stigmatum on the right foot. f. 93, two initials, Pietà and John the Evangelist accompanied by a bracket left type B border. ff. 91v, 92, 92v, 93 bracket left border of type B. Gold, blue, and magenta dentelle initials throughout. Guides for the insertion of miniatures written in the lower margins of the verso of the preceding folio; that on f. 18v indicates a miniature of Saint John the Evangelist, now removed.

Parchment. ff. iii + 166 + i. 204 × 140 mm (105 × 70 mm). Collation impracticable. Alphabetical leaf signatures mostly trimmed. Ruled in violet ink. Text written in 19 long lines, calendar in 33 long lines, both in gothic textualis quadrata formata. Headings in red in script of text.

Bound in dark brown calf, s. xv, stamped with the same panel four times, front and back incorporating the motto Sancta Maria Mater and with another smaller panel including a griffin, Margaret coming out of the dragon (?), a wyvern, a stag, a mermaid, an Agnus Dei, a unicorn, a lion, and a monkey.

Written and decorated in Bruges, c. 1455, for the English market as indicated by the phrase, "secundum consuetudinem Anglie" on f. 36. Saints and selections of texts are typically English. Texts 11, 12, 14, and 20 in the masculine form. Front pastedown: "The namys of the children of Wilham Gonstone and Benet his wif of the perisshe of Saincte Donistones in the est as hereafter ffolowith." List on flyleaf i. First entry: "Friday the xxiiii day of November being Saincte Clementis Day and the xxiiii yere of King Henry VIIth . . ."; last entry written in the "Sixt yere of our sayde souuerayne lorde King Henry the Eight." f. i^{v}–ii^{v}, list of the children of Thomas Mildmay (*sic*); births recorded in various hands to 1607. f. ii^{v}, name of Walter Mildmaye; cf. *DNB* 13:374. f. 8, a heraldic ownership mark drawn in pen in lower margin possibly that of Mildmaye. Stubbs following f. 166 indicate traces of other ownership notes, now removed. Erasures, masking, and scratching out of references to Thomas à Becket and indulgences date from English Reformation. Ownership attributed to Baron Fitzwalter (d. 1608) by Kessler, *French and Flemish Illuminated Manuscripts,* no. 5, not confirmable from the book. Acquired by the Newberry from Edward E. Ayer, 1920.

De Ricci, 1:536. *La Siècle d'or de la miniature flamande* (exhibition catalogue; Brussels, 1959), p. 164. Kessler, *French and Flemish Illuminated Manuscripts,* no. 5 (plates of 35v, 56v, and 90v).

f36

(Ry 20; I7406)

Alain Chartier, *Quadrilogue Invectif, Dialogus Familiaris, Traité de l'Espérance* (in English); Boethius, *De Consolatione Philosophiae* (in English and Latin); William of Tigonville, *Les Dits des Philosophes* (in English)

England [*Illustrated*] c. 1480

1. ff. 1–23 To the ryght high and excellent magister of princes . . . and rathir for profytyng by goode exortation than for repriefe to any persone.

Alain Chartier, *Quadrilogue invectif* (English translation), ed. Blayney, *Fifteenth-Century English Translations* 1:134–246.

2. ff. 23–32v A famylyer dialogue of the ffrende and þe ffellawe uppon the lamentacyon of the miserable calamyte of Ffraunce (in red). What is it my most trusty frende . . . And fere we both wele in the comon pece. Amen. Here endeth the Ffamylyer dialouge of the ffrende and the ffelaw upon the lamentable compleynt of the calamyte of Fraunce.

Alain Chartier, *Dialogus familiaris* (English translation), ed. R. A. Dwyer, Ph.D. dissertation, U.C.L.A., 1965. Blayney, *Fifteenth-Century English Translations* 1:11.

3. ff. 33–78 In the Xth yere of my sorofoule exile . . . But the prophecye of Danyell abideth yet for to come.

Alain Chartier, *Le Traité de l'espérance* (English translation). Blayney, *Fifteenth-Century English Translations* 1:3–132, line 24.

4. ff. 78–204

The whyle that Rome was reynyng in hys
flowres . . .
þat all þing do beholde plenerly.

Boethius, *De consolatione philosophiae,* English translation of John Walton, ed. M. Science, EETS, o.s., no. 170 (London, 1927). In this manuscript, the translation is interspersed with the original Latin text (written entirely as prose). Translator's prologue not present. See R. A. Dwyer, "The Newberry's Unknown Version of Walton's Boethius," *Manuscripta* 17 (1972): 27–30.

5. ff. 204–205 Tempore Theodorici regis insignis auctor Boecius claruit . . . quia iam non erat tantus amor sapiencie quantus prius fuerit.

Text related to *Vita Boethii,* ed. R. Peiper, *Philosophiae consolationis* (Leipzig, 1871), pp. xxx–xxxv. See F. Troncarelli, *Tradizioni perdute: la Consolatio philosophiae nell'alto medioevo* (Medioevo e umanesimo, 42; Padua, 1981), pp. 1–37.

6. ff. 205v–207v [R]ecapitulacio quinque librorum Boecii de consolacione philosophie; [C]armina (in red). In isto primo metro plangit Boecius . . . In fine monet nos euitare uicia et malum et adherere bona. Per dominum J. Clynton priorem scriptum. 148. (=? 1480).

Cf. C. Halm et al., *Catalogus codicum latinorum bibliothecae regiae monacensis,* vol. 2, pt. 2 (Munich, 1878), 15825.

7. ff. 207v–241 Incipit prologus de dictis philosophorum de gallica manca translata (in red). Syn yt ys so þat every naturalle creature . . . Incipit liber de dictis philosophorum translatus de gallica in anglica per Antonium Ryvers comes de Ryvers et cetera (in red). Sedethyas was þe fyrst phylysovyr . . . the fyrst was Esculapyus þe seconde Goryus.

f. 207v, in sixteenth-century cursive in upper margin, "Anthony Woodvile de la Riveux lord Stalles et cetera translated this work entire from Ffrench into thys old English."

ff. 241–242v blank.

William of Tigonville, *The Dictes and Sayings of the Philosophers,* translation of Anthony Rivers. Facsimile of the Caxton edition of 1477 (London, 1877). See C. F. Bühler, "The Newberry Library Manuscript of *The Dictes and Sayings of the Philosophers,*" *Anglia* 74 (1956): 281–91. Albert Hartung, *A Manual of the Writings in English 1050–1500* (New Haven, Conn., 1967), pp. 802–3.

Parchment. ff. i + 243. Modern foliation 1–241, two folios 201, last folio unnumbered. ff. 203 and 242, severely cropped. ff. 117–122, mutilated by removal of lower corners. f. 208, margin removed along outer line of ruling. Trimmed to 305 × 225 mm (200 × 150 mm). 1^{10} (1 wanting), $2–5^{10}$, 6^{12}, 7^{10}, $8–11^{8}$, $12–17^{12}$, 18^{10}, $19–25^{8}$, 26^{8} (2–7 stubs only). Some catchwords present. Quire 6 numbered on verso of the last leaf "vi." Quires 8, 9, and 18 on upper margins of ff. 72, 80, and 176, numbered respectively 1, 2, and 10 in arabic numerals. f. 96, quire 10, numbered "ii" in red in lower right corner. Cf. Blayney, *Fifteenth-Century English Translations* 2:9. Frame ruled in pen, prickings visible. Written by at least two hands. ff. 1–78, in secretary media incorporating many anglicana traits in 38–40 long lines; ff. 78–241 in a hybrida media incorporating many anglicana traits. Writing generally hung on the upper ruled line. Headings and names of *personae* in red in script of text. ff. 1–78, red initials historiated with human faces, acorns, and oak leaves in ink of text. Simple red initials and red paragraph marks throughout. In text 4, initial letter of each line of verse touched in red. ff. 78–235, in prose sections, red used as punctuation.

Bound in brown calf over cardboard, s. xvii, gilt stamping on spine.

Written in England, signed in red on f. 207v, by J. Clynton in 1480 (?), see above. Front pastedown, "Christoforus Lincolne Monachus" written in red in fifteenth-century textualis, final letter historiated with face of monk, possibly name of a scribe or rubricator [cf. Cottineau, 1:1622]; occasional notes, s. xv–xvi, in margins. In s. xvi, owned by Thomas Sowthen, an indenture between him and John Craven, dated 1574, written on outer margin of f. 98. f. 241v, "Thomas Sowthen dyed this last day of Aprill 1579" followed by these verses:

Mr. Thomas Sowthen did owne this boke
God gave him grace thereon to loke
and when he hath lokte to tak good hede
and marke the thinge that he doth rede
and I Isaac Frise will bere record
that it was Thomas Sowthens in the yere of our lord
1 thousand fyve hundred seventie and seven
and so god send vs all the blis of heaven
Amen qoth Isaac Ffrise, [his mark].

f. 242, date of 1575 in hand of Isaac Frise. f. 242v, acronym of Isaac Frise, see Blayney, *Fifteenth-Century English Translations* 2:10–11. Beginning of same acronym written on f. 242. f. 241, brief enigmatic notes for years 1571–81, by another hand. Front pastedown and f. 241v, signature of R. Alsen in an Elizabethan hand. In s. xx, in the library of Lord Clifford of Ugbrooke Park, Chudleigh, Devonshire. Sold to William H. Robinson. Acquired by the Newberry from William H. Robinson (cat. 60, 1936, item no. 39) in March 1937.

Second folio: vertu and lett.

Faye-Bond, pp. 148–49.

f37.1

Froissart, *Chroniques,* Book I (beginning)

Flanders s. XV[1] (after 1425)

1. ff. 1′–8′ Chi commenche la genealogie, de pluiseurs rois de Franche et de leurs hoirs . . . et ses fiex sen vinrent a Paris. Queres le remanant de ceste histore en l'autre livre apries cest ichi.

f. 8′v blank, followed by three unnumbered folios, entirely blank.

The genealogy of the kings of France which begins this text is the same as Brussels, BR, 11138–39, ff. 8v–9. It is followed immediately by the *Chronique normande du xiv*e *siècle,* ed. A. and E. Moliner (Paris, 1882), to the year 1317. Other manuscripts of this combined text: Lille, BM, 633, and Brussels, BR, 20628. See Saenger, "A Lost Manuscript Refound," pp. 15–26.

2. ff. 1–269v A fin que les grans merveilles et li biau fait d'armes . . . nous nos retournerons a parler dou duch de Lancastre.

Jean Froissart, *Chroniques,* Book I, sections 1–641 in the edition of S. Luce (Paris, 1869–), 1:1–7:191.

Paper with watermark, cf. Briquet 2988. ff. 282. Foliated 1–8, followed by three unfoliated leaves, 1–127, followed by one unfoliated leaf, 128, followed by one unfoliated leaf, 129–269. Trimmed to 370 × 258 mm (280 × 170–85 mm). 1^{12} (1 wanting), $2–5^{12}$, 6^{6}, $7–10^{12}$, 11^{14} (a leaf wanting), 12^{12}, 13^{12} (a leaf wanting), 14^{14}, 15^{10}, 16^{14}, 17^{10}, 18^{14}, 19^{10}, 20^{14}, 21^{10}, 22^{14}, 23^{10}, 24^{14} (14 wanting). ff. 1–54, catchwords present. Ruled in hard point and pencil. Prickings visible on inner margins. ff. 55–269, frame ruled in pencil and hard point. Written by two scribes: f. 1–54, in cursiva media in 60 lines in two columns; ff. 55–269, in cursiva media tending to currens in 41–57 lines in two columns by Johannis Caulier; see MS f37.2, f. 237v. Writing begins on the first ruled line throughout. ff. 1–54, incipits of each chapter in textualis media. f. 1v, heading in red written in script of text, partly trimmed. Guide letters to rubricators present throughout. Red initials and line fillers throughout.

Bound in black stained sheepskin, s. xviii. Spine title in gold: "Froissar (*sic*) Tom I."

Written in Flanders in the first half of the fifteenth century after 1425, the release from captivity of Raoul de Gaucourt alluded to in MS f37.2, text 4, partially in the hand of Johannis Caulier. Tipped onto front pastedown is the armorial bookplate of Cardinal Guilielmus van Hamme, dated 1659, possibly transferred from another book. In s. xviii, in the library of Abbé Jean Favier, sold at auction in Lille, 1765. See L. Delisle, "Notice sur un manuscrit perdu des chroniques de Froissart," *Bibliothèque de l'École des Chartes* 33 (1872): 286–88. De Lettenhove, *Oeuvres de Froissart,* pp. 433–35. Saenger, "A Lost Manuscript Refound," pp. 15–26. Sold by Sotheby's at auction of the Clumber Library, 12 June 1937, lot no. 945; *Colophons de manuscrits occidentaux,* 9205. Pencil notations on front pastedown, "244"; within a circle, "138" underlined; "24/c" written in pen. Acquired by the Newberry from Maggs Brothers, 1938.

Second folio: et xvii. Et quant.

Faye-Bond, p. 152.

f37.2

Froissart, *Chroniques,* Book I (conclusion) and Book II

Flanders s. XV[1] (after 1425)

1. ff. 1–237v Chi comenche li capellains de sainte Anne (in red, partially removed in trimming). Quant li dus de Lancastre se fu retrais en le ville de Calais . . . Ensy tresboche fortune ses amis et ennemis. Je me suis [–?] Jo[hannis] Caullier. Orate, pro huius partis scriptore (in red).

ff. 238–241v blank. Deletion on f. 237v in red.

Froissart, *Chroniques,* Book I, section 641 to the end; Book II (complete) in the edition of S. Luce (Paris, 1869–), 7:191–11:313.

2. ff. 242–246v Or wel iou parler et traittier de une grande matere qui fu moult merveilleuse. C'est de Jehan de Baiviere . . . Et s'en o rala cascuns en sen pays et en se plache.

This text describing the rebellion of the Liègeois against Louis of Bavaria also exists as a continuation of the *Chronique normande* in Brussels, BR, 11138–39, ed. Kervyn de Lettenhove, *Istore et chroniques de Flandres d'après les textes de divers manuscrits* (Brussels, 1879–80), 2:426–36.

3. ff. 247–248v Chi ensieut le bataille de Roussiauville (in red). En lan mille cccc et xv apries paskes . . . acompagnies de boines gens d'armes.

f. 249–249v blank.

A description of the Battle of Agincourt, composed after 1425. Editions: M. Quenson, "Battaile de Azincourt," *Archives historiques et littéraires du nord de la France et du midi de la Belgique* 4 (1834): 136–44, and P. A. Roger, *Noblesse et chevalerie du comté de Flandre, d'Artois et de Picardie* (Amiens, n.d.), pp. 161–73. For date of composition, see J. H. Wylie, *The Reign of Henry the Fifth* (Cambridge, 1914–29), 3:444.

Paper. Watermark identical to MS f37.1. ff. 249. Trimmed to 370 × 256 mm (283 × 170–80 mm). $1–2^{12}$, 3^{14}, $4–16^{12}$, 17^{12} (1 wanting), $18–20^{12}$, 21^{10} (9–10 stubs only). Catchwords present quires 1–13 only. ff. 1–182, quires 1–13, and ff. 242–249, quire 19, ruled in hard point and pencil. Prickings visible in inner margins. ff. 183–241, frame ruled in pencil and hard point. ff. 1–182 and 242–248v, written in gothic cursiva media in 60 lines in two columns by same scribe as copied MS f37.1, ff. 1–54. ff. 183–241, written in gothic cursiva media, tending to currens in 51–54 lines in two columns (see Examples of Selected Scripts) by Johannis Caulier, signed on f. 237v. Writing begins on first ruled line throughout. ff. 1–182 and 242–248v, incipits of each chapter in textualis media. Guide letters to rubricators present throughout. Red initials and line fillers throughout. f. 182v, red heading trimmed and rendered illegible.

Binding identical to MS f37.1. Spine title: "Froissar (*sic*) Tom 2."

Written in the first half of the fifteenth century, after 1425, in Flanders. Bookplate of Cardinal Guilielmus van Hamme, dated 1659, pasted to front pastedown. Provenance as for MS f37.1.

Second folio: se il voloit.

Faye-Bond, p. 152.

f38

(c 19171)

Book of Hours, Use of Rome

Low Countries c. 1450

1. ff. 1–5v Short Hours of the Cross, beginning imperfectly.

2. ff. 6–8v Short Hours of the Holy Spirit, beginning imperfectly.

3. ff. 9–13 Missa de beata uirgine Maria (in red). Salue sancta parens . . . Part of rubric may have been trimmed when margin was removed.

4. ff. 13–14 Inicium sancti euangelii secundum Iohannem . . . (in red). John 1:1–14.

5. f. 14–14v (addition s. xvi) Cento, beginning with Psalm 69:2, followed by Ave Maria and Psalm 29:1–2.

6. ff. 15–58v Hours of the Virgin, use of Rome, beginning imperfectly. Nine psalms at matins with rubrics for the days of the week; opening leaf of terce missing after f. 41; of sext after f. 44; of nones after f. 45.

7. ff. 59–64v Changed Office of the Virgin, beginning imperfectly.

8. ff. 65–73 Seven Penitential Psalms, beginning imperfectly.

9. ff. 73–75v Litany including Jeremiah and David among the patriarchs and prophets. Litany proper followed by [Deus a quo sancta desideria] . . . (beginning wanting), Ure igne sancti spiritus . . . , Fidelium deus omnium conditor . . . , Omnipotens sempiterne deus qui uiuorum dominaris simul . . . Folios with text removed after ff. 73 and 74.

10. ff. 76–100 Incipit officium mortuorum (in red). Use of Rome. Folio with text removed after f. 78.

11. ff. 100–103v Obsecro te . . . Et michi indigno famulo tuo impetres . . . dulcissima uirgo Maria, mater dei et misericordie. Amen.

Leroquais, *Heures* 2:346–47.

Parchment. ff. 103. An undetermined number of folios removed before f. 1; single folios of text or miniatures removed after ff. 5, 8, 14, 41, 44, 45, 58, 64, 73, 74, 75, and 78. ff. 9, 30, 39, 48–51, 55, 84–85, 102, margin all or in part removed. 118 × 80 mm (67 × 51 mm). 1^8 (1 and 7 removed), 2^8, 3^8 (1 removed), $4–5^8$, 6^8 (5 removed), 7^8 (1, 3, and 8 removed), 8^{10} (10 removed), 9^6, 10^9 (1, an inserted leaf), 11^8 (1, 3, and 5 removed), 12^8 (2 removed), 13^8, 14^8 (5 removed), 15^4. Ruled in violet ink. Written in Italian style gothic textualis rotunda media in 16 long lines. Headings in red in script of text. Gold, blue, and magenta dentelle initials. Minor blue initials with red flourishes and gold initials with black flourishes.

Bound in olive green deerskin (s. xvi?) with four brass corners on front and back, one back-to-front clasp; pouch for rosary at bottom. For a similar portable binding depicted in the hands of a Dominican friar, see E. Mâle and E. Pognon, *Jean Bourdichon: les heures de'Anne de Bretagne* (Paris, 1946), pl. xxi; cf. K. Haebler, *Deutsche Bibliophilen des 16 Jahrhunderts* (Leipzig, 1923), p. 9 and pl. 2; H. Lufting and H. E. Teitge, *Handschriften und alte Drucke* (Wiesbaden, 1981), p. 237; and E.-M. Hannebutt-Benz, *Die Kunst des Lesens* (Frankfurt am Main, 1985), pp. 19 and 42.

Written in the Low Countries, possibly in Bruges c. 1450 as indicated by the initials, ruling, and fragments of border decoration. Text 11 in the masculine form. Red double-edged oval stickers on front pastedown bear nos. 3 in ink, 86 in pencil. "Ad maiorem dei gloriam" written on blank portion of f. 103v in very black ink by the same early modern hand which has rewritten the incipit on f. 1. Acquired by the Newberry in 1924 from Alexander Greene, list 39, item no. 1.

Second folio: meris ad locum.

De Ricci, 1:541. D. Miner, *The History of Bookbinding 525–1950 A.D.* (exhibition catalogue; Baltimore, 1957), p. 56; W. H. Blumenthal, "Girdle Books for Waist Wear," *The American Book Collector* 13 (1963): 17–23; J. A. Szirmai, "The Girdle Book of the Museum Meermanno-Westreenianum," *Quaerendo* 18 (1988): 18–34.

39

(23872)

Book of Hours, Use of Rome (incomplete)

Bruges c. 1460

1. ff. 1v–14 (f. 2) Incipit confessio dicenda ante missam beate Marie (in red). In nomine patris et filii et spiritus sancti. Amen. Sancti spiritus adsit nobis gratia. Amen. Et introibo ad altare dei . . . (f. 5) Sequitur missa gloriosissime uirginis Marie (in red). Salue sancta Parens . . .

f. 1 blank; f. 1v, miniature.

2. ff. 14–16 *Inicium* sancti euangelii *Secundum Johannem* (only words in italics in red). Io 1:1–14.

3. ff. 16–19 Seguex se Te deum laudamus a honor de la gloriosa uerge Maria (in red). Te matrem dei laudamus, te matrem uirginem confitemur . . . ut nos deffendas in eternum.

Cf. Leroquais, *Heures* 2:456; *RH* 20156.

4. ff. 19–22 Seguex se lo Te deum laudamus lo qual feren los benauenturats sent Augusti e sen Ambros al lahor, gloria et honor de nostre senyor deu Ihesu Christ (in red). Te deum laudamus te dominum confitemur. Te eternum . . . (f. 21v) E pot se dir lo sobredit Te deum en lo offici de la gloriosissima uerge Maria ço es a saber ans de les laudes (in red).

f. 22v blank.

RH 20086.

5. ff. 23–72 Incipit officium crucifixi quod composuit ffrater Bonauentura (in red).

f. 72v blank.

Bonaventure, *Officium de passione domini, Opera omnia* 8:152–58.

6. ff. 73–78 Short Hours of the Cross. ff. 77v–78, Direu agenollada la Salue regina . . . (in red).

7. f. 78–78v Oratio (in red). Interueniat pro nobis quesumus, domine Ihesu Christe, nunc et in hora mortis mee apud clemenciam tuam, beata et gloriosa uirgo Maria . . . doloris gladius pertransiuit et in resurreccione tua nouus amor accendit. Qui uiuis et regnas cum deo patre in unitate spiritus sancti deus per omnia secula seculorum. Amen.

Leroquais, *Heures* 2:34.

8. ff. 79–83v Incipit officium sancti spiritus (in red). Short Hours of the Holy Spirit.

9. ff. 83v–88v Cimbolum Athanasi (in red). Quicumque uult saluus esse . . . Saluus esse non poterit. Gloria patri et cetera.

Leroquais, *Heures* 2:444.

10. ff. 88v–90 Seguexen se los nou miseferes a deu acceptes (in red). Miserere mei et exaudi oracionem meam . . . quia multum repleti sumus despeccione. Gloria patri et cetera.

Leroquais, *Heures* 1:186.

11. ff. 90–91 Los set uersos del glorios sent Bernat (in red). Illumina oculos meos neumquam (*sic*) obdormiam in morte . . . et consolatus est me. Gloria patri.

Leroquais, *Heures* 2:415.

12. ff. 91–92v Commemoracio beati Michaelis archangeli (in red). Princeps gloriosissime Michael dux celestium exercituum . . . (f. 92) Oracio (in red). Omnipotens sempiterne deus qui saluti humano generi ex summa clemencia tua . . . et tue excelse magestati beatifice presentari. Per . . .

Leroquais, *Heures* 2:80.

13. ff. 92v–94 Comemoracio omnium ciuium paradisi (in red). (f. 93) O gloriosissimi ciues paradisi eterni et ueri dei mundissima specula . . . (f. 95) Oracio (in red). Pater omnis creature, creator deus qui humanos actus et uitam per angelicam custodiam gubernari uoluisti . . . in illa celesti Hierusalem gloria. Per . . .

f. 94v blank.

f. 1v (a separate leaf) Full-page illustration of the Annunciation, full border of blue and gold acanthus with floral decoration and marginal figures, all of the variety associated with the workshop of Willem Vrelant in Bruges. f. 2, full border and blue, magenta, and gold initial 6 lines high. f. 5, full border with initial 6 lines high. ff. 23, 32, 39v, 43, 49, 55v, 63, 67, 73, and 79, full border with initials 4–5 lines high. f. 55v, King David playing a harp in the outer margin. Minor blue, magenta, and gold dentelle initials throughout, some with sprigs of border decoration.

Parchment. ff. 94. Formerly foliated [1]–34, 229–96 with numerous errors, refoliated 1–94. 178 × 124 mm (85 × 60 mm). Written space washed in yellow. 1^{1+8}, 2^8, 3^6 (6 wanting), $4–12^8$. Horizontal catchwords preceded and followed by a flourished dot. Ruled in violet. Written in Catalonian (i.e., Italian) style gothic textualis rotunda in 14 long lines. Headings in red in script of text. Incipits in mixed rustic capitals and uncials.

Bound in red morocco, s. xix, silver back-to-front clasps.

Written in Bruges, c. 1460, by a scribe with Catalonian training. Rubric at the end of text 6 in feminine form. Two other portions of this codex in Brussels, BR, IV. 35 and IV. 375. L. M. J. Delaissé, "A Spanish Scribe, a Dutch Miniaturist, and a Flemish Manuscript in the Newberry Library," *Library Bulletin* 4 (1957), 139–41 and plate of f. 1v. *Le Siècle d'or de la miniature flamande* (exhibition catalogue; Brussels, 1959), p. 165. L. Gilissen, "Membra disjecta d'un livre d'heures en latin et catalan," *Scriptorium* 14 (1960): 326–32. *Cinquantaire de la Société des bibliophiles et iconophiles de Belgique* (exhibition catalogue; Brussels, 1960), p. 7. H. Kessler, "A Book of Hours from the Atelier of William Vreland," *Scriptorium* 18 (1964): 94–99. *Vingt livres de la bibliothèque de feu M. Fernand J. Nyssen* (exhibition catalogue; Brussels, 1967), p. 3. Kessler, *French and Flemish Illuminated Manuscripts*, no. 7 (plate of f. 1). See also Warner, *Descriptive Catalogue*, no. 103, and Sotheby's sales catalogue of 1 December 1958, lot no. 78. No. 45 from the collection of Henry Probasco, acquired by the Newberry 1 December 1890.

Second folio: Incipit confessio.

De Ricci, 1:529.

f40

Pseudo Ludolf of Saxony,
Speculum humanae salvationis (in French)

Flanders c. 1455

ff. 1v–43 Ad ce doncques que nous ne resamblons pas Lucifer auant nous sommes reluisans . . . de l'amour divine et des felicites des cieulx ausquelz nous vueille produire le pere, le filz et le saint esperit. Amen.

ff. 1 and 43v–44v blank.

Ps. Ludolf of Saxony, *Speculum humanae salvationis* in the same abbreviated French translation as in the Hunterian Museum Library, University of Glasgow 60 (dated 1455) and Chantilly, Musée Condé 139 (c. 1500). Latin rubrics above the miniatures identify their subject, rubrics below the miniatures identify the sources. The translation omits the prologue and chapters 43–45 of the Latin text.

168 square miniatures: some fully colored, some partly grisaille, perhaps unfinished, within gold frames at the head of each column, following the iconographic conventions for chapters 1–42; cf. P. Pendrizet and J. Lutz, *Speculum humanae salvationis: texte critique, traduction inédite de Jean Miélot (1448)* (Leipzig, 1907). The style of the illumination is related to other manuscripts produced in Flanders in the mid-1450s. For a discussion of the artist, see H. L. Kessler, "The Chantilly *Miroir de l'humain salvation* and Its Models," in I. Lavin and J. Plummer, *Studies in Late Medieval and Renaissance Painting in Honor of Millard Meiss* (New York, 1977), p. 277, and A. and J. L. Wilson, *A Medieval Mirror, Speculum Humane Salvationis: 1324–1500* (Berkeley, 1984), pp. 77–80 with plates of ff. 1v, 3, 30v, and 37. Blue, green, and pink acanthus spray margins under the outer column of the verso of each folio in the presence of standard gold dentelle initials with white patterning on grounds of magenta and blue 4 lines high. Each initial extended to form a gold baguette in the outer left margin. Similar minor dentelle initials throughout.

Parchment. ff. 44. Modern foliation corrected in rebinding. 382 × 283 mm (210 × 155 mm). $1–3^{12}$, 4^{8}. Catchwords present. Ruled in violet ink. Written in *lettre bâtarde* media in 28 lines in two columns. Headings in red in script of text.

Bound in modern white calf over wooden boards. Formerly bound in red morocco by Niédrée, Paris, before 1844; see the manuscript annotations of the Crozet sales catalogue cited below.

Copied and decorated in Flanders, c. 1455. Formerly in the library of Philip the Good of Burgundy, recorded in the inventories of 1467 and 1485, J. Barrois, *Bibliothèque protypographique* (Paris, 1830), nos. 760 and 1620. Recorded in the Burgundian library until 1577; see the inventory of Vigilius printed in J. Marchal, *Catalogue des manuscrits de la Bibliothèque Royale des ducs de Bourgogne* (Brussels, 1842), 1:cclc. f. 1, "Le livre etoit intitulé de l'humaine salvation," written in an eighteenth-century hand. Sold at Maison Silvestre by Joseph Crozet to J. Techener, 20 December 1841; see the Newberry's annotated copy of the *Catalogue des livres composant le fonds de librairie de feu M. Crozet . . . publié avec des notes . . . de MM. Charles Nodier, G. Duplessis et Leroux de Lincy* (Paris, 1841), p. 2. According to the annotations, this manuscript sold by M. [Jules] G[allois] at Techoener's (*sic*), 13 May 1844. In 1853, said to be in the library of Robert S. Holford (1808–92), possibly recorded by G. F. Waagen, *Treasures of Art in Britain* (London, 1954), 2:221. Sold privately by his son Sir George Holford (1860–1926) to A. S. W. Rosenbach of Philadelphia; see De Ricci, *English Collectors*, pp. 115–16. Purchased by Louis H. Silver in 1952. Acquired by the Newberry from him in 1964.

Second folio: (rubric) Perceptum datur.
(text) Lieu n'estoit pas garni d'un arbre ne de deux.

Faye-Bond, p. 176. *Illuminated Books of the Middle Ages and Renaissance* (exhibition catalogue; Baltimore, 1949), p. 40. Kessler, *French and Flemish Illuminated Manuscripts*, no. 6. R. Achilles, ed., *Humanities' Mirror: Reading at the Newberry, 1887–1987* (Chicago, 1987), plate 14. R. A. Koch, *Miroir de la vie humaine: Newberry Library MS. f.40*, monograph in preparation.

– 41

(23487)

Book of Hours, Use of Paris

France c. 1480

1. ff. 2–13v Calendar of Orléans in French in red and black with major feasts in red including many of the feasts of Paris. Feasts include: Saincte Genevieve (3 January), Saint Maur (15 January), Saint Vincent (22 January, in red), Saint Flou, Saint Blaise (3 February, in red), Saincte Croys (4 May), La deliverance d'Orleans (9 May instead of 8 May, in red), Saint Germain (19 May), Saint Liphard (3 June), Saint Euvertre (12 June, in red), Saint Aignan (14 June, in red), Saint Avi (17 June, in red), Saint Martin (4 July, in red), Sainte Anne (26 July, in red), Saint Lo, Saint Gille (1 September), Saint Euvertre (7 September, in red), Saint Michiel (29 September, in red), Saint Francois (4 October, in red), Saint Denis (9 October, in red), Saint Mamert (13 October), Saint Aignan (17 November, in red), Saint Melinam (15 December).

2. ff. 14–20 Gospel sequences, that of John followed by prayer Protector in te sperancium . . .

f. 20v blank.

3. ff. 21–25 Obsecro te domina sancta Maria . . . Et michi famulo tuo . . . uirgo Maria, mater dei et misericordie. Amen.

Leroquais, *Heures* 2:346–47.

4. f. 25–25v Salue, regina, misericordie uita, dulcedo et spes nostra . . . O clemens, o pia, o dulcis Maria.

Leroquais, *Heures* 2:449. *RH* 18150.

5. ff. 25v–26 Concede nos famulos tuos, quesumus domine deus . . . a presenti liberari tristicia, et eterna perfrui leticia. Per . . .

SMRL 2:320.

6. f. 26–26v Alma redemptoris mater, que peruia celi porta manens (*sic*) et . . . ab ore sumens illud aue peccatorum miserere.

RH 861.

7. f. 26v Aue regina celorum; aue domina angelorum . . . et pro nobis semper Christum exora.

RH 2070.

8. f. 26v Antiphona (in red). Regina celi, letare, alleluya. Quia quem meruisti portare . . . deum alleluya.

RH 17170. The text is followed by the versus, Surrexit dominus, and the responsorium, Qui pro nobis perpendit.

9. f. 27 Interueniat pro nobis, quesumus domine Ihesu Christe, nunc et in hora mortis . . . et in resurrectione tua nouus amor accendit. Per . . .

Leroquais, *Heures* 2:34.

10. f. 27–27v Inuiolata, integra et casta es, Maria . . . sola inuiolata permansisti.

RH 9094.

11. ff. 27v–28 Quant on va reposer au soyr on doit dire ceste petite oraison (in red). Gratias ago tibi domine deus omnipotens, qui me in hac die . . . tibi ualeam seruitium exibere, Qui uiuis . . .

Leroquais, *Heures* 1:99, 2:33.

12. f. 28–28v Devote oraison a dire a son lever faicte par saint Edme de Pontyny; Oraison (in red). Gratias ago tibi, domine Ihesu Christe, qui me indignum famulum tuum in hac nocte custodisti . . . ad finem me peruenire fecisti, Qui uiuis . . .

Cf. Leroquais, *Heures* 1:234, 2:108.

13. ff. 29–84 Hours of the Virgin, use of Paris.

ff. 84v–85v blank.

14. ff. 86–99v Seven Penitential Psalms.

15. ff. 99v–105v Letania (in red). Includes Ambrius, Evurtius, and Anianus among the confessors and Columba and Bridget among the virgins. Litany proper followed by two short prayers: Deus cui proprium est . . . and Fidelium deus omnium conditor . . .

16. ff. 106–110 Short Hours of the Cross.

17. ff. 110–113v Short Hours of the Holy Spirit.

18. ff. 114–174v Office of the Dead, use of Paris.

19. ff. 175–181 Les XVe joyes nostre dame (in red). Doulce dame de misericorde, mere de pitie, fontaine de tous biens . . . la voulonte de dieu soit faicte en ciel en terre et en mer. Amen.

Leroquais, *Heures* 2:310–11. Sonet, 458.

20. ff. 181–188 Cy apres ensuivent les heures de la conception de la vierge Marie . . . (in red).

Texts for terce and vespers only. Leroquais, *Heures* 2:392.

21. ff. 188–190v Cy apres ensuit oraison devote primo modo (in red). Saint Gregoire estant en vie en chantant messe, nostre signeur luy apparut en semblance de sa passion. Le quel meu en devotion, a donne a tous vrais confes et repentans de leurs peches qui diront devotement devant l'ymage de dieu, les genoulz flechis a terre, cinq pater noster et ave Maria avec les oraisons qui apres ensuivent, chacun iour quatorze mille ans de vray pardon et plusieurs aultres papes y ont adiouxte grant somme de pardons qui se montent en tout vingt mille et douze ans de pardons . . . O domine Iesu Christe, adoro te in cruce pendentem . . . et omnibus fidelibus defunctis miserere, et propicius esto michi peccatori. Amen. Pater noster. Aue Maria.

Leroquais, *Heures* 2:346; no. 3 in the printed text here in the sixth position.

22. ff. 190v–192v Oraison devote a dieu (in red). Mon benoit dieu, ie croy de cueur et confesse de bouche . . . avec tous les sainctz et sainctes de paradis. Amen.

Leroquais, *Heures* 2:330–31. Sonet, 1150.

23. ff. 192v–198 O dieu createur du ciel et de la terre, roy des roys, seigneur des seigneurs qui m'aves daigne faire et creer . . . amis et af-

fins, familierz et biensfacteurs. Amen. Benedicamus domino. Deo gracias.

Leroquais, *Heures* 2:433. Sonet, 1313.

24. ff. 198–199 Sire dieu tout puissant, tout voyant, toutes choses congnoissant . . . Ie povre pecheresse ay fait . . . ma vie et ma mort. Amen. Credo in deum patrem et cetera.

Leroquais, *Heures* 2:339. Sonet, 2007.

25. ff. 199–207v Quicumques dira ceste oraison qui s'ensuit tous les semadis (*sic*), il verra nostre dame cinqu foys devant quil meurge (*sic*) en son aide (in red). Missus est Gabriel angelus ad Mariam uirginem . . . iudicare uiuos et mortuos et seculum per ignem . . .

A long text interspersed with the prayers Ave Maria and Dominus tecum; described by Leroquais, *Heures* 2:429.

26. ff. 207v–208v Oratio (in red). Te deprecor ergo mitissimam, piissimamque, misericordissimam, castissimam spectiosissimam dei genitricem Mariam . . . et participem me facias celestium gaudiorum. Prestante eodem domino nostro Ihesu Christo . . .

Leroquais, *Heures* 2:20, 26, 250.

27. ff. 208v–209 On doit dire l'oraison qui s'ensuit quant on se lieuve (in red) . . . Gratias ago tibi domine omnipotens deus qui me in hac nocte . . . obsequium seruitutis tue seruitutis tue (*sic*). Qui uiuis et regnas deus. Per Christum.

Leroquais, *Heures* 2:33.

28. f. 209 Quant tu orras sonner mydy, dy (in red). Sit nomen domini benedictum . . . Quant tu te leveras dy (in red). Surrexit dominus de sepulcro . . . pependit in ligno, miserere nobis.

SMRL 2:527.

29. f. 209v Quant tu ystras hors de ta maison, dy (in red). Dias (*sic*) tuas, domine, demonstra michi . . . ut non moueantur uestigia mea.

Five half-page illuminations: f. 29, the Annunciation, fantastic bird-serpent and duck-mammal in blue and violet acanthus margins on a compartmentalized gold, red, and brown ground; f. 86, David in prayer, a harp at his side, a fantastic mammal in a similar border on a compartmentalized clear and gold ground (remaining miniatures have similar borders); f. 106, the Crucifixion, bird of prey in the margin; f. 110v, Pentecost, a fantastic bird of prey in the margin; f. 114, Job on the dung heap with a bird of prey and bird-serpent in the margin. At the presence of initials 2 lines high, outer band margins decorated with thistles, violets, and small red flowers. Where appropriate they are traced on recto and verso. Minor gold initials on alternating red and blue grounds.

Parchment. ff. 199. Foliated, beginning with a modern flyleaf, 1–150 and 160–209. Trimmed to 123 × 85 mm (70 × 42 mm). Horizontal and vertical catchwords. $1–2^{6}$, 3^{8} (8 wanting), 4^{8}, 5^{10} (10 wanting), $6–13^{8}$, 14^{4}, $15–21^{8}$, 22^{8} (7–8 wanting), 23^{12} (11–12 wanting), 24^{8} (8 wanting), $25–26^{8}$. Plus mark after the middle of the quire sometimes present. Quire 24, numbered by an eighteenth-century hand in the lower left margin of the first folio, partially trimmed. Ruled in violet ink. Written in gothic textualis quadrata media in 15 long lines by at least two scribes; f. 90, an instance of change in ink and quite probably of hand.

Bound in gold-stamped brown calf, s. xviii; spine title "Horae romanae."

Written in France, possibly in Orléans; see calendar and litany, c. 1480. Prayers in texts 3, 12, and 21 in masculine form; in text 5 in masculine plural form. Text 24 in feminine form. Style of miniatures suggests influence of Tours. No. 26 from the collection of Henry Probasco, acquired by the Newberry 1 December 1890.

De Ricci, 1:527.

42

(23845)

Book of Hours, Use of Rouen

France c. 1450

1. ff. 1–12v Calendar of Rouen written in French in blue, red, and gold with principal feasts in gold. Feasts include: Saint Sever (1 February), Saint Ausbert (9 February), Saint Austrebert (10 February), Sainte Honorine (27 February), Translation Saint Ouen (5 May), Saint Laurens (10 May), Sainte Honorine (16 May), Saint Godart (8 June), Saint Ursin (12 June), Saint Martial (3 July, in gold), Saint Vivien (27 August), Saint Nigaise (11 October), Saint Michiel (16 October), Sainte Austreberte (20 October), Saint Mellon (22 October), Saint Romain (23 October, in gold), Saint Cler (4 November), Saint Ursin (30 December).

2. ff. 13–18v Gospel sequences, that of John followed by Protector in te sperancium . . . and Ecclesiam tuam quesumus . . .

3. ff. 18v–23 Obsecro te domina sancta

Maria . . . Et michy famulo tuo impetres . . . uirgo Maria, mater dei et misericordie. Amen.

Leroquais, *Heures* 2:346–47.

4. ff. 23–26v Oratio (in red). O intemerata et in eternum benedicta . . . de te enim filius uerus . . . et esto michi miserrimo peccatori propicia in omnibus auxiliatrix . . . uitam et requiem sempiternam. Amen.

Leroquais, *Heures* 2:336–37.

5. ff. 27–79 Office of the Virgin according to the use of Rouen. After lauds, suffrages to the Holy Spirit, Nicolas, and Catherine.

f. 79v blank.

6. ff. 80–85v Short Hours of the Cross.

7. ff. 86–91v Short Hours of the Holy Spirit.

8. ff. 92–104 Seven Penitential Psalms.

9. ff. 104–108v Le letanie (in red). Denis and Maurice among the martyrs, "Iudoce," Alexus, and Leonard among the confessors, Juliana and Bridget among the virgins. Followed by two short prayers, Deus cui proprium est . . . and Fidelium deus omnium conditor . . .

10. ff. 109–152v Office of the Dead as in Salisbury use.

11. ff. 153–157v Doulce dame de misericorde, mere de pitie . . . et pour tous trespasses qu'il aient pardon et repos. Ave Maria.

Les Quinze joies, Leroquais, *Heures* 2:310–11. Sonet, 458.

12. ff. 157v–160 Les vii requestes ensievent (in red). Doulx dieux, doulx pere, sainte trinite . . . Sire si comme che fu voir, aies vous pitie de moy. Pater noster.

Leroquais, *Heures* 2:309–10. Sonet, 504.

13. f. 160–160v Saincte vray crois auree qui du corps fus aournee (*sic*) . . . que vray confes puisse morir. Amen. Cues for Pater noster, Ave Maria, and Credo in deum patrem follow.

Prayer to the Cross which generally follows *Les Quinze joies* and *Les Sept requestes.* Sonet, 1876.

Fourteen half-page illuminations: f. 13, the Four Evangelists; f. 27, the Annunciation; f. 37v, the Visitation; f. 50, the Nativity; f. 56, the Annunciation to the Shepherds in the Field; f. 61, the Adoration of the Magi; f. 64v, the Presentation in the Temple; f. 68, the Flight to Egypt; f. 74, the Coronation of the Virgin; f. 80, Crucifixion between the two thieves; f. 86, Pentecost; f. 92, King David in prayer inspired by Divine Light, harp beside him; f. 109, last rites over a corpse, and above, Michael saving a naked soul from the devil; f. 153, stock female owner portrait in prayer before the enthroned Virgin and Child, an angel playing a harp. f. 1 and each illuminated folio, a full border combining acanthus spray and rinceaux decoration with gold, blue, and magenta initials 2 lines high. All other folios, outer floral borders, and similar borders in the inner margin of the rectos in the presence of gold dentelle initials with white patterning on grounds of magenta and blue, 2 lines high.

Parchment. ff. 158. Foliated 1–19, 20–21 on one leaf, 22–160 (f. 60 omitted). Trimmed to 210 × 151 mm (110 × 70 mm). French post-medieval quire numbering in lower margin of the recto of the first folio of each quire; also, in upper margin after the calendar. $1\text{–}2^{6}$, 3^{8}, 4^{6} (6 wanting), $5\text{–}6^{8}$, 7^{8} (8 wanting), $8\text{–}10^{8}$, 11^{6} (1 wanting), 12^{8}, 13^{4}, $14\text{–}15^{8}$, 16^{10} (10 wanting), $17\text{–}20^{8}$, 21^{4}, 22^{8}. Ruled in violet ink. Written in gothic textualis formata in 15 long lines. Headings in red in script of text.

Bound tightly in red morocco, c. 1965, by the Lakeside Press, Chicago.

Written in France, probably in Rouen, c. 1450; see Panofsky, *Early Netherlandish Painting,* p. 409. Prayers in texts 3 and 4 in the masculine form (cf. miniature on f. 153). Front pastedown, armorial bookplate of Comte François Potocki, Vilna. For the history and manuscripts of this family, see W. Semkowicz, *Przewodnik po zbiorze rękopisów wilanowskich* (Warsaw, 1961), and *SFRMP* 19 (1938), nos. 4, 12, and 13. No. 24 from the collection of Henry Probasco, acquired by the Newberry 1 December 1890.

De Ricci, 1:527. Kessler, *French and Flemish Illuminated Manuscripts,* no. 15 (plates of ff. 61 and 84).

43

(23846)

Book of Hours, Use of Rouen

France c. 1470

1. ff. 1–12v Calendar of Rouen with many feasts of Paris in French with a feast for every day of the year, written alternately in red and blue with major feasts in gold. Feasts include: Sainte Genevievfve (3 January), La Chandeleur (2 February, in gold), Saint Aubert (9 February), Saint Germain (28 May), Saint Landri (10 June), Saint Barnabe (11 June, in gold), Saint Jehan Baptiste (24 June, in gold), Saint Eloy (25 June, in gold), Saint Pierre (29 June, in gold), Sainte Anne (28 July, in gold), Saint Loys (25 August, in gold), Saint Mellon (22

October), Saint Romain (Bishop of Rouen, 23 October, in gold).

2. ff. 13–18v Gospel sequences. John followed by the prayers Protector in te sperancium . . . and Ecclesiam tuam quesumus . . .

3. ff. 19–22v Obsecro te domina sancta Maria mater dei . . . Et michi famulo tuo impetres . . . dulcissima Maria, mater dei et misericordie. Amen.

Leroquais, *Heures* 2:346.

4. ff. 22v–26v Oratio (in red). O intemerata et in eternum benedicta . . . de te enim unigenitus filius dei uerus . . . et esto michi miserrimo peccatori pia et propicia in omnibus auxiliatrix . . . cum electis suis uitam et requiem sempiternam. Amen.

Leroquais, *Heures* 2:336–37.

5. ff. 27–84v Hours of the Virgin, use of Rouen. Suffrages after lauds to: The Holy Spirit, Michael, John the Baptist, Peter, Lawrence, Nicholas, Catherine, Margaret, All Saints, Peace.

f. 54v (following lauds) blank.

6. ff. 85–98 Seven Penitential Psalms.

7. ff. 98–103v Letania (in red). Includes many saints of Paris. Litany proper followed by two short prayers, Deus cui proprium est . . . and Fidelium deus omnium conditor . . .

8. ff. 103–107v Hore sancte crucis (in red).

9. ff. 107v–110v Hore sancte spiritus (in red).

10. ff. 111–157v Office of the Dead as in Salisbury use.

f. 158–158v blank.

11. ff. 159–163 Prayers in French (addition s. xvi). Oraison pour dire apres la communion (in red). O pere celeste, dieu du saint corps du Jesu Christ . . . O vray viande angelique, O vray pain celeste des humains . . . O dieu tout puissant la vray reception de ton corps . . . Exercise pour bien et heureusement commencer la iournee (in red). Vous direz le matin, quand il se fault lever du lict. La grace du saint Esprit nous vueille assister . . . , and nine other prayers for different occasions. Texts appear to be post-medieval and are unrecorded by Sonet.

ff. 163v–164 blank.

Thirteen half-page miniatures accompanied by full acanthus spray borders decorated with many hybrid animal-men figures, exotic birds, and fantastic creatures. f. 13, the Four Evangelists in four panels. f. 27, the Annunciation. f. 38v, the Visitation. f. 55, the Nativity. f. 61, the Annunciation to the Shepherds in the Field; in margin, naked bird-man or -woman with long beak penetrating its own rectum and an elephant with cloven hooves. f. 65, the Adoration of the Magi; in lower margin, battle of a male and female human-beast; in outer margin, a camel. f. 69, the Presentation in the Temple; in margin, a male cripple courting a mermaid admiring herself in a mirror. f. 73, the Flight into Egypt; in the background, miracle of the cornfields and falling idol, the Holy Family accompanied by a girl with a basket of doves. f. 80, Coronation of the Virgin; in margin, man-dog shooting at unicorn-bird. f. 85, King David in prayer with a harp present; in margin, man with unsheathed sword. f. 104, the Crucifixion; in margin, four roundels depicting, from upper right to lower left: Christ in the Garden at Gethsemane, Christ bearing the Cross, Christ before Pontius Pilate, and Christ nailed to the Cross; in lower margin, a pelican in its piety, below the legend "Je meure pour vous." f. 108, Pentecost; in lower margin, an anal sexual encounter between two beast-men. f. 111, a burial in a churchyard; outer margin, a Dominican friar. Traced band borders throughout.

Parchment. ff. 164. ff. 159–164, paper (s. xvi). 196 × 150 mm (93 × 70 mm). 1^{12}, 2^{8}, 3^{6}, $4–10^{8}$, 12^{2}, $12–13^{8}$, 14^{8}, 15^{2}, $16–21^{8}$, 22^{6} (paper). Ruled in violet ink. Written in gothic textualis rotunda media in 14 long lines. Calendar ruled for 17 lines. Headings in red in script of text.

Bound in gold-stamped brown calf; on front and back, Jesus on the Cross between Mary and John the Evangelist and the inscription "Iesus nazarenus rex iudaeorum miserere nobis," c. 1630.

Written in France, probably in Rouen c. 1470. Prayers in texts 3 and 4 in masculine form. ff. 1–2 in margins, nine unidentified proverbs in Latin, Greek, and French, dated twice 1595, all by one hand, possibly the same as that which added prayers on ff. 159–163. Front pastedown, signature "A. Schinkel Anno 1843," sold at his sale, the Hague, 21 November 1864, lot no. 31, clipping from the catalogue pasted below the signature. No. 25 from the collection of Henry Probasco, acquired by the Newberry 1 December 1890.

De Ricci, 1:527.

44
(23481)
Book of Hours, Use of Rome

France c. 1450

1. ff. 3–14v Calendar of western France, probably of Angers, written alternately in blue

and red with major feasts in gold. A saint for each day including: Hylarii episcopi (13 January), Sancti Iuliani (27 January, in gold), Licini episcopi (13 February), Albini episcopi (1 March), Cypriani (14 July), Maurilii episcopi (13 September), Mauricii sociorumque eius (22 September, in gold), Michaelis in monte (29 September and 16 October, in gold), Benedicti confessoris (23 October), Gaciani episcopi (18 December).

ff. 1–2v, blank flyleaves.

2. ff. 15–19 Gospel sequences with that of Mark preceding Matthew.

ff. 19v–22v blank.

3. ff. 23–65 Hours of the Virgin, use of Rome. Terce and sext removed; see catchword f. 54v. Nine psalms at matins, divided for the nocturns, suffrages to All Saints at the end of each hour, lauds to compline.

4. ff. 66–71v Changed Office of the Virgin, ending imperfectly. A folio of text removed after f. 71.

5. ff. 72–74v Short Hours of the Cross, beginning imperfectly.

6. ff. 75–77v Short Hours of the Holy Spirit.

7. ff. 78–89 Seven Penitential Psalms.

8. ff. 89–97 Letania (in red). Litany for eastern France, probably Angers: Sergius, Bacchus, Symphorianus, and Timothy among the martyrs; Maurilius, Licinius, Renatus, Julianus, and Magnobod among the confessors; Euphemia and Radegundis among the virgins. Followed by three short prayers: Deus cui proprium est . . . , Absolue, quesumus domine . . . ; Fidelium deus omnium . . .

f. 97v blank.

9. ff. 98–127v Office of the Dead, use of Rome.

10. ff. 127v–131 Oracio beate Marie virginis (in red). Obsecro te domina sancta Maria . . . Et michi famulo tuo . . . et exaude me miserum peccatorem, dulcissima mater dei et misericordie. Amen.

Leroquais, *Heures* 2:346–47.

11. ff. 131–134 Alia oratio (in red). O intemerata et in eternum benedicta singularis atque incomparabilis uirgo dei genitrix . . . de te enim dei filius . . . et esto michi miserrimo peccatori in omnibus auxiliatrix . . . cum electis suis uitam et requiem sempiternam. Amen.

Leroquais, *Heures* 2:336–37.

12. f. 134v Oratio (in red). Deus qui in sancta cruce pendens pro salute nostra uirginem matrem . . . et in uitam eternam me introducant per te Ihesu Christe, saluator mundi . . .

Leroquais, *Heures* 1:34.

13. ff. 134v–136 Oratio (in red). Deus propicius esto michi peccatori et custos mei omnibus diebus uite mee . . . ✠ Christe, salua me in omni tempore et in omnibus diebus uite mee. In nomine patris . . .

Leroquais, *Heures* 2:397. This prayer often attributed to Augustine.

14. f. 136–136v Domine Ihesu Christe qui hanc sacratissimam carnem de gloriose uirginis Marie utero assumpsisti preciosum sanguinem tuum . . . et ab uniuersis periculis et in celis preteritis, presentibus et futuris. Amen.

Leroquais, *Heures* 2:400. See Wilmart, p. 378n (no. 10).

15. ff. 136v–137 Deus qui manus tuas et pedes tuos et totum corpus tuum pro nobis peccatoribus in ligno crucis posuisti . . . ueram scienciam, rectam spem usque in finem uite nostre. Per te . . .

Leroquais, *Heures* 1:xxiv and 2:396.

16. ff. 137–138v Prosa (in red). Stabat mater dolorosa, iuxta crucem lacrimosa . . . paradisi gaudia. Amen.

Leroquais, *Heures* 2:455. *RH* 19416. Wilmart, p. 509.

17. ff. 138v–139 De sancto Iohannes euangelista (in red). Obsecro te sancte Iohannes Baptista, precursor Christi et martyr . . . et militare sibi. Qui . . .

Leroquais, *Heures* 1:35.

18. f. 139–139v De santo Petro (in red). Sanctissime celestis regni clauiger, princeps apostolorum, pastor dominicorum ouium . . . portam regni celorum ualeam. Amen.

19. ff. 139v–140 De sancto Paulo (in red). Beatissime Paule, uas electionis . . . in azimis sinceritatis et ueritatis. Amen.

Leroquais, *Heures* 1:35.

20. f. 140–140v De sancto Andrea (in red), Gloriose saluatoris mei apostole Andrea, qui eiusdem ad primam uocationis obediens

extisti missionem . . . qui non uult mortem peccatoris sed ut conuertatur et uiuat. Amen.

21. ff. 140–141v De sancto Iohanne euangelista (in red). Sancte Iohannes apostole uirgo electe a domino . . . peccator sum . . . cui est pre ceteris apud eum familiaritatis fiducia.

f. 142–142v blank.

Nine half-page illuminations accompanied by full gold and blue acanthus borders, decorated with flowers: f. 23, the Annunciation; f. 40v, the Visitation; f. 51v, the Nativity; f. 55, the Circumcision; f. 58, the Presentation in the Temple; f. 63, the Flight into Egypt; f. 75, Gnadenstuhl Trinity; f. 78, King David in prayer, a harp at his side, rays of light streaming to his eyes; f. 98, a funeral with casket borne by friars of at least two orders, the Franciscans wearing brown habits and sandals. Four historiated initials accompanied by a similar bracket left marginal border: f. 15, the eagle; f. 16, the ox; f. 17, the lion; f. 18, the angel: symbols of the Four Evangelists with each holding a banderole with his name inscribed in French. ff. 128 and 131, full border decoration; f. 137, bracket left border. Blue initials filled with magenta alternating with magenta initials filled with blue, decorated with gold flora on gold grounds 2–4 lines high throughout. Gold dentelle initials with white patterning on grounds of blue and magenta, also throughout. Two miniatures probably removed as part of quire 8, a third removed after f. 78.

Parchment. ff. ii + 139 + i. Foliated 1–142, flyleaves included in foliation. 222 × 158 mm (113 × 69 mm). $1–2^{6}$, $3–7^{8}$, 8 (entirely removed with loss of text), $9–10^{8}$, 11^{8} (2 removed), $12–13^{8}$, 14^{4}, $15–18^{8}$, 19^{4}, 20^{8}. Catchwords in *lettre bâtarde*. Ruled in violet; flyleaves ruled in purple ink. Written in textualis quadrata formata of uneven quality in 16 long lines. Headings in red in script of text.

Bound in gold-stamped red morocco, s. xviii. Modern (American?) pencil note on front flyleaf records 147 leaves, 11 large, 4 small miniatures, and 18 full borders; therefore, 8 folios and 2 illuminations had been removed from this codex prior to its foliation; cf. ff. 54v and 72 above.

Written in western France, probably in Angers, to judge from the calendar and litany, c. 1450. Prayers in texts 10, 11, 13, and 21 in the masculine form. f. 98, three coats of arms with a black eagle on a gold field are visible on the wall depicted in the miniature. Formerly no. 20 in the collection of Henry Probasco, acquired by the Newberry 1 December 1890.

De Ricci, 1:526.

45

(23844)

Book of Hours, Use of Paris

France c. 1460

1. ff. 3–14v Calendar of the region of Paris in French written alternately in violet and blue with major feasts in gold, one saint for each day of the year. Very similar to Perdrizet, *Calendrier parisien*.

2. ff. 15–21v Gospel sequences, that of John followed by the prayer, Protector in te sperancium . . .

3. ff. 21v–26 Oratio beate Marie (in violet). Obsecro te domina sancta Maria mater dei . . . Et michi famulo tuo . . . mater dei et misericordie. Amen.

Leroquais, *Heures* 2:346–47.

4. ff. 26–30v Oratio (in violet). O intemerata et in eternum benedicta . . . de te enim dei filius . . . et esto michi miserrimo pecatori propicia in omnibus auxiliatrix . . . cum electis suis uitam et gloriam sempiternam. Amen.

Leroquais, *Heures* 2:336–37.

5. ff. 31–103 Hours of the Virgin, use of Paris. Nine psalms and lessons at matins with no intervening rubrics.

f. 103v blank.

6. ff. 104–117v Seven Penitential Psalms.

7. ff. 117–123v Letania (in violet). Includes Remigius and Hilary among the confessors. Ends with three short prayers: Deus cui proprium est . . . , Omnipotens sempiterne deus qui facis mirabilia . . . , Fidelium deus omnium conditor . . .

8. ff. 123v–130v Ad matutinas de cruce (in violet). Short Hours of the Cross.

9. ff. 130v–136 Ad matutinas de Sancto Spirito (in violet). Short Hours of the Holy Spirit.

10. ff. 136–186v Ad uesperas mortuorum (in violet). Office of the Dead, use of Paris.

f. 136v blank.

11. ff. 186v–193v Les XV joyes nostre dame (in red). Doulce dame de misericorde, mere de pitie, fontaine de tous biens . . . et pour tous les trespassez que dieu leur face pardon. Aue Maria.

Leroquais, *Heures* 2:310–11. Sonet, 458.

12. ff. 193v–197 Les V (*sic* for VII) reques-

tez nostre seigneur (in violet). Doulx dieu, doulx pere, sainte trinite, ung dieu . . . Sire si comme ce fut voir, ayez pitie et mercy de moy. Pater noster.

Leroquais, *Heures* 2:309–10. Sonet, 504.

13. ff. 197–197v

Sainte vraye croix aoree
Qui du corps dieu fus aornee . . .
Que vroy (*sic*) confes puisse morir. Amen.

Sonet, 1876. Generally follows *Les Quinze joies* and *Les Sept requestes*.

14. ff. 197v–207v Suffrages to the saints: De saint Michel, Iehan Baptiste, Iehan evvangeliste, saint Iaques, saint Christofle (prayer in the masculine form), saint Sebastien, saint Anthoine, saint Laurens, saint Denis, sainte Catherine, sainte Marguerite, sainte Barbe, sainte Geneviefve. Texts in Latin.

ff. 208–209v blank.

Fifteen half-page illuminations by at least two artists in a style reminiscent of Maître François, accompanied by full blue and green acanthus spray borders with various flora including thistles, roses, and berries on grounds of different geometrical gold patterns. f. 15, angel encouraging John, eagle holding ink pot; f. 31, the Annunciation; f. 57, the Visitation; f. 69, the Nativity; f. 75, the Annunciation to the Shepherds in the Field, one shepherdess shearing a sheep; f. 80, the Adoration of the Magi; f. 85, the Presentation in the Temple; f. 90, the Flight into Egypt, by a different artist; f. 97v, the Coronation of the Virgin; f. 104, King David in prayer, harp at his side, an angel with unsheathed sword above; f. 124, the Crucifixion between the two thieves; f. 131, Pentecost; f. 137, the three living and the three dead; f. 187, the Virgin and Child enthroned between two angels; f. 194, the Trinity, Father and Son wearing one cloak, dove between them. Sixteen smaller illuminations 5 lines high accompanied by an outer bracket border on a clear ground: f. 17, Luke; f. 18v, Matthew; f. 20v, Mark; f. 197v, Michael; f. 198, John the Baptist; f. 199, John the Evangelist; f. 199v, James; f. 200, Christopher; f. 202, Sebastian; f. 203v, Anthony; f. 204, Lawrence; f. 204v, Denis; f. 205, Catherine; f. 206, Margaret; f. 206v, Barbara; f. 207, Geneviève. Two 5-line historiated initials also accompanied by an outer bracket border. f. 21v, the letter O historiated with angels crowning the Virgin. f. 26, the letter O historiated with the Pietà. Gold dentelle initials with white patterning on grounds of blue and magenta throughout. Traced band borders on rectos and versos, facing folios, and on versos of facing folios.

Parchment. ff. ii + 205 + ii. Foliation 1–209 includes flyleaves. 162 × 112 mm (83 × 51 mm). Collation impracticable. Ruled in violet ink. Written in gothic textualis quadrata media in 16 long lines. Headings in violet in the script of the text.

Tightly bound in gold-stamped red morocco, s. xviii.

Written in France c. 1460. Prayers in texts 2, 3, and 4 in masculine form. Belonged successively to Pieter de Hubert, Heer von Burgt (1627–1697), Anna Elizabeth van Panhuis, Elizabeth de Hochepied; purchased at her sale, The Hague, 1842, by A. D. Schinkel, his note on provenance in Dutch on verso of front flyleaf, dated 28 March 1842; his sale, The Hague, 21 November 1864, no. 32. A loose four-page note in Dutch, s. xix. No. 22 from the collection of Henry Probasco, acquired by the Newberry 1 December 1890.

De Ricci, 1:527. Kessler, *French and Flemish Illuminated Manuscripts*, no. 16 (plates of ff. 75 and 194).

45.5

Roman Missal (Excerpts)

Northern Europe (Germany?) s. XIV²

1. ff. 1–2v Officium beate Marie (in red). *SMRL* 2:320 (*Concede nos*).

2. ff. 2v–4v Aliud officium beate Marie (in red). *SMRL* 2:319–20 (*Rorate celi*).

3. ff. 4v–6 Aliud officium beate Marie (in red). *SMRL* 2:320 (*Vultum tuum*).

4. ff. 6–8 Officium misse defunctorum (in red). *SMRL* 2:326, no. 63a, followed by secret and postcommunion of 63g.

5. f. 8–8v Missa pro femina (in red). *SMRL* 2:329, no. 63h.

6. ff. 8v–9 Pro patre et matre (in red). *SMRL* 2:329, no. 63m.

7. ff. 9–9v Pro omnibus fidelibus (in red). *SMRL* 2:329, no. 63o.

8. ff. 9v–10 Pro congregatione (addition in margin, heading wanting). *SMRL* 2:329, no. 63i.

9. ff. 10–15 Prefaces to the Mass accompanied by *infra canum* (*sic* for *infra canonem*): In natali domini prefacio, De epiphanie prefacio, De sancta cruce, De beate Marie, De quadragessima, De uigilia pasce, In die pasche, De ascensione, De pentecosten, De trinitate, De apostolis.

f. 11v blank.

10. ff. 15–21v Order and Canon of the Mass.

11. ff. 22–24v Mass without title = Ad missam maiorem [in natiuitate domini] statio ad sanctam Mariam maiorem. *SMRL* 2:212.

12. ff. 24v–28 Circumcisio domini officium (in red). *SMRL* 2:215.

13. ff. 28–29 In die sancto pasche officium (in red). *SMRL* 2:251.

14. ff. 29v–31v Die ascensionis officium (in red). *SMRL* 2:255.

15. ff. 31v–33v In die pentecosten (in red). *SMRL* 2:258.

16. ff. 33v–36v Officium de trinitate ad missam (in red). *SMRL* 2:261n.

17. ff. 36v–38v Officium corporis Christi (in red). *SMRL* 2:261n.

18. ff. 38v–40 Officium crucis (in red). *SMRL* 2:319.

19. ff. 40–42 Mass without heading, not in *SMRL*. Gaudeamus omnes in domino . . . Largire nobis, clementissime pater . . . In lectulo meo . . .

20. ff. 42v–44v Omnium sanctorum officium (in red). *SMRL* 2:303.

21. ff. 44v–47 In natiuitate beate Marie uirginis officium (in red).

22. ff. 47–49v In dedicatione sancti Michaelis archangeli (in red). *SMRL* 2:390.

23. ff. 49v–51v Katerine uirginis et martiris officium (in red); cf. *SMRL* 2:305.

24. ff. 51v–53v Missa pro euitenda (*sic*) mortalitate quam Clemens papa ordinauit in collegio cum dominis cardinalibus et concessit dicentibus et audientibus ccxl dies indulgentie . . . = *SMRL* 2:327, Votive Mass, no. 61.

f. 51v, 4 lines of text, probably noted, erased.

25. ff. 53v–54v Sancti Georgii martiris (in red). *SMRL* 2:280.

26. ff. 54v–55 Benedictions for water and salt.

f. 55v blank.

27. f. 56–56v De sancto Laurencio officium (in red); cf. *SMRL* 2:293.

28. ff. 56v–57v De sancto Gregorio (in red); cf. *SMRL* 2:278.

29. ff. 58–59 Noted introit Protexisti me deus. f. 59v ruled for music but blank.

Front flyleaf verso, Secundum Johannem. In illo tempore dixit Ihesus turbis iudeorum, Amen, amen, dico uobis . . . = *Lectio* from the Mass *In agenda defunctorum*, *SMRL* 2:328.

f. 15, historiated magenta initial on blue ground 8 lines high depicting Christ on the Cross between Mary and John the Evangelist in gold, pink, blue, and orange, extended to form partial border of orange and blue ivy decorated with a fantastic dragon.

Parchment. ff. ii + 59 + i. 274 × 185 mm (197 × 120 mm). 1^8, 2^{10} (1 wanting), $3–6^8$, 7^8 (7–8 stubs only), 8^4. Catchwords within rectangles with animal faces appended to the left ends. Prickings visible in outer margins. ff. 1–53v, ruled in pencil; ff. 54–57v, ruled in ink. f. 53v, partly reruled in ink; f. 55v, unruled; ff. 58–59v, frame ruled in ink (music ruling added mostly in red ink). Main body of text written in Italian gothic textualis formata in 18 long lines. ff. 51–53v, in a Northern gothic textualis media, with use of long terminal s and caroline type t; possible indication that this portion was copied from a pre-gothic exemplar. ff. 53v–59, in gothic textualis by three other hands. ff. 54–57v, in 31 long lines. Headings in red in scripts of the text. Red and blue initials, some patterned and some with violet flourishes, 2–4 lines high; simple alternating red and blue initials 2 lines high. Texts 23–27 have red initials only. Finger tabs on ff. 6 and 15.

Bound in original boards re-covered with dark morocco ruled with Saint Andrew's cross; fore-edge clasp.

Written in northern Europe in the second half of the fourteenth century by a scribe with Italian training. Completed with addition of texts 23–27, possibly in Germany. ff. 16v–19v, marginal notes in a fourteenth-century northern cursive script. f. 55v, pen trials, "1521," possibly a date. Front flyleaf has modern inscriptions "Bi. Rot 1687" and "Joachim Richard 1792." Acquired by the Newberry from Louis H. Silver, 1964.

Second folio: -pulus in suam.

46

(23871)

Book of Hours, Use of Rome

Flanders after 1450

1. ff. 1–6v Calendar of Bruges written in red and black. Feasts include: Amandi et Uedasti (6 February, in red), Eleutherii episcopi (20 February), Gertrudis uirginis (17 March), Barnabi apostoli (11 June, in red), Diuisio apostolorum (15 July), Arnulphi episcopi (18 July), Egidii hermite (1 September, in red), Remigii et Bauonis (1 October, in red), Donatiani episcopi (14 October, in red), Eligii episcopi (1 December, in red).

2. ff. 7–11v Incipiunt hore de sancta cruce (in red). Short Hours of the Cross.

3. ff. 12–15v Incipiunt hore de sancto spiritu (in red). Short Hours of the Holy Spirit.

4. ff. 16–19v Incipit missa beate Marie uirginis (in red) . . . Salue sancta parens . . .

5. ff. 19v–22v Gospel sequences, ending imperfectly at the end of the quire in Mark: nouis, serpentes tollent. Et si //

6. ff. 23–24v (begins imperfectly on the second leaf of the quire) // te commendauit sancto Iohanni apostolo . . . Et michi famule tue . . . Et exaudi me dolcisima Maria mater dei et misericordie. Amen.

The prayer *Obsecro te,* Leroquais, *Heures* 2:346–47.

7. ff. 25–26v O intemerata et in eternum benedicta . . . O Iohannes . . . ego miserima peccatrix . . . me ducat electorum suorum benegnissimus paraclitus. Qui cum patre et filio coeternus et consubstantialis cum eis et in eis uiuit et regnat omnipotens deus in secula seculorum. Amen.

Wilmart, pp. 488–90.

8. ff. 27–30v Suffrages to the saints: De sancto Michaele archangelo, De sancto Iohanne baptista, Memoria de sancto Petro apostolo, Memoria de sancto Paulo, Memoria de sancto Andree (*sic*), Memoria de sancto Nicholao, De sancta Barbara, De sancta Margareta.

9. ff. 31–70v Incipiunt hore beate Marie uirginis secundum usum romane curie (in red). Nine psalms at matins with rubrics for the days of the week. Prayers at the end of each hour, compline ending with the Salue regina, followed by its usual prayer, Omnipotens sempiterne deus qui gloriose uirginis. . . . Text disordered apparently in binding and should read 56, 61, 59, 57, 58, 60.

10. ff. 71–76v Changed Office of the Virgin.

11. ff. 77–84 Incipiunt septem psalmi (in red).

12. ff. 84–89v Letania (in red). Text disordered apparently in binding; f. 89 should follow f. 84. Denis, Maurice, and Eustachius among the martyrs, Bernardino among the confessors, Agatha, Gertrude, and Ursula among the virgins. Followed by Psalm 61, Saluos fac seruos tuos . . . and seven short prayers: Deus cui proprium est . . . , Exaudi, quesumus domine, supplicum preces . . . , Ineffabilem misericordiam tuam . . . , Deus a quo sancta desideria . . . , A protectione tranquilla . . . , Ecciones (*sic*) nostras . . . , Omnipotens sempiterne deus qui uiuorum dominaris simul. . . .

13. ff. 90–119v Incipiunt uigilie mortuorum ad uesperas (in red).

Nine small illuminations 8 lines high, accompanied by left bracket blue and pink acanthus and green vine leaf borders; f. 25, Virgin and Child on a crescent; f. 27, Nicholas and the children in the barrel (*sic,* suffrage is to Michael Archangel); f. 27v, John the Baptist; f. 28, Peter and Paul (*sic,* suffrage is to Peter alone); f. 28v, Paul; f. 29, Andrew; f. 29v, Michael the Archangel (*sic,* suffrage is to Nicholas); f. 30, Barbara; f. 30v, Margaret. Full borders accompany gold dentelle initials with white patterning on grounds of blue and magenta 6 lines high at the beginning of each text. Minor dentelle initials and blue initials with red flourishes, gold with black flourishes, throughout. Some pages with miniatures may have been removed.

Parchment. ff. 119. 159 × 112 mm (99 × 63 mm). Errors in binding in Hours of the Virgin and litany; original quires appear to have been violated in rebinding, which makes collation impracticable. Ruled in violet ink. Written in gothic textualis quadrata media in 21 long lines. Headings in red in script of text.

Bound in parchment over paper boards, s. xviii; spine title: "Officium B.M.V."

Written in the Low Countries, probably in Bruges, after 1450 (date of canonization of Bernardino). Prayers in texts 6 and 7 in feminine form. No. 44 from the collection of Henry Probasco, acquired by the Newberry 1 December 1890.

De Ricci, 1:529.

47

(23482)

Book of Hours, Use of Rome

France c. 1490

1. ff. 1–12v Calendar of Paris in French, corresponding to Perdrizet, *Calendrier parisien,* with the bold-faced feasts usually in blue. Other saints in a regular sequence in black, violet, and red. Feasts include: Saint Yves (19 May), Saint Germain (29 May), Saint Landri (10 June), Saincte Anne (28 July), Saincte Couronne (12 August), Saint Loys (25 August),

Saint Cloust (7 September), Saint Denis (9 October), Saincte Geneviefve (26 November).

2. ff. 13–20 Gospel sequences.

3. ff. 20–24 Oroison de nostre dame (in violet). Obsecro te domina sancta Maria mater dei pietate plenissima . . . Et michi famule tue . . . mater dei et misericordie. Amen.

Leroquais, *Heures* 2:346–47.

4. ff. 24v–25v Passio domini nostri Ihesu Christi secundum Iohannem . . . Apprehendit Pylatus Ihesum . . . uerum est testimonium euis.

Cento mainly from Io 19:1–34. For this and following text, see *Lyell Catalogue,* pp. 65–66. *Horae eboracenses,* p. 123.

5. ff. 25v–26 Deus qui manus tuas et pedes tuos . . . usque in finem per te, Ihesu Christe, saluator mundi et rex glorie. Qui . . .

f. 26v blank.

Leroquais, *Heures* 1:xxiv, 2:396.

6. ff. 27–106v Hours of the Virgin, use of Rome. Short Hours of the Cross and Holy Spirit incorporated. Nine psalms at matins with rubrics in French for the days of the week; suffrages to All Saints, lauds through compline. ff. 102v–103, Hours of the Virgin end with the Salue regina and its usual prayer, Omnipotens sempiterne deus qui gloriose uirginis . . .

7. ff. 107–116v Changed Office of the Virgin for Advent.

8. ff. 117–127 Seven Penitential Psalms.

9. ff. 127–135 Litany of saints with Quintinus and Eutropius among the martyrs, Silvester and Leo among the confessors. Litany proper followed by the usual series of ten short prayers as in the Roman breviary.

10. ff. 135–179 Vigilie mortuorum (in violet). Office of the Dead, use of Rome.

ff. 179v–180v blank.

11. f. 181 Aue uerum corpus natum de Maria uirgine . . . O dulcis, o pie, o Ihesum filii Marie.

Leroquais, *Heures* 2:382. *RH* 2175.

12. f. 181 Benedicat me imperialis maiestas, regat me regalis deitas . . . salus et proteccio. In nomine patris et filii et spiritus sancti. Amen.

Leroquais, *Heures* 2:68.

13. ff. 181v–183 Domine Ihesu Christe, adoro te in cruce pendentem et coronam spineam . . . et propicius esto michi peccatori . . . miserere mei sedentis in tenebris et umbra mortis. Amen. Pater noster. Aue Maria.

Leroquais, *Heures* 2:346 in this order with respect to the printed text: 1, 2, 4, 7, 3, 5, 6.

14. ff. 183–184 Illumina oculos meos ne unquam obdormiam in morte . . . et consolatus es me. Domine exaudi orationem meam; Et clamor meus ad te ueniat (in smaller letters).

Leroquais, *Heures* 2:415. This prayer often attributed to Bernard. For the versus and responsorium, see *Horae eboracenses,* pp. 27 and 97.

15. f. 184–184v Omnipotens sempiterne deus qui Ezechie regi Iudee . . . concede michi indigne famule tue . . . Secundum tuam misericordiam consequi merear. Per dominum.

Leroquais, *Heures* 2:348. Follows the preceding text in many manuscripts. See MS 83, text 14.

16. f. 185–185v Deus qui uoluisti pro redempcione mundi a iudeis reprobari . . . perduxisti tecum latronem crucifixum. Qui cum deo patre et spiritu sancto uiuis et regnas deus. Per omnia secula seculorum. Amen.

Horae eboracenses, p. 83. *Lyell Catalogue,* p. 64. Cf. MS 35, text 18, and MS 82, text 26.

17. ff. 186–197v Suffrages to the Holy Trinity, all angels, John the Evangelist, John the Baptist, James, the Apostles, Lawrence, Stephen, Cosmas and Damianus, Eutropius, all martyrs, Francis, the confessors, Mary Magdalene, Anne, Catherine, Barbara, Margaret, Susan, and All Saints.

18. ff. 198–199v

Stabat mater dolorosa
Iuxta crucem lacrimosa . . .
Paradisi gaudia. Amen.

Leroquais, *Heures* 2:455. *RH* 19416. Wilmart, p. 509.

19. ff. 199v–200 Interueniat pro nobis, domine Ihesu Christe, nunc et in hora mortis nostre apud tuam clemenciam . . . amor ascentit (?) qui uiuis.

f. 200, text effaced and portions illegible; f. 200v blank; f. 201–201v blank.

Cf. Leroquais, *Heures* 2:34.

Thirty-one half-page illuminations simply executed in a style reminiscent of Jean Bourdichon accompanied by elaborate full borders of blue, red, and green acanthus on grounds of gold, red, and black, often compartmentalized in intricate geometrical designs. Many flowers and fanciful creatures; gold, red, and blue initials 4 lines high. f. 13, John on Patmos, fantastic camel and dragon in margin; f. 15, Luke, centaur in margin; f. 17, Matthew; f. 19, Mark, a savage man in margin; f. 20v, Pietà; f. 27, the Annunciation (full page), beginning of text written as inscription on the architectural frame in Roman capitals; f. 44v, the Visitation; f. 55v, Christ betrayed by Judas; f. 57, the Resurrection depicted in the setting of Renaissance arches and columns; f. 58v, the Nativity; f. 63, Christ before Pilate; f. 64v, Mary Magdalene before the Risen Christ in a garden (Noli me tangere); f. 66, the Annunciation to the Shepherds in the Field; f. 70v, Christ bearing the Cross; f. 72, Christ at Emmaus; f. 73v, the Adoration of the Magi; f. 77v, Christ being nailed to the Cross; f. 79, Christ with doubting Thomas; f. 80v, Circumcision; f. 85, Christ on the Cross with Mary and John; f. 86v, Christ in heaven showing his wounds, surrounded by angels; f. 87v, Flight into Egypt with John the Baptist and his parents; f. 95, Descent from the Cross; f. 96v, Pentecost; f. 98, Coronation of the Virgin; f. 103v, the Entombment; f. 105v, the Resurrection of the Dead, Christ in the sky sitting on a rainbow judging the naked good and wicked; f. 117, King David watching Bathsheba in the bath, with her dress raised above her knees; f. 135v, the living encountering the dead; f. 181v, Gregory's vision at Mass with the sudarium held by an angel; f. 192v, Francis in a gray, half-gold habit receiving the stigmata. Other folios have decorated compartmentalized band border on outer margins. Minor gold initials on alternating grounds of red and blue. Inscriptions in miniatures on ff. 80v, 96v, and 117 in Roman capitals.

Parchment. ff. 201. f. 201v, heavily worn. 153 × 117 mm (85 × 51 mm). 1^{12}, 2^{8}, 3^{6}, $4–13^{8}$, 14^{10}, 23^{4}, $24–25^{8}$. Ruled in violet ink. Written in *lettre bâtarde* in 17 long lines. Headings in violet in script of text; true red used in calendar.

Bound in worn modern velvet over paperboard.

Written in France, possibly in Tours, as suggested by the miniatures, c. 1490. Prayer in text 3 in feminine form; prayer in text 12 in masculine form. Front pastedown, armorial bookplate c. 1727: "Ex bibliotheca Christ. Gottl. Schwarzii, Prof. P. Altorf" = Christian Gottlieb Schwarz (1675–1751), *ADB* 39:227–28. No. 21 from the collection of Henry Probasco, acquired by the Newberry 1 December 1890.

De Ricci, 1:526. Kessler, *French and Flemish Illuminated Manuscripts,* no. 19 (with plates of ff. 55v, 77v, and 87v). F. Avril, "Manuscrits à peintures d'origine française à la Bibliothèque Nationale de Vienne," *Bulletin monumental* 134 (1976): 335.

50
(324352)
Book of Hours, Use of Rome

Western France — c. 1500

1. ff. 2–4v Calendar of Western France in two columns, written in French in alternating violet and black ink. Major feasts in blue. A saint listed for each day of the year with feasts of Angers, Tours, and Le Mans. Feasts include: Saint Iulien (25 January), Saint Yves (19 May), Saint Gervais (19 June), Saint Martin (4 July), Saint Ernoul (18 July), Saint Morice (23 September), Saint Michiel (16 October), Saint Martin (11 November, in blue), Saint Brice (13 November), Saint Eloy (1 December), Saint Silvestre (31 December). For a similarly mixed calendar, see Leroquais, *Heures* 1:122. (In this calendar September has saints for 31 days.)

2. ff. 5–7 Gospel sequences.

3. ff. 7–8v De uirgine (in violet). Obsecro te domina sancta Maria . . . Et michi famulo . . . dulcissima uirgo Maria, mater dei et misericordie. Amen.

Leroquais, *Heures* 2:346–47.

4. ff. 8v–9v O intemerata et in eternum benedicta . . . O Iohannis . . . ego miserimus peccator . . . benignissimus paraclitus. Qui cum patre et filio . . .

Wilmart, pp. 488–90.

5. ff. 10–34 Hours of the Virgin, use of Rome. Nine psalms at matins, rubrics for the days of the week.

6. ff. 34v–37 Changed Office of the Virgin.

f. 37v blank.

7. f. 38–38v Short Hours of the Cross, beginning imperfectly.

8. ff. 39–40 Short Hours of the Holy Spirit.

9. ff. 40v–45v Seven Penitential Psalms.

10. ff. 45v–49 Litany. Vincent, Fabianus, and Sebastian among the martyrs; Martin, Louis, and Julianus among the confessors, followed by the standard set of ten short prayers as in the Roman breviary.

11. ff. 49v–67 Office of the Dead, use of Rome.

12. ff. 67v–71 Suffrages to Michael, John the Baptist, John the Evangelist, Peter, Paul,

Christopher, Sebastian, Nicholas, Mary Magdalene, Barbara.

ff. 71v–72v blank.

13. f. 73 De sanctissima trinitate (in red) . . . Omnipotens sempiterne deus qui dedisti famulis tuis in confessione uere fidei . . . ab omnibus semper tueamur aduersis. Per dominum.

14. f. 73–73v Sequitur oratio ad deum patrem (in red). Pater de celis, deus, miserere nobis. Domine sancte pater omnipotens eterne deus qui coequalem, consubstancialem et coeternum tibi . . . propter nomen sanctum tuum. Qui uiuis.

Leroquais, *Heures* 2:401. *PL* 101:1399. Texts 15 and 16 customarily follow this text as a series of suffrages. Cf. *Horae eboracenses,* pp. 122–25.

15. f. 73v Oratio ad filium (in red) . . . Domine Iesu Criste, filii dei uiui, qui es uerus et omnipotens deus, splendor et imago patris . . . sed salua et adiuua me propter nomen tuum.

Leroquais, *Heures* 1:313. *PL* 101:1399.

16. f. 73v Oratio ad spiritum sanctum (in red). . . . Domine spiritus sancte, deus qui coequalis, consubstancialis . . . et ignem sanctissimi amoris tui. Qui uiuis et regnas.

Leroquais, *Heures* 2:401. *PL* 101:1399.

17. ff. 73v–74 De sancta facie (in red). Salue sancta facies nostri redemptoris . . . omnes dicant, amen.

Leroquais, *Heures* 2:349–50. *RH* 18189.

18. f. 74 Oratio (in red). Deus qui nobis famulis tuis lumine uultus tui signatis ad instanciam Ueronice . . . securi uideamus te Christum dominum nostrum. Amen.

Leroquais, *Heures* 2:397. Van Dijk, *Origins,* p. 102, n. 9.

19. ff. 74–84 Suffrages to James, all apostles, Stephen, Lawrence, Denis, Eutropius, Maurice, Julianus, Vincent, Andrew, Blasius, "plurimorum martirum," Claudius, Anthony, Julianus, Martin archbishop, "De sancto Gaciano," "De sancto Maurilio," "De sancto Licinio," René, Martin of Vertou, Fiacre, "De sancto Armagilo," "De sancto Serenedo," Francis, Martialis the Apostle, "De sancto Iovino," Gregory, Augustinus, Anna, "De sancta Katherina," Margaret, Apolonia, "De sancta Auia," Geneviève, Agnes, Agatha, Lucy, Susanna, All Saints, the angels.

20. ff. 84–85 Secuntur (*sic*) orationes sancti Gregorii pape (in red). O domine Iesu Criste, adoro te in cruce pendentem . . . et propicius esto michi peccatori. Pater noster et cetera.

Leroquais, *Heures* 2:346, here in the same order as the printed text.

21. ff. 85–88 Deuotissima oratio ad beatam uirginem (in red). Missus est Gabriel angelus ad Mariam uirginem . . . qui deus et homo uenturus est iudicare uiuos et mortuos et seculum per ignem.

Leroquais, *Heures* 2:429.

22. f. 88 Oremus. Te deprecor ergo mitissima, piissima, misericordissima, castissima, speciosissima dei genitricem Mariam . . . et participem me facias celestium gaudiorum, prestate (*sic*) eodem domino nostro Iesu Cristo qui uiuit et regnat . . . Pater noster, Aue Maria.

Leroquais, *Heures* 2:20, 26, and 250.

23. f. 88 De sancta Maria (in red). Aue domina sancta Maria, mater dei, regina celi, porta paradisi . . . et ora pro peccatis meis. Amen.

Leroquais, *Heures* 2:380.

24. f. 88–88v Aue uerum corpus et sanguis domini nostri Iesu Cristi natum de Maria . . . O Iesu fili uirginis Marie nostri (*sic*), miserere. Amen.

Cf. Leroquais, *Heures* 2:382. *RH* 2175.

25. ff. 88v–89v In conceptione beate Marie uirginis antiphona (in red). Benedicta conceptio . . .

f. 90–90v blank.

Hours of the Conception (in short form) with texts for prime, sext, nones, and compline; Leroquais, *Heures* 2:392, cf. MS –41, f. 181.

Five half-page illuminations accompanied by full borders of blue and gold acanthus spray on various grounds of patterned gold. Below, gold, blue, and red illuminated initials 4 lines high except f. 4 which has a simple gold initial on dark red ground. f. 4, John the Evangelist, light rays streaming to his head, eagle holding ink pot; f. 10, the Annunciation; f. 39, Pentecost; f. 40v, David and Goliath; f. 49v, Job on his dunghill, marginal decoration on the ground of gold fleurs-de-lys. Seven historiated illuminations 16 lines high accompanied by outer bracket borders: f. 17v, the Visitation; f.

22v, the Nativity; f. 24v, the Annunciation to the Shepherds in the Field; f. 26, the Adoration of the Magi; f. 28, the Presentation in the Temple; f. 29v, the Flight into Egypt; f. 32v, the Coronation of the Virgin. Ten illuminations 12 lines high: f. 67v, Michael; f. 67v, John the Baptist; f. 68, John the Evangelist; f. 68v, Peter; f. 68v, Paul; f. 69, Christopher; f. 69v, Sebastian; f. 70, Nicholas; f. 70v, Mary Magdalene; f. 70v, Barbara. ff. 1–3v, in the lower margins of calendar pages four compartments depicting the occupation and the zodiac sign for each month. All other leaves except blanks accompanied by traced blue and gold acanthus spray band borders, those on ff. 73–89v more finely prepared. ff. 7 and 8v have bracket outer borders, all on clear grounds. Minor gold initials on alternating red and dark red grounds with occasional gold initials on blue grounds. Line fillers of gold on red and dark red grounds.

Parchment. ff. 89, foliated 1–90 including a modern front flyleaf. 179 × 100 mm (118 × 55 mm). Collation impracticable. Ruled in violet ink. ff. 2–71, written in gothic cursiva formata in 35 long lines; ff. 73–89v in *lettre bâtarde* media in 31 long lines. Headings in scripts of text, ff. 2–71 in violet, ff. 72–89v in red.

Bound in brown morocco c. 1560, according to De Ricci. Gold-stamped monograms MM and CC within wreaths. Front pastedown has traces of the mirror image of a French vernacular text written in fifteenth-century Burgundian *lettre bâtarde* script from a fragment now removed. It also bears notes in French and Latin, s. xvii. Rear pastedown, French verses, s. xvi–xvii, followed by 7 lines of prose by a second hand, dated 1629.

Written probably in western France, c. 1500, as indicated by the calendar and litany. Prayers in texts 3 and 20 in masculine form. Acquired by the Newberry from Edward E. Ayer, 1920.

De Ricci, 1:536.

50.5

Book of Hours, Use of Rouen

France c. 1450

1. ff. 1–12v Calendar of Rouen, written in French in red and blue, major feasts in gold. Feasts include: Saint Sever (1 February), Saint Marcial (24 February, in gold), Saint Godart (13 June), Saint Marceal (3 July, in gold), Saint Nigaise (11 October), Saint Mellon (22 October), Saint Romain (23 October, in gold), Saint Lorens (14 November), Saint Maclou (15 November), Saint Ursin (30 December).

2. ff. 13–17v Gospel sequences, followed by prayers, Protector in te sperancium . . . and Ecclesiam tuam quesumus . . .

3. ff. 17v–19v Passio domini nostri Ihesu Christi secundum Iohannem (in red). In illo tempore apprehendit Pylatus Ihesum . . . Cento taken mainly from John 19; see *Lyell Catalogue,* pp. 65–66. *Horae eboracenses,* p. 123. Followed by the usual prayer Deus qui manus tuas et pedes tuos et totum corpus tuum . . .

ff. 19v–20v blank.

4. ff. 21–60v Office of the Virgin, use of Rouen, beginning imperfectly. ff. 38v–40v, after lauds, suffrages to the Holy Spirit, Nicholas, Catherine, the Trinity, and All Saints.

5. ff. 60v–63v Messe du saint esperit (in red). Spiritus domini repleuit orbem . . .

6. ff. 63v–66v Messe de notre dame (in red). Salue sancta parens . . .

7. ff. 67–78 Seven Penitential Psalms.

8. ff. 78–82v Letania (in red). Romanus, Mellonius, Vivianus, and Audoenus among the confessors; Austreberta among the virgins. Ends with two short prayers: Deus cui proprium est . . . and Fidelium deus omnium conditor . . .

9. ff. 83–85v Short Hours of the Cross.

10. ff. 86–88v Short Hours of the Holy Spirit.

11. ff. 89–92 Obsecro te domina sancta Maria . . . Et michi famulo tuo . . . mater dei et misericordie. Amen.

Leroquais, *Heures* 2:346–47.

12. ff. 92v–96 O intemerata et in eternum benedicta . . . de te enim dei filius . . . et esto michi miserimo peccatori pia et propicia in omnibus auxiliatrix . . . cum electis suis uitam et leticiam sempiternam. Amen.

Leroquais, *Heures* 2:336–37.

13. ff. 96v–134 Office of the Dead, as in use of Salisbury.

f. 134v blank.

14. ff. 135–140 Doulce dame de misericorde, mere de pitie, fontaine de tous biens . . . et pour les trespasses qu'il aient merci et repos. Amen.

Les XV joies. Leroquais, *Heures* 2:310–11. Sonet, 458.

15. ff. 140–142v Doulx dieu, doulx pere, sainte trinite, ung dieu . . . me regardes en pitie. Pater noster.

Les Sept requestes. Leroquais, *Heures* 2:309–10. Sonet, 504.

16. ff. 143–145 O intemerata et in eternum benedicta . . . O Iohannis . . . uobis duobus ego miserimus peccator . . . optimus spiritus paraclitus. Qui cum substancialis et eternis cum eis et igneis (*sic*) uiuit et regnat per infinita seculorum secula. Amen.

Wilmart, pp. 488–90.

17. f. 145–145v Deo deuotissima oratio (in red). Domine Ihesu Christe qui hanc sacratissimam [carnem] de gloriose uirginis utero assumpsisti . . . et ab omnibus inmundiciis et ab uniuersis et perriculis mentis nunc et imperpetuum. Amen.

Leroquais, *Heures* 2:400. Wilmart, p. 378n (no. 10).

18. ff. 145v–146v Oratio deuota (in red). Succurite michi, queso omnes sancti dei, ad quorum ego m[i]scera et peccatrix patrocinia confugio . . . consummatio laudabilis et me adiuuate ut per uos ueniam. Prestante domino nostro Ihesu Christo qui cum patre et spiritu sancto uiuit et regnat deus. Per.

Leroquais, *Heures* 2:93.

19. ff. 147–153 Domine Ihesu Christe, qui in hunc mundum propter nos peccatores de sinu patris omnipotentis aduenisti . . . et misereatur michi omnipotens deus, omnia peccata mea presencia, preterita et fuctura (*sic*). Amen.

PL 101:476–79. Attributed to Augustine, *HUWHA* 1:1, 404; 2:i, 376. Barré, *Prières anciennes,* p. 55, n. 194.

20. ff. 153–154 Digna uirgo, flos, nubes, regina theototos . . . In delitiis tuis sancta dei genitrix.

Achten, *Lateinische Gebetbuchhandschriften,* nos. 1, f. 19v, and 6, f. 255v.

21. f. 154–154v O Maria, porta paradisi, tu linea celi, tu templum domini, tu p[a]lacium dei . . . perpetua interuentrix atque interuentrix (*sic*) auxiliatrix. Amen.

Cf. Leroquais, *Heures* 2:380.

22. ff. 154v–156 Chi ensieuent les v gaudes nostredame (in red). Gaude uirgo mater Christi que per aurem concepisti. Gabriele nuncio . . . in perhenni gaudio. Amen.

Leroquais, *Heures* 2:409. *RH* 7017.

22 bis. f. 156 Fructus floris uirginalis, fructus uite spiritualis . . . salus et redemptio.

This prayer follows text 22 without interruption.

23. f. 156–156v Sic zophuus (?) nutrix rorem rore florem querit . . . Deum et hominem genuit.

24. f. 156v Deus qui beatissimam uirginem Mariam in conceptu et partu . . . in celis piissima eius intercessione ualeamus peruenire. Per.

Leroquais, *Heures* 1:54.

Thirteen half-page illuminations by the Master of Sir John Fastolf: f. 30, the Visitation, Joseph in the background; f. 41, the Nativity; f. 46, the Annunciation to the Shepherds in the Field; f. 49, the Adoration of the Magi; f. 52, the Presentation in the Temple; f. 55, the Flight into Egypt, with the Massacre of the Innocents in the background; f. 57, the Coronation of the Virgin; f. 67, David in prayer, a harp at his side, receiving inspiration by Divine Light; in background, David and Goliath, David playing his harp, and David and Bathsheba; f. 83, the Crucifixion; f. 86, Pentecost; f. 89, Pietà; in background, Bearing of the Cross and Nailing to the Cross; f. 96v, funeral scene in a churchyard with abbot and monks; f. 135, Virgin and Child, red, blue, and gold checkered background. On each illuminated leaf, borders combine orange, magenta, blue, and green acanthus spray and rinceaux decoration, strawberries, violets, etc. Gold dentelle initials with white patterning on blue and magenta grounds 4 lines high.

Parchment. 156 ff. 179 × 130 mm (95 × 66 mm). Collation impracticable. Some catchwords present, often surrounded by penscrolls. Ruled in violet ink. Written in gothic textualis quadrata formata media in 16 long lines. Headings in red in script of text.

Bound in French gold-stamped calf over paper boards, s. xvi, re-covered with worn velvet. Two fore-edge clasps wanting.

Copied in France, probably in Rouen, c. 1450. Text 18 in feminine form. Texts 11, 12, and 16 in masculine form. Front pastedown, armorial bookplate of Henri Auguste Brölemann, early nineteenth-century book-collector in Lyons; his books sold by his great-granddaughter, Mme. Etienne Mallet, Sotheby's, 4–5 May 1926, lot 56 with plate of f. 55. Gift of Chester D. Tripp to the Newberry, 1969.

Kessler, *French and Flemish Illuminated Manuscripts,* no. 14 (plates of ff. 89 and 96v).

51

(23843)

Book of Hours, Use of Rouen

France c. 1450

1. ff. 1–12v Calendar of Rouen in French in red and blue with major feasts in gold.

Feasts include: les reliques sainte Anne (30 January), Saint Sever (1 February), Saint Ausbert (9 February), La translacion Saint Ouen (5 May), Saint Hyldevert (27 May), Saint Marcial (3 July, in gold), Saint Victrice (7 August), Saint Nigaise (11 October), Saint Michiel (16 October), Saint Mellon (22 October), Saint Romain (23 October, in gold), Saint Cler (4 November), Saint Laurens (13 November instead of 14 November), Saint Ursin (30 December).

2. ff. 13–16v De beata Maria; Oratio (in red). Obsecro te domina sancta Maria, mater dei . . . Et michi famulo tuo . . . mater dei et misericordie. Amen.

Leroquais, *Heures* 2:346–47.

3. ff. 16v–20 De beata Maria (in red). O intemerata et in eternum benedicta . . . de te enim unigenitus filius dei . . . et esto michi indigno peccatori . . . uitam et requiem sempiternam. Amen.

Leroquais, *Heures* 2:336–37.

4. ff. 20–25v Gospel sequences, that of John followed by the prayers, Protector in te sperancium . . . and Ecclesiam tuam quesumus . . .

5. ff. 26–64v Hours of the Virgin, use of Rouen, each hour except nones beginning imperfectly as a result of removal of illuminated leaves. Suffrages after lauds to Holy Spirit, the Trinity, John the Baptist, Peter, Lawrence, Nicolas, Margaret, Catherine, All Saints, and prayer for peace.

Folios with text removed after ff. 25, 34, 48, 52, 54, 59, and 60.

6. ff. 64v–76 Les Sept pseaulmes (in red).

Text beginning imperfectly on f. 65; a leaf with text removed after f. 64.

7. ff. 76–81v Letania (in red). Martialis as last apostle; Lawrence, Denis, Maurice, Nicasius, and Eustachius among the martyrs; Audoenus, Romanus, Vivianus, Hildebert, Marturinus, Victor, Lupus, and Clarus among the confessors; Anastasia, Juliana, and Austreberta among the virgins. Followed by two short prayers: Deus cui proprium est . . . and (ends imperfectly) Pretende, domine, famu[lo] //

A folio of text removed after f. 81.

8. f. 82–82v Short Hours of the Cross, beginning and ending imperfectly.

A folio of text removed after f. 82.

9. ff. 83–85v Short Hours of the Holy Spirit, beginning imperfectly.

f. 85v blank; a folio of text removed after f. 85.

10. ff. 86–114 Office of the Dead as in use of Salisbury, beginning imperfectly.

f. 114v blank; an undetermined number of folios removed after f. 114.

Two extant miniatures accompanied by full red, blue, and gold acanthus spray borders decorated with various flowers and fruits in the presence of blue, magenta, and gold initials 3 lines high: f. 47, Catherine (face repainted?); f. 57, the Presentation in the Temple (for the hour of nones). Eleven folios with miniatures removed after ff. 25, 34, 48, 52, 54, 59, 60, 64, 81(?), 82(?), 85, and 114. ff. 13, 16v, and 20v, bracket left borders all with blue, magenta, and gold initials 4 lines high. Minor similar initials throughout, occasionally extended to form rinceaux sprigs in margins. Gold, blue, and magenta dentelle initials and line fillers throughout.

Parchment. ff. 114. Folios removed listed above. 183 × 134 mm (95 × 63 mm). Collation impracticable. Ruled in violet ink. Written in gothic textualis quadrata media in 14 long lines.

Bound very tightly in modern red velvet.

Written in France, probably in Rouen, c. 1450. Prayers in texts 2, 3, and 6 in the masculine form. Rear pastedown in script of s. xvii "Boibasset Becdelievre a [entirely crossed out]; Aeternitas nec tempus est nec ulla temporis pars." In Germany in s. xix, notes of pagination "114 blatt" on front and rear pastedowns. "42432" written in brown ink on rear pastedown. No. 23 from the collection of Henry Probasco, acquired by the Newberry 1 December 1890.

De Ricci, 1:527.

52

(324349)

Book of Hours, Undetermined Use

France s. XV¹/s. XV med.

1. f. 1–1v (addition) Supplico te, virga sanctissima et martir Christi Barbara . . . indigno famulo tuo . . . Oremus. Misericordiam tuam, quesumus domine nobis clementer ostende . . . ac martiris tue placita deuotione gaudiamur. Per . . .

2. ff. 2–13v Calendar in French written in black and red with major feasts in red. A feast for each day. Feasts include: Saintes reliques (30 January), le candelier (2 February, in red), Saint Tymothe (21 August), Saint Michel (28 September, in red), Saint Remi (1 October), Saint Martin (11 November, in red), Saint Ed-

mont (19 November, in red), Saint Nichaise (14 December). Many similarities to the calendar of Paris, but not identical; cf. Perdrizet, *Calendrier parisien*.

3. f. 14 (addition) List of saints: "Crespin, Ladre, Flaman, Severin, Egile, Thomas, Victor, Bertin," and by another hand, "Thomas de Aquino."

f. 14v, miniature.

4. f. 15 (addition) Ueni, creator spiritus, mentes tuorum uisita . . . Qui paraclitus . . . nobisque mittat filius carisma sancti spiritus. Amen.

RH 21204.

5. f. 15 (addition) Angele de dieu qui est commis de moy garder des anemis. Je te prie fais en ton devoir . . . lassus en paradis portee. Amen.

Sonet, 71.

6. f. 15v (addition) O glorieus sains et sainctes de paradis . . . que mestier me sera. Amen.

Sonet, 1383. This prayer also in Poitiers, BM, 95 (s. xv), ff. 3v–4.

7. ff. 15v–16 (addition) O glorieuse vierge Marie, mere de Jhesu Crist, je vous prie merchi . . . que vous fustes temple et chambre de la glorieuse trinite. Amen.

8. ff. 16–17 (addition) O mon tres doulx dieu et createur, je te prie merchi. Je te prie que tu me donne memoire et souvenanche de ta benoite passion . . . en vostre saint paradis. Amen.

Sonet, 1456.

9. ff. 17–18 (addition) Je vous commans a dieu le roy tout puissant par ycelle meisme grasce que dieu commanda sa benoite mere a monseigneur saint Iehan evvangeliste. .N. je vous commande . . . le roy Nabugodonosor les vouloit faire arcoir. Amen.

Cf. Sonet, 837 and 919.

9 bis. f. 18–18v (addition) Christus rex uenit in pace deus homo factus est . . . (change of ink, probably of hand) Qui habitat in adiutorio altissimi in protectione dei celi . . . et ostendam illi salutare meum.

This text continues without interruption from text 9.

The second portion of this text also in Kornik, Polska Akademia Nauk, 1712 (s. xv–xvi); see Zathey, *Catalogus*, p. 552.

10. f. 19 (addition) Anima Christi sanctifica me. Corpus Christi salua me . . . et cum angelis laudem te in secula seculorum. Amen.

Lexikon für Theologie und Kirche 1:563–64. Leroquais, *Heures* 2:340. *RH* 1090.

11. f. 19–19v (addition) Antienne de sainte Anne (in red). Benedicta mater matrisque est mater sui patrisque ab angelo predictam peperisa (?) benedictam cuius benedictus fructus . . . Deus qui beate Anne tantam gratiam donare dignatus est . . . ad celestem Iherusalem peruenire mereamur. Per . . .

12. ff. 20–26v Gospel sequences.

13. ff. 27–29 Suffrages to John the Baptist, Anthony, and Martin of Tours. Rubrics in French.

14. f. 30 (addition) Orison a nostre dame qui tient son enfant ou droit brac et est pour les fievres.

Glorieuse vierge Marie
qui de l'angele fustes siervie . . .
et si recoif a le mort marme

15. f. 30v (addition) Orison de saint Pere de Luxembourg (in red). O dulcissime confessor dei, Petre lucemburgensis, tibi humiliter suplicamus ut dominum nostrum Ihesum Christum . . . (ends imperfectly, probably at the end of a quire) Oremus (in red) // Suffrage to Peter of Luxembourg; the collect is wanting.

16. ff. 31–83v Hours of the Virgin, uncertain use, leaves missing after f. 57(?), 72, and 78.

17. ff. 83v–87 Hore de sancta cruce (in red). Short Hours of the Cross.

18. ff. 87–92v Ci apres s'ensievent les quinze joies nostre dame (in red). Doulce dame de misericorde, mere de pitie, fontaine de tous biens . . . il vuelle avoir mercy de l'ame de moy. Ave Maria, gracia.

Leroquais, *Heures* 2:310–11. Sonet, 458.

19. f. 93–93v (addition) Memoire de sainte Margaritte antienne (in red). Cum autem Margareta duceretur foras ciuitatem dixit ei . . . Orison (in red). Deus qui beatam Margaretam uirginem martyremque tuam ad celos . . .

20. ff. 94–107 Septem psalmos (*sic*) penitentiales (in red).

21. ff. 107–112v Letania (in red). Lambert

and Philbert among the martyrs; Nichasius, Martin, Nicolas, Bertinus, Amandus, Germanus, Vedastus, Medardus, Gildard, and Cassianus among the confessors. Litany proper, followed by the short prayer, Deus cui proprium est . . .

22. ff. 113–157v Office of the Dead as in Salisbury use.

23. ff. 157v–160 Oratio (in red). Inclina, domine, aurem tuam ad preces nostras . . . ut animas famulorum famularumque tuarum quas de hoc seculo migrare . . . uitam et requiem sempiternam. Amen.

Leroquais, *Heures* 2:4.

24. ff. 160v–161 Memoire de sainte Appollone (*sic*) antienne (in red). Sancta Appollonia fuit uirgo inclita cuius dentes extracti fuerunt . . . Oratio (in red). Deus qui beatam Appolloniam gloriosam uirginem et martirem tuam excussione dentium pro tui nominis fide passam in celestibus coronasti tribue quesumus . . . et a periculis tam corporis quam anime liberari.

25. ff. 161v–162 Les cinq joies nostre dame (in red). Gaude uirgo, mater Christi, que per aurem concepisti Gabriele nuncio . . . in perhenni gaudio. Amen . . .

RH 7017. Leroquais, *Heures* 2:409.

26. f. 162v Oratio (in red). Deus qui beatissimam uirginem in conceptu et partu uirginitate . . . ualeamus peruenire. Per . . .

Leroquais, *Heures* 1:54.

27. ff. 163–166v (addition, beginning imperfectly, at least one leaf removed) // se eslecha en celle sainte heure . . . Et te plaise tres humble vierge Marie, mere de dieu et de misericorde, ouir et essauchier et en gre recepvoire ceste suppliante oreson, et moi donner vie pardurable a ma desraine, fin. Amen.

28. ff. 166v–173 (addition) Devote oreson (in red). Saincte glorieuse trinite, benoite glorieuse deite, benoite doulce humanite . . . durra tous jours sans fin pardurablement. Amen.

29. ff. 173v–175v (addition) De saint Nicaise un boin orison (in red). He me sire saint Nicaise, vrai martyr, a qui dieu donna grace . . . nom essauchier et loer. Followed by seven similar invocations.

30. f. 176 (addition) He sire saint Michel, archangele de paradis, conduisseur des ames et madame saincte Eutrope, seur a ce glorieux martyr et hastivel (?) me sire saint Nicaise . . . en le sainct compaignie de nostre sire Ihesu Crist . . .

31. f. 176v (addition) Oratio (in red). Infirmitatem nostram respice, omnipotens deus, quod (?) pondus proprie actionis grauat beati Nicasii martiris tui atque pontificis intercessio gloriosa nos protegat. Per Christum.

32. ff. 176v–179v (addition) Chy apres s'ensieuvent les sept requeste de nostre sire Jhesu Crist. Quiconques voeult estre bien conseille . . . Biaus sire dieu, regardes moy en l'onneur et pite . . . voir me regardes vous en pitie.

Leroquais, *Heures* 2:309; first stanza here omitted.

33. ff. 179v–181 (addition) Chi apres s'ensieut une moult bonne oreson qu'on doit dire pour lui et pour aultrui qui est ales en aucun voiage ou en prison ou en battaile et doit on nomer premierement le personne pour qui est que on le dist; Oreson. Biaus tres doulz Jhesu Crist en l'onneur de tres doulz Lorens dont vous fustes loies a l'estaque le jour du bon venredi . . . nous gardes de pechies et de mort soudaine. Amen.

34. ff. 181–182v (addition) Aouree sois tu saincte crois ou rechut mort Jhesus, ainsi comme che fu voirs et chou est nostre salut . . . et de la saincte crois soit avoec toy. Amen.

35. ff. 182v–184 (addition) De celle sainte beneichon soies tu huy beneis .N. dont dieu beney les trois roys qui Herode vouloit ochire . . . et tous les sains de paradis en ta garde. Amen.

36. ff. 184–189v (addition)

Royne des cieulx glorieuse
Fille et mere dieu gracieuse
Je vieng a toi merchi querir
Car tu es la plus heurieuse . . .
Ceste oreson chi portera.
Amen.

Sonet, 1793. Langförs, p. 347. Rézeau, "La Tradition des prières," no. 130.

37. ff. 189v–198v Chi apres s'ensieut une devote oreson a Jhesu Crist que fist maistre Jehan Gerson.

Glorieux dieu qui me feis
A ta semblance et a t'ymage . . .
Du tout en tout et desconfite

Sonet, 703, but not attributed to Gerson.

38. ff. 199–203v (addition) Suffrages to the saints: Mary Magdalene, Nicholas, Sebastian, Adrian, and Catherine.

39. f. 204 (addition) Inuiolata integra et casta es Maria . . . que sola inuiolata permansisti.

RH 9094.

40. f. 204 (addition) Deus qui de beate Marie uirginis utero uerbum tuum . . . apud te intercessionibus, adiuuemur per Christum.

SMRL 2:472.

41. f. 204 (addition) Aue regina celorum, aue domina angelorum, salue radix sancta . . . et pro nobis semper Christum exora.

RH 2070.

42. f. 204 (addition) Regina celi letare, alleluya. Quia quem meruisti portare, alleluya . . . Ora pro nobis deum, alleluya.

RH 17170.

43. f. 204v (addition) Salue regina misericordie, uita . . . O Ihesu dulcis Maria.

RH 18150.

44. f. 204v (addition) Omnipotens sempiterne deus qui gloriose uirginis Marie corpus et animam . . . a peste et a morte perpetua liberemur. Per Christum dominum nostrum. Amen.

This prayer usually follows the *Salve regina*.

45. f. 205 Memoria de sancto Michaele (in red).

46. ff. 205v–208 (addition) Short Hours of the Holy Spirit.

f. 208v blank.

Some miniatures are beginning to flake from the leaves. f. 14v (addition), full-page illumination of Christopher, symbols of the Four Evangelists in roundels at each corner. Twenty-two half-page illuminations in the presence of gold initials 2–3 lines high. The following are in square compartments accompanied by green, blue, orange, and purple acanthus border with floral decoration, vases, and angels in outer margin: f. 20, John the Evangelist with a devil emptying his ink pot; f. 21v, Luke sharpening his pen; f. 23v, Matthew with an angel holding his ink pot; f. 25v, Mark holding a pen in his mouth; f. 27, John the Baptist; f. 28, Anthony; f. 29, Martin with the beggar; f. 30, the Annunciation with the angel holding a scroll; light rays and the dove going from God above to the Virgin; f. 43v, the Visitation; f. 54v, the Nativity; f. 57v, the Annunciation to the Shepherds in the Field; f. 64v, the Adoration of the Magi; f. 68v, the Presentation in the Temple; f. 87v, the Virgin (reading) and Child, angel bearing a bowl of cherries, historiated initial of the Virgin; f. 94, David in prayer, historiated initial of a soldier, probably Uriah; f. 113, Michael the Archangel struggling with a demon for the soul of a dead man, historiated initial of a funeral; f. 160v, Appolonia. The following have slightly different margins decorated with jesters and animals and are in frames of various shapes: f. 200, Mary Magdalene; f. 201, Nicholas; f. 202, Sebastian; f. 203, Adrien; f. 204, Catherine with a bishop portrayed in the margin. Minor magenta, gold, and blue dentelle initials with similar line fillers; sprigs of floral decoration extend from larger initials. Miniatures removed after ff. 72 and 78.

Parchment. Contemporary sewing on some leaves. ff. 208 + i. Folios missing after 57(?), 72, 78, and 162. 163 × 120 mm (90 × 66 mm). Collation impracticable. Ruled in black and brown pencil and ink. Written in gothic textualis quadrata media in 13 long lines; calendar in 17 long lines. ff. 163–202v, additions in a similar script in 13 long lines. Other additions in textualis and cursiva hands in 14–22 long lines. Headings in red in scripts of text.

Bound in olive-green French morocco c. 1600, gold-stamped with interlaced monograms of C, B, MA, AV, Y, and closed S; and in the center, two interlaced C's surrounded by four closed S's. On the closed S as a sign of affection, see C. Dulong, "L'S fermé et les signes d'amour dans la correspondance Anne d'Autriche-Mazarin," *Revue française d'heraldique et de sigillographie,* No. 50 (1980): 31–38; G. Hobson, *Les Reliures à la fanfare et le problème de l'S fermé* (London, 1935). See also MS 83.

Written in France in the first half of the fifteenth century, quite possibly in northeastern France. Feast of Remy celebrated 1 October as at Reims. ff. 173–176, prayers to Nicaise, venerated at Reims. Cassianus, Bishop of Autun, listed in litany. Nicaise also in litany and calendar. Prayer in text 24 in masculine and feminine plural form. ff. 163–204v, addition written c. 1450. Other additions all s. xv, probably s. xv^2. In the first half of the sixteenth century, this book belonged to Jean Nicolas, Commissaire examinateur au Châtelet, rear flyleaf verso, "Ces heures apartiennent a moy, Jehan Nicolas, examinateur et commissaire ordinaire de par le roy notre sire ou Chastellet de Paris, demourant rue Montellerie, d'achapt par luy faict a douze solz tournois." This same Jean Nicolas mentioned in Paris, Archives Nationale register Y 17065, in a privilège de Franc-Salé (?) dating from 1536–41. f. 209v, inscription, s. xvi or xvii, "Confitebor tibi domine in toto corde meo." Rear flyleaf contains epistolary pen exercise, s. xvi, including: "Henry Roy de France. A nos ames et leaulx conseillers, les gens de nostre court de parlement de Bretagne . . ." f. 160, "Anno domini millesimo quingentesimo quinquagesimo octauo. Donne a Orleans l'an de grace." Acquired by the Newberry from Edward E. Ayer, December 1920.

De Ricci, 1:536.

–53

(324350)

Book of Hours, Use of Rome

Flanders c. 1475

1. ff. 1–12v Calendar of Tournai (?) in black with major feasts in violet. Feast days include: Bernardini confessoris (20 May), Basilii episcopi (14 June), Eligii episcopi (25 June, in violet), Amelberge uirginis (13 July), Clare uirginis (12 August), Bertini abbatis (5 September), Lamberti episcopi (17 September), Bauonis et Remigii (1 October, in violet), Francisci confessoris (4 October), Donatiani episcopi (14 October, in violet), Liuini episcopi et martiris (12 November), Eligii episcopi (1 December, in violet).

f. 13 blank and unruled; f. 13v, miniature for the following text.

2. ff. 14–86v Incipit officium beate Marie uirginis secundum usum romane curie (in violet). Nine psalms at matins with rubrics for the days of the week; prayers for protection, to All Saints, for peace, at the end of each hour from lauds through compline.

f. 87 blank and unruled; f. 87v, miniature for the following text.

3. ff. 88v–96v Incipit officium gloriose uirginis Marie quod dicitur per totum aduentum (in violet).

f. 97 blank and unruled; f. 97v, miniature for the following text.

4. ff. 98–147v Incipiunt uigilie mortuorum (in violet). Use of Rome.

f. 148 blank and unruled; f. 148v, miniature for the following text.

5. ff. 149–169 Incipit psalterium sancti Ieromini (in violet). Followed by usual prayer, Omnipotens sempiterne deus clementiam tuam suppliciter deprecor ut me famulum tuum .N. . . .

f. 169v blank; f. 170 blank and unruled; f. 170v, miniature for the following text.

Horae eboracenses, pp. 116–32. Leroquais, *Heures* 1:xxviii, 83, 275, 315, and 354. Text and prayer not recorded *BHM*. See MS 35, texts 31a–31d.

6. ff. 171–183v Seven Penitential Psalms.

7. ff. 183v–194 Letanie (in violet). Nicholas of Tolentino (canonized 1446) and Alexius among the holy monks and hermits; Elizabeth among the virgins. Followed by the ten standard collects as in the Roman breviary.

8. f. 194 (addition). Pro uno famulo oratio (in red). Inclina domine aurem tuam ad preces nostras . . . ut animam famuli tui . . . et sanctorum tuorum iubeas esse consortes. Per.

Leroquais, *Heures* 2:4.

9. f. 194–194v (addition). Pro patre et matre (in red). Deus qui nos patrem et matrem honorare precepisti . . . gaudio fac uidere.

SMRL 2:329. *Horae eboracenses,* p. 111. See MS 83, text 2.

10. f. 194v (addition). Pro anniuersario (in red). Deus imdulgenciarum (*sic*), domine . . . beatudinis luminis claritatem.

f. 195 blank; f. 195v, miniature for the following text.

SMRL 2:329. Andrieu, *Ordines romani* 1:558.

11. ff. 196–202v Incipit officium de sancta cruce (in violet). Short Hours of the Cross.

f. 203 blank and unruled; f. 203v, miniature for the following text.

12. ff. 204–207v Incipit officium de sancto spiritu (in violet). Short Hours of the Holy Spirit.

f. 208 blank and unruled; f. 208v, miniature for the following text.

13. ff. 209–215v Incipit missa beate Marie uirginis (in violet). Salue sancta parens . . .

14. ff. 215v–221 Gospel sequences.

f. 221v blank; f. 222 blank and unruled; f. 222v, miniature for the following text.

15. f. 223–223v De sancto Sebastiano antiphona (in violet). O beate Sebastiane, magna est fides tua . . . tuis precibus liberari . . . Oratio (in violet). Omnipotens sempiterne deus, qui meritis beati Sebastiani gloriosi martiris tui quandam generalem pestem . . . in corpore liberemur. Per Christum dominum nostrum. Amen.

Leroquais, *Heures* 2:81.

16. f. 224–224v De sancto sacramento (in

violet). O sacrum conuiuium in quo Christus sumitur . . . nobis pignus datur . . . Oratio (in violet). Deus qui pro nobis sub sacramento mirabili passionis tue . . . ut redemptionis fructum in nobis iugiter sentiamus. Per Christum dominum nostrum. Amen.

17. ff. 224v–225 Alia oratio de eodem (in violet). Aue uerum corpus natum de Maria uirgine . . . O clemens, o pie, o Ihesu fili Marie, miserere nobis.

Leroquais, *Heures* 2:382. *RH* 2175.

17 bis. f. 225 Aue caro Christi cara, immolata crucis ara, redemptoris hostia . . . fac redemptos luce clara, tecum frui gloria. Amen.

This prayer follows text 17 without interruption.

Wilmart, p. 379n.

18. f. 225–225v Oratio (in violet). Anima Christi, sanctifica me . . . ut cum angelis laudem te, in secula seculorum. Amen.

Lexikon für Theologie und Kirche 1:563–64. Leroquais, *Heures* 2:340. *RH* 1090.

19. ff. 226–229v Deuota oratio de domina nostra (in violet). Obsecro te, domina sancta Maria, mater dei . . . Et michi famulo tuo . . . mater dei et misericordie. Amen.

Leroquais, *Heures* 2:346–47.

20. f. 230–230v Alia oratio de sancta Maria (in violet). O intemerata sancta dei genitrix, obsecro te ut in hora exitus mei ex hac dulcissimam consolationem et visionem tuam (*sic*) atque . . . sine fine letari. Per Christum dominum nostrum. Amen.

21. ff. 230v–233 Beatus Augustinus sequentem orationem scripsit et reuelata fuit ei a spiritu sancto, ut quicumque eam qualibet die dixerit bono corde uel supra se portauerit, inimicus ei nocere non poterit, in illa die in igne non peribit nec in aqua nec in bello nec ueneno mortifero morietur. Et si quod iustum a domino petierit impetrabit, et non morietur morte subitanea et anima eius in infernum non appropinquabit; Oratio (in violet). Deus propitius esto michi peccatori et custos mei omnibus horis atque diebus et noctibus uite mee . . . in omni tempore et in omnibus horis atque diebus uite mee. ✠ In nomine patris et filii et spiritus sancti. Amen.

Attributed to Augustine, *HUWHA* 2:i, 374; 5:i, 422. Leroquais, *Heures* 2:396.

22. f. 233–233v (addition by same hand as above, f. 194–194v). Credo in deum patrem omnipotentem creatorem celi et terre . . .

f. 234–234v blank.

Sixteen full-page grisaille illuminations with pastel blue, pink, and gold (on inserted sheets with no writing on the recto) accompanied by full blue-grey acanthus frame. Full matching margins also on the opposite page separated from text by gold and blue baguettes. f. 13v, the Annunciation, Virgin reads from banner held by angel; f. 34v, the Visitation; f. 48v, the Nativity; f. 54v, the Annunciation to the Shepherds in the Field; f. 60v, the Adoration of the Magi; f. 66v, the Presentation in the Temple; f. 72v, the Massacre of the Innocents (vespers); f. 81v, the Flight into Egypt, Roman columns in background; f. 87v, the Coronation of the Virgin; f. 97v, Jesus raising Lazarus; f. 148v, Jerome as cardinal writing with left hand on a roll in his study (made from a reversed tracing); f. 170v, King David in prayer, a harp at his side; f. 195v, the Crucifixion; f. 203v, Descent of the Holy Spirit; f. 208v, the crowned Virgin with Child accompanied by two angels, one playing a harp; f. 222v, Sebastian. Gold, black, and white illuminated initials 4 lines high on folios facing the illuminations. Gold, black, and white dentelle initials on grounds of blue with white patterning throughout. Alternating blue initials with red flourishes and gold initials with black flourishes also throughout.

Parchment. ff. 234. 109 × 74 mm (58 × 34 mm). 1–2^{6}, 3^{9} (1 inserted), 4^{8} (5 wanting), 5^{10} (4 is a cancel), 6^{8}, 7^{10} (2 and 8 inserted), 8^{9} (4 inserted), 9^{10} (1 and 7 inserted), 10^{8} (5 inserted), 11^{9} (4 inserted), 12^{4}, 13^{9} (1 inserted), 14–15^{8}, 16^{8} (8 wanting), 17^{8}, 18^{10}, 19^{11} (2 inserted), 20^{8}, 21^{4}, 22^{9} (1 inserted), 23–24^{8}, 25^{10} (1 and 9 inserted), 26^{7} (4 inserted), 27^{8}, 28^{19} (3 inserted), 29^{6}. Catchwords surrounded by four flourished points. Ruled in violet ink. Written in Italian style gothic textualis rotunda media in 15 long lines. Headings in violet in script of text. f. 194–194v, headings in additions in red.

Bound in modern red velvet decorated with ten enamel roundels of the Crucifixion and the Seven Sorrows of the Virgin set in brass frames; one brass clasp wanting.

Written in Flanders, c. 1475; shows similarity to the style of Willem Vrelant. The manuscript postdates the canonization of Bernardino (1450) mentioned in the calendar. Prayers in texts 5, 8, 19, and 21 in masculine form. f. 13v, unidentified arms painted over original arms and initials (see color illustration). "V. F. V." in lower margin. Acquired by the Newberry from Edward E. Ayer, 1920.

De Ricci, 1:536. Kessler, *French and Flemish Illuminated Manuscripts,* no. 9 (plate of f. 56v).

54
(324351)
Book of Hours, Use of Le Mans

France c. 1450

1. 1–12v Calendar of Le Mans in black and violet with major feasts in violet. Feasts include: Guillermi episcopi (10 January), Hillarii episcopi (13 January), Iuliani episcopi cenomanensis (27 January, in violet), Albini (1 March), Turibii (15 April), Quiriacii (*sic,* 4 May), Cenericii (*sic,* 7 May), Yuonis confessoris (19 May), Bertranni episcopi (6 June), Liborii episcopi (9 June), Aniani episcopi (14 June), Cirici et Iulite (16 June), Geruasii et Prothasii (19 June, in violet), Karilephi abbatis (1 July), Pauacii (9 July), Pauacii (24 July), Iuliani episcopi cenomanensis (25 July, in violet), Ffrancisci (4 October), Romanni confessoris (7 November), Macuti episcopi (15 November), Aniani episcopi aurelianensis (17 November), Dompnoli (1 December), Corentini episcopi cenomanensis (12 December), Geruasii et Prothasii (13 December, in violet), Thome bituricensis archiepiscopi (*sic,* instead of "cantuariensis," 28 December).

2. ff. 13–64v Hours of the Virgin, use of Le Mans. f. 21, *RH* 20086 titled "Psalmus Bernardini." Short Hours of the Cross and the Holy Spirit incorporated.

3. ff. 64v–75 Sequuntur septem psalmi (in violet).

4. ff. 75v–78v Litany. Vincent and Cosmas among the martyrs; "Aniane" Julianus, Pavacius, Paduinus, Liborius, and Turibius among the confessors; Euphemia among the virgins. Litany proper followed by two short prayers: Deus cui proprium est . . . and Fidelium deus omnium conditor.

5. ff. 79–80v Secundum Iohannem (in gold). Gospel sequence from John only, followed by the prayer Protector in te sperancium . . .

6. ff. 80v–109 Sequuntur uigilie mortuorum (in violet). Use of Le Mans.

f. 109v blank.

7. ff. 110–112v Obsecro te domina sancta Maria . . . Et michi famule tue . . . dulcissima Maria mater dei et misericordie. Amen. Pater noster. Aue Maria.

f. 113–113v blank.

Leroquais, *Heures* 2:346–47.

ff. 13, 65, 81, blank space reserved for half-page miniatures with full rinceaux border decoration in the presence of gold, blue, and red initials 5 lines high. ff. 33v, 41, 47, 52v, 55v, bracket left margins. f. 52v, bracket left margin with acanthus spray; f. 60v, left rinceaux margin. ff. 21–104, gold dentelle initials with white patterning on grounds of blue and magenta. ff. 1–12, 104v to end, gold initials on alternating red and blue grounds. ff. 13–20, alternating blue initials with red flourishes and red initials with black flourishes.

Parchment. ff. ii + 113 + iv. 156 × 109 mm (73 × 56 mm). 1^{12}, $2–9^{8}$, 10^{4}, 11^{8} (6 stub only), $12–13^{8}$, 14^{6}, 15^{4}. ff. 13–44, catchwords present. Ruled in violet ink. ff. 13–52v, written in cursiva formata; calendar and ff. 53–112v in *lettre bâtarde* media. Written in 14 long lines except for the calendar written in 17 long lines. Change of scribe for the last quire. Headings in violet in script of text.

Bound in original stamped calf over wooden boards; recto and verso bear same four panels which somewhat resemble playing cards: God the Father, Peter, John the Baptist, King David; two rear-to-front fore-edge clasps.

Written in France, probably in Le Mans, c. 1450. The last quire and the initials of the calendar and the final initials may be later additions. Bernardinus (canonized 1450) cited f. 21 but not qualified as a saint. Prayer in text 7 in feminine form. Acquired by the Newberry from Edward E. Ayer, 1920.

De Ricci, 1:536.

54.1
(Ry 56-50)
Collection of Musical Treatises

Pavia [*Illustrated*] 1391

1. ff. 1–6v (Begins imperfectly on the second leaf of the quire with table of proportions.) Capitulum 3^m de inuencione musice per Pictagoram philosophum (in red). Pictagoras nolens aurium iudicio de consonanciis adherere . . . Et per simile semibreuem alteram imperfici per minimum est tenendum.

Explicit explicite quod erat implicite.
Fons atrox eria pedalis truncus usya
Primi dant nomen benefactoris et omen.
Papie 2 scriptum octobris 1391 per fratrem G. de Anglia.

Petrus de sancto Dionysio, *Fragmentum tractatus de musica secundum Johannem de Muris,* ed. Michels, *Corpus,* pp. 56–83 and 147–59. Von Fischer has identified this text as an original compilation of G. de Anglia, based on Johannes de Muris's *Notitia artis musicae,* "Theoretikerhandschrift," pp. 23–33. Chapters 6 and 12 of this treatise were edited from a transcription of this manuscript by Coussemaker, *Scriptorum* 3:399–403.

2. ff. 6v–7 Contrapunctum magistri Phillipoti Andree artis noue (in red).

Post octauam quintam, si note tendunt in altum . . .
Et 5ªm 6ª erit, si fa mi re fuerit.

Dubious Philippus de Caserta, *De contrapunctu tractatus versificatus.* Coussemaker, *Scriptorum* 3:116–18. Other manuscripts listed by Michels, *Corpus,* p. 12.

3. ff. 7v–9 Tractatus magistri Phillipoti Andree artis noue; Capitulum 1 (in red). Quoniam sicut deo placuit scientiam musice in corda desiderantium graciose perlustrauit . . . numerus sic dificeret (*sic*). Sic itaque ad complementum huius temporis consequtus sum, ideo refero gracias deo. Amen.

Tractatus de diversis figuris. Coussemaker, *Scriptorum* 3:118–23. Attributed variously to Philippus de Caserta and Egidius de Murino. See G. Reaney, *Die Musik in Geschichte und Gegenwart,* vol. 3, cols. 1169–72; vol. 10, cols. 1202–3. Manuscripts listed by Michels, *Corpus,* p. 12. A new edition of this text prepared by Philip E. Schreur is in preparation.

4. f. 9 Diagram of note values identical to that of Johannes de Torkesy in Oxford, BL, Bodley 842, ed. G. Reaney, *Corpus scriptorum de musica* 12 (1966): 28.

5. f. 9v Sciendum est quod in superiori linea huius tabule subscripte . . . supertripartis (?).

Diagram follows with the heading in red: "Tabula magistri Alberti super proporciones."

6. f. 10 La harpe de melodie faite, saunz mirancholie (?) . . . de bone acort, une chanson.

Chanson of J. Senleches, found also in Chantilly, Musée Condé, 564 (s. xv), f. 44; *Chantilly: le cabinet des livres, manuscrits* (Paris, 1900), 2:292. The chanson is accompanied by music and is inscribed within an illumination of a harp. See Von Fischer, "Theoretikerhandschrift," pp. 30–31.

7. ff. 10v–33 Prohemium uel epistola (in red). Magnifico militi et potenti domino suo domino Raynerio . . . Incipit lucidarium Marcheti de Padua in arte musice plane; De inuencione musice tractatus primus et capitulum primum (in red). Qualiter Picth[ag]oras adinuenit musicam memorat Macrobius libro 2° post principium . . . hec uoces graues, acute et superacute necessario distinguuntur. Explicit lucidarium Marcheti de Padua in arte musice plane et mensurate, inchoatum Cesene Ueroneque perfectum (in red).

Marchetus de Padua, *Lucidarii tractatus,* I–XIV, ed. M. Gerbert, *Scriptores ecclesiastici de musica sacra potissimum* (Saint Blasien, 1784), 3:65–120.

8. ff. 33–42 Incipit pomerium Marcheti de Padua in arte musice mensurate epistola (in red). Preclarissimo principum domino Roberto dei gratia Ierusalem et Sicilie regi . . . Inter cunctos yerarchicos actus . . . (ends imperfectly in mid folio) tempus musicum superius diffinitum est primum quia.

f. 42v blank.

Marchetus de Padua, *Pomerium,* ending imperfectly in mid sentence in the second part of Book I, *Tractatus quintus,* chapter 2, ed. J. Vecchi, *Corpus scriptorum de musica* 6 (1961): 35–79. This manuscript not recorded.

9. ff. 43–49 Tractatus uenerabilis magistri Iohannis de Muris; Quilibet in arte practica mensurabilis cantus erudiri mediocriter affectans causa scribit diuisibiliterque sequutur summarum (*sic*) compilata secundum Iohannem de Muris; Capitulum 1ᵐ (in red). Partes prolacionis in musica sunt quinque . . . sufficiant in arte practica mensurabilis cantus anhelantibus introduci. Explicit musica uenerabilis magistri Johannes de Muris (in red).

Johannes de Muris, *Libellus cantus mensurabilis.* Coussemaker, *Scriptorum* 3:46–58. See Michels, *Die Musiktraktate,* p. 27.

10. f. 49 Hec sunt regule contrapuncti eiusdem magistri (in red). Sex sunt species speciales discantus, scilicet unisonus, semiditonus . . . Et hec sufficiant de regulis contrapuncti.

Anonymous, *Tractatus de musica,* ed. A. de la Fage, *Essais de diphthéographie musicale* (Paris, 1864; reprinted Amsterdam, 1964), 1:381–82, first paragraph only.

11. f. 49 Expositio specierum (in red). Nota quod semiditonus 1 tercia minor distancia est . . . Quintadecima est distancia 10 tonorum et 4 semitonorum.

Ps. Johannes de Muris, *Ars contrapuncti.* Coussemaker, *Scriptorum* 3:59. See Michels, *Die Musiktraktate,* pp. 40–42, on authorship.

12. ff. 49–50 Que et quot sunt species cantus et de declaratione earum (in red). Unde

sciendum est quod 9 sunt species . . . et ut fa que est dyatessaron.

Ps. Philippe de Vitry, Coussemaker, *Scriptorum* 3:23.

13. ff. 50v–52v Hebrew, Greek, Armenian, Saracen, Arabic, Persian, and Turkish alphabets and numerals with Latin transliterations.

14. ff. 52v–53 Incipiunt optime regule contrapuncti (in red). Septem sunt species consonanciarum . . . Et dissonancia et consonancia imperfecta pro eodem habentur.

Anonymous, *Ars perfecta in musica,* edited from a transcription of this manuscript by Coussemaker, *Scriptorum* 3:28–29. See Michels, *Corpus,* p. 13.

15. ff. 53–56v Tractatus iste (*sic*) super musicam composuit uenerabilis magister Philippus de Uitriaco (in red). Omni desideranti noticiam artis mensurabilis musice . . . tenens dimidium spatium ut hic [musical example follows]. Explicit ars perfecta in musica magistri Philippoti de Uitriaco (in red).

f. 57 blank.

Ps. Philippe de Vitry, *Ars perfecta in musica.* Edited from a transcription of this manuscript by Coussemaker, *Scriptorum* 3:29–35.

16. f. 57v Hungarian and Czech alphabets and numbers with Latin transliterations.

17. ff. 57v–58v Sicut se habent breuis et longa in modo perfecto, ita se habent . . . et potest ea commixti significare.

Anonymous summary of rules of notation.

18. f. 58v 0987654321. Primo loco posita significat se ipsum, secundo loco decies se, tercio, censies (*sic*) se . . . 10,000, 20,000, 30,000, 90,000.

f. 59–59v blank.

Explanation of values of numbers written to the base 10.

f. 10, full-page illumination of a harp in black, brown, and red, text 6 written within. f. 43v, table set between five Italian gothic columns and vaults in the same colors. ff. 7v, 10v, and 33, blue initials with red flourishes alternating with red initials with blue flourishes, both with intricate pen work in the interior, 7–10 lines high. f. 43, a similar red and blue initial 7 lines high. Simple alternating red and blue initials and red paragraph marks throughout.

Parchment of southern preparation. ff. 59. 249 × 180 mm (170 × 120 mm). 1^{16} (1 wanting), 2^{16}, 3^{8}, 4^{8} (4–8, stubs only), 5^{12}, 6^{8} (6–8, stubs only). Quires 2–4, numbered in roman numerals. Quires 3 and 4 numbered in roman numerals on the lower right recto of the first leaf. Catchwords on ff. 15v and 31v. First eight leaves in quires 1 and 2 signed 1–8 in arabic numerals. Ruled lightly in pencil. Quire 1, frame ruling in dark ink over original ruling. Diagrams and musical scores ruled in red. Written in Italian hybrida media in 34–40 long lines by an English scribe, G. de Anglia. Headings in red in script of text. The diagrams, tables, and music which usually accompany these texts written in both black and red ink.

Bound in Germany or Austria in stamped pigskin, s. xvi, heavily worn so as to make identification of stamps of border and interior difficult. Stamps on front cover include: right margin, Christopher, and lower margin, a friar with a nimbus of beams of radiating light. Shelfmark E embossed on front cover. Stubs of a twelfth-century Latin text (not Italian) visible in the front. Parchment fragments under each paper pastedown. Pastedown with watermark of coat of arms, dated Vienna, 1570; Briquet 1026.

Written in Pavia by Friar G. de Anglia, 2 October 1391, signed and dated on f. 6v. In the nineteenth century in the possession of a Vienna collector, known to Edmond de Coussemaker by a transcription provided by Ferdinand Wolf; Coussemaker, *Scriptorum* 3:xv–xvi. Acquired by the Newberry from C. M. Nebehay (Vienna), 1955. Acquisition announced by John F. Ohl, *Newberry Library Bulletin* 4 (1958): 192–93.

Second folio: ex eisdem in eadem.

Faye-Bond, p. 152.

54.5

(Ry 239; 63-1625)

Collection of Chronicles and Documents Pertaining to the Dukes of Burgundy

France or Belgium c. 1450

1. ff. 1–51v En l'an mil iii^{c} iiii^{xx} et vxi (*sic*) le Roy Richart rendy la ville et chastel de Brest au duc de Bretaigne . . . Je prie a dieu qui lui fasse vray mercy et a tous aultres trespasses.

Chronicque de la Traïson et Mort de Richart II Roy Dengleterre, ed. B. Williams (London, 1846). A. Molinier, *Sources de l'Histoire de France* (Paris, 1901–6), 3988.

2. ff. 52–120v En ce temps estripuy le roy de Ghonguerie et fist scavoir par ses lettres . . . Je prie a dieu qui mette son ame en sa glore de paradice. Amen.

Relation de la croisade de Nicopoli par un serviteur de Gui de Blois, ed. de Lettenhove in *Oeuvres de Froissart,* 15:439–508, 16:413–43 (edition based on this manuscript and a manuscript of Lord Ashburnham).

3. ff. 121–164v Par devers la tres haulte et tres noble maieste du roy comme vray subiet et obeissant au roy souverain seigneur . . . Explicit la justification de monseigneur le duc de Bourgoingne, conte de Flandres, d'Artois et de Bourgoingne sur le fait de la mort de feu le duc d'Orleans proposee publicquement a Paris en l'ostel du roy a Saint Pol par maistre Jaques (*sic*) Petit docteur en theologie et conseillier du duc de Bourgoingne le viii[e] jour dudit mois de mars l'an m cccc et vii en la presence du duc de Guienne . . . et grant multitude des gens de tous etas.

Jean Petit, *Justification de monseigneur le duc de Bourgogne,* ed. L. Douët d'Arcq, *Chronique de Monstrelet* (Paris, 1857–62) 1:178–242. A. Coville, *Jean Petit: la question du tyrannicide au commencement du XVe siècle* (Paris, 1932) pp. 133–68, does not list this manuscript. See also C. C. Willard, "The Manuscripts of Jean Petit's Justification: Some Burgundian Propaganda Methods of the Early Fifteenth Century," *Studi Francesi* 13 (1969): 271–80.

4. ff. 165–168v C'est ce qui fut advise sur le fait touchant le cas advenu en la personne de feu monseigneur d'Orleans dont dieu ait l'ame. Premierement que monseigneur de Bourgoingne sera par devers le roy a Chartres . . . Il donera la fille de mondit seigneur de Bourgoingne de la solde iiii[m] livres tournois rente par an.

Accord between the Duke of Burgundy and the children of Charles of Orléans. Isambert, *Recueil des anciennes lois,* vol. 7, no. 440.

5. ff. 168v–172v Lettres faites sur la paix concordee a Saint Mar des Fossez ou mois de decembre l'an mil cccc et xviiii. Charles par la grace de dieu roy de France savoir faisons a tous presens et advenir que comme par extropacion et appaisement des guerres, discors, et divisions . . . donne a Paris le xvi[e] jour de decembre l'an de grace mil iiii[c] et xviii et de nostre rengne le xxxix. Ainsi signe par le roy J. de Lespine.

Treaty of Saint-Maur-des-Fossés, December 1418. Unrecorded by Isambert, *Recueil des anciennes lois,* vol. 8, p. 607; cf. du Fresne de Beaucourt, *Charles VII* 1:108 and 113. This text also in Chantilly, Musée Condé, 879 (s. xv), f. 44.

6. ff. 172v–176v Copie des lettres du traictie de la paix faicte entre monseigneur le daulphin et feu monseigneur de Bourgoingne. Charles filz de roy de France et daulphin de Viennois, duc de Berry et de Thouraine et conte de Poitu et Jehan duc de Bourgoingne . . . assamblee sur le ponceau qui est a une lieue de Melun ou droit chemin de Paris assez prez de Poully le Fort, le mercredy xi[e] jour de juillet l'an de grace mil iiii[c] et xix.

Treaty of Pouilly-le-Fort, 11 July 1419, ed. *Mémoires pour servir à l'histoire* 1:255–58. Isambert, *Recueil des anciennes lois,* vol. 8, no. 675. Du Fresne de Beaucourt, *Charles VII* 1:146, n. 2.

7. ff. 176v–179 La confermacion du traictie de la paix faicte entre feu monseigneur de Bourgoingne et monseigneur le daulphin a Ponceau pres de Melun et abolicion generale le xie jour de juillet l'an mil quatre cens et xix Charles par la grace de dieu roy de France . . . donne a Ponthoise le xxixe jour de jullet l'an de grace mil cccc xix et de nostre rengne le xxxixe. Ainsi signe par le roy. J. de Rivel.

Royal confirmation of the Treaty of Pouilly-le-Fort, ed. *Mémoires pour servir à l'histoire* 1:265–69; *ORF* 12:263–66 (dated 18 July); cf. Isambert, *Recueil des anciennes lois,* vol. 8, no. 676, and de Fresne de Beaucourt, *Charles VII* 1:150 and 179.

8. ff. 179v–184v C'est assavoir que soubz umbre desdits paix et traictiez . . . le xe jour de septembre, l'an de grace mil cccc xix. Ainsi signes par monseigneur le daulphin en son conseil. Malive.

Letters of the dauphin specifying the terms of the Treaty of Pouilly-le-Fort. Isambert, *Recueil des anciennes lois,* vol. 8, no. 677, note 1. Cf. *ORF* 12:268–73.

9. ff. 185 and 188–192v (error in foliation, no folios 186 and 187). S'ensuyt la teneur des lettres envoyees par le Roy et fait publier en sa cite de Paris et allieurs en son royaume sur le fait du desloyal murdre fait en la personne de monseigneur le duc Jehan de Bourgoingne par le daulphin a Monstreau ont fault yonne cas par lesquelles le declare icellui daulphin inhabille a jamais succeder a sa courronne. Charle par la grace de dieu roy de France, a noz chiers et bien amez . . . le xxviie jour de janvier l'an de grace mil cccc et xix et de nostre regne le xlme. Ainsi signe par le roy en son conseil. Bordes.

Letters by which Charles VI in January 1420 (n.s.) disinherited the dauphin Charles (future Charles VII) prior to the Peace of Troyes, ed. M. Félibien, *Histoire de la Ville de Paris* (Paris, 1706), 5:264–67; *ORF* 12:273–77 (dated January 17). This text dated 27 January in Chantilly, Musée Condé, 879 (s. xv), f. 70.

10. ff. 193–202 Abstension de guerre entre monseigneur le duc Phelippe de Bourgoingne et le roy Charles de France. Phelippe par la grace de dieu duc de Bourgoingne . . . donne en nostre ville de Lille le xiiie jour de decembre l'an de grace mil cccc trente et ung. Ainsi signe par monseigneur le duc en son conseil ou quel vons . . . et pluseurs aultres estoient. G. de Lamandre.

ff. 202v–203v blank.

Ed. U. Plancher, *Histoire générale et particulière de Bourgogne* (Dijon, 1739–81), 4:ciia–cviib.

11. ff. 204–221v La paix entre le roy de France et monseigneur le duc de Bourgoingne faite a Aras l'an mil cccc xxxv. Phelippe et cetera. Savoir faisons . . . donne en notre ville d'Arras le xxi jour de septembre l'an de grace mille quatre cens trente et cincq. Explicit toutum.

f. 222–222v blank.

Philip the Good's letters of approbation of the Treaty at Arras, 1435, described by H. Beaune and J. d'Arbaumont, *Les Mémoires d'Olivier de la Marche* (Paris, 1883–88), 1:206, n. 2; cf. E. Cosneau, *Les grands traités de la guerre de cent ans* (Paris, 1889), pp. 116–51.

Paper. ff. 220. Modern foliation 1–185, 188–222. Trimmed to 253 × 185 mm (194–200 × 117–25 mm). $1–6^{20}$, 7^{10}, $8–10^{20}$, 11^{10}, 12^{20} (19 and 20 detached, 20 is rear pastedown). Catchwords at end of first five quires only. ff. 1–130, ruled in ink; ff. 131–219, frame ruled in pencil and hard point. Written by one scribe: ff. 1–130, in *lettre bâtarde* in 27 long lines; ff. 131–219, in cursiva media in 22–26 long lines. Writing begins on the first upper ruled line throughout. On the verso of the modern front flyleaf, "Cronique d'angleterre" is written in an eighteenth-century hand.

Bound in parchment over pasteboard, s. xviii with embossed arms of the Dukes of Arenberg on front and back covers.

Written in France or Belgium, c. 1450, probably before the death of Philip the Good, who is here still the living duke; see ff. 195 and 204, cf. 176v. This collection very similar in contents to Chantilly, Musée Condé, 879. Old spine label, "Chronique d'Angleterre manuscrit"; blue-edged printed sticker above with "No 1, 2me serie" written in red ink. Belonged to the Dukes of Arenberg in the nineteenth century; cf. *Bibliothèque de l'Ecole des chartes* 124 (1966): 163, 167–68, and 171–72. Acquired by the Newberry from William H. Schab (cat. 34, lot no. 2), in May 1963. Acquisition announced by H. Baron, *Newberry Library Bulletin* 6 (1965): 142.

Second folio: lieues pres de.

55

Geoffrey de Vinsauf, *De Arte Versificandi;*
Thomas Merke, *De Moderno Dictamine*

England s. XV med.

1. ff. 1–90v Tria sunt circa que cuiuslibet operis uersatur artificuum (*sic*) principium scilicet progressus et consummacio . . . de conclusione et quomodo sit sumenda. Hoc opus exegi; sit celi gracia regi.

Geoffrey de Vinsauf, *Documentum de modo et arte dictandi et versificandi*. Text varies greatly from the edition of E. Faral, *Les Arts poétiques du XIIe et XIIIe siècle* (Paris, 1923), pp. 265–320. For descriptions of the manuscripts, see E. Faral, "Le Manuscrit 511 du Hunterian Museum de Glasgow," *Studi medievali* 9 (1936): 26; N. Denholm-Young, *Collected Papers* (Cardiff, 1969), p. 49; R. A. B. Mynors, *Catalogue of the Manuscripts of Balliol College* (Oxford, 1963), p. 282. On f. 24, catchwords do not match initial words of f. 25; a quire of text is wanting. Explicit does not match Oxford, Balliol College, 263 or Glasgow, Hunterian Museum, 511, but is very close to Cambridge, Pembroke College, 287, f. 105 sqq.

2. ff. 91–107v Dilectissime frater in quodam amoris et timoris intersticio . . . prolixa distancia. Explicit tractatus.

Thomas Merke, *De moderno dictamine*. See J. J. Murphy, "Rhetoric in Fifteenth-Century Oxford," *Medium aevum* 34 (1965): 18, n. 96, and "A Fifteenth-Century Treatise on Prose Style," *Newberry Library Bulletin* 6 (1966): 205–10; Mynors, supra, p. 282. See also A. B. Emden, *Biographical Register: Oxford* 2:1263–64.

Parchment. ff. 107. f. 1 severely stained. Blank folio after f. 90, an addition to the original manuscript and correctly left unfoliated. Trimmed to 159 × 98 mm (116 × 55 mm). $1–7^{12}$, 8^{6}, 9^{12}, 10^{6} (6 wanting). Trace of old signatures gi–qv indicates that six initial quires of this manuscript are missing and that one quire from the first text was wanting at an early date. Horizontal catchwords, beginning with quire b within double rectangles. End of quire b (f. 24), two catchwords, neither matching f. 25 (see supra, text 1). This break correlates with a change in rubricating; i.e., rubrication not present after f. 24. Ruled in pencil, double boundary lines in brown crayon for first text, single crayon boundary lines for second text. Written in secretary cursiva media by two hands, one for each text, in 27 long lines. The first hand shows chancery influence; the second hand is more current. Blue initials with red flourishes throughout. f. 1, flourishes extended to form an outer and upper bracket border. ff. 1–24, names of authorities underlined in red; red touches used as punctuation. A few secretary and anglicana marginal notes, s. xv.

Bound in brown morocco, s. xix.

Written in England in the middle of the fifteenth century. Note on f. 100v referring to text "Nota hic de occisione Magistri Waltar Daychs." On front pastedown, clipping of an old sales catalogue describing this manuscript in its present binding as "Tractatus de rhetorica auctoris incertu (*sic*)." In 1879, Mrs. James F. Waterman of Sycamore, Illinois, presented this codex to the Chicago Historical Society, her signature and inscription commemorating her gift on the third front flyleaf. Old number 2549 above. A gift of the Chicago Historical Society to the Newberry, 1950.

Second folio: tum ab exemplo tripliciter.

De Ricci, 1:519. Faye-Bond, p. 156.

f55.5

Jacques Legrand, *Livre de Bonnes Meurs*; Jacques de Cessoles, *Liber de Moribus* (in French)

Flanders s. XV² (before 1478)

1. ff. 1–95 Cy commence la table des rubriches du livre de bonnes meurs intitule que composa freres Jaques le Grant religieux des freres hermittes sainct Augustin . . . (f. 5) Tous orgueilleux se veulent a dieu comparer . . . pou vault l'esperance de ceulx qui dient que le monde durra aincoires longuement. Amen. Amen. Explicit. Cy fine le livre intitule des bonnes meurs; Explicit; Amen (in red).

ff. 3v–4v and 95v blank.

Jacques Legrand, *Le Livre de bonnes meurs*, the author's French translation of the *Sophologium*, parts ii and iii. Hain, 10481; Copinger, 3749–53; and numerous sixteenth-century reprintings. See P. Glorieux, "Jacques Legrand," *Dictionnaire des lettres françaises* 1:401, and A. Coville, *Les Cabochiens et l'ordonnance de 1413* (Paris, 1888), pp. 127–28. Partial list of manuscripts, Zumkeller, *Manuskripte*, 431a.

2. ff. 96–152 Honnourable et discret Bertran Aubert escuier de Terreston, frere Jehan Ferron des freres prescheurs de Paris . . . que nous puissons vivre honnestement en ce monde et en paradiz regner pardurablement. Amen. Explicit.

ff. 152v–153v blank.

Jacques de Cessoles, *Libellus de moribus hominum et de officiis nobilium sive super ludo scaccorum*, translation of Jehan Ferron. A. Payen, "Jacques de Cessoles," *Dictionnaire des lettres françaises* 1:399–400. Kaeppeli, 2323.

Three half-page illuminations and twenty smaller one-column illuminations c. 12 lines high: f. 5, God the Father presiding over the fall of the angels (half page); f. 37v, elevation of the Host; f. 44v, an enthroned king with his court; f. 58v, a rich man dispensing alms; f. 78, a man on his deathbed with attendants; f. 96, Jehan Ferron presenting his translation to Bertran Aubert (half page); f. 100v, an enthroned king (half page); f. 102v, a queen; f. 106v, a judge; f. 109, a knight in full armor; f. 114, a royal officer; f. 120v, the first pawn or peasant; f. 122v, the second pawn, a carpenter; f. 124, the third pawn, a notary; f. 128, the fourth pawn, a merchant banker; f. 131, the fifth pawn, a physician; f. 134, the sixth pawn, an innkeeper; f. 136, the seventh pawn, a city watchman; f. 138, the eighth pawn, a messenger; f. 140v, a teacher explaining the game of chess. These miniatures have been attributed by Friedrich Winkler to the Master of Anthony of Burgundy in a letter dated 27 October 1951 in the files of the Newberry and in *Die Flämische Buchmalerei*, p. 261. Miniatures on ff. 5, 44v, 100v, and 126 published by Kessler, *French and Flemish Illuminated Manuscripts*, no. 10. ff. 5, 96, and 100, ornate gold dentelle initials with white patterning on grounds of blue and orange-red 2–4 lines high accompanied by margins with floral decoration in the presence of half-page illuminations. Similar dentelle initials 2 lines high and bracket acanthus spray margins in the presence of smaller illuminations. Each chapter begins with a standard gold dentelle initial with white patterning on grounds of magenta and blue. Alternating blue initials and paragraph marks flourished with red, and gold initials and paragraph marks flourished with black. Headings in red in script of text.

Parchment. ff. 153. 340 × 238 mm (200 × 150 mm). 1^4, 2^{12}, $3–4^8$, 5^8 (8 wanting), $6–18^8$, 19^{10}. Modern quire signatures in pencil inaccurate and misleading. Ruled in violet ink. Written in *lettre bâtarde* formata in 31 lines in two columns (see Examples of Selected Scripts). The script is typical of that used in the most deluxe books of the Burgundian court at the time of Philip the Good and Charles the Bold.

Bound in English restored calf over boards, c. 1520, stamped with two rolls, one with a medallion of a head of a man, a medallion of a head of a woman, and a growing flower, the other with the growing flower stamp only, similar to Oldham, *English Blind-Stamped Bindings*, CH, a (4), 577.

Written and decorated in Flanders before 1478 for Wolfart de Borsele, his arms painted on lower margin and on ff. 5 and 96 without the insignia of the Order of the Golden Fleece to which he was elected at the thirteenth chapter of the order, Bruges, 1478. See H. Martin and P. Lauer, *Principaux manuscrits à peintures de la Bibliothèque de l'Arsenal* (Paris, 1929), pp. 45–46; M. Pecqueur, "Manuscrits armoriés de l'Arsenal," *Bulletin de l'Institut de recherche et d'histoire des texts* 4 (1955): p. 133; A. W. Byvanck, "Les Principaux manuscrits à peintures conservés dans les collections publiques du Royaume des Pays-Bas," *SFRMP* 15 (1931): 107–8. Other Borsele manuscripts include Paris, Arsenal, 5169; Utrecht, University Library, 42; and Leningrad, State Public Library, F. V. XIV. 1. Bound in England, c. 1520. f. 1, "Ex libris D. Baliar (?) Bousers (?) 1526," crossed out. In 1918, this book was in the hands of a Berlin dealer; see Winkler, *Die Flämische Buchmalerei,* p. 161. Sold by H. P. Kraus to Louis H. Silver. Acquired by the Newberry from him in 1964.

Second folio: Comment les gens.

Faye-Bond, p. 176.

56

(324353)

Book of Hours, Use of Rome; Prayerbook of Margaret of Croy

Flanders and Holland c. 1430/c. 1450

1. ff. 1–6v Calendar of Bruges in black with major feasts in red. Feasts include: Amandi episcopi (6 February, in red), Cathedra sancti Petri (22 February, in red), Gertrudis uirginis (17 March), Basilii episcopi (14 June, in red), Eligii episcopi (25 June, in red), Diuisio apostolorum (15 July), Egidii abbatis (1 September, in red), Lamberti episcopi (17 September), Remigii et Bauonis (1 October, in red), Dionisii martiris (9 October, in red), Eligii episcopi (1 December, in red), Nichasii episcopi (14 December, in red).

2. ff. 7–12v Six miniatures on inserted leaves, versos unruled, with titles for the following illumination written in red on ff. 7v–11v only.

3. ff. 13–16 Missa beate Marie uirginis (in red). Salue sancta parens . . .

4. ff. 16–19 Gospel sequences.

5. ff. 19v–21v Hore sancte crucis (in red). Short Hours of the Cross.

6. ff. 22–23v Officium sancti spiritus (in red). Short Hours of the Holy Spirit.

7. ff. 24–64v Incipiunt hore beate Marie uirginis secundum usum romane ecclesie (in red). Nine psalms at matins with rubrics for the days of the week. At the end of each hour, prayer for protection, prayer to All Saints, and prayer for peace, entire text ending with the Salue regina followed by its usual prayer, Omnipotens sempiterne deus qui gloriose uirginis . . .

8. ff. 64v–70 Changed Office of the Virgin. f. 70v blank.

9. ff. 71–78 Incipiunt septem psalmi penitenciales (in red).

10. ff. 78–82v Litany of the saints. Barnabus among the apostles; Quintinus and Lambertus among the martyrs; Amandus, Bavo, Eligius, and Egidius among the confessors; Gertrude, Walburgis, and Ursula among the virgins. Litany proper followed by four collects. The first and fourth are the first and eighth of the usual sequence of ten in the Roman breviary. The two other short prayers are Omnipotens sempiterne deus, dirige actus nostros . . . *SMRL* 2:510, and Deus, qui nos patrem et matrem honorare precepisti . . . *SMRL* 2:329.

11. ff. 83–107 Office of the Dead, use of Rome.

ff. 107v–108v blank (f. 108–108v unruled).

12. ff. 109–111 Oratio deuota ad dominum nostrum Ihesum Christum ualde utilis (in red). Domine deus omnipotens, qui es trinus et unus . . . qui iudicas contra aduersorem fias defensor meus, qui es benedictus in secula seculorum. Amen.

Cf. Leroquais, *Heures* 1:73 and 247–49. Wilmart, pp. 99 and 573–77. Gjerlow, *Adoratio crucis,* p. 164.

13. ff. 111v–112v Oratio de mane dicenda deuote flexis genibus (in red). Domine sancte pater omnipotens qui me creasti, redemisti, custodisti specialiter tempore noctis huius . . . omnibus quoque fidelibus defunctis requiem eternam concedas. Qui uiuis et regnas deus.

Leroquais, *Heures* 1:85 and 230.

14. ff. 112v–113 Oratio ad idem (in red). In manus tuas domine Ihesu Christe et in misericordia tua commendo hodie nunc et semper animam meam, sensum meum, intellectum meum . . . Et me defendas a subitanea et improuisa morte. Qui cum deo patre in unitate spiritus sancti uiuis et regnas deus. Per . . .

Leroquais, *Heures* 2:416. Wilmart, p. 403n.

15. ff. 113–114v Oratio beati Ieromini de mane dicenda (in red). O domine Ihesu Christe, mane cum surrexero, intende ad me et guberna omnes actus meos, uerba mea et cogitationes meas . . . Eleuacio manuum mearum sacrificium uespertinum.

Ps. Jerome, *Oratio matutinalis,* shorter recension. *PL* 101:490–491. *BHM* 950.

16. ff. 114v–115v Oratio sancti Thome de Aquino que sequitur deuote dicenda (in red). Concede michi, misericors deus, que tibi placita sunt ardenter concupiscere . . . in patria frui per gloriam. Qui uiuis et regnas . . .

A. I. Doyle, "A Prayer Attributed to St. Thomas Aquinas," *Dominican Studies* 1 (1948): 229–38. Grabmann, *Die Werke,* pp. 112 and 370–72.

17. ff. 115v–117 Sequitur oratio deuotissima ad sanctam trinitatem (in red). Deus pater, deus filius, deus spiritus sanctus trinus et unus . . . Salua me et adiuua me, sancta trinitas, unus deus. Qui uiuis . . .

18. ff. 117–118v Deus qui de sinu patris in mundum uenisti peccata relaxare, afflictos reducere . . . Et concede michi indigne famule uestre graciam uestram. Et intercedite pro me ad dominum deum nostrum. Qui uiuit . . .

Leroquais, *Heures* 2:177. Cf. MS 82, text 18.

19. ff. 118v–121 Oratio deuotissima pro se ipso et pro omnibus uiuis et defunctis siue benefactoribus siue malefactoribus, flexis genibus deuote dicenda (in red). Domine Ihesu Christe, deus meus, generis humani conditor . . . Quem unum deum colimus, laudamus et adoramus in terris. Amen.

20. f. 121 Cum uolueris ire cubitum signans lectum, dicas cum deuocione flexis genibus ante lectum tuum que sequuntur (in red). Ore tuo Christe benedictus sit locus iste . . . gratiam tibi ualeam seruitium exhibere. Per Christum dominum nostrum gratiam tibi.

RH 31371.

21. ff. 121–122v Alia oratio ad idem (in red). Domine deus misericors, gracias ago tibi pro omnibus beneficiis tuis tam corporalibus quam spiritualibus que hodie michi peccatrici et indigne famule tue . . . et ego semper merear esse tecum. Qui es deus trinus et unus . . .

Leroquais, *Heures* 1:85 and 230.

22. ff. 122v–123 Oratio ad idem (in red). Me mundet et muniat illuminet et consignet et saluet triumphalis titulus Ihesus Nazarenus rex iudeorum . . . Et nomina omnium sanctorum et sanctarum dei sint benedicta in seculorum secula. Amen.

This text also in Kornik, Polska Akademia Nauk, 27 (France, s. xv), f. 18v; see Zathey, *Catalogus,* p. 79.

23. ff. 123–126v Oratio in qua continetur confessio generalis (in red). Domine Ihesu Christe inestimabilis misericordie et immense potestatis et pietatis . . . pro me, miserrima peccatrice, beatissima genitrice tua Maria cum omnibus sanctis tuis super quos uiuis et regnas deus trinus et unus qui es benedictus in secula seculorum. Amen.

Attributed to Alcuin, *PL* 101:524–26.

24. ff. 126v–129 Domine ne in furore, primum (in red). Qui tollis peccata mundi . . . Et tocius gregis tui quem effucione proprii cruoris redemisti.

Prayer on the Seven Penitential Psalms, Wilmart, *Codices reg. lat.* 1:701, followed by the antiphon Ne reminiscaris domine . . . *SMRL* 2:67.

25. f. 129–129v Oratio deuota (in red). Pie et exaudibilis domine Ihesu Christe, clemenciam tuam cum omni supplicatione . . . infidelibus ueram fidem et fidelibus defunctis requiem propicius donare digneris sempiternam. Qui cum deo . . .

Leroquais, *Heures* 1:46. A. Wilmart, *Precum libelli,* p. 93. See MS 82, text 49.

26. ff. 130–131 Ista oratio deuotissime dicenda est in presencia corporis et sanguinis domini (in red). In presencia corporis et sanguinis tui, domine Ihesu Christe, commendo tibi me famulam tuam Margaretam per uirtutem sancte crucis . . . et ad uitam perducat eternam te miserante qui uiuis et regnas cum deo patre in unitate spiritus sancti deus per omnia secula seculorum. Amen.

Wilmart, p. 378n (no. 11). *Horae eboracenses,* p. 71.

27. f. 131–131v Oratio sancta et deuota dicenda est in presencia corporis domini . . . (in red). Aue domine Ihesu Christe, uerbum patris, filius uirginis, agnus dei . . . uita perhennis.

Wilmart, pp. 412–13, text 3 and n. 2.

27 bis. ff. 131v–132 Aue principium nostre creacionis . . . aue premium nostre expectacionis, aue mundissima caro Christi filii dei

uiui, miserere mei et concede michi Margarete famule tue . . . et ueraciter accipere ualeam. Amen.

This prayer follows text 27 without interruption. Wilmart, p. 587.

28. f. 132–132v Bonifacius papa sextus dedit omnibus dicentibus sequentem oracionem infra eleuationem corporis domini et tercium agnus dei duo milia annorum de indulgenciis (in red). Domine Ihesu Christe, qui hanc sacratissimam carnem et preciosum sanguinem . . . quod modo in altari tuo tractatur ab omnibus immundiciis mentis et corporis periculisque et anime presentibus et futuris. Amen.

Leroquais, *Heures* 2:400. Wilmart, p. 378n (no. 10). *Horae eboracenses*, p. 177.

29. f. 132v Qui dicit istam orationem in honore domini nostri Ihesu Christi cotidie numquam morte subitanea morietur (in red). Ihesus nazarenus rex omnipotens iudeorum et omnium populorum semper amabilis atque laudabilis, glorificabilis et desiderabilis . . . sit nobis assiduus auxiliator et pius in omni tempore Christus mundi saluator beatissimus. Amen. A subitanea et improuisa morte et a morte perpetua liberet nos pater et filius et spiritus sanctus. Amen.

Same text in Lyon, BM, 784 (s. xv), f. 60.

30. ff. 132v–133 Oratio in presencia corporis domini (in red). Salue sancta caro dei, per quam salui fiunt rei . . . Et da michi sedem iustorum in secula seculorum. Amen.

Leroquais, *Heures* 2:348. Wilmart, p. 378n (no. 13). *RH* 18175.

31. f. 133–133v Oratio ante corpus domini (in red). Aue corpus Christi natum de Maria uirgine . . . o clemens, o pie, o dulcis fili Marie.

RH 2175.

32. f. 133v Alia ad idem (in red). Aue caro Christi cara immolata crucis ara, pro redemptis hostia . . . fac redemptos luce clara tecum frui gloria. Amen.

Wilmart, p. 379n.

33. f. 133v Alia ad idem (in red). Salue caro Christi que (*sic*) pro me passa fuisti . . . cui decantatur osanna.

RH 33066.

34. ff. 133v–134v Deus propicius esto michi peccatori et sis custos mei omnibus diebus uite mee . . . Crux Christi salua me, crux Christi protege me, crux Christi defende me. In nomine patris, et filii et spiritus sancti. Amen.

Leroquais, *Heures* 2:396. Same prayer in feminine form, text 100, below. This prayer often attributed to Augustine.

35. ff. 134v–136 Domine Ihesu Christe qui septem uerba die ultimo uite tue in cruce pendens dixisti . . . in regno meo epulari, iocundari et commorari per infinita seculorum secula. Amen.

Leroquais, *Heures* 2:342.

36. f. 136–136v Precor te, piisime domine Ihesu Christe, propter illam caritatem . . . propter magnam misericordiam tuam michi tribuere digneris. Qui uiuis . . .

Leroquais, *Heures* 2:443. Wilmart, p. 378n (no. 12).

37. ff. 136v–137 Papa Nicholaus concessit uuicumque (*sic* for cuicumque) dicenti istam orationem flexis genibus uiginti continuatis diebus confesso et contrito corde omnium peccatorum suorum absolucionem (in red). Deus qui uoluisti pro redemptione mundi a iudeis reprobari . . . quo perduxisti tecum crucifixum latronem. Qui uiuis . . .

Leroquais, *Heures* 1:153. *Horae eboracenses*, pp. 83 and 177. Cf. MS 35, text 18, and MS 82, text 26.

38. f. 137–137v Incipiunt deuotissime orationes sancte et adorande crucis in die ueneris sancta multum deuote flexis genibus dicende (in red). Domine deus sancte pater omnipotens, da michi digne accedere ad salutandam atque adorandam crucem . . . Et ab inflictis uulneribus euacuari ad uitam eternam, ualeam peruenire. Amen.

39. ff. 137v–138v Oratio ad idem (in red). Domine Ihesu Christe fili dei uiui, gloriosissime conditor mundi qui cum sis splendor glorie . . . tibi merear assistere mundus. Domine Ihesu Christe qui celum et terram . . . per caritatis uinculum. Amen.

Peter Damian, *Prayer 30*. Cf. *PL* 145:929. Final portion not in the printed text. Wilmart, p. 146.

40. ff. 138v–139 Ad idem oratio (in red). Domine Ihesu Christe fili dei uiui, obsecro te per crucem tuam ut dimittas peccata mea . . . et tribue michi uitam eternam. Amen.

Leroquais, *Heures* 2:91 at the explicit.

41. f. 139–139v Alia idem (in red). Tuam

crucem adoramus domine, tuamque sanctam resurreccionem laudamus . . . Crux michi uita, crux michi salus, crux michi resurreccio in uitam eternam. Amen.

Gjerlow, *Adoratio crucis,* p. 70. Followed by a cento beginning with Psalm 69:1.

42. ff. 139v–140 Oratio (in red). Deus qui tribus pueris mitigasti flammas ignium . . . nec dilanient nos suggestiones inmundorum spirituum. Amen.

SMRL 2:473.

43. f. 140 Alia ad idem (in red). Deus cuius preconium innocentes martires non loquendo . . . ut fidem tuam quam lingua nostra loquitur etiam moribus uita fateatur. Amen.

44. f. 140 Collecta (in red). Da nobis domine quesumus omnium beatorum martirum tuorum intercessione . . . incendia superare. Amen.

SMRL 2:469.

45. f. 140–140v Domina et mater misericordie que mundi edidisti saluatorem . . . absque dilacione misereatur mei. Amen.

46. ff. 140v–141 Incipit oratio deuotissima de sancta Ueronica flexis genibus dicenda (in red). Salue sancta facies nostri redemptoris . . . sed fruamur requie, omnes dicant amen.

Attributed to Giles of Rome. Zumkeller, *Manuskripte,* nos. 26 and 26A. Leroquais, *Heures* 2:349–50. *RH* 18189.

47. f. 141 Alia ad idem (in red). Aue facies preclara, pro nobis in crucis ara . . . in perhenni gloria. Amen.

Cf. *RH* 23474. Followed by a cento beginning with the cue for Psalm 66.

48. ff. 141v–142 Oremus (in red). Deus qui nobis signatum lumine uultus tui memoriale tuum ad instanciam Ueronice . . . Ut te tunc facie ad faciem uenturum super nos iudicem securi uideamus, dominum nostrum Iesum Christum filium tuum qui tecum uiuit et regnat in unitate spiritus sancti deus per omnia secula seculorum. Amen.

Van Dijk, *Origins,* p. 102n.

49. ff. 142–143v Ad ymaginem crucifixi (in red). Omnibus consideratis, paradysus uoluptatis . . . emendetur homo prauus in te qui spem habuit.

Jean de Limoges, *De passione Christi,* lines 1–69. *Analecta hymnica* 31:87–89. Wilmart, p. 584 (note to p. 527). Continuation below, text 57.

50. ff. 143v–144 Oratio (in red). Domine Ihesu Christe, creator celi et terre et omnium que in eis sunt, ego miser peccatrix suppliciter peto . . . ab omnibus impedimentis separantibus me a te.

51. f. 144 O bone Ihesu, intimo cordis affectu supplico in illa ultima hora . . . quibus iram tuam, domine Ihesu, misericordissime pater, prouocaui.

52. f. 144–144v Oratio (in red). Piissime pater, etiam rogo ut michi infundere digneris sapienciam regendi me . . . Ideo supplico, misericordissime Ihesu, ut michi propicius esse digneris.

53. f. 144v Oratio (in red). O bone Ihesu, concede michi desiderium plenum in corde meo . . . in hora separationis a corpore animam meam in custodiam et protectionem tuam suscipere dignemini suppliciter exoro.

54. f. 145–145v Oratio bona et deuota ad dominum Ihesum Christum (in red). O bone Ihesu, o dulcissime et piissime Ihesu, o Ihesu fili Marie plenus misericordia et pietate . . . et omnes qui inuocant hoc nomen sanctum quod est Ihesus. Amen. Pater noster et cetera.

Attributed to Richard Rolle. Allen, *Writings Ascribed to Richard Rolle,* p. 314. Leroquais, *Heures* 2:345.

55. f. 146 Domine Ihesu Christe fili dei uiui, per illam amaritudinem quam sustinuisti propter me in cruce . . . miserere anime mee in egressu suo.

Leroquais, *Heures* 2:100.

56. f. 146–146v Illumina oculos meos ne umquam obdormiam in morte . . . et consolatus es me.

Leroquais, *Heures* 2:415. This prayer often attributed to Bernard of Clairvaux.

57. ff. 146v–147v Ad sanctam Mariam (in red). Maria plasma nati . . . quem Christus eripuit. Amen.

Conclusion of Jean de Limoges, *De passione Christi,* line 70 to the end. Followed by a liturgical cento beginning with Kyrieleison and ending with Ualde honorandus est Iohannes euuangelista . . . *SMRL* 2:35–36, and the prayer Omnipotens sempiterne deus qui unigenitum filium tuum . . .

58. ff. 147v–148 Adorans tu crucem dic antiphonam (in red). Salue sancta crux . . . Uersus (in red). Adoramus te Christe . . . Oratio (in red). O crux benedicta redemptio

nostra, liberacio nostra, salus nostra . . . usque dum felicitate celesti perfrui merear ad laudem dei patris omnipotentis, qui in trinitate perfecta uiuit et regnat deus per omnia secula seculorum. Amen.

Leroquais, *Heures* 1:365.

59. ff. 148–149 Passio domini nostri Ihesu Christi secundum Iohannem (in red). In illo tempore apprehendit Pylatus Ihesum . . . est testimonium eius.

Cento drawn from John 19, etc. *Lyell Catalogue,* pp. 65–66. *Horae eboracenses,* p. 123. Followed by the usual prayer, Deus qui manus tuas et pedes tuos . . . See MS 47, texts 4 and 5.

60. ff. 149–150 Innocencius papa hanc oracionem de passione domini composuit (in red). Domine Ihesu Christe, fili dei uiui, fons uite et origo tocius bonitatis . . . tecum crucifixum latronem tibi sero confitentem in cruce. Auxilientur michi . . . ut me miseram peccatricem custodias protegas et defendas ab omnibus incursibus dyoboli et omnium inimicorum uisibilium et inuisibilium. Amen.

Leroquais, *Heures* 1:139.

61. f. 150–150v Oratio breuis et efficax beatissimi Gregorii quam iussit populo romano dicere qualibet die et dum mane surgeret, et dum sero dormitum iret (in red). Titulus triumphalis Ihesus nazarenus rex iudeorum . . . Sancta trinitas unus deus, miserere nobis.

Leroquais, *Heures* 2:457.

62. ff. 151–153v O intemerata et in eternum benedicta . . . de te enim dei filius . . . et esto michi peccatori . . . concedas michi misericorditer cum electis suis uitam et requiem sempiternam.

Leroquais, *Heures* 2:336–37.

63. ff. 153v–155v Oratio de domina nostra sancta Maria (in red). Obsecro te domina sancta Maria . . . et michi famule tue Margarete . . . uirgo Maria, mater misericordie. Amen.

Leroquais, *Heures* 2:346–47.

64. f. 156–156v Oratio de domina nostra, feria tercia dicenda (in red). Aue cuius concepcio, solempni plena gaudio . . . assumpcio nostra glorificacio.

Leroquais, *Heures* 2:380. *RH* 1744. Followed by the versus Ora pro nobis sancta dei genitrix . . . *Horae eboracenses,* p. 198.

65. f. 156v Oremus. Deus qui nos concepcionis, natiuitatis, annunciacionis . . . et cum ipsa gaudere mereamur in celis. Per Christum dominum nostrum.

Leroquais, *Heures* 1:91, and as listed by Zathey, *Catalogus,* p. 79.

66. ff. 156v–157 Oratio ad idem (in red). Gaude Maria dei genitrix, uirgo immaculata. Gaude que gaudium ab angelo suscepisti . . . in hora mortis nostre perpetua interuentrix.

Cf. Wilmart, p. 504n.

67. f. 157–157v Alia ad idem (in red). O pia domina dulcissima, ornamentum seculi, margarita celestis, sancta Maria, tu porta paradysi, tu ianua celi, tu templum dei, tu palacium Christi . . . et numquam me dimittas sine adiutorio. Amen.

Leroquais, *Heures* 2:380. Wilmart, *Codices reg. lat.,* vol. 1, MS 121, f. 219.

68. f. 157v Alia oratio feria tercia dicenda (in red). Gaude uirgo mater Christi, que per aurem concepisti . . . in perhenni gaudio. Aue Maria.

Leroquais, *Heures* 2:409. *RH* 7017. Followed by the versus Exaltata es sancta dei genitrix . . . *SMRL* 2:155–56.

69. f. 158 Omnipotens sempiterne deus qui diuina Gabrielis salutacione . . . et sempiternis gaudiis perfrui mereamur. Per eundem Christum dominum nostrum. Amen.

70. f. 158–158v Oratio (in red). O domina glorie, o regina leticie, o fons pietatis et misericordie . . . Tu benedicta in eternum, permanes cum Ihesu Christo filio tuo. Qui cum patre . . .

Leroquais, *Heures* 1:143.

71. ff. 158v–160v Oratio feria quarta. Quicumque hec septem gaudia in honore beate Marie uirginis semel in die dixerit C dies indulgentiarum obtinebit a domino papa Clemente qui hec septem gaudia proprio stilo composuit que sequntur (*sic;* in red). Uirgo templum trinitatis, deus summe bonitatis . . . ad eternum gaudium. O Maria tota munda . . . et duc tecum ad iocunda (*sic*) paradisi gloria (*sic*). Amen.

Philippe de Grève, *VII gaudia beatae Mariae.* Wilmart, p. 329, n. 1. Four lines of text at the end not present in MS 35, text 13.

72. ff. 160v–161 Oratio (in red). Te depre-

cor sanctissima Maria mater dei pietate plenissima . . . pro me peccatrice Margarete famule tue (*sic*) . . . et defunctis requiem sempiternam. Amen.

Leroquais, *Heures* 1:138. Cf. MS 35, text 14, and below, text 81.

73. ff. 161–162 Hec sunt nomina lxxii[a] beate Marie uirginis (in red). Diua, uirgo, flos, rubes (*sic*), regina, theototos . . . Alumpna Maria.

Achten, *Lateinischen Gebetbuchhandschriften,* nos. 1, f. 19v; 6, f. 255. Leroquais, *Heures* 2:208. Followed by an antiphon, two versi, and the collect Protege, domine, famulos tuos . . .

74. ff. 162–165v Feria quinta has uideas laudes qui sancta uirgine gaudes et uenerando piam studeas laudare Mariam, uirginis intacte cum ueneris ante figuram, pretereundo caue ne taceatur aue, inuenies ueniam sic salutando Mariam; Salue (in red). Salue uirgo uirginum, stella matutina, sordidorum . . . in gloria sua collocare. Amen.

Attributed to Bonaventure, *Carmina super canticum "Salue Regina."* Bonaventure, *Opera omnia* (Rome, 1596), 6:489. Glorieux, 305, bs. Followed by the versus Ora pro nobis sancta dei genitrix . . . and the collect Deus qui de beate Marie uirginis utero . . . *SMRL* 2:472. See MS 35, text 9.

75. ff. 165v–166 Oratio ad sanctam Mariam feria sexta flexis genibus dicenda (in red). Stabat mater dolorosa iuxta crucem lacrimosa . . . ut anime donetur paradisi gloria. Amen.

Leroquais, *Heures* 2:455. *RH* 19416. Wilmart, p. 509.

76. ff. 166v–167v Oratio beate Marie uirginis die sabbati dicenda (in red). Aue mundi spes, Maria; Aue mitis, aue pia . . . semper tecum sim mansurus. Per immortalia secula seculorum. Amen.

RH 1974. Followed by Adiuuet nos, quesumus, domine deus beate Marie semper uirginis . . . *Horae eboracenses,* p. 135.

77. ff. 168–170v Istam orationem confirmauit dominus Innocencius papa quartus et dedit omnibus eam deuote dicentibus quingentos dies indulgenciarum et unam carenam (in red). O domina mea sancta Maria, perpetua uirgo uirginum, mater summe benignitatis . . . et exaudi me in hac peticione mea. Audi nos nam te filius nichil negans honorat. Salua nos, Ihesu, pro quibus uirgo mater te orat. Lege predictos uersos ter et tria aue Maria flectendo genua tua ad terram rogando interim quod desideras (in red).

Leroquais, *Heures* 1:319, cf. 2:398. Wilmart, p. 516, n. 1.

78. ff. 170v–171v Ut sicut certus sum quod ille te nichil negans . . . et uiuis salubrem prosperitatem in hoc seculo et in futuro. Amen.

79. f. 171v Oratio de domina nostra sancta Maria (in red). Maria, o dilectissima est tibi tale oculum hunc audire uersiculum, Ave Maria, gracia plena, dominus tecum. Tociens enim o castissima oscularis . . . et perfecta caritate in extremis frui. Amen.

Cf. *Liber meditationum ac orationum devotarum* (Paris: Petrus Le Dru, 1502), f. 69.

80. f. 172–172v Innocencius papa fecit hanc orationem, et dedit omnibus eam deuote dicentibus ducentos dies indulgenciarum (in red). Saluto te, beatissima dei genitrix, uirgo Maria, angelorum regina . . . et perpetuam digne accipere merear beatitudinem. Per Christum dominum nostrum. Amen.

Leroquais, *Heures* 2:449.

81. ff. 172v–173v Innocencius papa hanc orationem dicentibus donauit iiii[or] annos indulgenciarum (in red). Deprecor te, sancta Maria, mater domini nostri Ihesu Christi pietate plenissima, summi regis filia . . . ut intercedas ante conspectum filii tul pro me peccatrice . . . cum electis et sanctis suis uitam et requiem sempiternam. Amen.

Leroquais, *Heures* 1:250 and 350, cf. 2:395. See above, text 72.

82. ff. 173v–174v Si quis istam orationem in honore beate Marie legerit, in finem uite sue ueram confessionem cum contricione et fonte lacrimarum faciet (in red). O sanctissima, o dulcissima, o piissima, o misericordissima . . . Et adiuua me, domina piissima uirgo Maria, ut in finem bonum et perseueranciam sanctam consequi merear. Amen.

Cf. Leroquais, *Heures* 1:320.

83. ff. 174v–187 Suffrages to Michael, John the Baptist, Peter, Paul, Andrew, John the Evangelist, James, all the apostles, Stephen, Lawrence, Cornelius, George, Christopher, Quirinus martyr, Sebastian, Erasmus, the ten thousand martyrs, all martyrs, Martin, Anthony the Great, Theobaldus, Nicholas,

Francis, Hubert, all the confessors, Mary Magdalene, Catherine, Barbara, Agnes, Apollonia, Margaret, Elizabeth, Ursula, the eleven thousand virgins, Cunera, Dorothy, all virgins, all saints.

84. ff. 187–188 Orison a monsigneur saint Sebastien contre l'epidemie (in red). Signum salutis pone, domine, in domibus istis ut non permittas . . . Collecta (in red). Omnipotens deus qui meritis beati Sebastiani martiris tui gloriosissimi quemdam generalem pestem epydemia hominibus mortiferam reuocasti . . . et ab omnibus tam uisibilibus quam inuisibilibus inimicis singulis diebus liberentur. Per Christum dominum nostrum. Amen.

For the first prayer, see Andrieu, *Ordines romani* 1:264. For the principal prayer, see *Horae eboracenses,* p. 130.

85. f. 188–188v ✠ Ihesus autem transiens per medium illorum ibat. Sic ego per uirtutem . . . ananisapta (?) dei, miserere mei.

86. ff. 189–190v Een deuoet ghebet tot onsen lieuen here Ihesum (in red). Uoer die uoeten uwer hoecheit bin ic gheuallen sondich mensche . . . Lof si den coninc der hemelscher glorien. Amen.

87. ff. 190v–192v Een deuoet ghebet an onsen here Ihesum Christum (in red). O here Ihesu Christe scepper hemelrijcs ende eertrijos ende aldat daer in is . . . ende regneert een god in ewicheit der ewicheiden. Amen.

88. ff. 192v–193v Een goet ghebeth (in red). O lieue heer wilt mi die sin uerlenen uwer passien . . . uanden rechtueerdighen rechter onse here Ihesu Christo.

89. ff. 193v–199 Een goede beuelinghe beghint aldus (in red). In den name des uaders ende des soens ende des heilighen gheests. Amen. Soe beueel ic huden op desen dach ende altoes dijn lijf ende dijn ziele . . . Dese woerde sijn also goet ende also waer als dat heilighe pater noster, dat si waer in gods namen. Amen. Collecta (in red). Protege, domine, famulum tuum .N. subsidiis pacis et beate Marie . . . a cunctis hostibus redde securis. Per Christum dominum nostrum. Amen. Here Ihesu Christe leuende gods soen, die in deser werelt quames om onse sonders te uerlossen uanden sonden . . . ende brenct mi tot dijn ewighe leuen. Amen. Here Ihesu Christe in teghenwoerdicheit uwes lichaems ende uwes bloedes beuele ic . . . bescermt ons uan allen lede ende brenct ons ten ewighen leuen. Amen.

90. ff. 199–200 Een ynnich ghebet tot onsen here Ihesu Christo (in red). O alre uolcomenste ende luchtichste exemplar alre duechden ende goeder wercken here Ihesu Christe . . . ende glorie alle dijnre heilighen.

91. f. 200 Een deuoet ghebet an onser urouwen (in red). Eya moeder der ontfermherticheit ioncfrouwe uan ongheliker puerheit regiert mi . . . ende die glorie dijnre hogher weerdicheit sien moghe in ewicheden. Amen.

92. ff. 201v–205v So wie dit ghebet dat hier na bescreuen staet der moeder gods Marien te eeren mit deuocien leest daghelix xxx daghe an een . . . (in red). O mijn alre liefste urouwe sunte Maria ewighe maghet der magheden moeder der ouerster goedertierenheit . . . Behoude ons Ihesu uoer wien die maghet ende moeder di bidt. Knielt neder ende leest drie, aue Maria; Ende bidt dar ghi begheert (in red). Want also als ic dat seker bin dat hi di eert . . . ende alre ghelouigher leuende of doot saligen uoerspoet inder tijt ende inder ewicheit. Amen.

93. ff. 205v–206 An dinen eyghen enghel een ghebeth (in red). O heilighe enghel gods een borgher des ouersten houes die uanden almachtighen god . . . ende presentierse gode den hemelschen uader inden ewyghen leuen. Amen.

94. f. 206–206v An sinte Peter apostel (in red). Wat dattu bijndes opter aerden dat sal ghebonden wesen . . . Collecta (in red). O God die dinen salighen apostel Petrum macht te bijnden ende te ontbijnden ghegheuen heues, wi bidden . . . Ouermids onsen here Ihesum Christum. Amen.

95. ff. 206v–207 An sinte Ian ewangelist (in red). O Iohannes ewangelist alre gemindeste apostel Christi bescouwer der heiligher drieuoudicheit ende . . . daer du regnieres in uolcomente glorien in ewicheit der ewicheit. Amen.

96. f. 207–207v Uan sinte Barbara orisoen (in red). Here god wi bidden di oetmoedelike toen ons goeder tierlike uwe ontfermherticheit

. . . ende uerdienste der saligher ioncfrouwen ende martelaersche sunte Barbara. Amen.

97. ff. 207v–209 Sunte Jorijs orisoen (in red). Dese bedinghe plach mijn here sinte Joriis te lesen doe hi leuede . . . (in red). Mitten heilighen monde daer Ihesus Christus mede sprac ende sijn ghebenedide moeder . . . daer wi alle comen moeten die u dienen mit deser grueten. Amen.

98. f. 209 Sunte Augustinus die gloriose leere seit . . . ende die uleyschelike begheerte uerwynnen.

99. f. 209v

Lieue ioncfrou bouen alle dinck
Sÿt gode bedienstich ende bemint . . .
Hi en uertroesten tot enighen uren.

100. f. 210–210v Deus tu propicius esto michi peccatrici et custos mei omnibus diebus et noctibus uite mee . . . Crux Christi protege me; crux Christi defende me. In nomine patris et filii et spiritus sancti. Amen.

Leroquais, *Heures* 2:396. A longer version in masculine form above, text 34. This prayer often attributed to Augustine.

101. ff. 210v–211 De sancta cruce (in red). Crucem tuam adoramus, te ueneramur, domine Ihesu Christe . . . uitam et gloriam sempiternam. Amen.

Leroquais, *Heures* 2:393.

102. ff. 211v–212v (addition). ✠ Ihesus autem transiens per medium illorum ibat et dixit pax uobis ✠ . . . Qui in trinitate perfecta uiuit et regnat deus per omnia secula seculorum. Amen.

Six inserted full-page miniatures, of which five are in the style of Otto von Mordrecht, accompanied by full rinceaux border with floral decoration: f. 7, the kiss of Judas, rabbit in outer margin, bird in lower margin; f. 8, Christ before Pilate; f. 9, the scourging of Christ; f. 10, Christ bearing the Cross; f. 11, Descent from the Cross (by another artist), bird in upper margin, dog in lower margin, fantastic bird with a human head in outer margin; f. 12, the Entombment; f. 13, not inserted but with similar border decoration, the Coronation of the Virgin; above, an angel blowing a horn bearing a pennant with the five wounds of Christ, a fantastic animal in the upper margin, a centaur in the lower margin blowing a horn bearing a pennant with a white cross on a red ground, another centaur in the outer margin. Thirteen half-page miniatures by at least two artists accompanied by full rinceaux borders of a different style, fantastic creatures of various sorts and blue initials on grounds of gold and magenta: f. 20, the Crucifixion with Mary and John; f. 22, Pentecost; f. 24, the Annunciation; f. 36, the Visitation; f. 43v, the Nativity; f. 47, the Annunciation to the Shepherds in the Field; f. 50, the Adoration of the Magi; f. 53, the Massacre of the Innocents; f. 56, the Presentation in the Temple; f. 61, the Flight into Egypt; f. 65, Dormition of the Virgin; Peter dressed as a Dominican friar; f. 71, King David in prayer, a harp at his side; f. 83, funeral scene in a church, two black monks in attendance.

Two half-page miniatures accompanied by full acanthus spray margins, magenta initials on gold grounds: f. 109, Gnadenstuhl Trinity, a centaur in outer margin, a fantastic dragon-bird in lower margin; f. 151, Margaret of Croy kneeling before the Pietà. Thirty-eight blue and magenta historiated initials on gold grounds 5 lines high: f. 174v, Michael, John the Baptist; f. 175, Peter; f. 175v, Paul; f. 176, Andrew, John the Evangelist; f. 176v, James; f. 177, all apostles, Stephen; f. 177v, Lawrence; f. 178, Cornelius, George; f. 178v, Christopher; f. 179, Quirinus, Sebastian; f. 179v, Erasmus; f. 180, the ten thousand martyrs; f. 180v, all martyrs, Martin; f. 181, Anthony the Abbot; f. 181v, Theoboldus, Nicholas; f. 182, Francis in a brown habit; f. 182v, Hubert, all confessors (in the front row, a Franciscan friar in a brown habit); f. 183, Mary Magdalene; f. 183v, Catherine, Barbara; f. 184, Agnes; f. 184v, Apollonia; f. 185, Margaret, Elizabeth; f. 185v, Ursula with her cloak above the eleven thousand virgins; f. 186, Cunera; f. 186v, Dorothy, all virgins; f. 187, All Saints; f. 187v, Sebastian.

ff. 1–107, gold dentelle initials with white patterning on grounds of blue and magenta with pieces of floral decoration mark sections of text; within text, alternating blue initials with red flourishes and gold initials with black flourishes. ff. 109–211, blue and magenta dentelle initials with white patterning on gold grounds 4 lines high with pieces of rinceaux border mark beginnings of major texts; gold dentelle initials with white patterning on grounds of blue and magenta mark shorter texts; gold initials with red flourishes within texts.

Parchment. ff. 1 + 212 + 1. 179 × 129 mm (105 × 70 mm). $1–2^{6}$, 3^{8} (an unidentified leaf wanting), 4^{4}, $5–14^{8}$, 15^{5} (5 inserted, s. xvi?), $16–28^{8}$, 29^{2} (2 is pastedown). Ruled in violet ink with change in shade beginning on f. 109. Prickings visible in outer margins. Written in gothic textualis quadrata media in 19 long lines by two hands. ff. 1–107, in a brown to black ink; ff. 109–211, in very black ink. Calendar ruled for 33 lines.

Bound in late s. xvi, stamped gilt calf over wooden boards. Gilt edges.

Original manuscript (ff. 1–6 and 13–107) written in Flanders, probably in Bruges c. 1430. Inserted miniatures on ff. 7–12 resemble those produced in Utrecht c. 1430. For related manuscripts, see J. D. Farquhar, "Identity in an Anonymous Age: Bruges Manuscript Illuminators and Their Signs," *Viator* 11 (1980): pp. 371–83, and Sotheby's sales catalogues of 21 June 1982, lot 15, and 23 June 1987, lot 121. ff. 109–211, added c. 1450, probably in Utrecht, note presence of Cornelius and Cunera in the suffrages; this section added for Margaret of Croy, daughter of Antoine of Croy (1385–1475), wife of Henry of Montfort (Holland). See de Vegiano, *Nobiliaire des Pays-Bas et du comté de Bourgogne* (Ghent, 1862–65), vol. 1, pt. 2, p. 570, no. 689. This manuscript confirms her name as Margaret; cf. Anselme, 5:637. f. 151, her arms within the illuminated initial; her name inserted into the prayers in texts 26, 27, 63, and 67. Texts 18, 21, 24, 50, 60, 81, and 100 also in feminine form. Texts 32 and 64 in masculine form. Margaret is also included among the suffrages. f. 1, three ink library stamps: the first oval with Virgin and Child, two others circular; f. 212v, another circular unidentified ink library stamp; f. 213, another ink stamp with a shield, possibly a serpent below the hat of a cardinal. Initials "G. B. S." (s. xviii?) on rear pastedown. Acquired by the Newberry from Edward E. Ayer, 1920.

De Ricci, 1:537. Panofsky, *Early Netherlandish Painting*, p. 406. Kessler, *French and Flemish Illuminated Manuscripts*, no. 3 (plates of ff. 12, 22, 71, and 151). W. H. Beuken and J. H. Marrow, *Spiegel van den Leven ons Heren* (Doornspijk, Holland, 1979), p. 96, n. 77. E. M. Gifford, "Pattern and Style in a Flemish Book of Hours: Walters Ms 239," *The Journal of the Walters Art Gallery* 45 (1987): 89–102 and fig. 38.

f57

(51-209; 36.1)
Collection

Belgium [*Illustrated*] c. 1462–64

1. f. i^v Proprietates rustici.

Cum inprecaris eum, surdescit non habet aures . . .
. . . nouit amare fidem.

Listed from this codex, Walther, *Initia*, 15229.

1 bis. f. i^v Quis continuit spiritum in manubus (*sic*) suis. Sex sunt quos odit dominus et septimum detestatur anima eius. Oculos sublimes, linguam mendacem . . . et eum qui sciat interficiens discordias.

2. f. ii Relacio ducis Burgundie dum diem suum clauderet extremum ad filium suum Karolum.

Imperium, Karole fili, grande tibi relinquo . . .
. . . dat iniquus iniquo.

f. ii^v blank.

3. ff. iii–vii Incipit tabula subsequencium tractatuum . . . Scripta est hec tabula per manus Io. Gherinx phisici, anno domini millesimo quadringentesimo sexagesimo quarto, augusti uicesimo nono, hora prima post meridiem.

Table of contents for entire codex referring to contemporary foliation.

4. ff. vii–x Ouidius de Uentre (in upper margin)

Concilium celebrant humani corporis artus . . .
Hic quoque uult finem carmen habere suum.
Finis Ouidii de uentre.

ff. x^v–xii blank.

Ps. Ovid, *De ventris membrorumque altercatione*, ed. F. W. Lenz, "Das Pseudo-Ovidische Gedicht *De ventre*," *Maia* 2 (1959): 169–211 (185–95). *PL* 99:1005–8. Walther, *Initia*, 3087.

5. f. xii^v

Memorie celebris maximi antistitum Pii . . .
Que si scire cupis, hunc, oro, lege libellum.

Ten verses in praise of Pope Pius II.

6. ff. 1–21v Incipit tractatus duorum amancium nuncupatus ab Enea Siluio tunc illustrissimi imperatoris cancellario, nunc papa Pio solemniter editus. Magnifico ac generoso militi domino Gaspari Slick domino noui castri Cesareo cancellario . . . Eneas Siluius poeta imperialisque secretarius salutem plurimam dicit Mariano Sozzino . . . quod longe plus aloes habet quam mellis. Uale. Io. Gherinx phisicus scripsit anno 1463° kalendas februarii in domo proprie habitacionis in Sancto Trudone tunc residenciam faciens.

Pius II (Aeneas Silvius Piccolomini), *De duobus amantibus historia*, prefaced by a letter of Aeneas Silvius to Kaspar Schlick, ed. Wolkan, *Der Briefwechsel* 1:353–93, text 154 followed by text 153.

7. ff. 21v–29v Mafeus Uegius fratri Eustatio salutem dialogus feliciter incipit. Dum repeterem nuper animo Eustachi frater . . . atque ego te sequor libens et sic est finis. Io. Gherinx medicorum minimus scripsit.

f. 30–30v blank.

Maffeo Vegio, *Dialogus veritatis et Philalethis ad Eustachium fratrem.* Editions: B. Remboldt and I. Waterloes (Paris, 1511); M. de la Bigne, *Maxima bibliotheca veterum patrum* (Lyon, 1677), 26:754–59. See also Raffaele, *Maffeo Vegio,* p. 113 sqq. and passim; A. C. Brinton, *Maphaeus Vegius and His Thirteenth Book of the Aeneid* (Stanford, 1950), p. 7; Prete, *Codices barberiniani latini,* vol. 1, MS 61, f. 30r.

8. ff. 31–47v Tractatus de miseriis curialium editus per sanctum dominum nostrum papam Pium .ii. dum in minoribus esset constitutus et dum imperatorum secretarius et consiliarius. Eneas Siluius poeta salutem plurimam dicit domino Iohanni de Aich perspicati (*sic*) et claro iuriconsulto. Stultos esse . . . Ex Pruck, pridie kalendas decembris, anno domini m° cccc° xliiii°. Finit tractatus Enee Siluii de miseriis curialium.

Pius II (Aeneas Silvius Piccolomini), *De miseriis curialium,* ed. W. P. Mustard (Baltimore, 1948). Ed. Wolkan, *Der Briefwechsel,* pp. 453–87.

9. ff. 48–59v Mafei Uegei laudensis de felicitate et miseria incipit feliciter. Obsecro te, O Charon, sine me iam ut nauim conscendam . . . salue, O Palinure, et uale.

f. 60–60v blank.

Maffeo Vegio, *De felicitate et miseria* (printed, Basel, 1518). Manuscripts and early editions frequently attribute this text to Lucian, translation to Rinucio Aretino. See Raffaele, *Maffeo Vegio,* p. 115 sqq. and passim; Lockwood, "De Rinucio Aretino," pp. 94–97; Prete, *Codices barberiniani latini,* vol. 1, MS 64, f. 219r.

10. ff. 61–84v Incipit liber primus de miseria hominis editus a Lothario diacono et cardinali qui postea dictus fuit Innocencius tercius et cetera. Domino patri karissimo Petro . . . sulphur et ignis ardens sine fine a quibus omnibus liberet nos qui est benedictus in secula seculorum. Amen. Explicit liber Lotharii dyaconi cardinalis qui postmodum dictus est Innocencius tercius de uilitate condicionis humane.

Innocent III, *De Miseria humane conditionis,* ed. R. Lewis (Athens, Georgia, 1978). This manuscript unrecorded.

11. f. 85–85v Augustinus de miseria hominis. Fratres carissimi, quam tremenda est dies illa . . . et procedent qui bona fecerunt in resurrectionem uite.

Ps. Augustine, *Tractatus de miseria hominis.* See *HUWHA* vol. 2, pt. 1, 378; Strasbourg, 31, *Catalogue général des départements,* series in 8°, 47, 22; Troyes, 1032, f. 42, *Catalogue général des départements,* series in 4°, 2, 426. Associated in last two manuscripts with the treatise of Innocent III. Also in *CLM* 5424, f. 135; cf. Ps. Augustine, *Sermo de iudicio extremo,* 251. *PL* 39:2210 (= Ps. Ambrose, *Sermo* 24. *PL* 17:651).

12. ff. 85v–92 Qualia fecit quisque talia recipiet. Tradunt doctores quod quantum spacium aeris occupauit aqua in diluuio . . . quia si malus remanes, deus malum male perdet. Explicit.

Attributed to Augustine by Johannes Gherinx above in the table of contents of this codex, f. iv^v^, cf. Cambridge, Corpus Christi College 481, p. 586; James, *Descriptive Catalogue of Corpus Christi College* 2:431.

13. ff. 92v–149 "Flosculi poetarum." Title given here taken from the table, f. iv^v^. Includes excerpts from Seneca, the Sibyl, Pythagoras, Socrates, Plato, Aristotle, Theophrastus, Demosthenes, Epicurus, Zeno, Plautus, Statius, Terence, Marcus Cato, Diogenes, Julius Celsus (i.e., Julius Caesar), Cicero, Sallust, Varro, Virgil, Horace, Sextus Pictagoricus (on the birth of Christ), and Ovid. Accompanied by notes and excerpts of historical texts. On ff. 136v–137v, a long note on the reign of Caesar Augustus.

14. f. 149

Uersus Marcialis de formica electro inclusa.
Dum Phatontea formica uagatur in
umbra . . .
Eiusdem de uipra.
Flentibus Eliadum ramis dum uipra
serpit . . .
Uipera si tumulo nobiliore iacet.

Martial, *Epigrammata,* VI, 15; IV, 59.

15. f. 149

Ludouici Bruni de rana.
Iam genus humanum cesset iactare
sepulcra . . .
Artificis nusquam tale videtur opus.

ff. 149v–150 blank.

On Ludovicus Bruni, see Chevalier, *Bio-Bibliographie* 1:711–12.

16. f. 150v Ex capitulo decimonono libri quartidecimi Iohannis Bocacii uatis celeberrimi cognomento de Cartaldo de geneologia deorum in laudem Francisci Petrarche. Franciscus Petrarcha a iuuentute sua celibem uitam ducens . . . plus ex moribus quam ex uerbis

traxisse doctrine, dixi. Iohannes Gherinx phisicus scripsit 1464 29 augusti.

Giovanni Boccaccio, *De genealogia deorum,* Book XIV, chap. 19, ed. V. Romano (Bari, 1951), 2:741–42.

17. ff. 151–157 Epistola Francisci Petrarche ad Sagremor de Pomeriis ex equite armate milicie cisterciensis cenobii monachum exhortatoria ut in felici sacri status proposito felicius perseueret. Semper et uiuis uocibus tuis . . . Uiue nostre amicicie memor et uale, Uenetiis xv kalendas aprilis . . . finit feliciter et uotiue, deo gracias. Amen.

Petrarch, *Epystola ad Sagromorum de Pomeriis (Rer. senil.,* X, i), ed. *Opera omnia* (Basel, 1554), 2:952–58. E. H. Wilkins, *Petrarch's Correspondence* (Padua, 1960), p. 146. Transcribed as a separate text, Mann, *Petrarch Manuscripts,* pp. 11 and 251.

18. ff. 157v–160v Epistola Pogii ad Leonardum Aretinum de morte Hieronimi heretici. Pogius Leonardo Aretino salutem dicit. Cum pridem ad balnea fuissem, scripsi . . . Uale, 3° kalendas iulii Hieronimus penas luit, scriptum anno domini m ccc lxxvi.

Poggio Bracciolini, *Epistola de morte Hieronymi Pragensis,* ed. Garin, *Prosatori latini,* pp. 228–40. Hain, 13206*–13211. Poggio, *Opera omnia* (Turin, 1964–69), 3:11–20, reprint of the text of Tonelli. The manuscript varies considerably from the printed text.

[19.] Text wanting. According to the table on f. vi^{v}, ff. 161–193 contained the *Liber scaccorum* of Jacques de Cessoles = Kaeppeli, 2066.

20. ff. 194–203v Titulus de nobilitate (in red). Aput maiores nostros sepenumero de nobilitate dubitatum est . . . in uestra sentencia relinquitur. Explicit controuersia de nobilitate inter Publium Cornelium Scipionem et Gayum Flamineum per legum doctorem egregiumque oratorem Bonacursum pistoriensem. E copiata per manus Io. Gherinx phisici anno domini 1462° in uigilia natiuitatis hora octaua in Sancto Trudone in domo proprie habitacionis.

Buonaccorso da Montemagno, *Controversia de nobilitate,* ed. G. B. Casotti, *Prose e rime de' due Buonaccorsi da Montemagno con annotazioni* (Florence, 1718), pp. 2–96; partial edition revised, Garin, *Prosatori latini,* pp. 138–65. In many manuscripts and early editions attributed to Leonardo Bruni; see Goldschmidt, *Medieval Texts,* p. 6; H. Baron, *The Crisis of the Early Italian Renaissance* (Princeton, 1956), 2:623–24; Prete, *Two Humanistic Anthologies,* p. 32, n. 35.

21. f. 203v Subsequuntur facecie Pogii poete laureati scripte ob animi (?) Io. Gherinx phisici nouitatem (ends imperfectly in mid quire) //

Table of contents, f. vii, lists this text as beginning on f. 204. The text itself is now wanting.

First folio is parchment and once served as a pastedown; subsequent folios are paper, watermarks of *tête de cerf,* cf. Briquet 15545. ff. 182. Foliation: i–xii in modern roman numerals followed by 1–160, 194–203 in contemporary arabic numerals. Significant portions of the manuscript removed after ff. 161 and 204. Trimmed to 214 × 185 mm (173 × 114 mm). 1^{6} (3–6 wanting), $2–18^{10}$, 19^{8} (1–2 wanting), 20^{10} (5–10 wanting). ff. 10v, 20v, 169v, some catchwords in decorative scrolls not removed by trimming. Ruled in pencil with double boundary lines on outer margins. Written in 34–39 long lines beginning on the first ruled line throughout. ff. iii–vii, 1–30, 150v, 194–203v, written by Johannes Gherinx; see *Colophons de manuscrits occidentaux,* nos. 5758 and 9826–29, and *Manuscrits datés (Belgique)* 3:69–70. Gherinx uses two scripts: the table on ff. iii–vii is written in gothic textualis formata showing influence of Italian gothic textualis rotunda; Gherinx's other script is a hybrida media showing humanistic influences, e.g., use of ct ligature, humanistic rustic capitals, and occasional use of half-uncial d. Remainder of manuscript written in hybrida media/hybrida currens by other hands. ff. 157v–60v written in gothic cursiva currens. Texts 1, 2, 4, 5, 13 (f. 92v only), 14, and 15 added following the preparation of the entire codex but before binding. Marginal corrections, index notes, and pointing fingers by the scribe. f. 1, gold illuminated initial accompanied by a sprig of floral decoration. Germanic red minor initials throughout, with violet flourishes in some portions of the manuscript.

Bound in contemporary geometrically ruled black leather with fleur-de-lys, an Agnus Dei (?) and other unidentifiable stamps within compartments over boards, severely deteriorated. Remains of two fore-edge clasps.

Written in Belgium, 1462–64, portions of text copied in St. Trond in 1462 and 1463 by Johannes Gherinx. Table of contents copied by Gherinx in 1464. f. 1, arms of the Nuti family (Florence). It is possible that some portions of this codex were written in Italy. f. i, pen trials; ". . . nomen eius" and "est negauit (?)." f. i^{v}, "Data quando leodienses subiciuntur principi Burgundie ad libitum eius et quando dominum episcopum Lodewicum de Borbon expulsum ui receperunt in dominum. Ecce quam faceti sunt nunc leodienses. 1467. Sich hoe saecht moedich sijn si nu di ludikers. Aliter. Elc mach wel claghen nu ter tijt." Portions visible only under ultraviolet light. Sold by Karl und Faber, September 1943, lot no. 30. Acquired by the Newberry from the auction of Dr. Ernst Hauswedell (Hamburg), catalogue 41, lot 3, 1950. Acquisition announced by H. Baron in *Renaissance News* 7 (1954): 146.

Second folio: -nes resista.

Faye-Bond, p. 153.

–58
(324347)
Book of Hours, Use of Rome

Flanders c. 1460

1. f. 1–1v De sancto Iohanne baptista antiphona (in violet). Inter natos mulierum non surrexit . . . Oratio (in violet). Perpetuis nos quesumus domine beati Iohannis baptiste . . .

f. 2–2v blank; f. 3 blank and unruled; f. 3v, miniature for the following text.

Suffrage to John the Baptist. *Horae eboracenses*, p. 44n.

2. ff. 4–10v Incipiunt hore de sancta cruce . . . (in violet).

Short Hours of the Cross.

3. ff. 11–14v Missa de sancto spiritu (in violet). Spiritus domini repleuit orbem . . .

f. 15 blank and unruled; f. 15v, miniature for the following text.

4. ff. 16–21v Hore de sancto spiritu . . . (in violet).

f. 22 blank and unruled; f. 22v, miniature for the following text.

Short Hours of the Holy Spirit.

5. ff. 23–29 Incipit missa beate Marie uirginis (in violet) . . . Salue sancta parens . . .

6. ff. 29–34 Gospel sequences.

f. 34v blank; f. 35 blank and unruled; f. 35v, miniature for the following text.

7. ff. 36–104v Incipiunt hore beate Marie uirginis secundum consuetudinem romane ecclesie . . . (in violet). Nine psalms at matins with rubrics for the days of the week. Prayers at the end of each hour, lauds through compline. Ends with Salue regina and its usual prayer, Omnipotens sempiterne deus qui gloriose uirginis . . .

f. 105 blank and unruled; f. 105v, miniature for the following text.

8. ff. 106–114v Changed Office of the Virgin.

9. ff. 115–118v Oratio de domina nostra (in violet). Obsecro te domina sancta Maria . . . Et michi famulo tuo . . . et exaudi me dulcissima Maria, mater dei et misericordie. Amen.

Leroquais, *Heures* 2:346–47.

10. ff. 119–121v Alia oratio de domina nostra (in violet). O intemerata et in eternum benedicta . . . orbis terrarum. Inclina mater . . . O Iohannes . . . ego miserrimus peccator . . . ad gaudia perducat omnium angelorum suorum benignissimus paraclitus. Qui cum . . .

f. 122 blank and unruled; f. 122v, miniature for the following text.

Wilmart, pp. 488–90.

11. ff. 123–134 Incipiunt septem psalmi penitentiales (in violet).

12. ff. 134–143v Litany. Damianus, Lupus, Amantius, Donatus, Erasmus, and Blasius among the martyrs; Francis, Eligius, and Egidius among the holy doctors and confessors; Clare, Elisabeth, Amelberga (*sic*), Juliana, and Ursula among the virgins, followed by the standard set of ten short prayers as in the Roman breviary.

f. 144 blank and unruled; f. 144v, miniature for the following text.

13. ff. 145–190v Incipiunt uigilie mortuorum (in violet). Use of Rome.

Thirteen illuminations on inserted leaves, each accompanied by a blue and gold acanthus spray border decorated with flowers and fruit. Matching border on the facing page in the presence of a gold, magenta, blue, and green initial, 5 lines high. A fourteenth illumination probably removed after f. 79. f. 80, at the beginning of text, border only without the preceding illuminated leaf. f. 3v, the Crucifixion; f. 4, bird in right margin; f. 15v, descent of the Holy Spirit depicted within a circular rainbow; f. 16, peacock in right margin; f. 22v, Virgin and Child enthroned in the presence of harp-playing angel; f. 23, a bird in the right margin; f. 35v, the Annunciation, Divine Light and rainbow above, white lilies in a vase before the Virgin; f. 36, pheasant in right margin; f. 56v, the Visitation; f. 68v, the Nativity; f. 74v, the Annunciation to the Shepherds in the Field; f. 85v, the Circumcision; f. 89v, the Massacre of the Innocents; f. 98v, the Flight into Egypt; f. 105v, the Coronation of the Virgin; f. 122v, King David in prayer, a harp at his side; above, God within the arc of a rainbow; f. 123, a green bird in right margin; f. 144v, the raising of Lazarus; f. 145, bird in the right margin. f. 1, gold, magenta, blue, and green initial 5 lines high accompanied by a full border. Sections of text marked by gold dentelle initials with white patterning on grounds of blue and magenta 2 lines high. Blue initials with red flourishes alternating with gold initials with blue-black flourishes.

Parchment. ff. 190. 105 × 70 mm (55 × 24 mm). 1^{10}, 2^{4}, 3^{10}, 4^{8}, 5^{9} (3 inserted), 6^{8}, 7^{9} (6 inserted), 8^{8}, 9^{10}, 10^{8}, 11^{10}, 12^{9} (5 inserted), 13^{9} (3 inserted), 14^{10} (a leaf wanting), 15^{11} (2 inserted), 16^{8}, 17^{9} (6 inserted), $18–21^{8}$, 22^{10} (a leaf wanting), 23^{2}. Ruled in violet ink. Written in gothic textualis media in 16 long lines. Headings in violet in script of the text.

Bound in French gold-stamped black morocco over paperboards c. 1810, stamped R. P. Chilliat on spine.

Written in Flanders, c. 1460. f. 1, effaced red, blue, gold, and green arms of original owner. Prayers in texts 9 and 10 in masculine form. Given to Edward E. Ayer by Martin and Carrie Ryerson, 16 November 1911, on the occasion of Mr. Ayer's seventieth birthday. His autograph note is on the second front flyleaf. "12/69" is written on the verso of the first flyleaf; "Femo" is written on the upper right-hand corner of the third back flyleaf. Acquired by the Newberry from Edward E. Ayer, 1920.

De Ricci, 1:536.

f58.1

(354567)

Latin Bible

Belgium [*Illustrated*] 1433

ff. 1–236v Latin bible in two parts in the usual order, beginning imperfectly in Genesis 5:6 and ending imperfectly in Job 29:11. Four leaves missing after f. 35 should have contained Exodus 38:26–Leviticus 8:18. Text as it stands accompanied by 8 of the 9 apposite prologues: Stegmüller, *Repertorium biblicum,* 311, 323, 328, 330, 332, 341 + 343, 344; 327 is wanting. f. 86–86v, section of text containing Joshua 14 out of sequence crossed out by the rubricator. Text accompanied by very sparse notes of s. xv–xvi by several hands.

f. 108v blank.

Paper. ff. 236. ff. 1–108v, an *arbre* watermark not in Briquet; ff. 109–235, a *raisin* watermark, cf. Briquet 12993, and a *croix à deux travers,* cf. Briquet 5762. These two sections were probably separate volumes as indicated by a colophon on f. 108 and an ownership note on f. 109; see provenance section below. Trimmed to 280 × 200 mm (205 × 150 mm). ff. 1–108, collation impracticable, but four pages removed after f. 35 with loss of text. ff. 109–236, $1–10^{12}$, 11^{12} (9–12 removed with loss of text). ff. 109–236, catchwords in lower right margin, sometimes underlined in red. Frame ruled in pencil, some portions very lightly. Written in gothic cursiva media in 42–51 lines in two columns by two hands with the break falling after f. 108; ff. 109–236, in darker ink. Headings of books in red in script of text, chapter numbers in red roman numerals. ff. 109–236, guides for chapter headings in outer margin, underlined in red like the catchwords; guides for numerals present throughout. ff. 1–108, running headings in upper margin in gothic capitals in red and black, a flourish in black or red on either side; ff. 109–236, running headings in larger gothic cursiva, underlined in red with a flourish in black ink on either side. Alternating red and blue initials. Guides for initials in ink of scribe present.

Bound in mottled calf over paperboard, Belgium, s. xviii. Parchment fragment bearing text visible in binding.

ff. 1–108 written by Gerard de Scurhoven in 1433, and the entire book willed by him to brothers of the third order [of Saint Francis] in Zepperen (near Saint-Trond) in 1456. Colophon on f. 108, "Scriptus est hic liber per manus Gerardi de Scurhoven presbiteri leodiensis diocesis pro tunc capellani cure beghinarum opidi Sancti Trudonis et finitus anno domini millesimo quadringentesimo tricesimo tercio mensis marcii die secunda, orate pro eo." Added in another hand, "Presertim pro animo eius cui domum fratrum 3[ii] [ordinis] in Zeppren (?) contulit hunc librum. Obiit eius prefatus dominus Gerardus anno xiiii[c] lvi[o] mensis iulii." ff. 109–236 written before 1456 by another hand. f. 109, lower margin, "Liber fratrum tertii ordinis in Zepperen legatus a domino Gerardo de Scurhoven bone memorie qui obiit anno domini xiiii[c] lxi[o] mensis iulii die X[m]." For another manuscript with a related provenance see *Manuscrits datés (Belgique)* 3:90, no. 379. Acquired by the Newberry from T. Thorpe, catalogue 41, item 50, in 1951.

Second folio: arche quam.

De Ricci, 1:540. Faye-Bond, 153.

59.1

Missal from the Church of Saint Michael, Ghent

Ghent c. 1470

1. ff. 3–8 Calendar in red and black of Tournai, about half full. Pharahildis uirginis (4 January, in red), Eleutherii episcopi confessoris (20 February, duplex, underlined in red), Translatio sancti Eleutherii episcopi et confessoris

(25 August, duplex), Egidii abbatis confessoris (1 September, duplex, underlined in red), Pyati martiris (1 October, in red, duplex), Translatio Piati (29 October), Willebrordi episcopi confessoris (8 November), Liuini (12 November), Egidii episcopi et confessoris (1 December, duplex), Nychasii episcopi et martiris (14 December, in red, duplex).

ff. 1–2v blank.

2. f. 9–9v Office for the benediction of salt and water as in MS 75, text 2, and MS 77, text 11.

3. f. 10 Oratio ante missam (in red). Ante conspectum diuine maiestatis tue, domine deus, reus assisto . . . da michi ueniam in carne constituto ut per penitentie labores uita eterna perfrui merear in celis. Per . . .

Wilmart, p. 113. This prayer frequently attributed to Ambrose.

4. f. 10 Alia ante missam dicenda (in red). Consciencia trepida, accedo ad sumendum misterium corporis et sanguinis tui domine . . . contra dyaboli infestationes et temptaciones firmissima tuicio . . .

Same text in Cambrai, BM, 276 (s. xv), f. 26–26v.

5. f. 10–10v Item oratio ante missam (in red). Omnipotens sempiterne et misericors deus, ecce accedo . . . quidem uelatum accidentibus suscipere propono, reuelata facie, contemplari.

Wilmart, p. 381, n. 2.

6. f. 10v Ante missam (in red). Deus qui non mortem sed penitentiam desideras peccatorum . . . in hac peregrinacione laudare mereamur. Per Christum.

Wilmart, p. 118n.

7. f. 10v Post missam oratio (in red). Gratias tibi ago piissime deus qui me ad offitium sacerdotale elegisti . . . a purgatorio digneris liberare, pater minarum, pro tua misericordia in eternum. Amen.

Cf. Wilmart, p. 381, n. 2.

8. ff. 1–124 and folio 1 of the third numerical sequence. Proper of Time from the first Sunday in Advent through the twenty-fourth Sunday after Pentecost followed by "Dominica quando agitur de trinitate," feria quarta and feria sexta. f. 12v, Mass for Pharahildis of Ghent added on a separate leaf following the feast of Silvester.

9. ff. 1–2v Sequitur de dedicatione ecclesie (in red).

10. f. 2v In dedicatione unius altais (*sic*, in red).

11. f. 3 Laus angelica (in red). Gloria in excelsis deo . . .

12. f. 3–3v Simbalus (in red). Credo in unum deum, patrem omnipotentem, factorem celi et terre . . .

13. ff. 4–6 Prefatio communis (in red). Followed by special prefaces for principal feasts: De natiuitate domini, In epiphania domini, In quadragesima, A dominica in passione usque in cena domini et in festo palmarum de cruce, In cena domini, In die pasche, In ascentione, De sancto spiritu, De sancta trinitate, De sancta Maria, De apostolis. Ends imperfectly in mid folio.

f. 6v blank.

14. ff. 7–11 Canon of the Mass. Begins imperfectly (one folio of text removed) // Christum dominum nostrum. Amen. Infra actionem (in red). Hanc igitur . . .

15. ff. 1–40v Proper of Saints, Andrew through Maximius. f. 29, translation of Eleutherius; f. 30v, Octave of Eleutherius; f. 35, feast of Piatus; f. 37v, translation of Piatus.

16. ff. 41–50 Incipit commune sanctorum . . . (in red).

17. ff. 50v–62v Votive Masses (titles in red): Per ebdamodam de trinitate, De sancto spiritu, Post lxx[a] usque pascha, De sancta cruce, Post trinitatem de sancta Maria, In aduentu de domina, Post natale de domina, Post purificationem de domina, In paschali tempore de domina (two Masses), De angelis, Pro peccatis, Presbiter pro semetipso, Pro amico fideli, Pro famulis et famulabus, Pro quacumque tribulatione, Pro febricitante pro infirmantibus, Pro infirmo morti proximo, Ad postulandam pluuiam, Pro serenitate aeris, Pro stabilitate loci, Pro pace, A[d] postulandam graciam, De omnibus sanctis, Pro sanctis in ecclesia quiescentibus, Pro pastore nostro, Pro rege nostro, Pro principibus nostris, Pro abbate et congregatione, Ad postulandam sapienciam, Ad postulandam caritatem, Ad postulandam humilitatem, Ad petendas lacrimas, Contra temptaciones carnales, Contra malas cogitaciones, Pro concordia fratrum, Pro

amico tribulato, Pro iter agentibus, Alia secundum aliquos, Pro omni gradu ecclesie, Pro pace ecclesie, Contra tempestatem, Pro inimicis, Contra pestem animalium, Contra hominum mortalitatem, Presbiter pro se ipso, Contra sterilitatem terre, Contra sterilitatem mulierum.

18. ff. 62v–66 Masses for the Dead (titles in red): Pro fidelibus defunctis, In depositione unius defuncti, In anniuersario unius defuncti, Pro uno defuncto, Pro femina defuncta, Pro uno penitente defuncto, Plurimorum defunctorum, Pro parentibus, Pro congregacione, In depositione unius sacerdotis, Pro anima sacerdotis, In depositione unius episcopi, Plurimorum prelatorum, Pro quiescentibus in cymiterio, Pro omnibus fidelibus defunctis, Tam pro uiuis quam defunctis, Tam pro uiuis quam defunctis generaliter.

19. ff. 66v–83 Sequences in order of the liturgical year: Sequitur sequentie ii de sancto Andrea (in red). Sacrosancta hodierne festiuitatis preconia . . . *RH* 17733. Gratulare ergo tanto patre, Achaya, illustrata . . . *RH* 27434. De sancto Eligio (in red). Eligentis et electi nomen habens . . . *RH* 5340. De sancta Barbara (in red). Festum presens recolentes . . . (f. 67), De sancto Nycholao (in red). Congaudentes exultemus uocali concordia . . . *RH* 3795. In conceptione beate Marie (in red). Stella maris, o Maria, expers paris parens pia . . . *RH* 19456. (f. 67v), Feria iiii[a] in aduentu quando dicitur missus (in red). Inuiolata, integra et casta es Maria . . . *RH* 9094. In natiuitate domini in galli cantu (in red). Letabundus exultet fidelis chorus . . . *RH* 10021. In aurora (in red). Hac clara die, turma festiua, det preconia . . . *RH* 7494. Ad summam missam (in red). Nato nobis saluatore, celebremus . . . *RH* 11891. (f. 68), De sancto Stephano prothomartire (in red). Magnus deus in uniuersa terra . . . *RH* 11032. De sancto Iohanne euangelista (in red). Trinitatem reserat aquila summus euangelista . . . *RH* 20574. De innocentibus (in red). Pura deum laudet innocentia . . . *RH* 15824. (f. 68v), De sancto Thoma (in red). Laureato nouo Thoma . . . *RH* 10485. De sancto Pharahilde (in red). Felici connubio regi regis filio nupsit . . . *RH* 5998. (f. 69), De epyphania domini (in red). Epiphaniam domino cantemus gloriosam . . . *RH* 5497. De sancto Uincentio martire (in red). Martiris egregii triumphos Uincentii . . . *RH* 11276. (f. 69v), In purificatione beate Marie (in red). Salue, mater saluatoris, uas electum, uas honoris . . . *RH* 18051. (f. 70), In die sancto pasche (in red). Fulget preclara rutilans per orbem . . . *RH* 6638. Feria secunda (in red). Dic nobis quibus e terris . . . *RH* 4567. Feria tercia (in red). (f. 70v), Aule lucide repertor, lux et ianua . . . *RH* 1579. Feria quarta (in red). Christe, rex bone domine . . . *RH* 2967. Feria quinta (in red). Concinat orbis cunctis, alleluya . . . *RH* 3714. Feria VI[a] (in red). Uictime paschali laudes intonent christiani . . . *RH* 21505. (f. 71), In octaua pasche et de sancta Maria Magdalena (in red). Mane prima sabbati surgens dei filius . . . *RH* 11064. In octaua Magdalene (in red). O Maria Magdalena, audi uota laude plena . . . *RH* 13193. De sancto Eutropio (in red). Uictima Cristi uictoris sanctus Eutropius . . . *RH* 21500. In inuentione sancte crucis (in red). Laudes crucis attolamus . . . *RH* 10360. (f. 71v), In exaltatione sancte crucis (in red). O crux, lignum triumphale . . . *RH* 12852. (f. 72), In die penthecostes (in red). Sancti spiritus assit nobis gratia . . . *RH* 18557. Feria II[a] (in red). In omnem terram deo laus personet dulcisona . . . *RH* 8711. (f. 72v), Feria tercia (in red). Almiphona iam gaudia rutilant . . . *RH* 919. Feria quarta (in red). Alma cohors domini nunc pangat nomina summi . . . *RH* 822. Feria quinta (in red). Ueni, sancte spiritus, et emitte celitus lucis tue radium . . . *RH* 21242. (f. 73), Feria sexta (in red). Laudes deo deuotas dulci uoce et sonora . . . *RH* 10370. De sancta trinitate (in red). Benedicta sit semper sancta trinitas . . . *RH* 2440. De sacramento (in red). Lauda, Syon, saluatorem, lauda ducem et pastorem . . . *RH* 10222. (f. 73v), In dedicatione ecclesie (in red). Quam dilecta tabernacula domini uirtutum . . . *RH* 16071. (f. 74), Per octauas dedicationis (in red). Clara chorus dulce pangat uoce nunc alleluia . . . *RH* 3297. Alia per octauas (in red). Gaude, uirgo mater ecclesia . . . *RH* 7024. Alia per octauas (in red). Rex Salomon fecit templum . . . *RH* 17511. (f. 74v), De natiuitate sancti Iohannis baptiste (in red). Gaude, caterua, diei praesentis celebrans . . . *RH* 6719. In octaua et decol-

latione Iohannis baptiste (in red). Fulgore perhenni ecce rutilat dies . . . *RH* 6646. (f. 75), De sancto Petro et Paulo (in red). Laude iocunda melos, turma, persona . . . *RH* 10265. Divisio in conuersione sancti Pauli (in red) Sacre Paule, ingere dogmata . . . *RH* 17643. In uisitacione beate Marie (in red). Ueni, precelsa, domina Maria . . . *RH* 21231. De sancta Anna electa (in red). Aue, preclara mater Anna . . . *RH* 2046. (f. 75v), Ad uincula Petri (in red). Gaude, Roma, caput mundi . . . *RH* 6928. In festo beate Marie de niue (in red). Hodierne lux diei celebris in matris dei . . . *RH* 7945. (f. 76), In transfiguratione domini (in red). De parente summo natum, sed a patre non creatum uerbum in principio . . . *RH* 4232. De sancto Laurentio martire (in red). Stola iocunditatis, alleluya . . . *RH* 19523. (f. 76v), In assumptione beate Marie (in red). A rea uirga prime matris Eue florens rosa processit . . . *RH* 16. De sancto Bartholomeo apostolo (in red). Laudemus omnes inclyta Bartholomei merita . . . *RH* 10306. (f. 77), De sancto Eleutherio (in red). Tornacensis ciuitas, laudes pange debitas . . . *RH* 20495. De sancto Augustino episcopo (in red). Interni festi gaudia nostra sonet armonia . . . *RH* 9054. (f. 77v), In natiuitate beate Marie (in red). Ille (*sic*, corrected by a later hand) celeste necnon et perhenne luya . . . *RH* 801. (f. 78), De sancto Lamberto (in red). Christi laudem predicamus . . . *RH* 3074. De sancto Michaele archangelo (in red). Ad celebres, rex celice, laudes cuncta clangat . . . *RH* 100. (f. 78v), De sancto Pyato martire (in red). Diem hanc leticie, regi gratam glorie, celebret ecclesia . . . *RH* 4595. De sancto Dyonisio (in red). Gaude prole, Grecia . . . *RH* 6912. (f. 79), De sancto Quintino martire (in red). Per unius casum grani . . . *RH* 14826. De omnibus sanctis (in red). Superne matris gaudia representet ecclesia . . . *RH* 19822. (f. 79v), In depositione et translatione sancti Martini (in red). Sacerdotem Christi Martinum . . . *RH* 17622. De sancta Katherina (in red). Nato patris sine matre . . . *RH* 11893. (f. 80), In octaua (in red). Audi pia (*sic*) congaudentes, serua tibi seruientes . . . *RH* 1476. Communes sequentie de apostolis (in red). Clare sanctorum senatus apostolorum, princeps orbis . . . *RH* 3336. Alia (in red). Celi solem imitantes . . . *RH* 3513. (f. 80v), Alia de apostolis (in red). Alleluya nunc decantet uniuersalis ecclesia . . . *RH* 815. De euangelistis (in red). Iocundare, plebs fidelis . . . *RH* 9843. (f. 82[1]), Plurimorum martirum (in red). Gaude, turma triumphalis . . . *RH* 6986. Sequenciam unius confessoris uel martiris non habent propriam se (in red). Hic sanctus, cuius hodie recensentur solempnia . . . *RH* 7836. Unius uirginis et martiris (in red). Exultemus in hac die festiua . . . *RH* 5765. (f. 82[1]v), Plurimarum uirginum (in red). Uirgines caste, uirginis summe . . . *RH* 21639. Genouefe uirginis (in red). Crebros saltus dat hic agnus inter illas . . . *RH* 3971. (f. 82[2]), Sequuntur sequentie indifferentes dicende de beata uirgine (in red). Beata es, uirgo, et gloriosa . . . *RH* 2330. Alia (in red). Benedicta es celorum regina . . . *RH* 2428. Alia (in red). Aue, mundi spes, Maria . . . *RH* 1974. Alia (in red). Maria preconio seruiat cum gaudio . . . *RH* 11162. (f. 82[2]v), Alia (in red). Uerbum bonum et suaue persomus (*sic*) . . . *RH* 21343. Alia de sancta Maria (in red). Aue, Maria, gratia plena . . . *RH* 1879. Alia (in red). Epitalamita dic sponsa . . . *RH* 5500. (f. 83), Alia (in red). Aue, stella marium, Maria . . . *RH* 2133. Alia (in red). Alma redemptoris mater quem in terris . . . *RH* 862. Pascali tempore (in red). Uirgini Marie laudes intonent christiani . . . *RH* 21660.

f. 83v blank. No leaves numbered 84 or 85.

20. f. 86–86v Table of sequences by incipit with references given to folios.

21. f. 86v Extract from Lc 7:11–16 followed by a Mass for Roche, added in a cursive hand, s. xvi.

f. 87–87v blank.

Five historiated initials in the Proper of Time only. f. 1, pink initial on a gold ground, historiated with the Coronation of the Virgin, 12 lines high. f. 9, blue initial P on a gold ground, historiated with the Nativity, 8 lines high. f. 77, blue initial R on a gold ground, historiated with the Resurrection, 10 lines high. f. 88, similar initial U, historiated with the Ascension, 8 lines high. f. 92, similar initial S, historiated with Pentecost, 8 lines high. In each instance, accompanied by a gold and red baguette and pieces of blue and gold acanthus spray border in the upper and lower margins.

Parchment. ff. 1 + 231. A small unnumbered leaf tipped in after f. 12. First ten leaves unfoliated; 1–124 foliated in contemporary roman numerals, verso and recto in red ink; 11 leaves foliated in modern pencil 1–11; second medieval foliation in roman numerals, verso and recto, 1–88 with no folios 81, 84, or 85, two folios 82. 330 × 235 mm (245 × 160 mm; Canon 230 × 154 mm). Folios signed, partially trimmed. 1^{10}, $2–16^{8}$, 17^{6}, 18^{6} (1 removed with loss of text), 19^{6}, $20–22^{8}$, 23^{10}, $24–28^{10}$ (last leaf serves as rear pastedown). Ruled in brown ink. Written in hybrida media in 36 lines in two columns. ff. 3–6, second numerical sequence in hybrida formata in 22 lines in two columns. Headings in scripts of text. Guides to the rubricator occasionally present. Alternating blue and red flourished and simple initials. ff. 19v and 28, green added to flourishes in Proper of Saints.

Bound in rebacked stamped calf over boards, s. xv². Central panel filled with ruled lozenges, each lozenge filled with a lozenge-shaped stamp of radiating foliage. Rectangular-shaped compartments surrounding central panel filled with stamps of a flower within a lozenge, a double eagle within a lozenge, a seated lion within a small square, and a rosette at each corner within a ruled square compartment. Each stamp repeated several times; same pattern front and back. Two rear-to-front clasps wanting. For a binding with similar stamps, see E. Dhanens, "Le Scriptorium des Hiéronymites à Gand," *Scriptorium* 23 (1969): pl. 136. Red and white fore-edge knots; three knotted place marks, all postdating the binding and probably modern.

Written probably in Ghent, c. 1470, by the Brethren of Jerome, as suggested by the binding and the calendar of the diocese of Tournai, for the use of a secular church. Proper of Saints and choice of sequences are to be found in printed Tournai missals. f. 1, rubbed out, visible under ultraviolet light: "Missale istud reuenit ad mensam sancti spiritus in ecclesia sancti Michaelis gandauensis." This church rebuilt 1480. Mass for Pharahildis on leaf inserted after f. 12 in the Proper of Time added for Ghent use. Signature "Bernarts," incorporating a notarial-like *signum*, s. xv² or xvi¹, on front pastedown. Gold-stamped armorial leather bookplate of Eduard Hailstone; see De Ricci, 3:196. Acquired from the Chicago Caxton Club by Louis H. Silver, his gift to the Newberry, 1960. f. 1, a modern hand has written "Tournai Missal, about 1470."

61

(23839)

Geert Groote, *Getijdenboek*

Holland after 1471

1. ff. 2–10v Calendar of Utrecht. Variants from the text printed in Van Wijk, *Het Getijdenboek*, pp. 25–35, include: Phileas martir (4 February), Anestorius biscop martir (26 February), Swidbertus biscop (1 March), Herebertus biscop (16 March), Eustacius abt (29 March), Tymeon dyake (19 April), Uictor paeus martir (20 April), Ioriis martir (23 April), Priuatus biscop martir (21 August), Satirus confessor (18 September), Fidis ionfer (6 October), Gummaer confessor (11 October, in red), Florentinus biscop (17 October), Uitalis agri martir (26 November).

2. ff. 10v–38v Hier beghinnen onse urouwe gehetiden (in red). Heir du selte op doen mine lippen . . . in enicheit des heilighen gheestes een god in ewicheit. Amen.

Text begins on f. 12. f. 39 blank and unruled; f. 39v, miniature for the following text.

Hours of the Virgin, Dutch translation of Geert Groote without the prologue; Van Wijk, *Het Getijdenboek*, pp. 36–70.

3. ff. 40–55v Hier beghinnen die ewige wijsheit ghetiden (in red). Mijn ziele heeft di begheert inder nachte ende . . . ende onse lichaem. Amen.

f. 56 blank and unruled; f. 56v, miniature for the following text.

Hours of Eternal Wisdom, Dutch translation of Geert Groote; Van Wijk, *Het Getijdenboek*, pp. 92–119, no. 10.

4. ff. 57–73v Hier beghinnen die lange cruus gheti (in red). O here Ihesu Christe des leuendighen godes zoen . . . Alle ghelouighe zielen moeten rusten in ureden. Amen.

f. 74 blank and unruled; f. 74v, miniature for the following text.

Long Hours of the Cross, Dutch translation of Geert Groote; Van Wijk, *Het Getijdenboek*, pp. 113–38.

5. ff. 75–86v Hier beghinnen die heilige gheest gheti (in red). Here du selte opdoen mine lippen . . . Alle guelouighe zielen moeten rusten in urede. Amen.

Hours of the Holy Spirit, Dutch translation of Geert Groote, Van Wijk, *Het Getijdenboek*, pp. 71–86.

6. ff. 87–104v Alle godes heilighen biddet uoir onser alze salicheit. Amen. Here du salte opdoen mine lippen . . . Alle ghelouighe zielen moeten rusten in ureden. Amen.

f. 105 blank and unruled; f. 105v, miniature for the following text.

Hours of All Saints in Dutch translation; R. A. Parmentier, "Een vijftiendeeuwsch getijdenboek . . ." *Annales de la Société d'Émulation de Bruges* 76 (1933): 108–12.

7. ff. 105v–112v Hier beghinnen die seuen

psalmen Dauids (in red). Here, in dijnre uerbolghentheit . . . Want ic dijn dieure bin.

Seven Penitential Psalms, Dutch translation of Geert Groote; Van Wijk, *Het Getijdenboek,* pp. 139–45.

8. ff. 112v–119v Letanien (in red).

f. 120 blank and unruled; f. 120v, miniature for the following text.

Litany of Geert Groote: "Sinte Sebastiaen," "Sinte Geruasius," "Sinte Iorijs," and "Sinte Yuo" among the martyrs; "Sinte Bauo" and "Sinte Gelijs" among the confessors; "Sinte Barbara" among the virgins and widows; cf. Van Wijk, *Het Getijdenboek,* pp. 145–50.

9. ff. 121–146v Hier beghint die uigeli inuitatorium. Mi hebben ombeuanghen die suchtene des dodes . . . ende regniert in enicheit des heilighen gheestes in ewicheit der ewicheden. Amen.

Office of the Dead, beginning on the second page of the printed text, Van Wijk, *Het Getijdenboek,* pp. 156–95, n. 11.

10. ff. 146v–148v Hier beghinnen die corte cruus ghetiden (in red). Here du salte opdoen mine lippen . . . Here Ihesu Christe des leuendighen gods et cetera.

Short Hours of the Cross, Dutch translation of Geert Groote; Van Wijk, *Het Getijdenboek,* pp. 87–91.

11. ff. 148v–149v Item alsmen ten heilighe sacramente willen gaen les dit ghebet (in red). Wes ghegruet alre heilichste lichaem ons heren onthouden inden heilighen sacramente . . . ende mi ten lesten een salich wtganc moet ghegeuen werden. Amen.

Meertens, *De Godsvrucht* 6:8, no. 13a.

12. ff. 149v–150 Here ic en bin niet weerdich dattu comest onder mijn dack . . . tot minem ghenadighen troester ende uerlosser. Amen.

Meertens, *De Godsvrucht* 6:23, no. 316.

13. f. 150–150v Item alsmen dat heilighe sacrament ontfanghen hebben les dan dit ghebet (in red). Danc segghe ic di almactighe god want du . . . daer dijn heilighe sacrament is in ghegaen. Amen.

Meertens, *De Godsvrucht* 6:21, no. 10c, etc.

14. ff. 150v–151 Item soe wie dit ghebet leset allmen dat heilighe sacrament opboert die uerdient ccc daghen aflaets (in red). Wes ghegruet waerachtich lichaem gheboren uander ioncfrouwen Marien . . . O suete kijnt Marie.

Meertens, *De Godsvrucht* 6:18, no. 186, etc.

15. f. 151 Tot onse here (in red). Gods ziel heilighe mi, Gods lichaem behoe de mi . . . dat ic di louen moet mitten enghelen ewelike. Amen.

Meertens, *Die Godsvrucht* 6:34, no. 20.

16. ff. 151–152 Hier begihnt een goet leringhe wander lijdsaemheit (in red). Het was een deuoet mensche die begheerde te weten uan onse lieue here waer an hi hem liefste dienen mochte . . . liden om minen wille. Onser heer seit inder ewangelien, in uwuer uerduldicheit selt ghi uwue zielen besitten.

An unidentified spiritual example.

17. ff. 152–153 Dit is sinte Ians ewangeli (in red).

Io 1:1–14 in Dutch translation.

18. f. 153–153v Tot dinen enghel een ghebet (in red). Heilighe enghel godes den ic beuolen bin om dattu mi uoersiende behoeden selste . . . onsen here Ihesum Christum. Amen.

Cf. Leroquais, *Heures* 2:13, and Meertens, *De Godsvrucht* 6:18, no. 20.

19. ff. 153v–154 Item Sixtus die uierde paeus heeft ghegheuen alle die in penitenciem staen die dit na ghescreuen ghebet leset mit deuocien die uerdient alle reise xi^{m} jaer aflaets (in red). Wes ghegruet alre heilichste Maria moeder godes coninghinne des hemels poerte . . . ende bid uoir mijn sonden. Amen.

Meertens, *De Godsvrucht* 6:21, no. 7a.

20. f. 154–154v Item die dese vii ghebedekijn mit seuen pater noster ende aue Maria leset al knielende uoir die wapenen ons heren die uerdient xlvi^{m} iaer ende xl daghen aflaets (in red). O here Ihesu Christe, ic anbede di hanghende anden cruce . . . in haer wtuaert. Pater noster (in red).

Dutch version of the *Adoro te;* Achten and Knaus, *Deutsche und Niederländische Gebetbuchhandschriften,* p. 36; cf. Wilmart, 361 sqq. and passim. For a related Latin rubric, see MS 104.5, text 25.

21. ff. 154v–156 Hier beghint een ghebet dat ghmaket (*sic*) ist in die eren ons heren aenschijn. Ende Iohannes die xxii paeus heeft ghegheuen alle kersten menschen alsoe dicke als sijt lesen mit berouwe hace sonden uan ghesetter penitencien cccc daghen aflaets ende alsoe menich karijn (in red). God gruet u, heilighe aenschijn ons heren in welken blinket die ghedaente des godliken lichtes . . . ende uer-

derue mi arme mensche niet . . . Collecte (in red). O god wanttu ons woudes laten ghetei-kent dat licht dijns aensichtes . . . ende regniert in ewicheit der ewicheden. Amen.

Meertens, *De Godsvrucht* 6:21, no. 16, and 12, no. 3.

22. f. 156–156v Item goet ende deuoet ghebet toe onse lieue urouwe Maria ende moder (in red). Weest ghegruet alre oetmoedichste dienstmaghet der heiligher drieuoldicheit Maria . . . soe ontfanghet mijn ziel ende offert die dijn alre soetsen zoen Ihesum Christum die mitti leuet ende regniert in ewicheit. Amen.

Meertens, *De Godsvrucht* 6:17 bis, no. 25.

23. ff. 156v–158 Een ghebet tot Maria (in red). O alre goedertierenste wtuercoren moder godes Maria. O alre sekerste troest . . . ontfanghet mine ziele na desen leuen in dat ewighe leuen. Amen.

Meertens, *De Godsvrucht* 6:21, no. 8.

24. ff. 158–162 Suffrages to Peter, Andrew, Erasmus, the ten thousand martyrs, Barbara, Appollonia, and Catherine as in Brussels, BR, 12081; Meertens, *De Godsvrucht* 6:21, 19a–d and 20a–c except here 20b precedes 20a.

25. f. 162–162v Item men uint ghescreuen alsoe wie dit naughescreuen ghebet leset uoer dat crucifix of in gheheuchnisse des lidens Christi die uerdient iii^{m} iaer aflaets ghegheuen uan die uierde paeus Bonifacio (in red). O naecte oetmodicheit, o grote martelie . . . wil ons helpen totten ewighen salicheit. Amen.

Meertens, *De Godsvrucht* 6:21, no. 7b, etc.

26. f. 162v Alsmen ouer een kerckhof gaeste (*sic*) les dit ghebet (in red). O here god doer iuwe barmherticheit wes ghenadich die zielen . . . sonden ende pinen. Amen.

f. 163–163v blank.

Meertens, *De Godsvrucht* 6:21, no. 7c.

Six crudely painted miniatures on inserted leaves, each within a silver flamboyant gothic arch frame, three silver balls at the top (partially trimmed): f. 11v, Virgin and Child surrounded by four angels; f. 39v, Gnadenstuhl Trinity; f. 56v, Christ on the Cross between the two thieves; below, Mary and John the Evangelist, two female figures and a man on horseback; f. 74v, the infant Jesus between Mary and Ann, the Holy Ghost above; f. 105v, the Buffeting of Christ; f. 120v, Pietà. Two miniatures removed before f. 87 and f. 147. Major divisions of the text begin with rather crude red and blue initials with red and blue flourishes touched with green, sometimes yellow, 9–10 lines high. Other divisions begin with red initials with blue tipped with green flourishes alternating with blue initials with red tipped with green flourishes, 3 lines high. Alternating minor simple red and blue initials with the text throughout.

Parchment. ff. i + 164. 165 × 121 mm (95 × 71 mm). 1^{4}, 2^{6}, 3^{9} (1 inserted), 4–5^{8}, 6^{9} (4 inserted), 7^{8}, 8^{9} (4 inserted), 9^{8}, 10^{9} (5 inserted), 11–12^{8}, 13^{10}, 14^{9} (1 inserted), 15^{6}, 16^{9} (9 inserted), 17–20^{8}, 21^{4} (4 serves as a pastedown). All inserted leaves are miniatures. Catchwords. Ruled in brown ink. Prickings visible in outer margins. Calendar ruled for three columns. Written in hybrida media in 21 long lines. Headings in red in script of text.

Bound in stamped black calf over boards with silver clasps, County of Holland, c. 1500. Ruled panel stamp with a large Agnus Dei within an oval medallion surrounded by the symbols of the evangelists, each within a roundel. Inscription on the outer edge of the oval medallion: "Siet dat lam Godes dat boert die sonden [d' uerl]." Four stamps of fleurs-de-lys within small lozenges around the outer margins. Entire pattern oriented toward the fore edge; same design front and back. This binding very similar to P. Verheyden, "Noord-Hollandse Boekbanden," *Het Boek* 31 (1954): 232–36 (type IIIc). Two back-to-front silver clasps.

Written in Holland, probably in Enkhuizen, whose patron saint Gummar is in red in the calendar, after 1471, date of the election of Sixtus IV, to whom text 19 is attributed. In choice of texts, size, initials, and number of written lines, this codex is very similar to Brussels, BR, 12081; Meertens, *De Godsvrucht* 6:21. Manuscript bound and miniatures inserted c. 1500. f. 56v, "1461" written in brown ink next to a miniature. This misconstrued to be a date by an eighteenth(?)-century hand, which has written "Anno 1461" and "No. 333" on the rear pastedown. A clipping from a nineteenth-century sales catalogue, almost certainly Dutch, pasted on what remains of the front pastedown, describes this codex in French as item no. 24. No. 14 from the collection of Henry Probasco, acquired by the Newberry 1 December 1890.

Second folio: Scholastica ionfer.

De Ricci, 1:526.

62

(52-15)

Collection of Humanistic Texts

Low Countries or Germany s. XV ex.

1. pp. 1–19 Incipit dyalogus Salomonys et Marcolfi. Cum staret Salomon super solium Dauid, patris sui, plenus sapiencia et diuiciis

. . . Et sic euasit manus Salomonys regis, post hoc domum remeans quieuit in pace. Explicit dyalogus Salomonys et Marcolfi.

Salomonis et Marcolfi dialogus, ed. W. Benary (Sammlung Mittellateinischer Texte, 8; Heidelberg, 1914). This manuscript unrecorded.

2. pp. 19–32 Incipit quoddam exemplum cuiusdam clerici uero amore amante quandam matronam Aroni coniugem et hoc morale. Erat Ianuensis urbs multum copiosa ciuibus . . . cum ieiunio abstinentiaque seruauit. Ffinit hoc dogma morale editum per Franciscum Petrarcham eminentem poetam laureatum.

Ps. Petrarch, *Historia de Arono et Marina,* ed. M. Hermann, "Die lateinische *Marina,*" *Vierteljahrschrift für Litteraturgeschichte* 3 (1890): 2–12. R. Penninck, *Twee uit het Latijn Vertaalde Middelnederlandse Novellen* (Zwolle, 1965), pp. 63–109. See also, Mann, *Petrarch Manuscripts,* p. 279.

3. pp. 32–49 Ffrancisci Petrarche poete laureati de uera sapiencia dialogus primus incipit feliciter. Orator enim et ydiota collocutores sunt. Conuenit pauper quidem idiota ditissimum oratorem in foro romano quem facete surridens sic alloquutus est . . . quod tibi et mihi concedat ipsa dei sapiencia semper benedicta. Amen. Ffrancisci Petrarche de vera sapiencia dyologus secundus (*sic*) explicit feliciter.

De vera sapientia [extracts from Petrarch, *De remediis utriusque fortune* and Nicholas of Cusa, *De sapientia*], *Opera Petrarchae* (Basel, 1554), 1:364–72. On early editions, see Goldschmidt, *Medieval Texts,* p. 133.

4. pp. 49–55 Ffrancisci Petrarche sequitur dyalogus perornatus et poeticus de romane curie euitacione. Cuius colloquentes Pilades sunt et Horrestes, hospes caupoque. Hoe (*sic*): Unde, mi Horestes . . . ad preparatas nobis sedes euolemus. Et huius libelli periocundi finis adest. Per Franciscum Petrarchum poetam deo gratias.

Ps. Petrarch, *De romana curia,* ed. L. Bertalot, "Eine Satire gegen die Roemische Curie aus dem XV Jahrhundert," *Archivum romanicum* 10 (1926): 428–38; reprinted by Kristeller, *Studien* 1:411–26. P. Piur, *Petrarcas Buch ohne Namen und die päpstliche Kurie* (Halle, 1925), pp. 107–8, n. 8.

5. pp. 56–60 Pii ii pontificis maximi de captione urbis Constantinopolitane tractatus incipit. Maomethes defuncto Amurate gubernacula regni ex uoto adeptus . . . qui ab ortu saluatoris Christi secundus et quinquagesimus supra millesimum quadringentesimumque concurrit. Et sic est finis.

Pius II, *De captione urbis Constantinopolitanae.* M. Pellechet, *Catalogue général des incunables des bibliothèques publiques de France,* ed. F. R. Goff (Nendeln, Liechtenstein, 1970), vol. 1, nos. 174 and 175 = *De Europa* (chapter 7) in Pius II, *Opera quae extant omnia* (Basel, 1551; reprinted Frankfurt, 1967), pp. 400–402.

6. pp. 61–65 Paulus Niauis artium magister uenerando uiro Thome Friberger plebano Friberge apud sanctum Petrum domino suo et fautori precipuo . . . Cogitaui, uir honorande, nuper quo studio . . . Dyalogus Luciani per Arispam de greco in latinum translatus de charone inferorum nauta. Sepe ac multum ea mente cogitaui que cladis tempore de morte funerali deque pompa contemnenda grauiter ac sapienter solitus es mecum disserere . . . (p. 62) Audite quo quidem pacto . . . atque uitam cuiusque examinare necesse est. Ffinis.

Lucian, *Charon,* trans. Johannes Aurispa (?), prefaced by a letter of presentation of Paulus Niavis. On Paulus Niavis's edition of this text, cf. Hain, 10269–70, and Copinger, 4402–3. Other manuscripts, Sabbadini, *Biografia documentata,* p. 201. This manuscript unrecorded. This translation also attributed to Rinuccio Aretino; cf. Bandini, *Catalogus codicum latinorum* 3:654, and Lockwood, "De Rinucio Aretino," pp. 97–100.

7. pp. 65–69 Alexandri magni, Hanibalis karthaginensis, Scipionis affricani, maiorum trium summorum ducum de artis imperatoria presidentia contentio, apud inferos, sub Minone iudice, ex Luciano autore greco per Iohannem Arispam in latinum conuersa feliciter incipit. Alexander: Me, o libice, preponi decet, melior equidem sum . . . neque hic quidem spernendus est. Telos.

pp. 69–72 blank.

Lucian, *Contentio de praesidentia P. Scipionis,* without the epistolary prologue, trans. Johannes Aurispa. Hain, 10275–76. Sabbadini, *Biografia documentata,* pp. 31 and 188. Bandini, *Catalogus codicum latinorum* 3:630. G. Martellotti, "La Collatio inter Scipionem . . . ," *Classical, Mediaeval, and Renaissance Studies in Honor of Berthold Louis Ullman* (Rome, 1964), 2:146.

Paper. ff. 36. Modern pagination 1–72. Two watermarks: a crowned fleur-de-lys above interlaced letters (p. 9), cf. Briquet 7251 sqq., and a P with a flower above (p. 69), cf. Briquet 8590 sqq. Trimmed to 209 × 143 mm (165 × 93 mm). $1–3^{12}$, leaf signature q and p in red ink visible in quires 2 and 3 indicating that this was once part of a larger codex. Prickings in outer margin. Catchwords present. Ruled in pencil. Written in hybrida media in 36 long lines. Red initials in Germanic style. Headings underlined in red.

Half bound in parchment over pasteboard.

Written probably in the Low Countries or in Germany at the end of the fifteenth century. Acquired by the Newberry from H. P. Kraus, 1951.

Second folio: Marcolfus: Olla bene.

Ullman, "Petrarch Manuscripts," p. 450, n. 19. Faye-Bond, p. 153.

63.1

(61-1308)

Questions on Aristotle's Nicomachean Ethics

Southern Germany s. XV²

ff. 1–24v (begins imperfectly at the beginning of the quire) // primo non est status rerum inquisicione consilii ex parte . . . (ends imperfectly at the end of the quire) et inuidia de bono proximi. Exemplum de operationibus //

Marginal corrections by the scribe. f. 8v, index note in red.

The second and fourth quires bound in reverse order, from unidentified questions on Aristotle's *Nicomachean Ethics*. Quire 1 contains the end of Book III and the beginning of Book IV. Questions on Book IV begin on f. 9, Sequitur quartus ethicorum circa quem queritur primo utrum liberalitas sit uirtus circa usum pecuniarum existens . . . Quire 2 contains end of questions on Book I and beginning of questions on Book II. Questions on Book II begin on f. 16, Utrum uirtus insit nobis a natura et dicitur quod non. Arguitur quod sic quia . . .

Paper, furry. ff. 24. Quire 1 contains watermark of a Greek cross, cf. Briquet 5464. Quire 2 contains watermark of six-lobed flower, Briquet 6515. 218 × 151 mm (140 × 100 mm). $1–2^{12}$. Quires numbered on verso of last leaf; quire 1, "quartus"; quire 2, "2us". Catchwords at the end of Book I, "Est celare (?)," do not match initial words on quire 2. Frame ruled in ink. Written in northern European gothic cursiva currens. Headings in Rhine Valley hybrida media. f. 16, heading for Book II in script of text. ff. 9 and 16, crude green initials on grounds of pink and magenta. f. 9, crudely penned floral decoration in lower margin.

Bound in old pasteboard with a label of s. xvi or xviii, "Commentarium in IV ethicorum Aristotelis."

Written in southern Germany, as indicated by texture of paper, watermarks, and initials, in the second half of the fifteenth century. The letter H written on the verso of the back cover, erased but still visible. Acquired by the Newberry from R. Rizzi (Milan, cat. 16, item no. 2) in 1961.

Second folio: secundum uerbum non et.

64

(324354)

Collectbook

Southern Germany [*Illustrated*] 1427

1. ff. 2–7 Calendar as in a Benedictine breviary with graded feasts in black, red, and blue: Brigidie uirginis commemoratio (1 February), Dorothee uirginis et martiris commemoratio (6 February), Gertrudis uirginis commemoratio (17 March), Gordiani et Epymachi martirum commemoratio (10 May), Bonifacii et sociorum eius martirum XII lectiones (5 June), Anne matris Marie (26 July, in blue), Willibrordi episcopi xii lectiones (7 November).

f. 8–8v blank.

2. ff. 9–85v Common of Time beginning with first Sunday of Advent. *Orationes* and *capitula* only. On the divisions of collectbooks, see C. Wordsworth and H. Littlehales, *The Old Service Books of the English Church* (London, 1904), pp. 123–29.

3. ff. 85v–97v Sequitur commune sanctorum . . . (in red). *Orationes* and *capitula* only.

4. ff. 97v–99 Dedicacione ecclesie . . . (in red). Three *orationes* and two *capitula*.

5. ff. 99–157v Incipiunt propria sanctorum (in red). Stephen through Thomas the Apostle. f. 116, Gordiani et Epymachi martirum. f. 117, Bonifacii et sociorum eius martirum. f. 144, Eufemie uirginis. f. 155v, Finitum est in die sancti Florini; O dilectissima dompna; Nolite obliuisci scriptricis in oracionibus uestris deuotis (in red and blue).

f. 156 blank. ff. 156v–157v, *oratio* and two *capitula* for Anne, out of calendrical sequence.

f. 1v Inserted portrait of a male owner wearing armor, in prayer, with a rosary, below crowned Virgin and Child on crescent moon, framed in a flamboyant gothic architectural motif. Owner facing his arms with helmet, mantle, crest, and horns. Legend below reads: "Poppo de Wildec dictus Seifert." f. 9, bracket outer rinceaux border with blue, violet, and orange flowers, decorated with small gold disks in clusters of three, an illuminated initial in same colors, 6 lines high. ff. 15v, 49v, 64, blue and magenta initials on gold grounds, 5 lines high, decorated with Schwarzenberg arms (cf. f. 1v). Alternating red and blue initials throughout.

Thick parchment. ff. 157. Erroneous modern foliation on the first leaf of each quire excludes f. 1. 225 × 160 mm (115 × 95 mm). 1^8 (1 inserted), 2^8 (1 wanting), $3–19^8$, 20^6. Traces of leaf signatures visible. Ruled in pencil. Prickings visible in outer margins. Written in gothic textualis quadrata formata, in 15 long lines, calendar in 30 long lines.

Bound in plain calf with five brass bosses front and back, back-to-front fore-edge clasp on long leather strap.

Written in south Germany in 1427. Colophon on f. 155v indicates a female scribe, but this may indicate the rubricator only, for according to a contemporary note, this book was written by Paul, a Carmelite friar, in 1427 for Poppo de Wildek (see f. 1v for his arms), who gave this book to a certain Henry. f. 1, "Anno domini mccccxxvii, frater in Christo perdilectus Poppo de Wildek cognominatus antecessorum more spontali opus hoc in maiorem dei omnipotentis glorioseque uirginis Marie honorem manu fratris Pauli Karmelite scribi curauit mihique Henrico in perpetuam fraterne amicitie memoriam kalendis ianuarii (illegible) dedit." *Colophons de manuscrits occidentaux,* 15003. Front pastedown, inscription, "V[endu] La Haye 1837 $NN" and sticker of Leo S. Olschki (Venice, dating from 1890–1897), no. 23490 (crossed out). Another Olschki sticker on spine, no. 23934. f. 1, tipped-in bookplate of A.T.P. (Paris). An old and inaccurate descriptive note, probably from a dealer, tipped on to a modern back flyleaf. Acquired by the Newberry from Edward E. Ayer, 1920.

De Ricci, 1:537.

64.1
(59-1218)
Latin Glossary

Germany 1407

ff. 1v–107v Incipit (in red). A littera sicut dicit Ysodorus primo libro libro (*sic*) etymolyarum (*sic*) ideo (4, 16) in omnibus ligwis (*sic* for linguis) est prior quia ipsa nascentium uocem aperit unde dicit magister in historiis (Peter Lombard, *Historia scholastica,* 1071) masculus recenter natus euilando (*sic*) dicit a, mulier uero e, unde omnes dicent e uel a . . . Alma interpretatur uirgo, item a secundum katholicum eandem uim habet quam habet ab. Ab est prepositio . . . Aaron . . . Zoticus . . . Zozima . . . Zucara, re uel zucarum, ri, id est, sucre et cetera. Explicit mamotractus uocabulorum sacre theologie sub anno incarnacionis domini m° cccc° vii° et cetera.

f. 1 blank, fragment of text on upper margin partially trimmed; f. 107v, inscription of the scribe: "Plures facti sunt sacerdotes, ideo quot morte prohibentur permanere, Ihesus (?) autem eo quod maneat in eternum, sempiternum habet sacerdotium, deo gratias"; below by the same hand, "Aliqui sunt mortui."

Latin glossary drawn largely from Johannes Balbus, *Catholicon* (Stegmüller, *Repertorium biblicum,* 4220); first entry from the *Summa britonis,* ed. L. W. and B. A. Daly (Padua, 1975), 1:4. Short entries, about 3,200 *lemmata.* This text appears to be related to *Vocabularius dicitur abbas Niger,* Metz, BM, 293 (s. xv), *Catalogue général des départements,* series in 4°, 5:127. It is unrelated to the *Mammotractus* of Johannes Marchesinus, O.F.M.

Paper. Watermarked with *cloche,* not in Briquet but similar to 3965 sqq. ff. 107. Trimmed to 283 × 215 mm (339 × 180 mm). $1–8^{12}$, 9^{12} (12 wanting). Quire 2 numbered "2us," quire 3 "3us," on lower margin of initial leaf. Frame ruled in brown ink for two columns and a special column for the initial letter of each entry. Written in gothic cursiva media in 45–49 lines in two columns. f. 107v, colophon in gothic textualis. Each alphabetical section begins with a simple Germanic red initial. Red line fillers and paragraph marks. Initial letter of each entry touched in red.

Bound in worn geometrically ruled contemporary stamped leather, not from another book, but large parts of contents taken out. Panel divided into diamond-shaped compartments decorated with stamps including, in the border, four radiating fleurs-de-lys within a double lozenge and a lamb with a pennant within a double roundel (cf. Weale, *Early Stamped Bookbindings* 4:18), and a rosette, all repeated. In the interior, smaller stamps including a single fleur-de-lys in a lozenge, a double circle, a cluster of three leaves within a lozenge, and a cluster of four leaves within a lozenge, one stamp within each compartment. All stamps repeated several times. Brass corners, two fore-edge clasps wanting, five bosses wanting front and rear. Old (s. xix?) spine label in black ink: "S.III MSS Vocabularius 1404 [i.e., misread vii on f. 107v as iiii], fol. 423."

Written in Germany in 1407, dated on f. 107v. Acquired by the Newberry from Bernard Rosenthal, item 9, p. 3, list dated 26 March 1959.

Second folio: abiuratio, onis.

f65

(19172)

Thomas Aquinas, Epitome of the *Summa Theologica, De Vita Christi;* Heinrich von Langenstein, *Responsum;* etc.

Germany or Austria s. XV[1]

1. ff. 1–7v Excerpta de tertia parte Thome (in red). Quia saluator dominus noster Ihesus Christus teste ewangelio et angelo populum suum saluum faciens . . . questionem 58[m] quere in fine huius libri (in red); ubi hoc [sign of a star, a tie mark to f. 117].

Marginal gloss by the hand of the scribe.

Thomas Aquinas, prologue of *Summa theologica,* part 3, followed by an epitome of the text, continued below on f. 117.

2. ff. 8–16v Abhominacio domini cogitationes male et peruerse malis uerbis et ociosis (followed by seven lines of text) . . . Incipiunt dicta Uegetii super ewangelium (in red). Cum appropinquasset Ihesus Ierosolimis et uenisset et reliqua (Mt 21:1). Domine Iesu Christe qui es triplex pax et uia ad pacem, qui pro nobis uenisti in carnem per unionem diuine nature . . . me ad te peruenire concedas. Amen. Explicit Beda per manus [name of scribe omitted].

Dubious Bede, *Orationes ex dictis evangeliorum.* Same text in Klagenfurt (Austria), Bibl. Episc., XXX, c22 (s. xv), ff. 71–92, and Klagenfurt, Studienbibliothek, Pap 106 (s. xv), ff. 66–77v; see H. Menhardt, *Handschriftenverzeichnis der Kärtner Bibliotheken,* vol. 1 (Vienna, 1927). Text and manuscript unrecorded by M. L. W. Laistner, *A Hand-List of Bede Manuscripts* (Ithaca, N.Y., 1943); cf. Bede, *Homeliarum evangelii libri ii, CC* 122 (1960): 201 sqq.

3. ff. 16v–19 Incipit determinacio magistrorum sacre theologie sancte uniuersitatis studii winensis et cetera (in red). Petrus apostolus Ihesu Christi, katholici gregis pastor et doctor . . . quantum ei sufficiebat pro immortali uita (?) unde et sanguinem circumcisionis non creditur resumpsisse et cetera et est finis illius operis.

Heinrich von Langenstein, *Responsum facultatis theologice studii generalis viennensis de thesibus circa materiam incarnationis et eucharistiae anno domini 1385 die 12 septembris in conventu fratrum praedicatorum Ulmae per magistrum Johannem Munzinger propugnatis.* This text ends with ten lines not in the text printed by J. Schelhorn, *Amoenitates literariae* (Frankfurt, 1725–31), 11:223–39. Manuscripts listed by A. Lang, "Johann Müntzinger, ein Schwäbischer Theologe und Schulmeister am Ende des 14. Jahrhunderts," in *Aus der Geisteswelt des Mittelalters: Studien und Texte Martin Grabmann zur Vollendung des 60. Lebensjahres von Freunden und Schülern gewidmet, BGPTM* supp. 3 (1935): 1208–9. T. Hohmann, "Initienregister der Werke Heinrichs von Langenstein," *Traditio* 32 (1976): 413.

4. ff. 19v–57v . . . (f. 20) Sanctus Thomas in librum de uita Christi (in very black ink). Christus Ihesus uenit in hunc mundum . . . unde Bernhardus ueniet dies iudicii ubi plus ualebunt pura corda quam astuta uerba et cetera. Amen. Et sic est finis liber de uita Christi.

Table of chapters precedes text on f. 19v. Marginal gloss by the hand of the scribe. Reworked chapter divisions, differing slightly from those of the printed text, noted in upper margins of the recto and verso of each leaf.

Ps. Thomas Aquinas, *De humanitate Christi,* chapters 1–25 inc.; formed from excerpts of Thomas, *Summa theologica,* see A. Galea, "Animadversio in dissertationes De Rubeis circa opusculum *De humanitate Christi,*" *Divus Thomas,* vol. 1 (Piacenza, 1880), pp. 227 sqq., and vol. 2 (1881), pp. 73–75, 82–92. Grabmann, *Die Werke,* p. 398. Thomas Aquinas, *Opera omnia* (Paris, 1952–73), 28:254–316.

5. ff. 58–107 Incipit prologus in sermonibus de aduentu domini (in red). Ihesu Christo Marieque matri sue gloriosissime ad laudem et gloriam michique et meis auditoribus ad edificacionem sub correccione . . . Incipit sermo dominice prime aduentus (in red). Penitenciam agite appropinquabit enim regnum celorum (Mt 3:2, 4:17). Quia uero beato apostolo attestante in epistola dominice prime . . . (ends abruptly at the end of the recto of the leaf) et hoc ipsum quod relictum in antepriori sermone est moralisare succincte.

ff. 107v–116v blank.

Unidentified collection of sermons for Advent.

6. ff. 117–125 De sessione Christi ad dexteram patris (in red). Sedere ad dexteram patris nichil aliud est . . . Quod nobis prestare dignetur dominus noster Ihesus Christus, qui cum deo patre et spiritu sancto eternaliter uiuit et regnat benedictus deus. Amen.

ff. 125v–127v blank.

Marginal comments as in text 1 above.

Continuation of the epitome of Thomas Aquinas, *Summa theologica,* part 3, above. Five-pointed star, a tie mark added in margin by scribe, corresponds to star after explicit on f. 7v.

Paper, three watermarks: *tête de boeuf,* cf. Briquet 17741; *cloche,* cf. Briquet 3971 sqq.; and *scorpion,* cf. Briquet 13610. ff. 127. Modern foliation erroneous after f. 20. 293 × 120 mm (213 × 152 mm). Collation impracticable. Frame ruled in pen for two columns. Written in gothic cursiva varying from currens to media in c. 45 lines. Headings in red in gothic cursiva and gothic textualis. German style initials in red, some wanting. ff. 58–107, guides for rubricator written in margin in script of text.

Bound in restored brown calf over boards, original brass bosses and label frame, s. xv; chain attached on top back board. Fore-edge clasp wanting.

Written in Germany or Austria in the first half of the fifteenth century. After f. 41, a loose small fragment in German, s. xv or s. xvi, possibly related to the history of the book. Old inscription, "Antonius parmenis . . ." recorded by De Ricci no longer visible on the book. Bookplate of E. Kroencke recorded by De Ricci and the files of the Newberry Library also no longer visible. Acquired by the Newberry before 1932.

Second folio: infinita gratia.

De Ricci, 1:541.

f65.1

(58-2589)

Johann von Neumarkt, *Hieronymusleben;* Saints' Lives and Sermons (in German)

Germany [*Illustrated*] 1451

1. ff. 1–40 Der durchleuchtigen fürstin und frawen . . . Daz ist der brief den sannd Ewsebius Damasio dem bisc[ho]f (in red) . . . Dem erwirdigen vater Damasio dem bischof . . . in ewigen frewden ewigklichen beleiben. Amen.

The "Widmung an Elizabeth" and translation of *Epistola Ps. Eusebii ad Damasum* from Johann von Neumarkt, *Hieronymusleben, Schriften,* pp. 6–242. Additional manuscripts in "Johann von Neumarkt," W. Stammler, *Die Deutsche Literatur des Mittelalters: Verfasserlexikon,* vol. 2 (Berlin and Leipzig, 1936), pp. 615–20. For the original Latin text, see *BHM* 903.

2. ff. 40–48v Dy vorred sannd Augustin (in red). Gewonndlich ist Rittern und Knechten . . . Hyenach volgent die episteln des heyligen herren sannd Augustin (in red). Nw hebend sich an die episteln sannd Augustin . . . ist ymmer and ewigklichen on ennde.

German translation of the *Epistola Ps. Augustini ad Cyrillum* from Johann von Neumarkt, *Hieronymusleben, Schriften,* pp. 245–88, cf. *BHM* 903.

3. ff. 48v–84v Daz ist di vorrede des bischofs von Olmuntz dez kaysers kanntzlers (in red). Der lewt ist genug auf erden die grossen heyligen . . . (f. 49) Nw hebent sich an die epistel sannd Cirilli . . . (ends imperfectly in chapter 106; one leaf removed after f. 84) dy er getan het und volbraht zu seinen wirden und eren. Darnach.

German translation of *Epistola Ps. Cyrilli ad Augustinum* from Johann von Neumarkt, *Hieronymusleben, Schriften,* pp. 289–498, cf. *BHM* 903.

4. ff. 85–88v Item von dem heyligen zwelfpoten sannd Peter (in red). Der lieb herr sannd Peter der zwelfpot . . . und nach disem leben komen yn daz ewig leben. Amen.

Life of Peter from the German version of the *Legenda aurea.* Hain, 9968–92. See Munich, Staatsbibliothek, Cgm. 208; Schneider, *Die Deutschen Handschriften,* p. 40.

5. ff. 89–103 Von dem heyligen herrn und ritter sannd Iörgen (in red). Ein graf waz zu Palastin . . . Und daz wir got mit im ewigklichen loben. Amen.

Life of George from the German version of the *Legenda aurea.*

6. ff. 103–112v Von sannd Pauls dem zwelfpoten (in red). Sannd Pawls der zwelfpot, der hiess des ersten Saulus . . . Und daz wir kömen nach disem leben zu dem ewigen frewdenreichen leben. Amen.

Life of Paul, not in the consulted printed versions of the German *Legenda aurea.*

7. ff. 112v–116 Von dem lieben heilign sannd Sebastian (in red). Der lieb heylig sannd Sebastian ist von Maylannt geborn und waz ein ritter . . . und daz er unns geb nach disem leben daz ewig.

Life of Sebastian from the German version of the *Legenda aurea.*

8. ff. 116–120v Von der heiligen jungkfrauen sannd Barbara (in red). In den zeitn do Maxencius kayser waz . . . und andaht daz er unnser gelaitt well sein von disem leben zu dem ewigen. Amen.

A text similar to that in the German version of the *Legenda aurea.*

9. ff. 120v–126 Von Allenheiligen (in red). Wir sullen billichen aller heiligentageren und sollen sie bitten daz sie uns umb got erwerben

. . . und daz wir uns mit got und ine ewigklichen frewen.

On All Saints from the German version of the *Legenda aurea*.

10. ff. 126v–129v Von allen gelaubigen seelen (in red). Die selen die mit rew on todsunde verfaren seien . . . und ein gutz ennde geb unnserm leben und nach diser zeit das ewigleben. Amen.

On All Believing Souls from the German version of the *Legenda aurea*.

11. ff. 129v–131v Von sannd Michel Ertzengel (in red). Es ligt ein stat yn walhen dy haist Sepaws, darynnen was ein reicher man der hiess Garganus . . . daz wir got mit euch erkennen und liebhaben ewigklichen. Amen.

Life of Michael, not in the usual printed versions of the German *Legenda aurea,* but included in *Der Heiligen Leben,* Munich, Staatsbibliothek, Cgm. 208, f. 1. Schneider, *Die Deutschen Handschriften,* p. 40.

12. ff. 132–138 Vor der Undankperkait (in red). Undankperkait ist ein solhe sündt und übel daz sy als sannd Bernhart spricht . . . (f. 132v) Die lerere sprechent und schreibent daz drey ordern der engele sind und derselben drey orden hat ieglicher drey orden . . . und in ewigklichen eren und loben auch niessen und sein reich mit im besitzen sollen yn gottes namen. Amen.

Anonymous sermon on the angels. Same text found in Munich, Staatsbibliothek, Cgm. 230 (s. xv), ff. 188–193, a manuscript of the German translation of *The Golden Legend* of Jacobus de Voragine; see Schneider, *Die Deutschen Handschriften,* p. 100, n. 8.

13. ff. 138–143 Hab got lieb (in red). Qui non renunciauerit omnibus que possidet non potest meus esse discipulus, Luce capitulo 13 (underlined in red). Es spricht der herr Jhesus Christus . . . daz verleich uns got im selb zu lob. Amen.

Anonymous homily on Luke 14:33; cf. Latin sermon attributed to John Chrysostom, Munich, Staatsbibliothek, CLM 10895, f. 130.

14. ff. 143–147 Von dem grossen Kaiser Karl (in red). Zw den zeiten do der grosz kayser Karel daz reich het do reichsnet und herschte . . . das wir auch frolichen komen yn das himlisch lannde. Amen. 1451.

f. 147v blank.

Life of Charlemagne from the German version of the *Legenda aurea,* see K. Schneider, "Die Deutsche Legende Karl der Grossen," *Zeitschrift für Deutsche Philologie* 86 (1967), Sonderheft, pp. 46–63.

Paper with watermark of *tête de boeuf;* cf. Briquet 14847. ff. 147 + i. Loose leaves at beginning and end. f. 147 repaired. Three folios removed after f. 84. 320 × 215 mm (205 × 136 mm). 1^{12} (1 wanting), $2–7^{12}$, 8^{12} (2 removed), $9–12^{12}$, 13^{12} (8–12 removed). ff. 142–144, folios loose. Catchwords present. Ruled in hard point. Written in gothic cursiva media in 36 lines in two columns. Headings in red in script of text. Red initials; red touches used as punctuation. Latin phrases and names underlined in red.

Bound in contemporary stamped pigskin. Front, one panel divided into six compartments. Stamps within include dragon inside tear-shaped ovals (cf. Weale, *Early Stamped Bookbindings* 15:2), star-shaped flower repeated several times, and a single rosette in the center. A similar rosette at each corner. Surrounded by oak leaves, acorns, and vine. Star-shaped flower and dragon repeated in outer margins accompanied by stag within a roundel and Maria written within a scroll, both repeated. Back, four panels of four compartments each, stag within roundel within each compartment above, dragon within each compartment below; border similar to the front. Two rear-to-front fore-edge clasps wanting; catches for clasps inscribed "uns." A single lozenge-shaped boss removed from center of front and back. Four corner bosses removed front and back. Chain mark, rear board, top center. Fragment of a colored metalcut on verso of front board.

Written in Germany in 1451 (f. 147). Trace of old monastic, possibly Franciscan, shelf-mark "A" in red on front cover; cf. E. Kyriss, *Verzierte otische Einbände im alten Deutschen Sprachgebiet* (Stuttgart, 1951–53), Tafelband, plates 44, 46, and 52. f. 1, inscription in black ink within red initial, "Iesus Maria 1594" and by the same hand in outer margin "Iesus Maria / Franciscus." Rear pastedown pen trials (?) "mo / Maria / 1594 / J." f. 1, lower margin and on the upper edge, library stamp "S.K.M." in circle, long stroke of K crossed to form a cross. Old label "S.P." and blue-edged dealer label on spine. Acquired by the Newberry from Ifan Kyrle Fletcher (London), August 1958.

Second folio: vil arbaitten ängsten.

–66

(Ry 29; J9951)

Antoninus, *Summa Confessionum,* etc.

Cologne [*Illustrated*] 1469

1. ff. 1–146 (begins imperfectly in the table of contents) // De interrogationibus circa magistros et doctores . . . Prologus super trac-

tatum de instructione seu directione simplicium confessorum, editum a domino Anthonio (*sic,* corrected to Anthonino) archiepiscopo Fflorentino et sequitur prologus (in red). Defecerunt scrutantes scrutinium, ait psalmista. Scrutantes aliorum peccata sunt confessores . . . a domino papa pro ultimo articulo mortis tue. In nomine patris et filii et spiritus sancti. Amen. Explicit summa confessionum seu interrogatorium pro simplicibus confessoribus; Editum ab archiepiscopo florentino uidelicit fratre Anthonio (*sic*) ordinis predicatorum; Et scripta sunt ista et completa per me Theobaldum de sancto Wandalino pro tunc uicario ad sanctam Brigidam in Colonia 1469 in profesto corporis Christi hora precise quinta (in red).

One folio of text removed after f. 33; two folios of text removed after f. 139.

Antoninus, *Summa confessionum* (shorter recension). This recension with identical rubrics printed by Ulrich Zell, Cologne, 1469, in which this text is followed by text 2 below. *GW* 2080–2101. For full bibliographical description, see Paris, BN, *Catalogue des manuscrits latins* 4 (1958), MS 3265; Kaeppeli, 256; Orlandi, *Bibl. Ant.,* pp. 313–19. Bloomfield, *Incipits,* 1501.

2. ff. 146v–151 Incipit sermo beati Iohannis Crisostomi de penitentia (in red). Prouida mente et profundo cogitatu cognosci debent . . . plena est penitencia tua atque perfecta promerebitur indulgentiam prestante uero domino nostro Ihesu Christo in secula seculorum. Amen et cetera.

Dubious John Chrysostom, *De poenitentia, GW* 2080–2101. Hain, *5026 and 5044. On this text, see A. Wilmart, "La Collection des 38 homélies latines de saint Jean Chrysostome," *Journal of Theological Studies* 19 (1918): 307, n. 1. For manuscripts and editions of this work attributed to Ps. Cyprianus, see H. von Soden, *Die Cyprianische Briefsammlung: Geschichte ihrer Entstehung und Überlieferung* (Texte und Untersuchungen zur Geschichte der altchristlichen Literatur, 25, pt. 3; Leipzig, 1904), pp. 228–29. For other manuscripts, see Bloomfield, *Incipits,* 4301.

3. ff. 151–153v Incipit sermo beati Augustini episcopi super oracionem dominicam primus (in red). Quoniam domino gubernante . . . et hic uos custodiat et in futuro dignos efficiat. Ipsi gloria in secula seculorum. Amen. Explicit sermo beati Augustini de oratione dominica (in red).

Ps. Augustine, *Sermo 65. PL* 39:1970–71. This and texts 4–6 below printed by Ulrich Zell, Cologne, 1467–c. 1479. *GW* 2995–97 (texts 4 and 5 inaccurately recorded as one). The printed text has identical rubrics.

4. ff. 153v–156 Incipit exposicio eiusdem super simbolum (in red). Queso uos fratres, ut nobis reserantibus exposicionem symboli . . . Quapropter, dilectissimi, bene uiuamus ut non ad penam sed ad eternam uitam resurgamus per Christum dominum ac redemptorem nostrum uiuentem et regnantem. Per omnia secula seculorum. Amen.

Sections headed in red: "Petrus," "Andreas," "Iacobus maior," "Iohannes," "Thomas."

Ps. Augustine, *Sermo 242,* recension different from *PL* 39:2191–93. For the same recension, see Augsburg, Staats-und-Stadtbibliothek, 35, ff. 362–66, A. Sottili, *I codici del Petrarca nella Germania occidentale* (Padua, 1971–78), 1:32. See also J. Madoz, *Le Symbole du XIe concile de Tolède* (Louvain, 1938), p. 44 and n. 1. *CPL* 91.

5. ff. 156–158 Sequitur alia exposicio super simbolum et cetera (in red). Oportet attendere, fratres karissimi . . . Si autem credideris eternis gaudiis inseraris per Christum dominum nostrum uenientem et regnantem cum patre et spiritu sancto nunc et semper et in omnes eternitates seculorum seculi. Amen. Explicit exposicio super simbolum (in red).

Ps. Augustine, *Sermo 243. PL* 39:2193–94.

6. ff. 158–160v Incipit sermo beati Augustini episcopi de ebrietate cauenda (in red). Licet propicio Christo, fratres karissimi . . . in pauperum refectionem proficiat, prestante domino nostro Ihesu Christo qui cum patre et spiritu sancto uiuit et regnat deus. Per omnia secula seculorum. Amen. Amen.

Ps. Augustine, *Sermo 294. PL* 39:2303–6.

7. f. 161–161v (addition by the same scribe) "Casus episcopales." List of thirty-nine moral and legal offenses.

8. f. 161v (addition by the same scribe) List of five senses, six corporal works of mercy, six spiritual works of mercy, and seven deadly sins; cf. MS 75.5, f. 103.

9. flyleaf (addition by the same scribe). List beginning imperfectly of thirteen books printed at Cologne by Ulrich Zell and others:

// [1] Item cantica canticorum 1471 [= Gregory I, *Commentum super cantica canticorum,* printed by Zell not after 1473, *B.M.*

Cat. of 15th-Century Books 1:192]. Voulliéme, 504.

[2] Item defensorium fidei, 1478 [cf. *GW* 8246].

[3] Item fformicarius, 1479 [= Johannes Nyder, *Formicarius,* printed by Zell, s.d., *B.M. Cat. of 15th-Century Books* 1:194]. Voulliéme, 848.

[4] Item uita Ihesu, 1479 [= Ludolpus of Saxony, *Vita Ihesu,* abridgement printed at Cologne, s.d., by Arnold Ther Hoernen, *B.M. Cat. of 15th-Century Books* 1:209]. Voulliéme, 758–59.

[5] Item liber septem sapientium [= Dicta septem sapientium Graeciae, printed at Cologne by Johann Guldenschaff, s.d., *B.M. Cat. of 15th-Century Books* 1:256]. Voulliéme, 370.

[6] Item manuale confessorum uenerabilis magistri Iohannis Nyder, 1480 [printed by Zell, s.d., *B.M. Cat. of 15th-Century Books* 1:185]. Voulliéme, 850.

[7] Item Cesarium anno 1481 [= Caesarius de Heisterbach, *Dialogus miraculorum,* printed by Zell, s.d., *B.M. Cat. of 15th-Century Books* 1:195]. Voulliéme, 300.

[8] Item copia.

[9] Item storia trium regum [= Johannes de Hildesheim, *Historia trium regum,* printed at Cologne in 1481 by Bartholomaeus de Unkel, *B.M. Cat. of 15th-Century Books* 1:241; for other Cologne printings, see 1:253, 254, and 257]. Voulliéme, 678–81.

[10] Item liber philossophorum (*sic*), 1482 [= *Pharetra doctorum et philosophorum,* printed at Cologne by Conrad Winters de Homborch, s.d., *B.M. Cat. of 15th-Century Books* 1:247]. Voulliéme, 938–40.

[11] Item regimen sanitatis, 1483 [= Arnoldus de Villanova, *Regimen sanitatis,* printed by Conrad Winters de Homborch at Cologne, s.d., *B.M. Cat. of 15th-Century Books* 1:250]. Voulliéme, 1002.

[12] Item duo psalteria. Cf. Voulliéme, 986–89.

[13] Item breuiarium in duobus uoluminibus. Cf. Voulliéme, 277–83.

Paper. Parchment flyleaf part of old limp binding. ff. 161 + i. Seven folios removed with loss of text: two folios before f. 1, one folio after f. 33, two folios after f. 139, two folios after f. 161. Trimmed to 142 × 102 mm (106 × 70 mm). 1^{12} (1–2 removed), 2^{12}, 3^{12} (12 removed), $4–11^{12}$, 12^{12} (1–2 removed), 13^{12}, 14^{12} (11–12 removed), 13^{12}, 14^{12} (11–12 removed). Quires numbered on recto of first folio and on verso of last folio, partially removed by trimming. Frame ruled in pencil. ff. 1–160, written in gothic cursiva currens by one hand in 30 long lines. Texts on ff. 161 and flyleaf, later additions by the same hand. Headings in red in script of text. Minor red German style initials. Red touches used as punctuation.

Bound in parchment formed from fragment of an unidentified liturgical text, s. xv.

Written in the church of Saint Bridget, Cologne [*DHGE* 13:303–4], by Theobaldus de Sancto Wandalino, text 1 dated 1469; text 9 added in 1483 or after. Texts 1–6 and 9 suggest a close connection to Cologne printers. Theobaldus de Sancto Wandalino also copied, in 1482, a portion of Paris, BN, lat. 11413, ff. 171–183 (this also a quire of twelve paper leaves containing sermons of Augustine et alia). See Samaran and Marichal, *Catalogue des manuscrits* 3:235 and plate ccii; *Colophons de manuscrits occidentaux,* 1764. On flyleaf, "Hunc librum manuscriptum e seculo xv emi Moguntiae an. MDCCCXXVII, Henricus Hoffmann Mogonus"; another note dated 1830 or 1836. f. 1 and passim, notes referring to pagination and missing folios in same hand. f. 1, note signed "H Hoffmann Mogonus." Front pastedown, armorial bookplate Bernard Brocas Beaurepaire. Acquired by the Newberry from Mrs. Douglas of Oak Park, Illinois, 1938.

Second folio: expossit ut.

Faye-Bond, p. 150.

66.1

(Ry 221; 60-1262)
Rufinus, *Historia Monachorum;*
Jerome, *Vitae Sanctorum;*
Hugues de Fouilloy, *De Claustro Animae;*
Hugh of Saint Victor, *De Institutione Novitiorum*

Germany s. XV med.

1. ff. 2–30v In nomine domini; Amen; Ieronimus de uita patrum prologus; Benedictus dominus (in red) qui uult omnes homines saluos fieri . . . Incipit uita et uirtutes sancti Johannis (in red). Primum igitur tamquam . . . et tanta ostendit nobis mirabilia Christi, gloria in secula seculorum. Amen.

Rufinus Aquileiensis, *Historia monachorum sive de vitis patrum*. Editions: *Tyrannii Rufini aquileiensis . . . opera omnia* (Verona, 1745), 115 sqq. ed. Rosweyd, *Vitae patrum* (Antwerp, 1615), reprinted with additional errors introduced *PL* 21:387–462. On attribution, see A. J. Festugière, "Le Problème littéraire de *l'Historia monachorum*," *Hermes* 83 (1955): 257–84; *Historia monachorum in Aegypto: edition critique du texte grec et traduction annotée* (Subsidia hagiographica, 53; Brussels, 1971), pp. v–vi. Late medieval manuscripts and incunable editions, e.g., Hain 8586 sqq. and Copinger 2598 sqq., attribute this text to Jerome.

2. ff. 31–40 Incipit prefacio sancti Ieronimi in uitam sancti Hilarionis (in red). In sanctis oracionibus tuis memento mei decus ac dignitas uirginum nonna Assella. Scripturus uitam beati Hilarionis eius inuoco spiritum sanctum . . . Hilarion ortus est uico Thardach . . . forsitan quia plus illum locum dilexerat.

Jerome, *Vita S. Hilarionis. Acta sanctorum,* Oct. 9:43–58. *PL* 23:29–54. See Oldfather, *Studies,* pp. 250–305; *BHM* 262. This manuscript not recorded. *CPL* 618. On the dedication to Asella, see M. McNeil, "The Latin Manuscript Tradition . . ." in Oldfather, *Studies,* pp. 253–54.

3. ff. 40–43 Incipit uita sancti Malchi (in red). Qui nauali proelio dimicaturi sunt . . . et hominem Christo deditum posse mori et non posse superari.

Jerome, *Vita Malchi. PL* 23:55–60; ed. C. C. Mierow in *Classical Essays Presented to J. A. Kleist* (Saint Louis, 1946), pp. 31–60. Oldfather, *Studies,* pp. 449–511. *BHM* 263. This manuscript not recorded. *CPL* 619. C. C. Mierow, "The Thirty-five Vatican Manuscripts of Jerome's *Vita Malchi:* Prolegomena to an Edition," *Speculum* 20 (1945): 468–81.

4. ff. 43–47 Incipit uita sancti Pauli primi heremite (in red). Inter multos sepe dubitatum est . . . quam regum purpuras cum regnis suis.

Jerome, *Vita S. Pauli. PL* 23:17–28. Oldfather, *Studies,* pp. 65–142. *BHM* 261. This manuscript not recorded. *CPL* 617.

5. ff. 47–77 Incipit prologus in uitam sancti Antonii (in red). Presbiter Euagrius Innocenti filio karissimo . . . Optimum, fratres, inistis certamen aut equare . . . explicit prologus; incipit uita sancti Antonii (in red). Igitur Antonius nobilibus religiosisque parentibus natus in Egypto . . . et tocius corrupcionis artiffices qui eos colunt. Regnante eodem domino nostro Iesu Christo cum patre et spiritu sancto in secula seculorum. Amen.

ff. 77v–78 blank.

Athanasius, *Vita S. Antonii,* translation of Evagrius, epilogue of Evagrius wanting. *PG* 26:838–976. *Acta sanctorum,* Jan. 2:120–41. Rosweyde, *Vitae patrum,* 35–60; reprinted, *PL* 73:125–70. *BHL* 609.

6. ff. 78v–109 Incipiunt capitula in librum Hugonis [– de sciencia et disciplina] de claustralibus . . . Incipit liber Hugonis de claustralibus (in red). Locutus, karissime, de hiis que addeficacionem (*sic*) claustri sunt materialia . . . tolle grabbatum tuum et ambula et cetera.

Words in brackets crossed out in red.

Hugues de Fouilloy, *Liber de claustralibus vel de sciencia et disciplina,* Books II and III, 1–9 (inc.). Table includes chapter for texts 6a and 6b, infra. *PL* 176:1051–1104C. This manuscript belongs to category IIB of Baron; see "Hugues de Saint-Victor," p. 287 sqq., and "Note sur le *De claustro,*" *Sacris erudiri* 15 (1964): 249–55. See also M. de Marco, "Codices Vaticani del *De claustro animae* di Ugo di Fouilloi," ibid., pp. 225–27. Goy, *Die Überlieferung,* p. 6 and 491–92. I. Gorby in *Dictionnaire de spiritualité* 7 (1969): 882.

7. ff. 109–123v Sequitur aliud capitulum (in red). De institucione nouiciorum capitulum 32 (in red). Quia, fratres, largiente domino de uana conuersacione . . . Bonitatem uero dei orate ut uobis det deus. Amen.

Prologue is numbered 32 as if part of text 6; text divided into 15 chapters, numbered 1–15.

Hugh of Saint Victor, *De instructione novitiorum.* Follows as part of *Liber de claustralibus* in text, titled *Liber de sciencia et disciplina* in the table on f. 78v. Explicit marked by a contemporary hand. *PL* 176:925–52. On attribution, see Baron, "Hugues de Saint-Victor," p. 274 sqq., and B. Hauréau, *Les Oeuvres de Hugues de Saint-Victor: essai critique* (Paris, 1886), pp. 116–24. For other manuscripts, see Goy, *Die Überlieferung,* pp. 340–67.

7 bis. ff. 123v–126v (follows preceding text without interruption) Ad viii ualet multiplicitas operum unius caritatis, Iocundat, stabilit, auget, peccata remittit, debilitat, remouet, roborat atque cauet (underlined in red) . . . et de intentione sua. Explicit liber Hugonis doctoris egregii de claustralibus; sit laus Christo (in red).

Includes chapters numbered 17–24, titled "De septem riuis Egypti," "De uana gloria," etc. This variant portion of the *De instructione novitiorum* unrecorded by Goy, *Die Überlieferung.*

Paper. ff. 125. Foliated 2–126. Trimmed to 289 × 214 mm (180 × 120 mm). Collation impracticable. Frame ruled in pencil. Written in gothic cursiva formata degenerating to cursiva media in 29–37 long lines. Headings in red in script of text. f. 2, green initial with yellow-brown flourishes 16 lines high extended to form bracket border on inner, upper, and lower margins. f. 79, similar initial 7 lines high also extended to form bracket border.

Bound in modern gray paper over pasteboard.

Written in Germany in the middle of the fifteenth century. Typed dealer's description tipped to front pastedown. Acquired by the Newberry from Ifan Kyrle Fletcher, 1960.

Second folio: futurus esset.

67.1
(53-990)
Heinricus de Ratisbona,
Vocabularius dictus "Lucianus"

Austria s. XV (before 1462)

ff. 2–252 Abba sicut dicit glosa ad galatas quarto hebraycum est et interpretatur pater . . . zona, e, id est cingulus . . . inde zonefractor et cetera. Explicit scartha, finita feria quarta, finita feria ii[a] post dominicam letare, et cetera.

Occasional additions and corrections by the scribe.

ff. 1–1v and 252v–253v blank.

Henricus de Ratisbona, *Vocabularius dictus "Lucianus."* Zumkeller, *Manuskripte,* p. 344. Stegmüller, *Repertorium biblicum,* 3224. This manuscript not recorded.

Paper. End pastedown has *tête de boeuf* watermark; cf. Briquet 14610. f. 1, parchment. ff. i + 253 + i. Small unnumbered bifolio formed from a slip of paper inserted after f. 249, writing on first recto only. 295 × 121 mm (220 × 160 mm). Portion of f. 253 removed. 1^{1+12}, $2\text{–}6^{12}$, 7^{14}, $8\text{–}20^{12}$, 21^{12} (10–12 stubs only). Catchwords present. Quires 1 and 2 signed "primo" and "2[us]" in the lower margin of the verso of the last leaf. Quires 12–20, numbered "1[o]–9[us]" on lower margin of verso of last leaf in arabic and roman numerals. Two-column frame ruling in brown ink. Written in gothic cursiva media in 38–42 lines in two columns. Ink varying from black to light brown, changing color on f. 136. Guide letters to rubricator present. Red Germanic initials throughout; red paragraph marks and punctuation sporadically present. f. 1, contemporary title "Interpres uocabulorum."

Bound in contemporary geometrically ruled whittawed leather, two rear-to-front brass clasps. Five bosses wanting front, one of five wanting rear. Front cover bears title on parchment label "[illegible] uocabulorum," s. xv, effaced by wear. Chain mark on rear board.

Written in Austria in the fifteenth century, before 1462. Formerly in the Benedictine abbey of Garsten [Cottineau, 1:1256–57], consecrated to the Virgin in 1107. f. 1, "Hunc librum dedit dominus Petrus Budatsth ad bybliothecam in Garstim ad honorem beate uirginis pro anime sue salute anno domini m[o] cccc[o] lxii[o]." This Garsten manuscript unrecorded, *Mittelalterliche Bibliothekskataloge Österreichs* 5:19–24. f. 1, old shelf numbers "Primo/E/Ultimo" and "2157," in pen. On front pastedown, "315," "Uocabularius breviloquus, $400, xv[e]s.," in pencil. Other pencil jottings by modern dealers. Acquired by the Newberry from Kroch's, Chicago, 1953.

Second folio: -tture et.

Faye-Bond, p. 153.

f67.2
(55-650)
Missal of Regensburg

Germany s. XIV

1. ff. 1–22 Votive Masses variously with sequences, prayers, secrets, graduals, communions, and postcommunions (titles in red): De sancta Maria, Tempore pascali de sancta Maria in aduentu domini, De angelis, De patronis, De sancto Benedicto, Pro peccatis, Missa propria sacerdotis, Pro defunctis, De corpore Christi, De sancto Emmeramo, De sancto Wolfgango, De sancto Dyonisio, Marie Magdelene, De sancto Leonhardo, Scolastice uirginis, De sancta trinitate, De sancto spiritu, De sancta cruce, De sancta Maria, In aduentu domini, Infra natalem domini, Post natiuitatem domini, Tempore pascali, De angelis, Missa generalis, Pro fundatore, Pro episcopo, Pro abbate sanctificato, Pro abbate, Pro nuper defunctis, In anniuersario, Pro famula, Pro fratribus et sororibus, Pro his sepultis, Pro parentibus, Pro commissis.

2. ff. 22–24v Lessons from the Old and New Testaments (titles in red): De sancta cruce, De sancta Maria, In aduentu domini, Post natiuitatem domini. Ends in red, Reliqua ewangelium require post canonem.

3. f. 25–25v Hymns to the Virgin and Votive Mass "Pro amico" taken from another book and attached to a stub.

4. f. 26–26v Benediction of the Chalice.

5. ff. 26v–30v Prefaces to the Mass for daily use and special feasts (titles in red): In natiuitate domini, In epyphania domini, In xl[a], In cena domini, In festo pasce, In ascensione domini, In pentecosten, De sancta trinitate,

De sancta cruce, De apostolis, De sancta Maria, Cottidiana, ends imperfectly.

6. ff. 31–46 Ordinary and Canon of the Mass.

7. ff. 46v–48v Continuation of lessons from f. 24v above: Tempore pascali, De angelis, De patronis, Benedicti abbatis, ends imperfectly.

8. f. 49–49v Separate fragment of Votive Masses similar to f. 25 above (titles in red): In dedicatione [ecclesie], Pro infirmis.

9. ff. 50–51v Masses by a different hand from ff. 1–24 above, beginning imperfectly in an unidentified Mass (titles in red): In natiuitate domini, In epiphania domini, De resurectione domini, Pro tribulatione.

10. f. 52–52v Four Votive Masses on a separate fragment similar to ff. 25 and 49 above (titles in red): Pro iter agentibus, Pro salute uiuorum, Pro serenitate, Pro pluuia, followed by Infra octauam Iohannis Baptiste.

11. f. 53–53v A fragment of a Mass for the Dead by a different hand from the above: Iste introitus cantatur pro uno queque (*sic*) defuncto exceptis episcopis et abbatibus (in red). Requiem eternam dona eis, domine . . . cf. *SMRL* 2:327–28.

12. ff. 54–56 Masses, same hand as ff. 50–51v (titles in red): In ascencione domini, In die sancto pentecostes, Pro pace, Goediani et Epymachi, Uitalis martirum uel de uno martire tempore pascali.

13. f. 56v (additions) [D]eus qui ad imitandum passionis tue exemplum decem milia martyres. Achatium et socios eius . . . Followed by a Mass for the Visitation of the Virgin added by a second hand.

The text of the prayer follows the *Passio Beati Achacii* (*BHL* 20/21) in Charville, BM, 59 (s. xv), ff. 99v; see J. van der Straeten, *Catalogue des manuscrits hagiographiques de Charville, Verdun, et Saint-Mihiel* (Subsidia hagiographia, 56; Brussels, 1974), p. 19.

Parchment. ff. 56. Foliated erratically in s. xv or xvi in a manner which cannot be fully explained: ff. 8–22, 25–28 = ff. 1–19; ff. 3–34 = ff. 22–26; f. 37 = f. 31; ff. 46–56, in a highly confused order. Undetermined number of folios missing at the beginning and after f. 48. A leaf of text removed after f. 30. 283 × 210 mm (210 × 130 mm). Sheets attached to ff. 25, 49, and 52 are 95–125 mm in width and may be formed from scraps of unused parchment, possibly cut from rolls. $1–3^6$, 4^8 (1 stub only), 5^8 (6 removed), $6–7^8$, $8–9^4$. Quires 1–7 numbered in roman numerals in lower margin of verso of last leaf. Prickings in outer margins. Ruled in pencil. ff. 1–24, 26–30v, 44v–48v, in gothic semiquadrata media in 20 long lines; ff. 31–44, in gothic textualis rotunda media in 27–29 long lines. Vertical strokes used as adjuncts to word separation by space. Headings in scripts of text. Directions for rubricator in right margins. f. 31, gold illuminated initial with red and blue flourishes. Alternating red and blue flourished and simple initials throughout.

Bound in red-stained geometrically ruled leather over boards, s. xvi, with a brass boss and four brass corners on front and back; corners bear legend "Maria gratia." Two rear end clasps wanting; catches on front cover bear inscription "O sa[ncta]." Fore-edge tabs removed. Paper pastedowns with a *cloche* watermark, clapper to one side. Trace of an older pastedown formed from a fourteenth-century vernacular German document visible at the end. This fragment similar to the stock used for mounting f. 49.

Written in Germany in the fourteenth century for a Benedictine abbey in or near Regensburg. Note presence of Emmeran and Wolfgang, both of Regensburg, and Benedictine saints in Masses on ff. 1–22. Front pastedown bears name of Joannes Hainricus Ebron zu Wildenberg (died June 1605) in note dated 4 February 1609 signed by his successor Christophorus de Stinglhaim, councillor of Ratisbonne, who gave this book to the chapel of Saint George in the castle of Wildenberg. The arms of both men with mantles and horned helmets are painted on the front pastedown. "R" written in a hand of s. xvi in upper right corner of rear pastedown. Acquired by the Newberry from Bernard Rosenthal, list 1, item no. 71, 17 January 1955.

Second folio: donis laudant.

Faye-Bond, p. 153.

67.3
(59-365)

Johannes Hagen, Collection of Extracts

Erfurt [*Illustrated*] 1460

1. ff. 2–37v Excerpts from Peter Lombard, *Four Books of Sentences*.

Stegmüller, *Rep. in sent. Petr. Lomb.*, 1; cf. Klapper, *Johannes Hagen* 2:124.

2. ff. 38–67v Ex scripto sancti Thome super iiii sentenciarum. Misit uerbum suum . . .

Excerpts from Thomas Aquinas, *Commentary on the Fourth Book of the Sentences of Peter Lombard*. Stegmüller, *Rep. in sent. Petr. Lomb.*, 846; cf. Klapper, *Johannes Hagen* 2:125.

3. ff. 68–73v, 62 (upper portion only) Ex quotlibeto Egidii de Roma . . . (f. 62) Expliciunt collecta de quotlibeto Egidii de Roma ordinis carmelitarum Augustini . . .

Summary of Giles of Rome, *Quodlibet* I, 1–VI, 20; *Quodlibet* VI, 21–25. See P. Glorieux, *La Littérature quodlibetique de 1260 à 1320* (Paris, 1925–35), 1:141–47. Zumkeller, *Manuskripte,* 58; cf. Klapper, *Johannes Hagen* 2:125.

4. ff. 74–77 Ex constitutionibus Groning[en]tii (?). Predicandi officium est amandum propter tria . . .

Extracts from an unidentified text.

5. ff. 77v–79v Rupertus abbas anno m° cx vii indictione decima scribit abbati Cuno sigerbensis montis in memoriam Michahelis . . .

Summary of an unidentified work of Rupert of Deutz.

6. ff. 80–99v Summary of Duns Scotus, *Commentary on the Sentences of Peter Lombard,* I–IV.

Stegmüller, *Rep. in sent. Petr. Lomb.,* 421; cf. Klapper, *Johannes Hagen* 2:125.

7. ff. 100–102v In nomine et auxilio Christi incipit de carena quid sit . . .

Unidentified sermons.

8. ff. 103–107v Extracts from Boethius, *De trinitate.*

CPL 890.

9. ff. 108–110v De uita christiana (in red). Boetius de fide christiana . . .

Extracts from *CPL* 893; cf. Klapper, *Johannes Hagen* 2:124.

10. ff. 111–112v De Maria Magdalena sermo. Succurre Christe cum Maria uirgine . . .

11. ff. 113–117 Origenes super leuitas . . .

Unidentified extract attributed to Origen; cf. Klapper, *Johannes Hagen* 2:124.

12. ff. 117v–119 Ex tractatu episcopi burgensis dyalogi Sauli iudei et Pauli fidelis christiani. Scrutamini scripturas . . .

Extracts from Paul of Burgos, *Dialogus qui vocatur scrutinium scripturarum libris duobus contra perfidiam Judaeorum.* Stegmüller, *Repertorium biblicum,* 6328; cf. Klapper, *Johannes Hagen* 2:124.

13. ff. 119v–123v Excerpta ex glosa ordinaria . . .

Extracts from the *Glossa ordinaria* for the books of Joshua, Judith, Esther, Tobit, and Judges; cf. Klapper, *Johannes Hagen* 2:125.

14. ff. 124–126 Wilhelmus parisiensis in uniuerso corporali, qui liber dicitur sapientialis . . .

Excerpt from William of Auvergne, *De universo.* Glorieux, 141w; cf. Klapper, *Johannes Hagen* 2:124.

15. ff. 126v–132 Excerpts from Jerome, *Contra Iovinianum.*

BHM 252; cf. Klapper, *Johannes Hagen* 2:125.

16. ff. 132v–139v Egidius de Roma, ordinis heremitarum Augustini scribit ad Philippum regem francorum (?) ob suam peticionem librum de dignitate principum . . .

Excerpts from Giles of Rome, *De regimine principum.* Zumkeller, *Manuskripte,* 54.

17. ff. 140–143 2ª ebdomada aduentus littera Ysaie xxi legitur in choro . . .

Unidentified homily.

18. f. 143v Extracts from Bernard of Clairvaux, *De diligendo Deo.*

PL 182:973–1000.

f. 144 blank.

19. f. 144v, unidentified extracts.

20. ff. 145–147v Extracts from William of Auvergne, *De universo,* Book II.

Glorieux, 141w; cf. Klapper, *Johannes Hagen* 2:125.

21. ff. 148–152 Rudimentum doctrine composuit frater Gilbertus de Tornaco ordinis minorum . . .

Extracts from Gilbert de Tournai, *Rudimentum doctrinae.* Glorieux, 311e. See also L. Baudry, "Wilbert de Tournai," *Revue d'histoire franciscaine* 5 (1928): 29.

22. ff. 152v–153v De proprietatibus quorumdam animalium Hugo in bestiario . . .

Extracts from Ps. Hugh of Saint Victor, *De bestiis et aliis rebus.* Goy, *Die Überlieferung,* p. 192.

23. f. 154–154v Liber puellarum compositus est a magistro Iohanne de Tambaco ordinis predicatorum et habet libros (*sic*) xv capitula . . .

= Johannes de Dambach, *Liber de consolatione theologiae,* Kaeppeli, 2256. The manuscript formerly in the Carthusian library at Erfurt is unique among recorded copies of the full text in giving this work the title "Liber puellarum"; see A. Auer, "Johannes von Dambach und die Trostbücher vom 11. bis zum 16. Jahrhundert," *BGPTM,* vol. 27, pts. 1–2 (1928), 12–13.

24. f. 155–155v Concilium basiliense deposuit Eugenium vii kalendas julii anno domini m° cccc 39 et anno domini m cccc 39 pridie nonas iulii pontificatus Eugenii, nouo in concilio florentino obtinuit unionem greco-

rum . . . (in mid f. 155) et patet hodie anno 1460, non esse antichristum . . .

Brief chronicle of events in the pontificate of Eugenius IV.

25. ff. 155v–159v Unidentified extracts from commentaries on the Old and New Testaments.

26. f. 159[1]v Egredimini, filie Syon, uidete regem Salomon . . . (Cant 3:11), karissimi fratres, sicut promissum est . . .

Unidentified sermon.

27. ff. 160–161v In nomine et auxilio Christi, incipit salutaris doctrina pro pastoribus . . .

Unidentified text.

28. f. 161v In nomine et gratia Christi incipit de confessione et absolucione in sacro ordine nostro . . .

This may be the treatise on this subject by Johannes Hagen; cf. Klapper, *Johannes Hagen* 1:1, no. 19, and 2:133.

29. ff. 162–163[1] Sanctus Bernardus ponit librum de xii gradibus humilitatis . . .

Summary of Bernard of Clairvaux, *Tractatus de gradibus humilitatis et superbiae*. *PL* 182:941–72.

30. ff. 163[1]v–165v Summary of Giles of Rome, *Theoremata de corpore Christi*.

Glorieux, 400i. Zumkeller, *Manuskripte,* 15.

31. f. 166–168 Ex prologo Ruffini in translacionem librorum sancti Gregorii nazanzeni (*sic*) . . .

Cf. *PG* 36:735–36. *CPL* 198g.

32. ff. 168v–171 Sermo 2[us] beati Augustini episcopi de uerbis apostoli. Cum timore et tremore et cetera (Tob 13:16). Et de carne et de sanguine Christi . . .

Unidentified text.

33. ff. 171–172 Liber de philosophia Marie . . .

This excerpt attributed to Johannes Hagen, *Mittelalterliche Bibliothekskataloge Deutschlands* 2:428.

34. ff. 172v–173v Hugo de claustro duplice . . .

Summary of Hugues de Fouilloy, *De claustro animae*. *PL* 176:1051–1104. This excerpt attributed to Johannes Hagen, *Mittelalterliche Bibliothekskataloge Deutschlands* 2:428.

35. ff. 174–175 Doctor Nicolaus Dinckelphuel wienensis scripsit super euangelia . . .

Extract of Nicolaus de Dinkelsbühl, *Commentary on the Gospels;* cf. Stegmüller, *Repertorium biblicum,* 5710–11.

36. f. 175v Bernardus de libero arbitrio dicit . . .

Extracts from Bernard of Clairvaux, *De gratia et libero arbitrio*. *PL* 182:1001–30.

37. f. 176–177v Ex libro Bernardi de precepto et dispensatione . . .

Extracts from Bernard of Clairvaux, *Liber de praecepto et dispensatione*. *PL* 182:809–54.

38. ff. 178–182 Ex scriptis Humberti circa regulam beati Augustini . . .

Extracts from Humbert of Romans, *Expositio regulae s. Augustini,* Kaeppeli, 2016. This extract and texts nos. 39–44 below attributed to Johannes Hagen, *Mittelalterliche Bibliothekskataloge Deutschlands* 2:428–29.

39. ff. 182v–187 Ex libro exameron beati Ambrosii episcopi. Opiniones fuerunt philosophorum de principiis . . .

Extracts from the works of Ambrose. *CPL* 123, 124, 128, 130, 131, 132, 135, 138, 127, 133, 143; cf. Klapper, *Johannes Hagen* 2:124.

40. ff. 187v–189v Gwilhelmus parisiensis scripsit summam de uirtutibus que diuiditur in tres partes . . .

Extracts from William of Auvergne, *Summa de virtutibus*. Glorieux, 141j.

41. ff. 190–192 Augustinus scribit 4[or] libros de doctrina christiana in quorum 2[o] dixit Ihesum filium . . .

Extracts from *CPL* 263.

42. ff. 192v–193v Ex tractatu sancti Thome de sacramento altaris . . .

Summary of an unidentified work attributed to Thomas Aquinas; cf. Mandonnet, *Opuscula omnia* 3:11–18.

43. ff. 194–196 Ex collacionibus patrum. Prima est abbatis Moysis . . .

Extracts from John Cassian, *Conlationes*. *CPL* 512.

44. ff. 196v–198 Augustinus scribit 13 libros confessionum . . .

Summary of *CPL* 251.

45. f. 198 Summary of Anselm, *Cur deus homo*.

PL 159:339–432.

46. ff. 198v–199v Instituta patrum composuit sanctus Iohannes Cassianus presbiter ad petitionem pape et episcopi Castoris . . .

Extracts from John Cassian, *De institutis coenobiorum*. *CPL* 513. This extract and texts nos. 47–52 below attributed to Johannes Hagen, *Mittelalterliche Bibliothekskataloge Deutschlands* 2:428–29.

47. ff. 199v–200 Cesarius episcopus monachis scripsit omelias . . .

Summary of ten homilies attributed to Caesarius of Arles.

48. ff. 200v–201v Augustinus scripsit duodecim libros de genesi . . .

Summary of *CPL* 266; cf. Klapper, *Johannes Hagen* 2:125.

49. ff. 202–278v Ex sermonibus Iacobi de Uoragine archiepiscopi ianuensis, ordinis predicatorum . . .

Sermon ending on f. 238 dated 1460.

Extracts from the *Sermones de sanctis et festis,* Kaeppeli, 2156; cf. Klapper, *Johannes Hagen* 2:126.

50. ff. 280–291 Excerpts from medical tracts including Galen, *Tegni,* and Johannitius, *Isagoge in Tegni;* cf. Klapper, *Johannes Hagen* 2:126.

51. ff. 291v–295 Ex lilio medicine . . .

Summary of Bernard Gordon, *Lilium medicinae,* Thorndike and Kibre, 772; = (?) "Liliature," cited by Klapper, *Johannes Hagen* 2:125.

52. ff. 295–296v "De regimine sanitatis."

Cf. Thorndike and Kibre, 1899, and Klapper, *Johannes Hagen* 2:125.

53. ff. 296v–298 Liber Iohannis Mesue sic incipit: In nomine dei misericordie cuius nutu . . .

Excerpts from John Mesue, *De consolatione medicinarum.* Thorndike and Kibre, 694 and 1688.

54. ff. 298v–299 Unidentified extracts.

55. f. 299v Prescriptions against various maladies.

Some of the leaves of this collection were originally written on by various hands for other purposes. f. 13v, rubric for the prayer *Adoro te,* "Sanctus Gregorius papa dedit multas indulgentias ad hanc figuram armorum Christi . . ."; f. 163[1], an unidentified liturgical fragment in Latin; an unnumbered leaf inserted after f. 198, the left half only of a letter in Low German of Johannes [Hagen], Prior of the Carthusian monastery of Erfurt, dated 1459; a narrow unnumbered oblong leaf inserted after f. 208, an inventory of sixteen books beginning, "Una biblia quasi integra . . ."; f. 218, an unidentified fragment in Low German on precious stones; an inserted leaf after 224[2], fragment of an unidentified text in Low German; an inserted leaf after f. 225, the draft of the will of a Carthusian friar in favor of the Carthusian monastery of Erfurt made in the presence of Prior Johannes [Hagen], the Monday before Advent.

Paper, watermarked with *tête de boeuf* with a six-lobed flower, cf. Briquet 14800 sqq., and *croix latine,* not in Briquet. ff. 319 Foliated 2–299 in contemporary arabic numerals with no leaf foliated 141, 222, 279, 288, 289, two leaves foliated 224 and 226. Four unnumbered leaves after f. 163[1]. Single unnumbered leaves of varying shape after ff. 10, 67, 126, 132, 136, 159, 198, 208, 217, 224, 227 (loose), 231, 241, 250, and 287. First leaf wanting. c. 220 × c. 155 mm (c. 210 × c. 145 mm). Collation impracticable but a portion of the text composed of single sheets instead of quires. Some sheets ruled in large squares. Written in gothic cursiva currens of uneven quality in 36 to 57 long lines, probably by one hand. Occasional headings in red in the beginning of the book. Quotations occasionally underlined in purple-red.

Bound in boards of the fifteenth century, very similar to Leiden, University Library MS BPL 2794, also from Erfurt Charterhouse. Back-to-front clasp wanting; rebacked and front board restored (oak), c. 1900. Traces of a front pastedown of a Latin text of the fourteenth century visible beneath modern paper. Spine title, "Loci communes theologiae." Pink stained leather index tabs of the fifteenth century.

Written in Erfurt by Johannes Hagen, prior of the Carthusian monastery of Mons salvatoris [*DHGE* 15:708–9], as indicated by rewritten fragments inserted following ff. 197 and 226, in 1460, this date appearing on ff. 155 and 278. Choice of texts corresponds closely to the inventory of study notes left by Johannes Hagen; see Klapper, *Johannes Hagen* 2:124–25. This codex recorded as "C142" in the late fifteenth-century inventory of the Carthusian Library at Erfurt, *Mittelalterliche Bibliothekskataloge Deutschlands* 2:428–29. Acquired by the Newberry in 1959 from Ifan Kyrle Fletcher (London).

Second folio: xii spiritus (?).

f68

Commentary on the *Decretales,* Books I and II

France — s. XV med.

ff. 1–204 (Begins imperfectly) bone memorie et cetera. Presbiter cardinalis postulandus est . . . (f. 77) Incipit secundus liber decretalium de Iudiciis. De Quouultdeo et cetera. Construitur hic littera et exponitur et secundum unam litteram ponitur hic casus pro casu . . . deo patriarche reuerenciam et obedienciam exhibere curetis et de suis iusticiis respondere. Explicit liber secundus.

Occasional marginal notes, s. xv. ff. 74v–76v and 205v–206v blank.

Unidentified commentary on the *Decretales,* I, 5, iii–II, 30, ix (last lemma, *Sua nobis*). A reference to Godfredus de Trano on f. 39.

Paper bearing a Y watermark, cf. Briquet 9173–85. ff. 206. Trimmed to 280 × 200 mm (195 × 150 mm).

Collation impracticable. Catchwords mostly removed. Traces of alphabetical leaf signatures visible on some rectos, a second sequence by a different hand visible on some versos beginning with Book II. Frame ruled in very light pencil. Written in gothic cursiva media in 39–44 long lines. f. 77, heading and incipit in *lettre bâtarde*. Running headings in script of text, underlined in red in upper outer margins. Alternating red and blue minor initials.

Bound in modern blue marble paper over pasteboard, quarter bound in blue calf. Spine title: *Decretales libri II* in gold.

Written in France in the middle of the fifteenth century. No. 616 in the collection of Joseph Barrois; "616" written on a faded green circular sticker on spine, same number on verso of front flyleaf. Sold to Lord Ashburnham in 1849, recorded *Catalogue of the Manuscripts at Ashburnham Palace* (London, 1862); *Eighth Report of the Royal Commission on Historical Manuscripts,* Appendix, part 3 (London, 1861), p. 96. Sold at Sotheby's 10 June 1901, lot no. 155; "155" written in blue crayon within a circle on verso of first front flyleaf; partially obscured by a clipping from a later English sales catalogue listing this book as item 1150; in the lower right, "494" in pencil with a cipher beneath it. On the Ashburnham sale, see De Ricci, *English Collectors,* p. 134. Acquired by the Newberry as a gift from George B. Utley, 1946.

Second folio: archiepiscopalis officii plenitudo.

+69
(23862)
Carthusian Missal

Spain after 1461

1. ff. i–vi verso Carthusian calendar with major feasts entirely or partially in red. Feasts include: sancti Thome de Aquino (7 March), Benedicti abbatis. Candele (21 March, in red), Ugonis episcopi et confessoris. XII lectiones (1 April, in red), Catherine uirginis de Senis (6 May), Anne matris domine nostre (26 July), Hugonis episcopi et confessoris. Candele (17 November, in red), Lini pape et martiris (26 November), Agricole et Uitalis (27 November), conceptio beate Marie. Candele (8 December, "conceptio" written over an erasure, "candele" in red).

2. ff. 2–140 Temporal beginning imperfectly in second Sunday of Advent ending with the twenty-fifth Sunday after Pentecost.

3. f. 140–140v Gloria and Credo with notes.

4. ff. 141–145v Ten noted prefaces: In natiuitate domini, In epiphania, In quadragesima, In resurrectione, De ascenssione, In pentecostem, De trinitate, De apostolis, De beata Maria, Sancte Crucis.

5. ff. 147–152 Ordinary and Canon of the Mass beginning imperfectly.

f. 152v blank.

6. ff. 153–200v Proper of Saints, Stephan through Thomas the Apostle. f. 198, "Hugonis episcopi," 11–23 November.

7. ff. 200v–202 Incipit comune sanctorum . . . (in red).

8. ff. 202–203 In aniuersario dedicationis (in red).

9. ff. 203–210 Votive masses: Pro pace et uictoria christianorum, Pro loco, Pro familiaribus, Per generalis, Pro prelatis, Pro papa uel pro episcopo, Pro amicis, Alia pro amicis, Pro familiaribus, Pro infirmo, Pro iter agentibus, Pro pace, Pro quacumque tribulatione, Item alia in tribulatione, Pro pace sancte ecclesie, Pro rege, In tempore belli, Contra paganos, Pro salute uiuorum, Pro mortalitate sedanda, Pro sacerdote propria (three Masses), Ad lacrimas postulandas (two Masses), Pro peccatis, Pro temptatione carnis, Ad gratiam sancti spiritus pro merenda, Ad malas cogitationes uitandas, Ad diligendum deum, Ad impetrandam pacientiam, Pro peste animalium, Pro pluuia, Pro serenitate, Contra tempestates.

10. ff. 210–214v Masses of the Dead: Ad offitium deffunctorum, Pro deffuncto, Pro pluribus deffunctis, Pro aniuersario, Alia pro sacerdote uel episcopo, Pro fratribus, Pro benefactoribus, Pro pluribus defunctis, Pro muliere, Pro sepultis in cimiterio, Pro patre et matre, Pro tranquilitate ecclesie, Alia generalis.

11. ff. 214v–215v Ad honorem gloriossissime uirginis Marie.

12. ff. 215v–217v Sequitur officium beate Marie in aduentu (in red).

13. ff. 217v–218 De sancte trinitatis offitium (in red).

14. ff. 218–219 De spiritu sancto (in red). Followed by lxx[a] usque ad pascha (in red).

15. ff. 219–220 Offitium sancte crucis (in red).

16. f. 220 Pro gratiarum actione (in red).

17. ff. 220v–221v Ordo for profession of a monk followed by an ordo for the profession of a lay novice. ff. 220v–221, "Ego frater illis promitto stabilitatem et obedientiam et conuersionem morum meorum coram deo et sanctis eius et reliquiis istius heremi, que constructa est ad honorem dei et beate Marie semper uirginis et beati Iohannis baptiste in presentia donni (*sic*) ille prioris." f. 221–221v, a similar profession.

18. f. 221v (addition s. xvi) Three prayers to Catherine of Alexandria followed by three prayers to Jerome.

ff. 153, 172, 176v, 183v, bracket acanthus margins in green, orange, violet, blue, and gold. f. 153, green dragon in upper margin, exotic birds in lower margin. f. 172, face of a man in lower margin. f. 176v, parrot in upper margin, exotic bird and purple dragon below. f. 183v, exotic bird and infant in left margin. f. 210, modern pen floral decoration added. Deep blue initials with red flourishes alternating with red initials with violet flourishes.

Parchment. ff. 223. Six unfoliated leaves, followed by leaves with original foliation in red roman numerals: 2–9, 11–145, 147–158, 160–221. Folios 1, 10, 146, and 159 removed; nine other folios mutilated: 94, 112, 158, 169, 170, 171, 172, 180, and 183. 323 × 225 mm (215 × 143 mm). 1^{8} (7–8 stubs only), 2^{10} (1 and 10 wanting with loss of text), $3–15^{10}$, 16^{12} (6 wanting with loss of text), 17^{8} (7 stub only with loss of text), $18–22^{10}$, 23^{10+1}. Catchwords begin with quire 4, preceded and followed by a point. Prickings in outer margins. Ruled in brown ink. Written in Spanish textualis rotunda formata in 31 long lines. Vertical line enders characteristic of Spain. Headings in red in script of text. Canon written in same script in larger letters in 16 long lines.

Bound in stamped Spanish red-brown calf, s. xv; the decorative patterns of the four rolls show Islamic influence; one of two fore-edge clasps present. Catches engraved with the cross and an urn. Resewn with green, yellow, and red thread. Contemporary (?) finger tabs.

Written in Spain after 1461, as indicated by transalpine feast dates of calendar, script, border decorations, and binding, for a Carthusian convent, as indicated by the calendar. f. 203, a sixteenth-century corrector has added to the Suffrage to All Saints, "adque (*sic*) beati Brunonis confesoris tui." Note also reference to *prior* and *heremus* on ff. 220v–221 above. f. 203v, in the Votive Mass, "Pro generalis," the same corrector has added, "Et famulos tuos, papam, regem, reginam et principes nostros cum prole regia et nos ab omni aduersitate custodi . . ." This is the same hand that added text no. 18. It is possible that this book comes from the convent at Aniago, founded in 1441 by Mary of Aragon, wife of John II of Castile; note references to Mary and John the Baptist on ff. 220v–221 above. No. 40 from the collection of Henry Probasco, acquired by the Newberry 1 December 1890.

De Ricci, 1:528.

70.5

(55-903)

Iacopo di Poggio Bracciolini, *Commento sopra el Triumpho della Fama di Francesco Petrarca*

Florence [*Illustrated*] 1480

ff. 1–93 Nel cor pien d'amarissima dolceza . . . El popolo romano superiore pelle sue singulari et inmense virtu . . . con grandissima gloria e beniuolentia inaudita de suoi populi. Finis laus deo semper. Transcriptus per me Bassianum de Uillanis et finitus die xxiiii° Octobris 1480, hora noctis quinta.

Occasional marginal index notes and corrections by the scribe in quires 2–4.

ff. 93v–94 blank.

Hain, 12789. Dedicatory prologue to Lorenzo de Medici wanting.

Paper, thick. Quires 2–4 with watermark of an *echelle;* cf. Briquet 5910. Quires 1 and 5–11 with a crowned bull's head quite distinct from Briquet 15220 sqq. ff. 102. Foliated 1–94, preceded and followed by four unfoliated leaves. 275 × 201 mm (173 × 113 mm). 1^{4}, $2–8^{10}$, $9–10^{12}$, 11^{4}. Ruled in dry point. Vertical catchwords except on f. 40 where horizontal. ff. 1–30, written in humanistic cursiva media by one hand, in 26 long lines, beginning on the second ruled line; ff. 31–97, the same type script of slightly inferior grade by Bassianus de Villanis in 28 long lines beginning on the first ruled line. Ink varying from brown to black. See inscription in his hand on f. i in provenance section below.

Bound for the Archinto collection in green stained parchment, s. xviii. Title on spine, "Estrat[to] della Storia Romana."

ff. 1–30 written in Florence by an unknown scribe. ff. 31–93 completed outside of Florence by Bassianus de Villanis, 24 October 1480. Signed and dated on f. 94. f. i, "Hic liber est mei Bassiani de Uillanis quem manu propria scripsi exceptis primis 3 qu[at]ernis, quos portavi ex Florentia, nam dono dati fuerunt." Also on f. i, in a fifteenth-century humanistic script pen trial (?), "In quello paese e honorato da lui intendendo essere Theseo limpero dal re, per lo quale benificio tornando ad Athene tutti li templi che la citta havea." Verso front flyleaf, armorial bookplate of Count Carlo Archinto (1669–1732) of Milan, his library sold at auction in Paris on 21 March 1863. J. Gelli, *3500 ex libris italiani* (Milan, 1908), pp. 20–21, no. 1. Rear pastedown, remnants of a French customs (?) declaration, s. xix. Various pencil notes and dealer numbers on front pastedown and flyleaf. Acquired by the Newberry from Mrs. Fletcher (Wimbledon, England), 1955. Acquisition announced by H. Baron, *Newberry Library Bulletin* 4 (1956): 80–81.

Second folio: di suoni.

Faye-Bond, p. 153. Ullman, *Petrarch Manuscripts in the United States,* p. 450.

71

(23819)

Breviary of the Congregation of Saint Justina
Central Italy after 1443

1. ff. 2–7v Benedictine calendar in red and black, graded with semi-duplex and duplex feasts. Feasts include: Anniuersario patris nostri domini Ludouici [Barbi] episcopi fundatoris congregationis sancte Iustine (19 September, in red). Sancte Iustine uirginis martiris duplex maius (7 October, in red). Sancti Romani abbatis confessoris (28 February) added by another hand.

2. ff. 8–13 Incipit rubrica generalis breuiarii monastici secundum ritum et consuetudinem monachorum congregationis sancte Iustine ordinis sancti Benedicti (in red) . . . Aduentus domini semper celebrari debet . . . explicit rubrica generalis. Cf. *SMRL* 2:14–21.

3. ff. 13–17 Incipit tabula qui dicitur paresina . . . In anno illo in quo natiuitas domini, in dominica uenerit (in red) . . . Ad ix, antiphona (in red). Magnificatus. *Parisian Table of Anthems before Christmas,* given here in tabular form with added entries; cf. *SMRL* 2:401–8.

4. ff. 17–19 Incipiunt letanie secundum ordinem monachorum congregationis sancte Iustine (in red). Justina fourth among the virgins. Ends with full set of ten prayers from the Roman Breviary: Deus, qui proprium est misereri . . . , Exaudi, quesumus domine, supplicum preces . . . Ineffabilem nobis, domine, misericordiam tuam . . . , Deus cui culpa offenderis . . . , Omnipotens sempiterne deus, miserere famulo tuo . . . Deus, a quo sancta desideria . . . Ure igne sancti spiritus . . . Fidelium deus omnium conditor et redemptor . . . Actiones nostras, quesumus, domine . . . Omnipotens sempiterne deus qui uiuorum . . .

f. 19v blank.

5. f. 20 Incipiunt suffragia sanctorum quotidiana . . . (in red). Suffrages to the Virgin and Benedict.

f. 20v blank; f. 21 removed.

6. ff. 22–107 Liturgical Psalter beginning imperfectly in Psalm 6 (in the second folio of the quire) and ending with the Confiteor deo, Pater noster, Credo in deum patrem omnipotentem, special prayers and offices for Advent. Cf. Leroquais, *Psautiers* 1:iv.

7. ff. 107v–130v Canticles and hymns. f. 130v, Explicit (in red). f. 125v, hymn for feast of Justina.

f. 131 removed.

8. ff. 132–374 Proper of Time beginning imperfectly in the second folio of the quire. f. 374, Explicit tempus tocius anni (in red).

f. 374v blank; f. 375 removed.

9. ff. 376–560 Proper of Saints beginning imperfectly in Andrew through Catherine. f. 560–560v, In festo apostolorum Philippi et Iacobi (in red).

f. 561–561v blank; f. 562 removed.

10. ff. 563–605 Common of Saints beginning imperfectly in second folio of text. f. 605, Explicit commune sanctorum (in red).

11. ff. 605v–609 Incipit officium beate Marie uirginis secundum consuetudinem monachorum congregationis sancte Iustine de obseruantia (in red) . . . Explicit officium beate uirginis Marie (in red).

12. ff. 609–612 Incipit officium mortuorum . . . (in red). Cf. *GW* 5181–5186; Downside Abbey, 26526, see Ker, *Medieval Manuscripts* 2:423.

Parchment. ff. 598. Foliated with a modern flyleaf 1–612, ff. 21, 131, 375, and 562 removed after this foliation; stains on preceding versos indicate these leaves had illuminated margins and initials. f. 424, illuminated initial cut out, folio repaired. Errors in foliation: 2 folios 101, folio after f. 203 unnumbered, f. 316bis follows f. 316, unnumbered folio follows f. 373, f. 400 follows f. 389, 2 folios 428, no folio 542. 154 × 113 mm (90 × 65 mm). 1^{6+2}, 2^{10}, 3^{10} (2 wanting with loss of text), $4–11^{10}$, 12^{8}, 13^{12+1}, 14^{10} (1 wanting with loss of text), $15–28^{10}$, 29^{6}, $30–36^{10}$, 37^{8}, 38^{10}, 39^{10} (1 wanting with loss of text),

40–55[10], 56[8], 57[10] (1 wanting with loss of text), 58–60[10], 61[10 + 1]. Catchwords surrounded on four sides by a wavy line beneath a comma-like mark. Signatures of leaves mostly trimmed but traces of at least three alphabetical sequences remain. Ruled very lightly in brown ink. Written in Italian gothic textualis media with one-story a and trailing terminal s in 29 lines in two columns by three hands: ff. 2–19, 605v–612v by hand A (ruled for and written in 30 lines); f. 20 by hand B, the rest by hand C. Alternating red initials with violet flourishes and blue initials with red flourishes throughout. ff. 22–130v, simple alternating red and blue initials within sections of text. f. 502, small green, blue, and pink initials 7 lines high on gold grounds, floral decoration extending into margin. Minor initials touched with yellow.

Bound in modern blue velvet over boards.

Written in Italy, probably central Italy, as indicated by the minor initials, in the middle of the fifteenth century after 19 September 1443, date of the death of Ludovico Barbo. Old (s. xvi?) library shelf-marks: f. 423v, "592"; ff. 374 and 612, "1251." No. 10 from the collection of Henry Probasco, acquired by the Newberry 1 December 1890.

De Ricci, 1:524. Hughes, *Mass and Office,* p. 402 and pl. 6 (ff. 12v–13); pl. 25 is not from this manuscript.

72

(23834)

Francis of Meyronnes, *Commentary on Book I of the Sententiae of Peter Lombard*

Italy — s. XIV ex./XV

ff. 1–348v (begins imperfectly on the second leaf of the quire) // ergo et cetera. Confirmatur quia impossibile est adiectiuum esse sine substantiuo posito uel intellecto . . . (ends imperfectly on the penultimate leaf of the final quire) Dico ergo quod praticum addit . . . (last three lines of text illegible) //

Numbered place references in outer margin except for ff. 60–99. Marginal notes, s. xiv and xv, mostly in the first 120 leaves, primarily by two hands.

Francis of Meyronnes, *Commentary on Book I of the Sententiae of Peter Lombard,* beginning imperfectly in the *proemium* and ending imperfectly in question 49, a recension with many variants from the printed text of Hain, 10535. For other editions of s. xv–xvi and manuscripts, see Stegmüller, *Rep. in sent. Petr. Lomb.,* 218. This manuscript not recorded.

Parchment of southern preparation. ff. 348. 145 × 105 mm (95 × 74 mm). 1[10] (1 wanting), 2–34[10], 35[10] (10 wanting). Catchwords present, partially trimmed. Leaf signatures mostly trimmed. Prickings partially visible in outer margins. Ruled in ink with special columns for numbered place reference to serve as marginal index. Written in Italian gothic textualis media with one-story a; incipits in Italian gothic textualis formata with two-story a. ff. 60–69 written in humanistic cursiva formata including some gothic traits, e.g., trailing terminal s, in 36–38 lines in two columns throughout, beginning on the second ruled line. Ruled in very light pencil without column for abbreviations. Running headings in gothic and humanistic cursiva. Alternating red and blue initials and paragraph marks. ff. 1 and 348v, heavily worn.

Bound in modern red velvet over boards.

Written in Italy at the end of the fourteenth century, except for ff. 60–69, written in s. xv. Headings added in s. xv. On upper margin of f. 60, "YHS." Fifteenth-century marginal notes by an Italian hand. f. 348v, inscription, s. xvi (?), "Zinn de noculo (?)." No. 6 from the collection of Henry Probasco, acquired by the Newberry 1 December 1890.

Second folio: de deo et.

De Ricci, 1:526.

f72.1

(Ry 59-2465)

Roman Ceremonials

Italy — [*Illustrated*] — 1476–78

1. ff. 1–168 Modus qui seruari consueuit per dominos cardinales quando insistunt super electione summi pontificis et eligunt per uiam procedere compromissi (in violet). In nomine domini Amen. Anno domini et cetera die Iouis, vi die mensis talis. Nos episcopi presbyteri et diaconi sancte romanę eclesię cardinales omnes et singuli . . . prout domino uidebitur et camerario et cetera.

Roman ceremonial containing elements of a pontifical, related to Agostino Patrizi, *Rituum ecclesiasticorum . . . libri* (Venice, 1516) and his *Pontificale romanum* (Rome, 1485); Section "De diuersitate colorum quibus Romana ecclesia in sacris uestibus diuersis temporibus uti solet" (ff. 36v–53v) is exactly as in the latter work. ff. 1–28, ceremonies and liturgical ritual pertaining to the election and consecration of a pope. ff. 36v–127, the liturgical functions of the pope as bishop of Rome including imperial and royal coronation orders. ff. 28–36v and 127v–168, papal ceremonies and liturgical rituals pertaining to the cardinals. This treatise is a possible source for Patrizi's works; see V. Leroquais, *Les Pontificaux ma-*

nuscrits des bibliothèques publiques de France (Paris, 1937), 1:xxviii, n. 1.

2. ff. 168v–182 Augustinus Patricius senensis Ioanni Monelo (*sic*) Cremano salutem plurimam dicit (in violet). Et si non dubito te uel fama uulgari intellexisse . . . et non tam rem ipsam quam mentem metiri. Uale Romę, et cetera.

Agostino Patrizi, *Descriptio adventus Frederici III imperatoris ad Paulum II papam anno 1468,* ed. L. Muratori, *Rerum italicarum scriptores,* vol. 23 (Milan, 1723–51), pp. 205–16.

3. ff. 182–185v Ordo ad suscipiendum regem Dacię uenientem Romam deuotionis gratia (in violet). Primum respondeatur litteris missis per suam maiestatem . . . ut etiam recipiant eum in eclesiis suis.

Ceremony and liturgies for the arrival in Rome of King Christian I of Denmark, 1474; cf. Pastor, *History of the Popes* 4:258–60.

4. ff. 186–190 Incipit tabula rubricarum istius ordinarii secundum folia huius uoluminis (in violet).

Folios not marked. f. 190v blank.

Paper with *huchet* watermark; cf. Briquet 7682, 7697, etc. 285 × 215 mm (200 × 117 mm). ff. 190. 1–19[10]. Vertical catchwords surrounded on four sides by two points and a slash. Leaves signed a–1 through t–6. Ruled in hard point. Written in humanistic cursiva media in 30 long lines. Most headings in violet in script of text; some headings and some incipits in rustic capitals. f. 1, bracket inner blue, purple, gold, and green acanthus border, initial in same colors 6 lines high. Red initials with violet flourishes alternating with blue initials with red flourishes.

Bound in original stamped brown calf. Stamps include a net of interlaced circles within a panel, a six-pointed star repeated 22 times without. Marginal decoration formed by a roll of a four-lobed flower. Same pattern front and back. Four clasps on rear cover, one above, one below, and two on outer edge, the lower one missing the metal portion only. Catches in the shape of fleurs-de-lys.

Written in Italy, probably in Rome, between 1476 and 1478. Belonged to Pedro Ferriz, Bishop of Tarazona, created cardinal in 1476, died in 1478 (*DHGE* 16:1292). f. 1, lower margin, his arms below the hat of a cardinal with legend "Petri Ferrici cardinalis tirasonensis." Front flyleaf, bookplate: "au Comte Chandon de Briailles," in black ink: "MSS 10." Acquired by the Newberry from Lathrop Harper (New York), 30 September 1959.

Second folio: cardinalatus primo.

73
(23820)
Franciscan Breviary

Central Italy c. 1400

1. ff. 1–10v, 260–269v, 27–36v, 53–62v, 47–52v, 97–100v, 93–96v, 249–254v. Liturgical Psalter, defective and bound out of order.

2. ff. 11–21v In sancti Francisci ordinis minorum . . . (in red). Offices for thirteenth-century Franciscan feasts (Francis, Anthony of Padua, Louis IX, Clare, Ambrose), and Conception and Visitation of the Virgin Mary. Cf. Leroquais, *Bréviaires* 1:cvii–cviii.

3. ff. 21v–23v Aduentus domini celebretur . . . (entirely in red). *Rubricae generales,* ed. *SMRL* 2:114–21.

4. ff. 23v–24 Hec sunt festa semi duplica, scilicet festum sancti Nicholai, Lucie . . . (entirely in red). Rubric on feasts graded duplex minus and duplex maius, not recorded *SMRL*.

5. ff. 24–26 Prima tabula; In illo anno in quo natiuitas domini in dominica uenerit . . . (entirely in red). *Parisian Table,* ed. *SMRL* 2:401–8.

6. f. 26–26v Tabula de dominicis que [ue]niunt post pentecosten ut non erretur. In illo anno quando pasca uenerit octauo uel vii kalendas aprilis . . . (entirely in red). Tables for Sundays after Pentecost, *SMRL* 1:142n, 165, 230, 238, 244.

7. ff. 179–238v, 83–92v, 239–248v, 37–46v, 255–258v. (f. 179), Incipiunt festiuitates sanctorum . . . (in red). Proper of Saints (incomplete), beginning with Saturninus (f. 179) and ending with Catherine of Alexandria (f. 258v).

8. ff. 63–82v, 101–177. Proper of Time, bound out of sequence.

9. f. 177–177v Incipit tabula mensis septembris. In anno illo in quo mensis septembris die dominico uenerit ystorie dicti mensis sic ordinantur. Dominica prima ipsius mensis ponitur liber Iob . . . (in red).

f. 178–178v blank.

Parisian Table for the Scripture Reading of September, often attributed to Boniface VIII. *SMRL* 1:168, 181, 240, 242–44; Van Dijk, *Ordinal,* pp. 342–46.

10. f. 258v In conceptione uirginis Marie . . . (in red). Aue decus uirginum. Aue iubar

ethereum, nobis . . . (ending imperfectly with a catchword, in italics, in line 4 of the printed text) dat *perpes* // *RH* 1752.

11. f. 259 On a separate sheet, six concluding lines of an unidentified text ending, "ut Iohanes precursor domini in utero statim sanctificaretur. Explicit et cetera."

f. 259v blank.

12. ff. 270–278 Common of saints, beginning imperfectly.

13. ff. 278–282 Incipit ordo officii beate Marie . . . (in red).

14. ff. 282–284 Incipit ordo ad communicandum infirmum . . . (in red).

15. ff. 284–289 Ordo commendationis anime . . . (in red).

16. f. 289–289v Incipit officium pro defunctis particulis (*sic*) . . . (in red). f. 289v, additional *capitula* added by a later hand.

f. 1, historiated orange, blue, green, pink, and black initial on a gold ground 15 lines high showing God the Father with an open book displaying the letters alpha and omega. Also, in the right column, an initial in the same colors 12 lines high. Both initials extending to form a delicate floral border with blue, red, and green flowers, an exotic bird in lower right margin, a moth in the lower center margin. ff. 11, 62, 139v, 209, and 213, illuminated initials in the same colors 5–8 lines high.

Parchment of Italian preparation. ff. 289. Modern foliation in inner corners alone is accurate. 177 × 123 mm (110 × 76 mm). $1\text{–}2^{10}$, 3^{6}, $4\text{–}5^{10}$, 6^{6}, $7\text{–}9^{10}$, $10\text{–}11^{4}$, $12\text{–}19^{10}$, 20^{8}, $21\text{–}27^{10}$, 28^{6}, 29^{4+1}, $30\text{–}31^{10}$, 32^{8}, 33^{2}. Quires disturbed in rebinding, portions of Psalter and Proper of Saints wanting. Catchwords surrounded by four strokes. Prickings visible on outer edges. Ruled in pencil. Written in Italian gothic textualis media with one story a and trailing terminal s in 36 lines in two columns. Psalter written in very black Italian ink. Headings in red in script of text. Red initials with violet flourishes alternating with blue initials with red flourishes. Alternating red and blue minor initials. Minor initials touched with yellow.

Bound in modern green velvet over pasteboard.

Written in Italy, probably central Italy, as indicated by the minor initials, c. 1400. Brief note, s. xix, on verso of front flyleaf describes manuscript. "1361" and "11" written in pencil. No. 5 from the collection of Henry Probasco, acquired by the Newberry 1 December 1890.

Second folio: me, exurge.

De Ricci, 1:73.

+75

(23861)

Lectionary and Capitulary of the Charterhouse of San Lorenzo

Florence c. 1408

1. ff. 1–6v Carthusian calendar with major feasts in purple, green, blue, red, and brown. Feasts include: Benedicti abbatis candele (21 March, in green), Hugonis gratianopolitani episcopi et confessoris (1 April, in blue), Sancte Anne matris beate uirginis Marie (26 July, in brown, original grading erased, candele substituted, s. xvi), Brunonis confessoris (6 October, in red), Hughonis episcopi linconiensis et confessoris (17 November, in green), Sileae apostoli (28 November, erased). Additions, s. xv and s. xvi by several hands: Nominis Iesu (14 January, in red), Cathedra sancti Petri Romę missa et Priscę uirginis et martiris (18 January), Thomę de Aquino iii lectiones (7 March, in red), Catherinae de Senis uirginis iii lectiones et missa (6 May), 1443 Obiit reuerendissimus dominus dominus Nicolaus presbiter cardinalis titulus sanctę crucis (9 May = Niccolò Albergati, his tomb in the Charterhouse of San Lorenzo, see below f. 193), Zenobii episcopi florentini commemoratio iii lectiones (25 May), Sileae apostoli (13 July), Bonauenturę episcopi et confessoris xii lectiones (14 July, in red), Nicolai de Tolentino confessoris xii lectiones (10 September, in red), ✠ 1400 obiit dominus Luchinus de comitibus, magnus benefactor domus nostrę (30 September).

Blank, unnumbered modern folio inserted after f. 6.

2. ff. 7–9 Exorcismus salis (in red).

Office for the benediction of salt and water as in MS 59.1, text 2, and MS 77, text 11.

f. 9v blank; f. 10 removed.

3. ff. 11–101 Lessons for the Proper of Time for the Mass, very similar to the use of Rome (cf. *SMRL* 2:207–70), beginning imperfectly and ending with the twenty-fifth Sunday after Advent. f. 87v, lesson titled "Ad missam."

f. 101v blank.

4. ff. 102–116v [I]ncipiunt epistole de festiuitatibus sanctorum (in red).

Lessons for the Proper of Saints from Anthony the Abbot through Thomas the Apostle, ending with "In dedicatione ecclesie," for the Mass, but only remotely resembling the use of Rome. One lesson for each saint with many cross-references, with indication of folio, to the Common of Saints and the Votive Masses (texts 5 and 6, below).

5. ff. 117–118v Incipit comune sanctorum (in red).

Lessons for the Common of Saints with a cross-reference from the Common of Martyrs to the lesson for Thomas of Canterbury on f. 20v.

6. ff. 119–120 Epistole in missis mortuorum (in red); In missis de domina (in red); In missis de cruce (in red); In missis uotiuis de sanctissima trinitate (addition s. xvi, in red); In missis de beata Maria in aduentu.

f. 120v blank.

7. ff. 121–125v Noted litany. f. 123, Jerome, "Hugo," and Bruno inserted in small letters among the confessors.

8. f. 126–126v Lectio epistole beati Pauli apostoli, ad Romanos, ad Corinthios, . . . ecclesiastici, libri genesis . . .

Common tones for the epistles.

f. 127–127v blank; f. 128 removed.

9. ff. 129–135v *Capitula* of the Common of Time for the canonical hours, beginning imperfectly.

10. ff. 135v–140 Incipiunt capitula festiua (in red).

Capitula from the Proper of Saints for the canonical hours. f. 140, In dedicatione ecclesie (in red).

11. ff. 140–142v Incipit comune sanctorum (in red).

Capitula of the Common of Saints for the canonical hours.

12. ff. 143–165 Incipiunt orationes per anni circulum (in red).

Orationes of the Common of Time for the canonical hours.

13. ff. 165–180v Incipiunt orationes sanctorum per anni circulum (in red).

Orationes of the Proper of Saints for the canonical hours. Additions s. xv: f. 167v, cross-reference from Joseph to f. 186; f. 175v, *oratio* for Nicolaus de Tolentino.

14. ff. 180v–184v Incipiunt orationes comunes sanctorum (in red).

Orationes of the Common of Saints for the canonical hours.

15. ff. 184v–186v Commemorationes ad laudes . . . (in red).

Suffrages to the Cross (ad laudes), Mary, John the Baptist, Lawrence, All Saints, the Cross (ad uesperas), a second prayer to Mary, a second prayer to John the Baptist, a second prayer to Lawrence, a second prayer to All Saints, and a third prayer to All Saints (in aduentu). Additions s. xv: Catherine, Bruno, Catherine of Siena, Januarius, Joseph (two prayers).

16. ff. 187–204v Obituary calendar prepared with the book for recording eventual deaths and left blank. Notices to 1479 all by one fifteenth-century hand. f. 202, 8 November: "1366 obiit dominus Nicola de Acciaiuolis magnus seneschalchus regni Ierusalem et Sicilie qui fecit hedificari istud monasterium et ipsum dotauit." On Niccolò Acciaiuoli, see *DBI* 1:87–90. f. 194, 31 May: "1408 obiit reuerendissimus dominus dominus Angelus de Acciaiuolis . . ." On Angelo Acciaiuoli, see *DBI* 1:77. f. 193, 9 May: "1443 obiit reuerendissimus dominus dominus Nicola presbyter cardinalis tituli sancte ✠ qui in hac domo sua elegit sepulturam et donauit bibliam pulcerrimam et alia queddam librorum uolumina." This bible of Cardinal Niccolò Albergati cited by Vespasiano, *Memoirs* 3:3, as having cost 500 ducats. It was sold at the Chester Beatty sale, Sotheby's, 24 June 1969. For a description of this codex, see E. G. Millar, *The Library of A. Chester Beatty* (Oxford, 1927–30), 2:232–40 and plates 185–88. See also *DBI* 1:619–21 and P. de Toth, *Il beato cardinale Nicola Albergati e i suoi tempi 1375–1444* (Viterbo, s.d.), 1:481, n. 3. f. 196v, 18 July: "1479 obiit dominus Nicolaus de Corbicis canonicus maioris ecclesie Florentie (change of ink, possibly of hand) magnus benefactor huius monasterii pro quo multa bona nobis deuenerunt, precipue multa uolumina librorum, omnes uidelicet quos habebat qui excedunt lx^{m} numerum . . ." f. 188, 29 January: "1483 obiit dominus Franciscus de Pisis, monachus professus huius domus antiquior qui scripsit manu sua plures libros in uulgari ex sua sollicitudine ac uigilantia." For three manuscripts copied by Francesco da Pisa, see *Colophons de manuscrits occidentaux*, 4360–62.

17. Rear flyleaf, verso (additions s. xv) Verses from psalms 23–25.

Historiated magenta, yellow, blue, and green acanthus leaf initials on gold grounds 4–5 lines high extended to form blue and green acanthus spray outer bracket borders decorated with pink, blue, and yellow flowers. f. 140v, three apostles; f. 143, a Carthusian friar in prayer, his face badly worn; f. 155, Andrew; f. 181, Jesus with a closed book. ff. 1, 17v, 18, 67, and 129–185, numerous similar initials with blue and magenta interiors decorated with gold dentelle patterning, many also decorated with flowers 3–8 lines high. Those with flowers in the interior extended to form piece acanthus spray borders, also decorated with flowers. f. 162v, an initial with a gold chalice and white host in the interior. Red and blue minor initials with intricate flourishes in red, blue, violet, and painted gold throughout. Minor initials washed with yellow.

Parchment. ff. ii + 202 + ii. Foliated 1–204, ff. 10 and 128 removed, stub of f. 10 with traces of floral border still present. 320 × 234 mm (217 × 163 mm). 1^{6}, 2^{4} (4 wanting), 3^{10} (1, a numbered leaf, stub only with possible loss of text), $4–13^{10}$, 14^{18}, 15^{10} (1 removed with possible loss of text), $16–19^{10}$, 20^{10} (10 wanting), 21^{18}. Catchwords surrounded by pen flourish designs. Ruled in pen: quire 1 in 32 long lines, quires 2–19 in 21 lines in two columns, quire 20 in 50 long lines. Front pastedown and front and first rear flyleaves ruled as the text. Quires 2–13 and 15–19 written in Italian gothic rotunda formata in very black Italian ink in 21 lines in two columns; quire 6 written in the same script in 6 lines in two columns; remaining lines used for musical notation on six red four-line staves which do not follow the original ruling. Headings in red in script of text. Cross-reference to folios in blue ink.

Bound in gold-stamped brown morocco, s. xvii, five bosses front and back. Two fore-edge clasps wanting. Traces of an old parchment spine title: "Caret [illegible]?"

Written in Florence, c. 1408, date on which the feast of Anne was accepted by the Carthusian order, see ff. 1–6v above, for the Carthusian monastery of San Lorenzo in Galluzzo near Florence [Cottineau, I, 1158], founded by Niccolò Acciaiuoli, see above, f. 202. Note Lawrence twice among the suffrages. Calendar, litany, and additions to the Proper of Saints are clearly Carthusian. Second rear flyleaf verso, "magnus" written in an eighteenth-century hand. Carthusian obituaries entered through the seventeenth century. Entries for s. xviii and s. xix appear to be for popes and other non-Carthusians, last entry on f. 193, death of Pius VI, 10 May 1879 (*sic*). Verso of front flyleaf, brief description of this book, possibly by a dealer, dated 1805; below, "Cosimo duca dei Cosmè Ferrarese" written by a modern hand. No. 39 from the collection of Henry Probasco, acquired by the Newberry 1 December 1890.

De Ricci, 1:528.

75.1

(62-2462)

Feo Belcari, *Laudi* and *Sonetti*

Italy s. XV^{2}

1. ff. 1–2 (begins imperfectly on the first leaf of the quire)

// Spirito sono e semplice natura . . .
et pagomi del mio preçço infinito. Deo gratias.

Belcari, *Laude spirituali* (Florence, 1863), p. 1, no. 1, beginning in line 6. Tenneroni, *Inizii*, p. 90.

2. ff. 2–3 Come el figliuolo di dio in croce si lamenta del peccatore (in brown).

Tanta pieta mi tira e tant'amore . . .
a'me che son per te morto et piagato. Deo gratias.

Laude spirituali, pp. 1–2.

3. f. 3–3v Come el peccatore conforta se medesimo a pensare all'altra uita (in brown).

S'i pensassi a' piacer del paradiso . . .
(ends imperfectly on the last leaf of the first half of the quire) destat'adunque et pensa ll'altra uita.

Laude spirituali, p. 2, ending with line 32. Tenneroni, *Inizii*, p. 243.

4. f. 4 (begins imperfectly on the first leaf of the second half of the quire)

// Sperando fruir te infinit amore . . .
Sien tutti pien del tuo perfect'amore. Deo gratias.

La sopra scripta laude si canta come leggiadra damigella et come molto m'annoia dello mio messere.

Laude spirituali, pp. 4–5, no. 8, beginning in line 18. Tenneroni, *Inizii*, p. 117.

5. ff. 4–5v Laude di sancto Niccolo di Lytia decto sancto Niccolo di Bary (in brown).

Auendo cuor tutti pien di letitia . . .
et chi uuol gratia prenda su'amicitia. Deo gratias.

La sopra scripta laude si canta come Do che e quel che dentro a'me uanpeggia.

Laude spirituali, pp. 18–19.

6. ff. 5v–7v Laude di sancto Sebastiano (in brown).

Con ogni reuerentia . . .
riceue gratia per la tua clementia. Deo gratias.

La sopra scripta laude se canta come Piangente con Maria et come euangeli della quaresima.

Laude spirituali, pp. 19–20. Tenneroni, *Inizii*, p. 86.

7. ff. 7v–9 Lettera mandata a uno che si uoleua fare religioso (in brown).

O anima che'l mondo uuo' fugire . . .
d'esser in questa uita affaticato. Deo gratias.

La sopra decta si canta come Si fortemente son tracto d'amore.

Laude spirituali, p. 5. Tenneroni, *Inizii*, p. 166.

8. ff. 9–11v Euangelio delle beatitudini exposto (in brown).

Ogniun con puro core . . .
uedrete la mia faccia con dolçore. Deo gratias.

Cantasi come euangeli di quaresima et come Piangete con Maria.

Laude spirituali, p. 6. Tenneroni, *Inizii*, p. 181.

9. f. 11v ✠ Laude di nostra donna (in brown).

Giammai laudarti quanto degna se' . . .
ch'a llui ritorni con dirįcto pe'. Deo gratias.

Cantasi come Jamais tant que ie vous revoie.

Laude spirituali, p. 7. Tenneroni, *Inizii*, p. 117.

10. ff. 12–16v Cantico d'uno seculare padre di famiglia, della sua criminale stultitia (in brown).

Udite matta paççia . . .
Sanami de tal paççia. Deo gratias.

La sopra decta paççia si canta come Se non mi pare e cortesia.

Laude spirituali, pp. 146–47, no. 303, and pp. 143–44, no. 299. Tenneroni, *Inizii*, p. 253. This version is much longer than the two printed laudi, which end on f. 14, line 16. The unprinted section begins, "Prima si uuole el ben fare . . ."

11. ff. 16v–19v Laude della sancta stultitia (in brown).

Mosso da sancta paççia . . .
e a tua madre Maria. Deo gratias.

Cantasi come Se non mi pare e cortesia.

A laude attributed to Belcari by other manuscripts. Tenneroni, *Inizii*, p. 157.

12. ff. 19v–21 Laude della natiuita de Christo (in brown).

Facciam festa et giulleria . . .
se non t'ama tutta uia. Deo gratias.

La sopra scripta laude si canta come Se non mi pare et come Uerbum caro.

Laude spirituali, p. 105. Tenneroni, *Inizii*, p. 110.

13. ff. 21–22 Come el pensare a benefici di dio accende l'anima al diuino amore (in brown).

Quanto piu penso dio . . .
alla tua deita. Deo gratias.

Cantasi come Quanto piu penso amore alla tua nobilta.

Laude spirituali, pp. 46–47. Tenneroni, *Inizii*, p. 224.

14. f. 22–22v Meditatione di quello che Christo diceua con la mente sua a' giudei quando portaua la croce (in brown).

O insensata gente, acerba et cruda . . .
e questa cruda spinosa corona. Deo gratias.

Ed. Delucchi, *Alcune laudi inedite*, pp. 23–24.

15. ff. 22v–23v Come el seruire a dio dilecta l'anima (in brown).

Chi serue a dio con purita di core . . .
che fa giocondo ogni suo seruidore. Deo gratias.

Cantasi come O crucifixo che nel cel dimori et come Uiuo per te signor col cor sincero et come Amar non uo'te mondo pien di guai.

Laude spirituali, p. 7. Tenneroni, *Inizii*, p. 77.

16. ff. 23v–24 Laude dell'amor diuino (in brown).

Chi non cerca Iesu con mente pia . . .
per esser alfin messo in buona uia. Deo gratias.

Cantasi come Chi guasta l'altrui cose fa uillania.

Laude spirituali, pp. 7–8. Tenneroni, *Inizii*, p. 7.

17. f. 24–24v Del dolçe amor di Iesu (in brown).

Cantar uo' del dolç'amore . . .
(ends imperfectly on the eighth leaf of the quire) non disia causa mortale //

Delucchi, *Alcune laudi inedite*, pp. 14–15, ending in line 26. Tenneroni, *Inizii*, p. 73.

18. f. 25–25v (begins imperfectly on the tenth leaf of the quire)

// dell'uom ch'è facto degno . . .
con dolce canto e piu leggiadro stile. Deo gratias.

Cantasi come O rosa mia gentile et come O donna del mio core.

f. 25 (addition s. xvi) alle Maria.

Laude spirituali, p. 8, no. 14, beginning on line 11.

19. ff. 25v–26 Laude di nostra donna (in brown).

Genitrice di dio . . .
tutto mi dolga del mal ch'o fact'io (?). Deo gratias.

Cantasi come Regina del cor mio.

Laude spirituali, p. 8. Tenneroni, *Inizii*, p. 115.

20. ff. 26–27v Laude di nostra donna (in brown).

Madre uergine, sposa, amica, et figlia . . .
et ponga a sensi uirtuosa briglia. Deo gratias.

Laude spirituali, p. 9. Tenneroni, *Inizii,* p. 150.

21. ff. 27v–29 Laude di nostra donna (in brown).

Adnuntiata pel diuin consiglio . . .
da gloria et fama alla cipta del giglio. Deo gratias.

Queste due laude sopra scripte si cantano cone (*sic*) Madre che festi, et Furon facte per la adnuntiata de' serui.

Laude spirituali, pp. 9–10. Tenneroni, *Inizii,* p. 60.

22. f. 29–29v Laude di nostra donna (in brown).

Merçe te chiamo uergina Maria . . .
libera me pel tuo figliuol messia. Deo gratias.

Cantasi come merçe ti chiamo, dolçe anima mia.

Laude spirituali, p. 10. Tenneroni, *Inizii,* p. 54.

23. ff. 29v–31 Dell'amor diuino (in brown).

I' sento 'l buon Iesu dentro dal core . . .
la carita del mio dolçe signore. Deo gratias.

Cantasi come I' ueggio ben ch'amor m'e traditore.

Laude spirituali, p. 10. Tenneroni, *Inizii,* p. 128.

24. f. 31–31v Laude di nostra donna (in brown).

Dolce preghiera mia . . .
a chi con grande humilita le disia. Deo gratias.

Cantasi come O cançonecta mia.

Laude spirituali, pp. 11–12. Tenneroni, *Inizii,* p. 101.

25. ff. 32–33 Laude di sancto Bernardino (in brown).

Qualunque sente dell'amor diuino . . .
per chi ricorre a llui col pensier fino. Deo gratias.

Cantasi come Madre che festi et cetera.

Laude spirituali, p. 12. Tenneroni, *Inizii,* p. 221.

26. f. 33–33v Laude del paradiso (in brown).

I' rendo laude et gratie al sommo sire . . .
in questo puncto et poi al mio finire. Deo gratias.

Laude spirituali, p. 12. Tenneroni, *Inizii,* p. 221.

27. ff. 33v–37 Lodato sia Iesu Christo; Laude del beato Giouanni Colombini (in brown).

O beato Giouanni Iesuato . . .
et goderete ogni ben operato. Finis.

(In outer margin) Cantasi come Nella bellezza del sommo splendore.

f. 37v blank.

Laude spirituali, pp. 12–13. Tenneroni, *Inizii,* p. 167.

28. f. 38 Della nobilta dell'anima (in brown).

Alma che cerchi pace infra la guerra . . .
cercando dio ch'ogni piacer contene. Deo gratias.

Lanza, *Lirici,* p. 211.

29. f. 38v Del riccho auaro (in brown).

Con grande industria e con sottile indagine . . .
e su si mecte el corpo in tra la porpora. Deo gratias.

Lanza, *Lirici,* p. 212.

30. f. 39 Del riccho liberale (in brown).

Chi con uirtu sopra tesoro imperia . . .
la roba manda el buon Iesu ringratia. Deo gratias.

Lanza, *Lirici,* p. 212.

31. f. 39v Pheo Belcari a Giouanni di Mariotto Stecchuti (in brown).

Per non por freno al nostro primo fomite . . .
delle uirtu sequendo'l sancto studio. Deo gratias.

Lanza, *Lirici,* p. 213.

32. f. 40 Pheo Belcari, che si duole de paççi maluagi ch'anno la paççia nel cuore (in brown).

Cercato ho sempre uiuere in concordia . . .
ma sol la força e lor saluteuole. Deo gratias.

Lanza, *Lirici,* p. 213.

33. f. 40v Antonio Calçiuolo a Feo Belcari (in brown).

O eleuato ingegno immenso e diuo . . .
et a tte fama et gloria in mille carte. Deo gratias.

Lanza, *Lirici,* p. 214.

34. f. 41 Risposta di Feo (in brown).

L'honor che tu mi fai tanto eccessiuo . . .
quando aro ben del dire in uersi l'arte. Deo gratias.

Lanza, *Lirici,* p. 214.

35. f. 41v Franchesco del maestro Andrea a Feo Belcari (in brown).

Spirito suppremo pien di gentileçça . . .
[illegible] si puo saluare.

Lanza, *Lirici*, pp. 214–15.

36. f. 42 Risposta di Feo (in brown).

Certo mi rendo che la tua riccheçça . . .
dei magni santi il sommo cel donare. Deo gratias.

Lanza, *Lirici*, p. 215.

37. f. 42v Maestro Antonio di Guido a Feo Belcari (in brown).

Frondosa testa [illegible] natura . . .
[illegible] non peccaua. Deo gratias.

Lanza, *Lirici*, pp. 215–16.

38. f. 43 Risposta di Feo (in brown).

La sacrosancta degna alma scriptura . . .
carn immortale e'n gratia il confirmaua. Deo gratias.

Lanza, *Lirici*, p. 216.

39. f. 43v Francescho di Macteo Orafo a Feo Belcari (in brown).

Quel sol che 'n fra mortal lume resplende . . .
d'original peccato fu concetto. Deo gratias.

Lanza, *Lirici*, p. 216.

40. f. 44 Feo Belcari a Giou[anni] di Cosmo (*sic*, in brown).

Se tra' nomi excellenti io bene annouero . . .
per driççar gli erranti al sommo culmine.

Lanza, *Lirici*, p. 217.

41. f. 44v Trachalo da Rimino a Giouan[ni] di Cosimo de' Medici (in brown).

Poi che [illegible] . . .
che la diriççi per piu l[i]eta uia. Deo gratias.

Lanza, *Lirici*, p. 221.

Parchment. ff. 44. An undetermined number of folios missing at the beginning, after f. 3, and probably at the end. Severe water damage at the end, considerable portions of text illegible even under ultraviolet light. 218 × 148 mm (138 × 70 mm). 1^6 (central portion of quire missing), 2^{10}, 3^{10} (9 wanting with loss of text), 4^{10}, 5^6, 6^4 (4 wanting). Catchwords present. Ruled in hard point for 25 lines. Written in humanistic textualis formata in 20–25 long lines beginning on the first ruled line. Spaces between words omitted with notable frequency. Headings in script of text in brown ink which was probably violet when written.

Bound in modern quarter morocco over pasteboard.

Written in Italy, probably in Florence during the lifetime of Belcari (d. 1484). Front pastedown, pencil note by an American or English hand: "Raffaello Uccelli, Firenze giugno 1925 costa L. 200.00." Acquired by the Newberry from H. P. Kraus, 1962.

Second folio: et pagomi.

75.5

(51-1748)

Antoninus of Florence,
Summa Confessionum; etc.

Parma [*Illustrated*] 1466

1. ff. 1–49v Tractatus utilis sed compendiosus reuerendissimi patris fratris Antonini ordinis predicatorum; Nunc autem episcopi archiepiscopi florentini feliciter incipit prologus (in red). Defecerunt scrutantes scutinio, psalmo lxiii. Scrutinium quoddam est confessio, in qua et penitens scrutatur conscientiam suam et confessor cum eo . . . et hoc personis clare declarandum est. Finis. Laus omnipotenti deo clementissimo semper. Iohanes Malgarius de Parma scripsit anno domini nostri Iesu Christi M° cccc° lxvi°.

ff. 50–51v blank.

Antoninus, *Summa confessionum* (longer recension). *GW* 2088 and 2101. Kaeppeli, 256; this manuscript unrecorded. Orlandi, *Bibl. Ant.* 2:313–19. Bloomfield, *Incipits*, 1502.

2. ff. 52–55 Che cosa e peccato mortale (in red). Peccato mortale e una uoluntaria deliberata auersione da dio . . . in uno solo acto de uolunta o de opera.

ff. 55v–56v blank.

Italian translation of scholastic definitions of sin, citing Augustine, Alexander of Hales, Bonaventure, Thomas Aquinas, etc.

3. ff. 57–102v Interrogatione le quale prima se debeno fare che si domanda de gli peccati mortali (in violet). Domandi prima al penitente si alpertene a sua iurisditione . . . tale cose non po corregere debe lassare tale cura del monasterio, chuom se lege de sancto Benedetto. Finis (in violet).

Unidentified manual for a confessor, in Italian.

4. f. 103 (addition s. xv) Outline, in Latin, of three theological and four cardinal virtues, seven corporal and seven spiritual works of mercy, seven sacraments, and seven gifts of the Holy Ghost, cf. MS −66, f. 161v.

ff. 103v–104v blank.

Parchment of southern preparation. ff. 104. 150 × 105 mm (85–100 × 65 mm). 1–5[10], 6[6], 7–10[10], 11[8]. Ruled in pen. ff. 1–49v, written in humanistic textualis media with many gothic traits in 29 long lines beginning irregularly on the first and on the second ruled line. Incipits and proper names in capitals; headings in red in script of text. ff. 52–55, in humanistic textualis media in 32 lines in two columns in black, typically Italian ink beginning on the first ruled line. ff. 57–102v, in humanistic cursiva media in 28 long lines beginning on the first ruled line. Headings in rustic capitals in violet. f. 103, addition in humanistic cursiva formata by a later hand in very black ink. f. 1, gold initial with red flourishes 8 lines high. ff. 1v–19v, alternating minor red initials with violet flourishes and blue initials with red flourishes. ff. 57–102v, red initials with violet flourishes.

Bound in dark brown morocco over pasteboard, s. xix, signed by R. de Coverley.

Written in Italy. ff. 1–49v in Parma, by Johannes Malgarius de Parma in 1466, signed and dated on f. 49v; cf. *Colophons de manuscrits occidentaux,* 10871. Other sections possibly written somewhat later. Acquired by the Newberry in 1951 from an unrecorded source.

Second folio: inde est, quod.

Faye-Bond, pp. 153–54.

76
(23874)
Hieronymite Breviary

Central Italy [*Illustrated*] 1471–84

1. ff. 1–12v Ungraded calendar of the Roman court (1260), cf. *SMRL* 2:365–76, with additions, many from northern Italy. Major feasts in red. Feasts include: Sancti Herculani episcopi et martiris (1 March), Sancti Uincentii confessoris ordinis predicatorum (6 April), Sancti Petri martiris (29 April), Sancti Ubaldi episcopi et confessoris (16 May), Sancti Bernardini confessoris (20 May), Sancti Antonii confessoris (13 June, in red), Sancte Marie ad Niues (5 August, in red), Sancti Augustini episcopi et doctoris (in red) et sancti Hermetis martiris (28 August), Sancti Nicolai de Tolentino (10 September), Sancti Hieronymi presbyteri (30 September, in red), Sancti Francisci confessoris et sancti Petronii episcopi et confessoris (4 October), Sancti Sauni episcopi et martiris (30 October), Sancte Helysabeth uidue (19 November), Sancti Syri episcopi et confessoris (9 December).

2. f. 13–13v Ymnus iste scilicet, Primo dierum̄ dicitur in dominicis diebus a kalendis octobris usque ad auentum (*sic*) domini . . . (in red), Primo dierum omnium, quo mundus extat conditus . . . *RH* 15450. (f. 13v) Iste due (*sic*) ymni sequentes dicitur (*sic*) ab octaua pentecostes usque ad kalendas octobris dominicis diebus ad nocturnum et ad laudes (in red). Nocte surgentes uigilemus omnes semper in psalmis . . . *RH* 12035. Second hymn not present, cues for nocturnal antiphons and psalms follow.

3. ff. 14–145 Liturgical Psalter.

4. f. 145–145v Ymnus quem angeli cantauerunt quando dominus natus est (in red). Gloria in excelsis deo . . . For this and texts 5–7 below, see Leroquais, *Psautiers* 1:lv.

5. f. 145v Oratio dominica (in red). Pater noster qui es in celis . . .

6. ff. 145v–146 Isti sunt duodecim articuli de fide, quos fecerunt apostoli duodecim (in red). Credo in deum patrem, creatorem celi et terre . . .

7. f. 146–146v Secundus (in red). Credo in unum deum, patrem omnipotentem, factorem celi et terre . . .

8. ff. 146v–150 Incipiunt [li]tanie feliciter (in red). Followed by the standard ten short prayers as in the Roman breviary. f. 149v, prayer 5 begins: Omnipotens sempiterne deus miserere famulo tuo Francisco pontifice nostro (i.e., Sixtus IV, Francesco della Rovere) . . .

9. f. 150–150v (addition by two hands) Unidentified office, [U]enite ascendamus ad montem domini . . . Not recorded *SMRL*.

10. ff. 151–167v In dominica prima de aduentu domini ad uesperas hymnus (in red). Hymnal as in the Roman breviary through the feast of Michael; hymn for the feast of George the Martyr substituted for the remainder.

11. ff. 168–216v Incipit commune sanctorum secundum romanam curiam (in red).

12. ff. 216v–222 In dedicatione ecclesie (in red).

13. ff. 222–223 In festo uisitationis beate Marie uirginis ad uesperas ymnus (in red). Prayers for vespers, matins, and lauds are given in this and remaining texts.

14. ff. 223–224v In sancti Uiti martiris (in red).

15. ff. 224v–225 In festo sancte Moniche (in red).

16. ff. 225–226v In conuersione sancti Augustini episcopi (in red).

17. ff. 226v–227v In festo prime translationis sancti Augustini episcopi (in red).

18. ff. 227v–228v In secunda translatione sancti Augustini que celebratur die ultima februarii (in red).

19. ff. 228v–229v In sancte Anne matris uirginis Marie (in red).

20. ff. 229v–230v In sancte Marthe uirginis (in red).

21. f. 230v In sancti Hieronymi presbyteri et confessoris (in red). Ends imperfectly. Catchword erased. Finis deo written in an early modern Italian hand.

f. 13, blue, green, and violet initial on a gold ground historiated with a red poppy 4 lines high; f. 14, initial in same colors 8 lines high. Full Ferrara style border of blue and pink flowers, acanthus, thistles, small radiating gold disks. ff. 151, 168, and passim, initials in similar but not identical style and colors. Red initials with violet flourishes alternating with blue initials with red flourishes at the beginning of sections of text. Alternating minor simple red and blue initials throughout. Headings in red. Guides to rubricator visible.

Parchment of Italian preparation, ff. 151–230 notably stiffer. ff. 230. Trimmed to 146 × 105 mm (94 × 73 mm). 1^{12}, $2–14^{10}$, 15^{8}, $16–23^{10}$. Beginning with quire 9, vertical catchwords. Ruled in pen (ff. 1–150v) and pencil and hard point (ff. 151–230v). Written in Italian gothic textualis media formata in 24 lines in two columns in very black to brown Italian ink by several hands. Headings in red in script of text.

Bound in stamped yellow-brown Italian morocco with handmade patterned endpapers as pastedowns over pasteboard, s. xviii. Two fore-edge cloth clasps wanting.

Written in Italy, possibly in central Italy, as indicated by the calendar, between 1471 and 1484, i.e., during the pontificate of Sixtus IV, see above f. 149v. Northern and central Italian saints in calendar include Herculanus (Perugia), Sabinus (Sienna), Petronius (Bologna), and Ubaldus (Perugia). The supplemental offices, texts 13–21, indicate that this Roman breviary was probably prepared for friars of the Hieronymite order; Jerome and Augustine in red in the calendar. Cf. *GW* 5141. f. 230v, possible ex libris erased and not legible under ultraviolet light. No. 27 from the collection of Henry Probasco, acquired by the Newberry 1 December 1890.

De Ricci, 1:530.

77

(23816)

Camaldolese Breviary

Central Italy c. 1463

1. f. a Calendrical table 1463–1554 with space for additions.

2. f. a^{v} Table of golden numbers and dominical numbers, movable feasts, etc.

3. ff. b–g^{v} Graded Camaldolese calendar in red and black. Sancti Romualdi abbatis (18 June, in red).

4. f. h–h^{v} Calendrical table similar to a–a^{v}.

5. f. i Diagram of a human hand with instructions in Italian for calculating dates on fingers, dated 1463, 1464, 1465.

6. f. i^{v} Benedictions (all titles in red): Ad nones (?), festiuitatibus beate Marie uirginis, In festiuitatibus sanctorum, In festiuitate unius martiris, Benedictio omnium comestibilium.

7. ff. 1–10v In nomine sanctissime Trinitatis. Incipit breuiarium secundum ordinem camalduensem (in red) . . . Ecce dies ueniunt dicit dominus. Proper of Time, initial portion only. Continuation of text missing after 10v; for the printed text, see *GW* 5191 (f. 156).

8. ff. 11–88 Liturgical Psalter, beginning imperfectly in Psalm 4 and ending with the hymn Quicunque uult saluos esse, the Pater noster, the Credo in deum, patrem et omnipotentem, and the Canticle of Moses, etc. Cf. Leroquais, *Psautiers* 1:lv.

9. ff. 88–90 Incipit letania (in red). Followed by seven prayers: Deus quam (*sic*) proprium est misereri . . . Omnipotens sempiterne deus qui facis mirabilia . . . Deus qui beatum Petrum . . . Defende, quesumus domine deus, intercedente beata et gloriosa dei genitrice Maria . . . Ure igne sancti spiritus . . . , Ineffabilem misericordiam tuam . . . Deus qui es sancorum (*sic*) tuorum splendor . . .

10. ff. 90–106 Incipit hymnarium (in red).

11. ff. 106–107 Incipit benedictio aque (in red). Office for the blessing of salt and water as in MS 59.1 and MS +75.

12. ff. 107–109 Incipit officio mortuorum (in red).

13. ff. 1–197v In nomine et indiuidue trinitatis et gloriose uirginis Marie incipit breuia-

rium secundum ordinem Camaldulensis (in blue and gold). Proper of Time (complete).

f. 198–198v blank.

14. ff. 199–321v Proper of Saints.

15. ff. 321v–340 Common of Saints.

16. ff. 340–350v Incipit ordo ad ministrandum infirmum (in red).

17. ff. 350–351 Instructions for receiving Holy Communion.

18. ff. 351–355v Tabula de adventu (in red). Quando natiuitas domini uenerit die dominico . . . Antiphona (in red) Gande (*sic*) e[t] letare.

19. ff. 355v–357v Tabula officii (in red). Cf. *GW* 5191.

20. ff. 357v–358 Benedictions (all headings in red): Benedictione (*sic*) in nocte natiuitatis domini; In circumcisione . . . In epiphanio domini benedictione (*sic*); In resurrectione domini; In ascensione domini benedictio; In pentecostes benedictio; In festo corporis Christi benedictio; In sancta Maria benedictio; In omnium sanctorum benedictio.

21. f. 358–358v Oratio pro defunctis (in red). Deus indulgentiarum, domine, da animabus famulorum famularumque tuarum quorum anniuersarium . . . *SMRL* 2:329. Quesumus, domine, ut animabus (*sic*) famulorum famularumque tuarum quorum obitus . . . *SMRL* 2:328. Deus uenie largitor et humane salutis amator, quesumus clemenciam tuam ut nostre congregationis fratres et sorores . . . *SMRL* 2:329. Deus qui nos patrem et matrem honorare . . . *SMRL* 2:329. Fidelium deus omnium condicor (*sic*) et redemptor . . . *SMRL* 2:330.

22. ff. 359–363 (addition s. xvi) Office of the Virgin.

f. 363v blank.

23. f. 364–364v (addition s. xvi) Deus propitius esto mihi peccatori, custos mei omnibus horis . . . In omni tempore et omnibus diebus uite mee, in nomine patris . . .

Leroquais, *Heures* 2:396.

f. 1, pink, blue, and green initial, historiated with what appears to be David holding a psaltery, 7 lines high; bracket floral border in same colors, in lower margin a cherub astride an erased olive wreath intended for a coat of arms. f. 1 (second numerical sequence), magenta, blue, and green initial, historiated with a half-length portrait of the Virgin (?) holding a book, 7 lines high; full border with olive leaf wreath for arms containing some gold paint, but mostly blank. ff. 11v–109v, red initials with violet flourishes alternating with blue initials with red flourishes. Minor simple red and blue alternating initials. ff. 1–355 (second numerical sequence), red initials with violet flourishes (toward the very end blue flourishes) and blue initials with red flourishes only. Minor initials touched with yellow in the second half of the manuscript.

Parchment of southern preparation, last quire paper. ff. 482. Foliated a–i (modern); 1–10, s. xvi probably from another codex; 11–109 (modern) and every tenth leaf. Medieval roman foliation 1–350, beginning on what would be f. 110 of the preceding numerical sequence. Final folios unnumbered. In the last foliation, leaf after f. 49 not numbered, no f. 179, two f. 235, and no ff. 275 and 302. 142 × 109 mm (86 × 60 mm). Second quires smaller and originally from a different book, 139 × 102 mm (76 × 60 mm). 1^{10} (1 wanting), 2^{10}, 3^{10} (1 wanting with loss of text), $4–6^{10}$, 7^{8}, $8–11^{10}$, 12^{12}, $13–31^{10}$, 32^{8}, 33^{12}, $34–47^{10}$, 48^{4}, 49^{14} (4 wanting), 50^{6}. Catchwords surrounded by four strokes except quire 2 which is in a decorated rectangle. Ruled in pencil. Written in Italian gothic textualis in 29 lines in two columns (quire 2 ruled for and written in 25 lines) by several hands with occasional evidence of humanistic influence. Ink varies from brown to very black.

Bound in rebacked dark brown Italian stamped calf over boards, s. xv. Interior of panel and outer border decorated by the same small rope motif stamp, repeated many times. Same pattern front and back. Two foreedge clasps wanting.

Written in central Italy, the decoration suggests in or near Florence c. 1463–65, dates cited in calendrical tables above, text 1. f. 358v (second numerical sequence), erased colophon in red ink under second column, illegible under ultraviolet light. In lower margin, contemporary ex libris, "Iste liber est mei Siluestrie Ioanis s[er] Francisci de Anglario" (= Anghiari, *prope* Arezzo). Another possible ex libris in lower right margin entirely illegible. No. 7 from the collection of Henry Probasco, acquired by the Newberry 1 December 1890.

De Ricci, 1:524.

77.1

(59-41)

Latin Dictionary

Germany — s. XIV med.

ff. 1–98 A (in red) Hec littera in omnibus gentibus ideo prior est quod ipsa nascentibus uocem prior apperiat, hec Papias . . . Abatis dicitur ab atis . . . Ab accidentibus . . . Abauus pater pro aui . . . Tristicia . . . Turgens . . . Triticum a tritura est . . . uulgo semen dicitur, ibidem.

Additional entries added in margins, c. 1400 by another hand, written in hybrida currens with a two-story a and a long terminal s. Index of entries added in lower margin in the beginning of the fifteenth century, by an Italian hand; guide letters through the second letter added in upper margins.

f. 98v blank.

Latin dictionary containing about 5,500 *lemmata,* drawing heavily from Papias but also citing Isidore, Cassiodorus, and others. Arranged in rough alphabetical order through the second letter with frequent violations.

Parchment; flyleaves parchment of southern preparation; f. 98, outer and lower margins removed. ff. i + 98 + i. Foliation of s. xv or xvi, mostly arabic, on verso of each folio in upper margin center. 315 × 225 mm (235 × 166 mm). $1–8^{12}$, 9^{2}. Catchwords present. Leaves of the first quire signed. Prickings visible in outer margins. Ruled in pen. Written in gothic textualis media in 45 lines in two columns. Additions in Italian hybrida currens. Marginal index in Italian cursiva media. Germanic red initials 2 lines high throughout; entry points underscored in red in text and additions.

Quarter bound in calf over fifteenth-century wooden boards. One fore-edge clasp of Italian pink leather wanting; catch in the shape of a fleur-de-lys, inscribed "Aue," the letter s below. Modern spine label, "Vetustissimum dictionarium latinum seculi xiv," a mistaken reference to Papias, the incipit of which is almost identical to this text.

Written in Germany in the middle of the fourteenth century. Additions also written in Germany in s. xiv. Marginal index written in Italy in early s. xv. f. 98v, inscription of s. xiv, "Liber fratris Philippi de Alemania" or "Alcania" followed by a cipher (perhaps a shelfmark); below, an inscription in Italian textualis rotunda, s. xiv, "Amor amoris / Anthonio de Pol de Zotte." Front flyleaf is a notarial diploma dated 25 August 1401 recording a transaction in which a piece of land is sold for 16 ducats to a woman from Vinenza, living in Chioggia: "In nomine dei eterni amen. Anno ab incarnacione domini nostri Yesu Christi millesimo quadrigentesimo primo, die uigesimo quinto mensis Augusti, indicione nona, Clugie. Testificor ego Laurencius Panerio, curie Clugie decanus, quod eodem predicto die, de mandato egregii et sapientis uiri domini Nicolai Foscari, honorabilis potestatis Clugie . . ." Signed by two notaries, Iohannes de Andre and Petrus de [illegible], a notarial *signum* below. f. 98v, inverted drawings (Italian, c. 1400) of a man and a woman, labeled Pretrus (*sic*) and Margaretha with a pen trial in the same hand (not inverted), "Pater noster in omni omnium tribulacione et a[n]gustia et in omni." Second rear flyleaf verso, an inverted inscription worn and now illegible. Front flyleaf verso, inscription, s. xvi, in very black ink, "Vetustissimum dictionarium latinum *aliisque linguis insertum,*" words in italics crossed out apparently by the same hand. Acquired by the Newberry from H. P. Kraus in 1959.

Second folio: id est diabolus priuauit penam peccatorum.

78
(23811)
Bartholomew of San Concordio alias of Pisa, *Summa de Casibus Conscientiae*

Milan [*Illustrated*] 1466

1. ff. 11–369 (begins imperfectly) // [ex]communicati alium deueniant, extra, de officio legati, excommunicantis (*Decretales,* I, 30, 9). Legatio uero . . . ut dictum est supra inuidia scilicet ii°. Finis (in red).

Unidentified marginal gloss in a humanistic script, rubricated like the text. A reader's note written by the same hand on a small rectangular scrap of paper was found loose in the book and is now on file at the Newberry.

Summa de casibus conscientiae, beginning in chapter "Absolutio II." *GW* 3450–56. Bloomfield, *Incipits,* 5052. Kaeppeli, 436.

2. ff. 369v–370 A (in red). Ac. Accurs[i]us; Al. Albertus . . . ad confirmandum ponuntur.

Alphabetical table of abbreviations which usually accompanies the *Summa de casibus conscientiae,* ed. G. Fumagalli, *Rivista delle biblioteche e degli archivi* 6 (1896): 185–88. The text is followed by the same brief note, not in the printed edition, found in MS 90.1, text 3.

3. ff. 370–374 Alphabetical table of the *lemmata* of the text.

4. ff. 374v–381v Rubrice iurisdictionis ciuilis et canonici . . . (in red). Rubrics for the corpus of civil and canon law ending imperfectly in the rubrics of book V of the *Codex.* The initial of the first noun of each rubric written in red in a column to the left of the rubrics.

Parchment of southern preparation. ff. 371. Ten folios removed at the beginning. Original arabic foliation in red ink, ff. 11–381. 158 × 110 mm (102 × 57 mm). ff. 112 and 116, repaired. Lower portions left blank on ff. 11v–118, possibly for diagrams or illuminations. 1^{10} (entirely removed), $2–39^{10}$, 40^{1} (a single leaf, matches catchword on f. 380v). Vertical catchwords preceded and followed by a dot. Ruled in pencil, special column for the gloss. Written in semi-gothic textualis media with occasional use of humanistic d, g, and long terminal s in 31 lines in two columns beginning on the second ruled line. Incipits of chapters in rustic capitals with letters alternately in red and black ink. Headings in red in script of text. Red initials and paragraph marks; red touches used for punctuation even in catchwords, e.g., f. 370v.

Bound in modern green velvet over boards.

Written by friar Gabriel de Prato Alboyno in the Franciscan convent of Sant'Angelo in Milan in 1466. f. 369, "Hanc summam pisanam per me inceptam in loco s. Marię de angelis apud Mediolanum foras muros portę Cumanę condito expleui in eodem loco, ego frater Gabriel de Prato Alboyno ordinis minorum professor anno domini millesimo quadringentesimo sexagesimo sexto, viii° kalendas septembris, id est xxv° die augusti hora xx^ma^ anno ętatis meę xxxv°, mense decimo, conuersionis uero ad religionem anno xv et mense vii°, cuius *summe usus est michi fratri Bernardino de Martinengo concessus per reuerendum patrem fratrem Ludouicum a Turri uicarium prouincie Brixie*" (words in italics written by a humanistic hand before 1498 over the latter portion of the original inscription which is erased and illegible). On Ludovicus della Torre, see M. Ferrari, "Per una storia delle biblioteche francescane a Milano nel Medioevo e nell'Umanesimo," *Archivum franciscanum historicum* 71 (1979): 452–53. *Colophons de manuscrits occidentaux,* 3179. No. 2 from the collection of Henry Probasco, acquired by the Newberry 1 December 1890.

Second folio: -me paragrapho laici.

De Ricci, 1:523.

78.1

(Ry 61–1744)

Humanistic Miscellany

Central Italy s. XV med.

1. ff. 1–72 Francisci Arhetini in Phalaridis tyranni agrigentini epistulas prohemium (in violet). [U]ellem Malatesta nouelle princeps illustris tantam mihi dicendi facultatem dari . . . (f. 5) Phalaris Alciboo (in violet). Policletus messenius quem proditionis apud ciues tuos . . . sed summae bonitatis premium accepissent . . . Scripsisti ad me Francisce patauine uir eximie . . . doctorum iudicium non amplius formidabo. Uale. Laus deo (in red).

Letters numbered by a later hand, see below, ff. 104–105.

Ps. Phalaris, *Epistolae* (with epilogue), translated from the Greek by Francesco Griffolini of Arezzo. Text with the dedicatory letter to Francesco Pellato as in Hain, 12880 and 12889; cf. *Epistolarum laconicarum atque selectarum farragines duae* (Basel, 1554), 1:216–342. See G. Mancini, *Francesco Griffolini cognominato Francesco Aretino* (Florence, 1890), pp. 17–18. For manuscripts, see Prete, *Codices barberiniani latini,* pp. 111–12; Ruysschaert, *Codices vaticani latini: 11414–11709,* pp. 288–99. To these lists, add Vatican, Ottob. Lat. 1164 and 1785, ff. 142–91, and Vatican, Chigi, I, iv, 127, ff. 1–40v.

2. f. 72 Martialis (in violet).

Hoc iacet in tumulo raptus puerilibus annis . . .
Artificis leuior non potes esse manu.

Martial, *Epigrammata,* VI, 52.

3. f. 72 Martialis (in violet).

Saepe salutatus numquam prior ipse salutas
Sic eris, aeternum, Pontiliane. Uale.

Martial, *Epigrammata,* V, 66.

4. ff. 72v–79 Leonhardi Arhetini interpretatio Aristotelis opusculi de re familiari, Ad Cosmum de Medicis florentinum incipit (in violet). Pretiosa sunt interdum corporis exigui . . . (f. 73v) Res familiaris et res publica inter se differunt non solum quantum domus et ciuitas; haec enim sunt earum subiecta . . . sic enim parata non requirentur. Finis.

Ps. Aristotle, *Oeconomica,* preface and Book I only. Preface edited by Baron, *Leonardo Bruni Aretino,* pp. 120–21. Editions: *GW* 2433–39, 2341, 2347, 2349, 2367, 2370–71; Venice, 1501; and as listed by Cranz, *Bibliography of Aristotle Editions,* p. 133. For the manuscript tradition, see H. Baron, *Humanistic and Political Literature in Florence and Venice at the Beginning of the Quattrocento: Studies in Criticism and Chronology* (Cambridge, Mass., 1955), p. 166 sqq.; and J. Soudek, "The Genesis and Tradition of Leonardo Bruni's Annotated Latin version of the Ps. Aristotelian Economics," *Scriptorium* 12 (1958): 260–68; "Leonardo Bruni and His Public: A Statistical and Interpretative Study of His Annotated Latin Version of the Ps. Aristotelian Economics," *Studies in Medieval and Renaissance History* 5 (1968): 51–136, especially 57–58, 124 (no. 187), 128, and 130; "A Fifteenth-Century Humanistic Bestseller: The Manuscript Diffusion of Leonardo Bruni's Annotated Latin Version of the Ps. Aristotelian Economics," *Philosophy and Humanism: Renaissance Essays in Honor of Paul Oskar Kristeller* (New York, 1976), pp. 116–28.

5. f. 79 Hieronimi presbiteri dictum (in violet). Ad Titum Liuium lacteo eloquentiae fonte manantem . . . urbem quaererent.

Excerpt from Jerome, *Epistula 53 ad Paulinum*, ed. I. Hilberg, *CSEL* 54 (1910): 443–44. Same excerpt in Vatican, Arch. S. Pietro C.132, f. 1v, *Manuscrits classiques latins* 1 (1975): 36.

6. ff. 79v–80 Epistola Guarini (in violet). Guarinus ueronensis suo Christofolo (*sic*) salutem plurimam dicit. Si tardior in mittendis ad te commendaticiis litteris fui . . . deque familia scire opto. Uale, Uenetiis.

Guarino Veronese, *Letter to Christophoro Scarpa*, 18 July 1418, ed. R. Sabbadini, *Epistolario di Guarino Veronese* (Venice, 1915–19), 1:200. In the margin opposite "Alexandrum" in the text, the rubricator has written "Iocose" in violet; cf. ibid., 3:85.

7. f. 80 Epytaphium Caesaris optimatis (in violet). In Macedum campis ultus iam Caesaris umbras . . . et sidera summa reliqui.

f. 80v blank.

Epitaph of Caesar Augustus, six lines written as prose, ed. Riese, *Anthologia latina*, vol. 1, pt. 2, p. 309. See L. Bertalot, "Die älteste gedr. Epitaphiensammlung," *Collectanea Variae Doctrinae Leoni Olschki Oblata* (Munich, 1921), p. 11, reprinted by Kristeller, *Studien*, 1:269–301. Walther, *Initia*, 8980.

8. ff. 81–103 Lactantii Firmiani de iustitia dei fragmentum foeliciter incipit (in violet). [N]am si iustitia est ueri dei cultus . . . uel coronam fidei uel premium immortalitatis adipisci. Finis. Laus deo (in violet).

Lactantius, *Epitome divinarum institutionum*, 51–68, ed. S. Brandt and G. Laubmann, *CSEL* 19 (1980): 730–61. *CPL* 86.

9. f. 103 (addition s. xv)
Ignes interiorem edunt medulas . . .
Impia non uerita diuos scelerare parentes.

f. 103v blank.

Unidentified poem of ten lines.

10. ff. 104–105 (addition s. xv ex. or xvi in.) Alphabetical table of the *Epistles* of Ps. Phalaris. The same hand as numbered the letters in text 1 above.

f. 105v blank.

Paper with griffin watermark, cf. Briquet 7464. ff. 105. 195 × 134 mm (132 × 70 mm). $1–10^{10}$, 11^{6} (1 stub only). Ruled in pencil. Written in humanistic cursiva formata in 24 long lines. Headings in pale violet in script of text with running marginal index notes of proper names and topics also in the same script; nota signs, pointing hands, all in violet.

Bound in limp parchment with spine title "Francisci Arethini in Phalaridem" in script of s. xvi^{2} or xvii.

Written in central Italy, probably in Florence, as suggested by the selection of texts and the watermarks, in the middle of the fifteenth century. Front flyleaf, "Marino Bertoia" written by a hand of s. xviii–xix. On verso, in pencil, "510 Bertoja Marino." "Lire 600" written lightly in pencil by another hand. Note in pencil on front pastedown, "Cat XII / 35." Acquired by the Newberry from Bernard Rosenthal, catalogue 12, item no. 35, 1961.

Second folio: eorum laudibus.

79
(83870)
Rule of Saint Benedict (in Italian)

Italy s. XV^{2}

ff. 1–57v In nomine domini nostri Ihesu Christi; Incomincia el prologo ne la regula del padre nostro sancto Benedecto (in red). Ascolta o figliola li commandamenti del maestro e inclina la orechia del cuore tuo . . . le quale di sopra hauemo dicto siando dio tuo protectore. Amen.

Commentaries incorporated in the text under red *lemmata*, "Declaratio."

ff. 58–61v blank.

The Rule of Saint Benedict, in Italian, prepared for nuns, note "figliola" in incipit; "monache" and "abbadessa" mentioned in the text. Text to be compared to the incunable editions described by Zambrini, *Le Opere volgari*, cols. 860–61, and *GW* 3833–35. This translation differs from the text edited by E. Lisi (Florence, 1855). See also O. L. Kapsner, *A Benedictine Bibliography* (Collegeville, Minn., 1962), 2:31.

f. 1, historiated initial depicting Benedict reading his rule, monks to his right, nuns to his left, framed in dull gold 10 lines high. Alternating blue initials with red flourishes and red initials with violet flourishes.

Parchment of southern preparation. ff. 61 + i. Foliated 1–62. 225 × 165 mm (155 × 108 mm). $1–4^{8}$, $5–6^{10}$, 11^{10} (8, stub only). Catchwords written in black or red ink, surrounded by four dots. Ruled in light brown ink. Written in Italian gothic textualis rotunda formata in 30 long lines in very black Italian ink. Headings in red in script of text.

Bound in contemporary stamped black Italian calf over boards. Inner panel framed by repeated rectangular stamp of an interlaced rope motif, within it 4 stamps of a flower within a rope lozenge motif, decorated with smaller stamps of 3 leaf clusters, repeated numerous times; same pattern front and back. Upper and fore-edge clasps; lower clasp wanting; 5 bosses front and back.

Written in Italy in the second half of the fifteenth century. A sixteenth-century pen trial on the rear pastedown. Acquired by the Newberry from Edward E. Ayer, 1899.

Second folio: del quale regno.

De Ricci, 1:532.

80
(23821)
Franciscan Repertory of Papal Bulls
Central Italy [*Illustrated*] 1464–71

1. ff. 1–99 Absolutionis et dispensationis beneficium (alphabetical and topical table of contents with reference to folios) . . . (f. 16v) Bonifacius octauus in sexto de sententia excomunicationis, suspensionis et interdicta; Recipe in capitolo 9, libro quinto [*Liber Sexti Decretalium,* V, 22, 24] (in red). Alma mater ecclesia plerumque non nulla rationabiliter ordinat et consulte . . . de regimine uero et cura predictorum de obseruancia nuncupatorum se aliter non intromittat nulli ergo. Datum Rome aput sanctum Petrum anno incarnationis dominice 1446, 10 augusti pontificatus nostri anno 16. Laus deo. Amen. Horetis (*sic*) deum pro scriptore. Finis.

Pointing hands in red in margins. Marginal additions to the table of contents by a contemporary hand.

Bullarium ordinis minorum. Collection of extracts of papal bulls drawn from the *Corpus juris canonici* and the original documents; cf. *Bullarium franciscanum,* ed. J. H. Sbaralea and C. Eubel (Rome 1759–1904). Entries include short historical notes on canonizations, confirmations of the rule, etc. f. 22v, canonizations of Francis and Anthony.

2. ff. 99–100v Pontifices romani (in red). Chronological table of popes through Paul II (1464–71) with additions by several hands through Paul III. Preceded by a note stating that Peter sat in Antioch in A.D. 38 and in Rome in A.D. 45.

Parchment of southern preparation. ff. ii + 100 + i. Original arabic and roman foliation in red 1–100. 200 × 153 mm (148 × 103 mm). $1–10^{10}$. Catchwords present: 1–2 horizontal within four dots; 3–5 within scrolls; 6–9 vertical within red dots. Leaves signed a1–g5, traces afterward. Ruled in ink. ff. 1–58v, written in humanistic textualis media, quires 1–2 by one hand; quires 3–6 (to f. 58v) by another. ff. 58v–100, written in Italian gothic textualis media, with one-story a and trailing terminal s beginning on the first ruled line throughout. ff. 1, 11, and 16v, humanistic, i.e., square roman capitals illuminated in magenta, blue, or gold, decorated with green acanthus spray. Alternating red and blue minor rustic capital initials, washed with yellow throughout.

Bound in contemporary stamped pigskin. Panel, front and back, decorated with stamps of clusters of three circles, parallel bars of rope motif, and a roll of rope motif around the outer edge. Early sixteenth-century shelf-mark, "P.n. 15 Bancho 3" written in red on paper label affixed over an older paper label on the back cover. Numbers 22 and 40 added by a modern hand. Two cloth fore-edge clasps wanting; one brass catch remains in the shape of a fleur-de-lys with the initial s. Chain mark front cover, center bottom.

Written in central Italy during the pontificate of Paul II (1464–71). Note of s. xv on rear flyleaf "Omnes isti summi pontifices a sancto Petro usque ad Sixtum 4^{m}, cc^{il} XX^{ti} s^{ex}," confirmed by table, above ff. 99–100v. From the collection of Henry Probasco, 4 and 12 written on flyleaf. Acquired by the Newberry 1 December 1890.

Second folio: minores et predicatores.

De Ricci, 1:525.

80.1
(60-339)
Martial, *Epigrammata*
Italy s. XV ex.

ff. 1–88v (begins imperfectly) // O quanta est gula, conties (*sic*) comesse . . . Cum se uentorum scribet amica tibi.

Text accompanied by extensive marginal glosses.

Martial, *Epigrammata:* V, 70, line 5–V, 72; III, 64–IV, 3, line 7; lacuna of two folios; IV, 15–IV, 34; IV, 69–V, 26; V, 28–V, 56; V, 58–V, 61; V, 57; V, 62–V, 67; V, 73–VI, 31; VI, 33–VI, 36; VI, 32; VI, 37–VI, 61, line 7; lacuna of 36 folios; X, 7–X, 12; X, 20; X, 13–X, 19; X, 21–X, 53; X, 55–XI, 48; XI, 50–XI, 52; XI, 49; XI, 53–XI, 63; XI, 65; XI, 64; XI, 69; XI, 67; XI, 66; XI, 68; XI, 70–XII, 4; XII, 7; XII, 5–XII, 6; XII, 8–XII, 21; XII, 23; XII, 22; XII, 24–XII, 25; XII, 27–XII, 28; XII, 26; XII, 29–XII, 45; XII, 47–XII, 48; XII, 46; XII, 49–XII, 50; XII, 52; XII, 51; XII, 53–XIV, 6, line 2; cf. edition of J. P. Postgate, *Corpus poetarum latinarum,* vol. 2 (London, 1905), pp. 434–53. B. L. Ullman, in a memorandum dated 15 December 1959, on file at the Newberry, identified the gloss as an original fifteenth-century composition, different from that of the incunable editions.

Parchment. ff. 88. Ink foliation, s. xix. 7–12, 15–40, 77–132; more recent foliation, 1–88. Quires 2, 3, and 4, numbered 6, 7, and 8 by a modern hand on upper margins of first folios. Therefore, 3 initial quires and part of fourth lost prior to s. xix. 6 folios before f. 1, 2 folios after f. 6, and 36 folios after f. 32, removed more recently. ff. 85–88, badly stained; f. 88v, formerly served as limp parchment cover and is badly worn and stained. 185 × 110 mm (120 × 72 mm). 1^{10} (1–2, 9–10 wanting with loss of text), $2–3^{10}$, 4^{10} (7–10 wanting with loss of text), 5^{8}, $6–8^{10}$, 9^{8}, 10^{10}. Vertical catchwords. Modern quire numbers occasionally preceded and followed by two dots. Prickings visible in outer margins. Ruled in hard point. Written in humanistic cursiva formata in 26 long lines beginning on the first ruled line. Initial letter of each line in rustic capitals. Initial of each stanza and headings in red or violet in script of text. Gloss written in humanistic cursiva with *lemmata,* some in red or violet identical to that of headings in the text, some underlined in the same colors. Text and gloss written by a single scribe.

Quarter bound in brown calf over pasteboard, s. xix. On spine, blue-edged round sticker with "147" written in red ink.

Written in Italy in the last third of the fifteenth century. Acquired by the Newberry from Bernard Rosenthal, 1960.

Second folio: Exuimur, nudos.

81
(23855)
Psalter Hymnal

Italy s. XV² (after 1461)

1. ff. 1–149v Liturgical Psalter. Psalms numbered in red.

2. ff. 149v–162v Eleven hymns, Pater noster, Gloria in excelsis, and Apostles' creed as listed in Leroquais, *Psautiers* 1:lv, nos. 1–14.

3. ff. 162v–164v Compendium Athanasii de fide catholica (in red). Leroquais, *Psautiers* 1:lv, no. 16.

4. ff. 164v–165 Salutatio deuota beate uirginis Marie pro uenia impetranda dicenda ante letaniam (in red). Aue, stella mattutina, peccatorum medicina, funde preces, lux diuina . . . funde preces dei mater pro nobis ad filium. Cf. *RH* 2135 and 35746.

5. f. 165 Oratio (in red). Omnipotens et misericors deus cui magis proprium est parcere quam punire . . . in afflictione positis pepercisti. Per eundem Christum dominum nostrum. Amen.

6. f. 165–165v Psalmi penitentiales sunt infrascripti (in red). Incipits of the Seven Penitential Psalms with their usual numbers written in red for reference use to text 1. Followed by the antiphon Ne remiscarris, which usually follows the Penitential Psalms in books of hours and breviaries, cf. *SMRL* 2:67.

7. ff. 165v–170 Letania (in red). Barnabas last among the apostles; Ignatius and Denis among the martyrs; Remigius, Bernard, Hugh, Francis, Dominic, and Thomas Aquinas among the confessors; Ursula, Brigida, Catherine of Siena, Blandina, and Euphemia among the virgins. Thomas Aquinas and Catherine of Siena written partially in red. Litany proper followed by the seven short prayers: Deus cui proprium est . . . , Absolue, quesumus, domine nostrorum uincula peccatorum . . . , Pretende domine famulis et famulabus tuis . . . , Deus qui iustificas impium . . . , Deus qui nos patrem et matrem honorare . . . , Fidelium deus omnium conditor et redemptor . . . , Omnipotens sempiterne deus qui uiuorum dominaris simul et mortuorum.

8. ff. 171–183v Secuntur cantica festiualia. See Leroquais, *Psautiers* 1:lvi.

9. ff. 183v–198v Incipit hymnarius in aduentu domini. Ad uesperas hymnus (in red). Conditor alme siderum . . . *RH* 3733. (f. 184), In natale domini hymnus ad uesperas et nocturno (in red). Uenit redemptor gentium . . . *RH* 21294. (f. 184v), In xl[a] ad uesperas tamen ymnus (in red). Audi be[ni]gne conditor . . . *RH* 1449. (f. 185v), In resurrectione domini ad uesperas et nocturno (in red). Hic est dies uerus dei . . . *RH* 7793. (f. 186v), In acensione domini ad uesperas et nocturno (in red). Optatus uotis omnium sacratus illuxit dies . . . *RH* 14177. (f. 187), In pentecostes domini (in red). Ueni, creator spiritus, mentes tuorum uisita . . . *RH* 21204. (f. 188), Ad nocturnum tamen dicitur (in red) Iam Christus astra ascenderat, regressus unde uenera (*sic*) . . . *RH* 9216. (f. 188), Ad laudes tamen dicitur (in red). Impleta gaudent uiscera . . . *RH* 8506. (f. 188v), In solempnitate corporis Christi . . . (in red). Pange, lingua, gloriosi corporis, misterium sanguinis . . . *RH* 14467. (f. 189v), Ad nocturnum tamen dicitur (in red). Sacra solempnis iuncta sint gaudia . . . *RH* 17713. (f. 190), Ad laudes tamen dicitur (in red). Uerbum supernum prodiens nec patris linquens dextera . . . *RH* 21398. (f. 190v), In natiuitate sancti Iohannis baptiste ymnus ad uesperas di-

citur tamen (in red). Ut queant laxis resonare fibris . . . *RH* 21039. (f. 191), In festo sancte crucis ad uesperas et nocturnum (in red). Crux fidelis inter omnes . . . cf. *RH* 4018. (f. 191v), In solemnitate omnium sanctorum, reliquiarum apostolorum Petri et Pauli et in festiuitatibus martirum, confessorum, uirginis xii uel ad uesperas tamen (in red). Christe, redemptor omnium, conserua tuos famulos . . . *RH* 2959. (f. 192), Ad laudes tamen dicitur (in red). Ihesu, saluator seculi, redemptis ope subueni . . . *RH* 9677. (f. 192v), Dominicis et ferialibus diebus ad uesperas (in red). Deus, creator omnium polique rector, uestiens . . . *RH* 4426. (f. 193v), Ad nocturnum dicitur (in red). Eternum rerum conditor . . . *SMRL* 2:484. (f. 194), Ad laudes tamen (in red). Splendor paterne glorie . . . *RH* 19349. (f. 194v), Ad primam semper dicitur (in red). Iam lucis orto sidere . . . *RH* 9272. (f. 195), Ad tertiam semper dicitur (in red). Nunc sancte nobis spiritus . . . *RH* 12586. (f. 195v), Ad sextam semper dicitur (in red). Rector potens, uerax deus, qui temperas rerum uices . . . *RH* 17061. (f. 195v), Ad nonam semper dicitur (in red). Rerum, deus, tenax uigor inmotus in te permanens . . . *RH* 17328. (f. 196), Ad complectorium semper dicitur (in red). Christe, qui lux es et dies . . . *RH* 2934. (f. 196v), Ad omnes horas beate Marie (in red). Memento, salutis auctor . . . *RH* 11446. (f. 197), Ad nocturnum tamen (in red). Antra deserti teneris sub annis . . . *RH* 1213. (f. 197v), Ad laudes tamen dicitur (in red). O nimis felix meritique celsi . . . *RH* 13310. (f. 198), In solempnitate beate Marie (in red). Aue, maris stella, dei mater alma . . . *RH* 1889. (f. 198v), Ad nocturnum (in red). Misterium ecclesie, hymnum Christo referimus . . . *RH* 11828. (f. 198v), Ad laudes (in red). Ends imperfectly without the beginning of the hymn.

Parchment. ff. 198. Trimmed to 161 × 111 mm (99 × 73 mm). $1–12^{10}$, 13^{2}, $14–19^{10}$, 20^{8}, 21^{6}, 22^{2}. f. 1 remounted on thicker parchment obscuring text of f. 1v. Catchwords surrounded by four flourishes, 2 points, and a stroke. Traces of leaf signatures visible on some folios. Ruled in brown ink. Written in Italian gothic textualis media, headings in red in script of text. f. 1, bracket right floral border in purple, green, and blue. Olive leaf wreath contains initials YHS. f. 1v, two modern miniatures of the scourging of Christ in a sixteenth-century style, pasted in. Red initials with violet flourishes and blue initials with red flourishes throughout. Alternating red and blue minor initials.

Bound in Spanish calf over pasteboard, s. xix.

Written in Italy after 1461, date of the canonization of Catherine of Siena listed in the litany. Saints of litany suggest Dominican affinities. No. 33 in the collection of Henry Probasco, acquired by the Newberry 1 December 1890.

Second folio: Tunc loquetur.

De Ricci, 1:527.

82

(324359)

Book of Hours, Use of Rome

(Order of Saint Francis)

Gubbio s. XV[1]

1. f. 1–1v Infrascripti sunt xii dies ueneris sancti boni et honorandi ut infra (in red). Ego Clemens romanus pontifex . . . ad honorem xii apostolorum.

Primus dies ueneris mensis martii . . .

Helia et omni tribu filiorum Ysrael.

2. f. 2–2v Easter Table.

3. ff. 3–14v Calendar with a saint for almost every day, all feasts in black. Feasts include: Sancti Gilberti et sancti Gellasii confessoris (4 February), Sancti Ugolini episcopi (7 February), Sancti Gagi episcopi (20 February), Sancti Fradii martiris (11 March), Sancti Petri martiris (29 April), Translatio sancti Francisci (25 May), Sancti Francisci confessoris (4 October), Translatio sancte Reparate (8 October), Sancti Cerbonii (10 October), Sancte Helisabeth (19 December). Accompanied by verse, Prima dies Iani timor est et septima uani . . . Walther, *Initia,* 14561. Dedicatio basilice noted for 29 September and 9 and 18 November.

4. ff. 15–58 Office of the Virgin, use of Rome. Text beginning imperfectly after the third lesson of matins. Prayers for protection, for peace, and to all saints at the end of each hour, lauds through compline. Ends with the Salue regina followed by the usual prayer, Omnipotens sempiterne deus qui gloriose uirginis . . .

5. ff. 58–66 Six psalms with rubrics for the days of the week.

6. ff. 66–75 Changed Office of the Virgin. f. 75, Explicit officium beate uirginis Marie (in red).

7. ff. 75–77 Oratio in honorem sancte Marie et omnium sanctorum (in red). Per beate dei genetricis Marie et omnium angelorum archangelorum, patriarcharum . . . digneris custodiam. Per dominum nostrum et cetera.

f. 77v blank.

8. ff. 78–91 Incipiunt septem psalmi penitentiales (in red).

9. ff. 91–101 Letania (in red). Crisentinus (*sic*), Marianus and Jacobus, and Ubaldus among the martyrs. Ubaldus crossed out in red, listed also among the confessors. Followed by the standard set of ten short prayers as in the Roman breviary, and two others: Inmense misericors deus, pater omnipotens, qui per os Dauid ellecti tui . . . Concede, queso, michi indigno famulo tuo . . . Leroquais, *Heures* 1:48, and Ne reputes, piissime domine, peccata . . .

10. ff. 101v–105v Incipit officium sancte crucis [quod cuilibet deuote dicenti papa Iohannes xii dedit quadraginta dies indulgentie pro qualibet hora] . . . (in red, portion within brackets struck out in black ink). Short Hours of the Cross.

11. ff. 106–136v Incipit officium mortuorum (in red). Use of Rome.

f. 137–137v blank.

12. ff. 138–139v Incipit missa beate uirginis (in red). Salue sancta parens . . .

13. ff. 140–145 Gospel sequences, John omitted.

14. ff. 145–148 Symbolum Athenasii (in red).

15. f. 148–148v Credo in deum, patrem omnipotentem, creatorem celi et terre . . .

16. ff. 149–150v Oratio sancti Ieronimi (in red). Benedictum nomen tuum, domine deus, patrum nostrorum qui cum natus fueris misericordiam facis et in tempore tribulationis peccata dimittis . . . saluator mundi deus qui uiuis et regnas in secula seculorum. Amen.

Prayer unrecorded *BHM*.

17. ff. 150v–152v Domine Ihesu Christe qui septem uerba die ultimo uite tue . . . Per infinita secula seculorum. Amen.

Leroquais, *Heures* 2:342 and 400. This prayer often attributed to Bede; see MS 35, text 16.

18. ff. 152v–160v Inquisitio sancti Augustini de infrascripta oratione, ut in quacumque die cantetur nec diabolus nec malus homo impedimentum facere poterit, et quod iustum petierit a domino, dabitur illi et si anima de corpore egredietur inferno non recipietur (in red, entirely struck out in black ink). Domine Yhesu Christe qui in hunc mundum propter nos peccatores de sinu summi patris aduenisti . . . aduertas iram tuam a me famulo tuo .N. . . . indulgeat michi omnia peccata mea hic et in futuro seculo. Amen.

PL 101:476–79. Leroquais, *Heures* 1:318. Attributed to Augustine, *HUWHA*, vol. 1, pt. 1, p. 404, and vol. 2, pt. 1, p. 376. Barré, *Prières anciennes*, p. 55, n. 94. This expanded version mentions Ubaldus, Criscentinus (*sic*), Dominic, Peter Martyr, Thomas Aquinas, and Francis.

19. ff. 160v–163 Oratio ad filium (in red). Domine Yhesu Christe, filii dei uiui creator et restaurator generis humani . . . equalis est maiestas. Per gloriam in secula seculorum. Amen.

Leroquais, *Heures* 1:321. Attributed to Augustine, *HUWHA*, vol. 1, pt. 1, p. 404.

20. ff. 163–165v Oratio ad spiritum sanctum (in red). Domine sancte spiritus, coeterne et cum substantialis patri et filio qui super eundum dominum nostrum Yhesum . . . gloria patri qui fecit nos et gloria filio qui saluauit nos, gloria spiritui sancto qui renouauit nos. Per infinita secula seculorum. Amen.

Cf. Wilmart, *Codices reg. lat.*, 1:646.

21. ff. 165v–166v Oratio ad sanctam trinitatem (in red). Domine deus omnipotens qui in trinitate perfecta dominaris et regas (*sic*) . . . ad suam sanctam misericordiam perducat qui uiuit et regnat in secula seculorum. Amen.

Related texts in Paris, Bibliothèque Mazarine, 3636 (s. xv), f. 86v, and Stuttgart, Württembergische Landesbibliothek, HB. VII.5. (s. xii), ff. 23v–24.

22. ff. 166v–171v Oratio sancti Gregorii [quam quicumque dixerit deuote omni die sicut ipse Gregorius dicit, sciat que nec diabolus nec malus homo nunquam nocere ei poterit nec animam neque ad (*sic*) corpus. Et si de hac luce migrauit in infernum non descendet] (in red, portion within brackets struck out in black). Domine, exaudi orationem meam quia

iam cognosco tempus meum prope est . . . ut exaudias deprecationem meam. Qui uiuis et regnas in secula seculorum.

Leroquais, *Heures* 2:287 and 399.

23. ff. 171v–173v Oratio ad crucifixum deuotissima et utilis (in red). Concede michi, misericors deus, que tibi placita sunt ardenter concupiscere . . . et tuis gaudiis in patria frui per gloriam. Amen.

Doyle, "Prayer Attributed to Saint Thomas," pp. 229–38. Grabmann, *Die Werke*, pp. 112 and 370–72.

24. f. 174–174v Saluatio saluatoris (in red).

Aue Yhesu Christe, uerbum patris, filius uirginis,
Agnus dei . . .
Pacis dulcedo requies mea et uita perhennis. Amen.

Wilmart, pp. 412–13. *RH* 1844.

25. ff. 174v–175 Salutatio ad sudarium (in red).

Salue sancta facies nostri redemptoris . . .
Sed fruamur requie, omnes dicant, Amen.

Leroquais, *Heures* 2:449. *RH* 18189.

26. ff. 175v–176 Alia oratio ad crucifixum (in red). Deus qui pro redemptione mundi uoluisti a iudeis reprobari . . . tecum latronem crucifixum. Qui cum patre et spiritu sancto uiuis et regnas deus in secula seculorum. Amen.

Leroquais, *Heures* 1:45. See MS 35, text 18, and MS 56, text 37.

27. f. 176–176v Oratio dicenda quando eleuatur corpus domini (in red). Domine Yhesu Christe qui hanc sacratissimam carnem . . . et anime preteritis presentibus et futuris. Qui uiuis et regnas in secula seculorum. Amen.

Wilmart, p. 378n (no. 10).

28. f. 177 Alia oratio quando eleuatur corpus domini (in red). Aue caro Christi cara, immolata crucis ara . . . tecum frui gloria.

Wilmart, p. 379n.

29. f. 177–177v Oratio quando fit comunio (*sic*, in red). Deus qui nos per singulos dies in sacramento altaris corpus et sanguinem tuum in panis et uini spetie . . . in regno tuo participes esse mereamur. Qui uiuis . . .

30. ff. 177v–178 Alia oratio ad corpus Christi (in red).

Christi corpus aue de sancta uirgine natum
Uera caro . . .
Per loca salua me me (*sic*) rege quaque die.

RH 3050. Second stanza different from the version in Mone, 1:281.

31. ff. 178–180v Oratio pro afflictis (in red). Domine Yhesu Christe qui de sinu patris missus es in mundum relassare peccata, afflictos redimere in carcerem positos, soluere dispersos . . . Absalon contra Dauid regem. Qui uiuis et regnas in secula seculorum.

Cf. Leroquais, *Heures* 2:177. See above, text 18.

32. ff. 180v–182v Oratio pro inimicis omni die (in red). Te deum creatorem meum Yhesum Christum filium dei uiui, rogo et peto pro inimicis meis . . . te decet laus magna nunc atque per cuncta secula. Amen.

33. ff. 182v–183 Confessio optima de octo principalibus uitiis (in red). Multitudinem criminum et enormitatem scelerum meorum . . . mea culpa, mea maxima culpa. Amen.

Same text in Paris, Bibliothèque Mazarine, 512 (s. xi), f. 2, and 513 (s. xiii), f. 7.

34. f. 183v Oratio quando transis coram ymagine crucifixi (in red). Domine Yhesu Christe per illam amaritudinem passionis tue . . . anime mee in egressu. Amen.

Leroquais, *Heures* 2:100.

35. ff. 183v–184v Alia oratio ante crucifixum (in red). Domine Yhesu Christe qui neminem uis perire et cui nunquam sine spe misericordie tue aliquod postulator . . . qui es gloriosus et benedictus in secula seculorum. Amen.

36. ff. 184v–185v Oratio ad proprium angelum (in red). Sancte angele dei qui ad custodiam fragilis uite mee deputatus es . . . et eius merear hic et ubique protectione deffendi. Per Christum dominum nostrum. Amen.

Cf. Wilmart, pp. 552 and 581.

37. f. 186 Oratio quando surgis de mane (in red). Gratias tibi ago, domine, sancte pater, omnipotens sempiterne deus, qui me miserum peccatorem dignatus es in hac nocte . . . tibi placeat servitus mea. Amen.

Cf. Leroquais, *Heures* 1:199 and 2:33.

38. f. 186v Oratio quando uadis dormitum (in red). Gratias tibi ago, sancte pater, omnipotens sempiterne deus, qui me miserum

peccatorem dignatus es . . . tibi ualeam exhibere.

Cf. Leroquais, *Heures* 1:51.

39. ff. 186v–187 Oratio Benedicti pape xii cum indulgentia ccc dierum deuote dicentibus (in red). Benedicat me imperialis dei maiestas, protegat me regalis diuinitas, custodiat me sempiterna deitas . . . sit michi ista inuocatio salus et protectio. Amen.

Cf. Leroquais, *Heures* 2:68.

40. ff. 187v–191 Obsecro te domina sancta Maria, mater dei pietate plenissima . . . et michi famulo tuo . . . Audi, exaudi dulcissima uirgo Maria, mater dei et misericordie. Amen.

Leroquais, *Heures* 2:346–47.

41. f. 191–191v

Aue Maria totum (*sic*) sanctissima
Mater dei pietate plenissima . . .
Nunc et in hora mortis mei (*sic*) perpetua
interuentrix. Amen.

42. ff. 191v–193v Alia oratio (in red). Domina glorie dei genetrix beata Maria et omni laude dignissima, o domina mundi regina letitie . . . semper succurrere digneris in omnibus necessitatibus et angustiis meis. Amen.

43. ff. 193v–195v Ad laudem et reuerentiam gloriose uirginis (in red). Gaude uirgo mater Christi que per aurem concepisti, Gabriele nuntio . . . In perhenni gaudio. Aue Maria (in red).

Leroquais, *Heures* 2:409. *RH* 7017.

44. ff. 196v–197v [C]um beatus Thomas canturiensis (*sic*) hec supernotata septem gaudia singulis diebus repeteret, apparuit ei beata uirgo Maria . . . et dixit:

Gaude flore uirginali que honore
speciali . . .
Non cessabunt nec decrescent per eterna
secula.
Amen. Ave Maria et cetera (in red).

Leroquais, *Heures* 1:xxvii, 2:409. *RH* 6810. On the attribution to Thomas, see Wilmart, p. 329, n. 1.

45. f. 197v Uerba beate uirginis (in red). Quicumque me cum istis gaudiis uenerabitur cotidie deuoto corde, huic apparebo in finem uite sue et eterna gaudia sibi a domino impetrabo, et hoc expertum est.

46. ff. 197v–198v Alia oratio ad beatam uirginem (in red). Sancta dei genitrix Maria, domina mea, spes mea, dulcedo mea, misericordia . . . et gloriam eiusdem filii tui domini nostri Yhesu Christi. Qui cum patre et spiritu sancto uiuit et regnat in secula seculorum. Amen.

D. H. Turner, "A Twelfth-Century Psalter from Camaldoli," *Revue Benedictine* 72 (1962): 123.

47. ff. 199–200

Domina sancta Maria in Bethelem
dormiens
Illuc accessit dominus, dulcis mater
inquiens . . .
. . . penas euadet inferni.
Non amittendo gloriam.

48. f. 200v Alia oratio ad eandem (in red). Aue et gaude domina mea sancta Maria, spes et solatium omnium . . . o clemens, o pia, o dulcis uirgo Maria. Amen.

49. ff. 201–202 Oratio in honorem omnium sanctorum pro omni populo christiano (in red). Pie et exaudibilis domine deus noster Yhesu Christe, clemenciam tuam cum omni supplicatione deposcimus . . . requiem propitius donare digneris. Qui cum patre et cetera.

Leroquais, *Heures* 1:46. Barré, *Prières anciennes,* pp. 11 and 30. See MS 56, text 25.

50. f. 202–202v Alia oratio ad precedentem (in red). Misericors pater, largire michi fidem, opus bonum scientiam abstinentiam . . . Et fac me esse participem uite eterne. Saluator.

51. ff. 202v–203 Alia oratio ad filium (in red). Domine Yhesu Christe, rex uirginum, integritatis amator . . . et possum cunctis diebus uite mee complacere tibi. Qui uiuis et cetera.

Wilmart, p. 116n. Wilmart, *Precum libelli,* p. 140.

52. ff. 203–204 Alia oratio ad sanctam trinitatem (in red). Sancta trinitas et uera unitas omnipotens et sempiterne deus, spes unica mundi . . . ut nulla umquam obliuione deleatur. Qui uiuis et cetera.

53. f. 204–204v Oratio pro patre et matre et pro omni progenie seu familiaribus (in red). Omnipotens et misericors deus, respice propitius peccatam meam et exaudi me pro famulo tuo . . . et eos conseruare in nomine tuo. Qui cum patre et spiritu sancto uiuis et regnas in secula seculorum. Amen.

54. f. 205–205v Quando despiciet tibi peccata tua et in peccatis fueris ita profunda-

tusque tam multitudine quam magnitudine quam consuetudine tibi non posse tibi a peccatis continere, dic ut cumsequitur (in red). Peccaui supernumerum arene maris et multiplicata sunt peccata mea . . . et malum coram te feci.

This text also in Paris, Sainte Geneviève, 2778 (s. xv–xvi), f. 5.

55. ff. 205v–211 Confiteor deo beate Marie et beato Francisco et omnibus sanctis quia peccaui . . . Primo contra deum per ignorantiam . . . orare pro me.

Franciscan prayer of confession, cf. *Horae eboracenses,* p. 26.

56. f. 211 Misereatur michi omnipotens deus et dimittat michi omnia peccata mea . . . et perducat me ad uitam eternam.

Horae eboracenses, p. 26.

57. f. 211–211v Psalm 129, followed by Gloria patri, Kyrieleison . . . , Pater noster, and Et ne nos, cues only.

58. ff. 212–213v Sequitur uersus (in red). Miserere mei, domine, quoniam tribulor (Ps 30:10). Tribulor quia fomite peccati succendor . . . Ideo miserere mei secundum eloquium tuum. Followed by Domine exaudi, cue only.

59. ff. 213v–214 Deus qui uoluisti pro mundi redemptione a iudeis reprobari . . . perduxisti latronem crucifixum. Qui uiuis et regnas cum patre et spiritu sancto in secula seculorum. Amen.

f. 214v blank.

Leroquais, *Heures* 1:153.

60. f. 215–215v Cum uolueris perigrinari ut deus iter tuum faciat prosperum, dic ut sequitur (in red). Omni tempore benedic deum et pete ab eo . . . Confiteor deo omnipotenti beate Marie uirgini beato Francisco et omnibus sanctis quia peccaui . . . orare pro me.

Franciscan prayer of confession; cf. text 55.

61. ff. 215v–216 Psalmus Dauid (in red). Psalm 53.

62. ff. 216–217 A cento formed from psalms 118:1–6, 24:5, etc.

63. f. 217v Adesto supplicationibus nostris omnipotens deus, uiam famulorum tuorum . . . semper protegamur auxilio.

64. ff. 217v–218 Oratio (in red). Deus qui beatum Petrum ambulantem in fluctibus . . . gloriam consequamur. Per dominum nostrum Yhesum Christum filium tuum qui tecum uiuit et regnat in unitate spiritus sancti deus. Per omnia secula seculorum.

65. f. 218–218v Cum uis orare ut deus te liberet uel perseueret a persecutione linguarum (in red). Circundederunt me uiri mendaces sine causa . . . Confiteor deo omnipotenti beate Marie semper uirgini, beato Francisco et omnibus sanctis . . . Miserere michi omnipotens deus et dimittat in omnia peccata mea . . . perducat me in uitam eternam. Amen.

Franciscan prayer of confession, cf. text 55.

66. ff. 218v–221 Deinde dicantur infrascripti psalmi (in red). A cento including Psalm 139.

67. ff. 221–224v Sequntur letanie usque ad Te rogamus, audi nos et tunc dicatur ut sequitur (in red). Ut a linguis deridentibus nos custodias. Te rogamus, audi nos . . . Ut a linguis et uerbis turpiloquii nos custodias. Te rogamus, audi nos . . .

68. ff. 224v–225v Domine, libera animam meam a labiis iniquis et a lingua dolosa . . . Et clamor meus ad te ueniat.

69. f. 225v Oratio (in brown). Deus qui in tantis nos periculis . . . in unitate spiritus sancti deus. Per omnia secula seculorum. Amen.

Twelve Milanese style historiated magenta initials in the same style on gold grounds 4 lines high depicting a male figure engaged in the activities of the four seasons: f. 3, January, seated before a fire; f. 4, February, pruning; f. 5, March, blowing a double horn; f. 6, April, smelling flowers; f. 7, May, with a falcon; f. 8, June, cutting grain with a sickle; f. 9, July, thrashing grain; f. 10, August, making a barrel; f. 11, September, picking grapes; f. 12, October, picking fruit; f. 13, November, drawing wine; f. 14, December, preparing the carcass of an animal. A miniature probably removed after f. 19. Eleven similar initials 5–7 lines high: f. 16v, the Nativity; f. 27, the Annunciation to the Shepherds in the Field; f. 32, the Presentation in the Temple; f. 36v, the Adoration of the Magi; f. 40v, the Flight into Egypt; f. 45, Christ and the Doctors; f. 52v, the Baptism of Christ; f. 78, King David in prayer; f. 101v, the Crucifixion; f. 106, funeral Mass, participants in white habits; f. 138, Madonna and Child. Each smaller initial accompanied by sprigs of gold ivy decoration. Larger initials accompanied by bracket borders decorated with red, blue, and magenta flowers. Gold, blue, and magenta initials 2 lines high throughout, accompanied by gold ivy spray extending into the margin. Minor red initials with violet flourishes alternating with blue initials with red flourishes.

Parchment. ff. 225. 166 × 120 mm (98 × 68 mm). A leaf removed after f. 14. Collation problematic. Catchwords present surrounded by a variety of decorative pen flourishes. Leaves signed alphabetically with roman numerals sometimes in red, mostly trimmed. Ruled in pencil. Written in Italian gothic textualis rotunda media in 16 long lines, calendar in 18 long lines. Headings in red. Guides for the rubricator present, see f. 72 and elsewhere.

Bound in parchment over pasteboard, s. xviii.

Written in central Italy, probably in Gubbio, in the first half of the fifteenth century, probably for a member of the Franciscan order, as indicated by the calendar and the formulas of confession in texts 55, 60, and 65. Note Ubaldus of Gubbio listed twice in the litany; Marianus and Jacobus, patrons of the cathedral in Gubbio, also in the litany. Other saints of Umbria and central Italy in the litany and the calendar. The dates of "dedicatio basilice" correspond to those of Michael and Salvatore and Theodore in the calendar of Gubbio, see M. Sarti, *De episcopis eugubinis* (Gubbio, 1755). Texts 9, 18, 37, 38, and 40 in masculine form. Front flyleaf iii, inscription "Ludovicus Bertivey," s. xviii (?). Acquired by the Newberry from Edward E. Ayer, 1920.

De Ricci, 1:538.

83

(23873)

Prayer Book of Anne of Brittany

Florence [*Frontispiece*] after 1499

1. ff. 1–13 Incipiunt septem psalmi penitentiales (in red).

2. ff. 13–22v Letanie (in red). Mary and Denis among the martyrs, Benedict and Louis among the confessors, and Anne among the virgins, all written in red. Margaret among the virgins, written in black in large letters. Other saints in litany include: Martialis as the last apostle, Cletus, Maurice, Eustachius, Eutropius, and Quintinus among the martyrs, Nichasius, Remigius, Eligius, Egidius, Çenobius, Maurus, Lubin, Sulpice, Leonard, and Guillermus among the confessors. Litany followed by Psalmus XL (*sic,* for LXIX) and standard set of ten short prayers as in the Roman breviary, with the additional prayer Deus qui nos patrem et matrem honorare precepisti . . . *SMRL* 2:239; *Horae Eboracenses,* p. 111, inserted after the ninth prayer. See above MS –53, text 9. f. 22v, Expliciunt vii psalmi penitentiales (in red).

3. ff. 23–25v Suffrages to the Trinity, God the Father, God the Son, and the Holy Spirit.

4. ff. 25v–26 Johannes papa XXII dedit indulgentiam cuilibet dicenti trium milium dierum criminalium et mille uenialium dierum; Oratio (in red). Anima Christi sanctifica me, corpus Christi salua me . . . laudem te dominum saluatorem meum in secula seculorum. Amen.

Lexicon für Theologie und Kirche 1:563–64. Leroquais, *Heures* 2:377. *RH* 1090.

5. f. 26–26v Alia oratio (in red). Aue uere sanguis domini nostri Iesu Christi qui de latere eius cum aqua fluxisti . . . in futuro seculo per infinita seculorum secula.

Leroquais, *Heures* 2:340. Wilmart, p. 378n (no. 6). *RH* 2171.

6. ff. 26v–27

Salue sancta caro dei
per quam salui fiunt rei . . .
Da mihi fidem iustorum
qui regnas in secula seculorum.

Wilmart, p. 378n (no. 13). *RH* 18175.

7. ff. 27v–28 Quilibet dicenti infrascriptam orationem inter eleuationem corporis Christi et agnus dei concessus est duo milia annorum de indulgentiam (*sic*) per papam Bonifatium quartus (*sic*) ad instantiam Philippi regis; Oratio (in red). Domine Iesu Christe qui hanc sanctissimam carnem . . . et regnas deus in secula seculorum. Amen.

Leroquais, *Heures* 2:400. Wilmart, p. 378n (no. 10).

8. ff. 28v–29v Oratio ante communionem (in red). Omnipotens et misericors deus ecce accedo ad sacramentum corporis et sanguinis . . . Da michi famule tuae Annae . . . reuelata tandem faciem contemplari. Qui . . .

The name of Anne is written in red.

Leroquais, *Heures* 2:437. Wilmart, p. 381, n. 2.

9. f. 30–30v Oratio ad patrem ualde utilis et deuota cui papa Bonifatius concessit xl[a] dierum indulgentiam post perceptionem corporis Christi . . . (in red). Gratias tibi ago, domine sancte pater, qui me famulam tuam nullis meritis sed sola miseratione satiare dignatus es . . . ubi tu Christe lux es sanctis tuis et sempiternum gaudium. Per eundem Christum dominum nostrum.

Leroquais, *Heures* 1:156, etc. Wilmart, p. 381, n. 2.

10. ff. 31–33v Oratio sancti Thome de Aquino qua singulis diebus genibus flexis crucifixum orabat . . . (in red). Concede mihi queso, omnipotens et misericors deus, que tibi placita sunt ardenter concupiscere . . . in patria perfrui per gloriam.

Doyle, "Prayer Attributed to Saint Thomas." Grabmann, *Die Werke*, p. 112.

11. ff. 33v–35 Johannes papa III concessit pro omni uice cuilibet deuote dicenti infrascriptam orationem de indulgentia pro remissionem suorum peccatorum sex mille sex centos sexaginta sex annos ut dicitur apparere in sacra Romana ecclesia (in red). Oro te, piissime domine Iesu Christe, propter tuam magnam caritatem . . . ad bona ac gaudia uite eterne, qui uiuis et regnas cum deo patre in unitate spiritus sancti deus per omnia secula seculorum. Amen.

12. ff. 35–37 Hec oratio habet indulgentiam annorum uiginti milium et xii et dierum xxiii. Ita patet Rome in capella Cardinalis Hostiensis sita in ecclesia sancti Petri, et in secundo libro pontificatus Calisti iii, folio ccxiii, qui die xvii iunii 1456, eam confirmauit, et addidit duas ultimas orationes (in red). O domine Iesu Christe, adoro te in cruce pendentem . . . et propitius esto mihi . . . deprecor te, misere mei. Amen. Pater noster, aue Maria. Et quinquies ante imaginem pietatis (in red).

Leroquais, *Heures* 2:346, in the order 1, 2, 4, 7, 3, 5, 6 with respect to the printed text.

13. ff. 37–38 Uersus sancti Bernardi abbatis electis (*sic*) ex omnibus psalmis. O bone Iesu (in red). Illumina oculos meos ne umquam obdormiam in morte . . . et consolatus es me.

Leroquais, *Heures* 2:415.

14. f. 38–38v Oratio (in red). Omnipotens sempiterne deus qui Eçechie regi Iude te cum lacrimis deprecanti uite spatium protendisti, concede michi indigne famule tue Anne . . . secundum tuam misericordiam consequi merear. Per Christum dominum nostrum. Amen.

The name of Anne is written in red.

Wilmart, *Codices reg. lat.*, 1:687. Follows the *Versus sancti Bernardi* in other manuscripts. See MS 47, text 15.

15. ff. 38v–40 Oratio sancti Augustini ualde utilis et deuota. Quicumque eam semel in die dixerit non peribit mala morte. Et si de hac uita decesserit contritus et compunctus anima eius inferno non appropinquabit. Et qui iustum petierit impetrabit; Oratio (in red). Deus propitius esto mihi peccatrici et custos omnibus horis et diebus uite mee . . . salua me in omni tempore et diebus uite mee. Amen.

Attributed to Augustine, *HUWHA*, vol. 2, pt. 1, p. 374, and vol. 5, pt. 1, p. 472.

16. ff. 40–41 Uersus reperti in longinquis partibus sub imagine crucifixi (in red). Huc me sydereo descendere iussit Olimpo . . . dilige pro tantis sat mihi solus amor.

Identified as a work of Maffeo Vegio, E. E. Lowinsky, "Josquin des Prez and Ascanio Sforza," *Atti del Congresso Internazionale sul Duomo di Milano*, ed. M. L. Gatti Perer, 2 vols. (Milan, 1968), 2:18. Attributed to Johannes Trithemius, F. W. E. Roth in *Romanische Forschungen* 6 (1891). Walther, *Initia*, 8510.

17. ff. 41v–45v Oratio deuotissima ad beatissimam uirginem dei genitricem Mariam (in red). Obsecro te domina mea sancta Maria, mater dei pietate plenissima . . . et mihi famule tue . . . audi et exaudi me, dulcissima uirgo Maria, mater dei et misericordie. Amen.

Leroquais, *Heures* 2:346–47.

18. ff. 45v–46 Sequens oratio dicitur data a deo cuidam heremite, et omnes eam deuote dicentes dicuntur habere undecim milia annorum de indulgentia; Ita fertur inueniri in cronicis romanis. Oratio (in red). Aue sanctissima Maria, domina mea, mater dei, regina celi, porta paradisi, domina totius mundi . . . et ora pro peccatis meis. Amen.

Leroquais, *Heures* 2:381.

19. ff. 46–47 Oratio de uirgine Maria facta a sancto Bernardo abbate . . . (in red). Memento dulcissima mater et domina illius memorande stationis . . . propter illum qui amore mei nudus pependit in cruce, Iesus Christus, filius tuus, dominus noster. Amen.

20. ff. 47–48v Septem gaudia beate uirginis, composita per sanctum Thomam martirem et archiepiscopum cantuariensem, cui dicitur apparuisse beata uirgo et laudasse opus suum pollictamque esse presentiam suam ante obitum illius qui celebrauerit quotidie memoriam eius his gaudiis . . . (in red). Gaude flore uirginali quem honore spetiali . . . et florescent per eterna secula. Amen.

Leroquais, *Heures* 1:xxvii, 2:409. *RH* 6810. On the attribution to Thomas, see Wilmart, p. 329, n. 2.

21. ff. 48v–49 Oratio (in red). Dulcissime Iesu Christe qui beatissimam genitricem tuam . . . feliciter perueniamus. Qui uiuis.

Leroquais, *Heures* 1:282.

22. f. 49–49v Commemoratio conceptionis uirginis Marie contra pestem. Antiphona (in red). Conceptionem uirginis Marie . . . Oratio (in red). Deus ineffabilis misericordie qui prime pia clara mulieris . . . et uirgo peperit dominum nostrum Iesum Christum filium tuum, Amen.

23. ff. 49v–52v Oratio habita per beatum Leonardum qua liberata fuit regina Francie, que in partu deficiebat nec parere poterat iam desperata; Et est maxime uirtutis quoties deuote legitur et attente auditur cum mulier est in partu; Oratio (in red). Deus omnipotens solus sine fine et initio . . . glorificare nomen tuum. Qui est benedictus in secula seculorum.

24. ff. 52v–57v Suffrages to Margaret, guardian angel, Raphael archangel, Louis (King of France), Anne, Benedict, Sebastian.

25. ff. 57v–58v Protestatio fidei hortodoxe (in red). Coram te domine Iesu Christe dulcissime redemptor meus, corde protestor et ore confiteor . . . signo salutifere crucis. In nomine patris et filii et spiritus sancti. Amen.

f. 59 blank.

Wilmart, p. 378n, no. 9.

26. ff. 59v–60 Deus alpha et omega omnium rerum principium et finis huic libello ad salutem regine Francie finem inponatur. Et qui eam primam integris reginam constituit, eam in celis post longam uitam dignetur recipere. Amen. (Entirely in gold.)

f. 60v blank.

f. 1, blue initial "D" 9 lines high decorated with green and magenta acanthus spray on a gold ground, historiated with King David in prayer; note presence of descending rays of Divine Light and a psaltery. In two oval roundels on left and right, the Annunciation. In border above, two putti holding roundel with Greek inscription, an abbreviation for Christ, gold letters on blue ground; below, two angels holding arms (repainted). Two birds and other putti in border of gold acanthus spray on a ground of red, blue, or gold. f. 35v, gold filigree initial "O" 2 lines high within a frame 7 lines high, on a dark red ground, historiated with Christ on the Cross, arms free with bleeding wounds and the instruments of torture. f. 40v, illumination of Christ crucified, 10 lines high. ff. 2, 3v, 10v, 13, 20v, and 21, blue, gold, and magenta initials 2 lines high with piece floral border decoration with magenta and green acanthus spray, blue flowers, and small radiating gold discs, in the style of Francesco d'Antonio. Gold filigree initial 2 lines high on an alternating blue and red ground; simple gold initials 1 line high and paragraph marks on red, blue, and green grounds throughout. All gold decoration painted except a burnished initial on f. 59v.

Parchment. ff. 60. 202 × 132 mm (116 × 70 mm). 1–6^{10}. Catchwords surrounded by varying intricate geometrical pen borders. Ruled in black-brown ink. Written in Italian gothic textualis rotunda formata in 17 long lines in black Italian ink. Headings in red in script of text; ff. 59v–60, entirely in irregular roman capitals in gold ink.

Bound in sixteenth-century French gold-stamped olive morocco; elaborate monogram composed of EECE and two lambda (one inverted) in center accompanied by a field of closed S and interlaced lambda. The closed S is a sign for love; the lambda is a sign for life and the inverted lambda is a sign for *fidelitas*. For a similar binding and bibliographic references, see MS 52.

Written in Florence, as indicated by the decoration and presence of Zenobius in the litany, after 7 January 1499, the date of the marriage of Louis XII and Anne of Brittany. Note prominence of Louis IX and Anne in the litany and suffrages. Anne's name in texts 8 and 14. Arms repainted with those of Duchess Renée of Lorraine, c. 1520–30. Monogram of the binding painted under the arms. No. 46 from the collection of Henry Probasco, acquired by the Newberry 1 December 1890.

Second folio: -gabo. Turbatus est.

De Ricci, 1:530.

84

(23869)

Book of Hours, Use of Rome

Italy [*Illustrated*] 1474

1. ff. 1–12v Calendar in red and black, major feasts in red. Feasts include: Sancti Uincentii ordinis predicatorum (5 April), Sancti Petri ordinis predicatorum (29 April), Festum niuis et sancti Dominici confessoris (5 August), Sancti Petroni (*sic*) episcopi et Sancti Francisci (4 October, in red), Sancti Homoboni confessoris (13 November), Sancte Helysabeth uidue (19 November), Sancti Syri episcopi et confessoris (9 December).

2. ff. 13–43 Incipit officium beate uirginis

secundum consuetudinem romane curie (in red).

3. ff. 43–49 Six psalms for matins of the Office of the Virgin with rubrics for the days of the week.

4. ff. 49–55 Changed Office of the Virgin.

5. f. 55v (addition s. xvi) Oratio ad Iesum domini Gregorii papę in fine psalmorum pęnitentię. O bone Iesu uerbum patris, splendor paternę glorię . . . et suauis iucunditas ubi Iesu deus cum patre et spiritu sancto uiuis et regnas per omnia sęcula sęculorum. Amen.

6. ff. 55v–57 (addition s. xvi) Alia oratio ad Iesum. O bone Iesu, o pyssime Iesu, o dulcissime Iesu, o Iesu fili Marie uirginis plene misericordia et pietate . . . et omnes qui inuocant nomen tuum quod est Iesus.

Leroquais, *Heures* 2:79. Attributed to Richard Rolle; Allen, *Writings Ascribed to Richard Rolle,* p. 314.

7. ff. 57–65 Incipiunt septem psalmi penitentiales (in red).

8. ff. 65–72 Incipiunt letanie (in red). Petronius among the confessors; Francis and Bernard among the monks and hermits; Clare and Elizabeth among the virgins. Litany proper followed by the ten short prayers as in the Roman breviary. The fifth in the series begins Omnipotens sempiterne deus, miserere famulo tuo S. (= Sixtus IV) nostro et dirige eum . . .

9. ff. 72v–95v Incipit officium mortuorum (in red). Use of Rome.

10. ff. 95v–98v Incipit officium sancte crucis (in red). Short Hours of the Cross with marginal additions of s. xvi by the same hand as above, ff. 55v–56v.

11. ff. 99–100v Missa in honorem beate uirginis Marie. Salue sancta parens . . . hec tue optulimus maiestati. P.S. 1474.

12. ff. 100v–102 (addition s. xvi) Litanię B.V.M. Same hand as above, ff. 55v–56v.

13. f. 102–102v (addition s. xvi) Sub tuum presidium infra quesumus sancta dei genitrix . . . and by another hand the postcommunion, Gratiam tuam, quesumus domine . . . and the benediction, Diuinum auxilium . . . *SMRL* 2:229, 320, and 340. On the prayer Sub tuum presidium . . . , see Barré, *Prières anciennes,* p. 20, etc.

Front flyleaves (addition s. xvi) Oratio ante missam (partially effaced), liturgical responses, the Gloria in excelsis deo . . . , and the Credo in deum, patrem omnipotentem, factorem celi et terrę . . .

Five historiated magenta, green, and blue initials 5–6 lines high on gold grounds accompanied by full gold filigree borders decorated with green and blue flowers. f. 13, the Virgin and Child, a hare within a roundel in right margin; f. 57, David in penance, a heron-like water bird within a roundel in lower margin; f. 72v, a human skull, a white rabbit with a white bird flying above it within a roundel in the lower margin; f. 95v, the Cross with the instruments of torture on it; magenta laurel leaves form right margin; f. 99, a priest celebrating Mass accompanied by an inner bracket margin only. Magenta, blue, and green initials on gold grounds at the beginning of texts accompanied by outer bracket margins. Gold dentelle initials with white patterning on grounds of magenta, blue, and green 3 lines high in the calendar accompanied by similar but simpler inner margins. The beginnings of major sections of texts marked by gold, magenta, blue, and green dentelle initials accompanied by piece border decoration. Simple alternating blue and gold initials within the texts, alternating line fillers of the same colors within the litany.

Parchment. ff. ii + 102. 104 × 75 mm (63 × 43 mm). 1^{12}, $2–6^{8}$, 7^{4}, $8–11^{8}$, 12^{10}, 13^{4}. Catchwords present, f. 72v, visible behind an illuminated roundel. Leaf signatures partially trimmed. Ruled horizontally in pen. Written in Italian gothic textualis rotunda media in 17 long lines. Partially retraced in s. xvi by the hand of the additions on ff. 55v–56v. Running headings in upper margin added by the same hand. Headings within the text in red in the script of the text.

Bound in dull Italian brown morocco, s. xviii. Silver rear-edge clasp with the scallop of St. James.

Written in northern or central Italy, possibly in Bologna, in 1474 by the scribe P.S., signed with date on f. 100v. Saints in the calendar include Peter of Verona, Syrus (Pavia, Liguria, and Piedmont), Homobonus (Cremona), and Petronius (Bologna); Petronius also in the litany. f. 13, unidentified partially effaced arms (see color illustration). No. 47 from the collection of Henry Probasco, acquired by the Newberry 1 December 1890.

De Ricci, 1:529.

–85

(23870)

Book of Hours, Use of Rome

Italy s. XV² (after 1482)

1. ff. 1–11v Calendar written in black and red, most feasts in red. Feasts include: Barnabe

apostoli (10 June, perhaps in a different shade of red), Sancte Marie ad niues (5 August, in red), Transfiguratio domini (6 August, in red), Sancte Clare uirginis (12 August, in red), Remigii episcopi et confessoris (1 October, an addition), Sancti Francisci (4 October, in red).

Leaf containing November missing after f. 10.

2. ff. 12–58 Hours of the Virgin, use of Rome, beginning imperfectly. Prayers for protection and to All Saints after each hour after matins, ending with the Salue regina, followed by its usual prayer Omnipotens sempiterne deus qui gloriose uirginis . . .

3. ff. 58v–65v Six psalms for matins with rubrics for the days of the week. Rubrics give total of six psalms, but the rubric for the third of the second three has been omitted.

4. ff. 66–73v Changed Office of the Virgin. f. 73v, Finit officium beate Marie uirginis secundum consuetudinem romane curie (in red).

5. ff. 73v–74 Papa Sixtus quartus concessit cuilibet deuote dicenti infrascriptam orationem undecim milia annorum de uera indulgentia pro qualibet uice (*sic*); Oratio (in red). Aue sanctissima Maria, mater dei, regina celi, porta paradisi, domina mundi . . . et ora pro peccatis meis. Amen.

Leroquais, *Heures* 2:381.

6. f. 74–74v Specialis salutatio ad beatam uirginem Mariam (in red). Aue ancilla trinitatis, aue filia sempiterni patris . . . in omnibus tribulationibus meis. Amen.

Leroquais, *Heures* 2:380. *RH* 1692.

7. ff. 74v–85 Incipiunt vii psalmi. Text begins imperfectly on f. 75 in Psalm 6:9.

8. ff. 85–95 Letanie (in red). Bonaventure among the confessors, Bernardinus among the holy monks and hermits. Clare and Elizabeth among the virgins. Litany proper followed by the usual set of ten short prayers as in the Roman breviary, cues, and: Benedictio (in red). Exaudiat nos omnipotens et misericors dominus . . .

f. 95v blank.

9. ff. 96–139v Office of the Dead, use of Rome, with text beginning imperfectly.

10. ff. 139v–142 Incipit officium sancte crucis (in red). Short Hours of the Cross beginning imperfectly.

11. ff. 142v–145 Incipit officium sancti spiritus (in red). Short Hours of the Holy Spirit beginning imperfectly on f. 143.

ff. 145v–146v blank.

Parchment. ff. 146. Folios with text removed after ff. 10, 11, 74, 95 (stub bearing traces of marginal decoration present), 139 (stub bearing traces of marginal decoration present), and 142. 126 × 69 mm (72 × 40 mm). 1^{12} (11 wanting), 2^{10} (1 wanting), $3–7^{10}$, 8^{4}, 9^{10} (1 wanting), 10^{10}, 11^{10} (3 wanting), $12–14^{10}$, 15^{10} (8 wanting), 16^{6} (2 wanting). Vertical catchwords on the initial leaf of each quire matching last words on the preceding quire. Ruled in brown ink. Written in Italian gothic textualis in 16 long lines. Red initials with violet flourishes alternating with blue initials with red flourishes. Simple red and blue initials within sections of text.

Bound in limp parchment.

Written in Italy, probably after 14 April 1482, date of the canonization of Bonaventure, listed in the litany, and certainly after 1471, date of the succession of Sixtus IV, cited on f. 73v. Calendar, litany, and attribution of text 5 suggest possible Franciscan affinities. No. 43 from the collection of Henry Probasco, acquired by the Newberry 1 December 1890.

De Ricci, 1:529.

– 86

(234360)

Book of Hours, Use of Rome

Northern Italy s. XV²

1. ff. 3–14v Calendar written in black with major feasts in red. Feasts include: Sigismundis regis (2 May), Gotardi episcopi (5 May), Sancti Bernardini confessoris (20 May, in red), Iustini martiris (1 June), Sancti Antonii confessoris (13 June), Iustini presbyteri (5 August), Sancte Clare uirginis (13 August), Ludouici episcopi (20 August),Nicolai de Tolentino (10 September), Sancti Francisci seraphici (4 October), Sancte Iustine uirginis (7 October), Sancti Prodocimi episcopi (7 November), Sancte Helisabeth (19 November).

ff. 1–2v blank, serve as flyleaves; f. 15 blank and unruled; f. 15v, miniature.

2. ff. 16v–88v Hours of the Virgin, use of Rome. Two leaves wanting after f. 31; text ends imperfectly on the Te Deum of matins with the words "Et laudamus nomen." Lauds begins in Psalm 92:2 on f. 32.

f. 16 blank; f. 81 blank and unruled; f. 81v, miniature.

3. ff. 88v–97 Six psalms for matins with rubrics for the days of the week.

4. ff. 97–111 Changed Office of the Virgin. f. 111, Explicit officium beate Marie uirginis secundum consuetudinem curie romane feliciter (in red).

5. ff. 111–129 Incipiunt septem psalmi penitentiales (in red). Text beginning imperfectly on f. 112v in second word of Psalm 6.

ff. 111v–112 blank.

6. ff. 129v–143v Incipiunt letanie (in red). Francis, Anthony, and Dominic among the monks and hermits; Clare and Elizabeth among the virgins. Litany proper followed by the usual set of ten prayers as in the Roman breviary, and two other prayers as in Roman votive Masses for the dead: Oratio pro patre et matre (in red). Deus qui nobis patrem et matrem . . . *SMRL* 2:329; and Oratio pro omnibus fidelibus defunctis (in red). Deus cuius miseratione anime . . . *SMRL* 2:329.

f. 144 blank.

7. ff. 144v–200v Office of the Dead, use of Rome.

8. ff. 200v–206 Incipit officium sancte crucis (in red). Short Hours of the Cross with text beginning imperfectly in the second sentence on f. 201v.

f. 201 blank.

9. ff. 206–211v Incipit officium sancti spiritus (in red). Short Hours of the Holy Spirit with text beginning imperfectly in the second sentence on f. 207v.

ff. 206v–207 blank.

10. ff. 211v–215v Ad missam beate Marie uirginis (in red). Text beginning imperfectly in the fourth word of the Salue sancta parens on f. 212v.

f. 212 blank; ff. 216–217v blank, serve as flyleaves.

Two inserted miniatures in early sixteenth-century Venetian style. f. 15v, the Annunciation; f. 81v, the Massacre of the Innocents (compline). A modern hand on f. 1v has attributed these to Giulio Clovio, but they are not likely his. Probably to be attributed to a follower of Cima da Conegliano; cf. M. Salmi, *Italian Miniatures* (New York, 1956), pl. lxix b, and W. Smith, *The Farnese Hours: The Pierpont Morgan Library* (New York, 1976).

Parchment. ff. 216. Foliated 1–61, 63–217. Two leaves of text removed after f. 31. 73 × 54 mm (38 × 26 mm). 1^{2}, 2^{12}, 3^{13} (1 inserted), 4^{10} (5–6 removed), $5–7^{10}$, 8^{12} (4 inserted), 9^{13} (3 inserted), $10–11^{10}$, 12^{12}, $13–14^{10}$, 15^{12}, $16–21^{10}$, 22^{2}. Catchwords present. Leaves signed alphabetically, partially trimmed. Ruled in green ink. Written in Italian gothic textualis formata in 13 long lines. Blank leaves within the text intended for illuminated miniatures and incipits. Border decorations in blue, green, and red ink of architectural motifs, with many birds and a rabbit (f. 51v) present. Blue initials with red flourishes alternating with red initials with blue flourishes throughout, 2 lines high at beginning of sections of text, 1 line high within the text.

Bound in modern brown morocco, two silver scallop clasps.

Written in northern Italy, possibly in Padua, note presence of Justina, Anthony, and Prosdocimus in the calendar. The calendar also suggests Franciscan affinities. "Siena" written in modern pencil in upper margin of f. 216. f. 1v, old sticker, probably of a dealer, with number "1354" and "tra" in black ink and "rax" in red ink; "17" written in pencil on the flyleaf itself. Acquired by the Newberry from Edward E. Ayer, 1920.

De Ricci, 1:538.

f87.1

(56-68)

Venetian Chronicle to 1434

Venice s. XV med. (after 1434)

1. ff. 1–217v Qui uederemo chome Atilla flazelum dei pagani crudelisisimo . . . (ends imperfectly in mid folio) i qual son do sapientissimi homini, e foi fato grando //

Marginal additions on ff. 19–21 and 55v–57 by the same hand which copied texts 2 and 3 below; occasional index notes and dates by another hand, s. xv^{2}.

ff. 218–225v blank.

A recension of the usual anonymous fifteenth-century *Chronicle of Venice,* in Italian, beginning with the invasion of the Huns and here ending imperfectly 15 January 1434 with the arrival in Venice of two ambassadors of Pope Eugenius IV, described by H. Baron, "A Forgotten Chronicle of Early Fifteenth-Century Venice: The Copy in Newberry Manuscript f. 87.1," *From Petrarch to Leonardo Bruni: Studies in Humanistic and Political Literature* (Chicago, 1968), pp. 178–95; and Carile, *Cronachistica veneziana,* p. 111.

2. ff. 226–228v (addition s. xv ex.) [Qu]este sono le chaxade di nobelli che uano a conseio, e doue le uene e de che partte e de che condizion, e chomo fo el so orizene e chi fo edifichadori de algune giexie che sono per Ueniexia . . . E per simelle alguni portamentti fatti de utelle de la tera fatti per alguni e per algune uere la signoria de Ueniexia ano proue-

zudo in diuerssi tenpi de farne de consseio de Ueniexia, chomo sono questi sotto notadi: cha' Barixan, cha' Benedetto, Cha' Rezi . . . Cha' Uituri, Cha' Gay.

f. 229–229v blank.

Notes on the great families of Venice, closely related to texts found in other Venetian chronicles; cf. Carile, *Cronachistica veneziana,* p. 22, and A. Prost, "Les Chroniques vénitiennes," *Revue des questions historiques* 31 (1882): 520–21.

3. f. 230–230v (addition s. xv ex.) Questa he la refudaxion de l'ixolla de Candia et Sallonichi, fatta per U. Marchexe de Monteferato al doxe miser Rigo Dandollo et al chomun de Ueniexia. [A]nno en la incarnazione del nostro signor Yhesu Christo mcciiii al tempo de Inozenzio papa . . . Sequitta del dito Marchexe de mile marche d'arzentto. In nomine domini nostri Yhesu Christi anno ab incharnazione eiusdem m°cc°iiii° fatto in la zitta de Andrenopolli . . . actum die xii intrando agosto in presenzia de questi testimonii, silizet miser Bonachorso de Frigiano e miser Henrigo de Fizido e miser Pegeratto da Uerona e miser Guilberto da Uerona et Iachobo Gregori. Et io Bonus Amichus sachri palazii de duzia notario, tuto che de sopra se leze chon la mia mane scripissi.

Two documents in Italian translation pertaining to the transfer of Crete to Venice after the sack of Constantinople in 1204, closely related to the Venetian chronicle tradition; cf. Carile, *Cronachistica veneziana,* pp. 103–4 and 405–6.

Paper, watermarked with crossed arrows; cf. Briquet 6269 sqq. ff. iii + 230 + i. Arabic foliation of s. xv or xvi; ff. 1–207, with two leaves foliated 195, begins on f. 11 and ends on f. 218. ff. 1–230 modern pencil foliation. 330 × 225 mm (225 × 150 mm). $1–23^{10}$. Catchwords within decorative borders, mostly rectangular. Ruled in pen. ff. 1–10v, written in Italian hybrida media in 41 long lines beginning on the second ruled line. ff. 11–217, written in Italian gothic textualis rotunda media incorporating occasional humanistic traits (note, for example, the presence of long terminal s on f. 41, lines 9–10) in 42 long lines beginning on the first ruled line. ff. 226–228v and 230–230v, additions written in humanistic cursiva media in 49 lines in two columns beginning on the first ruled line. Ducal arms painted within roundels added in late s. xv or early s. xvi, occasionally covering the marginal notes by the second hand in text 1. Alternating simple red and blue initials throughout, some initials with red flourishes. Additions in the text marked with red paragraph marks; ff. 228–228v and 230–230v, additions marked with alternating red and blue paragraph marks.

Bound in half calf with rules over wooden boards, s. xv^2 or xvi^1; two fore-edge clasps wanting.

Written in Venice, c. 1450, certainly after 15 January 1434, last date mentioned in the text. In early s. xix, in the library of Lorenzo Antonio da Ponte, his engraved bookplate with the number "cod. ccxiv c" and "LL. 4" by another hand on the inside of the front cover. "Cronica uen[etia], bibl[ioteca] de Ponte, n. 9" written in a hand of s. xix on second front flyleaf. In 1821 sold with his library to Adolfo Cesare; see E. A. Cigogna, *Saggio di bibliografia veneziana* (Venice, 1847), p. 75. Sold by Cesare to Frederick North, Fifth Earl of Guilford (1766–1827); see De Ricci, *English Collectors,* pp. 94–95 and 122. Sold by North to Sir Thomas Phillipps, number "7503" in his collection printed on label pasted on the spine; recorded C. Castellani, *Elenco dei manoscritti veneti della collezione Phillipps* (Venice, 1890); see also Munby, *Phillipps Studies* 3:162. On spine, "232/3" written on a circular white label; "1697" written by a modern hand on the front flyleaf. Acquired by the Newberry from H. P. Kraus, November 1957.

Second folio: longe in mundo.

+88
(23859)
Franciscan Capitulary

Venice after 1403

1. ff. 1–6v Franciscan calendar of Venice with major feasts in red. Feasts include: Sancti Marci euuangeliste, duplex minus (25 April, in red), Octaua sancti Anthonii, semi-duplex (20 June, in red), Sancte Lucie uirginis et martiris, semi-duplex (13 December, in red).

2. ff. 7–113v In nomine domini, amen. Incipit ordo manualis fratrum minorum secundum consuetudinem romane curie.

Noted Common of Time from Haymo of Faversham, *Order of the Breviary. SMRL* 2:7–114. For the relation of this text and those that follow to the capitulary, see Van Dijk, *Origins,* pp. 321–25; this manuscript listed p. 325, n. 3.

3. f. 113v Incipit tabula siue rubrica maior breuiarii (in red) . . . Aduentus domini . . . (ends imperfectly in mid folio) in utrisque uesperis.

General Rubric of the Breviary, 1–3 (inc.). *SMRL* 2:114.

4. f. 113v (addition s. xv^2) In sanctorum martirio Berardi, Petri, Accursii, Adiuti, et Ottonis. Largire nobis, quesumus, domine,

beatis martiribus tuis Berardo, Petro, Accursio, Adiuto, et Ottone intercedentibus cęlestia semper et Christum amare quorum glorioso martirio ordinis minorum initia consecrasti. Per eum.

Invocation to the five Franciscan protomartyrs.

5. ff. 114–165 Incipiunt festiuitates sanctorum per anni circulum (in red).

Noted Proper of Saints from Haymo of Faversham, *Order of the Breviary. SMRL* 2:121–73.

6. ff. 165–168v Incipit tabula siue rubrica maior breuiarii . . . ; Aduentus domini . . . scilicet, o sapiencia et cetera (entirely in red).

A revised version of the *General Rubric of the Breviary;* cf. *SMRL* 2:114–21. Section 23 expanded to 22 feasts. Section 24 omitted, in its place a long list of 22 duplex minor feasts including that of Mark, 20 semi-duplex feasts including that of Lucy, and a rubric on absolutions and benedictions. After section 26, an added rubric on the "Te deum laudamus."

7. ff. 168v–169 Infrascripta tabula siue rubrica edita fuit per dominum Clementem papam vi^m^ (entirely in red) . . .

Decree of Clement VI on Franciscan feasts; cf. *SMRL* 1:166–67.

8. f. 169 Item alia rubrica de dominicis ab octaua pentecostes usque ad aduentum domini; Notandum quod ab octaua pentecostes usque ad aduentum . . . Et sic numquam errabitur in dominicis precedentibus uel communibus faciendis (entirely in red).

Parisian Rubric for the Sundays after Pentecost. SMRL 1:181–82, 183, 202, and 242.

9. f. 169–169v Infrascripta tabula est ordinata pro dominicis que ueniunt post pentecosten ut non erretur. In illo anno quando pasca uenerit viii° et vii° kalendas aprilis . . . de qua fieri debet sicut dicit rubrica breuiarii. Similiter quando festum omnium sanctorum uenerit in dominica secundum rubrica breuiarii, nichil debet fieri de dominica. Explicit tabula de dominicis ponendis post pentecosten ut non erretur (entirely in red).

Table for the Sundays after Pentecost. SMRL 1:244.

10. ff. 169v–170v Infrascripta rubrica est ordinata pro hystoriis ponendis in mense septembrio sequitur; In anno quo kalendis (*sic*) septembris die dominico uenerint, ystorie dicti mensis sic ordinentur . . . Feria vi^a^ proxima sequente ponitur liber Hester (entirely in red).

Parisian Table for the Scripture Reading of September, often attributed to Boniface VIII. *SMRL* 1:168, 240, 242–44, and Van Dijk, *Ordinal,* pp. 342–46.

11. ff. 171–185 Noted Common of Saints from Haymo of Faversham, *Order of the Breviary. SMRL* 2:173–85.

12. ff. 185–191 Incipit ordo officii beate uirginis (in red).

Noted Office of the Virgin from Haymo of Faversham, *Order of the Breviary. SMRL* 2:185–91.

13. ff. 191–195v Incipit officium in agenda defunctorum (in red).

Noted Office of the Dead from Haymo of Faversham, *Order of the Breviary,* with an additional section at the end, beginning with the prayer Deus cui proprium est . . .

14. ff. 196–219v Common tones for invocations, collects, epistles, gospels, the hours of compline and matins, absolutions, and benedictions.

15. ff. 219v–222v Incipit ordo ad benedicendum mensam per totum annum; Congregatis fratribus (in red) . . . (ends imperfectly in mid quire) et letemur in ea //

Haymo of Faversham, *The Order of Grace, SMRL* 2:197–203, with a full musical setting; square notation on four-line staves.

Two historiated magenta, blue, green, and orange initials 7 lines high extended to form partial upper left bracket acanthus spray borders in the same colors decorated with blue and magenta flowers and clusters of three gold radiating disks: f. 7, Paul with a sword; f. 171, Paul with a sword and Bible. Quire 17 only, gold dentelle initials with gold patterning on grounds of blue, olive, green, and dark red 4 lines high. Red, blue, gold, and silver initials with red, blue, violet, gold, and silver flourishing, with gold and silver less prevalent after the litany of Holy Saturday and ending completely after f. 59v. ff. 1–41, flourishing occasionally extended to form partial borders decorated with gold and silver radiating disks.

Parchment of southern preparation. Paper pastedowns. ff. i + 222 + i. 347 × 245 mm (243 × 155 mm). 1^{8} (7–8 wanting), $2–9^{10}$, 10^{8}, 11^{10}, 12^{10} (10 wanting), $13–16^{10}$, 17^{10} (10 wanting), 18^{8} (leaves removed from the end and reinserted so that sewing precedes 7–8), $19–22^{10}$, 24^{2} (an undetermined number of leaves wanting with loss of text). Quires 16–19, numbered i–iiii in lower right margin of the recto of the first leaf. ff. 196–222, entirely reruled in red ink for musical notation. Calendar ruled for 36 long lines; text ruled for 28 lines in two columns in ink. Written in Italian gothic textualis rotunda formata in very black Italian ink in 28 lines in two columns.

Bound in contemporary brown calf with rules over wooden boards. Two cloth fore-edge clasps wanting. "Manuale Chorale" written on spine.

Written in northeast Italy, probably in or near Venice, as suggested by the calendar and the additions to text 6, probably after 20 June 1403 as indicated by the inclusion of the Octave of Anthony of Padua in the calendar. Additions on f. 113v by a scribe of s. xv ex. with northern training. No. 37 from the collection of Henry Probasco, acquired by the Newberry 1 December 1890.

De Ricci, 1:528.

89.1

(Ry 222; 60-1686)
Aulus Persius Flaccus, *Saturae;*
Antonio Loschi, *Carmina;*
Cicero, *Partitiones Oratoriae*

Milan s. XV[1]

f. iv Continentur autem in hoc libro: Flaci Persii satirę omnes, Antonii Lusci Uicentini poetę epistularum liber, et partitiones oratorię Marci Tullii Ciceronis.

Title page, s. xv.

1. ff. 1–11v Persei Lucilli Auli Flacci poetae satirici liber foeliciter incipit; Persei prologus (in red and violet).

Nec fonte labra prolui cabalino (*sic*) . . .
Inuentus, Crisippe, tui finitor acerui [–amoris]. Tellos (last 3 words written by another hand).

Text accompanied by an interlinear and a marginal gloss. Gloss 1 begins: Hedera est herba ex una parte uiridis . . . Gloss 2 begins: O curas hominum: Hęc est sathira prima, in 5 partes diuisa, primo rei nouitatis admirationem ponit . . .

ff. 12–14 blank; f. 14v, pen trials on verso of last folio of quire.

Aulus Persius Flaccus, *Saturarum liber,* ed. W. V. Clausen (Oxford, 1956), pp. 1–33.

2. ff. 1–2 Antonii Lusa (*sic*) uicentini poete epistolarum liber incipit. Ad reuerendissimum patrem dominum dominum Petrum de Candia cardinalem mediolanensem ipsius digna comendatio, ob id quod illustrium dominorum uicecomitum confirmandi et pacif[ic]andi status curam onusque susceperit.

Magne pugil fidei, rerum fons alte sacrarum . . .
Natura est genus anguigerum dominabile terris.

Da Schio, *Carmina,* pp. 45–47.

3. ff. 2–3

[C]arule (*sic*), magnanimis sate progenitoribus, unum . . .
Stabit et innocui fratres sua sceptra tenebunt.

Antonio Loschi, *Ad Carolum de Malatestis.* Da Schio, *Carmina,* pp. 59–61.

4. ff. 3–5

[L]etus amiciciam, tua cuius epistola nuper . . .
Et rapere affectus et pectora uoluere fundo.

Antonio Loschi, *Ad amicum,* ed. Zaccaria, "Le Epistole," pp. 441–42.

5. ff. 5–7v

[F]ama per Italiam celeri delapsa uolatu . . .
Ultima pontificis ueniat sibi cura supremi.

Antonio Loschi, *Ad Nicolum de Spinellis et Cavallium de Cavallis.* Da Schio, *Carmina,* pp. 7–11.

6. ff. 7v–9v

[Q]ue mouet ethereos si causa portentior orbes . . .
Hec uia tranquillo poterit nos sistere portu.

Antonio Loschi, *Ad Jacobum Livicum Furliviensem.* Massera, "Iacobo Allegretti da Forlì," pp. 202–3.

7. ff. 9v–11v

[N]atus in Italie est medio flos aureus agro . . .
Inter odora uomens nociturum lilia uirus.

Antonio Loschi, *Ad Pasquinum de Capellis.* Da Schio, *Carmina,* pp. 12–15.

8. ff. 11v–12v

[O]lim ego dum sacro, dux o clarissime, tecum . . .
Consilia, et uanas sparsere nocentia terras.

Antonio Loschi, *Ad ducem Mediolanensem,* Da Schio, *Carmina,* pp. 24–26.

9. ff. 12v–13v

[O] Felix, cui per placidam uidisse quietam . . .
Nec dignum lauro nec uatis honore superbum.

Antonio Loschi, *Francisco de Ricchaneto.* Da Schio, *Carmina,* pp. 22–23.

10. ff. 13v–14v

[O] Firmane, preces mea dura silentia tandem . . .
(f. 14, line 12) Pyeridum sanctasque domos uagus error et ingens
Musarum me ducat . . .

Si quod habat (*sic*) placitum tibi parua potentia rebus.

Antonio Loschi, *Ad Jacobum Firmanum,* initial portion only edited by Zaccaria, "Le Epistole," p. 443.

11. ff. 14v–16

[M]axime dux ligurum, quo sceptra tenente, quietem . . .

Quos decet et sanctum est hostili a fraude tueri.

Antonio Loschi, *Ad ducem Mediolanensem.* Da Schio, *Carmina,* pp. 27–29.

12. ff. 16–17

[E]st tua, crede michi, maiori digna teatro . . .

Talibus, hic regi grates aget, hostibus alter.

Antonio Loschi, *Ad Antonium de Romagno Feltrensem.* Da Schio, *Carmina,* pp. 17–18.

13. ff. 17–18v Ad egregium et amicum musis uirorum (*sic*) Matheum de Orglano uicentinum Antonii Lusci uicentini epistola aurea de Petrarce fontibus sumpta materia que ex auro nisa nobilia (*sic*), et quod ad maiorem nominis dignitatem omni rei nobili per antiquos fiat aureum (in red).

Ut nichil in terris fuluo preciosius (*sic*) auro . . .

Uiue sed ut ualeas sacro sis ditior auro.

Antonio Loschi, *Mateo Orglanensi Vincentino.* Zaccaria, "Quattro epistole," pp. 24–26.

14. ff. 18v–20

[E]loquii tuba celsa itali dignissime lauro . . .

Credite et insignis uestre nitor additur arti.

Antonio Loschi, *Ad Laurentium Monacum Venetum.* Zaccaria, "Quattro epistole," pp. 19–21.

15. ff. 20–21v

[U]na uetus patrie laus est et gloria nostre . . .

Hanc etiam nostris seruare nepotibus equum est.

Antonio Loschi, *Egregiis ac fidelibus civibus Vicentinis.* Da Schio, *Carmina,* pp. 42–44.

16. ff. 21v–23v

[M]iles ab audaci dura in certamina gallo . . .

Iam superis promissa colent sua uota puelle.

Antonio Loschi, *Virtuoso atque fortissimo militi singulari domino Galeatio de Grumello.* Da Schio, *Carmina,* pp. 3–6.

17. ff. 23v–29

[S]i qua olim in dubiis uatum sententia rebus . . .

Fama mouet, sacro uenit hostia digna labori.

Antonio Loschi, *Ad Jacobum Livicum Furliviensem.* Massera, "Iacopo Allegretti da Forlì," pp. 193–202.

18. ff. 29–30

[F]ecit ut aspicerem tua dulcis epistola quantus . . .

Pan facit armentum custosque paterque locorum.

Antonio Loschi, *Ad Leonardum Roellum de Monte Sabatino.* Zaccaria, "Le Epistole," pp. 430–31.

19. f. 30v

[M]agnanimi heroes, Itale tria sidera terre . . .

Desinet insidiis Latiam turbare quietem.

Antonio Loschi, *Ad dominum Mantuanum, dominum Pandulfum et dominum Malatestam de Malatestis.* Da Schio, *Carmina,* pp. 30–31.

20. ff. 31–32v

[I]acobe, militie decus et lux una latine . . .

Hanc facerent in qua proprie nil laudis haberent.

Antonio Loschi, *Ad Jacobum de Verme.* Da Schio, *Carmina,* pp. 32–34.

21. ff. 32v–34

O scelus et plus quam crudeli morte luendum . . .

Euolat ingenii tua mira scientia pennis.

Antonio Loschi, *Petro Cretensi episcopo Novariensi.* Zaccaria, "Le Epistole," pp. 425–26.

22. ff. 34v–35

[I]am uaga diffuse nec fessa licentia fame . . .

Nomen, et Italie moueat quem cura relicte.

Antonio Loschi, *Petro Cretensi episcopo Novariensi apud Cesarem,* ed. A. Corbellini, "Appunti sull'Umanesimo in Lombardia," *Bollettino della società pavese di storia patria* 16 (1916): 164–65.

23. ff. 35v–36

[S]i patris ante oculos natum laudare liceret . . .

Implicito, et tenui uix respondente Camena.

Antonio Loschi, *Ad Franciscum de Brunis bononiensem.* Da Schio, *Carmina,* pp. 20–21.

24. ff. 36–37

[S]epe ego cum magnas bellando uiceris urbes . . .

Spirantis uultus atque ora simillima uiuis.

Antonio Loschi, *Ad Jacobum de Verme*. Da Schio, *Carmina*, pp. 48–50.

25. ff. 37–39v

[S]oluerat auricomos nimpharum turba iugales . . .

Et sacram hostili uexabant agmine Romam.

Antonio Loschi, *Francisco de Fiano*. Da Schio, *Carmina*, pp. 55–58.

26. ff. 39v–40v

Uere pater patrie, Michael, iustissime princeps . . .

Illam inconcussa florentem pace relinquas.

Antonio Loschi, *Ad dominum Michaelem Steno ducem Venetiarum*. Da Schio, *Carmina*, pp. 62–64.

27. ff. 40v–42

Egregie, O iuuenis, quem clara ex indole natum . . .

Culmen utraque uia celsum uirtutis adibis.

Antonio Loschi, *Ad Johannem de Nogarolis*. Da Schio, *Carmina*, pp. 65–67.

28. f. 42–42v

[P]an tuus anguigera multis cum laudibus aula . . .

Atque uale et letam nostri memor exige uitam.

Antonio Loschi, *Ad Antonium de Romagno Feltrensem*. Da Schio, *Carmina*, p. 16.

29. ff. 42v–47v

[S]eptimus hybernum iam uersat aquarius annum . . .

Fer, precor, aut nostro, uelut altera Pallas, Ulixi.

Antonio Loschi, *Ad Colucium Pierium*. V. Zaccaria, "A. Loschi e Colucio Salutati," *Atti dell'Istituto Veneto di scienze, lettere ed arti* 129 (1971): 380–87.

30. ff. 47v–48v

[M]usa sepulta diu ligurum cum principe cuius . . .

(ends imperfectly at the end of the quire)

Durior obstabat felicibus obuia signis.

Brisia (catchword) //

Antonio Loschi, *Philippo Marie Vicecomiti duci Mediolanensi*. Zaccaria, "Le Epistole," pp. 437–38, line 61.

31. ff. 1–32 Partiones (*sic*) oratorię Marci Tulli Ciceronis. Studeo, mi pater . . . multisque ex tuis preclarissimis muneribus nullum maius expecto. Finis (in violet).

Text corrected by a humanistic hand on f. 2 only.

ff. 32v–34v blank.

Cicero, *Partitiones oratoriae*, ed. H. Bornecque (Paris, 1960).

Paper. ff. 1–14 bear serpent watermark; cf. Briquet 13625. ff. 1–48 bear *fleur* watermark; cf. Briquet 6592. ff. 102. Foliated in the following manner: 4 folios unfoliated, 1–14 (1 folio after f. 1 and 1 folio after f. 2, unfoliated), 1–48, 1–34. 201 × 141 mm (125–50 × 90–105 mm). 1^4, $2–9^8$, $10–12^{10}$, 13^4. Quires 2–3, vertical catchwords (floral mark above and below) in lower right margin; quires 4–9, horizontal catchwords (3 dots above and below, floral mark on either side) in center of bottom margin; quires 10–12 (except 10), vertical catchwords in rectangles in lower right margin. Quires 10–13 numbered 7–10 in roman numerals on upper right recto of the first folio. Quires 2–9 ruled in pencil, quire 10 unruled, quires 11–13 ruled in hard point. Text written by at least two different hands: quires 2–3 in Italian gothic textualis media incorporating occasional humanistic traits in 26 long lines beginning on the second ruled line; two glosses, one by same hand in same script as the text, the other in humanistic cursiva by another hand. Headings in red and violet in humanistic textualis. f. 1, red flourished gothic initial, other minor rustic capital initials in red. Quires 4–9 in a similar Italian gothic textualis media, with one-story a and trailing terminal s, in 24 long lines beginning on the second ruled line. ff. 1 and 17, headings in red in script of text. ff. 1, 17, 32v, 39v, 40v, red initials 2 lines high; ff. 1, 17, 25, 33, initial letter of each line touched in red. Blurring on f. 25 has confused a modern reader who numbered the "Epistole metriche" incorrectly. Quires 11–13, in humanistic textualis media changing to Italian hybrida media. Quire 10 written in 18–23 long lines with the minims of the first written line hung from the first ruled line. Quires 11–12 written in 21 long lines beginning on the second ruled line. Names of interlocutors in red. Headings in red in the same script.

Bound in "furry" calf over pasteboard, s. xv or xvi. Modern spine label, "Persii Satyrae et Cic. Orat."

Written in Italy, texts and paper indicate in or near Milan, c. 1430. Pen trials on f. 14v of the first sequence of foliation suggest that at least text 1 circulated separately before binding. Back cover has effaced black stamp with cardinal's hat over an eagle. f. 31 of the second foliation, sixteenth-century ex libris "Hic liber est Flaminii Cribelli." Formerly in the library of Ercole Silva of Milan (1756–1840). Front pastedown bears armorial bookplate "Ex libris Herculis de Silva"; see J. Gelli, *3500 Ex Libris italiani* (Milan, 1908), pp. 376–77. f. iv^v, "Dulac, 1872." Acquired by the Newberry in 1960 from J. Thiébaud, catalogue 334, item no. 57.

Second folio: text 1, a[d]sensere uiri; text 2, ad mare; text 3, uel auspiturm (corrected to aruspicum).

f90

(49-1571)

Aulus Gellius, *Noctes Atticae*

Northern Italy [*Illustrated in Color*] 1445

1. ff. 1–244v Auli Gellii commentario primo hęc insunt (in red). Quali proportione quibusque collectionibus Plutarchus ratiocinatum esse Pithagoram philosophum dixerit . . . (f. 18) Auli Gellii noctium atticarum liber primus incipit feliciter . . . (in red). Plutarchus in libro quem scribit G. quantum inter homines animi corporisque ingenio atque uirtutibus intersit . . . ut iam statim declaretur, quid quo in libro quęri inuenirique possit. Finis. Per Milanum Burrum 1445.

Aulus Gellius, *Noctes atticae;* cf. ed. P. K. Marshall (Oxford, 1968). This text in the recension of Guarino da Verona, Books I–VII and IX–XX, table of *capitula* includes Book VIII. Prologue follows the text. See H. Baron, "Aulus Gellius in the Renaissance and a Manuscript from the School of Guarino," *Studies in Philology* 48 (1951): 107–25.

2. ff. 245–272v Auli Gellii tabula per librorum et capitulorum numerum et ordinem alphabeti per litteras duas (in red).

Subject index "Absurduit" through "Transgressum," ends imperfectly at the end of a quire. Reference given to book and chapter.

Parchment. ff. 272. Original arabic foliation in red. Trimmed to 252 × 170 mm (164 × 94 mm). $1–34^8$. Quires numbered with arabic numerals on lower margin of verso of last folio. Catchwords present. Ruled in light pen. Written in humanistic textualis media in 35 long lines beginning on the second ruled line. Greek added in a different and lighter ink. Headings of chapters in red in script of text; leaves signed alphabetically, traces visible. Headings of principal divisions of the books in red in rustic capitals incorporating "Byzantine" elements, notably in the capital M. Running headings of book numbers in red arabic numerals in upper margin; running headings of chapter numbers in red roman numerals in outer margin. f. 1 and the beginning of each book except the first, gold initials decorated with white vine stem on grounds of pink, magenta, blue, green, and yellow 8 lines high. f. 18, blue initial on gold ground 17 lines high with a piece of green and gold ivy border, decorated with pink flowers. Alternating red initials with violet flourishes and blue initials with red flourishes throughout. Alternating simple red and blue initials in the initial section of *capitula*.

Bound in ruled calf, s. xviii.

Written in northern Italy, 1445, by Milanus Burrus, signed and dated f. 244v. For other manuscripts by this scribe active in the circle of the Visconti family, see H. Baron, "The Scribe of the Newberry Gellius of 1445: A Supplementary Note," *Studies in Philology* 49 (1952): 248–50; S. Morison, *Byzantine Elements in Humanistic Script Illustrated from the Aulus Gellius of 1445 in the Newberry Library* (Chicago, 1952); *Colophons de manuscrits occidentaux,* 13827–29. f. 18, arms of Finardi family of Bergamo, V. Spreti, *Enciclopedia storico-nobiliare italiana* (Milan, 1928–32), 3:182, painted over an effaced earlier coat of arms, cf. D. Miner, "The Manuscripts of the Grenville Kane Collection," *Princeton University Library Chronicle* 11 (1949–50): 41–44. f. 2, initials "B. R. S. L. R.," the "S" written over a triple cross, by an early modern hand. Before 1914, in the Biblioteca Molza (Modena). Acquired by the Newberry from Ulrico Hoepli (Milan), 7 July 1949.

Second folio: loquacitas et.

90.1

(59-1217)

Franciscan Collection

Umbria [*Illustrated*] 1456/1461–1469

1. ff. 1–4 In hiis expendimus tempus nostrum ubi es, o superbia et uanitas mea . . . integram et plenam confessionem se preparet et disponat.

Anonymous penitential text.

2. ff. 4–5 Modus cognoscendi se ipsum. Ad hoc notandum est quod quicumque uult ad perfectam sui cognitionem . . . Primo examinat cor suum . . . nisi interueniat gratia mediatoris dei et Christi Iesu domini nostri.

Anonymous penitential text.

3. f. 5 Ac. = Accurs[i]us . . . ad confirmandum ponuntur. Deo gratias. 1466 28 die aprilis in Parauis[in]o (?), in die sancti Uitalis, hora xvi.

Alphabetical glossary of legal abbreviations which usually accompanies Bartholomew of San Concordio, ed. G. Fumagalli, *Rivista delle biblioteche e degli archivi* 6 (1896): 185–88. The text is followed by a brief note on legal abbreviations, not in the printed edition, which is also found in MS 78, text 2.

4. ff. 5v–6 Solus papa. Primus casus est uotum ultramarium seu sancti sepulchri . . .

A list of reserved cases of papal excommunication followed by a list of episcopal excommunications.

5. ff. 7–8v, 6v, 9–12 Incipiunt constitutiones Martini quinti reducte sub compendio

cum suis remissionibus quantum ad communem utilitatem fratrum. Quia gaudent breuitate moderni et est facilius memorie commendare . . . quando leguntur constitutiones Martini deo gratias 1466 v die mensis maii hora xv[a]. Finis.

Compendium of the reform decrees of the Franciscan Chapter General of 1430 followed by the "Constitutiones familiae," prepared by the Chapter General of Osimo, 6 May 1461. See J. Moorman, *A History of the Franciscan Order* (Oxford, 1968), pp. 447–48 and 508.

6. f. 12–12v Iste sunt prime laxate secundum canones. Que prima sit pro singularis pecatis iniungenda recipe secundum Raymundum § xliii sequitur et se et Hostiensem § xxiii quia prima circa hac sunt diuerse opiniones . . . omnia Raymundi.

Anonymous penitential canons.

7. ff. 13–20 Est bona laudare et praua culpare, leges impellunt ipse igitur . . . Prudentia est calliditas . . . ut uulnus detegas.

Latin and Italian florilegium drawn from the works of the ancients, church fathers, and humanists. Authors include Ovid, Cicero, Augustine, Ambrose, Isidore, Dante, and Petrarch. Text divided into thirty-four chapters titled "De prudentia," "De pace," "De iustitia," "De luxuria," "De superbia," "De consilio petendo," "De uxore non capienda propter dotem," "De mutabilitate fortune," et cetera.

8. f. 20v Brief extracts in Latin from the tragedies of Seneca, Lucan, Boethius, and Ovid.

9. ff. 20v–21v Dante. In cantica inferni.
Et ella ad me nision (*sic*) maior dolore . . .
De trar l'ochi for delle toe onde
Explicit opusculum 1467 in uigilia Bartholomei in Escol[anens]e.

Extracts from Dante, *Divina commedia,* beginning with *Inf.*, 5, 121 and ending with *Par.*, 27, 123. Extracts from Boethius worked in.

10. ff. 21v–22v [G]eneroso et felici militi domino Raymundo Castri sancti Ambrosii Bernhardus in seruum deditus (*sic*) salutem. Doceri petis a nobis de cura et modo rei familiaris utilius gubernande . . . ad quem eam perducant merita sue dampnabilis senectutis et cetera. Deo gratias.

Ps. Bernard of Clairvaux, *Epistola de gubernatione rei familiaris*. *GW* 3960–81. *PL* 182:647–51. R. Avesani, *Quattro miscellanee medioevali e umanistiche* (Rome, 1967), pp. 42–43.

11. f. 22v Demostenes in oratione ad Alexandrum. Nihil habes Alexander uel fortuna tua . . . et formam sumpsisti et cetera.

Beginning only of Pietro Marcello, *Oratio Demosthenis ad Alexandrum*. Sabbadini, "Antonio da Romagno e Pietro Marcello," p. 243.

12. f. 22v Quicquid ad sum[m]um uenit . . .

Brief excerpts from an unidentified work attributed in the margin to Seneca.

13. f. 22v ✠ Christe filii dei uiui miserere ei ✠ deinde istos Christus . . . dicant ter pater noster cum aue Maria et cetera.

Cf. *SMRL* 2:465.

14. f. 22v Non tam sum demens ut egrotare culpam . . . et bonum est et obtabile quicquid ex huius geritur imperio. Uale.

Unidentified text titled "Sapiencia" (?) in the margin.

15. f. 23–23v Speculum anime beati Augustini (in red). O ueritas, lumen cordis mei, non tenebre mee loquantur mihi. Defluxi enim abs te . . . a gratia uero transeamus ad gloriam. Amen. Explicit speculum sancti Augustini de anima (underlined in red).

Attributed to Augustine, *HUWHA,* vol. 1, pt. 2, p. 406, and vol. 2, pt. 1, p. 381. Also titled *Speculum animae beati Augustini* in Holkham Hall 479 (s. xv), ff. 133–34, and Rome, Biblioteca Casanatense 3560 (s. xiii), ff. 43v–48; see V. Saxer, "Le Manuscrit 3560 de la Bibliothèque Casanatense de Rome," *Miscellanea codicologica F. Masai dicata* (Ghent, 1979) 1:282, where this sermon also precedes Augustine, *Sermo 350*. This is not one of the texts of the same title usually associated with Augustine, i.e., *GW* 3024–27 and *PL* 40:968 and 983.

16. ff. 23v–24 Incipit sermo Augustini episcopi de laude caritatis (underlined in red). Diuinarum scripturarum multiplicem habundanciam latissimamque doctrinam sine ullo errore comprehendit . . . appareat in nostris moribus. Amen, amen. Explicit sermo sancti augustini de laude caritatis (underlined in red).

Augustine, *Sermo 350 De laude caritatis*. *PL* 39:1533–35. *CPL* 284.

17. ff. 24–25v Augustinus de gaudio electorum et de supplicio dampnatorum (underlined in red). Tria sunt sub omnipotentis manu dei habitacula . . . et sine fastidio clamore cordis laudabunt deum omnipotentem, benignum et misericordem cui honor et gloria et nunc et per omnia secula seculorum. Amen. Explicit tractatus beati Augustini episcopi de

gaudio electorum et supplicio dampnatorum (underlined in red).

Ps. Augustine, *De triplici habitaculo liber I.* A. Gwynn, *Scriptores latini Hiberniae,* vol. 1 (Dublin, 1955), pp. 106–24. *CPL* 1106. *PL* 40:991–98.

18. ff. 25v–26 Sermo sancti Augustini de sancto Ioseph (underlined in red). Quoties uobis, fratres karissimi, lectiones de testamento ueteri recitantur . . . istos ualeat excusare correcta . . . qui uiuit et regnat deus per omnia secula seculorum. Amen. Finis sermonis beati Augustini de sancto Ioseph.

Ps. Augustine, *Sermo 13 De beato Joseph. CPL* 368. *PL* 39:1765–67.

19. ff. 26v–28v Regula e uita delli amatori de Ihesu Christo ordinata per magistro Antonio de Massa dell ordine de San Francesco fundata . . . Regula e uita delli amadori de Ihesu Christo e honesta zoe de obseruare el sancto euangelio dello nostro signore . . . alla dritta mano del padre sempiterno per infinita secula seculorum. Amen. Qui finissce la regola delli amadori de Ihesu. Amen.

Antonio da Massa, *Regola e uite degli amatori di Iesu Cristo,* edited in *Rime e prose del buon secolo della lingua tratte da manoscritti e in parte inedite* (Lucca, 1852), pp. 121–24. *DBI* 3:555–56. Zambrini, *Le Opere volgari,* col. 35.

20. ff. 28v–29 Incipit tenor ualoris misse. Paulus. Missa precellit rem dignior ceteris omnibus sicut Christus, qui est caput nostrum, est dignior . . . cum ueneris ante figuram pretereundo caue ne sileatur aue.

Unidentified text.

21. f. 29–29v Confiteor deo omnipotenti beate Marie semper uirgini, beato Francisco et omnibus sanctis . . . et peto misericordiam et absolutionem a domino deo et a uobis patres. Amen.

Franciscan prayer of confession.

22. f. 30 Pater noster, Ave Maria, all in Italian, titles in Latin.

f. 30v blank.

23. ff. 31–39 [I]ste liber uocatur stimulus amoris . . . [C]urrite gentes undique et miremini contra nos caritatem dei . . . in pace perpetua ad quam et cetera.

Ps. Bonaventure, *Stimulus amoris* (some versions attributed to James of Milan). This recension is the same as the edition of Cologne 1502, prologue omitted, to the end of chapter 4 only. On the variant recensions of this text, see *Bibliotheca franciscana ascetica medii aevi* 4 (1905): pp. vi–ix, and I. Fischer, *Handschriften der Ratsbücherei Lüneburg,* vol. 2, pt. 1 (Wiesbaden, 1972), p. 138. Glorieux, 305cx.

24. ff. 39v–40v Incipit epistola Bonauenture ualde notabilis. In nomine Ihesu fratri dilecto Petro frater eius Bonauentura in domino. Qualiscumque in ueteri homine iam exuto . . . nolite iudi quisquam.

Bonaventure, *Epistola viginti quinque memorialium,* in *Opera omnia* (Quaracchi, 1892–1901), 8:491–98. Glorieux, 305ac. This recension ends with 24 lines of text not in the printed edition.

25. ff. 41–44 De turbationibus occurrentibus in missa. [T]urbatur autem missa aut propter scandalum sacramenti aut propter scandalum sacerdotis . . . (f. 44) De diuinis officiis. Hoc tenendum est quod quamuis omni tempore tenemur laudare deum . . .

Florilegium of excerpts on the Mass drawn from Monaldus of Dalmatia, Thomas Aquinas, Gregory the Great, and Augustine.

26. ff. 44v–47. Ecce descripsi eam tripliciter prouerbiis xxii. Cum omnis scientia . . . amplexanda per osculum et dilectorum et hoc seraphin et cetera. Finis. Explicit paruum bonum Boneuenture (*sic*) ordinis minorum 1465 sabbato, infra octauam corporis Christi, infra xvii et x8 horas in Tuscanella, frater Uolfgangus de Austria ordinis minorum.

Bonaventure, *De triplici via* in the recension as in *GW* 4706 (titled "Regimen conscientie vel Parvum bonum"). Cf. *Opera omnia* (Quaracchi, 1892–1901), 8:3–27. Glorieux, 305am.

27. ff. 47v–50v Incipit tractatus infantium de ordine predicandi. Quam spetiosi sunt pedes euangelizantium pacem in Christum Ihesum qui est pax uera . . . in nomine domini incipit tractatus infantium de ordine predicandi et sermonizandi qui in quinque partes diuiditur . . . et estimo eum fuisse plusquam martir.

Anonymous, *Tractatus infantium de ordine predicandi.*

28. ff. 51–54v Superbia est proprie excellentie appetitus ut dicit Bernardus cuius 4[or] sunt species secundum Gregorium . . . (f. 53) Quid sit spes et quomodo differt a fide . . . (f. 53v) De iustitia et speciebus eius . . . (f. 54v) De 7 beatitudinibus et quomodo perficiunt animam . . . et possint recurrere et cetera ut dicitur. Frater Uolfgangus ordinis minorum de

Austria, capellanus monialium [Sancte Clare] in prouincia Marchie Anconitane ad Sanctum Genesium, tunc temporis scripsit hec, 1469, 1° kalendas marcii.

Anonymous treatise on the virtues and vices, unrecorded by Bloomfield, *Incipits*.

29. f. 55–55v Quotations from the Bible with reference to chapters, beginning: Ecclesiasticus 51, a lingua iniqua. Ends: 1 Cor 13, si linguis hominum loquor et angelorum.

30. ff. 55v–58v Petite cum cordis puritate . . . pro ultimo articulo mortis tue. Amen. (f. 56) Quintum peccatum mortale est auaritia, si fecit usuram si retinet pignora . . . michi penitentiam et absolutionem. Explicit 1.4.68 xii die mensis marcii.

Two folios of text removed after f. 55, another after f. 58.

Treatise on the seven vices, unrecorded by Bloomfield, *Incipits*.

31. f. 58v List of terms related to the virtues and vices.

32. ff. 59–66 Cases of papal excommunication; same as text 4 above to f. 60; followed by cases of episcopal excommunication differing from those in text 4.

33. ff. 66–68v Bull, beginning "Religiosus" of Eugenius IV, dated at Bologna "m°cccc tricesimo septimo quinto kalendas aprilis," i.e., 18 March 1438 (n.s.).

34. ff. 68v–71v De Regulis iuris. Beneficium ecclesiasticum non possit sine institutione canonica obtineri . . . Certum est, quod is committit in legem, qui, uerba legis complectitur, contra legis nititur uoluntatem.

Boniface VIII in *Liber Sextus*, lib. V, tit. xii, ed. A. Friedberg, *Corpus iuris canonici* 2:1122–24. This text transcribed separately in many manuscripts.

35. ff. 72–75v Incipit ordinatio misse. Indutus planeta sacerdos stet ante gradum altaris . . . Qua completa benedicit populum dicens, Benedicat et custodiat uos omnipotens deus pater et filius et spiritus sanctus. Amen. Explicit ordinatio misse, deo gratias, Ihesus. Questo libro nel quale sonno alcune operette sie ad usu di frate Antonio da Uiterbo et adpartene al luoco di Santa Maria del Paradiso adpresso a Uiterbo. 1456.

Haymo of Faversham, *The Order of Action and Speech for Private and Ferial Public Masses, SMRL* 2:1–14.

Paper, one bifolium (= ff. 71–72) parchment of southern preparation. ff. 75. 144 × 118 mm (c. 115 × 90 mm). 1^{14} (13–14 wanting), 2^{10}, 3^{10} (9–10 wanting), 4–5^{10}, 6^{10} (6 and 8 removed with loss of text), 7^{8}, 8^{10} (10 wanting). Quire 5 has catchwords on leaves 1, 2, 8, and 9. Quires 1–3, 5, and 6, frame ruled in pencil. Quire 4, frame ruled in hard point. Quires 7–8, frame ruled in hard point. Quires 1–6, written in northern European hybrida currens with a long terminal s, reflecting humanistic influence, by Friar Wolfgang of Austria. Quire 1, written in c. 52–62 lines in two columns; quire 2, written in 33–39 long lines; quire 3, written in 42–58 lines in two columns; quire 4, written in 42–73 long lines; quires 5 and 6, written in 39–43 long lines. Quires 2, 3, and 6, headings in red in Italian gothic textualis rotunda media. Writing begins on or above the upper ruled line. Quires 7–8, written in Italian hybrida with trailing terminal s in very black ink beginning on the second ruled line.

Bound in Italian stamped calf over paperboard, s. xv. Ruled panel decorated with a roll of a rope motif, semicircular rope motif stamps, and simple small double-circle stamps. Two fore-edge clasps wanting. Modern parchment spine label, "Varia MS 1466."

Quires 7 and 8 written in 1456 for Antonio da Viterbo of the Franciscan convent of Santa Maria del Paradiso in Viterbo, dated on f. 75v above. Quires 1–6 written in 1461–69 by Friar Wolfgang of Austria, a northern scribe, revealing only minimal Italian influence. He also copied Rome, Biblioteca Angelica, 140, in 1468–69, *Colophons de manuscrits occidentaux*, 18910. This manuscript dated or signed by Wolfgang on ff. 5, 12, 21, 47, 54v, and 58v; f. 5 dated in Parravicino (?), f. 21 dated in Ascoli, f. 47 dated in Tuscanella, f. 54v dated in San Ginesio (near Ancona). For information on the mendicant book trade in Viterbo and Tuscanella, see J. Ruysschaert, "La Bibliothèque des franciscains observants de Tuscanella au XVe siècle," *Bulletin de l'Institut de recherche et d'histoire des textes* 15 (1967–68): 251–66. f. 75v, pen trial of s. xvi or xvii, "Quis seris." Acquired by the Newberry in 1959 from Bernard Rosenthal.

Second folio: Ad tamen.

–91

(349631)

Jerome, *Epistolae;*

Pseudo Augustine, *Opuscula;* etc.

Central Italy 1484

1. ff. 1–27v Hieronymi doctoris eximii ac sacrosanctae ecclesię presbyteri cardinalis epistola ad Eustochium uirginem romanarum nobilissimam lares adhuc domesticos excolentem

e[t] de uirginitate seruanda incipit deuote (in red). Audi filia et uide et inclina aurem tuam . . . concupiscet rex decorem tuum. In psalmo xliiii° Deus ad animam loquitur . . . et flumina non cooperient eam. Finis.

Jerome, *Epistola ad Eustachium*. *BHM* 22. This text and texts 3, 5, and 6 only recorded by Lambert.

2. ff. 27v–37v Hieronymi epistola ad Rusticum monachum super penitentia exhortatoria (in red). Nihil est christiano foelicius cui promittuntur regna caelorum. Nihil laboriosius . . . sed magna sunt premia. Finis.

Jerome, *Epistola ad Rusticum monachum*. *BHM* 125.

3. ff. 38–46 Hieronymi epistola ad Pammachium de dormitione Paulinę coniugis suę consolatoria (in red). Sanato uulneri et in cicatricem superductę cuti si medicina colorem reddere uoluerit . . . tu duarum medius ad Christum leuius subuolabis. Finis.

ff. 46v–48v blank.

Jerome, *Epistola ad Pammachium*. *BHM* 66.

4. ff. 49–85v Eximii doctoris ac sacrosanctae Romanę ecclesię presbyteri cardinalis beati Hieronymi normulę uitae apostolicae ad Eustochium et coeteras uirgines deuote incipit prologus. Tepescens in membris procliuum corpus ad terram . . . Senectutem uestri deuoti Hieronymi sanctis uestris iuuate orationibus. Finis.

Ps. Jerome, *Regula monacharum ad Eustachium sacram deo virginem*. *BHM* 560. *PL* 30:391–426 (403–38).

5. ff. 86–93 Hieronymi epistola ad Paulam de dormitione Blesillae filię consolatoria. Quis dabit capiti meo aquam (Ier 9:1) . . . et plorabo non ut Hieremias ait, Uulneratos populi mei, nec ut Iesus, Miseram Ierusalem, sed plorabo sanctitatem, misericordiam, innocentiam, castitatem . . . audiet me semper loquentem cum sorore, cum matre. Finis.

Jerome, *Epistle 39*. *BHM* 39.

6. ff. 93v–99v Hieronymi epistola ad Eliodorum de contemptu mundi exhortatoria. Quanto studio et amore contenderim ut pariter in heremo moraremur . . . ut hęc tibi, frater, dicerem, ut iis interesse contingat quibus nunc labor durus est. Finis.

Jerome, *Epistle 14*. *BHM* 14.

7. ff. 99v–107v Hieronymi epistola obiurgatoria in Susannam Christo consecratam, de commisso adulterio siue sacrilegio et exortatoria ad penitentiam et tristitiam seruandam (in red). Quid taces, o anima Susannę; quid cogitationibus ęstuas . . . ab illo solo quaere remedium.

Dubious Niceta of Remesiana, *De lapsu virginis*, 1–38, ed. Gamber, pp. 25–34. *CPL* 633 and 651. *BHL* 320.

8. ff. 107v–108v Hieronymi epistola ad adulterum siue sacrilegium prenotatę Susannę exortatoria ad penitentiam (in red). De te autem quid dicam, fili serpentis . . . secundum quod gessit, bonum siue malum.

Dubious Niceta of Remesiana, *De lapsu virginis*, 39–42, ed. Gamber, pp. 34–35.

9. ff. 108v–110v Hieronymi epistola ad Susannam exortatoria ad penitentiam et consolatoria (in red). Quis consoletur te, uirgo filia Syon, quia magna facta est . . . et amplius non ero. Finis.

Dubious Niceta of Remesiana, *De lapsu virginis*, 43–51, ed. Gamber, pp. 35–37.

10. ff. 111–118v Hieronymi epistola ad Oceanum de morte Fabiolae consolatoria perpulchra (in red). Plures anni sunt quod super dormitione Blesillae Paulam uenerabilem foeminam recenti adhuc uulnere consolatus sum . . . Cui plus demittitur, plus amat. Finis.

Jerome, *Epistola ad Oceanum*. *BHM* 77.

11. f. 119–119v Consanguinitas beatae Marię secundum beatum Hieronymum (in red). Anna et Hesmeria fuerunt sorores . . . tres ergo uiros habuit Anna, scilicet Ioacchim, Cleopham et Salome.

Ps. Jerome, *De consanguinitate beatae Mariae*. *BHM* 672.

12. f. 119v Versus.

Anna solet dici tres concepisse Marias . . .
Tertia maiorem Iacobum uolucremque
  Ioannem.
Finis.

De genealogia III Mariarum. Hain, 8593, f. 22. Walther, *Initia*, 1060. *RH* 23006.

13. ff. 120–132 Diui Augustini episcopi hypponensis scala paradisi (in red). Cum die quadam corporali manuum labore occupatus de spiritualis hominis exercitio cogitare caepissem . . . habebunt gaudium, quod nemo tollet ab eis et pacem incommutabilem, pacem in id ipsum. Finis.

Marginal readers' notes, s. xvi or xvii.

Guigo II, Ord. Cart., *Scala claustralium*, ed. E. Colledge and J. Walsh, "Lettre sur la vie contemplative ('l'Échelle des moines')," *Sources chrétiennes,* vol. 163 (Paris, 1970), pp. 81–120. Bloomfield, *Incipits,* 1082. *PL* 40:997–1004; 184:475–84. Printed as a work of Augustine, *GW* 2863–66, 2868, and 2970.

14. ff. 132–140v Deuoti doctoris beati Bernardi oratio quam fecit quando imago saluatoris solutis brachiis de cruce amplexata est eum et primo ad pedes oratio (in red).

Salue, mundi salutare
Salue, salue, Iesu chare . . .
In cruce salutifera. Finis.

f. 141–141v blank.

Bernard of Clairvaux, *Rhythmica oratio ad unum quodlibet membrorum patientis et a cruce pendentis. PL* 184:1319–24. B. Hauréau, *Sur les poèmes latins attribués à saint Bernard* (Paris, 1882). Walther, *Initia,* 17126. *RH* 18073.

15. ff. 142–153 Incipit manuale beati Augustini episcopi de aspiratione animę ad deum; Capitulum primum (in red). Quoniam in medio laqueorum sumus positi . . . choros uirginum speculando; coelum et terra et omnia quae in eis sunt mihi dicere non cessant, ut deum meum diligam (end of chapter 25 in this codex).

Ps. Augustine, *Manuale. PL* 40:951–62 (chapters 1–24). This recension continuing through f. 158 below printed as one text, *GW* 2962–66.

15 bis. ff. 153–158 Capitulum xxvi (in red). Anima mea, si uis amari a deo . . . gratia lachrymarum, quam scientia litterarum, coelestium potius contemplatione, quam terrestrium occupatione. Explicit.

f. 158v blank.

Ps. Augustine, *Liber de dulci admonitione animae* = Ps. Bernard, *De interiore domo,* 38–41, *PL* 184:546–52.

16. ff. 159–200v Soliloquiorum beati Augustini; Capitulum primum de inestimabili dulcedine dei (in red). Cognosscam te, domine cognitor meus. Cognoscam te uirtus animę meę . . . sed iubilare facis omnia ossa mea, et reuiuiscere facis ut aquilę canos meos. Deo gratias. Diui Augustini liber soliloquiorum explicit (in red).

f. 201–201v blank.

Ps. Augustine, *Soliloquia. PL* 40:863–98.

17. ff. 202–209v

Frater Iacopone de Tode (in red).
Amor de charita
Perche m'hai si ferito . . .
Abassame in amore. Amen.

M°cccc° lxxxiiii°, viiii° kalendas februarii (in red).

ff. 210–211v blank.

Jacopone da Todi, *Laude,* 89, ed. F. Mancini (Rome, 1974). Tenneroni, *Inizii,* p. 54.

18. ff. 212–225v Incipit libellus ualde elegans beati Ioannis Chrysostomi de laudibus diui Pauli apostoli. Nihil prorsus errauit qui pratum quoddam insigne uirtutum ac paradisum spiritualem animam dixerit Pauli . . . quia per ipsos euangelii magis flamma crescebat. Explicit.

John Chrysostom, *De laudibus sancti Pauli.* Text follows that of the translation of Anianus, *PG* 50:471–514 through col. 478 only.

19. ff. 226–238v Doctoris seraphici sancti Bonauenturę ad confratrem et familliarem suum Petrum epistella deuota. In Christo Iesu fratri dilecto Petro frater eius Bonauentura in domino. Qualicunque ueteri homine iam exuto, Christo uiuere et mori mundo . . . Uale, frater in domino Iesu Christo sine quo omnia nihil ualent.

Bonaventure, *Epistola viginti quinque memorialium,* in *Opera omnia* (Quaracchi, 1883–1902), 8:491–98. Glorieux, 305ac.

20. f. 238v (addition s. xv)

Unum crede deum, cuius iurare caueto . . .
Contentusque tuis non aliena petas.

Ten precepts; cf. Walther, *Initia,* 19669.

21. ff. 239–245 In nomine domini. Amen. Perche secundo la doctrina de san Thomaso . . . della quale parlando sancto Bernardo dice, Nescire ignorantia est; nolle scire, superbia. Finis.

ff. 245v–246v blank; f. 247–247v blank and frame ruled only.

Advice (in Italian) for Franciscan friars drawn from the writings of Thomas Aquinas, the Franciscan Rule, Bartholomew of San Concordio, Bonaventure, Bernard, etc.

22. ff. 248–307v Illustris doctoris beati Ioannis Chrysostomi de reparatione lapsi; Primum capitulum. Quis dabit capiti meo aquam et occulis meis fontem lachrymarum (Ier 9:1). Opportunius nanque nunc a me quam tunc a propheta dei dicetur. Licet enim non urbes multę, nec gens integra lamentanda mihi sit . . . alia ultra medicamenta non queras. Explicit.

John Chrysostom, *Paraenesis,* in a translation differing from *PG* 47:277–308. The same recension as in this codex is anonymous in Tours, BM, 408 (s. xv), f. 38.

23. ff. 308–309 Chrysostomus de exitu animę. Pensandum quippe est, quom iam peccatrix anima uinculis incipit carnis absolui, quam amaro terrore concutitur . . . indeclinabiliter custodire. Haec ille.

ff. 309v–315v blank.

Dubious Peter Damian, *Epistola de die mortis.* = *Institutio monialis* (6 only). *PL* 144:460; 145:737–38. Hauréau, *Initia* 4:272.

24. f. 316 (addition s. xv, probably by one of the principal scribes of the text) Sanctus Bernardus. Si uis dominum honorare, ueniam impetrare . . . ualeat possidere. Haec ille.

Unidentified fragment, attributed to Bernard of Clairvaux; cf. Stockholm, Royal Library A234 (s. xv), f. 120–120v.

25. f. 316v (addition s. xv)

Martialis a morte Alcini (*sic*) amici sui.
Alcine (*sic*) quem raptum domino
crescentibus annis . . .
Non aliter cineres mando iacere meos.

Gloss on *Labycana* in margin.

Martial, *Epigrammata,* I, 88.

Paper, flyleaf parchment. ff. 315 + i. Modern foliation 1–316. 132 × 100 mm (110 × 64 mm). 1^{12} (1 wanting), $2–11^{12}$, 12^{10} (9 wanting), $13–15^{12}$, 16^{10}, $17–26^{12}$, 27^{12} (3–4 stubs only, text of s. xvi removed). Horizontal catchwords. Quires with red headings, surrounded by 8 radiating flourishes in yellow, black, and red; similar decoration for "finis" when it falls at the end of a quire. In quires with black headings, catchwords surrounded by four flourishes, touched with yellow. Ruled in pencil. Written in humanistic cursiva formata in 21–24 long lines by at least four scribes (hands change with change in catchword decoration, visible breaks on ff. 49, 142, 146v, and 212) in 24 long lines beginning on the first ruled line on ff. 1–209; in 21 long lines beginning on the second ruled line on ff. 212–307; in 22 long lines beginning on the first ruled line on ff. 308–309. Headings in red or black in script of text. Pointing hands and other *nota* symbols added by scribes. Incipits in square capitals interlaced in "Byzantine" fashion, notably in the quires of the first hand. Corrections added by another hand. f. 1, gold initial with violet flourishes 8 lines high. Alternating red and blue initials; red paragraph marks. ff. 212–307, initials in black. Minor initials often touched with yellow. ff. 278v and 279, blank leaves left in mid text, "Nihil deficit" written horizontally across leaves by the scribe. Other leaves intentionally left blank in mid quire include ff. 48, 48v, 141, 141v, 158v, 201v, 211, and 211v. See C. Bozzolo and E. Ornato, *Pour une histoire de livre manuscrit au Moyen Age: trois essais de codicologie quantitative* (Paris, 1980), p. 165 sqq.

Bound in parchment over cardboard, s. xviii. Spine title, "Variarae lectiones."

Written in central Italy in 1484 or 1485, dated on f. 209v. f. 311, a male bust with the inscription, "Ego sum qui hunc librum scripsit," written in a different script from the text, probably after 1500. ff. 120–132, notes of s. xvi or s. xvii in Latin. Text of s. xvi removed after f. 309; stubs only remain, traces of writing visible on stubs. Acquired by the Newberry from Davis and Orioli, 1926.

Second folio: -cta quę nouit et.

De Ricci, 1:539.

+92

(23880)

Rodrigo Sánchez de Arévalo,
Compendiosa Historia Hispanica

Italy [*Illustrated*] s. XV (after 1470)

1. ff. 2–246 (Original codex begins imperfectly with f. 2) // a principali orbis porta incepere . . . (f. 226) et subditos in uiam pacis et salutis eterne dirigat eo prestante. Qui est benedictus in secula. Amen. De mandato reuerendissimi patris domini Roderici episcopi Palentini auctoris huius libri ego Udalricus Gallus sine calamo aut pennis eundem librum impressi (in red) . . . (f. 227) Incipit tabula materiarum et rerum contentarum in hac historia hispanica (in red) . . . Explicit tabula materiarum et rerum in hoc libro contentarum. Finis (in red).

f. 246v blank.

Hain, 13955. See also *Diccionario de historia eclesiastica de España* (Madrid, 1972–75), 4:2169–70.

Parchment. ff. 245. Foliated 2–246. f. 1, a nineteenth-century insertion of missing text. f. 2, inscription "Rodericus episcopus palentinus de rebus Hispaniae" in a cursive eighteenth-century hand indicates that the original first folio was already wanting at that date. 218 × 215 mm (210 × 110 mm). Collation impracticable. Ruled in hard point. Written in humanistic textualis formata in 26 long lines beginning on the first ruled line. The acute accent used to denote monosyllabic prepositions. Roman style gold initials with white vine stem on grounds of blue, green, and red decorated with clusters of gold radiating disks throughout, 3–5 lines high. ff. 16v–17, gold dentelle initials with gold and white patterning on fields of blue and green.

Bound in Spanish gold-stamped red morocco, s. xix.

Written in Italy, probably in Rome, apparently copied from the Rome, 1470, printed edition of Ulrich Gallus, see colophon of Hain, 13955; *B.M. Cat. of 15th-Century Books* 4:20. For a possibly closely related manuscript in a Spanish library, see *Colophons de manuscrits occidentaux,* 18214. No. 57 from the collection of Henry Probasco, acquired by the Newberry 1 December 1890.

Second folio: Hispanię laudes.

De Ricci, 1:531.

92.5
(49-1571)
Collection

Italy s. XV[2]

1. f. 1 Begins imperfectly with final portion of Ps. Bernard, *Epistola ad Raimundum* (in Italian). Hain, 2879. Janauschek, *Bibliographia bernardina,* no. 12. Zambrini, *Le Opere volgari,* col. 65. Erased, possibly by a dealer to make the manuscript appear to be complete. Text illegible even under ultraviolet light. Title listed in table on f. 85.

2. ff. 1–7v Copia d'una epistola mandata ad uno amico sanato d'una grauissima infermita (in brown). Onde nasce dilectissimo mio tanto spirito e tanta sanctimonia di tua uita . . . Et onde questo nasca tu stesso lo giudica. Nec plura, uale cum domino.

Unidentified Italian text, discussing the Epistle of Paul to the Romans, including consideration of the problems of translation, citing Augustine, Jerome, Bede, Gregory, and Dante.

3. f. 8–8v Lettera scripta per Lentulo uficiale romano in Giudea dello aduenimento di Christo (in brown). Al tempo di Octauiano Cesare con cio fussi cosa che di diuerse parti del mondo . . . e figliuoli degli huomini.

Ps. Publius Lentulus, *Epistola ad Romanos de Christo Jesu* (in Italian). Editions: *Laudi del B. Jacopone* (Venice, 1514), p. 119, and *Testi de lingua inediti tratti da' codici della biblioteca vaticana* (Rome, 1816), p. 80; cf. F. Palermo, *Raccolta di testi inediti del buon seculo della favella toscana* (Naples, 1840), pp. 80–81; Leone del Prete, *Lettera inedita del Presto Giovanni all'imperatore Carlo IV ed altra di Lentuolo ai senatori romani . . .* (Lucca, 1857), p. 7. Zambrini, *Le Opere volgari,* cols. 591–93.

4. ff. 8v–30v Comincia uno tractato di nobilita composto per Bonacorso da Montemagno (in brown). Spesse uolte appresso de nostri antichi e stato dubbio . . . nella uostra sententia si rimette.

Buonaccorso da Montemagno, *De nobilitate* (in Italian), ed. G. B. Casotti, *Prose e rime de' due B. Buonaccorsi da Montemagno* (Florence, 1718), pp. 1–97. See Garin, *Prosatori latini,* pp. 1128–29.

5. f. 31–31v Oratio Massinisse (*sic*) in fine uitę sue (in brown). Io ti riceuetti o piccolo, o Giugurta, nel mio regno hauendo tu perduto tuo padre . . . che quegli che io ho generati.

Oration of Micipsa, Sallust, *Bellum Iugurthinum,* chapter X (in Italian). Not from the translation of Bartholomew of San Concordio.

6. ff. 32–35

Portando in collo il tuo supplicio
 auinto . . .
Per cui l'uman lignagio e fatto degno.
Finis.

Unidentified poem in Italian in terza rima described in the table on f. 85 as "Oratione in uersi della sanctissima Croce."

7. ff. 35v–43

Se mai priego mortal la su s'intese . . .
Se mai pregho mortal la su s'intese.
Telos.

Unidentified poem in Italian, described in table on f. 85 as "Oratione simile della sanctissima Annuntiata."

8. ff. 43v–48 [Q]uid commisisti, dulcissime puer, ut sic cruciareris. Quid fecisti, amantissime iuuenis . . . sed tua inextimabili pietate ad uisionem dei perueniat. Amen.

Dubious Bernard of Clairvaux, *Tractatus de passione Christi.* Two other manuscripts: Paris, Arsenal, 369, f. 13v; A. M. Bandini, *Bibliotheca leopoldina laurentiana* (Florence, 1791–93), supp. 1, p. 30. Text on ff. 43v–44, line 3, ending: compatitur Maria = Augustine, *Meditatio VII* (initial portion), *PL* 40:906 = Anselm, *Oratio II, PL* 158:861. See Wilmart, p. 128, n. 1.

9. ff. 48–56 Incipit lamentatio beatę uirginis et beati Bernardi (in red). [Q]uis dabit capiti meo aquam et oculis meis imbrem lacrimarum (Ier 9:1) ut possim flere per diem et per noctem . . . benedicti sint omnes qui diligunt eam et super omnia sit benedictus filius eius iste Christus dominus noster qui cum patre et spiritu sancto uiuit et regnat in secula seculorum. Amen.

Ps. Bernard of Clairvaux, *Planctus beatae Mariae.* Also attributed to Augustine and Anselm. *PL* 182:1132–42 (defective at beginning). Caillau, *S. Augustini sermones inediti,* vol. 2 (1842), p. 238. *GW* 4055–60. See Janauschek, *Bibliographia bernardina*, p. viii and passim. Wilmart, p. 422, n. 1, and p. 517, n. 1. Additional manuscripts: Hauréau, *Notices et extraits* 5:145; *Initia* 5:111; Paris, BN, *Catalogue des manuscrits latins, table des tomes I et II* (Paris, 1968), p. 130, and *table des tomes III à VI* (Paris, 1981–83), pt. 3, p. 817; Warner, *Catalogue of Royal Manuscripts* 1:164.

10. ff. 56–60v De quatuor uirtutibus Senecę (in red). [Q]uatuor uirtutum species multorum sapientum sententiis deffinitę sunt . . . contempnat ignauiam.

Martin of Braga, *Formulae vitae honestae*. Text attributed to Seneca in the twelfth century and after; ed. Barlow, *Opera omnia*, pp. 237–50. Bloomfield, *Incipits*, 4457. This manuscript unrecorded. *CPL* 1080.

11. ff. 60v–64 Tractatus [–Senecę] de quatuor uirtutibus (in red). [H]eę (*sic*) quatuor uirtutes dicuntur cardinales uel initiales uel principales quia principia sunt aliarum uirtutum . . . (ends imperfectly in mid leaf) Concordia est uirtus continens compatiens idemptitate iuris instituens uel correptionis spontaneę. Dignitas est.

f. 60v, "Senecę" deleted by the rubricator.

A treatise on the virtues, unrecorded by Bloomfield, *Incipits*.

12. ff. 64v–84v Incipit liber de perfectione iustitię beati Augustini (in red). [S]anctis fratribus et coepiscopis Eutropio et Paulo Augustinus. Caritas uestra, quę in nobis tanta est . . . et ore omnium anathematiçandum non dubito. Deo gratias. Explicit liber Augustini de perfectione iustitię.

Augustine, *De perfectione iustitiae hominis*, ed. C. Urba and J. Zycha, *CSEL* 42 (1902): 3–48. *PL* 44:291–318. *CPL* 347.

13. f. 85 (addition s. xviii) Table of contents, titled "Indice," signed "fatto da me Adriano Lazzeri Pisano Dottor di Legge." Titles of works following f. 43 added by another hand. Space for folio references not filled in.

Pastedowns are palimpsests of an unidentified Italian notarial text in humanistic script. ff. 69v, 81v–82, etc., margins repaired with palimpsest fragments from a register written in Italian gothic textualis rotunda; writing visible only under ultraviolet light.

Parchment of southern preparation. ff. ii + 85. 231 × 145 mm (c. 145 × 75 mm). 1^8 (1 wanting), $2–3^{10}$, 4^8, $5–9^{10}$. Two codices combined to form this manuscript, apparently at an early date. Table on f. 85 lists texts 1–7; seven more texts are listed by another sixteenth-century hand of which only the last five are now present. "De quatuor uirtutibus Senecae" and an "Oratio ad Iesum Christum" are wanting. Text 8 is the first of those listed in the table by the second hand which is now present. The break between the two former codices falls in mid quire, and it is quite possible that this fusion was done by a modern dealer who also erased text 1. Catchwords present: ff. 17v and 22v, surrounded by dots; ff. 55v and 65v, bracket in red on left. Ruled in hard point shifting to light brown ink for quires 8 and 9. Prickings visible in outer margin on ff. 1–44 only. Leaves signed in two alphabetical sequences, changing at the same breaking. Upper portion of f. 1 bleached to make manuscript appear to begin with text 2. ff. 16, 21, 35, and 73–76, margins restored. ff. 1–43, recto written in humanistic cursiva formata in 26 long lines; ff. 43v–84v, in humanistic cursiva media by two scribes with the second hand beginning on f. 66 in 27 long lines. Beginning on the second ruled line throughout. Headings written in script of text on ff. 1–43 in brown, probably violet when written; on ff. 43v–84v, in red. ff. 1, 1v, 8v, 9, and 31, gold dentelle initials on grounds of green, blue, and pink, 2–3 lines high. f. 35v, white vine stem initial. ff. 43v–84v, spaces for initials left blank. ff. 48, 56, and 60, guide letters present.

Bound in stamped calf, s. xv, panel decorated with a single stamp of a rope motif, repeated many times on front and back. Two fore-edge clasps repaired. This binding possibly taken from another book.

Written in Italy in the second half of the fifteenth century. Acquired by the Newberry from Ulrico Hoepli (Milan), 1947.

Second folio: amo riprendogli.

Faye-Bond, p. 147.

f93

(324557)

Leonardo Bruni, *De Bello Punico* (in Italian); Giovanni de' Bonsignori, *Compendium of Roman History*

Italy s. XV^2

1. ff. 1–116v Maternum prohemium primi belli punici a Leonardo Arretino editi in latinum posteaque in maternum conuersi (in violet). E parra forse a molti che io uadi dirieto a cose troppo antiche . . . Et non molto da poi tolto loro le possessioni constrecti furono in gran parte abbandonare il paese. Finis (in violet).

Running marginal index notes in violet.

ff. 117–118v blank.

Leonardo Bruni, *De bello punico* (in Italian), ed. A. Ceruti in *Scelta di curiosità letterarie inedite o rare* 165 (Bologna, 1878). Baron, *Leonardo Bruni Aretino,* p. 167.

2. ff. 119–40 Ioannis Tiphernatis de origine regum imperatorumque urbis Romae eorumque gestis breue compendium lege (in violet). Fino al presente puncto abbiamo assai cose narrate per conchiudere . . . essendo a Bonconuento nel contado di Siena passo della presente uita anni domini m ccc xiiii in uenerdi adi xxiiii di agosto a hora di nona. Finis.

f. 104v blank.

Giovanni de Bonsignori (of Città di Castello = lat. *Tiphernatis*), a compendium of Roman history to the death of the Holy Roman Emperor, Henry VII. This text usually follows the *Libro imperiale;* see G. Ballistreri, *DBI* 12:407–9.

f. 1, full gold and white ivy stem initial 6 lines high and full border on ground of blue and red, framed in gold, decorated with putti and exotic birds, one in lower margin eating a fly drawn with great detail; see H. Lehmann-Haupt, "The Microscope and the Book," in *Festschrift für Claus Nissen* (Wiesbaden, 1973). Six similar white vine stem initials 3–5 lines high accompanied by partial borders: f. 2v; f. 43, with an exotic bird; f. 75, with two birds; f. 95, with two birds; f. 97v, with three birds; f. 119, with three birds. f. 18v, gold dentelle initial on blue field, decorated with sprig of gold ending in cluster of gold rayed disks and an exotic bird.

Parchment. ff. i + 140. 250 × 163 mm (153 × 86 mm). $1–11^{10}$, 12^{8}, 13^{10}, 14^{12}. Vertical catchwords. Traces of leaf signatures visible at the end. Ruled in pen. Written in humanistic cursiva formata in 23 long lines. Headings and incipits in rustic capitals, headings in violet; running marginal index notes in violet in script of text.

Bound in contemporary stamped calf over boards. Front and back panels decorated with border of ivy leaves; in the interior, stamps of clusters of four circles and motif of interlaced rope. Two fore-edge clasps wanting.

Written in Italy in the second half of the fifteenth century. The decoration is similar to Paris, BN, lat. 7237 prepared for Louis XI at Rome. f. 1, unidentified arms borne by putti (see color illustration). Rear pastedown, clipping from a French catalogue describing this manuscript as item no. 37, and identifying the second text as a work of Giovanni Tifernate (*sic*). Front pastedown, sticker of "Leonis S. Olschki, Bibliopolae Veneti no. 23691, Serin 71." Acquired by the Newberry from the collection of Edward E. Ayer, December 1920.

Second folio: -mi, et molto.

De Ricci, 1:537.

93.1

(67-1116)

Collection of Humanistic Texts, etc.

France c. 1500

1. ff. 1–12v Liber de proprietatibus terminorum Ciceronis iuxta ordinem alphabeti compendiose editus incipit feliciter. Inter polliceri et promittere hoc interest . . . uesperum neutri generis secundae declinationis. Liber de proprietatibus terminorum Ciceronis Explicit.

Ps. Cicero, *Differentiae verborum* (interpolated version); cf. M. L. Uhlfelder, *De proprietate sermonum vel rerum: A Study and Critical Edition of a Set of Verbal Distinctions* (American Academy in Rome, 1954). f. 3, entries begin in alphabetical order starting with "abundare." Text differs from the versions listed by G. Brugnoli, *Studi sulle "Differentiae verborum"* (Rome, 1955), p. 41 sqq. *CPL* 1226.

2. ff. 13–19v Incipit tractatus de successionibus ab intestato. Ex quo materia successionum cuius notitia utilis est et saepe in multis casibus necessaria . . . Excoquitur, quicquid capitur, dum pauca docentur (= Walther, *Prov.*, no. 27213). Explicit tractatus de successionibus ab intestato.

Dubious Cino da Pistoia, *De successionibus ab intestato,* ed. G. Tellini (Pistoia, 1970), a reprint of *GW* 7048. *Tractatus universi juris,* vol. 8, pt. 1, ff. 319–21v. For other sixteenth-century editions, see F. K. von Savigny, *Geschichte des Römischen Rechts im Mittelalter* (Heidelberg, 1826–34), 6:83. This text also in St. Dié, BM 33(2) and Freiburg im Breisgau, Universitätsbibliothek 168. On the attribution to Cino da Pistoia, see D. Maffei, *La "Lectura super Digesto veteri" di Cino da Pistoia: studio sui MSS Savigny 22 e Urb. lat. 172* (Milan, 1963), pp. 57–59, and E. Altieri and G. Savino, *Cino da Pistoia: mostra di documenti e libri* (exhibition catalogue, Biblioteca comunale Forteguerriana di Pistoia; Florence, 1971), pp. 39–42.

3. ff. 19v–20 Casus breues trium partium tractatus successionum. De descendentibus. Si sunt descendentes . . . in eorum ordine aptissimo.

Summary of text no. 2 printed in *Tractatus universi juris,* vol. 8, pt. 2, f. 321v. This summary also follows in Freiburg im Breisgau 168. See W. Hagenmaier, *Die Lateinischen mittelalterlichen Handschriften der Universitätsbibliothek Freiburg im Breisgau* (Wiesbaden, 1974), p. 152.

4. f. 20 (addition s. xvi) Extract from a letter in French.

f. 20v blank.

5. ff. 21–40v Francisci Barbari ueneti de re uxoria liber incipit foeliciter ad Laurentium de Medicis ciuem florentinum. Maiores nostri, Laurenti carissime . . . uel quod ad (*sic*) optima fide ac animo certe tibi deditissimo proficiscitur.

f. 41 blank.

Francesco Barbaro, *De re uxoria*. A. Gnesotto, *Atti e memorie della Reale Accademia di Scienze, Lettere ed Arti in Padova*, n.s. 32 (1915): 23–100. Garin, *Prosatori latini*, pp. 104–37.

6. ff. 41v–44 Nicolao dei gratia reuerendissimo antistiti capuano ac urbis Romae praesidi Raynucius facultatem (*sic*). Ut si, reuerende pater, turba rerum perturbatione ac temporum difficultate te negociis publicis ita implicitum esse conspicio . . . (f. 41v) Explicit Prohemion. Incipiunt commentaria uitae Demosthenis oratoris latina per Raynuncium oratorem facta. Demosthenis oratoris uitam recognoscere operae precium est hiis . . . pecunia donatus est. Expliciunt commentaria super Demosthenis uita.

Rinuccio Aretino, trans., *Vita Demosthenis*, preceded by a prologue to this work and the Olynthian orations below, texts 7–9. Those texts mentioned by Rinuccio in his *Oratio ad Philippi epistolam* but not known to be extant by Lockwood, "De Rinucio Aretino," pp. 55 and 87 (lines 45–48). Text of the *Vita Demosthenis* (without prologue) in Montecassino, Biblioteca della Badia, 864; Kristeller, *Iter italicum*, 1:395.

7. ff. 44–46 Incipit argumentum super prima oratione Demosthenis pro Olinthiis in Philippum. Olinthus Thraciae ciuitas fuit . . . Incipit oratio prima pro olinthiis in Philippum habita in senatu. Pro grandi quidem pecunia, uiri athenienses . . . optimum esse duco.

Demosthenes, *Oratio Olynthiaca I*, translation by Rinuccio Aretino.

8. ff. 46–48v Argumentum super orationem secundam pro olynthiis in Philippum feliciter incipit. Athenienses accepta olinthiorum legatione eis auxilia . . . (f. 46v) Oratio Demosthenis secunda pro olynthiis in Philippum habita in senatu incipit feliciter. Non multa sunt, uiri athenienses, quibus uideor . . . pulcherrimum est.

Demosthenes, *Oratio Olynthiaca II*, translation by Rinuccio Aretino.

9. ff. 48v–50v Argumentum super oratione 3ª Demosthenis. Athenienses olinthiis auxilia contra Philippum . . . Oratio tertia Demosthenis pro olinthiis in Philippum habita in senatu, lege feliciter. De qua (?) quarum eadem mihi uideor intelligere, uiri athenienses, cum res ipsas uideo et cum uerba nonnullorum ipse mecum reputo . . . uos autem sequamini quod res publicae et nobis omnibus profuturum sit.

Demosthenes, *Oratio Olynthiaca III*, translation of Leonardo Bruni, ed. H. Wolfius (Genoa, 1607). C. Stornajolo, *Codices urbinates latini III (nos. 1001–1779)* (Rome, 1921), p. 182; Bandini, *Catalogus codicum latinorum* 2:614 and 3:192–93; Baron, *Leonardo Bruni Aretino*, pp. 128, 171, and 178.

10. ff. 50v–51v Dialogus in quo introducuntur dissonentes (*sic*) Minos, Hannibal, Alexander Magnus, et Scipio Aphricanus. Incipit Alexander. Me, o libice, praeponi decet, melior equidem sum . . . neque hic quidem spernendus est.

Lucian, *Contentio de praesidentia P. Scipionis*, without the epistolary prologue, translation of Johannes Aurispa. Hain, 10275–76. Sabbadini, *Biografica documentata*, pp. 31 and 188. Bandini, *Catalogus codicum latinorum* 3:630. G. Martellotti, "*La Collatio inter Scipionem . . .*," *Classical, Medieval and Renaissance Studies in Honor of Berthold Louis Ullman* (Rome, 1964), 2:146.

11. ff. 52–57v Leonardus Aretinus de re militari ad Raynaldum Albicium militem. Fateor, clarissime uir . . . Quę cum ita sint finem dicendi aliquando faciamus.

Leonardo Bruni, *De militia*, ed. C. C. Bayley, *War and Society in Renaissance Florence: The "De militia" of Leonardo Bruni* (Toronto, 1961), pp. 368–89. Baron, *Leonardo Bruni Aretino*, pp. 166–67.

12. f. 58 Final five lines of text referring to Cicero, Caesar, Cato, and Catiline ending, "in Hyspaniam profectus (?) eam domuit," crossed out by the scribe. The leaf before f. 58 removed, stub has traces of text.

13. ff. 58–59v In Demosthenis orationem de seruanda pace argumentum per Leonardum Aretinum. Uideo, athenienses, et cetera. Oratio ista que de seruanda pace . . . Oratio Demosthenis de seruanda pace. Uideo, athenienses, praesens quidem tempus difficultatem maximam et turbationem habere . . . proinde (?) delphis umbra bellum suscipere.

Demosthenes, *De pace conservanda*, translation of Leonardo Bruni. Baron, *Leonardo Bruni Aretino*, p. 178. Bertalot, "Forschungen über Leonardo Bruni Aretino," p. 304.

14. f. 59v Oratio habita in senatu atheniensi de recipiendo Alexandro an armis repellendo. Heschines. Reminiscor, athenienses, Alexandrum . . . si non obsequentes sibi supplicesque inuenerit.

Pietro Marcello, *Oratio Heschinis ad Athenienses*. Sabbadini, "Antonio da Romagno e Pietro Marcello," p. 241. For prior editions, see L. Bertalot, "Uno zibaldone umanistico latino del quattrocento a Parma," *Bibliofilia* 38 (1936): 77–78. For manuscripts of this and the two succeeding texts, see Prete, *Two Humanistic Anthologies*, p. 20. Ruysschaert, *Codices vaticani latini*, pp. 286–87.

15. f. 59v Demadoes (*sic*). Admirans uehementer admiror, athenienses . . . et consiliis uiribusque uacuam facilius diripiat.

Pietro Marcello, *Oratio Demadis*. Sabbadini, "Antonio da Romagno e Pietro Marcello," pp. 241–42.

16. ff. 59v–60 Demosthenes. Apud uos in questione ueteri uideor uidere . . . Nec dicamus nos nolle parere Alexandro qui seruiuimus Philippo.

Pietro Marcello, *Oratio Demosthenis*. Sabbadini, "Antonio da Romagno e Pietro Marcello," p. 242.

17. f. 60–60v Demosthenis ad Alexandrum oratio. Nihil habet, rex Alexander, uel fortuna tua maius quam ut possis . . . cum hec feceris consecutus es.

Pietro Marcello, *Epistola vel oratio Demosthenis ad Alexandrum*. Sabbadini, "Antonio da Romagno e Pietro Marcello," p. 243. This text attributed to Leonardo Bruni by Baron, *Leonardo Bruni Aretino*, p. 179.

18. ff. 60v–62 Philippus macedonum rex atheniensi senatui plebique salutem. Quoniam sepe iam legatos misi . . . et diis testibus inuocatis pro meis rebus pugnabo.

Philip of Macedonia, *Epistola ad Athenienses*, printed in *Epistolae regum, principum . . .*, pp. 210–16. Translation attributed to Leonardo Bruni. Baron, *Leonardo Bruni Aretino*, pp. 171 and 178. Bertalot, "Forschungen über Leonardo Bruni Aretino," p. 304.

19. ff. 62v–68v Leonardi Aretini in Xenophontis tyrannum ab ipso traductum. Epistola ad Nicolaum de Medicis [–aut Cosimam]. Xenophontis philosophi quendam libellum, quem ego ingenii exercendi gratia e graeco sermone in latinum conuerti . . . (f. 63) Cum ad Hyeronem tyrannum Simonides poeta . . . Felix enim cum sis nemo tibi inuidebit. Explicit tyrannus Xenophontis.

"Aut Cosimam" struck out by the scribe.

Xenophon, *Hiero*, translation by Leonardo Bruni. Hain 16225 sqq. Prologue edited by Baron, *Leonardo Bruni Aretino*, pp. 100–101; see also p. 161. Bertalot, "Forschungen über Leonardo Bruni Aretino," p. 288.

20. f. 68v Cesar imperator Ciceroni salutem. Recte auguraris de me . . . Nihil enim malo quam mei similem esse et illos sui.

Caesar, *Epistola ad Ciceronem* = excerpt from Cicero, *Epistola ad Atticum*, IX, 16, ed. E. O. Winstedt (Cambridge, 1962–67), 2:260–62. Other examples listed, *Manuscrits classiques latins*, vol. 1, Chigi H vi 181, etc. This text also in MS Wing ZW 1.4b.

21. ff. 69–73v Basilius e graeco in latinum per Leonardum Aretinum traductus. Ego hunc librum, Coluti . . . Multa sunt filii quae hortantur me . . . quo uos non patiamini nunc recta consilia aspernantes.

f. 74–74v blank.

Basilius, *Epistola ad nepotes de utilitate studii librorum gentilium*, translation of Leonardo Bruni. *GW* 3700–18. Prologue edited by Baron, *Leonardo Bruni Aretino*, pp. 98–100. This manuscript unrecorded by Schucan, *Das Nachleben*.

Paper. Watermark of *lettres assemblées;* cf. Briquet 9711 sqq. ff. 74. 186 × 132 mm (165 × 112 mm). 1^{8}, 2^{12}, 3^{10}, $4–5^{8}$, 6^{10}, 7^{12} (2 stub only), 8^{10} (7–9, stubs only). ff. 46v, 56v, and 67v, catchwords present. Ruled in hard point. Written in humanistic cursiva currens incorporating numerous traits of northern European gothic cursiva in 42 long lines beginning on the first ruled line. Short Greek phrases written at the end of many texts. Headings variously in northern gothic *lettre bâtarde* media with occasional rustic capitals and in script of text.

Bound in parchment over pasteboard.

Written in France, c. 1500. f. 20v, sixteenth-century inscription, "Marguerite Rolin de Suisse Regina Coeli," a simple table formed from the letters of her name written vertically in three columns. Acquired by the Newberry from W. Schab (New York), 1967.

Second folio: consuetudine hoc inter.

93.2

(66-3874)

Pseudo Ptolemaeus, *Centiloquium*, with Commentary of George of Trebizond; George of Trebizond, *De Antisciis*

Naples and Rome 1456

1. ff. 2–12v Liber Claudii Ptolomei (*sic*) qui uocatur fructus ad illustrissimum Alfonsum regem Aragonum et utriusque Sicilie a Georgio Trapezuntio ex gręco in latinum uersus (in violet). [I]am pridem perutiles ad preuidendum operationes stellarum . . . sin uero

non mouentur, hostis indigena erit. Finis (in violet).

f. 1–1v blank.

Ps. Ptolemaeus, *Centiloquium,* translation by George of Trebizond (printed, Rome, 1540; Basel, 1550). Thorndike and Kibre, 649. Monfasani, *Collectanea Trapezuntiana,* pp. 750–51.

2. ff. 13–90v Commentarii et expositiones Georgii Trapezuntii in aphorismis libri fructus Ptolomei ad Alfonsum regem Aragonum et utriusque Sicilie. [L]ibellus hic quem de gręco traductum nomini tuo dedicauimus, illustrissime rex . . . qui dicendi modus nec oratoribus quidem ignotus est.

Commentary on the *Centiloquium* by George of Trebizond with autograph corrections on ff. 20, 22, 26, 29–29v, 42v, 43, 51–51v, 57v, 60v, 62v, 64v, 65, 68, 75, 84v, 87v, and 90–90v. Printed with his translation supra (Basel, 1550). The explicit differs here from the printed text. Monfasani, *Collectanea Trapezuntiana,* pp. 99–100 and 689–95.

3. ff. 90v–106 Georgii Trapeçuntii breuis de antisciis tractatus (in violet). [N]unc quoniam rationem antisciorum quam maxime licet dissimulanter sequi Ptolomeus uidetur . . . ita ut nec potentioris dignitas negligatur nec commoda miscendi ratio quasi uana pretereatur.

f. 106v blank.

George of Trebizond, *De antisciis* (Cologne, 1544), ff. 21v–25 (Venice, 1525); partially printed, Gervasius Marstaller, *Artis divinatricis . . . encomia* (Paris, 1549), pp. 148–65; partially edited, this codex collated, Monfasani, *George of Trebizond,* pp. 341–42, and *Collectanea Trapezuntiana,* pp. 695–97. See also L. Thorndike, *A History of Magic and Experimental Science* (New York, 1922–58), 4:395, n. 20. Thorndike and Kibre, 966.

Paper, watermarked: ff. 1–93, *ciseaux,* cf. Briquet 3666; ff. 98–107, *échelle,* cf. Briquet 5904. ff. ii + 107. Contemporary arabic foliation partially trimmed. Trimmed to 210 × 140 mm (138 × 80 mm). 1^{12}, $2–9^{10}$, 10^{6} (6 stub only), 11^{10} (10 used as pastedown). Horizontal catchwords surrounded by four flourishes in violet or ink of text. No catchwords at end of quires 1 and 10. Quires 1–10, ruled in hard point and written in humanistic textualis media in 22 long lines beginning on the first ruled line by a scribe who appears to be the same who wrote Vat. lat. 2926 for Alphonso the Magnanimous. See letter of Msgr. José Ruysschaert to H. P. Kraus, 18 September 1965, at the Newberry. Autograph corrections by the author in humanistic cursiva media; cf. examples of Trebizond's hand, G. Mercati, *Codici latini Pico Grimani Pio* (Studi e Testi, 75; Vatican City, 1938), plate IIIB. Headings of texts 1 and 2 and initial two lines of text 2 also autograph. Other headings in violet in script of text. f. 97v, last ten lines struck out by the author. Tie mark links text to f. 98. Quire 11 ruled in hard point, written entirely by Trebizond in humanistic cursiva in 26 long lines beginning on the first ruled line; citations shown by quotation marks in margin.

Bound in contemporary limp parchment.

Texts 1 and 2 must have been written in Naples and Rome between 1453 and 1455. See Monfasani, *George of Trebizond,* pp. 118–19, and *Collectanea Trapezuntiana,* pp. 13–14 and plate III. On f. 93, Trebizond in referring to his age wrote 60 over 58 (visible under ultraviolet lamp) indicating that text 3 certainly was written between 1453–56, since Trebizond was born 3 April 1395. On f. 103, the year 1456 is mentioned. Old numbers "29" and "612" on spine, traces of blue and white (Olschki?) labels. Acquired by the Newberry from H. P. Kraus, May 1966.

Second folio: mundando arandoque.

93.3

(69-505)

Francesco Barbaro, *De Re Uxoria;*
Poggio Bracciolini, *De Nobilitate;* etc.

Northern Italy s. XV med. (after 1440)

1. ff. 1–44v Francisci Barbari ueneti ad insignem uirum Laurentium de Medicis ciuem florentinum de re uxoria incipit feliciter (in red). [M]aiores nostri, Laurenti (alternately in red and black) carissime, beneuolentia uel necessitudine sibi coniunctos in nuptiis donare consuerunt (*sic*) . . . uel quod ab optima fide ac animo certe tibi deditissimo proficiscitur.

Six unnumbered folios after f. 44 blank on rectos and versos.

Francesco Barbaro, *De re uxoria,* ed. A. Gnesotto in *Atti e memorie della Reale Accademia di Scienze, Lettere ed Arti in Padova,* n.s. 32 (1915): 23–100. Garin, *Prosatori latini del Quattrocento,* pp. 104–37.

2. ff. 45–68v [N]on dubito, prestantissime pater, nonnullos esse futuros qui hunc meum laborem non quidem aperte reprehendant . . . uisendumque fluuium quem iste nobis sepius ob fertilitatem piscium laudauit. Finis. Liber Poggii florentini de nobilitate explicit.

Poggio Bracciolini, *De nobilitate,* printed in *Opera omnia* (Basel, 1538), pp. 64–83; reprinted in *Opera omnia,* ed. R. Fubini (Turin, 1964), 1:64–83. Kristeller, *Lauro Quirini umanista* (Florence, 1977), pp. 21–42.

3. ff. 68v–71v [P]oggius plurimam salutem dicit uiro insigni Gregorio Corario sedis apostolice prothonotario. [O]ptarem, mi Gregori amantissime, ut libellus quem de nobilitate composui . . . uideatur. [U]ale, et me, ut facis, ama. Florentie viii die viii (*sic*) aprilis, 1440. Finit.

Letter of Poggio Bracciolini to Gregorius Corriarius, ed. T. Tonelli, *Poggio, epistolae* (Florence, 1832–61), 2:223–28; reprinted in *Opera omnia*, ed. R. Fubini (Turin, 1964), vol. 3, pt. 2, pp. 223–28. Kristeller, *Lauro Quirini*, pp. 21–42.

4. ff. 71v–73v Caroli Arretini ad Poggium uirum eruditissimum de nobilitate carmen incipit.

[Q]uid sit nobilitas scribere liberis . . .
Metas, nauigiis est male preuium.

f. 74–74v blank.

Carlo Marsuppini, *De nobilitate*. Printed in *Carmina illustrium poetarum italorum* (Florence, 1719–26), 6:282–84. Walther, *Initia*, 15904. Kristeller, *Lauro Quirini*, pp. 21–42.

Parchment of southern preparation. ff. ii + 79 + ii. Modern foliation 1–44, five unfoliated leaves, 45–74. 250 × 171 mm (175 × 100 mm). $1–7^{10}$, 8^{10} (10 wanting). Ruled in hard point with double boundary lines. Prickings in outer margins. Text 1 written in humanistic textualis media characterized by gothic proportions and occasional gothic traits in 29 long lines with writing on the first ruled line, remainder of the book in 27 long lines beginning on the second ruled line; in very black ink throughout. One fifteenth-century corrector or reader has added index notes, punctuation, and *prosodiae* as well as pointing hands. f. 1, heading in red and a red marginal index note. Index notes, mostly proper names, added by several hands in the remainder of the manuscript. Space for initials left blank. Beginning in text 3, guide letters present.

Bound in contemporary rebacked deerskin over wooden boards. Two rear-to-front clasps with two letters (?) on each brass catch. A bottom rear-to-front clasp removed, front cover repaired; five bosses, front and back. Front pastedown and flyleaf formed a bifolium, thirteenth- or early fourteenth-century Italian cartulary recording documents dated 1244, 1248, 1278, and 1282; the last referring to "Sonellus, monachus Sancte Marie de Gauello" [Cottineau, 1261].

Written in northern Italy, certainly after 1440, the date of the composition of text 3. Front flyleaf, inscription in Hebrew, possibly a pawn note. "39662" written in pencil on rear pastedown. Acquired by the Newberry from E. P. Goldschmidt, December 1968.

Second folio: prudentia consiliis.

93.5

(Ry 192)

Terence, *Comedies*

Florence c. 1415–20

1. f. 1

Natus in excelsis tectis Cartaginis altę . . .
Hoc quicumque leget, sic puto cautus erit.

Epitaphium Terentii, ed. Riese, *Anthologia latina*, vol. 1, pt. 2, p. 40. Walther, *Initia*, 11627.

2. ff. 1–26 Argumentum (in red). Sororem falso creditam meretriculę . . . Explicit Andria.

Terence, *Andria*, preceded by the usual *argumentum*, ed. Prete, *Comoediae*, pp. 55–83.

3. ff. 26–54v Incipit Eunuchus; Argumentum (in red). Meretrix adolescentem cuius mutuo amore tenebatur . . . Explicit eunuchus.

Terence, *Eunuchus*, preceded by the *argumentum* as printed by Prete, *Comoediae*, p. 178n.

4. ff. 54v–81v Incipit heutontumerumenon (*sic*). Argumentum (in red). In militiam proficisci gnatum Cliniam . . . Terentii Afri heutontumerumenon (*sic*) explicit feliciter (in red).

Terence, *Heauton timorumenos*, preceded by the usual *argumentum*. Prete, *Comoediae*, pp. 115–74.

5. ff. 81v–104v Incipit adelphos (*sic*; in red). Acta ludis funeribus . . . Duos cum haberet Demea adolescentulos . . . Terentii Afri adelphos (*sic*) explicit feliciter (in red).

Terence, *Adelphoe*, preceded by the usual *argumentum*. Prete, *Comoediae*, pp. 349–98.

6. ff. 104v–122v Incipit eundem hęchyra (in red). Acta ludis Romanis . . . Uxorem duxit Pamphylus Phylomenam . . . Terentii Afri hęchyra explicit feliciter (in red).

Terence, *Hecyra*, preceded by the usual *argumentum*. Prete, *Comoediae*, pp. 301–45.

7. ff. 122v–146 Incipit Phormio (in red). Acta ludis romanis . . . Chręmetis frater aberat peregre Demipho . . . Terentii Afri Phormio explicit feliciter; Deo gratias; Amen (in red).

f. 146v blank.

Terence, *Phormio,* preceded by the usual *argumentum.* Prete, *Comoediae,* pp. 241–98.

Parchment. ff. 146. 209 × 128 mm (155 × 75 mm). 1–18^8, 19^2. Horizontal catchwords. Prickings visible in outer margin on f. 1 only. Ruled in pencil. Written in humanistic textualis media in 32 long lines beginning on the second ruled line. Headings in red in script of text. Running headings in upper margin in rustic capitals in violet ink. Gold initials decorated with white vine stem 5 lines high at the beginning of each play. Each initial on a rectangular ground of blue, violet, and green; similar to early Florentine initials described by Pächt and Alexander, *Illuminated Manuscripts,* no. 214 and plate xix. Blue minor initials throughout.

Bound in modern green morocco with gold stampings, signed by F. Bedford.

Written in Florence, c. 1415–20; this date and place indicated by the initials. f. 1, lower margin, apparently a note of ownership erased; traces of a rustic capital M still visible. f. 146, old library stamp, "Bibliotheque de Bourgogne," i.e., Bibliothèque Royale of Brussels. Belonged to Henry Huth (1815–78): his oval label cut from red leather, embossed with gold, "Ex Museo Huthi." De Ricci, *English Collectors,* pp. 151 and 154. Sold by Sotheby's, *Catalogue of the Famous Library of Printed Books, Illuminated Manuscripts, Autograph Letters, and Engravings Collected by Henry Huth and Since Maintained and Augmented by His Son* (8 July 1919), p. 2019, lot no. 7299. Acquired by the Newberry from Bernard Quaritch, 1951.

Second folio: mihi propterea quod.

Faye-Bond, p. 154.

93.6

(79-36837)
Humanistic Collection

Italy [*Illustrated*] 1464

1. ff. 1–5v Huius primi uoluminis hec erit tabula et suorum capitulorum (in red).

ff. 6–12v blank.

Table of contents to text 2 with references to folio numbers.

2. ff. 13–122v Iesus (in upper margin). Sacro principi domino Martino quinto pontifici maximo (in violet). Etsi mea deuotio quę dignitati tuae exigitur ab omnibus maxima se tibi merita largitione quanta qualis ut sit reserare non ualet, ego tamen . . . (f. 14) etiam pro comoditate totius super omnes Ioannem affectare. De regibus Albanis et generatione Romuli (in violet). Troia decenni gręcorum pręlio comsumpta princeps Ęneas inde profugus ad Italiam migrans . . . qua proborum tranquilitas effloreat ęternis profecto laudum tuarum uirtutumque cumulis nihil usquam addiciendum esse meminero. Telos. Ioannes de Criuellis scriptor apostolicus se ipsum ad pedum oscula beatorum.

Johannes de Crivellis, *Compendium historiae romanae.* A chronicle from Aeneas to the Holy Roman Emperor Sigismund, ending with a chapter titled "Inuectiua contra tirannos et malos regentes sicuti fuerunt plurimi." Kristeller, *Iter italicum* 2:10 (a manuscript of s. xv which also contains Salutati's *Lucretia*). This text also in Vat. lat. 5261 (s. xv), ff. 103–160.

3. ff. 123–140 Ioui magno tonanati (*sic*); Ioui optimo maximo; Messalae Coruinii disertissimi oratoris ad Octauianum Cęsarem Augustum de progenie sua et urbis Romae regiminibus breue compendium (in violet). Cum ferequenter (*sic*) me digna moueat postulatio tua . . . et non nihil te imperante haud superesset indomitum. Aeternum, uale, tui saeculi perenne ac immortae (*sic*) decus, Caesar Auguste; Die iouis decimo quinto kallendas nouembris 1464 (in violet).

Ps. Messala Corvinus, *De Augusti progenie.* Printed as an appendix in many editions of Eutropius, e.g., *Breviarium historiae romanae* (Lyon, 1729), pp. 727–55, see F. L. A. Schweiger, *Handbuch der classischen Bibliographie* (Leipzig, 1830–34), vol. 2, pt. 2, p. 614. For other manuscripts, see H. Jordan, "Über das buch *Origo gentis romanae,*" *Hermes* 3 (1869): 426–28, and Kristeller, *Iter italicum* 382, 586, and 601. To these, add Paris, Bib. Maz. 1599, Vat. Chigi H.V. 164, Vat. Urb. 986, and CLM 78. A. Sottili, *Codici del Petrarca nella Germania occidentale* (Padua, 1971–78), 3:348.

4. ff. 140v–142v Uita Publii Uirgilii poetę Maronis maximi feliciter incipit. Publius Uirgilius parentis (*sic*) modicis fuit et pręcipue patre . . . interrumpens Uirgilius, Audi, inquit, quo pacto id coniitio, quoniam quedam enuntiarim.

Vita Virgilii, the first portion drawn from Suetonius, *Vita Virgilii,* ed. J. Brummer, *Vitae virgilianae* (Leipzig, 1912), pp. 1–2; cf. ed. K. Bayer, *Vergil-Viten* (Munich, 1981), p. 214 sqq. After line 24, this recension departs from the printed text and ends with a conversation between Virgil and Caesar Augustus.

5. ff. 143–147v Collucius Florentinus (in blue). Lucretia spurii Lucretii filia et Collatini Tarquinii uxor . . . et sibi persuadeant impudicis licitam fore uitam. Telos.

ff. 148–153v blank.

Coluccio Salutati, *Lucretia*. Attributed to Pius II in his *Opera omnia* (Basel, 1551; reprinted Frankfurt am Main, 1967), pp. 959–60. Other editions listed by B. L. Ullman, *The Humanism of Coluccio Salutati* (Padua, 1963), p. 34, n. 2.

6. ff. 154–163v Ihesus (in upper margin). De cognitione litterarum in quadris antiquis. A [=] Aulus, Aug [=] Augustus, AA [=] Augusta . . . a natiuitate Abram usque ad natiuitatem Christi MDX.

Anonymous, alphabetical table of Roman abbreviations followed by an explanation of word ordering in Roman names, an explanation and table of Roman numerals, brief chronological notes on creation, the flood, and the birth of Christ.

7. ff. 164–172v Feci, mi suauissime Lucherine, quod a me tam uehementer petieras, quę enim Dyonisius alicarnaseus de nuptiis ac natalitiis dicenda gręce tradidit, ea tibi latine traduxi . . . (f. 164v) atque oblectatio uideatur singularis noster amor efficiet. Uale, Mantuę, idibus quinti 1444. Est mihi profecto iocundissimum tuis istis interesse nuptiis mi carissimum caput . . . (168v) Sequitur oratio quę in natiuitatibus dici solet. Natiuitas enim matrimonium sequitur necesse est . . . et materiam orationum huius modi iterum habeamus. Telos.

ff. 173–178v blank.

Unidentified translation of Dionysius of Halicarnassus, *Ars rhetorica,* II and III, dated Mantua, 1444.

Paper. Quires 1–12 with the watermark of a *oiseau,* central portion obscured by the binding; quires 13–14 and 16–18 with a *tête humaine,* cf. Briquet 15619; quire 15 with *monts* within a circle, cf. Briquet 11844 sqq. ff. 178. Texts 1 and 2 with original arabic foliation in two sequences. Modern pencil foliation erroneous by one leaf, beginning 124 = 123, et seq. 203 × 139 mm (143 × 85 mm). 1^{12}, $2–14^{10}$, 15^{12} (1 wanting), 16^{10} (1 wanting), 17^{10}, 18^{6} (entirely blank). Quires 2–4 lettered A–C on verso of last leaf in lower right margin. Quires 3–4 numbered in violet ii–iii on the recto of the first leaf in the upper margin. Quires 5–7 numbered in black roman numerals in the same position. Catchwords on quires 4–11 surrounded by four dots; on quire 13 surrounded by flourishes on either side, one beneath. Ruled in hard point. Texts 1–4 and 6–7, written in humanistic textualis formata in 21 long lines. The acute accent used to denote monosyllabic prepositions. Text 5, written in humanistic cursiva formata also in 21 long lines. Beginning on the second ruled line throughout. Headings in scripts of text: text 1 and text 2, ff. 65v–122v, in red; text 2, ff. 13–65, in violet; text 3, headings and index notes in violet; texts 4 and 6, in ink of text; text 5, in blue. Text 2, simple blue square capital initials; texts 4 and 7, simple red rustic initials. ff. 124 and 143 (texts 3 and 5), blue square capital initials with brown flourishes. All initials 2 or 3 lines high.

Bound in parchment over pasteboard, s. xviii. Spine title, "Miscellanea," summary contents, and shelf-mark "No. 6." Blue and gold floral decorated endpapers, s. xviii.

Written in Italy, possibly in Rome, as suggested by the colophon of text 2. Texts 1 and 2 written by "Iohannes de Criuellis scriptor apostolicus," signed on f. 122v. Texts 3–5 and 7 in a similar script, possibly by the same hand. Text 3 dated 18 October 1464 on f. 140. Original foliation on texts 1 and 2 only suggests that these quires were not initially bound as one volume. In the library of Matteo Luigi Canonici of Venice (1727–1806): his summary table of contents on slip affixed to the verso of the front endpaper; see J. Mitchell, "Trevisan and Soranzo: Some Canonici Manuscripts from Two Eighteenth-Century Venetian Collections," *Bodleian Library Record* 8 (1969): 134–35, and *Lyell Catalogue,* p. 247. One of 915 Canonici manuscripts purchased by Rev. Walter Sneyd in 1835; his bookplate on the front pastedown. Pencil note on the second flyleaf, "Lot 377 N/-" is the number of this codex in the Sneyd sale at Sotheby's, 16 December 1903; see De Ricci, *English Collectors,* pp. 136–37. The codex is misdated in the sales catalogue. Acquired by the Newberry in 1979 from Bernard Rosenthal.

Second folio: De ciuili bello per.

–94

Sallust, *Bellum Iugurthinum, Catilinae Coniuratio*

Brescia [*Illustrated*] 1477

1. ff. 1–63v Crispi Salustii historici celeberrimi de Iugurthino bello liber foeliciter incipit; prohemium (in violet). Falso queritur de de (*sic*) natura sua humanum genus . . . spes atque opes ciuitatis in illo sitę sunt. Telos. Crispi Salustii omnium tam gręcorum quam latinorum Quintiliano teste historici celeberrimi opus Iugurthini belli foeliciter expletum est per me Tadeum Solacium tercio decimo kalendas iunias auditumque a preceptore Nicolao Botano omnium tum grauitate tum doctrina hac in ętate dignissimo idibus iuniis.

Contemporary corrections, glosses, notes, and *nota* marks by several Italian humanistic hands.

Sallust, *Bellum iugurthinum,* rev. ed., A. Kurfess (Leipzig, 1954).

2. ff. 64–96 Crispi Salustii historici celeberrimi de Catilinę coniuratione opus fęliciter incipit; prohemium (in violet). Omnis homines qui sese student pręstare cęteris animalibus . . . luctus atque gaudium agitabantur. Telos. Crispi Salustii historici celeberrimi de coniuratione Catilinę opus foeliciter transcriptum est per me Tadeum Solacium xv kalendas octobres anno millesimo quadragentesimo (*sic*) septuagessimo (*sic*) septimo, Eustachio prętore ac Iohanne Emo Brixię pręfecto.

Occasional pointing hands in margins.

ff. 96v–100v blank.

Sallust, *Catilinae coniuratio,* rev. ed., A. Kurfess (Leipzig, 1954).

Paper, watermarked with crescent and flower somewhat similar to Briquet 5296–97. ff. 100. 150 × 105 mm (97 × 60 mm). $1–3^{10}$, 4^{8}, $5–6^{10}$, 7^{12}, $8–10^{10}$. Vertical catchwords. Ruled in hard point and pencil. Written in humanistic textualis formata in 25 long lines beginning on the first ruled line. Headings in violet in rustic capitals; incipits in rustic capitals in ink of text. f. 1, gold dentelle initial with white patterning on a violet ground, severely damaged by moisture. f. 64, gold dentelle initial with white patterning on a violet ground, historiated in the interior with a scroll.

Bound in parchment over pasteboard with marble paper end leaves, s. xviii.

Written in Brescia by Tadeus Solacius in 1477, signed and dated on f. 96. Tadeus Solacius also copied Oxford, Bodl. Can. Lat. 261; see *Colophons de manuscrits occidentaux,* 17609, which has a colophon very similar to that of text 2 above. f. 96v, inserted into the colophon in humanistic cursive in violet ink, "Ego Hyeronimus Robertus ab infrascripto Tadeo emi librum istum." Another mention of this same Robertus in Bologna, Biblioteca Univ. 2395, f. 152. See *Studi italiani di filologia classica* (Florence, 1893–1915), XVII, 139, no. 1216; *Colophons de manuscrits occidentaux,* 7179. Sold by William Pickering in London, 12 December 1854, lot no. 163, to Henry G. Bohn. Belonged to Henry Allen: his bookplate on a front pastedown. Sold by his son Samuel Allen at Sotheby's, 30 January 1920, lot no. 97 of 115 Allen items offered for sale. See De Ricci, *English Collectors,* p. 159. Purchased by Hugh W. Davis; see De Ricci, ibid., pp. 179–80. Sold, Leighton Catalogue 1 (1920), lot no. 353; Catalogue 5 (1924), lot no. 77 to J. T. Adams. Sold by Adams at Sotheby's 7 December 1931, lot no. 212, to McLeish. Old label, edged in blue, with "40" written in black ink on front pastedown. Acquired by Philip Hofer, his bookplate also on front pastedown; his gift to the Newberry, 1935.

Second folio: quidem regere patriam.

De Ricci, 2:2280–81.

f95

(324356)

Petrarch, *De Vita Solitaria, De Otio Religioso*
Lombardy [*Illustrated*] s. XV med. (before 1464)

1. ff. 1–87 Clarissimi poetae laureati Francisci Petrarcae de [– ocio religioso] uita solitaria liber primus (corrected in black ink). Paucos homines noui quibus opusculorum meorum tanta dignatio tantusque sit amor . . . (f. 34v) Clarissimi poetae laureati Francisci Petrarcae de [– ocio religioso] uita solitaria liber secundus (in violet, correction in black). Sentio tamen adhuc aliquid deesse . . . bene suades, recte consulis, uerum dicis.

Corrections in the headings by the scribe. Sporadic marginal notes by several hands, s. xv–xvi, some of these in violet by the scribe to serve as index notes.

Petrarch, *De vita solitaria.* Text lacks chapter on Romualdus. No chapter headings or numbers; ed. G. Martellotti, *Prose* (Milan, 1955), pp. 286–590. This manuscript described by B. L. Ullman, "Petrarch's De vita solitaria," *Studies in the Italian Renaissance,* 2d ed. (Rome, 1973), pp. 159, 165, and 169.

2. ff. 87–159v Clarissimi poetae laureati Francisci Petrarcae de ocio religioso liber tertius (*sic;* in violet). Dignum erat o felix Christi familia . . . et mei memores ualete. O felices, si uos ipsos et bona uestra cognoscitis. Telos (in violet).

Petrarch, *De otio religioso,* ed. G. Rotundi (Studi e Testi, 195; Vatican City, 1958).

f. 1, gold initial decorated with white vine stem on ground of green, red, and blue, historiated with a bust of Petrarch, accompanied by full white vine stem and laurel leaf border 14 lines high; two putti bear coat of arms in lower margin, another above in upper right. Three similar gold initials decorated with white vine stem 7 lines high on ff. 38 and 87, 4 lines high on f. 88. Minor blue rustic capital initials with red flourishes and red initials with violet flourishes throughout.

Parchment. ff. i + 159 + i. Some minor water damage. Flyleaves are old pastedowns; rear flyleaf inverted. Trimmed to 278 × 196 mm (198 × 120 mm). $1–19^{8}$, 20^{8} (8 stub only). Vertical catchwords. Ruled in hard point.

Written in humanistic textualis formata slightly cursive in 33 long lines beginning on the first ruled line. Headings in rustic capitals in red. Some headings in violet. Incipits in rustic capitals in ink of text.

Bound in brown morocco by the Newberry in 1973, signed Frost; for the previous Archinto binding see De Ricci. Green staining visible on flyleaves.

Written in Lombardy before 1464. f. 1, putti bear arms of Borromeo family and initials CO FI = *Comes Filippus* = Filippo Borromeo (d. 1464). From the library of Conte Archinto (Milan), his armorial bookplate on rear flyleaf. On the Archinto Collection, see notes on MS 70.5. Purchased by Edward E. Ayer from L. S. Olschki in 1901. Acquired by the Newberry from Edward E. Ayer, December 1920.

Second folio: nisi rationem habeam.

De Ricci, 1:557. Faye-Bond, p. 147. Ullmann, "Petrarch Manuscripts in the United States," p. 450, no. 21. M. Jasenas, *Petrarch in America* (Washington and New York: Folger and Morgan Libraries, 1974), pp. 14, 35 and plate 18.

95.1

(59-1219)

Proverbs (in Italian)

Central Italy s. XV med.

ff. 1–4v

Non e si piccol sancto che non uenga la sua festa . . .

Chi e luxurioso poco li uale oro o topatio.

Ninety-six proverbs in stanzas of four rhyming lines (in Italian), ed. M. Masi and D. Bommarito, "The Italian Proverbs of Newberry Library MS 95.1," *Manuscripta* 24 (1980): 28–30.

ff. 4 One quire of four leaves, possibly from a larger codex. Paper, bears a circular watermark with an anvil (?) in the interior, partially obscured by the binding. 194 × 146 mm (151 × 89 mm). Ruled in hard point, left boundary line in pencil. Written in gothic textualis media, incorporating numerous humanistic traits, including ampersand, humanistic g, and ct ligature, in 24 long lines beginning on the second ruled line. Initials marked in violet, every eighth line marked with a simple violet cross.

Bound in modern cardboard.

Written in central Italy in the middle of the fifteenth century. A capital C with a point on either side on f. 3 in left margin and on f. 4v in lower margin. Acquired by the Newberry from Bernard Rosenthal, 1959.

Second folio: Lo falcione.

95.5

(65-3067)

Virgil, *Bucolics, Georgics, Aeneid*

Italy s. XV²

1. ff. 1–14v Publii Uirgilii Maronis liber bucolicorum feliciter incipit (in red).

Tityrę (*sic*), tu patulę recubans sub tegmine fagi . . .

Ite domum sature, uenit Hesperus, ite capellę.

Explicit liber bucholicorum.

Virgil, *Bucolics*. Mynors, *Opera,* pp. 1–28.

2. ff. 15–50v Publii Uirgilii Maronis liber Georgicorum feliciter incipit (in red).

Quid faciat lętas segetes, quo sidere seruet agricola

Quid faciat letas segetes quo sidere terram . . .

Tityre, te patulę cerini (*sic*) sub tegmine fagi.

Telos. Publii Uirgilii Maronis liber georgicorum explicit.

Virgil, *Georgics*. Mynors, *Opera,* pp. 29–101. Each book preceded by Ps. Ovid, *Argumenta Georgicon,* I–IV. Riese, *Anthologia latina,* vol. 1, pt. 1, pp. 16–17.

3. f. 51

Qualis bucolicis, quantus tellure domandi . . .

Contineat quę quisque liber, lege carmina nostra.

Ps. Ovid, *Argumenta Bucolicon et Georgicon*. Riese, *Anthologia latina,* vol. 1, pt. 1, p. 16.

4. f. 51

Primus habet Libyam ueniunt ut Troes in urbem . . .

Ultimus imponit bello Turni nece finem.

Basilius, *De XII libris Aeneados*. Riese, *Anthologia latina,* vol. 1, pt. 2, pp. 100–101.

5. f. 51

Aeneas primo Libye depellitur oris . . .

Ęxcidium Troię iussus narrare parabat.

Ps. Ovid, *Argumenta Aeneidis,* I. Riese, *Anthologia latina,* vol. 1, pt. 1, pp. 8–9.

6. ff. 51v–210v Publii Uirgilii Maronis liber primus Ęneidos feliciter incipit (in red).

Ille ego qui quondam gratili modulatus auena . . .

Arma uirumque . . .

Uitaque cum gemitu fugit indignata per umbras. Finis.

Virgil, *Aeneid*. Mynors, *Opera*, pp. 103–422, preceded by the *Praefatio* beginning "Ille ego." See Mynors, *Opera*, p. xii. R. G. Austen, "Ille ego qui quondam . . . ," *Classical Quarterly*, n.s. 18 (1968): 107. H. Goezler, *Virgile Énéide, livres I–VI* (Paris, 1936), p. 6n. G. Ianell, *Virgilii opera* (Leipzig, 1930), p. xvi. Books II–X of the *Aeneid*, prefaced by Ps. Ovid, *Argumenta Aeneidis*, II–XII; Riese, *Anthologia latina*, vol. 1, pt. 1, pp. 9–15. Marginal and interlinear gloss written by two humanistic hands beginning Musę: filię Iouis et memorię et fuerunt numero nouem . . . Gloss ends at the beginning of Book IX, 380, on f. 160v. This gloss clearly related at many points to that attributed to Giulio Pomponio Leto, edited in *Virgilius, opera omnia* (Basel, 1544), citing Leto explicitly on f. 65v. ff. 51v–160v, marginal index notes in violet.

Parchment of southern preparation. ff. 210. Trimmed to 230 × 150 mm (158 × 94 mm). $1–20^{10}$, 21^{12}. Vertical catchwords preceded and followed by a flourish. Leaves signed alphabetically al, etc., occasionally visible. Ruled horizontally in pen, vertically in pencil. Written in humanistic textualis formata in 31 long lines beginning on the second ruled line. Marginal corrections by a second hand. Incipits and initial letter of each verse in rustic capitals. Headings of chapters and running headings in red rustic capitals. Heading for the *Aeneid* on f. 51v written without word separation. ff. 51–210v, gloss in humanistic cursiva media by at least two hands, *lemmata* underlined in violet. ff. 51v–160 (= quires 6–16), index notes in rustic capitals; *nota* signs and pointing hands, all in violet. Gold initials decorated with white vine stem on grounds of blue, green, and red 6–8 lines high at the beginning of texts 1 and 2 and at the beginning of each book of the *Aeneid*. f. 1, initial extended to form inner and upper bracket margin with a cluster of three gold radiating disks at each end.

Bound in gold-stamped brown calf, s. xix.

Written in Italy, probably in or near Rome, in the second half of the fifteenth century. f. 1, lower margin, arms of the Maffei family of Volterra. Formerly in the library of Mario II de Maffei. f. 1, partially obliterated and barely legible under ultraviolet lamp, "De fig[liuoli] et ered[i] di Messer Mario Maffei," in script of end of s. xvi or beginning s. xvii. An old shelf-mark visible under ultraviolet lamp on f. 1, right margin, appears to read "L45." On the Maffei library, see J. Ruysschaert, "Recherches sur les deux bibliothèques romaines Maffei des XVe et XVIe siècles," *Bibliofilia* 60 (1958): 306–55. This manuscript listed as no. 59, p. 332. In the library of Anthony Askew (1722–74); *DNB* 1:664–65. De Ricci, *English Collectors*, pp. 52–53. Sold at Sotheby's, 7 March 1785, *Bibliotheca askeviana manuscripta* . . . , lot no. 536. Front pastedown, armorial bookplate of Sir George Schuckburgh (d. 1804), *Franks Collection of Book Plates*, 26854. Sold at Christie's, 4 May 1962, lot no. 14. Rear endpaper, "2, 16, on Chr. list," written in pencil; front pastedown, "16°" on a circular white sticker. Acquired by the Newberry from H. P. Kraus, 1962.

Second folio: Hinc alto sub.

f96

(51-2134)

Aristotle, *De Ethica ad Nicomachum*,
Translation of Johannes Argyropolus

Italy s. XV^{2}

ff. 1–135v Prefatio Ioannis Argiropili biçantii pro libro Aristotelis de moribus ad Nicomachum ad prestantissimum uirum Cosmam Medicem florentinum incipit feliciter (in violet). Ioannes Argyropylus byçantius magnificio uiro Cosmę Medici salutem plurimam dicit. Si ea mihi seruanda sunt erga te, quę iam olim institui, sapientissme Cosma, ea tantum sunt a me tibi offerenda . . . (f. 4v) Liber moralium primus, tractatus primus (in violet). Omnis ars omnisque doctrina atque actus itidem et electio bonum quoddam appetere uidetur . . . quibusue legibus utens ac moribus erit optime constituta. Hęc itaque aggredientes, deinceps dicamus. Liber decimus Aristotelis ad Nicomachum, quem Iohannes Argyropylus byçantius gratia magnifici Cosmę Medicis florentini traduxit, explicit fęliciter (in violet).

Contemporary marginal index notes and schematic diagrams.

GW 2359, 2361, and 2364; cf. H. W. Chandler, *A Catalogue of Editions of Aristotle's Nicomachean Ethics* (Oxford, 1868), nos. 3, 4, 21, 28, 30, 39, and 47. For other manuscripts, see C. Frati, "Le Traduzioni Aristoteliche di G. Argiropulo e un'antica legatura Medicea," *Bibliofilia* 19 (1917): pp. 1–25; Kristeller, *Iter italicum* 1:105 and 185; E. Garin, "Le Traduzioni umanistiche di Aristotele nel secolo XV," *Atti e memorie dell'accademia fiorentina di scienze morali la Colombaria* 16 (1947–50): 82–86 and 102.

Parchment of southern preparation. ff. 135. Trimmed to 279 × 209 mm (183 × 119 mm). $1–5^{10}$, 6^{6}, $7–13^{10}$, 14^{8}, 15^{1} (a single leaf, first words match catchwords on f. 134v). Horizontal catchwords throughout. Ruled in pen. Written in humanistic textualis formata in 30 long lines beginning on the first ruled line; parentheses present. Running headings in upper margins. Chapter headings in rustic capitals in violet. Eleven gold initials decorated with white vine stem on grounds of green, blue, and pink, 8–11 lines high, placed at the beginning of the prologue and of each of Aristotle's ten books. f. 1, initial extended to form an inner border ending in clusters of three gold radiating disks, decorated at the top with a pen drawing of a bird. f. 4v, initial decorated with two clusters of three gold radiating disks. Alternating simple red and blue rustic capital initials 3 lines high throughout.

Bound in modern gold-stamped brown morocco.

Written in Italy, possibly Florence, in the second half of the fifteenth century. A possible old ex libris erased on f. 1 in lower margin, center. Belonged to James P. R. Lyell (d. 1949). "DVVV 8/4/42" written over an erasure on front pastedown, Lyell's code for dealer and price of purchase. "120" written within a circle refers to post mortem inventory of his library; his bookplate, gold letters embossed on black leather, on front pastedown. See *Lyell Catalogue,* p. xxix. Acquired by the Newberry from Bernard Quaritch, 1951.

Second folio: legendo (fit.

Faye-Bond, p. 154.

+97

(23877)

Plato, *De Republica,* Translation of Antonio Cassarino; etc.

Naples s. XV med.

1. ff. 1–19 Plato atheniensis patre Aristone natus est, matre Perrictione quae Solonem generis auctorem nuncupabat . . . Haec autem sunt quae labore multo et studio quaecunque de Platone et aliis dicta fuerant excerpendo de uiro colligere potuimus. Finis.

ff. 19v–21v blank.

Diogenes Laertius, *Vita Platonis,* translation of Antonio Cassarino, partial edition from this codex, Volger, "Plato's Republik," pp. 197–200. See also Resta, "Antonio Cassarino," p. 262.

2. ff. 22–24v Plaerosque (*sic*) satis esse non dubito qui me interdum, etsi non culpent, parum certe laudent . . . Itaque hoc primum, inde Socratem disputantem audiemus.

Antonio Cassarino, *Isagogicon in Platonis vitam et disciplinam,* ed. Resta, "Antonio Cassarino," pp. 258–62.

3. ff. 25–229 Platonis de republica liber primus ab Antonio Cassarino siculo e graeco in latinum conuersus feliciter incipit (in gold). Hesterna die in Pireum descendi cum Glaucone Arystonis ut deam comprecarer . . . hic et in mille annorum itinere de quo diximus bene et feliciter agamus.

Laus tibi summe pater atque fili
Quique procedis simul ex utroque
Spiritus sancte deus unus idem
Laus tibi semper.

Praecipiti uentus quum strauit turbine malos
Et summa euertit classis carchesia regis
Arnaldi edicto, codex perfectus in Acre
Oui perque manum scriptus fuit iste Masulli (in violet).

f. 229v blank.

Plato, *The Republic,* translation of Antonio Cassarino for Alfonso the Magnanimous of Naples. Extract edited by Volger, "Plato's Republik," pp. 200–204. See also Resta, "Antonio Cassarino," pp. 269–70, and E. Garin, "Ricerche sulle traduzioni di Platone nella prima metà del sec. XV," in *Medioevo e Rinascimento: studi in onore di Bruno Nardi* (Florence, 1955), 1:357–60.

Parchment of southern preparation. ff. i + 229 + i. Modern paper flyleaves. Erroneous arabic foliation, s. xv or xvi, corrected in s. xx. 278 × 200 mm (197 × 110 mm). 1–28^{8}, 29^{8} (6–8 wanting). Vertical catchwords. Ruled in hard point. Written in humanistic textualis formata in 27 long lines beginning on the first ruled line. Accent marks present. f. 25, heading in gold in rustic capitals with points between words. Incipits in script of text in ink of text. f. 229, colophon written in violet ink in script of text. Texts 1 and 2 and each book of text 3 commence with a gold initial with white vine stem decoration on grounds of blue, red, and green accompanied by gold radiating disks 6–8 lines high. f. 25, white vine stem decoration extended to form inner border. Two putti bear arms with a decorative pattern in lower margin accompanied by floral decoration of different hues than those of the decoration in the rest of the book and, therefore, possibly a later addition.

Bound in rebacked Neapolitan stamped calf over boards, s. xv. Front and back panels decorated with two rolls of rope motifs, stamps of a third rope motif decorate a lozenge compartment in the center. Surrounding triangular compartments each containing a cluster of three small double circular stamps. Two cloth fore-edge clasps, a top and a bottom front-to-back clasp, all wanting. Top brass catch in the shape of a fleur-de-lys; other catches in the shape of a twelve-lobed leaf decorated with three cloverleaf cutouts. For closely related stamps and catches, see De Marinis, *La Biblioteca napoletana dei re d'Aragona,* vol. 1, plates 53 and 54; vol. 3, plate 140. On back cover, parchment label of s. xv, "Plato atheniensis de republica," first two words in Italian gothic rotunda formata; second two words in much smaller humanistic textualis media. Binding repaired in s. xviii or xix.

Written in the middle of the fifteenth century by Masullus in the Castel dell'Ovo in Naples for the library of King Alfonso the Magnanimous, King of Naples and Aragon, signed on f. 229. This manuscript known to De Marinis (*La Biblioteca napoletana dei re d'Aragona* 1:40), only from the notice of Beer, "Handschriftenschätze," p. 19. The binding, undescribed by Beer, confirms that the book was in fact in the royal library. Front pastedown, an inverted inscription of s. xv, possibly an old pressmark:

XXV slo(?) doe
P.

and an inverted Latin sixteenth-century pen trial. In 1858, in the library of Don Miguel de Mayora, Vice-Consul of Mexico in Barcelona, recorded by Volger, "Plato's Republik." Subsequently in the library of Don Luis Mayora, recorded by Beer, "Handschriftenschätze." "100" written on front pastedown, right side up. No. 54 from the collection of Henry Probasco, acquired by the Newberry 1 December 1890.

Second folio: -demia inde in.

De Ricci, 1:530.

97.1

(54-1374)

Stefano Fieschi, *Sinonima Sententiarum, De Compositione Stili Adornandi*

Italy [*Illustrated*] 1463

1. ff. 2–89 Stephanus Flischus de Soncino uiro peritissimo Iohanni Meliorantio ornatissimo, ciui uicentino, canzelario patauino (in violet). Cum superiora uerborum synonima tibi breuiter absoluissem . . . et ut me te alterum esse ducas uehementer exopto.

f. 1, in upper margin, sixteenth-century inscription "Stephanus Fliscus de Soncino de compositione stili adornandi atque collupletandę elocutionis et orationis 1463" refers to text 2; cf. colophon, f. 144.

f. 89v blank.

Stefano Fieschi, *Sinonima sententiarum*. Hain, 7136–54. See also T. Foffano, "Charles d'Orléans e un gruppo di umanisti lombardi in Normandia," *Aevum* 41 (1967): 455.

2. ff. 90–144 Stephani Flischi de Soncino de compositione stili adornandi et commode orationis atque colluplectande elocutionis ad sapientissimum uirum dominum Francischum Patrinum de Cremona inclitum militem comitemque palatinum ac perspicacissimum medicine doctorem liber incipit (in violet). Cum post multas diuturnasque studiorum pertrac[ta]tiones acuratius essem mecum perscrutatus, sapientissime mi Francisce, quę res potissimum collustrassent homines illos . . . per te missum facient. Stephani Flischi de Soncino liber de compositione stili adornandi et commode orationis atque colluplectande elocutionis explicit feliciter per me Iacobum Mafeum die 4 octobris 1463.

Stefano Fieschi, *Liber de compositione stili adornandi*. Other copies of this text recorded by Kristeller, *Iter italicum* 1:31 and 391, 2:395 and 591.

3. ff. 144v–145v List of synonymous Latin phrases.

ff. 146–147v blank.

Stiff parchment of southern preparation. ff. i + 146. Modern foliation begins with the flyleaf. 203 × 144 mm (130 × 98 mm). $1–2^{10}$, 3^{8}, $4–12^{10}$, 13^{8}, $14–15^{10}$. Catchwords surrounded by four marks, in some instances letters of the alphabet, n, d, u, w, and a. Ruled horizontally in pen and vertically in pencil. Written in Italian gothic cursiva formata incorporating many humanistic traits, notably half-uncial d and e with cedilla for ae diphthong, in 26 long lines beginning on the first ruled line. Headings in violet in script of text. ff. 138v–142, index notes in violet, also in script of text. f. 1, green square capital initial decorated with flora on a dark red ground 5 lines high; f. 90, red square capital initial on a green ground 5 lines high.

Bound in stamped quarter pigskin over wooden boards, s. xvi[1]. Four large rectangular stamps in two columns front and back. Stamps in order from top to bottom: Paul carrying the gospel with interlaced initials HD to the left of his head, R to the right of his head, titled Paulus; the Virgin and Child (half portrait), titled Maria; King David with his harp, titled Davidt (*sic*); Isaiah, carrying the legend "Puer natus erit," titled Isaiah. Above and below, two rectangular compartments with a stamp of a leaf on either side of a rosette. Two rear-to-front clasps. Old spine label removed.

Written in Italy by Jacobus Maffeus, 4 October 1463, signed on f. 144. f. 2, in lower margin, unidentified arms with a wreath of laurel leaves with initials "C" and "A" on either side. f. 147v, inscription of s. xvi, "Hac (*sic*) liber est o[illegible]," scratched out and erased. "Petrus Martiris," written twice, s. xvi, first signature very faded. Below, fragment of c. 1500, jottings in Italian and Latin. f. 1, inscription of s. xvi, "IHS" within circle of radiating beams and the inscription "Hic est nomen Iesu"; upper left, old pressmark, visible only under ultraviolet lamp "A II 24," "2" written above by another hand. Front pastedown, "407" in red crayon in upper left corner and pencil note of s. xviii (?), "Di Zatta P[illegible] N. 10 (?)." Acquired by the Newberry from A. L. Van Gendt (Blariacum, The Netherlands), 1954.

Second folio: Deus accessiones.

Faye-Bond, p. 154.

97.2

Leonardo Bruni, *De Primo Bello Punico* (in Italian)

Florence [*Illustrated*] 1464

ff. 1–115v Christus; Christus; Christus; Christus; Incomincia de primo bello punico in uolghare (in red). [E] parra forse a molti che io uada drieto a chose troppo antiche . . . E non molto di poi tolto loro le posessioni constrecti furono in grande parte habandonare il paese. Finis amen. Finito deo gratias; Amen (in red) . . . et fu fatta questa opera ouero libro in latino da messere Leonardo d'Areçço poeta laureato et sepellito in Firençe nella chiesa di sancta crocie in una sepoltura marmorea bellissima et ornatissima allato alla porta che ua ne chiostri di detta chiesa. Finis. Amen. Finis; Amen . . . (in red) . . . Io Iachopo de Franciescho di Lorenço di Niccolo da Soci di Casentino, al presente in Firençe, ho transcripto e chopiato questo libro di mia propria mano, e chomincia'lo a scrivere il sicondo di di quaresima, cioe a di sedici di março 1463 (*sic* = February 1463, i.e., 1464 new style), et finilo oggi, questo di sei di março prossimo, pure nel 1463 (i.e., 1464 new style), in detta quaresima. Et scripsilo in chasa di Domenicho di Belfrale di Firençe, nel popolo di Sancta Trinita. Il quale libro ho scripto a Bartolomeo di detto Domenicho di Belfrale. Finito. Amen.

Leonardo Bruni, *De bello punico,* in Italian, ed. A. Ceruti in *Scelta di curiosità letterarie inedite* 165 (Bologna, 1878). Baron, *Leonardo Bruni Aretino,* p. 167.

Paper, thick, stiff, and furry. Watermarked, cf. Briquet 3385. Flyleaves and pastedowns, parchment of southern preparation, ruled for two columns. ff. ii + 115 + ii. Portion of f. 81 restored in s. xvii. 210 × 145 mm (136 × 85 mm). $1–9^{10}$, 10^{8}, 11^{10}, 12^{10} (8–10 wanting). Catchwords within rectangles. Written in humanistic cursiva formata with less than average care. Headings in red in script of text.

Bound in contemporary stamped calf over wooden boards. Front and back, panel margin decorated with a roll of laurel leaves; interior decorated with a field of lozenge-shaped designs formed from two small stamps, one a double circle, the other a cross. Two fore-edge clasps wanting, two catches shaped as fleurs-de-lys remain.

Written in Florence, in 1464, by Iacopo di Francescho di Lorenzo di Nicolo da Soci di Casentino, cf. *Colophons de manuscrits occidentaux,* 7739. Rear flyleaf, inscription dated 1470 in a cursive hand, "A uno che dolesse i denti fa dire a quello tale tri patri nostri e tre aue marie in gienochie nudi, a laude e reuerenzie dela Santa Trinita, e po fa quiste cinque o o o o o in carta bambaxina, e toi uno chi[o]do novo e uno martello de ferro e di queste parole: Al fe'd[i]o, qui est principium et fine, e mitte el chiodo in uno de quiste o e di: Dolte el dente e lui dixe de si e alora da la botta in su el chiodo e fa cosi cinque uolte, cio di quelle parole, e cosi da in sul chiodo a ci[o] esche d'uno de quisti o, e subitto guarira. E questo uide prouare in la rochea de Soma Cologna (E. Repetti, *Diz. geogr. d. Toscana* [Florence, 1833–46] 5:424–25) in Garfagniana piu e piu uolte. 1470 a di primo de nouembre. Dio ne sia lodato." Front pastedown, notes of s. xv, erased and illegible. A bibliographical note of s. xviii identifying the text and analyzing and transcribing the colophon is tipped on to the front flyleaf. Acquired by the Newberry from H. P. Kraus, 1963.

Second folio: -ginesi uno che.

97.3

Leonardo Bruni, *Cicero Novus, Vita Demosthenis*

Northern Italy [*Illustrated*] c. 1450

1. ff. 2–49 Leonardi in Ciceronis uitam argumentum (in violet). Ocioso mihi nuper ac lectitare aliquid cupienti oblatus est libellus quidam ex Plutarcho traductus . . . (f. 3) ut uehementer exoptem a multis de hoc ipso scribentibus superari. (f. 3v) Ciceronis uita mores res gestae; Tulliorum familia, quae (in violet) et Ciceronis postea cognomentum recepit . . . misere tandem ignominioseque perierunt.

First unnumbered leaf and ff. 1–1v and 49v blank.

Leonardo Bruni, *Cicero novus seu Ciceronis vita* (an expanded version of Plutarch's life of Cicero) with the prologue to Nicolò Niccoli, ed. A. Mai, *M. Tullii Ciceronis sex orationum partes ante nostram aetatem ineditae . . .* (Milan, 1817), pp. 255–301; prologue and extracts edited in Baron, *Leonardo Bruni Aretino,* pp. 113–20 and 163–64.

2. ff. 50–74 Demosthenis uita; Demostenis pater De (in green and violet alternate letters)

-mosthenes ut Theopompus historicus tradit inprimis honestus ac uir probus fuit . . . quod sępe praedicenti Demostheni credere noluerat.

ff. 74v–77v blank.

Plutarch, *Vita Demosthenis,* translation of Leonardo Bruni. Hain 13124–13127. Baron, *Leonardo Bruni Aretino,* p. 163.

Parchment of southern preparation. ff. 78. Modern foliation begins with second leaf. 153 × 95 mm (97 × 55 mm). 1^{2}, $2–8^{10}$, 9^{4}, 10^{2}. Catchwords in lower right margins. Ruled in hard point. Written in humanistic cursiva formata in 22 long lines beginning on the first ruled line. Written in brown ink, omitted portion of text added in violet ink in margins by the scribe and by Bernardo Bembo; see provenance section below. ff. 3v and 50, four lines written in large violet (f. 3v) and alternating violet and green (f. 50) capitals so as to form title pages.

Bound in stamped brown goatskin over boards, s. xv. Panel decorated with rope motif, in the interior five small double circular stamps; outer margin formed by stamp "Ihs Maria" repeated numerous times; same pattern front and back. "Vitae" written across the fore-edge.

Written in northern Italy, c. 1450, probably for Bernardo Bembo (1433–1519) of Venice, see *DBI* 8:103–9. On the inside of the back cover, "Codex Bernardi B[em]bi" written in black by a fifteenth-century hand, rubbed out but visible under ultraviolet light. On the books in Bembo's library, see Alexander and De la Mare, *Italian Manuscripts,* pp. xxix, n. 6, and 108; P. de Nolhac, *La Bibliothèque de Fulvio Orisini* (Paris, 1887); C. H. Clough, *Pietro Bembo's Library as Represented Particularly in the British Museum* (rev. ed.; London, 1971); N. Gianetto, "I codici dell Eton College provenienti della Biblioteca di Bernardo Bembo," *Atti dell'Accademia Nazionale dei Lincei* 378 (1981), sez. 8, *Rendiconti, Classe di Scienze morali* 36 (1982): 219–37. Occasional corrections and notes in violet and differing shade of black ink (f. 68, in the presence of a pointing hand), some of which appears to be by the hand of Bembo, cf. C. Frati, "Un codice autografo di Bernardo Bembo," in *Raccolta di studi critici dedicata ad Alessandro d'Ancona* (Florence, 1901), figs. 1 and 2, facing p. 196. Modern note on flyleaf indicates that another manuscript belonging to Bembo, no. 61 in the Chester Beatty sale (Sotheby's, 9 May 1933; see De Ricci, *English Collectors,* pp. 171–72), had violet corrections of the text similar to those in this manuscript; see also BL Add. 41068A. f. 74v, "Memoriae felicissimae" written in square capitals in very black ink, s. xv. f. 1v, "Ciceronis uita, Demosthenis uita," written in humanistic cursiva, s. xv. "50" written on the front cover and "no. 50" written on f. i, both by an early modern hand (s. xviii?). Acquired by Thomas Edward Marston from C. A. Stonehill in 1958; formerly no. 178 in the Marston library, New Haven, Connecticut, his bookplate on the inside of the front cover. Bequeathed to Yale University. Sold at Sotheby's, 9 December 1974, lot 46, plate 8 (ff. 3v–4) where it was acquired by Bernard Quaritch for the Newberry.

Second folio: descripsimus. Est autem.

Faye-Bond, p. 84.

97.5

(63-107)

Antonius de Carlenis de Neapoli, O.P., *Questiones in Libros I–II Analyticorum Posteriorum Aristotelis;*
Thomas Aquinas, *Super Periermenias*

Naples [*Illustrated*] 1468

1. ff. 2–47v Queritur primo utrum subiectum libri posteriorium sit sillogismus demonstratiuus, et arguitur primo quod non, nam de subiecto demonstratur . . . Impono hiis super primum et secundum posteriorum analeticorum questiunculis finem. Amen. Expliciunt questiones super primum et 2um posteriorum edite per reuerendissimum dominum Antonium quondam archiepiscopum amalfitanum scripte per me Petrum anno domini millesimo cccc° lxviii mensis augusti, complete in nocte sancti Martini. Scripsit has questiones Petrus de Afelatro de Neapoli 5° anno sui studii in hiis artibus.

Marginal glosses, index notes, and pointing hands by the scribe.

f. 47v, table of questions.

ff. 1–1v and 48–49v blank.

Antonius de Carlenis, *Questiones in libros I–II analyticorum posteriorum Aristotelis.* This commentary not listed by Lohr, "Medieval Commentaries," *Traditio* 23 (1967): 365. Kaeppeli, 284, lists this manuscript as the only known example. On Antonius de Carlenis, see G. Meersseman, "Antonius de Carlenis O.P. Erzbischof von Amalfi," *Archivum fratrum praedicatorum* 3 (1933): 81–131; "Ergänzung zum Schrifttum des Antonius de Carlenis von Neapel, O.P.," ibid. 5 (1935): 357–63.

2. ff. 50–67v Dilecto sibi preposito louaniensi frater Thomas de Aquino salutem et uera sapiencie incrementa . . . (ends in Book II, cap. x, lect. 2, sect. 14, in middle of first sentence) dicit enim quod id quod in supra dic-

tis dictum est intelligi potest. Finis. Finitur expositio super peryamenias Aristotelis secundum angelicum diuum doctorem Thomam de Aquino quam ut dicitur non compleuit nec plus inuenitur. Hoc opusculum scripsi ego Petrus de Afelatro de Neapoli quod in pascatis uigilia hora prima noctis compleui. Finis deo laus.

Marginal glosses, index notes, and pointing hands by the scribe.

f. 68–68v blank.

Thomas Aquinas, *Super periermenias,* in *Opera omnia* (Rome, 1882), 1:7–84. Grabmann, *Die Werke,* pp. 272–74.

f. 1, purple dentelle initial with white patterning on a ground of yellow, blue, and green, historiated with a feline or dog-like animal, accompanied by a piece of yellow floral spray border decorated with radiating gold disks, some in clusters of three. Alternating red and blue minor initials throughout.

Paper, watermark of a *oiseau;* cf. Briquet 12146. ff. 68. 286 × 206 mm (209 × 155 mm). 1^{12} (12 wanting), 2^{10}, 3^{10} (7 wanting), 4^{10}, 5^{10} (7 wanting), 6^{10}, 7^{10} (an undetermined leaf wanting). Vertical catchwords. Leaves signed. Ruled in pen. ff. 2–47v, written in humanistic cursiva media tending to currens; ff. 50–67, in humanistic cursiva media, all by one hand beginning on the first ruled line in 46 lines in two columns with written lines centered on ruled lines.

Bound in parchment bearing traces of an unidentified Hebrew text, over pasteboard, s. xviii (?).

Written in Naples by Petrus de Afelatro de Neapoli in 1468, signed and dated on ff. 47v and 67v; the paper is Neapolitan. Petrus de Afelatro was professor of philosophy and medicine at the University of Naples; *Storia della Università di Napoli* (Naples, 1924), pp. 185, 325, 330, and 336. f. 50, sixteenth-century inscription placed before incipit, "Nil difficilius est quam amicitiam usque ad extremum uitę diem permanere." f. 68v, signature, "Ego frater Hyacynthus a Murano," a seventeenth-century Dominican friar, province of Calabria; *Monumenta ordinis praedicatorum historica* 13:236. Rear pastedown, "319" written within a circle in modern pencil. Acquired by the Newberry from Bernard Rosenthal, 1962.

Second folio: quam est.

H. F. Dondaine and H. V. Schooner, *Codices manuscripti operum Thomae de Aquino,* vol. 1 (1967), no. 1002E. McGinn, *Tradition of Aquinas and Bonaventure,* p. 6.

97.7

(79-44062)

Lorenzo Valla, *Antidotum Primum, Dialogus contra Pogium, Antidotum Secundum*

Southern Italy s. XV²

1. ff. 4–108v Laurentii uallensis uiri clarissimi aduersus Pogium terrinouanum defensio (in violet). Non eram nescius iam inde ab initio . . . estimanda dicere debuisti.

Lorenzo Valla, *Antidotum primum in Pogium,* ed. A. Wesseling (Assen, 1978).

2. ff. 109–143v [A]udio Pogium alteram in me composuisse inuectiuam . . . sed cur eum iam loqui paratum impedimus. Guarinus (*sic*).

Lorenzo Valla, *Dialogus contra Pogium,* printed in *Opera omnia* (Basel, 1540; reprinted Turin, 1962), 1:366–89.

3. ff. 144–162 [T]andem aliquando Podii (*sic*) altera in nos inuectiua in manus uenit . . . (ends in mid folio in mid sentence) sed qui legerit cui crimini et in qua causa.

f. 162v blank.

Lorenzo Valla, *Antidotum secundum in Pogium* (inc.), printed as Book IV of text 1 above (Basel, 1540), 1:325–37.

4. f. 163 (addition s. xvi) Notes on the powers of the prince to legislate.

ff. 163v–181v blank.

5. ff. 196v–182 (addition 1539; written from back to front and inverted) Aduersaria quottidianarum lectionum in iure ciuili Ioannis Francisci Russi troiani obiter contractarum in hunc codicem, Neapoli viii° iunii mdxxxix° sub uico Sangrio.

f. 197–197v blank. An insertion into this text by the same hand, also inverted, has been written on the rear pastedown.

Notes on the civil law beginning with references to the Pandects, Martial, Cicero, and Guillaume Budé. This text written in the book after it was bound.

Paper, quires 1–17 watermarked with a *château,* not in Briquet; quire 18 watermarked with a *huchet,* cf. Briquet 7608; quires 20–21 watermarked with a *oiseau,* cf. Briquet 12145. ff. iii + 194. Modern foliation begins on flyleaves. Trimmed to 213 × 144 mm (138 × 90 mm). 1^{10} (1 removed), $2–10^{10}$, 11^{8}, $12–16^{10}$, 17^{10} (3 stub only with a trace of sixteenth-century script), 18^{10}, 19^{4} (1 stub only), $20–21^{8}$ (8 serves as pastedown). Catchwords. Ruled in hard point. Written in humanistic cursiva media in 24 long lines beginning on the second ruled line. f. 4, heading in violet in script of text. Quotations underlined in red. Marginal finding notes by at least two fifteenth-century hands.

Bound in wooden boards, s. xv or xvi, back wanting, bands of spine exposed. Two fore-edge clasps wanting; brass catches in the shape of fleur-de-lys. Title written on front board, legible under ultraviolet lamp, "Laurentii Valla invectiva in Pogium." Short title also written across the fore edge.

Written in Italy in the second half of the fifteenth century; the paper and early ownership marks indicate Naples. Belonged to Callimacho de Monteverde (fl. 1475). f. 1, "Liber Callimachi Siculi" written by a fifteenth-century hand above his arms, drawn in pen. f. ii, "Ex munere Ioannis Philocali, Troiani ciuis et praeceptoris eruditissimi, Neapoli die xxii aprilis mdxxxviii," written in the hand of Giovanni Francesco Russo (see above, f. 196v) who added text 4 in June 1539. Another note by his hand struck out and now illegible. f. 1v, "carissimo mio," a pen trial of s. xv^2 or xvi^1. Another pen trial on the rear pastedown. In 1973, this manuscript in the possession of H. P. Kraus; see two letters at the Newberry of Giuseppe Billanovich to H. P. Kraus dated 23 October and 29 October 1973. Acquired by the Newberry in 1979 from William Salloch, catalogue 357, item no. 113.

Second folio: uir ut.

98

(Ry 4; 11339)

Cicero, *De Officiis*

Italy s. XV

ff. 1–70v Marci Tulii Ciceronis arpinatis consulisque romani ad filium offitiorum liber primus incipit; Prooemium (in violet). Quamquam te, Marce fili . . . si talibus monimentis praeceptisque letabere. Marci Tulii Ciceronis de officiis liber tertius et ultimus finit (in violet).

Marginal corrections by at least two humanistic hands.

Ed. C. F. W. Mueller, *Scripta quae manserunt omnia* (Leipzig, 1893–1936), pt. 4, vol. 3, pp. 2–130.

Parchment of southern preparation. Flyleaves prepared for use as palimpsests; flyleaves retain traces of erased unidentified inverted text of s. xii. ff. i + 70 + i. Trimmed to 234 × 153 mm (170 × 95 mm). 1–7^{10}. Vertical catchwords. Ruled in brown ink with double ruling on left to create a locus for minor rustic capitals at the beginning of paragraphs. Text written in humanistic textualis formata in 31 long lines beginning on the second ruled line. *Lemmata* incorporated into text, occasionally extending into outer margins, written in script of text in violet. f. 1, gold initial decorated with white ivy stem on a blue, green, and red ground. Same but discrete decoration forms inner and upper bracket marginal border framed in gold. ff. 30 and 48, gold dentelle initials with gold and black patterning on grounds of violet and green. Verso of rear flyleaf bears inscription, "Marcii Tulii Ciceronis arpinatis consulisque romani ad Marcum filium officiorum codices perbelle scriptos misit," written in very black ink by one of the hands which corrected the text.

Bound in parchment over pasteboard, s. xviii or xix.

Written in Italy, probably in northeastern Italy, in the fifteenth century. On modern front flyleaf, "Biblioteca Canal," crossed out, refers to the collection of P. Canal (1807–83) at Crespano. This manuscript recorded by P. Canal, *Bibliotheca scriptorum classicorum graecorum et latinorum nunc . . . exstans Crispani* (Bassano, 1884–85), I, 47. "77" written on front pastedown; "34. I^2" on rear pastedown. Acquired by the Newberry in 1931 from E. P. Goldschmidt, catalogue 23, item no. 4. Clipping from this catalogue affixed to front pastedown.

Second folio: bonitate unicatur neque.

De Ricci, 1:541.

98.1

(552791)

Giovanni de Bonsignori, *Libro Imperiale*

Italy [*Illustrated*] 1476

ff. 1–60v Incipit liber qui dicitur imperialis (in violet). [A]ltissimo, omnipotente et eterno padre cum lo adiutorio del tuo altissimo nome ad te recurro che presti gratia e força . . . ne l'anno m° ccc xiii di uenardi a di xiiii di agosto hora di nona. Explicit feliciter die ultima septembris 1476 (in violet).

Name of the author not given in chapter 3.

Giovanni de Bonsignori, *Libro imperiale*. Incunable editions (which omit the chronicle of Rome forming the final portion of the text) listed by Zambrini, *Le Opere volgari*, cols. 607–9; cf. *B. M. Cat. of 15th-Century Books*, 7:1133. Other manuscripts, G. Mazzatinti, *Inventari dei manoscritti delle biblioteche d'Italia*, 10 (1900): 197–99. For the attribution to Bonsignori, see G. Ballistreri, *DBI* 12:407–9.

Paper, watermark of the Agnus Dei; cf. Briquet 18 sqq. Front flyleaf parchment. ff. ii + 60 + i. Severe worm damage on ff. 57–60, small portion of text destroyed. 238 × 169 mm (166 × 111 mm). 1–6^{10}. Leaves signed a^1–f^5. Horizontal catchwords surrounded by 8 dots and dashes, 4 in ink of text and 4 in violet. Written in humanistic cursiva media in 32–36 long lines. Headings in violet in script of text. ff. 8–14, running headings in violet. Chapters 1–33 of text numbered in arabic numerals in violet; minor violet initials throughout.

Bound in original half calf and wooden boards. Part of original clasp remaining. Title on front board in large letters, "Cesario." Front pastedown and flyleaf formed from a fragment of a chant book, s. xii, containing a noted office for Palm Sunday; rear pastedown for the Sunday after Easter, cf. *SMRL,* II, 81 and 91. The form of musical notation is French.

Written in Italy in 1476, dated on f. 60v. Acquired by the Newberry from H. P. Kraus, 1955. Acquisition announced by H. Baron, *Newberry Library Bulletin* 4 (1958): 79.

Second folio: -gliuolo di Pompilio re di Egipto.

Faye-Bond, p. 154.

98.5
(59-1858)
Lucan, *Pharsalia*

Italy s. XV med.

1. f. 1

Corduba me genuit, rapuit Nero, prelia dixi . . .
Que tractim serpant, plus mihi coma placet.

Epitaphium Lucani. Riese, *Anthologia latina,* vol. 1, pt. 2, p. 139.

1 bis. ff. 1–71v

Proponit primus liber, inue[h]it inuocat atque . . .
Bella per Hemathios plus quam ciuilia campos . . .
(ends imperfectly at the end of a quire)
Hoc solum metuens incauto ab hoste timeri //

Intermittent gloss and interlinear and marginal notes, including index notes, by at least three Italian hands of the fifteenth century. Gloss to first *argumentum* begins: In istis uersibus comprehenditur totius primi libri sententia. Gloss to the text begins: In hac parte Lucanus incipit librum suum qui diuiditur in partes decem . . .

Lucan, *Pharsalia,* I–IV, line 719, ed. C. Hosius, *Belli civilies libri decem* (Leipzig, 1913), pp. 1–118. Each book preceded by *argumenta* in verse, Riese, *Anthologia latina,* vol. 1, pt. 2, pp. 278–80.

Paper. ff. 71. 290 × 220 mm (151 × 85 mm). 1^{8} (1 wanting), $2\text{–}3^{8}$, $4\text{–}7^{10}$, 11^{8}. Catchwords surrounded by four flourishes. Ruled in pencil. Written in gothic textualis media with one-story a, trailing terminal s, incorporating an increasing number of humanistic traits toward the end, in 21 long lines, no writing on the last ruled line. Pseudo-gothic decoration and pen drawing, c. 1900, throughout.

Bound in a leaf of an early printed missal over pasteboard, modern parchment spine.

Written in Italy in the middle of the fifteenth century. f. 1, upper margin, signed Ascanio Mignini (s. xvii?). Acquired by the Newberry from Bernard Rosenthal, 1959, catalogue no. 9, item no. 45 (illustrated with plate of f. 29).

Second folio: Regna deis.

99.1
(59-2402)
Ludovicus de Ferraria (Valencia), O.P.,
Compendium Ethicorum Aristotelis

Italy after 1483

ff. 1–75v Reuerendissimo in Christo patri et domino domino Oliuerio Carafe episcopo sabinensi, cardinali neapolitano, protectori ordinis predicatorum, frater Ludouicus de Ferraria sacre theologie professor et eiusdem ordinis procurator salutem dicit (in red). Ethicorum liber ab Aristotile editus, reuerendissime domine, mihi tradere uidetur quicquam ad humanam uitam bene instituendam possit pertinere . . . (f. 2v) sciam nec offitium nec diligentiam me pretermisisse. Uale. Primus; Incipit compendium ethicorum Aristotilis quo eius sententie referuntur et probantur . . . (in red). Bonum interpretamur esse quod omnia appetunt, nam non est aliud quam finis. Finis autem est terminus appetitus . . . quomodo unaquisque res publica sit instituta. Explicit liber ethicorum decimus deo summo laus (in red).

ff. 76–79, table of chapter headings.

f. 79v blank.

Ludovicus de Ferraria (Valencia), O.P., *Compendium ethicorum aristotelis.* J. Quetif and J. Échard, *Scriptores ordinis praedicatorum,* vol. 1 (Paris, 1719–23; reprinted New York, 1959), p. 882, recorded a "Commentaria in ethicam" of Ludovicus de Ferraria; cf. Lohr, "Medieval Commentaries," *Traditio* 27 (1971): 321. This text not known to Kaeppeli, 3:42–44. For other works dedicated to Oliviero Carafa, see *DBI* 14:595.

Paper. Water damage severe toward the end. ff. 76–79, folios reset on modern paper. ff. i + 79 + i. 260 × 200 mm (143 × 116 mm). 1^{10} (9 stub only), 2^{1} (a single leaf with catchwords on verso), 3–8[10], 9[10] (10 wanting). Horizontal catchwords surrounded by four fleur-de-lys-type flourishes; note catchword on ff. 9v and 10v. Ruled in pencil. Written in northern European *lettre bâtarde* in 25 long lines. Headings in red in script of text. Occasional marginal notes in Italian humanistic cursiva. f. 1, gold dentelle initial with white patterning on a ground of green, blue, and red 5 lines high. Discrete full border of blue, green, and red acanthus spray decorated with radiating gold disks. Gold dentelle initials with white patterning on grounds of green and blue 4 lines high at the beginning of each chapter, some decorated with a trace of acanthus spray bearing radiating gold disks. Alternating red and blue minor initials throughout.

Bound in stamped calf over pasteboard, s. xv, much deteriorated, with ruled rectangular panels, a single stamp of a floral ornament twice at each corner and eight times in the center, front and back.

Written in Italy by a scribe trained in northern Europe, after 31 January 1483, date on which Oliviero Carafa became bishop of Santa Sabina (Rome), see above, f. 1. f. 1, unidentified cardinal's arms placed beneath a bishop's miter, on either side, the initials "O" and "F" (see color illustration); these arms are not those of Oliviero Carafa, cf. Pächt and Alexander, *Illuminated Manuscripts* 2:37, n. 372. Front pastedown, signature of Henry Cestole, s. xviii. Acquired by the Newberry from Lucien Goldschmidt (New York), 1959.

Second folio: sagacem, recte.

101
(51-63)
Naldo de' Naldi,
Elegia ad Ludovicum Patriarcham

Italy s. XV[2]

ff. 1–5 Reverendissimo patri et domino domino Ludouico presbitero cardinali ac patriarche et cetera Naldus de Naldis.

Nunc mihi Phoebe nouo iam . . .
Audebo numeris mihi inseruisse nouis.
Telos.

ff. 5v–6v blank.

Text with many variants from *Elegiarum libri III ad Laurentium Medicen*, ed. L. Juhász (Leipzig, 1934), II, 4, pp. 31–34. This manuscript unknown to Juhász. The final eight lines, which he did not print, have been edited from this codex by W. L. Grant, *Naldo de Naldi, Bucolica volterrais hastiludium carmina varia* (Florence, 1974), p. 139.

Parchment. ff. i + 6. 160 × 115 mm (103 × 70 mm). Ruled in hard point. Written in humanistic cursiva media in 17 long lines beginning on the first ruled line. Initial letter of each verse in rustic capitals. f. 1, gold initial decorated with white vine stem on ground of blue, pink, and green decorated with radiating gold disks.

Bound in limp parchment. Trace of mirror image of writing, probably from the pastedown of an earlier binding, visible on the flyleaf.

Written in Italy in the second half of the fifteenth century. Acquired by the Newberry from Davis and Orioli (London), 1950.

Second folio: arbos leta nouas.

Faye-Bond, p. 148.

102
(52-15)
Leon Battista Alberti, *De Commodis Litterarum atque Incommodis, Descriptio Urbis Romae*

Italy s. XV med.

1. ff. 1–24v Leonis Baptistȩ Alberti de commodis litterarum atque incommodis incipit. Ad Carolum fratrem (in violet). Laurentius Albertus parens noster, uir cum multis in rebus . . . et dubitet nemo uel solam a nobis esse quesitam sapientiam.

Leon Battista Alberti, *De commodis litterarum atque incommodis,* ed. L. G. Carotti (Florence, 1976). This manuscript is one of the two used for the edition.

2. ff. 25–28v Leonis Baptistae Alberti (in violet). Murorum urbis Romȩ et fluminis et uiarum ductus . . . (f. 26) id feci breuitatis causa.

Key to Alberti's map of the city follows on ff. 26v–28v.

Leon Battista Alberti, *Descriptio urbis romae,* ed. R. Valentini and G. Zucchetti, *Codice topografico della città di Roma* (Rome, 1940–46), 4:209–22.

Paper, watermark of cardinal's hat; cf. Briquet 3387 sqq. ff. 28. Trimmed to 273 × 191 mm (191 × 125 mm). 1[10], 2[12], 3[6]. Catchwords present. Written in humanistic cursiva media in 32 long lines beginning on the second ruled line. Occasional marginal notes in humanistic cursiva currens. ff. 1, 1v, 25, and 25v, simple blue, red, and violet initials 2 lines high. f. 25, diagrams similar to those of the printed text in violet and ink of text.

Bound in modern limp parchment.

Written in Italy in the middle of the fifteenth century. Acquired by the Newberry from H. P. Kraus, 1951.

Second folio: cupiditate ununquenque auertere.

Faye-Bond, p. 154.

102.1
(55-2812)
Sicco Polenton, *Vitae Sanctae*

Northern Italy s. XV[1]

1. ff. 1–18v (begins imperfectly) // oculte [–h]ac deuia per loca redeunti fit obuia (*sic*, over an erasure) femina filium puerum pedibus manibusque contractum . . . (f. 5) oblata dispensent. Hec de uita sancti, nunc eius miracula uideamus . . . Caeci illuminati capitulum primum. Puerima infans sex menses supra annum nata carebat lummine occulorum . . . ut uidemus perdere potius certando cum eo quam luctary possemus.

Vita et miracula Sancti Antonii de Padua, beginning on p. 12 of the edition of the *Vita* by P. Saviolo, *Arca del Santo di Padova* . . . (Padua, 1653). *BHL* 598. Explicit of the *miracula* falls on f. 41v of Hain, 13212. *BHL* 599. This manuscript not recorded by Ullman, *Sicconis Polentoni,* p. xlvi.

2. ff. 18v–33v Siconis Polentoni prefatio ad Lazarum filium in beatorum Antonii peregrini ac [–H]elene monialis uitas incipit feliciter. Solicitare me soles precibus, Lazare fili . . . ut decet, ad dei laudem coles. 1437. Et sic est finis.

Vitae beatorum Antonii peregrinii ac Helene monialis. BHL 3791–92. Edited as two separate texts: "Vita helenae," *Acta sanctorum,* Nov., vol. 2, pt. 1 (1894), pp. 512–17; "Vita beati Antonii peregrini," *Analecta bollandiana* 13 (1894): 417–25. This manuscript not recorded by Ullman, *Sicconis Polentoni,* p. xlvi.

f. 34–34v blank.

Paper, soft and furry. ff. 34. An undetermined number of folios missing before f. 1. Trimmed to 210 × 145 mm (155 × 118 mm). $1–3^{10}$, 4^{10} (5–10 wanting). Horizontal catchwords in center of lower margins. Frame ruled in pencil. Written in Italian hybrida media in 32–36 long lines, the first written line hung from the first ruled line. Script similar but not identical to the autograph of the author; cf. Ullman, *Sicconis Polentoni,* p. xxi and plate II, b and c. A. Segarizzi, *La Catinia, le orazioni e le epistole di Sicco Polenton* (Bergamo, 1899), plate facing p. xxiv; Guido Billanovich, "Antichità padovane in nuove testimonianze autografe di Sicco Polenton," in *Medioevo e rinascimento veneto con altri studi in onore di Lino Lazzarini* (Medioevo e Umanesimo, 34–35; Padua, 1979), 1:293. Capitals occasionally reflect humanistic influence. Red initials with violet flourishes alternating with blue initials with red flourishes. f. 1, crude red bracket marginal decoration added to give a defective manuscript the appearance of completeness and thus conceal the loss of leaves before f. 1.

Bound in nineteenth-century half calf over pasteboard, spine title "De Anto. et Helena, MS MCCCCXXXVII." Old spine label: "[3]389" (Phillipps number).

Written in northern Italy. Date of 1437 on f. 33v may be date of composition or the date of this transcription. ff. 33v–34, notes on an early Italian owner in humanistic cursiva. Front flyleaf, signature "Henry Drury, 1822"; see De Ricci, *English Collectors,* pp. 98 and 122. Flyleaf, "Phillipps MS 3389" written in black ink. Munby, *Phillipps Studies* 3:53–54 and 151. Acquired by the Newberry from H. P. Kraus, 1955. Acquisition announced by H. Baron, *Newberry Library Bulletin* 4 (1958): 79–80.

Second folio: sanctus duas.

Faye-Bond, p. 154.

102.2
(61-692; Ry 226)
Jerome, *Epistolae*

Ancona [*Illustrated*] 1459

i. ff. 1–2 Tabula epistolarum presenti in libro contentarum editarum ordinatarumque per sanctissimum et eloquentissimum doctorem sacroque sancte romane eclesie cardinalem beatum Ieronimum confexorem clarisimum (in red). . . .

f. 2v blank.

The table divides texts into ten books under headings generally abbreviated from the text. The headings from the text are as follows: Book I, "Ad diuersos de uirginitate et castitate" (f. 3), texts 1–16. Book II, "Ad diuersos de uita et sciencia clericorum et monachorum et de contentu (*sic*) mundi et de perfectione uite uirtuose" (f. 62), texts 17–26. Book III, "Ad diuersos de commendatione et consolatione super infirmitate et morte sanctarum personarum que grece uocantur epitaphia" (f. 95v), texts 27–37. Book IV, "Ad diuersos de explanatione plurium questionum sacre scripture" (f. 123), texts 38–56. Book V, "Ad Damasum papam . . . de eadem explanatione sacre scripture et questionum dubiarum propositarum et de fide catholica contra hereticos" (f. 168), texts 57–71. Book VI, "Contra Ruffinum presbiterum Aquileie et calumpniarum suarum eiusdem libri . . . et ad quosdam alios contra eum et Uigilantium et alios sectatores Origenis et hereticos et dictorum peruersis opinionibus . . ." (f. 198), texts 72–99. Book VII, "Ad Augustinum et e conuerso de quibusdam questionibus sacre scripture et opinionibus uariis eorundem et aliis controuersiis questionum" (f. 241), texts 100–124. Book VIII, "Ad Marcellam de suis detractoribus . . ." (f. 274v), texts 125–145. Book IX, "Ad diuersos de sacris doctoribus et eorum doctrina et de libris suis . . ." (f. 293), texts 146–163. Book X, "Ad diuersos de dilectione et amicitia et mundi contemptu et pacientia in aduersis" (f. 316), texts 164–189.

ii. f. 3 Hyeronimus Eusepii filius Stridoni opido natus . . . obiit anno domini m°c°xxii (*sic*) ultima septembris hora completorii (entirely in violet).

Written entirely in rustic capitals, words separated by points.

Brief life of Jerome, ed. Warner, *Descriptive Catalogue,* p. 165 and plate lxvii; cf. *BHM* 902.

iii. f. 3

Sepulchri Epythaphium
Hic dux doctorum iacet et flos
  presbiterorum . . .
Dic ueniens aue desuper ire caue (entirely in
  violet)

Epitaphium Sancti Hieronimi, ed. *BHM* 928. To Lambert's list of manuscripts add Vat. Reg. 1793, f. 49v (s. xv) and Vat. Chigi A. VI, 188 (1481).

1. ff. 3–9 De Marie uirginitate perpetua confutatoria contra Enlupidium (*sic*) hereticum contrarium asserentem epistola prima beati Ieronimi (in red). Si perrogatus ut aduersus libellum . . . et caninam facundiam seruus domini pariter experiatur cum matre.

Jerome, *Adversus Heluidium de Mariae virginitate perpetua. PL* 13:183–206 (190–216). *BHM* 251.

2. ff. 9–16v De assumptione uirginis ad Paulam et Eustochium (in red). Hic theotkos (*sic*) sacre ueneratur sermo Marie . . . Cogitis me, o Paula et Eustochium, ymmo caritas Christi me compellit . . . cum Christo et uos appareatis in gloria. Amen.

f. 9 in margin, xviii Kalendas augusti.

Paschasius Radbertus, *Ad Paulam et Eustochium de Assumptione Mariae virginis,* standard text preceded by six lines of verse, A. Ripberger, *Der Ps.-Hieronymus-Brief IX "Cogitis me": ein erster Marianischer Traktat des Mittelalters von Paschasius Radbert* (Spicilegium Friburgense, 9; Fribourg, Switz., 1962), pp. 57–113. *CPL* 633. *BHM* 309. See MS 3, text 23.

3. ff. 16v–26 Epistola Ieronimi ad Eustochium uirginem filiam sancte Paule exortatoria de uirginitate (in red). Audi, filia, et uide et inclina aurem tuam . . . concupiscet rex decorem tuum quia ipse est dominus tuus. In psalmo xliiii . . . et flumina non cooperient eam.

BHM 22.

4. ff. 26–29 Epistola Ieronimi ad Alletam nurum eiusdem sancte Paule exortatoria et instig[ato]ria Pauline filie eius uirginis deo ab infancia dedicate (in red). Apostolus Paulus scribens ad corintheos . . . erudiam regnis celestibus offerendam.

BHM 107.

5. ff. 29–34 Epistola Ieronimi ad Demetriadem uirginem exhortatoria de seruanda uirginitate (in red). Inter omnes materias . . . quarum imitacio forma uirtutis est.

BHM 130.

6. ff. 34v–36 Epistola Ieronimi exortatoria de uirginitate et uite perfectione (in red). Ignoti ad ignotam scribimus . . . et denitent (*sic*) conscientias plurimarum hoc uidemus et patimur.

BHM 130 (extracts, 2, 1, through 19, 8); cf. *CSEL* 56 (1918): 176–201.

7. ff. 36–39 Epistola Ieronimi ad Furiam uiduam exortatoria de uiduitate et castitate seruanda (in red). Obsecras litteris et suppliciter deprecaris ut tibi rescribam, ymmo scribam . . . de secundis nuptiis cogitabis.

BHM 54.

8. ff. 39–43 (Heading omitted.) In uetere uia nouam semitam querimus . . . is (*sic*) libellus de monogamia sub nomine tuo titulum possidebit.

BHM 123.

9. ff. 43–46 Epistola Ieronimi ad Saluinam uiduam consolatoria de morte uiri et exortatoria de uiduitate seruanda (in red). Uereor ne officium putetur . . . et occultum iudicium legentium pertimesco.

BHM 79.

10. ff. 46–48v Epistola Ieronimi ad matrem et ad filiam in Galia exortatoria de castitate seruanda et obiurgatoria de suspicione non bene seruate castitate (*sic;* in red). Retulit mihi quidam frater e Gallia se nostrem (*sic*) habere sororem uirginem et matrem uiduam . . . ignoscat uel tempori.

BHM 117.

11. ff. 48v–51v Epistola Ieronimi ad Rusticum coniugatum exhortatoria de castitate promissa seruanda et reprehensiua de non bene

seruata et prouocatiua ad penitenciam (in red). Quod ignotus ad ignotum audeo scribere . . . mandata tua non sum oblitus.

BHM 122.

12. ff. 51v–52v Epistola Hieronimi ad Letham institutiuam filie sue et inductiua ad uirginitatem seruandam (in violet). Omnis gloria eius filie regis ab intus. Loquatur . . . que per auie amiteque uirtutes nobilior est sanctitate quam genere.

BHM 107 (7, 2, through 13, 10). *CSEL* 55 (1912): 298–304.

13. ff. 52v–53 Epistola Hieronimi ad Eustochium uirginem de transmissis muneribus exhortatiua ad abstinentiam et castitatem (in violet). Parua specie sed caritate magna sunt munera . . . Christi ancilla non essem.

BHM 31.

14. ff. 53–56 Epistola Hieronimi ad Susannam ob[i]urgatiua de lassu (*sic*) eius uirginitatis et exhortatiua ad penitentiam et castitatem seruandam (in violet). Puto leuius esse crimen . . . Quid agis, Susanna, ab ipso solo te conuenit in die iudicii expectare remedium.

Dubious Niceta of Remesiana, *De lapsu virginis,* 1–30, ed. Gamber, pp. 25–34. For the incipit, see E. Cazzaniga, *De lapsu Susannae incerti auctoris* (Turin, 1948), p. 2n. *CPL* 633 and 651. *BHM* 320.

15. f. 56 Epistola Hieronimi declaratiua de consanguinitatis (*sic*) beate uirginis Marie (in violet). Anna et Exmeria fuerunt sorores . . . tres ergo uiros Anna habuit, scilicet Ioachim, Cleophas et Salome.

Ps. Jerome, *De consanguinitate beatae Mariae. BHM* 672.

16. ff. 56v–62 Epistola Hieronimi ad filiam Mauricii uirginitatis commendatiua et ad eam exhortatiua (in violet). Quantam in celestibus beatitudinem uirginitas possideat . . . et ipse sit dignus.

Pelagius, *Ad filiam Mauritii laus virginitatis. CSEL* 1 (1866): 225–50. *CPL* 741. *BHM* 313.

17. ff. 62–66v Epistola Hieronimi ad Rusticum monachum exhortatoria de uita mona[s]ticha (*sic;* in violet). Nichil est cristiano felicius cui promittuntur regna celorum. Nihil laboriosius . . . sed magna sunt premia.

BHM 125.

18. ff. 66v–69v Epistola Hieronimi ad Paulinum de studio litterarum et de mundi contentu (*sic;* in violet). Frater Ambroxius tua mihi munuscula preferens detulit et suauissimas litteras . . . qui se semper cogitat moriturum.

BHM 53.

19. ff. 69v–72 Epistola Hieronimi ad eundem Paulinum exhortatoria de litterarum studio et perfectione uite monastice (in violet). Bonus homo de bono thesauro cordis . . . per te salutari uolo.

BHM 58.

20. ff. 72–73v Epistola Hieronimi ad Occeanum institutoria de uita clericorum (in red). Eusebius Hieronimus Occeano suo salutem. Deprecatus es . . . ut bonorum operum testificatio casto confirmetur effectu.

Ps. Jerome, Epistle 42. *BHM* 342.

21. ff. 73v–77v Epistola Hieronimi ad O[c]ceanum declaratiua de episcopo unius uxoris uiro eligendo quia post baptismum hoc sit tantummodo intellegendum (in red). Numquam, filii Occeane, fore putabam . . . quod concessum est.

BHM 69.

22. ff. 77v–81 Epistola Hieronimi ad Sabinianum diaconum lapsum exhortatiua de promissa castitatis seruanda et inductiua ad penitentiam de non bene seruata (in red). Et Samuel quondam lugebat Saulem . . . cuius consumatio in combustionem.

BHM 147.

23. ff. 81–85v Epistola Hieronimi ad Nepotianum presbiterum Aquileye exhortatoria de uita clericorum (in red). Petieras a me, Nepotiane carissime, de litteris transmarinis . . . quod talis sit confitetur.

BHM 52.

24. ff. 85v–88 Epistola Hieronimi ad Heliodorum monachum exhortatoria de clericorum et monachorum uita (in red). Quanto studio et amore contenderim ut pariter in heremo moraremur . . . labor durus est.

BHM 14.

25. ff. 89–90v Epistola Hieronimi ad Presidium diaconum exhortatiua ad uitam solitariam et ad contemptum mundi incitatiua (in red). Nulla res inquit comicus tam facilis est . . . tamquam formica sub ea conditione quam nosci. O quotienscumque hanc epistolam legeris tociens te scias quo pollicitus es esse ueniendum.

BHM 155, with the explicit as recorded *PSL* 2:19; cf. G. Morin, *Bulletin d'ancienne littérature et d'archéologie chrétiennes* 3 (1913): 51–60. *CPL* 621.

26. ff. 90v–95v Epistola Hieronimi pulcerrima uite et morum institutiua (in red). Decus (*sic*) scripture celebrata sententia ideo esse pudorem quo gloria . . . quia non inchoasse sufficit sed perfecisse iustitia est.

BHM 148.

27. ff. 95v–100 Epistola Hieronimi ad Heliodorum patriarcham Aquileie epythaphium seu epistola consolatoria super morte prefati Nepotiani nepotis eius et comendatiua uite eius (in red). Grandes materias ingenia parua non sufferunt et in ipso conatu ultra uires ausa succumbunt . . . de eo loqui numquam desinamus.

BHM 60.

28. f. 100–100v Epistola Hieronimi ad quemdam amicum suum egrotum consolatoria super eius infirmitate (in red). Sanctus filius meus Eradius (*sic*) diaconus mihi retulit quod cupiditate nostri Cissam usque uenisses . . . libenter suscipiam dispensationis mora magnitudinem fenoris duplicatam.

BHM 68.

29. ff. 100v–101v Epistola Hieronimi ad Tirasium consolatoria seu epithaphium super morte filie sue (in red). Benedicto et dilectissimo parenti Tyasio (*sic*) Hieronimus. Caritatis tue scripta percepi . . . (1 Thess 4:12) adducet cum eo.

Caelestius, *Ad Turasium super morte filiae suae consolatoria* (section 10 omitted). *PL* 4:434–39, 30:278–82. *CPL* 64, 633, and 769. *BHM* 340.

30. ff. 101v–103v Epistola Hieronimi ad Iulianum consolatoria super morte Artemie uxoris et filiarum et prouocatiua ad contemptum mundi (in red). Filius meus frater tuus Ausonius in ipso iam articulo profectionis . . . et tibi sit tanti dux femina facti.

BHM 118.

31. ff. 103v–105 Epistola Hieronimi ad Innocentium commendatoria de quadam muliere septies iniuste a carnifice percussa et morti exposita et a domino sanata (in red). Sepe a me, Innocenti karissime . . . ut redditam uite redderet libertati.

BHM 1.

32. ff. 105–107 Epistola Hieronimi ad Oc[c]eanum seu epithaphium consolatorium et conmendatorium de morte et uita Fabiole uidue (in red). Plures anni sunt quibus super dormitione Blexille uenerabilem Paulam feminam recenti . . . Cui plus dimittitur, plus amat.

BHM 77.

33. ff. 107–109v Epistola Hieronimi ad Pamachium epithaphium consolatoria de morte Pauline eius uxoris et filie sancte Paule (in red). Sanato uulneri et in cicatricem superducte cuti si medicina colorem reddere noluerit (*sic*) . . . tu duarum medius ad Christum leuius subuolabis.

BHM 66.

34. ff. 109v–111v Epistola Hieronimi ad Paulam predictam consolatoria super morte Blexille alterius sue filie (in red). Quis dabit capiti meo aquam (Ier 9:1) . . . audiet me semper loquentem cum sorore, cum matre.

BHM 39.

35. ff. 111v–119v Epistola Hieronimi ad Eustochium uirginem consolatoria de morte sancte Paule predicte et commendatoria uite ipsius (in red). Si cuncta mei corporis membra uerterentur in linguam . . . diebus xx^{ti} et uno.

BHM 108.

36. ff. 119v–121v Epistola Hieronimi ad Principiam uirginam (*sic*) consolatoria et commendatoria sancte Marcelle uidue (in red). Sepe et multum flagitas . . . et deo et legentibus placere desiderans.

BHM 127.

37. ff. 122–123 Epistola Hieronimi ad Euagrium presbiterum de quodam lęuita qui lapsum fecerat et a nemine est consolatus inuectiua de omissa consolatione et consolatoria (in red). Nisi uererer, beatissime frater . . . ita expulsione eius abluimur.

Bachiarus Monachus, *Epistola ad Ianuaricum* or *De lapsu*. *CPL* 569 and 1143a. *BHM* 358.

38. f. 123 Epistola Hieronimi ad eandem Principiam expositorius (*sic*) psalmi 44^{i}, scilicet Eructauit, et inductiuus (*sic*) ad uirginitatis obseruantiam (in red). Otio me, Principia, in Cristo filia, a plerisque reprehendi quod interdum scribam mulieres et ad fragiliorem sexum . . . excoquant et salutari igne eiciant proditorem.

BHM 65 (1–12, excerpts); cf. *CSEL* 54 (1910): 616–30.

39. ff. 123–124v Epistola Hieronimi ad Eugenium expositoria de Melchisedech (in red). Misisti mihi uolumen grecum (*sic,* followed by a blank space) et nescio utrum tu de titulo nomen subtraxeris an ille qui scripsit . . . nocuerit corporis ualitudini.

BHM 73.

40. ff. 124v–127 Epistola Hieronimi ad Dardanum expositoria de terra promissionis (in red). Queris, Dardane christianorum nobilissime nobilium christianissime . . . quorum alterum pudoris, alterum caritatis est.

BHM 129.

41. ff. 127–131v Epistola Hieronimi ad Fabiolam uiduam supradictam explanatoria de uestibus sacerdotalibus et tabernaculi (*sic*) et aliis legis cerimoniis (in red). Usque hodie in lectionem ueteris testamenti super faciem Moysi uelamen positum est . . . sed meis sum uiribus extimandus.

BHM 64.

42. ff. 131v–133 Epistola Hieronimi [blank] de tribus uirtutibus scilicet fortitudine, sapiencia et prudentia secundum Hieremiam prophetam planatorius (*sic;* in red). Tres quodammodo uirtutes dei assumens propheta . . . Cui est gloria et uirtus et imperium in secula seculorum.

Origen, *De tribus virtutibus*. *PL* 15:625–32. *CPL* 633. *BHM* 308.

43. f. 133–133v Epistola Hieronimi ad Ebiduam uiduam exhortatoria de uiduitate et explanatoria (in red). Ignota uultu, fidei mihi ardore notissima es . . . Aperi os tuum et ego adimplebo illud.

BHM 120 (preface only). *CSEL* 55 (1912): 472–73.

44. ff. 133v–143v Epistola Hieronimi ad Algasiam xii questionum noue legis ex euangeliis et apostoli epistolis, octaua epistola seu tractatus explanatorius (in red). Filius meus Apodemius qui interpretrationem (*sic*) nominis sui longa ad nos nauigatione signauit . . . id est antichristum, suscepturi sunt.

BHM 121.

45. ff. 143v–147v Epistola Hieronimi ad Alexandrum et Mineruum monachos duarum questionum de resurrectione mortuorum secundum apostolum ad chorintheos et thesalonicos (in red). In ipso iam perfectionis articulo sancti fratris nostri Sisimii (*sic*) qui uestra mihi scripta detulerat . . . quorum qui sensus sit supra diximus.

BHM 119.

46. ff. 147v–148 Epistola Hieronimi ad Dardanum presbiterum declaratiua uerbi Pauli, Omne peccatum quod fecerit homo extra corpum (*sic*) qui autem fornicatur in corpus suum peccat (in red). Quesiuisti de beati apostoli Pauli prima ad chorinthios epistola in qua loquitur: Omne peccatum . . . cum autem rerum omnium finis aduenerit et singuli sanctorum omnes uirtutes habeant ut sit Christus totus in cunctis.

Extracts from *BHM* 55 (beginning in 2, 1). Cf. *CSEL* 54 (1910): 487–91. See below, texts 48 and 154.

47. f. 148 Epistola Hieronimi ad Tranquillum demonstratiua quomodo Origenem legere debeat (in red). Maiora spiritus uincula esse quam corporum si olim ambiebas (*sic*) nunc probabimus . . . Sanctus frater Tacianus diaconus impendio te resalutat.

BHM 62. See below, text 146.

48. f. 148 Epistola Hieronimi ad Auriundum presbiterum declaratiua questionis an mulier relicto uiro adultero et sogdomita et alio per uim accepto possit absque penitentia communicare ecclesie (in red). Reperi (*sic*) iunctam epistole et conmentariolo tuo breuem cartulam . . . cui alterum uirum accipere non licet.

BHM 55 (4, 1). *CSEL* 54 (1910): 492–93. See texts 46 and 154.

49. ff. 148–150v Epistola Hieronimi de duobus filiis frugi et luxurioso declaratiua eius parabole (in red). Omnium quidem de scripturis questionum absolutio illi soli . . . coheredes esse domini nostri Iesu Christi quia ipsa est gloria et uirtus cum patre et filio et spiritu sancto . . . Amen.

Dubious Gregorius Illiberitanus, *De duobus filiis, frugi et luxurioso,* ed. A. C. Vega, *España sagrada* 56 (1957): 109–16. *CPL* 766. *BHM* 335.

50. ff. 150v–158v Epistola Hieronimi ad Ceratiam (*sic*) de uera circumcisione declaratiua circumcisionis multum eleganter (in red). Superiori (*sic*) epistola . . . eris in paradiso.

Eutropius Presbyter, *Epistola de vera circumcisione*. *CPL* 566. *BHM* 319. Cf. H. Savon, "Le *De vera circum-*

cisione du prêtre Eutrope et les premières editions imprimées des Lettres de saint Jérôme," *Revue d'Histoire des Textes* 10 (1980): 165–197. This manuscript not recorded.

51. ff. 158v–159 Epistola Hieronimi de quadragesima exhortatiua ad ieiunium et abstinentiam (in red). Quomodo miles semper exercetur ad prelium . . . et carnis ac sanguinis agni Christi Iesu.

Ps. Jerome, *Sermo de quadragesima*. *CPL* 600 and 638. *BHM* 228.

52. ff. 159–161v Epistola Hieronimi de membris dei alias assentia (*sic*) dei (in red). Omnipotens deus pater et filius et spiritus unus atque trinus . . . manifeste demonstrare.

De essentia divinitatis (a cento formed from Eucherius Lugdunensis, *Formulae spiritalis intelligentiae*). *PL* 42:1199–1206. *CPL* 488. *BHM* 314.

53. ff. 161v–162 Epistola Hieronimi ad Dardanum de aliquibus generibus musice et significatiua eorum secundum spiritualia (in red). Cogar a te, ut tibi, Dardane . . . et est minima sapiencia legis ueteris in manu iudeorum.

Dubious Rabanus Maurus, *Ad Dardanum de diuersis generibus musicorum,* ending incompletely in chapter 9. *PL* 30:213–15B. *CPL* 633. *BHM* 323.

54. ff. 162–163 Epistola Hieronimi de generibus leprarum declaratiua secundum sensum suum (in red). Admirabile diuine dispositionis examen . . . in uasis fictilibus. In stamine autem paratum se in hominibus deo prebeat ut mercedem ab ipso consequi mereatur et in die iuditii securus inueniatur, si nulla dei offensa in eo reperiatur.

Dubious Gregorius Illiberitanus, *De diuersis generibus leprarum* (1–7 only). A. C. Vega, *España sagrada* 56 (1957): 103–7. *PL* 30:245–47C. *CPL* 633. *BHM* 334.

55. ff. 163–164 Epistola Hieronimi declaratiua decem temptationum quas filii Israel in deserto contra dominum habuerunt (in red). Hec sunt uerba que locutus est Moyses ad omnem Israel . . . me misit Moyses ad terram considerandam.

Ps. Jerome, *De decem temptationibus populi Israel in deserto*. *PL* 23:1319–22. *BHM* 409.

56. ff. 164–168 Epistola Hieronimi declaratiua quarumdam questionum et reprehensiua (in red). Presumptionem meam excusare conaret (*sic*) . . . ex quo conmortui uiuimus ex uirtutibus consureximus in Christo.

Pelagius, *Ad Thesiphontem de divina lege*. *CPL* 633 and 740. *BHM* 307.

57. f. 168–168v Epistola beati Damasi pape ad Ieronimum consultoria v questionum legis ueteris (in red). Dormientem te et longo iam tempore legentem potius quam scribentem . . . deceptus errore benedixit.

BHM 35.

58. ff. 168v–169v Epistola Hieronimi ad Damasum papam de tribus questionibus legis ueteris expositorius (*sic;* in red). Beatissimo pape Damasio (*sic*) Hyeronimus. Postquam epistolam tue sanctitatis accepi, confestim accito notario, ut exciperet, imperaui . . . sciens Origenem duodecimum et tertium decimum in genesi librum de hanc (*sic*) tanta questione dictasse.

BHM 36 (1–9). *CSEL* 54 (1910): 268–75.

59. ff. 169v–178 Epistola Hieronimi ad Damasum papam super canticis duarum omeliarum Origenis tractatuum trium exclamatorius (*sic;* in red). Beatissimo pape Damasio (*sic*) Hieronimus. Origenes cum in cęteris omnes uicerit libris . . . ut digni efficiamur sponsi sermone et sapientia Yhesu Christi cui honor est et gloria in secula seculorum.

f. 175v, text on the palimpsest legible, see below, p. 208.

Origen, *In canticum canticorum homiliae II,* trans. Jerome, ed. W. A. Baehrens, *Origenes' Werke,* vol. 8 (Leipzig, 1925), pp. 26–60. *PL* 23:1173–96. *BHM* 206.

60. ff. 178–182v Epistola Hieronimi ad Damasum papam uisionis Ysaye prophete et calculi seraphim (in red). Et factum est in anno quo mortuus est rex Ozias, uidi . . . Antequam de uisione dicamus pertractandum uidetur quid sit Ozias . . . tantum studeamus et lingua.

BHM 18a.

61. ff. 182v–184 Epistola Hieronimi ad Damasum uisionis eiusdem Ysaie, tractatus quintus explanatorius (in red). Septuaginta, Et missum est ad me unum de seraphin . . . cum Siluanum in actibus apostolorum non legamus.

BHM 18b.

62. f. 184 Epistola Damasi ad Ieronimum consultoria de Osanna (in red). Dilectissimo filio Hieronimo Damasus episcopus in domino salutem. Commentaria cum legerem greco latinoque sermone in euangeliorum interpreta-

tione . . . sicut et de multis tibi curę nostrę in Christo Yesu gratias referant.

BHM 19.

63. ff. 184–185v Epistola Hieronimi ad Damasum explanatoria de Osanna secundum euangelistas (in red). Multi super hoc sermone diuersa finxerunt, e quibus noster Hylarius in commentariis . . . accomodare sermoni quam de aliena lingua alibi falsam referre sententiam.

BHM 20.

64. ff. 185v–192 Epistola Hieronimi ad Damasum papam parabole secundum Lucam de filio prodigo et luxurioso (in red). Beatitudinis tuę interrogatio disputatio fuit et sic quesisse querendo uiam est dedisse quesitis . . . non queruntur uerba sed sensus id est panibus sit uita sustentanda non siliquis.

BHM 21.

65. ff. 192–193v Epistola Hieronimi ad Damasum papam de simbolo fidei catholice contra hereticos (in red). Credimus in deum patrem omnipotentem cunctorum uisibilium et inuisibilium conditorem . . . uel etiam non catholicum nomine hereticum comprobabit.

Text on the palimpsest legible, see below, pp. 208–9.

Pelagius, *Libellus fidei ad Innocentium papam. PL* 45:1716–18. *CPL* 731. *BHM* 316.

66. ff. 193v–196 Epistola Hieronimi de simbolo fidei Nicei concilii quod creditur ab eodem fuisse translatum de greco in latinum (in red). Credimus in unum deum, patrem omnipotentem . . . qui (*sic*) fides inuisibilium rerum est non uisibilium . . . et regnum celorum hereditatione ambigua sunt sortiti.

Anonymous, *Explanatio fidei ad Cyrillum,* ed. C. Turner, *Ecclesiae occidentalis monumenta iuris antiquissima,* I, ii, 1 (Oxford, 1913), pp. 358–68. *CPL* 1746. *BHM* 317.

67. ff. 196–197 Epistola Hieronimi ad Damasum declaratoria de fide et omonsion (*sic*) contra arianos et cui debent communicare in fide (in red). Quoniam uetusto oriens inter se populorum furore collisus . . . cum antiquo sensu predicent.

BHM 15.

68. f. 197–197v Epistola Hieronimi ad Damasum declaratoria fidei eiusdem contra arianos (in red). Importuna in euangelio mulier tandem meruit audire et clauso cum ser[u]is hostio . . . pro qua Christus mortuus est.

BHM 16.

69. f. 197v Epistola Hieronimi ad Damasum declaratiua de panibus uel aliis oblationibus per quos sint utenda (*sic;* in red). Nouerit sancta auctoritas tua, papa uenerandę (*sic*), quia de questione . . . cum ipsi non debeant pro populo orare.

Ps. Jerome, *Epistle 43,* last sentence of the printed text omitted. *BHM* 343.

70. ff. 197v–198 Epistola Hieronimi ad Damasum deprecatiua ut in fine cuiuslibet psalmi iungi faciat gloria patri et cetera et de quibusdam aliis (in red). Beatissimo pape Damasio (*sic*) sedis et apostolice urbis Rome Hieronymus suplex. Legi litteras apostolatus uestri et secundum simplicitatem septuaginta interpretem (*sic*) . . . uox ista laudis canatur in aleph quid (*sic*) est alleluia hebrayce prologus, latine autem prefatio dicitur.

Ps. Jerome, *Epistle 47,* ed. Bruyne, *Préfaces de la Bible latine,* pp. 65–66. *BHM* 347.

71. f. 198 Epistola Damasi ad Ieronimum petetiua (*sic*) ut psalterium traducat secundum sententiam lxx interpretum (in red). Damasus episcopus fratri et conpresbitero Hieronimo in domino salutem. Dum multa corpora librorum in meo arbitrio oblata fuissent . . . aperiri uestigium. Missa quinto kalendas nouembris per Bonifatium presbiterum ierosolomitarum (*sic*).

Ps. Jerome, *Epistle 46,* ed. Bruyne, *Préfaces de la Bible latine,* p. 65. *BHM* 346.

72. ff. 198–205v Epistola Hieronimi ad Pamachium contra Ruffinum prefatum de libris contrario (?) Iuuinianum (*sic*) hereticum ab eodem calumpniatis excusatiuus (*sic;* in red). Quod ad te huc usque non scripsi, causa fuit silentii tui (*sic*) . . . in nostro arbitrio est uel Lacarum (*sic,* no cedilla) sequi uel diuitem.

BHM 49.

73. ff. 205v–206v Epistola Hieronimi ad Pamachium de eiusdem libris contra Ruffinum predictum calumpniatorem declaratiua et excusatiua dictorum librorum (in red). Christiani interdum pudoris est . . . sed uniuerso loquatur hominum generi.

BHM 48.

74. ff. 206v–208 Epistola Hieronimi ad Dominionem de eorundem librorum calumpniacione contra Ruffinum predictum defensiua et excusatiua (in red). Litterę tuę et amorem sonant pariter et querelam . . . uxores ducere.

Spaces for Greek left blank.

BHM 50.

75. ff. 208–212v Epistola Hieronimi ad Pamachium de optimo genere interpretandi declaratiuus (*sic*) et inuectiuus (*sic*) contra dictum Ruffinum et contra epistolas Epliphanii (*sic*) contra eum missas et a Hieronimo translatas calumniatis (in red). Paulus apostolus presente Agrippa rege . . . et Tulii philippicas scribere.

BHM 57.

76. ff. 212v–216 Epistola Epiphanii missa ad Iohannem Crisostimum (*sic*) patriarcham Constantinopolis contra dictum Ruffinum et alios Origenis sectatores (in red). Domino dilectissimo fratri Iohanni episcopo Epiphanius. Oportebat nos, dilectissime, clericatus honore non abuti in superbia . . . ne forte aliquos de populo tibi credito ad peruersitatem sui inducat erroris.

BHM 51.

77. f. 216–216v Epistola Pamachii et Occeani inuectiua ad Hieronimum contra translationem Ruffini prefati de libris periarchon Origenis peruerse factam et de calumpnia super hoc Hieronimo imposita (in red). Sanctus aliquis ex fratribus cedulas ad nos cuiusdam detulit quę Origenis uolumen quod periacon (*sic*) scribitur . . . consensisse uidearis.

BHM 83.

78. ff. 216v–217 Epistola Ruffini super dictos libros Origenis translatos fidei catholice derogatiuus (*sic*) et Hieronimi calumpniatiuus (*sic;* in red). Scio quamplurimos fratrum scientię scripturarum prouocatos, proposisse (*sic*) ab aliquantis uiris eruditis . . . maiores obscuritates legentibus generet.

BHM 80.

79. ff. 217–220v Epistola Hieronimi ad Pamachium et Occeanum reprehensiua et inuectiua contra Origenis sectatores et dicti Ruffini translationem et excusatoriarum (*sic*) impositarum calumpniarum (in red). Scedule quas misistis honorifica me afficere contumelia sic ingenium predicantes . . . qui seruare uelit eloquii uenustatem.

BHM 84.

80. ff. 220v–225 Epistola Hieronimi ad Auitum declaratiua omnium errorum Origenis in dictis libris periarchon contentorum translatis iterato a Ieronimo presbitero (in red). Ante annos circiter decem sanctus uir Pamachius ad me . . . que sibi cauenda sunt nouerit.

BHM 124.

81. f. 225 Epistola Hieronimi ad Ruffinum prefatum commonitoria de predictis calumpniis et impositis (in red). Diu te Rome moratum sermo proprius indicauit nec dubito spiritualium parentum ad patriam reuocatum desiderio . . . qui possint figuratis laudibus delectari.

BHM 81.

82. ff. 225–226 Epistola Ruffini ad Anastasium super dictis obiectionibus excusatiua et sue fidei et translationis peryarchon defensiua (in red). Audiui quosdam . . . propter inuidiam solam generant et liuorem.

Rufinus, *Apologia ad Anastasium,* ed. Simonetti, *CC* 20 (1961): 19–28. *PL* 21:623–28. *CPL* 198.

83. ff. 226–227v Epistola Hieronimi ad Uigilantium presbiterum sectatorem eiusdem Origenis et Ruffini et calumpniatorem Hieronimi confutatoria errorum eiusdem et excusatiua obiectorum (in red). Iustum quidem fuerat nequaquam tibi litteris satisfacere qui tuis auribus non credidisti . . . ut audias et taceas et intelligas et sic loquaris.

BHM 61. See below, text 89.

84. ff. 227v–228v Epistola Hieronimi ad Riparium presbiterum contra dictum Uigilantium et blasphemias eius confutatiua et declaratiua errorum eius (in red). Acceptis primum litteris tuis, non respondere superbie est, respondere temeritatis . . . et in ignem mittetur.

BHM 109.

85. ff. 228v–232v Epistola Hieronimi ad Uigilantium et eius errores (*sic*) confutatiua (in red). Multa in orbe monstra generata sunt . . . maritos earum Christi misterio arbitrantur indignos.

Jerome, *Contra Vigilantium. PL* 23:339–52. *BHM* 253.

86. ff. 232v–234 Epistola Hieronimi ad Thesiphonem declaratiua et confutatiua contra Porphirium an quis possit esse sine peccato si uelit (in red). Non audacter ut falso putes (*sic*), sed amantum (*sic*) studioseque fecisti, ut nouam mihi ex ueteris (*sic*) mitteres questionem . . . cum manus (*sic*) sentire aliud comprobentur.

BHM 133.

87. ff. 234–235v Epistola Hieronimi ad Pamachium et Occeanum inuectiua contra eorum errores et auaritie detestatiua (in red). Qui Ethiopem inuitat ad balnea . . . et iuditium eternum magis timere quam hominum.

Pelagius, *De renuntiatione seculi*. *PL* 30:239–42 (247–49). *CPL* 742. *BHM* 332.

88. f. 235v Epistola Hieronimi ad Ruffinum excusatiua de reprehensione sibi illata et supplicatiua ut suo iuditio sit contemptus (in red). Quod quereris stomacho suo . . . secundum mala peccantium multitudo non parit errori patrocinium.

Same text attributed to Jerome in Vat. lat. 367 (s. xv), ff. 249–250; cf. *BHM* IA, pp. 36 and 297.

89. ff. 235v–237 Epistola Hieronimi enucleatiua errorum Origenis et inuectiua contra hereticos (in red). Utile quidem fuerat necquaquam tibi litteris satisfacere qui tuis auribus non credidisti . . . ut audias et taceas et intellegas et sic loquaris.

Spaces for Greek left blank.

BHM 61. See above, text 83.

90. f. 237 Epistola Epiphanii ad Ieronimum suasiua ad persequendos hereticos ut consueuit (in red). Domino amantissimo filio ac fratri Hieronimo presbitero Epiphanius in domino salutem. Uenerabilis epistola . . . et tecum et per te plurimum salutamus.

BHM 91. See below, text 100.

91. f. 237–237v Epistola Theophili ad Epiphanium suasiua ad resistendum hereticis qui Constantinopolim nauigabant perresuscitanda heresi Origenis quoniam extincta erat (in red). Domino dilectissimo fratri suo coepiscopo Epiphanio Theofilus in Christo salutem. Dominus qui locutus est ad prophetam . . . est in domino salutat.

BHM 90.

92. f. 237v Epistola Hieronimi de prefatione Didimi de spiritu sancto ad Paulinum inuectiua contra eum Didimum (in red). Cum in Babilone uersarer . . . tam sensuum lumine quam simplicitate uerborum.

Prologue of Jerome to his translation of Didymus Alexandrinus, *De spiritu sancto*. *BHM* 258.

93. ff. 237v–238 Epistola Hieronimi ad Riparium exhortatiua ad persistendum hereticis et declaratiua mutationis locis suis propter hereticos (in red). Domino uere sancto atque omni mihi atque affectione uenerabili Ripario Hieronimus in Christo dicit salutem. Christi aduersum hostes catholice fidei dei bella bellare tuis litteris . . . tueatur omnipotens, domine uere sancte et uere munde frater.

BHM 138.

94. f. 238–238v Epistola Hieronimi ad Cromatium et Heliodorum de translatione cuiusdam libelli peruerse heresis demonstratiui (in red). Dominis uero sanctis et beatissimis Cromatio et Heliodoro episcopis Hieronimus exiguus Christi seruus in domino salutem. Qui terram auri consciam fodit . . . per nostram obedientiam potuerunt peruenire.

Ps. Jerome, *Epistle 49*, ed. C. Tischendorf, *Evangelia apocrypha* (Leipzig, 1876), pp. 50–52. *BHM* 349.

95. f. 238v Epistola Hieronimi ad Theophilum exhortatiua ut heresim quam patitur extirpet (in red). Beatissimo pape Theophilo Hyeronimus salutem. Meminit beatitudo tua quod eo tempore, quo tacebas, numquam ab officiis meis primo cessauit . . . et facti (*sic*) robustior fiat.

BHM 63.

96. f. 238v Epistola Theophili ad Ieronimum responsiua super eadem heresi (in red). Dilectissimo et amantissimo fratri Hieronimo Theophilus episcopus. Sanctus episcopus Agato cum dilectissimo dyacono Athanasio . . . et omnes nouas sopire doctrinas.

BHM 87.

97. ff. 238v–239 Epistola Hieronimi ad Theophilum responsiua superiori super eadem heresi (in red). Beatissimo pape Theophilo Hieronimus. Duplicem mihi gratiam beatitudinis tuę littere prestiterunt quod et sanctos et uenerabiles . . . ut ipse significas, succidere falce non cessent.

BHM 88.

98. f. 239 Epistola Theophili ad Ieronimum responsiua superiori super eadem heresi (in red). Domino dilectissimo et amantissimo fratri Hieronimo presbitero Theophilus episcopus. Didici et quod sanctitas tua nouerit . . . meo nomine salutari uolo.

BHM 89.

99. ff. 239–241 Epistola Hieronimi ad Pamachium contra Iohannem episcopum hierosolimitanum et Ruffinum presbiterum Origenis assequutores (in red). Si iuxta Paulum

apostolum, quod sentimus orare non possumus . . . quam aperte quod tectum fuerat confiteri.

Jerome, *Contra Ioannem Hierosolymitanum ad Pammachium* (1–6). *PL* 23:355–60. *BHM* 254.

100. f. 241 Epistola Hieronimi ad Theophilum commendatiua eius de Origenis et ceterorum hereticorum extirpatione (in red). Uenerabilis epistola que ad omnes catholichos scripta est . . . et tecum et per te plurimum salutamus.

BHM 91. See above, text 90.

101. ff. 241–242v Epistola Augustini ad Hieronimum obiurgatiua super translatione eiusdem ueteris testamenti de hebraico in latinum et super reprehensione Petri a Paulo et obseruatiua legalium simulatoria (*sic*) et uere exposita a Hieronimo in epistola ad galathas (in red). Domino uere dilectissimo et cultu sincerissime (*sic*) caritatis obsequendo atque amplectendo fratri et conpresbitero Hieronimo Augustinus. Numquam ęque quisquam tam facile cuilibet innotuit quam mihi tuorum in domino studiorum quieta letitia . . . quam iustam intulisse sententiam.

BHM 56.

102. ff. 242v–244 Epistola Augustini ad Ieronimum reprehensiua de predictis (*sic*) translatione et Petri reprehensione et legalium obseruatione et de libro illustrium uirorum consultiua (*sic;* in red). Domino dilectissimo . . . Augustinus. Habeo gratiam quod pro scripta salutatione mihi plenam epistolam reddidisti . . . in nostris regionibus existimationi bonum coram deo testimonium perhibemus.

BHM 67.

103. ff. 244–245 Epistola Augustini ad eundem excusatiua super predictis inuectionibus contra Hieronimum factis de dictis omnibus et litteris contra eum missis et publicatis (in red). Domino uenerando et desideratissimo fratri et compresbitero Hieronimo Augustinus in domino salutem. Quamuis existimem . . . melius tumor capitis dolet, dum curatur, quam dum ei parcitur non sanatur.

BHM 110 (to 4, 1). *CSEL* 55 (1912): 356–59. See below, text 106 bis.

104. f. 245–245v Epistola Hieronimi ad Augustinum reprehensiua predictarum inuectionum Augustini et litterarum contra eundem Hieronimum et declaratiua responsionum contra Ruffinum eidem Augustino missarum (in red). Super (*sic*) cum Reticii augustudunensis (*sic*) episcopi, qui quondam a Constantinopolitano imperatore . . . et Amos pastor caprarum in sacerdotium princeps inueniatur (*sic*).

BHM 37.

105. f. 245v Epistola Hieronimi ad Augustinum de recommendacione Presidii diaconi (in red). Domino uere sancto et cetera Hieronimus in Christo salutem. Anno preterito per fratrem nostrum Asterium ypodiaconum dignitationi (*sic*) tuę epistolam miseram . . . domine uere sancte et suscipiende papa.

BHM 103.

106. ff. 245v–246 (line 3) Epistola Augustini ad prefatum Presidium de translatione suarum litterarum Hieronimo (in red). Domino beatissimo et merito uenerando fratri et consacerdoti Pręsidio Augustinus in domino salutem. Sicut presens rogaui sinceritatem tuam, nunc quoque commoneo ut litteras meas sancto fratri et conpresbitero nostro Hieronimo mittere non graueris . . . si meam culpam ipse cognouero.

BHM 111. See below, text 122.

106 bis. ff. 246 (line 3)–247v Cur itaque conor contra tractum fluminus et non potius ueniam deprecor. Obsecro . . . ad pristinam concordiam reuertisse.

Text follows without interruption from the preceding letter.

BHM 110 (beginning in 3, 1). *CSEL* 55 (1912):358–66. See above, text 103.

107. ff. 247v–248 Epistola Hieronimi ad Augustinum inuectiua contra eius reprehensiones et ad ueram amicitiam prouocatiua (in red). Domino uere sancto et beatissimo pape Augustino . . . Crebras ad me . . . ad me primum facias peruenire.

BHM 105.

108. ff. 248–249 Epistola Augustini ad Ieronimum de duplici translatione eiusdem Hieronimi ex hebreo scilicet et greco in latinum facta de ueteri testamento consultiua et reprehensiua (in red). Domino uenerabili et desiderabili sancto fratri et conpresbitero Ieronimo . . . Ex quo cępi ad te scribere aut tua scripta desiderare numquam mihi melior

occurrit occasio . . . quantum potueris presentiam tuam.

BHM 104.

109. ff. 249–255 Epistola Hieronimi ad Augustinum super predictis questionibus de libro illustrium uirorum et de reprehensione Petri et obseruantia legalium et de soa (*sic*) triplici translatione (in red). Domino uere sancto et beatissimo pape Augustino . . . Tres simul epistolas ymo libellos breues . . . mihi sufficit iam auditore et lectore pauperculo in angulo monasterii susurare (*sic*).

BHM 112.

110. f. 255 Epistola Hieronimi ad Augustinum depredictis reprehensionibus translationis sue responsionum contra Ruffinum excusatiua (in red). Domino uere sancto et beatissimo pape Augustino Hieronimus in Christo salutem. Cum a sancto fratre nostro sollicite quererem . . . domine uere sancte et beatissime papa.

BHM 115. See below, text 120.

111. ff. 255–262 Epistola Augustini ad Ieronimum declaratiua siue excusationis super responsione contra Ruffinum reprehensa ab eodem Augustino et super translatione noui testamenti de greco accepta et etiam ueteris testamenti de greco in latinum traducta (in red). Domino dilectissimo et in Christi uisceribus honorando sancto fratri et conpresbitero Hieronimo . . . Iam pridem tue caritati prolixam epistolam misi . . . profecto maior est, sed melius hec minor quam nulla est.

BHM 116.

112. ff. 262–267v Epistola Augustini ad Hieronimum de anima humana consultoria utrum sit extraductionem (*sic*) an per infusionem et qua dei iustitia paruulis sine baptismo decedentibus pena iehenne debeatur (in red). Dominum deum nostrum qui nos uocauit in regnum suum et gloriam et rogaui et rogo ut hoc . . . posse liberari.

BHM 131.

113. ff. 267v–271v Epistola Augustini ad Ieronimum de uerbo Iacobi apostoli, si quis totam legero, consultatoria et sue opinionis declaratoria (in red). Quod ad te scripsi . . . ut id nobiscum communicare digneris.

BHM 132.

114. ff. 271v–272 Epistola Hieronimi ad Augustinum declaratiua super dictis duabus questionibus de anima et de uerbo Iacobi sue responsionis ad tempus impedito (in red). Domino uere sancto et beatissimo pape Augustino Hieronimus in domino salutem. In ipso perfectionis articulo sancti filii nostri Asterii ypodiaconi necessarii mei beatitudinis tue ad me littere superuenerunt . . . frater suppliciter te salutat.

BHM 102.

115. f. 272–272v Epistola Hieronimi ad Marcellinum et Anasachiam (*sic*) responsiua super anime statu et de eius infusione corpori humano quinque opinionum declaratiua (in red). Dominis uere sanctis atque omni officiorum caritate uenerandis filiis Marcellino et Annaphisichie Hieronimus in Christo salutem. Tandem ex Affrica uestre litteras humanitatis accepi et non penitet impudentie . . . domini uere sancti.

BHM 126.

116. f. 272v Epistola Hieronimi ad Augustinum et Alippum (*sic*) episcopos commendatiua eorum constantie contra hereticos et ad amicitiam prouocatiua (in red). Dominis uere sanctis . . . Sanctus Innocentius presbiter . . . atque omni affectione uenerabiles patres.

BHM 143.

117. ff. 272v–273 Epistola Hieronimi ad Augustinum de eadem amicitia et constantia contra hereticos commendatiua (in red). Multi utroque claudicant et ne factis quidem ceruicibus . . . et ibi seruitute pereat sempiterna.

BHM 142.

118. f. 273 Epistola Augustini ad Ieronimum excusatiua de suo sensu contrario et se correctioni beati Ieronimi subiectiua (in red). Domino carissimo et desideratissimo. Si forte aliqua in aliquibus scriptis meis reperiuntur . . . et scripta quamuis rara non spernere.

BHM 101 (beginning in 2, 2, and ending in 3, 2). *CSEL* 55 (1912): 233–34.

119. f. 273 Epistola Ieronimi ad Augustinum collaudatiua eius et inductiua ad amorem suum (in red). Domino sancto et beatissimo pape Augustino Hieronimus in domino salutem. Omni quidem tempore beatitudinem tuam eo quo decet honore ueneratus sum . . . domine uenerande et beatissime papa.

BHM 141.

120. f. 273 Epistola Hieronimi ad Augustinum de questione cucurbite et inuitatoria ad ludum in campo scripturarum (in red). Si legisti librum explanationum in Yonam . . . sine nostro inuicem dolore laudamus.

BHM 115 (beginning in 4). *CSEL* 55 (1912): 397. See above, text 110.

121. f. 273–273v Epistola Hieronimi ad Augustinum de impedimento responsionis sue ad tempus et prouocatiua ad ueram amicitiam et exhortatiua contra hereticos (in red). Uenerabili pape Augustino Hyeronimus in Christo salutem. Uirum uenerabilem fratem meum . . . ob fraudem cuiusdam amisimus.

BHM 134.

122. f. 273v Epistola Augustini ad Presidium deprecatiua ut litteras suas ad Ieronimum mittat (in red). Domino beatissimo et merito uenerando fratri . . . Sicut presens . . . ut litteras meas sancto fratri et conpresbitero nostro Hyeronimo mittere non graueris . . . si meam culpam ipse cognouero.

BHM 111. See above, text 106.

123. ff. 273v–274 Epistola Hieronimi ad Augustinum laudatiua eius sanctitatis et commendatiua Theodore (in red). Illum te oculum habere letor . . . ut Ay et Hasor quondam corruant pulcerrime ciuitates.

BHM 76 (beginning in 2, 1, and ending in 3, 2). *CSEL* 55 (1912): 35–36. See below, text 165.

124. f. 274–274v Epistola Hieronimi ad Paulinum excusatiua cur non responderit questionibus suis quia scribit in Danielem (in red). Uoce me prouocas ad scribendum, terres eloquia (*sic*) et in epistolari stilo propie Tullium representas . . . et munere et muneris auctore letatus.

BHM 85.

125. ff. 274v–275v Epistola Hieronimi ad Pamachium et Marcellam contra suos detractores inuectiua et Origenis sectatores et de epistolis Theophili patriarche Alexandrini contra eosdem scilicet missis et a Ieronimo de greco in latinum translatis (in red). Rursum orientalibus uos locupleto . . . per illius studium longo tempore arefacta moriantur.

BHM 97.

126. ff. 275v–276 Epistola Ieronimi ad Marcellam contra suos detractatores inuectiua (in red). Post priorem epistulam in qua de hebreis uerbis . . . ubi bos et asinus calcant.

BHM 27.

127. f. 276–276v Epistola Hieronimi ad Marcellam de quodam Onaso detractatore inuectiua (in red). Medici quos uocant cyrugicos (*sic*) crudeles putantur et miseri sunt . . . atque ita et formosus et discretus uideri poteris.

BHM 40.

128. ff. 276v–277v Epistola Hieronimi ad Asellam uirginem contra suos etiam detractatores inuectiua (in red). Domine ac sancte mater (*sic*) Aselle. Si tibi putem a me gratias referri posse . . . fluctusque maris tuis precibus mitigas.

BHM 45.

129. ff. 277v–278 Epistola Hieronimi ad Marcellam consolatiua et conmendatiua super morte et uita uirtuosa predicte Aselle uirginis (in red). Nemo reprehendat . . . scusipiant (*sic*) sacerdotes.

BHM 24.

130. f. 278–278v Epistola Hieronimi ad Marcellam de morte Lee uidue consolatoria (in red). Cum hora ferme tertia hodiernae diei septuagesimum secundum psalmum . . . ut possimus esse perpetui.

BHM 23.

131. ff. 278v–279v Epistola Hieronimi ad Marcellam de egrotatione Blexillie uidue filie sancte Paule predicte roboratiua ad pacientiam et consolatiua (in red). Abraham temptatur in filio . . . cum dominus eius dictus sit Belçebub.

BHM 38.

132. ff. 279v–282v Epistola Paule et Eustochie ad eandem Marcellam exhortatoria de urbe secedendo et ad loca sacra uisitanda (in red). Qensuram (*sic*) caritas non habet . . . et non dimittam illum.

BHM 46.

133. ff. 282v–283 Epistola Hieronimi ad Marcellam de secedendo de urbe (in red). Ambrosius quo chartas sumptus notarios ministrante tam in innumerabiles libros uester Adamancius . . . doleamus in terra.

BHM 43.

134. ff. 283–284 Epistola Hieronimi ad Marcellam de alphabeti hebraici litteris misti-

cis (in red). Nudius tertius . . . sub pedibus nostris uelociter.

BHM 30.

135. f. 284–284v Epistola Hieronimi ad Marcellam de nominibus hebraicis sacre scripture expositis (in red). Nuper dum pariter essemus non per epistolam ut ante consueueras . . . que tacta (*sic*) sunt.

BHM 26.

136. f. 284v Epistola Hieronimi ad Marcellam de decem nominibus ebraicis dei declaratis (*sic;* in red). Nonagesimum psalmum leges in eo loco quo scribitur . . . Salonas.

BHM 25.

137. ff. 284v–286v Epistola Hieronimi ad Marcellam de Teraphin et Ephot expositione (in red). Epistolare officium est de re familiari aut de quotidiana conuersatione aliquod scribere . . . etiam minora perdentes.

BHM 29.

138. ff. 286v–287 Epistola Hieronimi ad Marcellam de diapsalmate explanatoria (in red). Que acceperis reddenda cum fenore sunt sortisque dilatio usuram parturit. De diapsalmate nostram sententiam flagitaras . . . quam stultam habere scientiam nescientium.

BHM 28.

139. ff. 287–288v Epistola Hieronimi ad Marcellam de psalmo [126], Nisi dominus edificauerit domum (in red). Beatus Pamphilus martir cuius uitam Eusebius cesariensis episcopus tribus ferme uoluminibus explicauit . . . frustraretur infirmitas.

BHM 34.

140. ff. 288v–289 Epistola Hieronimi ad Marcellam de spiritu (*sic*) sancti blasphemia irremissibili secundum Matheum (in red). Breuis est questiuncula quam misisti et aperta responsio est . . . quam conmentariolum dictaremus.

BHM 42.

141. f. 289–289v Epistola Hieronimi ad Marcellam de dogmate nostro contra Montanum secundum uerba Iohannis euangeliste (in red). Testimonia de Iohannis euangelio congregata tibi quidam Montani sectator ingessit . . . a me uolueris scissitari (*sic*).

BHM 41.

142. ff. 289v–290v Epistola Hieronimi ad Marcellam de quinque questionibus legis noue; prima questio (in red). Magnis nos prouocas questionibus et torpens otio ingenium . . . apud quos esse dignatur et cetera.

BHM 59.

143. ff. 290v–291 Epistola Hieronimi ad eandem excusatiua sue breuitatis in scribendo ei propter translationem prophetarum (in red). Uitam (*sic*) paruam epistolam scriberem causa duplicis fuit . . . simul diligatur et mater.

BHM 32.

144. ff. 291–292v Epistola Hieronimi ad Marcellam uiduam persuasiua ad ipsam uiduitatis seruandam (in red). Magna (*sic*) humilitati nostre fiduciam scribendi ad uenerationem tuam Christi caritas dedit . . . instans nocte et die.

Pelagius, *Ad Marcellam viduam de sufferentia temptationum. CPL* 738. *BHM* 303.

145. ff. 292v–293 Epistola Hieronimi ad Marcellam de eisdem muneribus misticis (in red). [U]t absentiam corporum spiritus confabulatione solempniter faciat unusquisque quod preualet . . . sit gratum.

BHM 44.

146. f. 293 Epistola Hieronimi ad Tranquillinum de Origenis doctrina heretico (*sic*) quo modo sit legenda (in red). Maiora spiritus uincula esse quam corporum; si olim ambiebas (*sic*) nunc probauimus . . . Sanctus uero frater Tacianus diaconus inpendio salutat.

BHM 62. See above, text 47.

147. f. 293v Hieronimi epistola ad Desiderium de uiris illustribus et doctoribus ecclesie et de libris suis (in red). Letus sermo dignationis tuę . . . si uolueris.

BHM 47.

148. ff. 293v–294v Epistola Hieronimi ad Enagrium (*sic*) de duodecim doctoribus ecclesie et eorum doctrina (in red). Uis nunc acriter . . . ideo quasi umbra secus hominem sunt.

Ps. Jerome, *Epistle* 57. *BHM* 357.

149. ff. 294v–296 Epistola Hieronimi ad Magnum oratorem urbis Rome doctoribus ecclesiasticis et eorum doctrina (*sic;* in red). Sebesium nostrum tuis monitis profecisse, non tam epistola tua . . . finienda est.

BHM 70.

150. ff. 296–297 Epistola Hieronimi ad Ciprianum declaratoria psalmi [89], scilicet, Domine refugium (in red). Frater charissime

Cypriane, scito prenoscens quia si scribatur . . . dei auxilio deseritur.

BHM 140 (beginning in 16, 1). *CSEL* 56 (1918): 285–89.

151. ff. 297–298 Epistola Hieronimi ad Uitalem presbiterum de Salomone et Achaz quomodo dicantur xii (*sic*) annorum filios se generasse (in red). Symmo (*sic*) Salomon et Achaiz xi annorum genuisse dicantur filios. Çenon nauclerus . . . per Desiderium missa suscipe.

BHM 72.

152. f. 298 Epistola Hieronimi ad Ruffinum monachum declaratoria iudicii Salomonis (in red). Multum in utramque partem crebro fama mentitur et tam de bonis mala et quam de malis bona falsorum ore concelebrat . . . preoccupassem sermonem tuum.

BHM 74 (1 only). *CSEL* 55 (1912): 23–24.

153. ff. 298–299 Epistola Hieronimi ad Enagrum (*sic*) de sacerdotibus dyaconis et episcopis quomodo differant secundum apostolum (in red). Legimus in Ysaya, Fatuus fatua loquitur (*sic*) . . . hoc sibi episcopi et presbiteri et dyaconi in ecclesia uindicet (*sic*).

BHM 146.

154. ff. 299–300 Epistola Hieronimi ad Amandum presbiterum de quatuor questionibus legis noue (in red). Breuis epistole longus (*sic*) explanare non non (*sic*) ualet et in arctum multa concludens . . . non parcit medicus ut parcat seuit ut misereatur.

BHM 55. See above, texts 46 and 48.

155. ff. 300–301v Epistola Hieronimi ad Lucinum Beticum hyspanum heremitam de ieiunio et eucharistia secundum ritum primitiue ecclesie assumendis et de libris suis et de uita heremitica (in red). Non opinanti mihi subito littere tue reddite sunt . . . uicissitudine sentiamus.

BHM 71.

156. ff. 301v–303v Epistola Hieronimi de corpore et sanguine Christi declaratiua (in red). Magnitudo celestium beneficiorum . . . piis uos operibus preparare dignetur, qui uiuit et regnat in secula seculorum. Amen.

Eusebius Gallicanus, *De corpore et sanguine Christi*. *BHM* 338.

157. f. 303v Epistola Cromati et Eliodori ad Ieronimum deprecatiua ut de hebreo in latinum traducat librum de infantia saluatoris et uirginis Marie (in red). Dilectissimo fratri Hyeronimo presbitero Cromatius et Heliodorus episcopi salutem in domino. Ortum Marie uirginis regine . . . Uale in domino et ora pro nobis.

Prologue to the *Liber de ortu beatae Mariae et infantia salvatoris*, ed. C. Tischendorf, *Evangelia apocrypha* (Leipzig, 1876), pp. 51–52. *PL* 30:369–71. *BHM* 348.

158. f. 304 Epistola Hieronimi ad Summanum (*sic*) et Fretellam in psalterio qui lxx interpretum et dictione corruptus est (in red). Dilectis fratribus Sumnie (*sic*) et Fretelle et ceteris qui uobiscum domino seruiunt . . . Uere in nobis (*sic*) apostolicus . . . sed feritas discat simplicitatem.

BHM 106 (1 only). *CSEL* 55 (1912): 247–48.

159. ff. 304–306 Epistola siue tractatus Hieronimi de sanctis uigiliis expositiuus (*sic*; in red). Dignum est fratres aptumque prorsus satisque conueniens . . . cum omnibus nobis. Amen.

Niceta of Remesiana, *De obseruatione vigiliarum*, ed. C. H. Turner, *Journal of Theological Studies* 22 (1921): 306–12. A. E. Burn, *Niceta of Remesiana* (Cambridge, 1905), pp. 55–67. *CPL* 633 and 648. *BHM* 331.

160. f. 306–306v Epistola Hieronimi de libri pascalis translatione eiusdem libri eloquentie laudatiua et tarditatis sue excusatiua (in red). Beatissimo pape Theophilo Hieronimus salutem. Ex eo tempore beatitudinis tue accepi litteras epistolas (*sic*) . . . uel uertendos transmitte. Uale.

BHM 99.

161. ff. 306v–307 Epistola Hieronimi ad Paulam et Eustochium de noua psalterii emendatione et translatione secundum lxx[a] interpretes (in red). Psalterium dudum Rome positum (*sic*) emendaram et iuxta septuaginta interpretes . . . quam de purissimo fonte potare. Ualete.

BHM 157. Editions: *Biblia sacra*, vol. 10, *Liber psalmorum* (Rome, 1953), pp. 3–4, and De Bruyne, *Préfaces de la Bible latine*, p. 46.

162. ff. 307–314v Epistola Hieronimi a (*sic*) declaratiua questionis quare dies celebrandus dominice passionis reuoluto anno ad eundem non redeat diem sicut traditur natalis domini (in red). Lectis litteris tuis, ubi me commouisti (*sic*) . . . non emulatur, hanc epistolam multis daturam atque lecturam.

Augustine, *Epistle 55,* ed. A. Goldbacher, *CSEL* 34 (1898): 169–213. *PL* 33:204–23. *CPL* 262.

163. ff. 314v–316 Epistola Hieronimi reprehensiua eorum qui nolunt inter Pauli epistolas recipi ea que ad Philomenem (*sic*) scribitur et probatiua quod eius sit (in red). Qui nolunt inter epistolas Pauli . . . quo priuatas etiam sui commendatrices ad dominum litteras sumpserat.

Jerome, *Commentaria in epistolam sancti Pauli ad Philemonem* (prologue and the beginning portion of the text). *PL* 26:635–42B. *BHM* 219.

164. ff. 316–317v Epistola Ieronimi ad Theodoram sororem Lucini de morte eius et amicitia (in red). Lugubri nunctio consternatus super sancti ac uenerabili (*sic*) mihi dormitione Lucinii (*sic*) . . . et cor meum uigilat.

BHM 75.

165. ff. 317v–318 Epistola Hieronimi ad Ambigarum (*sic*) hispanum de amicitia et pacientia et cecitate (in red). Quamquam mihi multorum sim conscius peccatorum . . . per te opido (*sic*) salutamus.

BHM 76. See above, text 123.

166. f. 318–318v Epistola Hieronimi ad Florentinum de amicitia et mundi contentu (*sic*) et libris sancti Hilari (in red). In ea mihi parte heremi commoranti . . . negotium prosequatur.

BHM 5.

167. f. 318v Epistola Hieronimi ad eundem Florentinum de amicitia (in red). Quantus beatitudinis tue . . . chatene languoris innector.

BHM 4.

168. ff. 318v–319 Epistola Hieronimi ad Exuperantium de amicitia (in red). Inter omnia que mihi sancti fratris tui Quintiliani amicitie prestiterunt . . . si aperueris nos crebro habebis hospites.

BHM 145.

169. ff. 319–320 Epistola Hieronimi ad Cromatium, Iouinianum et Eusebium monachos de amicitia (in red). Non debet carta diuidere quos amor mutuus copulauit . . . amor ordinem nescit.

BHM 7.

170. f. 320–320v Epistola Hieronimi ad Theodosum (*sic*) et alios monachos inneruos (*sic*) commorantes de amicitia (in red). Quam uellem nunc uestro interesse conuentui . . . et ad portum optati littoris me prosequatur.

BHM 2.

171. ff. 320v–321 Epistola Hieronimi ad Paulum monachum concordie de amicitia (in red). Humane uite breuitas dampnatio delictorum est et in ipso sepe lucis exordio . . . nauigabunt.

BHM 10.

172. f. 321 Epistola Hieronimi ad Grisogonam monacham de amicitia (in red). Qui circa te affectus meus sit . . . quod scripseris.

BHM 9.

173. f. 321–321v Epistola Hieronimi ad Iulianum dyaconum Aquileie de amicitia (in red). Antiquus sermo est . . . reddas sermonibus lectiorem (*sic*).

BHM 6.

174. ff. 321v–322 Epistola Hieronimi ad Marcum presbiterum Calcidie de amicitia et fide catholica contra hereticos (in red). Decreueram quidem utendum mihi psalmiste uoce dicentis . . . plurimum salutamus.

BHM 17.

175. f. 322–322v Epistola Hieronimi ad Niteam subdyaconum Aquileie de amicitia (in red). Surpilius (*sic*) comicus tractans diuicissitudine (*sic*) litterarum . . . uel indignantis accipiam.

BHM 8.

176. f. 322v Epistola Hieronimi ad Antonium monachum Hemonie de amicitia [et] reconciliatione (in red). Dominus noster humilitatis magister disceptantibus de dignitate . . . conseruus impertias. Uale in deo.

BHM 12.

177. ff. 322v–323 Epistola Hieronimi ad uirgines Emonie de reconciliatione amicitie et dilectionis (in red). Carte exiguitas indicium solitudinis est . . . quare oculus tuus nequam est.

BHM 11.

178. f. 323 Epistola Hieronimi ad Castorinam materteram de dilectionis reconciliatione (in red). Iohannes apostolus idem et euangelista ait in epistola sua . . . cum lecta fuerit absoluet.

BHM 13.

179. f. 323–323v Epistola Hieronimi de honorandis parentibus exhortatiua et addit (*sic*)

obligatos esse uniuersos demonstratiua (in red). Parentum meritis subiugans . . . ut illa germanitas ęterno collegio firmaretur.

Ps. Jerome, *Epistle 11* (abbreviated version); cf. *PL* 30:145–47. *BHM* 311.

180. ff. 323v–325 Epistola Hieronimi ad Ruffinum monachum de Bonoso et eius uite lauditiua (*sic*) et exhortatiua ad perfectam amicitiam et conseruandam (in red). Plus deum tribuere quam rogatur . . . numquam uera fuit.

BHM 3.

181. ff. 325–327v Epistola Hieronimi ad Epiphanium collauditiua (*sic*) uere pacis (in red). Epistola tua hereditatis dominice te iudicans possessorem . . . ne remordentes inuicem confirmamur (*sic*) ab inuicem.

BHM 82 (in the usual recension, addressed to Theophilus).

182. ff. 327v–329 Epistola sancti Iohannis Crisostomi quam in exilium deportandus composuit contemptatiua ipsius exilii et suasiua ad persistendum in fide Christi (in red). Multi quidem fluctus . . . pro hiis gratias agamus deo, cui est gloria in secula seculorum. Amen.

John Chrysostom, *Homilia 38*. *PG* 52:431–36.

183. ff. 329–331 Epistola Hieronimi ad Creatiam de testamento Yeronti patris creatu (*sic*) et sororum exhortatiua ad illud executioni (*sic*) mandandum (in red). Cuncti sensus mei affectu uobis uoco (*sic*) . . . uos requiem prophetarum.

Eutropius Presbyter, *Ad Geruntii filias de testamento Geruntii*. *CPL* 565. *BHM* 302.

184. ff. 331–333v Epistola Hieronimi exhortatiua ad supportationem obbrobriorum et iniuriarum cum summa pacientia (in red). Diuersorum obprobria . . . admonere. Salutate omnes qui diligant . . . et in omnia secula seculorum.

Ps. Jerome, *Epistle 41*. *BHM* 341.

185. ff. 333v–334 Epistola Hieronimi ad Seuerum qua scribit cupere cum (*sic*) uidere (in red). Cum in urbem anteriori tempore commeassem . . . benedicte patris mei percipe regnum.

Anonymous *Epistola ad Augustinum* = Augustine, *Epistle 270*. *CPL* 633. *BHM* 352.

186. f. 334 Epistola Hieronimi ad Propanum qua plurimum condolet de domus euersione et suasiua ut inde abiens sancta loca petat (in red). Nescio qua temptacione diaboli factum sit, ut tuus labor et sancti Innocentii presbiteri industria et nostrum desiderium . . . quam fidem frangere seu perdere.

BHM 139.

187. ff. 334–335v Epistola Hieronimi inuectiua contra eum qui dicit se penitentem et in seculo moratur (in red). Ad te surgo . . . in ignem eternum.

Pelagius, *De homine poenitente*. *CPL* 743. *BHM* 333.

188. ff. 335v–336v Epistola Hieronimi ad Theodorum de superbia carnis inductiua ad humilitatem et superbie obiurgatiua (in red). Ad te manum meam extendo . . . et animam humiles (*sic*) exaltauit, ipsi honor et gloria in secula seculorum.

Ps. Jerome, *Epistle;* cf. *PL* 40:1074, cap. 64. *BHM* 360.

189. ff. 336v–337v Epistola Paulini et Therasii ad Sebastianum eius uite solitarie laudatiua (in red). Sancto et merito dilectissimo fratri Sebastiano Paulinus et Therasius (*sic*) in Christo domino salutem. Benedictus dominus deus Israhel qui elegit et assumpsit te in uas electionis et segregauit ab utero matris . . . abba, pater, benedicti domino fili pietatis et luminis et cetera.

Explicet liber decimus et ultimus epistolarum Hieronimi (in red).

Epi finito stolarum dextera sistat
Hieronimi libro quem frequens lectio gustet
Qui mundi exhaustos pacienter ferre labores
Uelit et eterni regnum conscendere poli (in red).

Iohannes Petrus Mathei de Anchona scripsit hunc librum m° cccc° lix° die xxiii[a] mensis aprilis (in red).

f. 338–338v blank.

Paulinus of Nola, *Epistle 26,* ed. W. von Hartel, *CSEL* 29 (1894): pp. 234–36. *CPL* 202.

Front pastedown, a fragment of Accursius, Ordinary Gloss on the *Digest;* s. xiv.

Entire manuscript written on reused parchment; the original fourteenth-century text is visible at many places and can be identified at these points:

a) f. 175v, Dynus de Mugello, *Super digesto novo,* tit., De confessis (Lyon, 1513).

b) f. 192, Jacobus de Arena, *Super digesto novo,*

tit., De privilegiis creditorum, printed in his *Commentaria in universum ius civile* (Lyon, 1541), f. 182.

f. 3, illuminated purple and dull gold initial decorated with green, blue, and purple acanthus spray on a checkered ground of gold, purple, and blue, 14 lines high. The acanthus spray extends into a full gold ivy border decorated with red, blue, and green tulip-shaped flowers, a peacock, putti, a wolf, and various fantastic animals; in the lower margin, a miniature of Jerome in a red robe writing on a scroll in his study. Text, initial, and illumination framed by a gold compartment filled with red, green, and blue. This leaf reproduced by Warner, *Descriptive Catalogue,* plate lviii. Red initials with blue flourishes and blue initials with red flourishes at the beginning of each book after the first, 8–10 lines high. Two initials also have pale yellow flourishes. Smaller blue initials with red flourishes alternating with red initials with blue flourishes at the beginning of each epistle.

Palimpsest formed from parchment of southern preparation, s. xiv. ff. i + 338. 340 × 232 mm (225 × 130 mm). 1^{2}, 2^{8}, $3–11^{10}$, 12^{8}, $13–35^{10}$. Catchwords surrounded by a varying pattern of points and flourishes. Prickings visible in outer margins; on f. 90, two rows of prickings present. Ruled in hard point. Written in Italian hybrida media with trailing terminal s, humanistic form of the g, occasional humanistic use of the e with cedilla for ae diphthong, and occasional use of the ampersand, in 40 long lines beginning on the first ruled line, by several very similar hands. The life of Jerome (f. 3) written in rustic capitals; the "Sepulcri epythaphium" (f. 3) written in humanistic cursiva. Headings written in violet (humanistic) on ff. 51–69v and in red (gothic) elsewhere, all in script of text. Incipits of the first letter of each book written in rustic capitals. Space for Greek left blank.

Bound in Italian calf over boards, s. xv. Decorated with identical patterns of ruled concentric lozenges, back and front. Four front-to-back clasps (two on the fore edge) wanting. Three catches bear a king seated, the upper catch bears an Agnus Dei, surrounded in each catch by a rosette; three bosses on each corner, one at the center and two at the corners, bearing the inscription: "O mater dei misereri m[ei]."

Written in Ancona by several scribes including Johannes Petrus Mathei de Anchona, signed and dated 23 April 1459 on f. 337v; *Colophons de manuscrits occidentaux,* 10945. In 1460, Nicolas of Ancona presented this book to the Franciscan convent of Ancona (*DHGE* 2:1533). f. 337v, "Has sacras epistolas deuotissimi Yieronimi sacrarum scripturarum grecarum et ebreicarum interpetris (*sic*), cuius laboribus ecclesia erudita extitit, Nicolaus Ankonitanus, legum doctor, conlocauit in sacrastia sancti Francisci de Ankona conscrictas et alligatas. Iussitque et mandauit inde nullo pacto admoueri posse per quemcumque, dominiumque et proprietatem earundem sibi et suis heredibus reseruauit, utendas et fruendas fratribus et aliis quibuscumque reseruauit; alienationem uero earundem omnino prohibuit interminatione diuini iuditii pro anima sua et filiorum suorum et Baldassarris sui consobrini. Ad laudem summi dei, amen. Anno domini 1460, in die natiuitatis domini hic posite fuerunt." f. 3, two unidentified coats of arms (see color illustration); reproduced by Warner, *Descriptive Catalogue,* plate lxviii. In the nineteenth century, in the library of George Reid: his bookplate on front pastedown, annotated in black ink, "bought in Rome by George Reid." Sold by Reid in 1904 to C. W. Dyson Perrins; see De Ricci, *English Collectors,* pp. 171–72; his armorial bookplate on the front pastedown. Also on the front pastedown, a blue and white circular "Perrins Collection" sticker with "65" written in black ink; this is the number of this manuscript in Warner, *Descriptive Catalogue,* pp. 165–66. Another black and white circular "Dyson Perrins" sticker with "115" written on it on the rear pastedown. This manuscript exhibited by Dyson Perrins at the Burlington Fine Arts Club in 1908, the catalogue description (no. 198) tipped onto a modern front flyleaf. Acquired by the Newberry at the Dyson Perrins sale, Sotheby's, 29 November 1960, lot no. 124 and plate 33.

Second folio (of the text): autem a nullo.

+102.5

Jerome, Letters and Tracts

Padua c. 1450

1. ff. 1–4 In nomine domini nostri Iesu Christi incipiunt epistolę et alia quędam opuscula pręfulgidi luminaris ecclesię beatissimi Hieronymi presbyteri ad orthodoxę fidei confirmationem et diuersarum hęreseon confutationem pertinentia; Et primo diffinitio fidei symbolique niceni concilii ab eodem de gręco in latinum translata sermonem (in red). Credimus in unum deum, patrem omnipotentem, omnium uisibilium et inuisibilium creatorem et in unum dominum nostrum Iesum Christum filium eius natum . . . et regnum caelorum hereditatione non ambigua sunt sortiti.

Ps. Jerome, *Explanatio fidei ad Cyrillum,* ed. C. Turner, *Ecclesiae occidentalis monumenta iuris antiquissima,* I, ii, 1 (Oxford, 1913), pp. 355–68. *PL* 30:176–81 (182–87). *BHM* 317. This codex known to Lambert, *BHM* (IB: 1113 and IVB: 163, as a Silver manuscript) but individual texts not recorded.

2. ff. 4–5v Diffinitio fidei beati Hieronymi ad Damasum papam (in red). Credimus in

deum patrem omnipotentem, cunctorum uisibilium et inuisibilium conditorem . . . non me hęreticum comprobabit.

Ps. Jerome, *Explanatio fidei ad Damasum*. *BHM* 316.

3. ff. 5v–6v Hieronymi ad Damasum papam de nouo nomine trium / hypostaseon subsistentiarum / (in red). Quoniam uetusto oriens inter se populorum furore collisus . . . cum antiquo sensu praedicent.

BHM 15.

4. ff. 6v–7 Hieronymi ad Damasum papam de fide et cui apud Antiochiam communicare debeat (in red). Importuna in euangelio mulier tandem meruit audiri et clauso cum seruis hostio . . . pro qua Christus mortuus est.

BHM 16.

5. f. 7–7v Hieronymi ad Marcum presbyterum Calcide super postulata fide (in red). [D]ecreueram quidem utendum mihi psalmistae uoce . . . plurimum salutamus.

BHM 17.

6. ff. 7v–18 Altercatio Luciferiani et orthodoxi a beato Hieronymo edita (in red). Proxime accidit, ut quidam Luciferi sectator . . . quam persuaderi.

Jerome, *Altercatio Luciferiani et orthodoxi*. *BHM* 250.

7. ff. 18–26 Hieronymi libellus aduersus Heluidium de beatae Mariae uirginitate perpetua (in red). Nuper rogatus a fratribus ut aduersus . . . seruus domini pariter experiatur cum matre.

Jerome, *Adversus Helvidium de Mariae virginitate perpetua*. *BHM* 251.

8. ff. 26–31 Hieronymi ad Occeanum de unius uxoris uiro (in red). Nunquam, fili Occeane . . . quod concessum est.

BHM 69.

9. f. 31–31v Hieronymi ad Euagrium presbyterum qualiter diaconus presbytero subiiciatur (in red). Legimus in Isaia . . . Audio quendam in tantam erupisse uaecordiam . . . et diaconi in ecclesia uendicent.

BHM 146.

10. ff. 31v–33v Hieronymi ad Euagrium presbyterum de Melchisedech (in red). Misisti mihi uolumen / anonymon sine nomine / et nescio utrum tu . . . nocuerit corporis ualitudini.

BHM 73.

11. ff. 33v–63v Hieronymi liber primus aduersus Iouinianum hęreticum (in red). Pauci admodum dies sunt, quod sancti ex urbe fratres cuiusdam . . . uiros esse desinere. Hieronymi liber primus aduersus Iouinianum hęreticum feliciter explicit (in red).

Jerome, *Adversus Iovinianum liber I*. *PL* 23:211–82. *BHL* 252.

12. ff. 63v–87v Incipit secundus (in red). Secunda propositio est . . . quam sub consulibus Epicuri luxuriam susceperunt.

Jerome, *Adversus Iovinianum liber II*. *PL* 23:282–338. *BHL* 252.

13. ff. 87v–88 Hieronymi prologus ad Pammachium super apologetico librorum ab eo contra Iouinianum aeditorum (in red). Christiani interdum pudoris est . . . sed uniuerso loquatur hominum generi. Explicit prologus (in red).

BHM 48.

14. ff. 88–97 Incipit apologeticus eiusdem (in red). Quod ad te huc usque non scripsi, causa fuit . . . uel Lazarum sequi uel diuitem.

BHM 49.

15. ff. 97–99 Hieronymi ad Domnionem contra Rufinum (in red). Litterae tuae et amorem sonant pariter et quaerelam . . . uxores ducere.

BHM 50.

16. ff. 99–100v Hieronymi aduersus Uigilantium presbyterum eius blasphemias arguentis (in red). Iustum quidem fuerat nequaquam tibi litteris satisfacere qui tuis auribus non credidisti . . . et sic loquaris.

BHM 61.

17. ff. 100v–101v Hieronymi ad Riparium presbyterum terraconensem pro scismate Uigilantii (in red). Acceptis primum litteris tuis non respondere superbiae est, respondere temeritatis . . . et in ignem mittetur.

BHM 109.

18. ff. 101v–107 Hieronymi libellus aduersum Uigilantium (in red). Multa in orbe monstra generata sunt . . . maritos earum Christi mysterio arbitrantur indignos.

Jerome, *Contra Vigilantium ad Riparium et Desiderium presbyteros*. *BHM* 253.

19. ff. 107–111v Epistola beati Epiphanii ad Iohannem hierosolymitanum episcopum per beatum Hieronymum de graeco in latinum translata sermonem (in red). Domino dilectissimo fratri Iohanni episcopo Epiphanius. Oportebat nos, dilectissime, clericatus honore

non abuti in superbiam . . . ad peruersitatem sui inducat erroris.

BHM 51.

20. ff. 111v–117 Hieronymi libellus ad Pammachium de optimo genere interpretandi (in red). Paulus apostolus presente Agrippa rege de criminibus responsurus . . . et Tullii philippicas scribere.

BHM 57.

21. ff. 117–118 Praefatio Rufini presbyteri in libros / periarchon de principiis / Origenis, quos de gręco transtulit in latinum (in red). Scio quamplurimos . . . maiores obscuritates legentibus generet.

BHM 80.

22. f. 118–118v Pammachii et Occeani ad Hieronymum super praefata interpretatione Rufini (in red). Sanctus aliquis ex fratribus scedulas ad nos cuiusdam detulit quae Origenis uolumen quod / periarchon de principiis / scribitur . . . consensisse uidearis.

BHM 83.

23. ff. 118v–122v Hieronymi ad Pammachium et Occeanum responsiua (in red). Scedulae quas misistis honorifica me affecere contumelia sic ingenium praedicantes . . . qui seruare uelit eloquii uenustatem.

BHM 84.

24. ff. 122v–141v Hieronymi ad Pammachium contra Iohannem hierosolymitanum episcopum et Rufinum Origenis sectatores (in red). Si iuxta apostolum Paulum . . . totumque nostrę paruitatis teste (*sic*) est monasterium.

Jerome, *Contra Ioannem Hierosolymitanum ad Pammachium*. *BHM* 254.

25. ff. 141v–145 Hieronymi ad Theophilum papam qui obsecrans scripserat ut pacem cum Rufino haberet (in red). Epistola tua haereditatis dominicae te indicat possessorem . . . consumamur ab inuicem.

BHM 82.

26. f. 145–145v Hieronymi ad Tranquillinum quomodo legere debeat Origenem (in red). Maiora spiritus uincula esse quam corporum si olim ambigebamus, nunc probauimus . . . impendio te resalutat.

BHM 62.

27. ff. 145v–146 Hieronymi ad Paulinum quur non scripsit in Danielem commentarios (in red). Uoce me prouocas ad scribendum, terres eloquentia . . . et muneris auctore letatus.

BHM 85.

28. ff. 146–147v Apologia Rufini quam pro se misit ad Anastasium romanę urbis episcopum (in red). Audiui quosdam quum apud beatitudinem tuam . . . propter inuidiam solam generant et liuorem.

Rufinus, *Apologia ad Anastasium,* ed. M. Simonetti, *CC* 20 (1961): 19–28. *PL* 21:623–28. *CPL* 198.

29. ff. 147v–185v Rufini liber primus contra beatum Hieronymum blasphemantis (in red). Relegi scripta, Aproniane fili carissime . . . siue aduersus tuos datam.

Rufinus, *Apologia contra Hieronymum,* ed. M. Simonetti, *CC* 20 (1961): 29–123. *PL* 21:541–624. *CPL* 197.

30. f. 185v Hieronymi ad Theophilum papam super corrigendis haereticis (in red). Beatissimo papae Theophilo Hieronymus. Meminit beatitudo tua, quod eo tempore, quo tacebas, numquam ab officiis . . . et facti robustior fiat.

BHM 63.

31. ff. 185v–186 Theophili ad Hieronymum ut moneat sermonibus emendatos ab haeresi Origenis (in red). Dilectissimo et amantissimo fratri Hieronymo Theophilus episcopus . . . et omnes nouas sopire doctrinas.

BHM 87.

32. f. 186 Hieronymi ad Theophilum (in red). Beatissimo papę Theophilo Hieronymus. Duplicem mihi gratiam beatitudinis tuae litterae praestiterunt quod et sanctos ac uenerabiles . . . non cessent.

BHM 88.

33. f. 186–186v Theophili ad Hieronymum quod fugati sunt sectatores Origenis et quod caueat ab hypocrytis (in red). Domino dilectissimo et amantissimo fratri . . . meo nomine salutari uolo.

BHM 89.

34. f. 186v Hieronymi ad Theophilum papam super uictoria haeresis Alexandrinę (in red). Beatissimo papae Theophilo Hieronymus. Nuper beatitudinis tuae scripta percepi emendantia uetus silentium . . . in aliquo laedere.

BHM 86.

35. f. 187–187v Theophili ad Epiphanium,

ut congregatis episcopis suae insulae condemnet Origenem et eius opera, et contra sectatores Origenis scribat episcopo constantinopolitano (in red). Domino dilectissimo fratri et coepiscopo Epiphanio Theophilus in domino, salutem . . . quae nobiscum est in domino salutat.

BHM 90.

36. ff. 187v–200v Hieronymi liber primus ad Pammachium et Marcellam pro se contra Rufinum defensiuus. Et uestris et multorum litteris didici . . . Ergo qui non facit, iam corruit in aeternum. Hieronymi ad Pammachium et Marcellam pro se contra Rufinum liber primus defensiuus explicit (in red).

Jerome, *Apologia adversus libros Rufini liber I. BHM* 255.

37. ff. 200v–216 Incipit secundus (in red). Hucusque de criminibus immo pro criminibus meis . . . quam hostem latentem sub amici nomine sustinere.

Jerome, *Apologia adversus libros Rufini liber II. BHM* 255.

38. f. 216 Epiphanii episcopi ad beatum Hieronymum (in red). Uenerabilis epistola quę ad omnes catholicos . . . et per te plurimum salutamus.

BHM 91.

39. ff. 216–232v Hieronymi ad Rufinum eius calumniis responsiua et in eundem inuectiua (in red). Lectis litteris prudentię tuae . . . ilico pax sequitur.

Jerome, *Liber tertius adversus libros Rufini. BHM* 256.

40. ff. 232v–233v Anastasii romanae urbis episcopi ad Iohannem hierosolymitanum episcopum super nomine Rufini haeretici (in red). Probatae quidem affectionis est . . . Ipse denique uiderit ubi possit absolui.

Anastasius I, *Epistola ad Ioannem Hierosolymitanum*, ed. E. Schwartz, *Acta conciliorum oecumenicorum* vol. 1, pt. 5 (Berlin, 1924–25), pp. 3–4. *PL* 20:68–73, 21:627–32, 48:231–40. *CPL* 1640.

41. ff. 233v–234 Hieronymi ad Rufinum (in red). Diu te Romae moratum sermo proprius indicauit nec dubito spiritalium parentum ad propria reuocatum . . . qui possint figuratis laudibus dellectari (*sic*).

BHM 81.

42. ff. 234–240 Hieronymi ad Auitum de erroribus Origenis in libris peri archon / de principiis / (in red). Ante annos circiter decem . . . cauenda sunt nouerit.

BHM 124.

43. ff. 240–241 Hieronymi ad Pammachium et Marcellam contra suos detractores et Origenis sectatores (in red). Rursum orientalibus . . . tempore arefacta moriantur.

BHM 97.

44. f. 241 Hieronymi ad Riparium (in red). Domino uere sancto atque . . . Christum aduersum hostes catholice fidei bella bellare tuis litteris . . . et suscipiende frater.

BHM 138.

45. f. 241–241v Hieronymi ad Apronium (in red). Nescio qua temptatione diaboli factum sit, ut et tuus labor et sancti Innocentii . . . quam fidem perdere.

BHM 139.

46. ff. 241v–284v Incipit prephatio sancti Hieronymi in dyalogum contra pellagianos hereticos sub nominibus Attici et Chritoboli, ubi commendatur gratia dei (in red). Scripta iam ad Thesiphontem epistola, in qua ad interrogata respondi . . . in hac parte errorem sequamini. Explicit.

Jerome, *Dialogi contra Pelagianos libri III. BHM* 257.

f. 1, gold initial historiated with Jerome as a cardinal in his study, decorated with white vine stem on a blue and pink ground 14 lines high in the presence of a full white vine stem border, decorated with gold on a ground of pink and blue. Lower margin center, within a roundel, Christ with cross standing in the tomb; lower margin left, half portrait of Justina; lower margin right, half portrait of Prosdocimus (?) as bishop. This leaf reproduced, Warner, *Descriptive Catalogue,* plate 78 and pp. 196–97. For a closely related manuscript with the same provenance, see Alexander and De la Mare, *Italian Manuscripts,* plate 52. ff. 147v, 187v, and 200v, gold initial with white ivy stem decoration 10 lines high in the presence of an outer white ivy stem margin; the border on f. 187v has a human head and a stag's head at the extremities. White vine stem initials 4–6 lines high throughout.

Parchment of southern preparation. ff. 285. ff. 1–240, original arabic foliation in red; ff. 241–284, modern pencil; last leaf unnumbered. Trimmed to 373 × 255 mm (230 × 148 mm). $1–28^{10}$, 29^{6} (6 wanting). Catchwords surrounded by four flourishes with many minor variations. Written in humanistic textualis formata, in 37 long lines, beginning on the second ruled line, by more than one scribe. ff. 201–217v, quotation marks frequently used. Accents present, a distinction made between the form of accent mark used for the tonic syllable and that used to denote the letter i. Headings in red in rustic capitals and in script of text. Upper margins, running headings in red in script of text. Greek words generally omitted in text, written by the scribe in Latin transliteration in margin with Latin interlinear translations. Some Greek words added in the blank spaces in s. xv.

Bound in red morocco and signed by Charles Lewis (d. 1836).

Written and illustrated in Italy at Padua c. 1450 for the library of the monastery of Santa Giustina [Cottineau, 2:2168–69]. ff. 1 and 284v, written in humanistic textualis media: "Iste liber est monachorum congregacionis sanctę Iustinę ipsi monasterio Sanctę Iustinę patauii deputatus," with number "325" and pressmark "B 15." Recorded as no. 325 in the library catalogue dating from 1453–84 in Padua, Museo Civico, B.P. 229, ed. L. A. Ferrai, in appendix to G. Mazzatinti, *Manoscritti italiani delle biblioteche de Francia* (Rome, 1886–88), 2:604. For other Manuscripts of this library, see Delisle, *Le Cabinet des manuscrits,* 2:414; E. P. Goldschmidt, *Gothic and Renaissance Bookbinding* (Boston, 1928), pp. 7 and 128–32; G. M. Boyce, *Italian Manuscripts in the Pierpont Morgan Library* (New York, 1953), no. 62; Alexander and De la Mare, *Italian Manuscripts,* pp. 115–88. This codex, on verso of front cover, printed label "From the library of Lawrence W. Hodson, Compton Hall near Wolverhampton." Sold at Sotheby's, 3–5 December 1906, lot no. 300. Sold by Quaritch in 1909 to C. W. Dyson Perrins, his armorial bookplate on front pastedown as well as round black Dyson Perrins sticker with "86" written in pen. This manuscript no. 86 in Warner, *Descriptive Catalogue.* Sold at Sotheby's, 9 December 1958, lot no. 29 and plate 33. Acquired by the Newberry from Louis H. Silver, 1964.

Second folio: filius non ex.

103.5

(48-453)

Ovid, *Tristia;* Pseudo Ovid, *De Pulice;* Horace, *Sermones*

Italy c. 1500

1. ff. 1–89v

[P]arue, nec inuideo, sine me liber ibis in urbem . . .

Laudat et hortatu comprobat acta suo. Finis. Telos.

f. 90–90v blank.

Ovid, *Tristia,* ed. R. Merkel, *P. Ovidius Naso* (Leipzig, 1902–4), 3:1–102.

2. f. 91–91v Publii Ouidii Nasonis de pulice opusculum incipit quamquam non putatur Ouidii opus a quibusdam.

[P]arue pulex et amara lues inimica puellis . . .

Et iam nil mallet quam sibi me sotium.

ff. 92–93v blank.

Ps. Ovid, *De pulice libellus,* ed. F. W. Lenz, *Maia* 16 (1962): 313 ff., manuscripts and editions, pp. 304–12; cf. Walther, *Initia,* 13752.

3. ff. 94–138v

[Q]ui fit, Moecenas (*sic*), ut nemo quam sibi sortem . . .

Canidia afflasset peior serpentibus afris . . . Finis deo gratias.

Marginal and interlinear gloss of the scribe in violet and ink of text, on f. 94 only, begins: Stultitiam nostrę inconstantię reprehendit . . .

ff. 139–141v blank.

Horace, *Sermones,* rev. ed., F. Klingner, *Opera* (Leipzig, 1970), pp. 161–239.

Paper. ff. 1–93, watermark of *arbre,* cf. Briquet 772; ff. 94–141, watermark of a *oiseau,* placed within a circle, cf. Briquet 12202 sqq. ff. 141. 207 × 140 mm (136 × 75 mm). 7^{12} (1 wanting), 8^{12} (11–12 wanting), $9–14^{8}$. ff. 1–93, ruled in hard point; ff. 94–141, ruled in pen. Vertical catchwords throughout. ff. 1–91v, written in humanistic cursiva by two hands; ff. 94–138v, perhaps slightly later. ff. 1–91 in 40 long lines. Beginning on the first ruled line throughout. Gloss on f. 94 only, partially written in violet ink.

Bound in brown calf, s. xviii. Trace of an illegible title (?) and pressmark (?) "CXII" written in pen on front cover.

Written in Italy, ff. 1–91v at end of s. xv as suggested by script and watermark; ff. 94–138v, slightly later. Formerly in the library of Richard Heber (1773–1833); *Bibliotheca heberiana,* vol. 11 (Evans), item no. 918, p. 193. See De Ricci, *English Collectors,* pp. 102–5, and W. Y. Fletcher, *English Book Collectors* (London, 1902), pp. 336–41. "Bibliotheca heberiana" stamp not present. Sold 10 February 1836 to J. B. Yates. 9 November 1909, sold by J. Martini at the Anderson sale, New York, item no. 318, clipping of sales catalogue affixed to the verso of the front cover. Bought by P. Wach. Acquired by the Newberry from Ernest F. Detterer, Custodian of the Wing Collection, 1948. "114" written in pencil within a circle on verso of front cover.

Second folio: Iudicis officium est.

De Ricci, 1:603. Faye-Bond, p. 146.

103.8

(Ry 237; 63-140)

Francesco Filelfo, *Odae;* Priscian, *Periegesis*

France s. XV^2

1. ff. 1–102 Francisci Philelphi carminum; Apollo carmen primum (in violet).

Scio qui se dederint inerti . . .

Ferte nouellum.

Text accompanied by occasional contemporary marginal glosses, written by the scribe of the text. f. 93 written in Greek with an interlinear Latin translation in violet ink. ff. 85v–86 "Carmen Tertium" (to Melpomene) includes Greek words with interlinear glosses in violet.

Francesco Filelfo, *Odae*. Five sections of ten poems each, attributed in succession to "Apollo," "Clio," "Euterpe," "Thalia," and "Melpomene." Preface to Francesco Sforza not present. Hain *12954. *B.M. Cat. of 15th-Century Books,* 7:978. Another edition (Paris, c. 1510). Manuscripts listed by G. Benadduci, "Contributo alla bibliografia di Francesco Filelfo," *Atti e memorie della Regia Deputazione di Storia Patria per le Provincie delle Marche* 5 (1901): 501–3. This manuscript unrecorded.

2. ff. 103–122v Prisciani interpretatio ex Dionisio de situ orbis.

[N]ature genitor, que mundum continet omnem . . .

(f. 122v) Omnipotens pro quo genitor mihi premia donet.

Finis felix.

f. 123 with lines 932–83, recto and verso, should follow f. 119.

Priscian, translation of the *Periegesis* of Dionysius, P. van de Woestijne, *La Périégèse de Priscien, édition critique* (Bruges, 1953). This codex unrecorded, M. Passalacqua, *I codici di Prisciano* (Rome, 1978), pp. 382–85.

3. ff. 124–125 (addition c. 1500) Themistoclis uox quam Pindarus Artemisii . . . Levi momento adducti reges nunc habent nunc illum tollunt demittuntque. Datum propterea gallicum prouerbium est (?): Principibus obsequi hereditarium non esse.

Eight lines written as verse, perhaps beginning imperfectly, followed by a commentary in prose; last two lines of text on f. 124 destroyed by water damage. ff. 124v and 125v blank. Proverb in explicit unrecorded by Walther, *Prov*.

Paper, three different watermarks present: ff. 1–48, 86–97, and 124–125, fleur-de-lys, cf. Briquet 7251; ff. 49–85, *tête de boeuf,* cf. Briquet 14223 sqq.; ff. 98–102, letter W, cf. Briquet 9173 sqq. ff. 125. Trimmed to 205 × 148 mm (162 × 88 mm). $1–6^{12}$, 7^{14} (5 stub only), 8^{12}, 9^6 (6 wanting), 10^8, 11^{14} (13 should follow 9, 14 wanting), 12^2. Horizontal catchwords visible on some quires. Ruled in hard point and pencil. Written in gothic cursiva media in 25 long lines beginning on the first ruled line. Headings in violet in script of text. Initials of the odes and sections of the *Periegesis* in red, many omitted. Guide letters for the rubricator throughout. A modern hand has filled in many of the missing initials in pencil, and on f. 82 an initial has been added in modern yellow. Initials of each line of verse washed in yellow; f. 8v, initial of each line of verse touched in red.

Bound in modern parchment over paperboard.

Written in France in the second half of the fifteenth century. f. 125, on a single remounted fragment of paper is written in a hand of s. xvii or xviii, "88 12^m r.o. bien complet," "124" added by a later hand. On another remounted fragment "4719" is written in an eighteenth-century hand. Acquired by the Newberry from B. Weinreb (London), 1963.

Second folio: Quem cruces omnes.

104.5

(56-2424)

Penitential Psalms, Prayers, Hymns, etc.

England s. XIV^2

1. ff. 7–23 (begins imperfectly at the beginning of the quire) // -mine, quoniam infirmus sum . . . quoniam ego seruus tuus sum. Gloria patri. Sicut erat. Kyrieleyson . . . Pater noster. Et ne. Ora pro nobis beate Ieronime. Ut digni. Domine exaudi. Et clamor meus (?).

Seven Penitential Psalms, beginning in 6:3, followed by cues related to the litany of the saints.

2. f. 23–23v Liberator animarum, mundi redemptor Ihesu Christo (*sic*) deus eterne rex immortalis, supplico ego conpeccator immensam clemenciam tuam et per magnam misericordiam tuam . . . eripe me ab omni impedimento mali . . . Amen.

Prayer to be said after the psalms, attributed variously to Bede and Alcuin. *PL* 94:529, 101:493. P. Salmon, *Analecta liturgica* (Studi e Testi, 273; Vatican City, 1974), p. 164, no. 386.

3. f. 24–24v Deus qui liberasti Susannam de falso crimine et Ionam de uentre ceti . . . nisi tu solus, qui in trinitate perfecta uiuis et regnas in secula seculorum. Amen.

Horae eboracenses, p. 73. J. Leclercq, "Anciennes prières monastiques," *Studia monastica* 1 (1959): 391. Wilmart, *Codices reg. lat.,* vol. 1, MS 121, f. 113v.

4. ff. 24v–25 Omnipotens sempiterne

deus, respice propicius preces ecclesie tue . . . ut uiriliter currentes in tuum feliciter mereamur introire regnum. Amen.

Wilmart, *Codices reg. lat.*, vol. 1, MS 12 (England, s. xi), f. 165. See below, text 26.

5. ff. 25–27 Quicumque se cum hac benedictione quotidie deuote benedixerit . . . a papa Bonifatio tres annos indulgencie obtinebit; Oracio (in red). Signum sancte crucis defendat me a malis preteritis, presentibus et futuris . . . ut hic et in eternum saluari merear. Amen. Hoc signum crucis erit in celo et cetera.

See Wilmart, "Prières médiévales," p. 39. Achten, *Lateinischen Gebetbuchhandschriften*, no. 9, f. 57. The same text is in an English book of hours, Cambridge, Saint John's College, 129 (s. xv), f. 94.

6. f. 27 Oratio (in red). Sanctifica, domine, famulum tuum signaculo sancte crucis ut fiat in obstaculum . . . et per pretium iusti sanguinis tui in quo me redemisti, qui cum deo patre et spiritu sancto uiuis et regnas deus per omnia secula seculorum. Amen.

Abbreviated version of *Horae eboracenses*, p. 73. Wilmart, "Prières médiévales," p. 36.

7. f. 27–27v Ad honorem faciei Ihesu Christi (in red). Aue facies preclara pro nobis que in crucis ara facta es . . . deitatis in perenni gloria. Amen.

RH 1787.

8. ff. 27v–28 Deus misereatur . . . Signatum est super nos lumine uultus tui . . . in corde meo (Ps 4:7). Kyrieleyson . . . Pater noster. Aue Marie. Et ne. Sed libera. Fac mecum signum in bono . . . Tibi dixit cor meum . . . domine requiram. Domine exaudi. Et clamor meus.

Cf. *Horae eboracenses*, p. 175, for this text and text 9.

9. f. 28–28v Oratio (in red). Deus qui nobis signatis lumine uultus tui memoriale tuum ad instanciam Ueronice . . . iudicem facie ad faciem secure uideamus dominum nostrum Ihesu Christum qui cum patre et filio et spiritu sancto uiuit et regnat deus per omnia secula seculorum. Amen.

Van Dijk, *Origins*, p. 102, n. 9.

10. ff. 28v–31 Sanctus Leo Rome apostolus fecit hanc oracionem et misit ad regem Carolum et dixit quod quicumque hanc oracionem dixerit uel uiderit illo die non dubitabit de morte subitanea nec morte armorum nec ueneno nec sub inimico, ne de carcere, nec ullo die uictus erit et nullus inimicus super eum illo die habebit superiorem manum; et scias quod si istud breue siue ista nomina quinquiens dixerit uel in mente habuerit, illo die non potest mori mala morte; et scias quod istud breue est utile super feminam parientem; liga istud breue super eam et statim pariet sine periculo; et scias quod qui istud secum deportauerit non dubitabit suum inimicum nec aliquod periculum nec in uia, nec in aqua, nec in bello uictus, nec in turnamento, nec coram iudice, sed semper superiorem manum habebit; Oracio (in red). Domine Ihesu Christe, fili dei, miserere mei et defende me famulum tuum . . . et gaudium habere imperpetuum firmiter speramus.

Cf. *Horae eboracenses*, p. 126.

11. f. 31–31v Oratio (in red). Quesumus, omnipotens et misericors deus, ut qui redempcionis nostre insignia temporaliter ueneramur . . . mereamur. Per Christum dominum nostrum. Amen.

Leroquais, *Heures*, 1:322. *Horae eboracenses*, p. 177. Same text below, text 37.

12. ff. 31v–37 Oratio ad beatam Mariam uirginem sequitur (in red). Sancta Maria, dei genitrix misericordissima, per amorem unigeniti filii tui domini nostri Ihesu Christi cum omnibus sanctis et electis dei ueni in adiutorium meum et dignare intercedere pro me peccatore . . . et nunquam dimittas me sine adiutorio tuo. Amen.

Prior portion (ff. 31v–32) closely related to Barré, *Prières anciennes*, pp. 115–16, n. 84. Leroquais, *Heures*, 1:318, cf. 230.

13. ff. 37–39 Salutacio dei, aue Maria (in red). Aue uirgo uirginum, flos et maris stella lumen gestans . . . et regnemus singuli celo coronati.

RH 2267.

14. ff. 39–40 Quicumque hanc oracionem quotidie deuote dixerit et humiliter ante ymaginem beate Marie uirginis apparebit ei beata Maria facie a facie ante tempus et diem mortis sue et habebit C dies indulgencie lx per papam Clementem in concilio letronence (*sic*); Oratio (in red). Deprecor te, domina mea sancta Maria, mater dei sanctissima, mater gloriosissima, mater orphanorum, consolatio desollatorum . . . et omnibus fidelibus uiuis et de-

functis uitam et requiem eternam concedat. Amen.

Leroquais, *Heures,* 1:34, 40, 51, 240, and 350; *Bréviaires,* 4:213. Wilmart, *Codices reg. lat.* 1:637.

15. f. 40 In nomine et honore domini nostri Ihesu Christi et sancte Marie uirginis et sancti cruci (*sic*) . . . et ministret nobis uite necessaria utriusque. Amen.

16. ff. 40–41 Has quicumque sequentes orationes beate uirginis Marie singulis diebus cum 1 Pater noster et 1 aue Maria deuoto puroque corde dixerit ab omnibus tribulacionibus secure liberabitur (in red, names of prayers in black). Maria dulcis (crossed out by scribe) miseros nos audi loquentes . . . post hanc uitam animas duc ad celi rorem.

RH 11102.

17. f. 41–41v Oratio (in red). O Maria, uirgo uirginum, consolatrix miserorum, precamur te per istas quinque tristicias . . . conregnare qui tecum uiuit.

18. f. 41v–42v Sciendum est quod quicumque hos uersus quotidie dixerit et eos secum portauerit nullo modo morietur inconfessus, per illos enim beata uirgo Maria quemdam scolarem saluauit qui in truncato capite et a corpore remoto mori non potuit donec perfecte et integre confessus fuerat; Istud miraculum fuit factum in Orogausa anno domini millesimo cc°lixxx; ix uersus (in red). Mater digna dei . . . pro pietate dei.

RH 11335. Editions of first five lines: W. von Hartel, *Sitzungsberichte, Akademie der Wissenschaften in Wien (Philosophisch-Historische Klasse)* vol. 112 (1886), p. 727, cf. H. A. Daniel, *Thesaurus Hymnologicus* (Halle, 1841–56), 1:349. Walther, *Initia,* 10755.

19. f. 42v Oratio (in red). Supplicacionem seruorum tuorum, deus miserator, exaudi ut qui sancte dei g[e]nitricis et uirginis Marie . . . a subitanea morte liberemur. Per eundem dominum.

20. ff. 42v–43 De sancta Maria antiphona (in red).

Gaude uirgo que de celis.
Per os dulce Gabrielis . . .
Ffac ut tecum gaudeamus.
In perenni gloria. Amen.

RH 27220.

21. f. 43–43v Oratio (in red). Deus qui salutis eterne beate Marie uirginitate fecunda . . . auctorem uite suscipere dominum nostrum Ihesum Christum filium tuum. Qui tecum.

SMRL 2:473. Cf. Kornik, Polska Akademia Nauk, 30 (s. xv–xvi), f. 76, where it forms part of the Office of the Virgin; see Zathey, *Catalogus,* p. 97.

22. ff. 43v–44 De sancto Christoforo (in red). O sancte Christofore, martir Ihesu, qui pro eius nomine penas pertulisti . . . Oratio (in red). Omnipotens sempiterne deus, qui beato Christoforo martiri tuo tantam gratiam contulisti quod ipsum sanctum corpus . . . concede nobis famulis tuis . . . ualeamus. Per Christum.

Leroquais, *Heures* 2:49.

23. f. 44 De sancto Georgio antiphona (in red).

O Georgi martir pie.
Christi miles et Marie . . .
Ut saluemur mortis hora.

24. f. 44–44v Oratio (in red). Deus qui nos beati Georgii martiris tui meritis et intercessione letificas . . . dona tue gratie consequemur. Per Christum.

25. ff. 44v–45v In illo tempore quo sanctus Gregorius in Roma fuit praesul, una die dum cantabat missam quando uoluit consecrare corpus domini nostri Ihesu Christi apparuit sibi dominus in tali effigie qua depingitur et ex magna compassione quam habuit quando uidit eum in ista figura, concessit omnibus illis qui talem figuram ubicumque fecit depicta deuote flexis genibus aspexerit dicendo quinquies *Pater noster* et quinquies *Aue Maria* xiiii mille annos indulgenciarum, summa omnium dierum xx milia; Istud registtum est in capella de uirgine Marie (*sic*) de Iherusalem in templo; Oratio (in red; words in italics in black). Domine Ihesu Christe fili dei uiui qui pendens in cruce pro peccatoribus dixisti patri, Pater dimitte illis . . . ad salutem quam noueris qui uiuis et regnas cum patre et spirito sancto.

A space of 7 lines separates the rubric from the text.

A prayer related to the *Adoro te;* see *Horae eboracenses,* pp. 80–81.

26. ff. 45v–46 Omnipotens sempiterne deus, respice propicius ad preces meas et da michi fidem rectam . . . ut uiriliter in tuo sancto seruicio concurrens feliciter ad tuum regnum merear peruenire. Amen.

A different recension of text 4 above.

27. f. 46 Oracio ad crucifixum (in red). Domine Ihesu Christe, rex glorie, qui es uerus agnus pro nobis . . . precioso sanguine tuo.

Leroquais, *Heures* 2:91–92.

28. f. 46–46v Oracio ad pedes (in red). Domine Ihesu Christe qui pedes tuos in cruce perforari passus es . . . ad opera sancta et salutifera.

Leroquais, *Heures* 2:91.

29. f. 46v Oracio ad quinque plagas Christi (in red). Domine Ihesu Christe qui te lancea uulnerari contra cor tuum . . . laude et honore semper et ubique. Amen.

Leroquais, *Heures* 2:91.

30. ff. 46v–47 Oracio ad brachia (in red). Domine Ihesu qui tua brachia in cruce extendisti . . . ad opera sancta et salutaria.

Leroquais, *Heures* 2:92.

31. f. 47 Oracio ad os Ihesu Christi (in red). Domine Ihesu qui fel ori tuo oblatum gustasti sed bibere noluisti . . . et abstinenciam.

Leroquais, *Heures* 2:92.

32. f. 47–47v Oratio ad labia (in red). Domine Ihesu Christe qui in cruce labia tua aperuisti . . . et aliis utilia sunt et accepta.

Leroquais, *Heures* 2:92.

33. f. 47v Oratio ad odoratum (in red). Domine Ihesu Christe cuius odoratus semper fuit purus et ordinatus . . . quod odoratu pecaui.

Leroquais, *Heures* 2:92, where this prayer is combined with the *Oratio ad aures Christi*.

34. ff. 47v–48 Oratio ad aures (in red). Domine Ihesu Christe cuius aures contumelias et opprobria pacienter audierunt . . . sed bona et utilia.

Leroquais, *Heures* 2:92.

35. ff. 48–49v Innocencius papa quartus hanc orationem composuit et omnibus eam deuote dicentibus tres annos indulgentie donauit ut sequitur (in red).

Culter uirga cum flagello.
Fforceps, claui cum martello . . .
Mereamur propere. Amen.

A space of 8 lines separates the rubric from the text. Innocentius IV, *Arma Christi*. *RH* 25116.

36. f. 49v Cruci, corone spinee, flagellis, clauis lancee . . . imperpetuum firmiter speramus.

Arma Christi. Leroquais, *Heures* 1:186, 322, 2:207.

37. ff. 49v–50 Quesumus, omnipotens deus, ut qui redempcionis nostre insignia temporaliter ueneramur . . . et sempiternis gaudiis perfrui mereamur per Christum dominum nostrum. Amen.

Same text above, text 11.

38. f. 50–50v De crucifixo (in red).

Aue Ihesu nobilis natus
Dextra palma penetratus . . .
Uultus tui cernitur. Pater Noster (in red).

RH 23555. Stanza 3 of the text as published in *Analecta hymnica* 15:44 omitted. Pater Noster written in red at the end of each verse.

39. f. 51 O quam dulcis memoria . . . nobis Ihesu honor et gloria.

40. f. 51 Deus qui in nomine Ihesu unigeniti tui quod est super omne nomine . . . eius passione ab omni aduersitate protegi et eiusdem in futuro gloria sanari. Qui uiuit.

Same text in Copenhagen, Royal Library, Gl. Kgl. 5. 1596 40, f. 52v (s. xiv–xv).

41. ff. 51–52 De sancta Anna (in red).

Anna sancta Ihesu Christi
Matris mater protulisti . . .
. . . celsi templi gloriam.

RH 1105.

42. f. 52 Deus qui sanctam Annam beate Marie uirginis genitricis tue templum . . . et regnat in unitate spiritus sancti deus per omnia secula seculorum. Amen.

43. ff. 52v–53v Trium puerorum. Benedicite sacerdotes domini . . .

A long list of benedictions interspersed with cues.

44. f. 53v Pater noster. Full text.

45. ff. 53v–54 Ave Maria. Full text.

46. f. 54v Three prayers associated with the preparation for the Mass: Deus qui tribus pueris . . . Ure igne spiritus sancti . . . Acciones nostras, quesumus domine . . .

Cf. Van Dijk, *Ordinal,* p. 177.

47. ff. 54v–55v Oratio (in red). Gracias tibi ago clementissime pater una cum sancto spiritu et tibi domine Ihesu Christe qui me miserrimum et indignissimum peccatorem ad sacerdotalem dignitatem peruenire fecisti . . . et ab omnibus aliis peccatis et negligenciis meis digneris absoluere. Qui cum deo. Per . . .

Cf. Wilmart, p. 381, n. 2.

48. flyleaf, fragment of an unidentified spiritual treatise, s. xv[1].

ff. 45 and 48, spaces left blank for miniatures of the vision of Gregory and the arms of Christ.

Parchment. ff. 49 + 1. Modern foliation 7–55. Paper flyleaf folded to fit in binding (possibly a pastedown from the original binding). Trimmed to 111 × 83 mm (103 × 65 mm). Collation impracticable. Ruled in pen. Written in gothic textualis media in 16 long lines, varying from semiquadrata to quadrata. Vertical strokes used as adjunct to word separation by space. Headings in red in script of text. Punctuation in red on final folios. f. 25, gold dentelle initial with white patterning on ground of magenta and blue, very deteriorated from moisture. Alternating red and blue minor initials. Blue initials with red flourishes mark beginning of some texts.

Bound in modern red morocco.

Written in England in the second half of the fourteenth century. Many of the texts are found in books of hours of English origin. ff. 28v–29, notes on Leo X written in English in an italic script, dated 1513. Acquired by the Newberry from Stanley Morison, 1956.

Faye-Bond, p. 154.

105

(Ry 58-1498; 212)

Collection of Historical and Religious Texts and Prayers

Italy s. XV[2]

f. 1 Diue Lucretie (in gold) de Alagno de Neapoli, clare uirgini et nobilissime domine sue, hunc libellum de uita clarissimarum mulierum romanorum Petrus Cola de Lauro de Spoleto dono dedit quem suum esse tribuit monumentum et pignus amoris.

f. 1v blank.

Contemporary title page. On Lucrezia Alagno (c. 1430–1478), see *Dizionari biografici e bibliografici Tosi* (Rome, 1946), 10:17–18.

1. ff. 2–10v De uita clarissimarum mulierum romanorum. [F]abius consul salutem dicit plurimam Quintiane uirginis. Collegi compendiose iamque pluribus uerbis dicerent (?) et de uita clarissimarum mulierum romanorum, ut sic legendo . . . [S]emphronia romana, Cornelio genere, castimoniam fecit, que non solum claustro noluit cludi cum aliis uirginibus, uerum sibi perpetuam carcerem constituit ut uirginitas non solum factis . . . in coronis et laudibus mulierum clarissimarum nemine (?) aduersante scribi fecerunt.

Unidentified text.

2. ff. 11–12 (addition s. xviii) Pater noster. Sanctissime pater noster, creator noster, redemptor noster, saluator noster qui es in celis, in angelis, in sanctis illuminans eos . . . Sed libera nos a malo preterito, presenti, et futuro. Amen.

f. 12v blank.

Dubious Francis of Assisi, *Expositio in Pater noster,* ed. K. Esser, "Die dem hl. Franziskus von Assisi zugeschriebene Expositio in Pater Noster," *Collectanea Franciscana* 40 (1970): 241–47. See also K. Esser and R. Oliger, *La Tradition manuscrite des opuscules de saint François d'Assise* (Rome, 1972). Stegmüller, *Repertorium biblicum,* 8928; Bloomfield, *Incipits,* 8654.

3. ff. 13–16v Tempore illo quo dominus ad passionem uenire debebat inter multa uerba . . . Et ego dei famulus .N. deprecor assidue ut . . . in adiutorium meum . . . et oret pro nobis suum piissimum filium dominum nostrum Yesum Christum qui cum patre et cum spiritu sancto uiuit et regniat (*sic*) in eternum. Amen.

Ps. Josephus ab Arimathea, *Transitus beatae Mariae,* C. Tischendorf, *Apocalypses apocryphae* (Leipzig, 1876), pp. 113–23. *BHL* 5350.

4. ff. 16v–21v [In] urbe alexandrinorum erat quedam puella annorum duo de uiginti . . . nam et de minimis ossibus que de sarchofago cum oleo effluunt . . . passa est ergo . . . cui est laus et gloria per infinita secula seculorum. Amen.

Vita et passio S. Catherinae, ed. E. Einenkel, *The Legend of St. Katherine,* EETS, o.s., 80 (London, 1884), pp. 6–123. Hain, 5480, ff. 52–65, and 9759, ff. 72–80, etc. *BHL* Supp. 1666a.

5. f. 22 [G]aude uirgo mater Christi, tu que sola meruisti, o uirgo dulcissima . . . per eterna secula. Aue Maria. O Maria mater munda, a peccatis nos emunda per hec septem gaudia, et secundo nos fecunda et duc tecum ad iocunda, paradisi menia. Amen. Spetiosa facta es et suauis. Responsorium. In delitiis tuis sancta dei genitrix. Oratio. Supplicationem seruorum tuorum deus miserator exaudi . . . deus per omnia secula seculorum. Amen.

Suffrage to the Virgin Mary. *Gaude virgo,* ed. Mone, 2:176–77 (contains three lines at the end not in the printed text). *RH* 7021. Van Dijk, *Ordinal,* pp. 368, 372, and 436.

6. f. 22v Aue uirgo Katerina, aue martyr et regina, aue sponsa Christi uera . . . qui uiuit

et regniat (*sic*). Amen. Uersus: Diffusa est gratia in labiis tuis. Responsorium: Propterea benedixit te deus in eternum. Oratio: Omnipotens sempiterne deus ineffabilem misericordiam tuam suppliciter deprecamur ut sicut liquor de membris . . . et omnia mala a nobis clementer auertat . . . Amen.

Suffrage to Catherine of Alexandria, *Ave virgo Catherina,* ed. Mone, 176–77. *RH* 2180.

7. ff. 23–26v Conditores urbis Romę. [I]anus filius Iaphet et nepos Noe edificauit manseolum (*sic*) in quodam monte . . . Ends with a list of the bridges of Rome.

Monuments including theaters, temples, etc., of ancient Rome.

8. f. 27 Italia. Ytalie longitudo que ab Augusta Pretoria per urbem Capuamque porrigitur usque ad oppidum regium . . . quatrigies centena sunt.

Geographic description of Italy citing Varro as a source.

9. f. 27v Septem etates mundi. [P]rima etas mundi fuit ab Adam usque ad Noe, secunda etas fuit a Noe . . . septima usque ad finem mundi.

Brief outline of the ages of the world. Similar texts found in many manuscripts.

10. f. 27v Septem etates hominis. [P]rima etas est infantia et durat usque ad septem annos . . . et durat usque ad mortem.

Cf. Cambridge, University Library, Ggl.1. (s. xiv), f. 393v.

11. f. 28 Prima etas et primi parentes fuerunt Adam [et] Eua, Abel et Caym fratres . . .

First paragraph of text similar to no. 12 infra, apparently intentionally erased.

Lower portion f. 28 and f. 28v blank.

12. ff. 29–38 Prima ętas, a mundi creatione. Primi parentes fuerunt Adam et Eua, Abel et Caym fratres . . . finis operis usque ad annum domini m°ccclxxxv.

f. 38v blank.

Universal chronology of the seven ages of the world including dates of emperors, popes, kings, and men of letters, both classical and medieval.

13. f. 39–39v Crux ✠ Christi sit mecum, crux ✠ Christi est quam semper adoro, crux Christi est uera salus . . . crux ✠ Christi descendat super me et meum maneat semper. Amen.

"IHS" written in violet in the upper margin on f. 39. Leroquais, *Heures* 2:12.

14. f. 39v Nomen dei patris et filii et spiritus sancti sit benedictum in me, fiat michi dominus, queso, fides firma in corde . . . et perseuerantia in bonis operibus usque in finem. Amen. Benedictum sit nomen . . . ut dignus merear exaudiri a te. Per.

15. f. 40 [D]omine Yesu Christe fili dei uiui quia tua potentia est ita magna quod multi surgunt de mane . . . ego miserrimus peccator . . . te adiuuante et conseruante, qui cum patre et spiritus sancto uiuis et regnas deus. Amen.

16. f. 40v [I]uste iudex, Yesu Christe, rex regum et domine qui cum patre semper regnas et cum sancto flamine . . . Tibi uirtus sit perhennis, honor in perpetuum. Amen.

Leroquais, *Heures* 1:155 and 340.

17. f. 41–41v [D]eus omnipotens pater et filius et spiritus sanctus, da mihi famulo tuo .N. uictoriam contra omnes inimicos meos . . . sit mihi ista inuocatio salus et eterna protectio. Amen.

Cf. Leroquais, *Heures* 1:329. *Lyell Catalogue,* p. 373, no. 88.

18. f. 41v [B]eatus est rex Abagaron quia me non uidisti et credidisti . . . me liberum esse concedas qui cum patre. Amen.

Leroquais, *Heures* 2:318.

19. ff. 41v–42v [O] saluator mundi salua me, ✠ domine Yesu Christe filius dei adiuua me ✠ . . . ac defendat nunc et in perpetuum. Amen.

20. ff. 42v–43 [E]go auctem (*sic*) constitutus sum in martiriis sanctorum eius et ipsi predicant preceptum eius ✠ . . . ab insidiis diaboli et omnium maligniorum (*sic*) spirituum me .N. custodiat et defendat. Amen.

21. ff. 43–44v [O] nazarenus rex iudeorum, filius uirginis Marie, miserere mihi peccatori . . . Yesus Christus ab omnibus predictis et ab omni aduersitatis genere me defendat. Amen.

22. ff. 44v–46 [A]ngelus Michael ✠ angelus Gabriel ✠ angelus Raphael . . . succurrite mihi .N. famulo eius . . . non confundor in eternum, alleluya, alleluya, alleluya. Amen.

This text in Troyes, BM, 1372 (s. xv), f. 24v.

23. ff. 46–47 [I]n nomine domini amen, ✠ in nomine patris ✠ et filii et ✠ spiritus sancti.

Amen. ✠ In nomine sanctissime trinitatis et indiuidue unitatis . . . ✠ Yesus autem transiens per medium illorum ibat. Amen.

24. ff. 47v–48v [O] nazarenus rex iudeorum, miserere mihi .N. et in uiam pacis dirige me . . . ut non possis ledere me dei famulum .N. Amen. Fiat. Amen.

25. ff. 48v–50v In infrascripta oratione, in principio ipsius, depicta erat linea longitudinis dimidii palmi; exinde sequebatur rubrica dicens quod erat mensura longitudinis Christi qui quidem fuit quindecies altitudinis linee eiusdem, et ultra multas uirtutes in dicta rubrica contentas. Sequebatur oratio tenoris sequentis quam composuerat sanctus Augustinus ad honorem spiritus sancti, uidelicet. [A] morbo Christi pietate caduco ✠, Leonum ✠, . . . ✠ radix Dauit alleluya ✠ Fiat. Amen.

For the rubric, see notes on the provenance of MS 20.

26. ff. 50v–52v [O] rex in pace uenit ✠ deus homo factus est et uerbum caro factum est . . . Maria regina celi adiuua me .N. ne peream intermedio iuditio. Amen.

27. f. 53–53v [I]n nomine patris et filii et spiritus sancti. Amen. ✠ Deus Abraham, ✠ deus Isaac . . . Christe, miserere mei, Amen.

28. ff. 54–55 Benedicat me, deus pater qui ex nihilo cuncta creauit . . . Exultabit cor meum in salutari tuo, cantabo domino qui bona tribuit mihi et psallam nomini domini altissimi, gloria patri et cetera. Amen.

Horae eboracenses, p. 36.

29. f. 55 [O] Marie filius salus mundi, dominus sit mihi propitius et clemens . . . Libera me .N. a peste. Amen.

30. f. 55–55v [O] Ihesu Christe, saluator mundi, salua me et defende me ab omni malo et presta mihi famulo tuo . . . Da mihi sedem sanctorum tu qui uiuis et regnias (*sic*) in secula seculorum. Amen.

31. ff. 55v–56 [O] uos iudices mei qui me iudicatis uel intenditis iudicare, represento uobis sanguinem Christi . . . in pace dormiam et requiescam.

32. f. 56–56v [In] nomine patris et filii et spiritus sancti. Amen. Sancta Maria mater dei domini nostri Yesu Christi, sancte Iohanne baptista . . . ita pone amorem inter .N. et uxorem eius .N. et letifica animum, cor, et mentes eorum ut in perpetuum bono animo et recta mente inter se diligant et colent. Amen.

33. ff. 56v–57 [In] nomine patris et filii et spiritus sancti. Amen. In nomine beate Marie uirginis in nomine omnium angelorum . . . ✠ Agyos ✠ O Theos ✠ Yschiros ✠ Athanatos ✠ Eleysonymas. Fiat.

34. f. 57–57v In nomine patris et filii et spiritus sancti. Amen. ✠ In nomine inuisibilis trinitatis, ✠ in nomine dei omnipotentis contra malum et dolorem matroni (*sic*) quod habuit sex radices . . . Ac ille dixit, Qui ymmo beati qui audiunt uerbum dei et custodiunt illud, deo gratias. Fiat. Amen.

35. ff. 57v–58v [In] nomine domini nostri Ihesu Christi saluatoris nostri. Amen. Coniuro te matricem per patrem et filium et spiritum sanctum et per uirginem Mariam matrem domini . . . libera hanc .N. famulam tuam ab omni infirmitate et dolore matricis. Amen. ✠ In nomine patri et filii et ✠ spiritus sancti.

36. f. 58v Ego sum uermis et non homo obprobrium hominum et abiectio plebis (Ps 21:7) ✠ Ihesus Christus . . . ut me .N. famulum eius . . . et amplius corpus meum non noceatis, nec in eo permanere ualeatis. Amen. Fiat. Amen.

37. f. 58v Deus ✠ dominus ✠ homo ✠ genitus . . . sicut laberasti beatum Petrum de febre Pater noster et Aue Maria et cetera.

38. f. 59–59v Domine deus meus Ihesu Christe, si ego miser fragilis et abominabilis peccator . . . cum tu domine domine Ihesu Christe sit uerus Yhesus et non est alius. Qui cum. Amen.

39. f. 59v [D]ominus Yesus creator saluator et redemptor meus, ego gaudeo et confiteor me esse creaturam tuam et non esse alienam . . . in me penitenti peccatore quod tuum est et absterge quod alienum est. Qui uiuis. Amen.

40. ff. 59v–60 [O] itaque sciens omnia que uentura erant super eum processit et dixit eis . . . extendisti manum tuam et saluum me fecit dextera tua ✠.

41. f. 60 [O] Christe nazarene crucifixe, respice ad meas miserias et meas tribulationes et angustias . . . ut liberes me ab angustiis et necessitatibus neis (*sic*). Fiat.

42. f. 60 [O] que ferebat datan (*sic*) de corduba ✠ . . . et super uestem meam miserunt sortem. Amen ✠.

43. f. 60v [O] Christus ✠ O Theos ✠ Yschiros ✠ Athanatos . . . absque penitentia et inimicos non timebit.

44. f. 60v [Ad] expellendem demonem ab aliquo eum uexante . . . carmina supradicta scripsit angelus dei in quodam lapide cuidam homini qui filium demoniacum habebat.

45. f. 60v [Co]ntra omne uenenum et contra morsum serpentum, scribe in tassia a parte interiori . . . spiritus sanctus ✠ gratia ✠. Amen.

Parchment. Composite book of the fifteenth century. ff. 60. 167 × 105 mm (100–35 × 70–84 mm). Collation impracticable. Ruled in hard point and pen. Texts 1 and 7–12 written in humanistic cursiva in 12 long lines in light brown ink. The remainder of the medieval book written in humanistic cursiva in very dark ink in 31 long lines, some initials in violet. Text 2 in humanistic cursiva by an eighteenth-century hand.

Bound in Spanish red morocco, s. xviii; arms on the cover include those of Spain and Este (Ferrare) and are perhaps those of the Guzman-Medina family.

Written in Italy in the second half of the fifteenth century. f. 1, three unidentified coats of arms: reading from the left, the arms of a cardinal of the Orsini family (Rome), the arms of the Pagni family (Florence), and unidentified arms (see color illustration). Texts 15, 17, 21, 22, 24, 29, and 35 in masculine form. Text 34 in feminine form. Summary table of contents in French on the front pastedown, s. xix (?); the initials "CN" written below a cross. Acquired by the Newberry from Lathrop Harper, 1958.

Second folio: -ssimis contra mulieres.

Ayer 740

Ptolemy, *Cosmographia*, etc.

Italy — s. XV med.

1. ff. 5–116v Beatissimo patri Allexandrini quinto pontifici maximo Iacobus Angelus (in violet). [A]d tempora Claudii et (*sic*) Ptolomei uiri allexandrini . . . (f. 6) Claudii Ptholomeii cosmographie liber primus habet (in violet) . . . [C]osmographia designatrix imitatio est totius cogniti orbis . . . uersus boream usque ad utrosque polos zodiaci. Claudii Ptolomei uiri allexandrini cosmografie octauus et ultimus liber explicit et cetera (in violet).

Marginal index notes and pointing hands added by a humanistic hand, s. xv.

ff. 1–4v and 117–120v blank.

Ptolemy, *Cosmographia*, tr. Jacobus Angelus. For early editions and manuscripts, see Thorndike and Kibre, 63 and 271, and Thorndike, *History of Magic and Experimental Science*, 1:106. Fischer, *Geographiae codex*, tomus prodromus. To the recorded manuscripts add Brussels, BR, 3942.

2. f. 121 Geometrically drawn astronomical diagram.

f. 121v blank.

3. ff. 122–123v [C]uiuslibet arcus propositi sinum rectum inuenire . . . (f. 122v) et duplicatum est arcus istius corde. Additions of s. xv ex. and two tables of Johannes de Lineriis follow.

ff. 124–128v blank.

Johannes de Lineriis, *Canon on Primum Mobile* (inc.), ed. M. Curtze, "Urkunden zur Geschichte der Trigonometrie im Christlichen Mittelalter," *Bibliotheca mathematica* 1 (1900): 391–93 and 411. Thorndike and Kibre, 276. Thorndike, *History of Magic and Experimental Science*, 3:255–57. This manuscript not recorded.

4. ff. 129–130 [H]oc instrumentum factum est pro inueniendo gradum ascendentium dicitur itaque . . . (f. 129v) paulo minus et cetera. Prima domus uitam censum notat inde secunda, tercia germanos . . . cuique modum seruare suis uelod infrascriptum (?) altis (?).

Cf. *Canones horoscopi instrumenti* in Oxford, BL 19993 (s. xv), f. 1–1v. Thorndike and Kibre, 631.

5. f. 130v (addition s. xvi) Omina (*sic*) igitur instrumentorum sunt hec, primum est armilla suspenssoria ad capiendum altitudinem . . . tabule autem ab hac signate sunt hec.

ff. 131–134v blank.

Nine lines of unidentified text.

6. ff. 135–141 [C]irculus ecentricus dicitur uel egresse cuspidius uel eggredientis centri . . . de reflexione est gradus (?) 1 in minuta 4 et cetera. Et sicut est finis laudetur deus et sanctus Bartholomeus.

Dubious Gerard of Cremona, *Theoria planetarum*, ed. F. J. Carmody (Berkeley, 1942). This codex collated. Thorndike and Kibre, 223. Thorndike, *History of Magic and Experimental Science*, 3:523.

7. f. 141v Astronomical diagrams of the eclipse of the sun and moon.

f. 142–142v blank.

8. f. 143 Astronomical diagram, s. xvi.

ff. 143–144v blank.

9. ff. 145–147v (addition c. 1500) Ad probamdum (*sic*) circa quamlibet speciem numeri utrum bene operatum fuerit utendum est hoc modo generali . . . (f. 147) Quadratum circulo circumscriptum habet se in proportione ad circulum scriptum sicut 14 ad ii . . . 3^m et diuide per primum.

Unidentified scientific text.

ff. 148–149v blank.

10. ff. 150–155v Tractatus de fluxu et refluxu aque maris. Secundum Aristotelem 4° (*sic*) metheororum de his que sunt manifesta sensui putamus sufficienter demonstrasse . . . quare nec motus aquarum ita certo incedunt ordine. Hec de diuersis motibus aque maris opinione Iacobi de Dundis Padauii ciuis et explicit tractatus de diuersis motibus accessus et recessus aque maris compilatus a magistro Iacobo de Dundis.

Corrections in margins, s. xvi.

Jacobus de Dondis, *De fluxu et refluxu maris,* ed. P. Revilli, "Il trattato della marea di Jacopo Dondi," *Rivista geografica italiana* 19 (1912): 200–283. This text also in Milan, Biblioteca Ambrosiana, N334 sup. (s. xv), ff. 1–12.

11. ff. 155v–156 Diagrams of the tides, s. xvi.

ff. 156v–159v blank.

Paper with watermarks of *monts* and *licorne,* not in Briquet. ff. 159. Trimmed to 300 × 315 mm (c. 195 × c. 145 mm). 1^4, $2–12^{10}$, 13^{10} (8–10 wanting), 14^{4+1}, $15–16^8$, 17^8 (an unidentified leaf wanting), 18^6, 19^4. Leaves signed in at least three sequences. Catchwords for text 1 within rectangular decoration, sometimes touched with violet. ff. 5–117 ruled in hard point; ff. 122–122v and 127v–134v ruled in pen; ff. 135–142v ruled in pencil; ff. 143–144v frame ruled in pencil; ff. 150–159v ruled in hard point. Other folios unruled. ff. 5–116v written in Italian hybrida media in 35 lines in two columns; f. 122–122v written in Italian hybrida media in 40 lines, this and following portion only beginning on the first ruled line; ff. 129–130 written in Italian hybrida currens in 44 lines in two columns; ff. 135–141 written in Italian hybrida media with trailing terminal s in 44 long lines; ff. 150–155v written in Italian hybrida media in c. 35 long lines. ff. 5–116, 122–122v, and 150–156 all by one scribe, in brown ink now eating into the paper. All other texts written by a different hand for each. ff. 45–97v, running headings in upper margins written in rustic capitals. ff. 5–123v, headings in violet ink.

Binding identical to Ayer 744.

Written in Italy in the middle of the fifteenth century. f. 5, "Yhesus Maria," written below a hollow pen cross, touched with violet. f. 1, "Cosmographia Claudii Tholomei," written by an Italian hand, s. xviii–xix; below, a circular white sticker, partially removed, with "°38" (?) written in black ink. "CHJ" written in black ink in the lower inner corner on the verso of the last leaf. Front pastedown, printed bookplate of Edward E. Ayer as in Ayer 744. From the Stevens Ptolemy Collection.

Second folio: In quo differt.

De Ricci, 1:548 (no. 36). Butler, *A Check List of Manuscripts in the Edward E. Ayer Collection,* p. 89.

Ayer 741

Ptolemy, *Cosmographia*

Italy s. XV^2

ff. 1–173v Beatissimo patri Alexandro quinto pontifici maximo Angelus. Ad tempora Claudi (*sic*) Ptolomei uiri alexandrini . . . (f. 2) Claudii Ptolomei primus haec capitula habet (in blue) . . . (f. 2v) Claudii Ptolomei liber primus cosmographie incipit feliciter (in violet). Et primo dicit in quo differt cosmographia a corographia (in blue). Cosmographia designatrix imitatio; est tocius cogniti orbis . . . uersus boream atque austrium usque ad utrosque polos zodiaci. Claudii Ptolomei uiri alexandrini cosmographiae octauus et ultimus liber a Iacobo Angelo e graeco in latinum traductus finit felicissimae; Uale qui legis (in alternate lines of blue and violet).

Sparse marginal notes, s. xv ex. or s. xvi.

Translation of Jacobus Angelus. For early editions and manuscripts, see Thorndike and Kibre, 63 and 271, and Thorndike, *History of Magic and Experimental Science* 1:106. Fischer, *Geographiae codex,* tomus prodromus. See also MS Ayer 740.

Paper (exceptionally glossy) with a *fleur* watermark; cf. Briquet 6686–90. ff. 173. Contemporary arabic foliation preceded and followed by a point. 290 × 198 mm (215 × 118 mm). $1–17^{10}$, 18^4 (4 wanting). Parchment anchor strips in center of outer and inner sheets. Leaves signed alphabetically a1 etc. Vertical catchwords preceded and followed by a point. Ruled in hard point. Written in slightly cursive humanistic textualis media in 31 long lines beginning on the second ruled line. Headings in faded violet and blue in script of text. Book divisions marked in roman numerals in black ink in upper margins. f. 1, white initial washed with yellow, c. 8 lines high, decorated with white ivy stem on a ground of faded blue and green, extended to form an inner and upper bracket border. Six similar initials, without yellow wash, 4–10 lines high at the beginning of each book. Minor red rustic humanistic capital initials throughout.

Bound in contemporary dark Italian stamped and ruled calf over wooden boards; an outer rectangular panel formed by a roll of a flower within a beaded lozenge, an inner panel formed by at least two different rope motif stamps one of which also forms a central decorative design; small circular stamps throughout. Same pattern front and back. Two front-to-back fore-edge clasps wanting; fleur-de-lys-shaped catches removed.

Written in Italy, probably central Italy, in the second half of the fifteenth century. Front pastedown, inscription of s. xv ex. or xvi, "No 69 Cosmographia Ptolomei." Back pastedown lower left, "CHJ" written in black ink.

Second folio: Sed nos in cosmographiam.

Butler, *Check List,* p. 89. De Ricci, 1:548 (no. 38).

Ayer 744

Ptolemy, *Quadripartitum,* with the Gloss of Haly ibn Ridwan

Italy s. XV med.

1. ff. 1–226v Incipit liber quadripartiti Ptholomei. [S]cire et intelligere gloriosum est . . . (f. 2) Prologus Haly (in violet). [U]erba que dixit sapientissimus Ptholomeus . . . (f. 4v) Incipit liber 4^{or} partium qui dicitur quadrupartitus (*sic*) Ptholomei philadelphi . . . Res, o Misori quibus perficiuntur pronosticationes . . . Ptholomeus inspexit in omnibus . . . deus te dirigat in uiam rectam, uolui probare utrum iste actor iudicaret . . . secundum tabulas mathematicas et inueni sic. Explicit liber Ptholomei astrologie cum commento Haly.

Marginal index notes and running headings by the scribe and the rubricator. Additional finding notes, glosses, and pointing hands added by several humanistic hands of the second half of the fifteenth century and the first half of the sixteenth century.

Ptolemy, *Quadripartitum,* translated from the Spanish version by Aegidius de Tebaldis, accompanied by the "glosa" of Haly ibn Ridwan, printed Hain 13544 and (Venice, 1519). Thorndike and Kibre, 1351, 1406, and 1687. M. Steinschneider, *Die Europäischen Übersetzungen aus dem Arabischen bis Mitte des 17. Jahrhunderts* (Vienna, 1905; reprinted Graz, 1956), p. 3. A. A. Björnbo, "Die Mittelalterlichen Übersetzungen aus dem Griechischen," *Archiv für Geschichte der Naturwissenschaften und der Technik* 1 (1909): 385–94. To the manuscripts listed add: Limoges, BM, 9 (28), f. 44; Aberdeen, University Library, 36.4 (1426), f. 2; Escorial, Monastery Library, lat. e. III. 4, f. 5; Paris, Bibliothèque de l'université, 593, which has the same explicit as this codex.

2. ff. 227–233v [Q]uia secundum Ptholomeum in secunda parte quadripartiti capitulis primo et 4° . . . de Cartoz et sui termini.

Marginal glosses by the scribe.

A commentary of Haly ibn Ridwan on the *Quadripartitum.* This text follows text 1 above in Cambridge, University Library, KK. IV. 7 (s. xv), ff. 88–91, according to Thorndike and Kibre, 1230.

3. f. 234–234v De partibus Asye et eius regionis notandum est pro expositione secundi quadripartiti quod regnum Cathay est maius regnum . . . in cuius summitate nemo habitare potest.

Unidentified text.

Paper with a watermark of a *tête de cerf,* cf. Briquet 15557, and an undetermined watermark not in Briquet. ff. 234. Original arabic foliation partly visible. 238 × 215 mm (205 × 137 mm). $1–2^{12}$, 3^{10}, $4–6^{12}$, 7^{6} (catchword on f. 76v matches text on f. 77v; text on f. 77 and part of 77v canceled by the scribe), $8–20^{12}$, 21^{2}. Catchwords throughout. Frame ruled in pencil for two columns. Written in northern hybrida media with Italian traits in 28–35 lines, the minims of the first written line hung from the upper ruled line; f. 5v, the scribe, in writing the text of Ptolemy, has lapsed into a northern gothic textualis media. Headings written in humanistic textualis media in violet. Guide letters for the rubricator present. ff. 223v and 225, space for an illumination left blank.

Bound in gold-stamped black morocco in the second half of the nineteenth century by W. Pratt; the name of the binder given on the bookplate of Edward E. Ayer.

Written in Italy (the paper suggests northern Italy) by a northern scribe. According to the information reproduced on the bookplate of Edward E. Ayer, on the front pastedown, Henry Stevens (or his son Henry Newton Stevens) purchased this manuscript for the Ptolemy collection from Quaritch between 1868 and 1898, when it was purchased by Mr. Ayer. Rear flyleaf verso, "Quaritch unb. £8.00." Acquired by the Newberry in 1911 from Edward E. Ayer.

Second folio: Prologus Haly (in violet). Uerba que.

De Ricci, 1:548.

Ayer 746

Astronomical Texts (in Catalan)

Catalonia s. XV med.

1. ff. 2–33 Açi comença lo tractat del stralau del gran stroleck Tholomeu; Rubrica del present libre (in red) . . . (f. 3) Primo es lo anell et ha nom lo penjament et es aquell ab lo quel penja l'estrelu per pendra l'altitud . . . Et abtant ha compliment los tractac del stralau. A deus gracias.

Ps. Ptolemy, *Hispanoarabic Treatise on the Astrolabe.*

2. f. 33v Taula de eleccions segons lo signe en que es la luna (vertically in inner margin).

Astrological table for various activities according to the twelve signs of the zodiac.

3. ff. 34–44 Açi comença la practica de fer l'astralau del gran stroleg Tholomeu per set elims (in red). Volem fer hun superfici rodon pla per figurar en aquell a spera et les sues rodas et los seus punts segons que la obra raquer per aquells . . . per dar compliment a la obra et traure aquella en acte. Et abtant es complida la pratica de fer l'estralau. A deus gracias.

Ps. Ptolemy, *Treatise on the Use of the Astrolabe.*

4. ff. 44v–48v Si volem saber hun pou quant ha de pregont ho qual se vulla altre cosa semblant . . . (f. 45v) que vendria a cascun any lo seu moviment en torn sinquanta hun minut.

ff. 46–48v Tables and diagrams.

Anonymous directions for the use of the astrolabe for surveying.

5. ff. 48v–50v Si volem fer hun instrument per lo qual sapiam quina hora es del dia per la ombre del sol . . . con la ombra de la columpna caura sobra aquesta linia, sera mig jorn.

f. 50v, diagram.

Anonymous treatise on the sundial.

6. ff. 51–70 Dix Jacob, fill de David, fill d'en Bonjorn, per tal com la sciencia matematical entre les altres scencies es singular en fortitud . . . Senyor ver deus, converteix nos, illumina les tues faç et serem fers sans. Et est phinitum.

Canons and Tables of Jacob ben David ben Yomtob (in Catalan); cf. J. M. Millás y Vallicrosa, "Una traducción catalana de las tablas astronómicas (1361) de Jacob ben Yomtob de Perpiñán," *Sefarad* 19 (1959): 365–71. For manuscripts of the Latin version, see Thorndike and Kibre, 454.

7. f. 70v Tabula per saper quantes hores fa de mig jorn segons les latiduds.

8. ff. 71–73 Notes and diagrams on the eclipse of the sun and moon.

9. ff. 73v–102v Astronomical tables, the first dated 1361.

f. 103 blank.

10. ff. 103v–105 (addition s. xvi) Birth records of the children of Rafel and Francesch de Besalú, 1490–1501, sons of Berthomeu de Besalú and his wife, Johanna, see below, text 12. Births recorded in Florence and Venice.

f. 104 blank.

11. ff. 105–108v and the front pastedown (addition s. xv) Recipes in Catalan for medicinal drugs and plasters.

12. f. 109 Birth and death records of the children of Berthomeu and Johanna de Besalú, 1438–1456.

f. 109v blank.

Parchment of southern preparation. ff. 109. Modern foliation begins with front pastedown. 175 × 115 mm (108 × 73 mm). $1–6^{10}$, 7^{12}, $8–9^{10}$, 10^{8} (3 wanting). Catchwords present on quires 1–6. Frame ruled in hard point. Written in gothic cursiva media in 22–28 long lines, sometimes beginning on the upper ruled line, sometimes centered on the first ruled line. ff. 105v–109 written in gothic cursiva currens by one hand. Headings in red in script of text. f. 2, blue initial with red and violet flourishes 4 lines high. Alternating red initials with violet flourishes and blue initials with red flourishes 3 lines high throughout. Minor initials touched with yellow. Tables ruled in black, red, and violet inks.

Bound in contemporary dark brown calf over boards, 5 brass bosses front and back. Two fore-edge clasps wanting. Old spine label "123." Modern box by W. Pratt matches the bindings of Ayer 740 and Ayer 744.

Written in Catalonia in the middle of the fifteenth century. Text 10 added in Italy in the beginning of the sixteenth century. Formerly in the Ptolemy Collection of Henry Stevens (d. 1886); f. 1v, printed bookplate of Edward E. Ayer identical to Ayer 744. Acquired by the Newberry from Edward E. Ayer in 1920.

Butler, *Check List,* p. 89. De Ricci, 1:549.

Greenlee 2

Bernard and Pseudo Bernard of Clairvaux, *Opuscula;* etc.

Germany s. XV²

1. ff. 3–6v Parabola beati Bernardi abbatis de filio regis (in red). Rex diues et prepotens

deus omnipotens filium fecit sibi hominem . . . postremo prouidus et eruditus et perfectus in regno caritatis.

Bernard of Clairvaux, *Parabola I.* Leclercq and Rochais, *Sancti Bernardi opera* 6, pt. 2: 261–67. *PL* 183:757–60.

2. ff. 6v–9 Parabola beati Bernardi abbatis de fide, spe et caritate (in red). Rex nobilis et potens tres habuit filias, fidem, spem et caritatem . . . sed nisi dominus custodie[r]it ciuitatem, frustra uigilat qui custodit eam (Ps 125:1).

Bernard of Clairvaux, *Parabola V.* Leclercq and Rochais, *Sancti Bernardi opera* 6, pt. 2: 282–85. *PL* 183:770–72.

3. ff. 9–13v Parabola beati Bernardi abbatis de nuptiis filii regis et de ornamentis sponse sue (in red). Filius regis supercelestis Iherusalem egressus est ut contemplaretur . . . cum hec sponsa paciatur.

Bernard of Clairvaux, *Parabola VI. Sancti Bernardi opera* 6, pt. 2: 288–95.

4. ff. 14–17 Parabola beati Bernhardi de guerra inter Babilonem et Iherusalem (in red). Inter Babilonem et Iherusalem nulla pax est, sed guerra continua . . . et a dextra caritatis decem millia. Deo gracias (in red).

f. 17v blank.

Bernard of Clairvaux, *Parabola II.* Leclercq and Rochais, *Sancti Bernardi opera* 6, pt. 2: 267–73. *PL* 183:761–65.

5. ff. 18–35v Incipit apologeticum beati Bernardi abbatis ad Wylhelmum de detractione (in red). Uenerabili patri W[ylhelmo] frater B[ernardus] fratrum, qui in Clareualle sunt, inutilis seruus, salutem in domino. Usque modo si qua me scriptitare iussistis, aut inuitus . . . Et hec non est detractio, sed attractio, quod ut nobis a uobis fiat semper, omnino precor et supplico. Ualete. Amen. Finit apologeticum beati Bernardi abbatis (in red). Apologeticus autem id est excusatorius, responsorius, defensorius, negatorius in eodem sensu. Ab apos quod est re et logos sermo quasi sermonis relacio uel responsio. Item apologicus autem id est excusatorius uel reprehensorius.

Bernard of Clairvaux, *Apologia ad Guillhelmum.* Prologue wanting. Leclercq and Rochais, *Sancti Bernardi opera* 3:80–108. *PL* 182:898–918.

6. ff. 36v–37. Three concluding portions from Bernard of Clairvaux, *Sermones in Cantica canticorum,* nos. 47, 49, and 50, here numbered by the scribe 48, 50, and 51 respectively.

f. 37v blank.

7. ff. 38–61 Tractatus de institutione morum beati Bernardi clareuallensis abbatis (in red). Hortatur quidem timidam mentis mee impericiam quantum sepe fraterna caritas . . . et flebilis supplexque tu ora hoc modo.

ff. 61v–62v blank.

Ps. Bernard of Clairvaux, *Tractatus de ordine vitae. PL* 184:561–84; cf. 147:477.

8. ff. 63–67v Incipit Basilius de uita solitaria (in red). Libet de singularis uite meritis pauca perstringere . . . domus non manu facte sed etiam eterne in celis, ipso prestante qui cum patre et spiritu sancto in celis regnat per omnia secula seculorum. Amen.

Peter Damian, *Liber qui dicitur dominus vobiscum.* Chapter 19. *PL* 145:246–51. Attributed to Basil in many manuscripts.

9. f. 68–68v De solitudine beatus Bernardus super canticum sermo xli (*sic;* in red). O sancta anima sola esto, ut soli regi omnium serues teipsam . . . si accepisset in me similiter potestatem. Et cetera (in red).

Bernard of Clairvaux, extract from *Sermo 40 in Cantica canticorum.* Leclercq and Rochais, *Sancti Bernardi opera* 2:27. *PL* 183:983D–84C.

10. ff. 68v–75v Admonicio sancti Effrem de iudicio et compunctione eiusdem (in red). Uenite, dilectissimi fratres, exhortacionem meam suscipite et semper mementote consilii mei peccatoris et imperiti Effrem . . . que sunt edificia anime, fundamentum cordis, mentis illuminacio, ut omnis qui hec meditatur, trahatur ad uitam eternam. Amen.

f. 76 blank.

Same Latin translation in Metz, BM, 223 (s. xi); cf. Assemanus, *Ephraemi Syri opera omnia* 2:50–56.

11. f. 76v Ex psalmo, Natus in Iudea deus. Quoniam cogitacio hominis . . .

Unidentified commentary on Ps 75:11, etc.

12. ff. 77–99v Consciencia in qua anima perpetuo mansura est, edificanda est . . . malas a corde tuo expellere. Hec sepe cogita; Explicit liber confessionum (crossed out and corrected in the script of the following text to de consciencia) beati Bernhardi abbatis (underlined in red).

Chapters marked by scribe in left margins.

Cf. Ps. Bernard of Clairvaux, *De interiore domo*. Prologue wanting. *PL* 184:509 sqq.

13. ff. 99v–101 [Ex] Bernardus super canticum sermone xii (*sic*). [O]rigo fontium et fluminum omnium mare est . . . hoc ego ipsis uirtutibus mirabilius iudico.

Bernard of Clairvaux, extract from *Sermo 13 in Cantica canticorum*. Leclercq and Rochais, *Sancti Bernardi opera* 1:68. *PL* 183:833–35D.

14. f. 101–101v Idem infra in eodem sermone. Omnis igitur de bonis multiformis . . . et in iusticia exaltabuntur. Hic ille ubi supra.

Bernard of Clairvaux, extracts from *Sermo 13 in Cantica canticorum*. Leclercq and Rochais, *Sancti Bernardi opera* 1:73–74. *PL* 183:838A–B.

14 bis. f. 101v O quam felix et sapiens qui oblatum conuicium et illatum . . . Aliud est consciencia, aliud timor consciencie . . . ad aliquod faciendum uel non faciendum animi deliberacione firmata.

Unidentified excerpts.

15. ff. 102–104v Sermo beati Augustini episcopi de persecucione christianorum (in red). Frequenter diximus, fratres carissimi, quod semper christiani persecucionem patiuntur . . . me et uos ab omnibus insidiis diaboli tutos saluare. Qui uiuit in secula seculorum. Amen. Explicit sermo beati Augustini episcopi de persecutione christianorum (underlined in red).

Jerome, *Tractatus de persecutione christianorum*. *BHM* 241. Attributed to Augustine, Grégoire, pp. 57 and 313.

16. ff. 104v–110 Incipit liber beati Augustini episcopi de beato latrone. Deus erat in Christo mundum reconcilians sibi, id est diuinitas operabatur in corpore . . . memento mei, domine, cum ueneris in regnum tuum. Explicit liber beati Augustini episcopi de beato latrone (underlined in red).

Eusebius Gallicanus, *Homilia XXIV de beato latrone*, ed. F. Glorie, *CC* 101 (1970): 279–90.

17. ff. 110–118 Incipit liber beati Augustini de tribus habitaculis. Tria sunt sub omnipotentis dei manu habitacula . . . deum omnipotentem, benignum et misericordem. Cui honor et gloria et nunc et per omnia secula seculorum. Amen. Explicit liber beati Augustini de tribus habitaculis; Deo gracias (underlined in red).

f. 118v blank.

Ps. Augustine, *De triplici habitaculo liber I*. A. Gwynn, *Scriptores Latini Hiberniae,* vol. 1 (Dublin, 1955), 106–24. *CPL* 1106. *PL* 40:991–98.

18. ff. 119–133v Incipiunt septem capitalia uicia (in red).

f. 134–134v blank.

Schematic diagram of the seven deadly sins and their divisions and subdivisions.

Paper, ff. 76–77, 82–83, 88–89, 95–96, and 106 parchment. ff. 134. Modern foliation includes two front postmedieval flyleaves. 143 × 105 mm (100 × 65 mm). 1^{12} (12 wanting), $2–5^{12}$, 6^{14}, 7^{14} (the outer two and the center bifolia, parchment), 8^{12}, 9^{5} (2 an inserted parchment leaf), 10^{12}, 11^{16}. Catchwords present after f. 76; the catchword on f. 118v does not match the one on f. 119. Leaves of quire 10 signed b1–b6 in red. Frame ruled in ink. Written in gothic hybrida media in 25–27 long lines with minims of the first written line hung from the upper ruled line. Headings begin on the upper ruled line. Texts 11, 13, and 14 written in hybrida currens in 27–31 long lines. Headings written in red in script of text. ff. 1–76v, German style blue initials 5–7 lines high; ff. 77–118v, German style red initials 2–4 lines high.

Bound in contemporary parchment, like that used for the text. Table of contents written on the front cover, s. xv ex. or s. xvi in.

Written in Germany in the second half of the fifteenth century. On the front cover, an inscription of s. xv ex. or xvi in., "Liber domus sororum in Coesfuldia ordinis sancti Augustini." This convent unrecorded by Cottineau. Sold by M. Breslauer (Berlin) to William B. Greenlee in 1922. Acquired by the Newberry before 1935 from William B. Greenlee.

Second folio: coacta in.

De Ricci, 1:608.

Wing ZW 1.4a

(W 9619)

Antoninus, *De Censura Ecclesiastica*

Central Italy s. XV med.

ff. 1–100 Tractatus de censuris ecclesiasticis (in faded red). Incipit prologus in 4ta parte summe domini Antonini archiepiscopi de Florencia de materia excomunicacionis siue de censura ecclesiastica (in red). Excomunicacio dicitur exclusio a communione . . . (ends imperfectly at the end of the quire, words in italics are catchwords). Extra., de clamdestina [de]sponsatione, *cum inhibitio* (Decretales IV.3.3) //

Ends imperfectly in chapter 99. *GW* 2068–2071. Editions listed: Orlandi, *Bibl. Ant.*, p. 303 sqq. Manuscripts listed by Kaeppeli, 253; this manuscript recorded, p. 90. Cf. Antoninus, *Summa moralis*, tit., 24–29.

Parchment of southern preparation. ff. 100. 155 × 112 mm (102 × 71 mm). $1–10^{10}$. Leaves signed a1–k5. Catchwords underscored in red. Ruled in pencil. Written in Italian gothic rotunda media, showing humanistic influence, in 36 lines in two columns beginning on the first ruled line. Incipits touched with yellow. Headings in red in script of text. f. 1, red initial with blue and red flourishes 7 lines high. Smaller alternating red and blue initials with contrasting flourishes throughout. Initials in the text touched with yellow. Alternating red and blue paragraph marks.

Bound in parchment over paperboard.

Written in central Italy in the middle of the fifteenth century. f. 1, lower right margin, largely obliterated library stamp bearing a fleur-de-lys; upper left margin, "56" written in pen. Front flyleaf, "132" written on a round white sticker. Notes dating after 1926 in French on front pastedown. No. 4 in the *Checklist of the C. L. Ricketts Collection*. Acquired by the Newberry from the estate of C. L. Ricketts, 1942.

Second folio: non gaudet.

Faye-Bond, p. 156.

Wing ZW 1.4b

(W 9169)

Basilius, *Epistola ad Nepotes de Utilitate Studii in Libros Gentilium*, Translation of Leonardi Bruni; A Humanistic Selection of Classical and Pseudo-Classical Letters

Italy s. XV med.

1. ff. 1–24v Leonardi Aretini praefatio in Magnum Basilium de institutis iuvenum incipit (in violet). Ego tibi hunc librum, Coluci . . . (f. 2v) Praefatio finit. Incipit Basilius (in violet). Multa sunt filii que hortantur me . . . quod uos non paciamini recta consilia aspernantes. Finit (in violet).

Basilius, *Epistola ad nepotes de utilitate studii in libros gentilium*, translation of Leonardo Bruni, *GW* 3700–3719, prologue edited by Baron, *Leonardo Bruni Aretino*, pp. 98–100. On manuscripts, see Pastor, *History of the Popes* 1:10, n. 1 (list of 24 Vatican manuscripts); Baron, p. 98; Kristeller, *Iter italicum* 1:105, etc. This codex recorded by L. Schucan, *Das Nachleben*, p. 240.

2. f. 25 Phillus (*sic*) Aristoteli salutem dicit (in violet). Filium mihi genitum scito . . . et rerum istarum susceptione.

Ps. Phillip of Macedonia, *Epistolae ad Aristotelem*, ed. R. Hercher, *Epistolographi graeci* (Paris, 1873), p. 466, n. 7. *Epistolae regum, principum . . .*, p. 209. Prete, *Two Humanistic Anthologies*, p. 21.

3. f. 25–25v C. Fabritius consul romani (*sic*) salutem dicit Pyrro regi (in violet). Nos pro tuis iniuriis continuo animo commoti inimiciter bellare tecum studemus . . . Tu nisi caues iacebis.

Ps. Caius Fabritius, *Epistola ad Pyrrum*, printed in *Epistola regum, principum . . .*, p. 278. This text also in Milan, Biblioteca Ambrosiana, H 118 inf. (s. xv), f. 132v; see Sabbadini, *Scoperte dei codici latini*, p. 175, n. 14.

4. f. 25v Cesar imperator Ciceroni salutem (in violet). Recte auguraris de me . . . Nihil enim malo quam et me simile esse mei et illos sui.

Caesar, *Epistola ad Ciceronem* = excerpt from Cicero, *Epistola ad Atticum*, IX, 16, ed. by E. O. Winstedt (Cambridge, Mass., 1962–67), 2:260–62. This text also in MS 93.1. Cf. examples listed by *Manuscrits classiques latins*, Chigi H vi 181, etc.

5. f. 26 Uirgilius Augusto Cesari salutem dicit (in violet). Ego, ut frequentes epistolas a te accipio . . . ad id opus multaque quia potiora impertiar. Uale.

Virgil, *Epistola ad Caesarem Augustum*, excerpt from Macrobius, *Saturnalia*, I, 24, 11, ed. C. Nisard, *Oeuvres complètes* (Paris, 1883), p. 219. Printed separately in *Epistolae regum, principum . . .*, p. 204.

6. f. 26–26v Uirgilius Macenati (*sic*) suo salutem dicit (in violet). Rufum Pomponium libertum tuum nouelle uidi . . . Philelphum reconciliet, suus est. Uale.

Ps. Virgil (Pier Candido), *Epistola ad Maecenatem*, ed. L. Barozzi and R. Sabbadini, *Studi sul Panormita e sul Valla* (Florence, 1891), p. 23, n. 10. For other examples, see *Manuscrits classiques latins*, vol. 1, Barb. lat. 2087, etc.

7. ff. 26v–27v Plutarchus Traiano salutem dicit (in violet). Modestiam tuam noueram non appetere principatum . . . quod impernitiem (*sic*) imperii non pergis, autore Plutarco. Uale.

Ps. Plutarch, *Epistola ad Traianum*. Same text in Milan, Ambrosiana N. 30 sup., f. 35. See Sabbadini, *Scoperte dei codici latini*, p. 175, n. 14, and Florence, Biblioteca Laurenziana 89 sup. 37 (s. xv). Text different from that printed in *Epistolae regum, principum . . .*, pp. 131–32. See A. Momigliano, "Notes on Petrarch, John of Salisbury, and the Institutio Traiani," *Journal of the Warburg and Courtauld Institutes* 12 (1949): 189–90.

Parchment of southern preparation. ff. 29. Foliated 1–27, beginning with the third leaf. ff. 1–2, later additions; f. 1 grafted on old stub. 157 × 104 mm (111 × 69 mm). 1^{10} (1–3 removed, 2 and 3 replaced by blanks), $2–3^{10}$. Formerly part of a larger codex. Quires numbered on verso of last folio in middle of lower margin X^{m}–XII^{m}. Quires 1–9 missing since manuscript was bound in the eighteenth century. Note on front pastedown in pseudo humanistic script of s. xix, "Leonardo Salusti (*sic*) prefatio in magnum basilium, 27 feuillets." Horizontal catchwords on lower inner margins. Ruled in hard point. Written in brown ink in humanistic semi-cursiva in 20 long lines; f's and s's descend below line. Occasional use of cursive form of g and of hanging short terminal s. f. 1, headings in violet, written in rustic capitals, elsewhere also in violet but in script of text. Index notes of proper names in violet in script of text in outer margins. Two gold initials with white vine stems on grounds of green, blue, and magenta: on f. 1, 7 lines high, on f. 2v, 5 lines high.

Bound in stamped Italian red-brown morocco, s. xviii.

Written in Italy in the middle of the fifteenth century. Rear pastedown, "Pagine S.A." and "245," crossed out. Front pastedown, clipping from an English catalogue c. 1870, this manuscript item no. 79. "No. 14" written on the corner of a blue and white sticker; "22" written in pencil. "189," an old pressmark, written on spine label. f. 1, armorial bookplate of Henrici Alani, i.e., Henry Ellis Allen; sold by his son Samuel Allen, Sotheby's, 30 January 1920, lot 6; bought by Bernard Quaritch, see De Ricci, *English Collectors,* p. 189. No. 3 in the *Checklist of the C. L. Ricketts Collection;* his name on first flyleaf. Acquired by the Newberry from his estate, 1941.

Second folio: ut magnus.

De Ricci, 1:644.

Wing ZW 1.41

Latin Lexicon

Italy s. XV[1]

ff. 1–36v De modica immo nulla sciencia elargita michi diuinitus concupiscens aliquod exibere munusculum quoddam opusculum siue aggressurus in quo totaliter alfabetum . . . Ago plura significat . . . Alo, lis, id est nutrio . . . Arceo . . . Aspiro . . . Uado . . . Uigeo . . . Uro, si, stum, id est cremo . . . Finito libro referamus gratiam Christo.

Lexicon of c. 700 *lemmata,* alphabetized by first letter only. Illustrative examples present for the great majority of entries.

Parchment. ff. 36 + i. 204 × 153 mm (148 × 110 mm). $1–3^{8}$, 4^{12}. Ruled in pencil. Prickings in outer margins. Written in Italian gothic textualis media with one-story a in 37 lines in two columns. f. 1, red and blue flourished initial 6 lines high. Alternating minor red initials with blue flourishes and blue initials with red flourishes throughout. Alternating red and blue paragraph marks denote entry points.

Bound in original geometrically ruled brown calf over wooden boards.

Written in Italy in the first half of the fifteenth century. Rear pastedown, crude heraldic device drawn in pen, fifteenth-century grammatical notes in Latin, obscure note of s. xvi in Italian. f. 1, lower margin, ink stamp "MN" of Giovan Battista Niccolini (1782–1861), Florence. Reported by De Ricci to have been lot n. 200 in an English sale c. 1850, not confirmable from the manuscript, but traces of what may have been a catalogue clipping are visible on verso of front cover. Sold by Sotheby's at the Samuel Allen sale, London, 30 January 1920, lot no. 72 to Quaritch; on this sale, see De Ricci, *English Collectors,* p. 189. No. 1 in the *Checklist of the C. L. Ricketts Collection.* Acquired by the Newberry from the estate of C. L. Ricketts, 1941.

Second folio: et indicitur.

De Ricci, 1:653.

Wing ZW 1.45

(63-38)

Collection of Italian Prose and Verse

Italy s. XV

1. front pastedown
Canti zoiosi et dolci melodia . . .
Fame gustare de quello che se dice.

Edited in *Cinque laudi del buon secolo di nostra lingua ridotte a miglior lezione* (Modena, 1862). Zambrini, *Le Opere volgari,* col. 551. Tenneroni, *Inizii,* p. 74.

2. ff. 1–44 Con cio sia cosa che lo transito de la morte si e molto teribile . . . Domine paratus sum et non sum turbatus a cio che possiamo gaudere in eterno cum il signore il quale e benedicto e laudato in secula seculorum. Amen.

Ars moriendi, in Italian, a translation different from *GW* 2618–29; cf. M. C. O'Connor, *The Art of Dying Well* (New York, 1942), pp. 97–101 and 157–62.

3. ff. 44–45 Interogauit sanctum Antonium quidam dicens quid custodiens placebo deo . . . et sic perseuerauit cum magna austeritate usque ad mortem et requieuit in domino. Amen. Laus deo semper. Amen. Bap[tista].

Adhortationes sanctorum patrum, a version differing from the translation of Jerome, excerpts: I, 1 and 21; III, 21. *PL* 73:856, 858, and 863. *BHM* 570.

4. ff. 45–47v

[M]adre de Christo o gloriosa e pura . . .
Si che la possa ormay uicere (*sic*) in pace.

S. Serdini da Siena, "Capitolo a Maria vergine composto per la peste del 1390," ed. Emilo Pasquini, *Rime* (Bologna, 1965), pp. 105–9.

5. ff. 47v–50

[Q]uelle brace tue uirgine Maria . . .
Collunt, adorant, predicant et cetera.

Unidentified poem, in Italian, three of last four lines in Latin.

6. f. 50–50v

[O] uirgine matre figlia del tuo figlio . . .
Prieghi ti porgo, e prego non siano scarsi.

Bernard's prayer to the Virgin from Dante, *Paradiso,* XXXIII, 1–21 and 28–30.

7. ff. 51–52

[A]ue fuit prima salus . . .
Celi portas o Maria.

Jacopone da Todi (?), *Ave Maria. RH* 1801.

8. ff. 52–55

[U]irgine bella che de sole uestita . . .
Che acoglia il mio spirito ultimo in pace.
Amen.
Laus Christo. Amen.

ff. 55v–59 blank.

Petrarch, *Canzoniere,* 366, ed. G. Contini (Alpignano, 1974), pp. 281–85.

9. f. 59v (addition s. xviii)

Audi benigne conditor nostras preces . . .
Fusas quadragenario.

ff. 60–63v originally blank.

RH 1451, first stanza only accompanied by musical notation. f. 60, "aatten cor (?)" written by the same hand. f. 61, the incipit of a religious poem, s. xix.

Parchment of southern preparation. ff. i + 63 + i. 145 × 101 mm (96 × 65 mm). $1–6^{10}$, 7^{4} (1 wanting). Vertical catchwords. Ruled in light brown ink. Written in Italian gothic textualis rotunda media with pointed one-story a. f. 1, blue initial decorated with patterned red flourishes 7 lines high, flourishes extending into the margin. ff. 1–44v, simple red initials 2 lines high. Guide letters for rubricator present throughout.

Bound in rebacked stamped leather over wooden boards, s. xv. Front and back, ruled panels decorated by a margin of rope motif employing at least two different stamps. In the interior, two small and one large lozenge formed from two rope motif stamps, one of which is identical to one of the two used in the margins. The lozenges are decorated with small double circle stamps in clusters of three on each inner corner of the panels. Fore-edge clasp removed. Spine and fore-edge, repaired in s. xix or xx.

Written in Italy, possibly northeast Italy as indicated by the orthography, by Baptista, signed f. 45, in the middle of the fifteenth century. ff. 1, 44v (in red), 55, and 63v, scribe has written "YHS." Rear pastedown, an Ave Maria written in a hand of c. 1500. ff. 55 and 61, notes of s. xvi in praise of the Virgin Mary. Acquired by the Newberry from H. P. Kraus, *Bulletin,* no. 63 (8 October 1962).

Second folio: che lo nostro.

Wing ZW 1.467

(W 9619)

Pseudo Diogenes Sinopensis, *Epistolae,*
Translation of Francesco Griffolini Aretino

Italy [*Illustrated*] 1467

ff. 1–33 Francisci Aretini in Diogenis Cinici epistolas elegia ad beatissimum patrem Pium II pontificem maximum (in violet). [A]d uaticani prę̨clara palatia Petri uade, precor, nostri diui Thalia memor . . . (f. 2v) Incipit Prę̨fatio (in violet). [D]iogenis philosophi epistolas nuper a me e greco in latinum traductas . . . (f. 4) Crateti (in violet). [A]udio quam iniquo animo feras . . . Bonum nanque esse secundum . . . Polliceri autem perfacile. Telos, Amen. Neapoli Ioannes Marcus parmensis tranquille transcripsit, 1467 (in violet).

Unnumbered leaf before f. 1 and ff. 33v–34v blank.

GW 8397–98. Other manuscripts, Alexander and De la Mare, *Italian Manuscripts,* p. 75 and no. 1; *Catalogo dei libri,* pp. 11–12; Madrid, BN, 10037, f. 83v.

Parchment. ff. 35. 181 × 125 mm (125 × 68 mm). 1^{8+1}, $2–4^{8}$, 5^{8} (3–8 wanting). Quires signed 1–4 surrounded by radiating dashes and dots. Catchword present on quire 1, trace of a catchword for quire 3. Ruled in hard point. Prickings visible in outer margins. Written in humanistic textualis formata in 23 long lines beginning on the first ruled line. Headings in violet in rustic capitals. Incipit on f. 2v in rustic capitals with letters alternately in violet and black ink. Names of *personae* in violet in rustic capitals or in script of text.

Bound in restored Italian stamped calf over wooden boards, s. xv. Panel formed by two rope-motif stamps, each repeated twice, four small flower stamps in the center; decorated with rules; same pattern front and back. Fore-edge clasp wanting; catch with "Yhs" on the rear board. Additional space in spine indicates that several quires were removed from the end of the codex.

Written in Naples by Giovanmarco Cinico of Parma in 1467, signed and dated on f. 33. This codex one of four or five manuscripts of this text written by the same scribe. Manuscripts written by him listed in *Colophons de manuscrits occidentaux,* 10444 sqq.; this manuscript no. 10460. See also Alexander and De la Mare, *Italian Manuscripts,* p. 75, and *Catalogo dei libri,* pp. 11–12. This manuscript formerly in the library of Alfonso of Aragon in Naples; see De Marinis, *La Biblioteca napoletana dei re d'Aragona,* vol. 1, no. 5. in the list of Cinico manuscripts. This is not the manuscript of Diogenes copied by Giovanmarco which belonged to the Marchese Girolamo d'Adda and Charles Fairfax Murray; cf. De Ricci, 1:653. Purchased by C. L. Ricketts from de Marinis, described in his catalogue 8 (1908), lot no. 25 and plate viii and in catalogue 11 (1911), lot no. 32. No. 2 in the *Checklist of the C. L. Ricketts Collection.* Acquired by the Newberry from the estate of C. L. Ricketts, 1941.

Second folio: Paranusque biceps natus.

De Ricci, 1:653.

Wing ZW 141.46

(W 9618-48)

Italian Gothic Alphabet

Northern Italy s. XV ex.

Italian gothic display script alphabet of mixed rustic capitals and uncials followed by Italian gothic rotunda alphabet, all drawn geometrically in ink and filled with yellow on a square grid ruled in pen. One letter on each page. On this and related alphabets, see G. Mardersteig, "Leon Battista Alberti e la rinascita del carattere lapidario romano nel quattrocento," *IMU* 2 (1959): 298. To these add Mantua, Biblioteca Comunale, 2541BV6; see *Tesori d'arte nella terra dei Gonzaga* (exhibition catalogue; Mantua, 1974), no. 250.

Very thick paper. ff. 48. 300 × 200 mm. 1^2 (1 is the front pastedown), $2–3^8$, 4^6, $5–6^8$, 7^8 (8 is the rear pastedown).

Bound in parchment over pasteboard, s. xvi.

Written in northern Italy. Formerly in the library of the Benedictine abbey of Saint John the Evangelist in Parma [Cottineau, 2:2224]. f. 1, note of the last quarter of the fifteenth century written in humanistic cursiva, "Iste liber est monasterii [written over monachorum] congregationis sancte Iustine ordinis sancti Benedicti de obseruantia deputatus monasterio sancti Iohannis euangeliste de Parma [three preceding words written over an erasure], signatus numero 68." This monastery united to the congregation of Saint Justina in 1477. Vat. Urb. lat. 597 also belonged to this library.

Faye-Bond, p. 156. Collins, *Anglo-Saxon Manuscripts,* pp. 66–67.

Wing ZW 141.48

(W 9619)

Composite Model Alphabet Book

Northern Italy s. XV^2

Italian gothic rotunda and northern gothic textualis letters geometrically drawn in black ink and filled with yellow on a square grid ruled in hard point, one letter per leaf. ff. 2v, 3v, 4v, 5v, 7v, and 8v blank. ff. 1v, 9v, and 10v, gothic capital letters in black with violet flourishes, cut from another sheet of paper and pasted into position. f. 11v, roman square capitals A–T in pink and green, written on strips cut from another sheet and pasted in this codex; this leaf reproduced by J. Ryder, *Lines of the Alphabet in the Sixteenth Century* (London, 1965), p. 19.

Paper with a watermark of a *couronne;* cf. Briquet 4763. One disbound quire of 10 leaves, f. 11 loose on different paper from ff. 1–10. 213 × 145 mm.

Written in northern Italy, as indicated by the paper, in the second half of the fifteenth century. f. 1, "Milan, 1885" written in black ink. Sold by Jacques Rosenthal to C. L. Ricketts in 1907, no. 5 in the *Checklist of the C. L. Ricketts Collection.* Acquired by the Newberry from the estate of C. L. Ricketts, 1941.

De Ricci, 1:655. Collins, *Anglo-Saxon Vernacular Manuscripts in America,* pp. 66–67.

Wing ZW 141.481

(W 9619)

Roman Capital Alphabet

Northern Italy s. XV^2

Roman capital alphabet drawn geometrically in black ink on a rectangular grid ruled in pencil. One letter per folio, versos blank. On this alphabet, see F. W. Goudy, "The Roman Alphabet, Its Origin and Esthetic Development," *Ars Typographica* 2 (1926): 202–5 (plates of the letters G and R); R. Bertieri, "Gli studi Italiani sull' alfabeto nel Rinascimento," *Gutenberg Jahrbuch,* 1929, pp. 269–86; S. Morrison, *Fra Luca de Pacioli* (New York, 1933), p. 19; S. H. Steinberg, "Medieval Writing Masters," *The Library,* ser. 4, vol. 22 (1941), p. 14, and "A Hand-list of Specimens of Medieval Writing Masters," *The Library,* ser. 4, vol. 23 (1942), p. 193; M. Meiss, *Andrea Mantegna as Illuminator* (New York, 1957), pp. 97, n. 2, and 98, n. 15, and fig. 96; D. E. Miner, P. W. Filby, and V. I. Carlson, *2,000 Years of Calligraphy* (exhibition catalogue; Baltimore, 1965), no. 54 and plate of ff. 12v–13; D. M. Anderson, *A Renaissance Alphabet: Il Perfetto scrittore parte secunda di Giovan Francesco Cresci* (Madison, Wisconsin, 1971), fig. 7 (cf. f. 17).

Paper with an *arc* watermark; cf. Briquet 812. ff. 24. 190 × 145 mm. 1^8 (1, 2, 7, and 8 loose), 2^8 (1 loose), 3^8. Disbound.

Written in northern Italy. Formerly in the Andrea Teissier collection (Venice), his sale Munich, May 1900, lot no. 895. Purchased from Jacques Rosenthal by C. L. Ricketts in 1907; No. 7 in the *Checklist of the C. L. Ricketts Collection.* Acquired by the Newberry from the estate of C. L. Ricketts, 1941.

De Ricci, 1:655.

INDEX OF AUTHORS, TITLES, AND SUBJECTS

For the sake of simplicity and to facilitate consultation, all persons who died before 1500 have been listed under their Christian names.

INCIPITS OF LATIN PRAYERS AND UNIDENTIFIED OR DIFFICULT-TO-IDENTIFY TEXTS AND FRAGMENTS

INDEX OF SCRIBES, FORMER OWNERS, AND SELECTED CODICOLOGICAL CHARACTERISTICS

DATED AND DATABLE MANUSCRIPTS

★ = *black-and-white illustration.* † = *color illustration.*

Call No.	Date		Place
f1	s. xi^{1}	★	Saint Peter of Moissac (?)
f2	s. xi^{1}	†	Southern France
f3	s. xi^{2}		Novalesa
+7	before c. 1173	†	Southern Germany
24	c. 1230		Italy
24.1	1294	★	Verona
+27	1339–60	★	Florence
32.5	1454–56	★	Rimini
f36	1480 (?)	★	England
f37.1	after 1425		Flanders
f37.2	after 1425		Flanders
46	after 1450		Flanders
−53	after 1450		Flanders
54.1	1391	★	Pavia
f55.5	before 1478		Flanders
f57	1462–64	★	Belgium
f58.1	1433	★	Belgium
61	after 1471		Holland
64	1427	★	Southern Germany
f65.1	1451	★	Germany
−66	1469	★	Cologne
67.1	before 1462		Austria
67.3	1460	★	Erfurt
70.5	1480	★	Florence
71	after 1443		Central Italy
f72.1	1476–78	★	Rome (?)
+75	c. 1408		Florence
75.5	1466	★	Parma
76	1471–84	★	Central Italy
77	c. 1463		Central Italy
78	1466	★	Milan
80	1464–71	★	Central Italy
81	after 1461		Italy
83	after 1499	†	Florence (*Frontispiece*)
84	1474	★	Italy
−85	after 1482		Italy
f87.1	after 1434		Venice
+88	after 1403		Venice
f90	1445	†	Northern Italy
90.1	1456–69	★	Umbria
−91	1484		Central Italy
+92	after 1470	★	Italy
93.2	1456		Naples and Rome
93.3	after 1440		Northern Italy
93.6	1464	★	Italy
−94	1477	★	Brescia
f95	before 1464	★	Lombardy
97.1	1463	★	Italy
97.2	1464	★	Florence
97.3	c. 1450	★	Northern Italy
97.5	1468	★	Naples
98.1	1476	★	Italy
99.1	after 1483		Italy
102.2	1459	★	Ancona
Wing ZW 1.467	1467	★	Italy

88

Deillis aut̄· quos indurare dī misericdia
nō pmittit q̄d scriptū ē·: flagellat
ds̄ omnē filium quē recipit; Et ite
rū· Quē eñ diligit ds̄ & corripit;
De hac obduracione· & iā ppheta;
ex psona· ppli ad dm̄ clamat di
cens;· Indurasti cor nr̄m· ne time
rem te;· Q̄d utiq; nō est aliud· nisi
deseruisti cor nr̄m ne cōuertere
mur ad te;· Quam rem multis p̄
cedentib; sacri legiis· in ppło iudeo
rum impletū ēē cognouim;· Ne
mo ergo· cū paganis· aut maniche
is dī iusticiā rephendere· aut
culpare p̄sumat· sed certissime
credat q̄d pharahonē· nō dī uio
lencia· sed ppria iniquitas· et in
domabilis supbia cōtra dī pcepta·
ociens fecerit obdurari· Quidē
aut̄ q̄d dix̄ ds̄, ego indurabo cor
ei· sine cū ab illo ablata fuerit
grā mea· ab duret illū nequicia
sua. Et ut hoc euidencius· possit
agnosci· aliquā similitudinē
de reb; uisibilib;· caritatis ure
opponimus. Sic eñ quociens ni
mio frigore aqua constringitur·
solis calore sup ueniente resoluitur
& descendente eodē sole iterum
obduratur· ita nimio peccatorum
frigore refrigescit caritas mul

MS f1, fol. 88
(top and bottom margins trimmed)

MS 24.1,
fol. 67

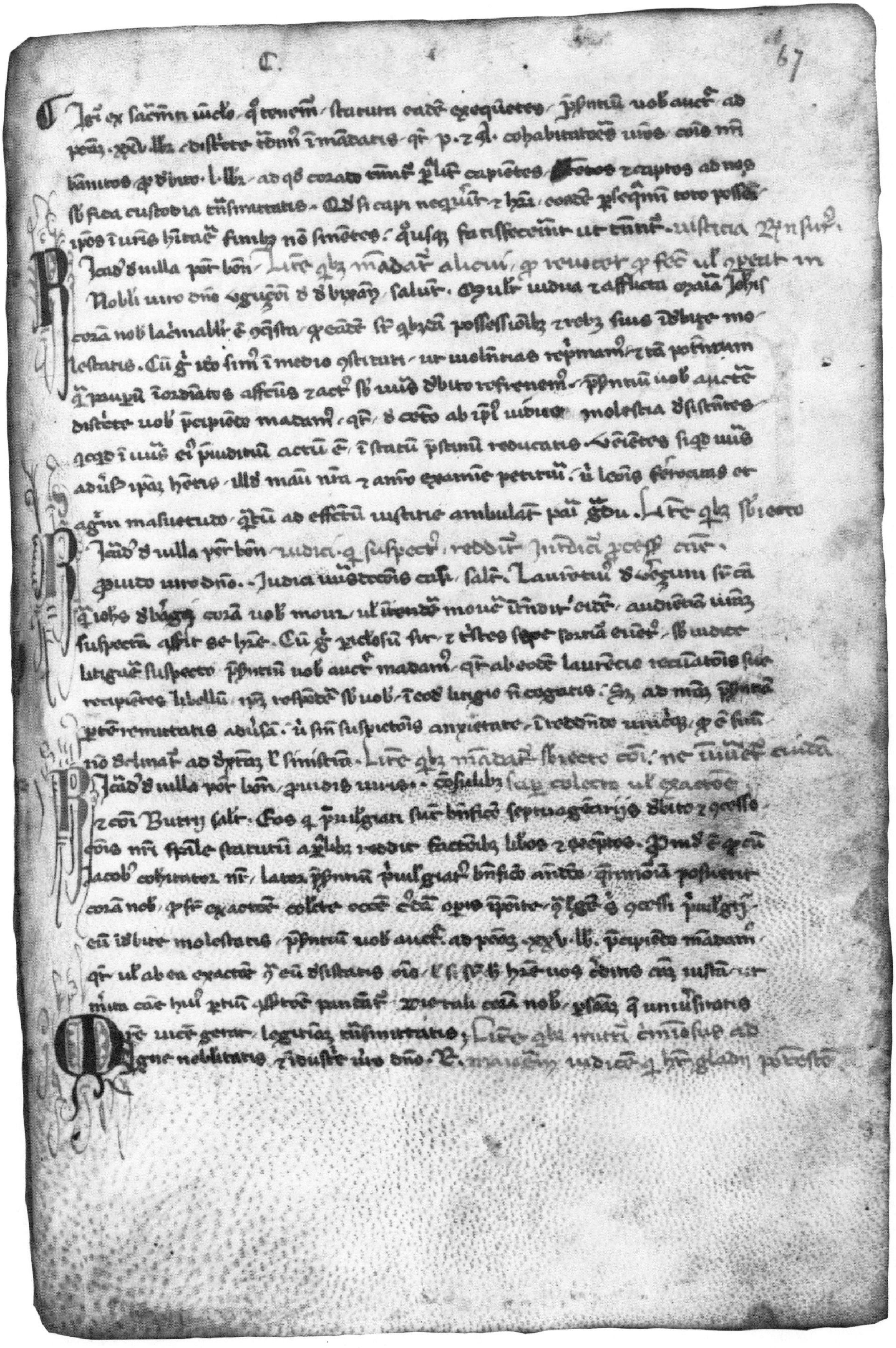

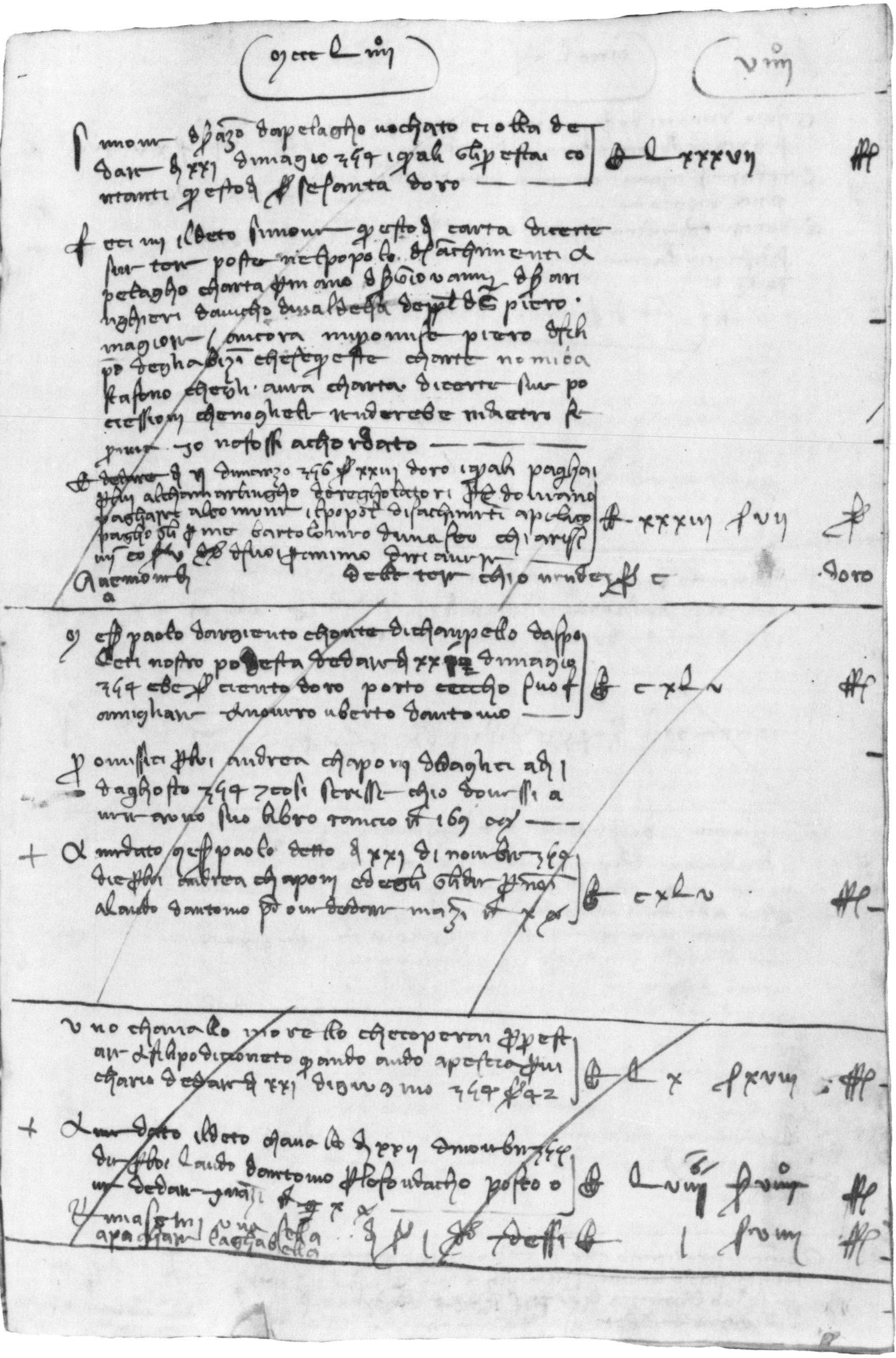

MS +27, fol. 9
(80% of actual size)

MS 32.5,
fol. 1

Facing page: MS f36, fol. 146
(*outside margins trimmed*)

ee q bonu e. Ita quidem. Cuncta igitur bonum petunt. Quod quidem ita describas licet ipsum
bonum esse quod desideretur ab omnibus. Nichil inquam verius excogitari potest. Nam vel
ad nichillum cuncta refiuntur & uno veluti vertice destituta sine rectore flu
itabunt. aut si quid est aliquid ad quod universa festinent id erit summum omnium bonorum.
Et illa. Nimium inquit o alumpne letor. ipsam enim medie veritatis notam mente fix
isti. Sed in hoc patuit tibi quod ignorare te paulo ante dicebas. Quid inquam. Quis esset
rerum omnium finis. Is profecto quod desideratur ab omnibus. Quod quia bonum esse colligi
mus. Oportet rerum omnium finem bonum esse ut fateamur.

To þis quod I must I nedys assent.
Zowr wordyse have bowndme so formeably. 9
Be reson of zowre sotel argument.
What yf þou know quod she verily.
I wold yt preyse att þe eynd quod I.
Yf I myth know god in þi man.
And yf I myth know hym perfyly.
I wold hym folow whyl I was here
That quod she os resonabyly.
Shew þe oppynly or we go.
So þat þoo þyngys stond ferme & stabyl.
Þat wych we be for þis have contentyd to.
And I may nat we go þer fro.
Have nat I schewyd þe pryvyly quod she.
Þat all þeys þyngys þat be desyryd soo.
Of many folke. ar full of vanyte.
And syn þey be dyverse it ys no nay.
Þey be nat goodys perfythly.
For whan on fro a nodyr ys a wey.
Nat ryth very godys utyrly.
To no wyght may þey bryng contenly.
But whan þey be asembyld in to on.
In warkyng & in forme verely.
Þan ys yt good or ellys ys yt non.
So þat þis power & þis suffycyans.
Þis gladnes. honowr & nobylyte.
Be þe same & on þyng in substans.
And yf þey lake very unyte.
Þer ys no cawse why þey schuld desyryd be.

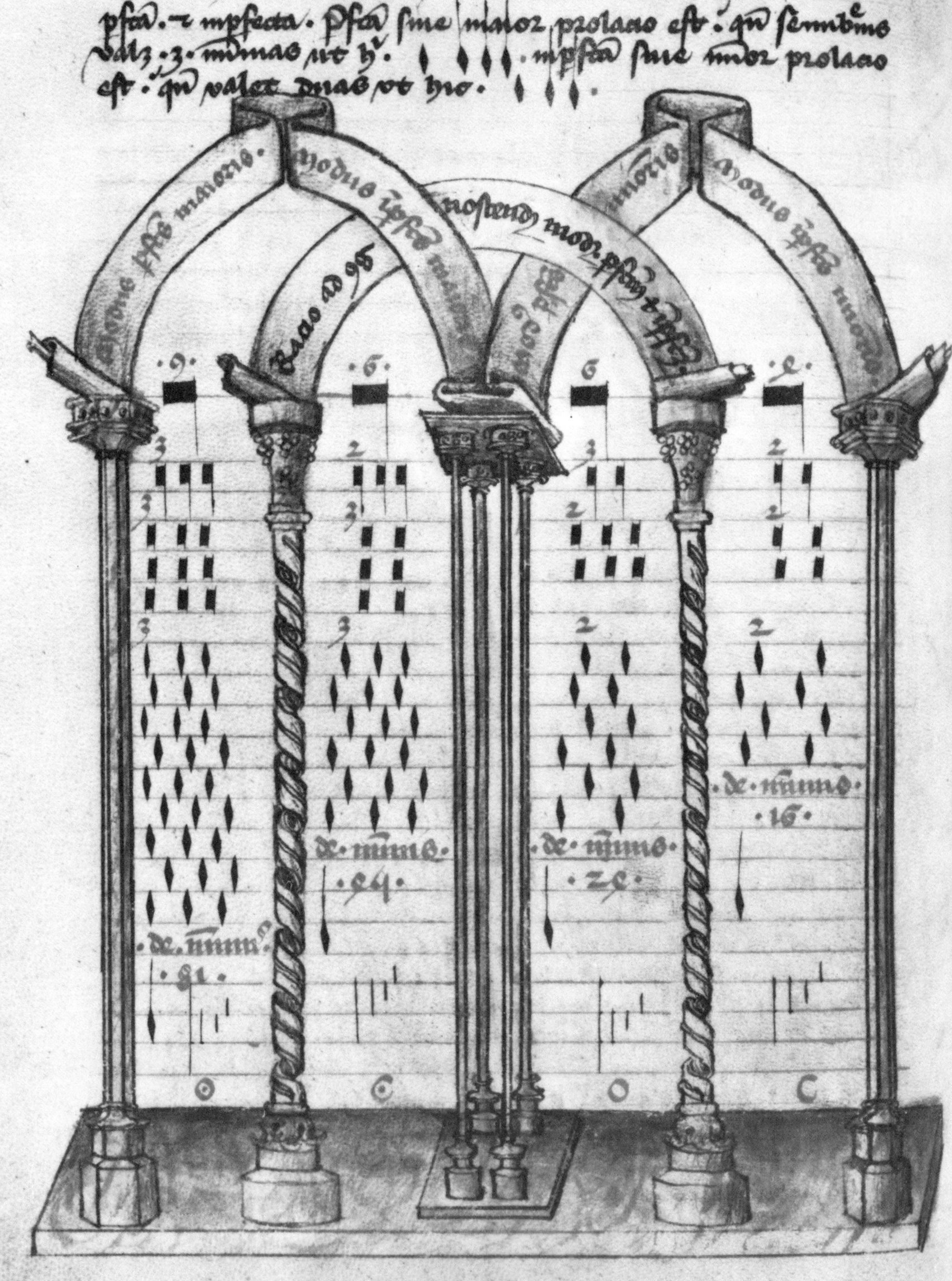

MS 54.1, fol. 43v

su recessit/ in terrā collapsa/ p famulos recepta/ et cubiliq3 data
donec resumeret spm̄. Ut vero ad se redijt/ vestes aureas et
purpuras/ et omnē leticie reclusit ornatū/ vilisq3 tunicis
usa. nūq̄ visa ridere. nullis facecijs/ nulloq3 gaudio nullisq3 um
q̄ iocis in leticiam potuit revocari. Quo in statu aliquādiu
pseueret/ egritudinē incidit. Et q2 cor suū aberat. nullaq3
menti dari consolacio poterat/ inter multū plorantes bra
chia matris/ ac collacrimantes et frustra consolacionis verb
utentes/ necessarios indignātē aīam exulavit. Eurialus vero
postq̄ ex ocīs/ nūq̄ amplius se visurus abijt. nulli iter eūdo
locutus/ solā in mente lucreciā gestabat. Et an umq̄ rever
ti possit meditabat. Venitq3 tandē ad cesarem pusij manē
tem q3 deinde ferrariā. mantuā/ tridētū. constanciā/ et ba
sileam secutus ē. ac demū i ungariā atq3 boemiā. Sz ut ipe
cesarem/ sic eū lucrecia sequebat in somnijs/ nullāq3 noctē
sibi quietam pmittebat. Q̄ ut obijsse verus amator agno
uit/ magno dolore promotus/ lugubrē vestē suscepit/ nec cō
solacionē admisit. nisi postq̄ cesar ex ducali sanguine virgi
nem sibi. tū formosā. tū castissimā atq3 prudentē matrimo
niunxit. Habes amoris exitū mariane mi amantissime/ nō
fictū. neq3 fallacem/ quā qui legerint/ piculū ex alijs faciāt
quod sibi ex usu fiet/ nec amatoriū bibere poculū studeant
quod longe plus aloes hēt q̄ mellis. Vale

Jo. gherinc phisicus scripsit Anno 1463°
klas februarij in domo ppe habitacionis
in sancto tritone tūc residēciā faciens

Mafeus vegius frī Eustatio salutē
Dialogus feliciter incipit

MS f57, fol. 21v (*margins trimmed*)

ex quo locutus est dominus ad moysen verbum istud quando ambulabat israel per solitudinem. hodie octoginta et quinque annorum sum sic valens ut eo valebam tempore quando ad explorandum missus sum illius in me temporis fortitudo usque hodie perseverat tam ad bellandum quam ad gradiendum. Da ergo mihi montem istum quem pollicitus est dominus me. Te quoque audiente in quo enacim et urbes magne atque munite si forte sit dominus mecum et potero delere eos sicut promisit mihi. Benedixitque ei iosue et tradidit ei ebron in possessionem. atque ex eo fuit ebron caleph filio iephone cenezeo usque in presentem diem quia secutus est dominum deum israel. Nomen ebron ante vocabatur cariatarbe. Adam maximus ibi inter enacim situs est et terra cessavit a preliis.

C. viii.

Dixit autem dominus ad iosue. ne timeas neque formides. Tolle tecum omnem multitudinem pugnatorum et consurgens ascende in oppidum hay. ecce tradidi in manu tua regem eius et populum. urbemque et terram. faciesque urbi hay et regi eius sicut fecisti iericho et regi illius. Predam vero et omnia animantia diripietis vobis. pone insidias urbi post eam. Surrexitque iosue et omnis exercitus bellatorum cum eo ut ascenderent in hay et electa triginta milia virorum fortium misit nocte. precepitque eis dicens. Ponite insidias post civitatem nec longius recedatis et eritis omnes parati. Ego autem et reliqua multitudo que mecum est accedemus ex adverso contra urbem. Cumque exierint contra nos sicut ante fecimus fugiemus et terga vertemus. donec persequentes ab urbe longius protrahantur. putabunt enim nos fugere sicut prius. Nobis ergo fugientibus et illis persequentibus consurgetis de insidiis et vastabitis civitatem tradetque eam dominus deus vester in manus vestras. Cumque ceperitis

succendite eam et sic omnia facietis ut [iussi]. Dimisitque eos et perrexerunt ad locum insidiarum. Sederuntque inter be[thel] et hay ad occidentalem plagam urbis hay. Iosue autem nocte illa in medio m[ansit] populi. Surgensque diluculo recens[uit] socios et ascendit cum senioribus [in] fronte exercitus vallatus auxilio pugnatorum. Cumque venissent et as[cen]dissent ex adverso civitatis steterunt [ad] septentrionalem urbis plagam inter quam [et] eos vallis erat media. Quinque [autem] milia viros elegerat et posuer[at] in insidiis inter bethaven et hay ex o[cci]dentali parte eiusdem civitatis. Omnis [vero] reliquus exercitus ad aquilonem di[ri]gebat aciem ita ut novissimi multitud[inis] occidentalem plagam urbis attingere[nt]. Abiit ergo iosue nocte illa et st[etit] in vallis medio. Quod cum vidisset [rex] hay festinavit mane et egressus [est] cum omni exercitu civitatis direxitque aciem contra desertum ignorans quod post tergum la[terent] insidie. Iosue vero et omnis multi[tudo] israel cesserunt loco simulantes metum et fugientes per viam solitudinis. At il[li] vociferantes pariter et mutuo cohor[tan]tes persecuti sunt eos. Cumque recess[issent] a civitate et nec unus quidem in urbe [hay] et bethel remansisset qui non p[ersequ]eretur israel sicut eruperant aperta o[ppida] relinquentes. Dixitque dominus ad iosue. Leva clipeum qui in manu tua est contra urbe[m] quoniam tradam eam. Cumque elevasset c[ly]peum ex adverso civitatis insidie que la[te]bant surrexerunt confestim et per[gen]tes ad civitatem ceperunt et succen[de]runt eam. Viri autem civitatis qui [per]sequebantur iosue respicientes et vide[n]tes fumum urbis ad celum usque co[n]scendere non potuerunt ultra huc illuc[que] diffugere. Presertim cum hi qui simula[verant] fugam et tendebant ad solitu[di]nem contra persequentes fortissime r[estitissent]. Vidensque iosue et omnis israel quod capta

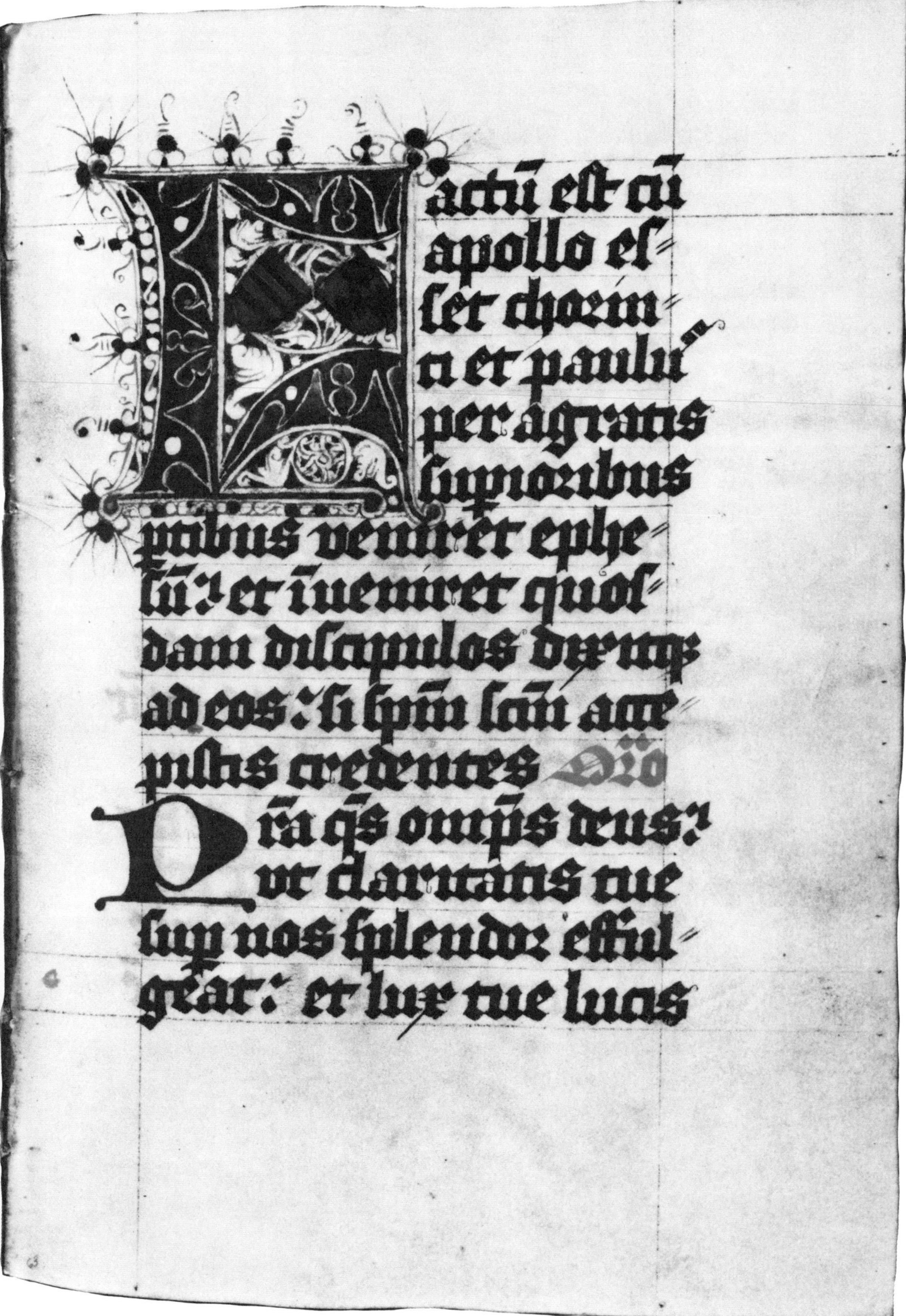

MS 64, fol. 63

Facing page: +58.1, fol. 86v (*bottom margin trimmed*)

MS f65.1,
fol. 19
(*margins trimmed*)

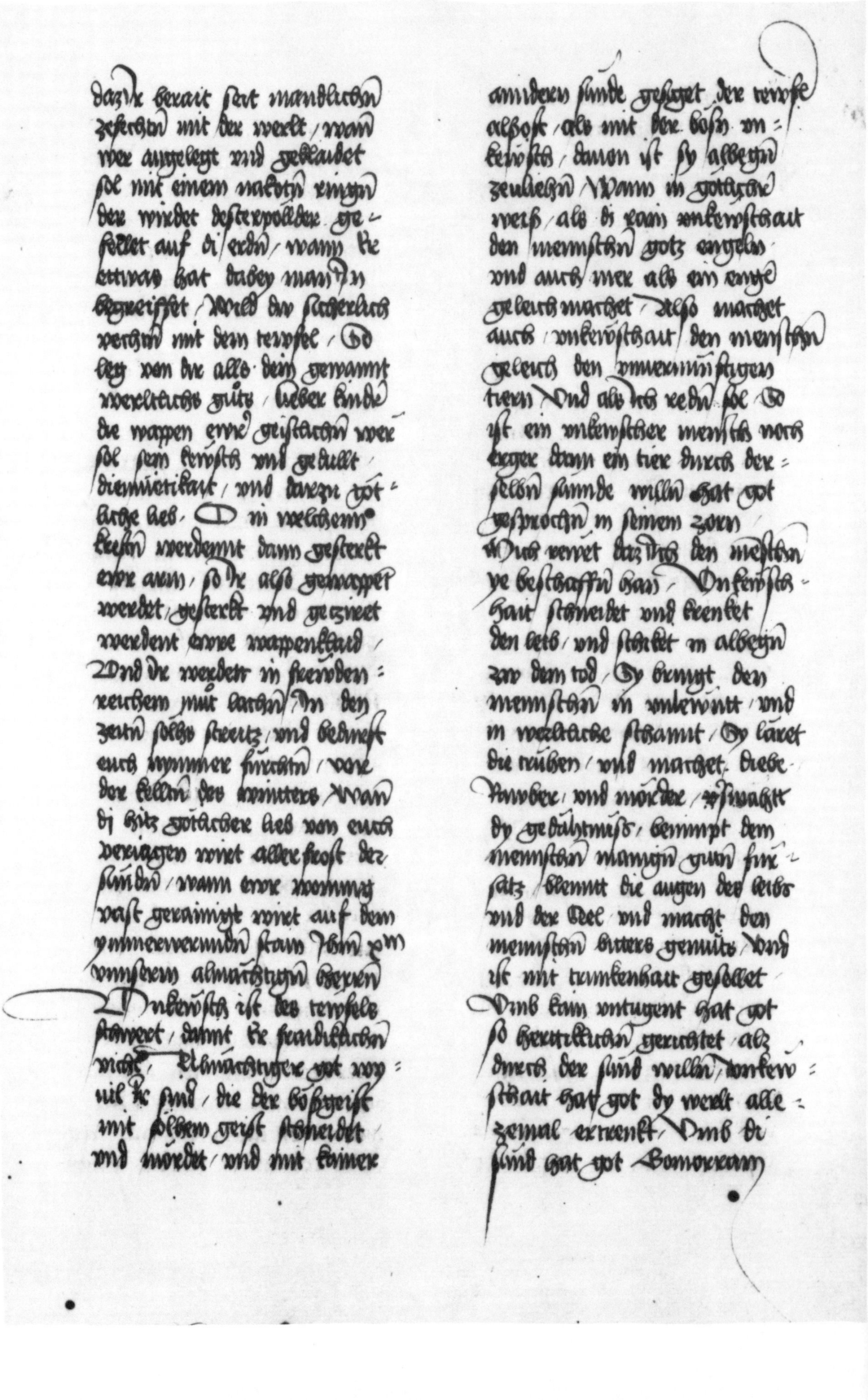

daz ir berait seit manlichen
zefechten mit der welt / wann
wer angelegt und geklaidet
sol mit einem nakchen ringen
der wirdet dester polder ge-
fellet auf di erden / wann er
ettwas hat dabey man in
begreiffet / Weil dir sicherlich
vechten mit dem teufel / So
leg von dir alls dein gewannt
werltlichs güts / lieber kinde
die wappen ewre geistlichen wer
sol sein kewsch und gedult
diemuetikait / und darzu got-
liche lieb / O in welchem
klaiden werdennt dann gesterckt
ewre arm / so ir also gewappet
werdet / gesterckt und geziert
werdent ewre wappenklaid /
Und ir werdett in frewden
reichen mit lachen / In den
zeiten solchs streitz / und bedurft
euch nymmer furchten / vor
der kellen des winters / Wan
di hitz gotlicher lieb von euch
veriagen wirt allen frost der
sünden / wann ewre wonung
vast geraimigt wirt auf dem
ymmerwerenden stain Ihesu xpo
unnserem almächtigen herren
Unkewsch ist des teufels
swert / damit er feindlichen
richt / Almächtiger got wie
vil ir sind / die der bösgeist
mit solhem geist schneidet
und mördet / und mit kainer

anndern sunde gesiget der teufel
alßoft als mit der bösen unkewsch / davon ist sy allerzeit
zeuliechen / Wann in göttlicher
weiß als di rain unkewschait
den menschen gotz engeln
und auch mer als ein engel
geleich machet / Also machet
auch unkewschait den menschen
geleich den unvernunftigen
tieren / Und als ich reden sol / So
ist ein unkewscher mensch noch
erger dann ein tier / durch derselben sunnde willen hat got
gesprochen in seinem zorn
Mich rewet daz ich den menschen
ye beschaffen han / Unkewsch-
hait swechet und krenket
den leib / und swechet in allzeit
zu dem tod / Sy bringt den
menschen in unkewsch / und
in werltliche schamt / Sy leret
die rauben / und machet diebe
rauber / und mörder / Sy swacht
dy gedächtnuss / benympt dem
menschen mangen guten fur-
satz / blennt die augen des leibs
und der sel / und macht den
menschen bitters gemüts / Und
ist mit krankenhait gefüllet
Umb kain untugent hat got
so herticlichen gerichtet alz
durch der sünd willen / unkewschait hat got dy welt alle-
zemal ertrenkt / Umb di
sünd hat got Sodomam

MS –66,
fols. 33v–34

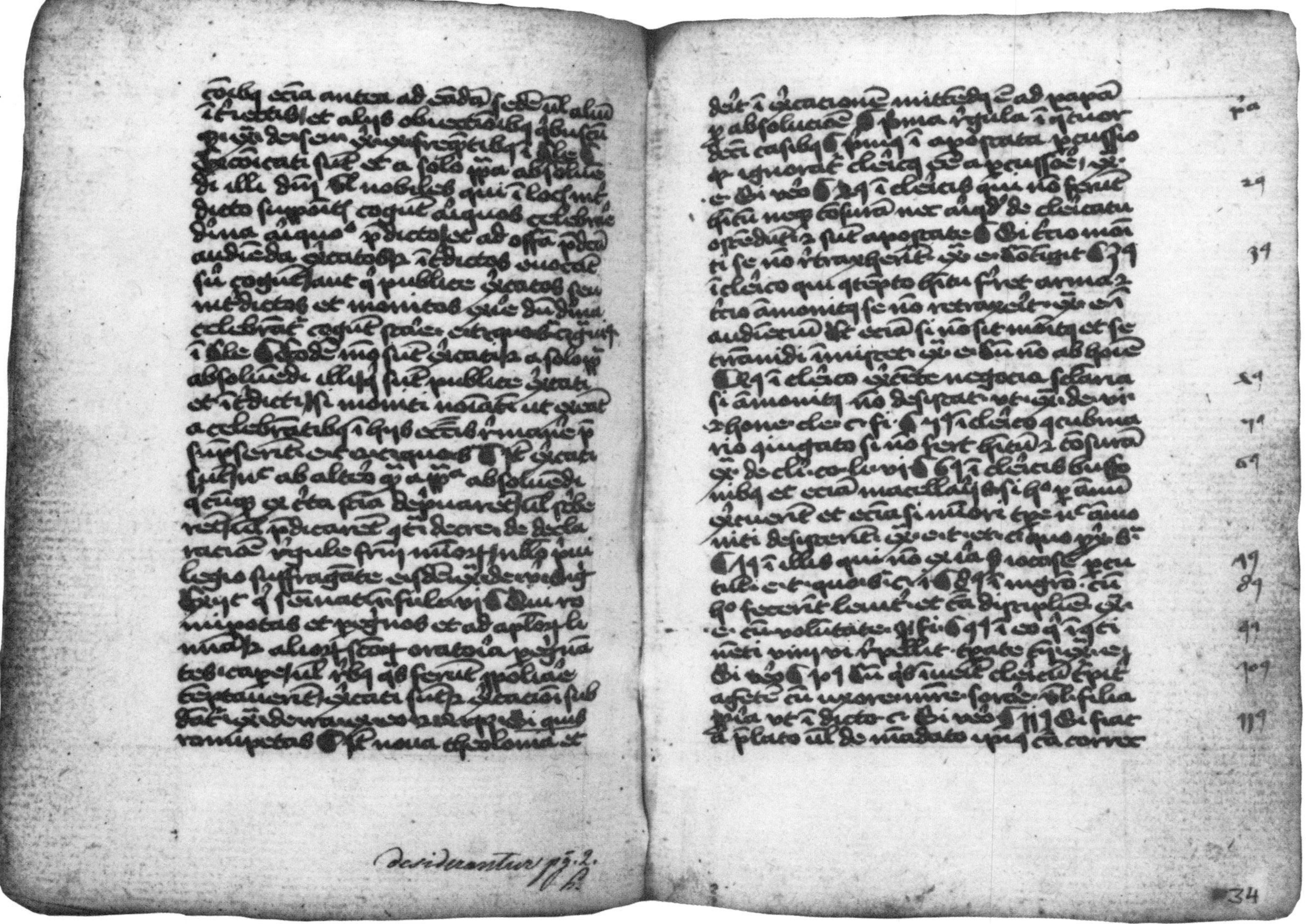

MS 67.3, fol. 67

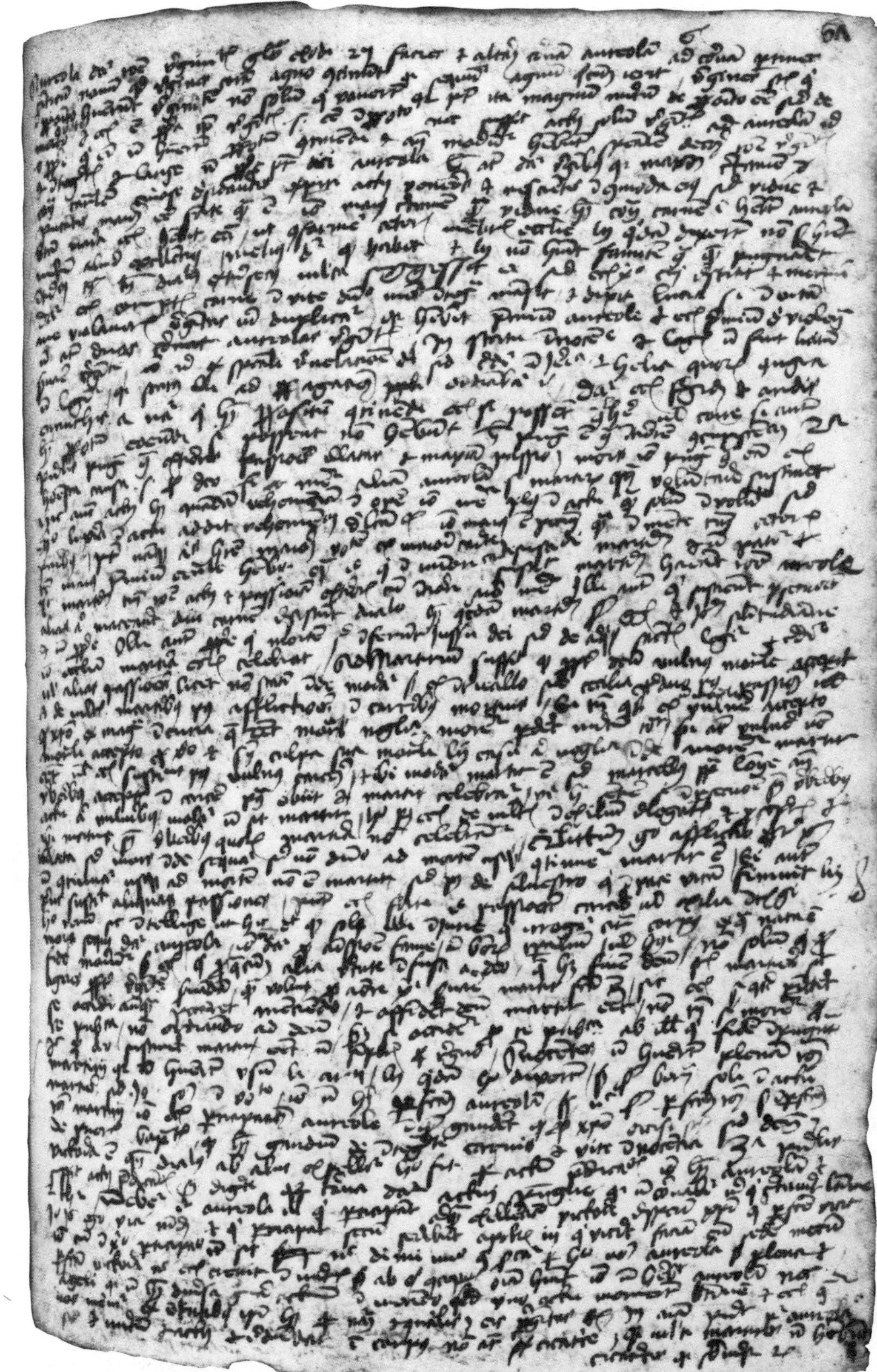

Facing page: 70.5, fol. 50

si facessi la pace, con conditione che pagassi le spese tutte che
li Romani haveano fatte in questa impresa: et lui lasciassi
tutta la signoria: che haveva di qua dal monte Tauro: che
era tanta che si dilatava per lungheza piu di XXX. giornate:
et piu di .X. per largheza. Per tanti meriti e suo edi Affri
cano, non fugi pero Scipione Asiatico, cosi dipoi chiamato:
e per la victoria: e perche fu el primo imperatore Ro. che con
lexercito passo in Asia. La medesima ingiuria che Affricano
sostenne: perche morto in exilio a Literno, come vogliono li piu
degli scriptori, non basto a nemici suoi havere veduto si in
degno fine di tale cittadino: se anchora el simile allo Asiatico
non facevano: Accusandolo del medesimo peccato che el fratello:
da la violenza di quali non si potendo defendere: per mezo
de Tiberio Graco tribuno della plebe: hebbe di gratia: che
tutti li suoi beni fossino venduti: et la persona sua rimanessi
libera. Per la qual cosa mandando li Questori a pigliare
la possessione de beni di Asiatico, non solamente non vi si tro
vo cosa alchuna: che sumptuosita o magnificentia mostras
si, di doni overo preda di Antiocho: come glera aposto:
ma non vi fu tanto che vendendolo agiugnessi alla somma
di che era damnato: la quale in niuno modo volle consentire
che li parenti o li amici pagassino. Ben fu contento che
tanto gli ricomperassino dal commune, quanto glera ne
cessario a vivere temperatamente: con la quale temperata
roba insino allultimo di si sostento: et cosi fu pagato lui
el fratello degnamente dal populo Ro. dellhavere quella patria
ricovrata da miserrima servitu, in dominatione di tutto
quello: che a loro piacque di aquistare. Questo perfecto:

ipsius genua flectere, et immediate post dationem annuli manum et pedem dicti domini pape osculari: et osculo per eum a domino papa recepto postea redire ad sedem suam.

Quid non possint facere novi cardinales

Novi cardinales annulos portare non debent etiam si antequam cardinales fierent, prelati existerent, quousque dominus papa in consistorio det eis titulos et annulos ut dictum est, nec deberent in capellis vel domibus propriis vel alienis dare benedictionem, quousque titulum et annulum receperint ut dictum est

De forma in apertione oris novorum cardinalium

Forma vero que antiquitus consuevit observari in apertione oris novorum cardinalium et assignatione titulorum et datione annulorum ut est infrascripta videlicet quod postquam sederint cardinales tam antiqui quam novi in ordine suo in consistorio tunc quando domino pape placebit dicat per eum novis cardinalibus quod secedant ad partem. Et ipsis absentibus dantur consilia circularia per cardinales antiquos. An ora ipsorum cardinalium novorum sint aperienda. Et si consulant quod sic revocantur ad consistorium iidem cardinales absentes et sedent in locis suis. Et tunc dominus papa proposita aliqua auctoritate si placet cum brevi vel modica et quasi nulla ipsius prosecutione ora ipsorum aperit dicendo. Nos aperimus tibi os

Facing page: MS f72.1, fol. 138

MS 75.5,
fols. 26v–27

MS 76,
fols. 152v–153

paruo qz lacte pastus +
est per quem nec ales +
esurit. Gaudet chorus
celestium et angeli can-
unt deo: palam q fit +
pastoribus pastor cre-
ator creator omnium.
Gloria tibi domine q
natus es de uirgine +
cum patre sancto spiri-
tu in sempiterna secu-
la. Amen.
In epyphania domi-
ni hymnus.
Hostis herodes +
impie christum
uenire quid times nō
eripit mortalia qui re-
gna dat celestia. Ib-
ant magi quam uide-
rant stellam sequentes
preuiam. lumen req-
runt lumine deum fa-
tentur munere. La-

uacra puri gurgitis +
celestis agnus attigit
peccata que non detulit
nos abluendo sustu-
lit. Nouum genus +
potentie aque rubesc-
unt ydrie uinū q ius-
sa fundere mutauit +
unda originem. Glo-
ria tibi domine qui ap-
paruisti cū patre sanc-
to spiritu i sempiter-
na secula. Amen.
Sabbato quadrage-
sime ad uesperas hy-
mnus.
Audi benigne cō-
ditor nr̄as pre-
ces cū fletibus in hoc
sacro ieiunio fusas +
quadragenario. Scr-
utator alme cordium
infirma tu scis uirtū
ad te reuersis exhibe

remisionis gratiam +
Multum quidem pec-
cauimus sed parce con-
fitentibus ad laudem
tui nominis confer +
medelam languidis. +
Sic corpus extra cō-
teri dona per abstinē-
tiam ieiunet ut mens
sobria a labe prorsus
criminū. Presta be-
ata trinitas concede
simplex unitas ut fru-
ctuosa sint tuis ieiuni-
orum munera. Am-
en. Ad nocturnū
hymnus.
Ex more docti my-
stico seruemus +
hoc ieiunium deno +
dierum circulo ducto
quater notissimō. Lex
et prophete primitus
hoc pretulerunt post-

modum christus sacra-
uit omnium rex atq
factor temporum. Uta-
mur ergo parcius uer-
bis cibis 7 potibus: so-
no iocis 7 artibus per-
stemus in custodia. +
Uitemus autem pes-
sima que subruunt +
mentes uagas: nulli
q demus callidum ho-
stis locum tyrannidi +.
Dicamus omnes cer-
nui clamemus atq si-
guli ploremus ante +
iudicem: flectamus
iram uindicē. Nostris
malis offendimus tu-
am deus clementiam
effunde nobis desuper
remissor indulgentiam.
Memento q sumus +
tui licet caduci plasma-
tis ne des honorē nois

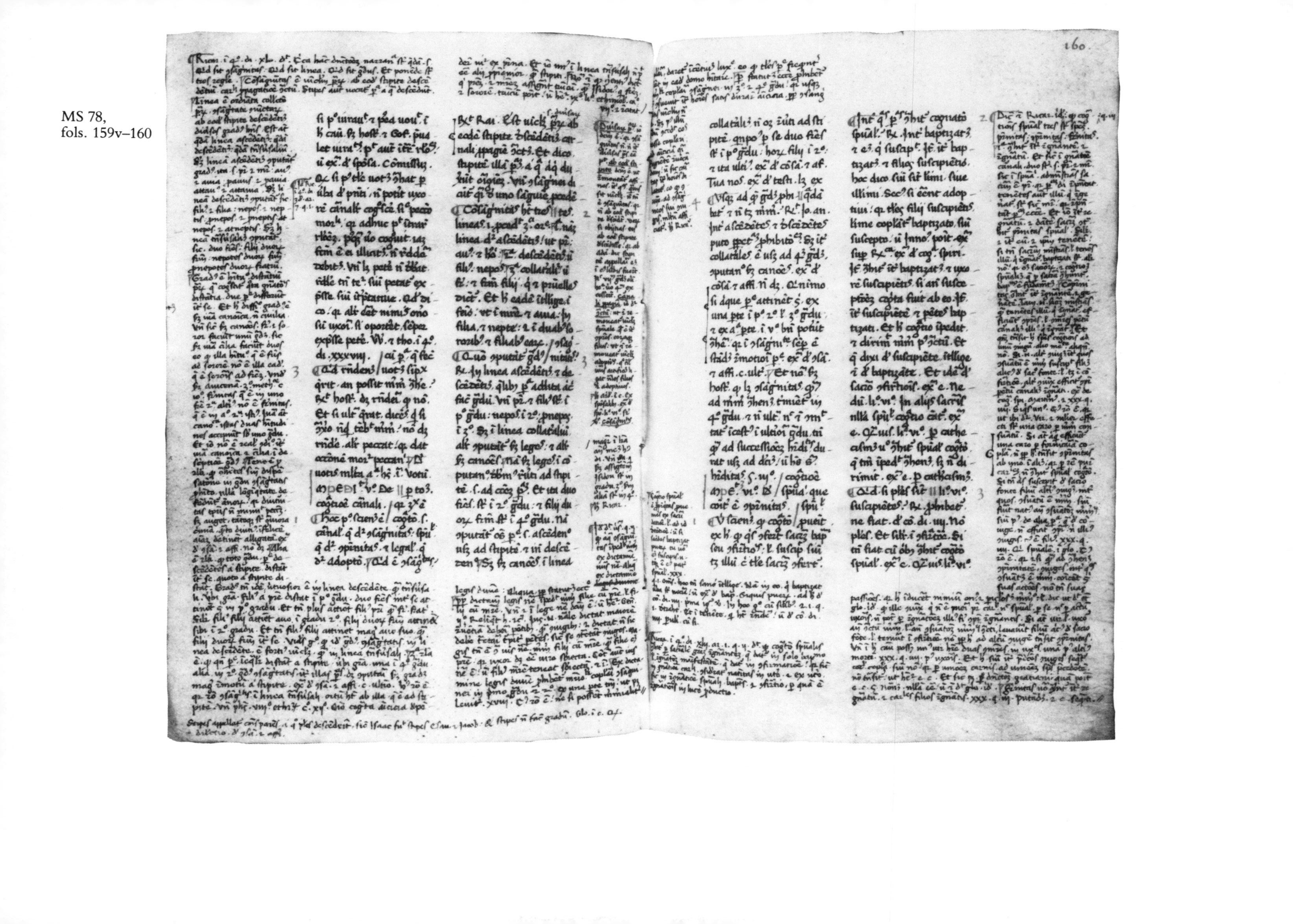

MS 78,
fols. 159v–160

MS 80,
fols. 58v–59

MS 84, fols. 61v–62

Facing page: MS +92, fol. 226 (*top and bottom margins trimmed*)

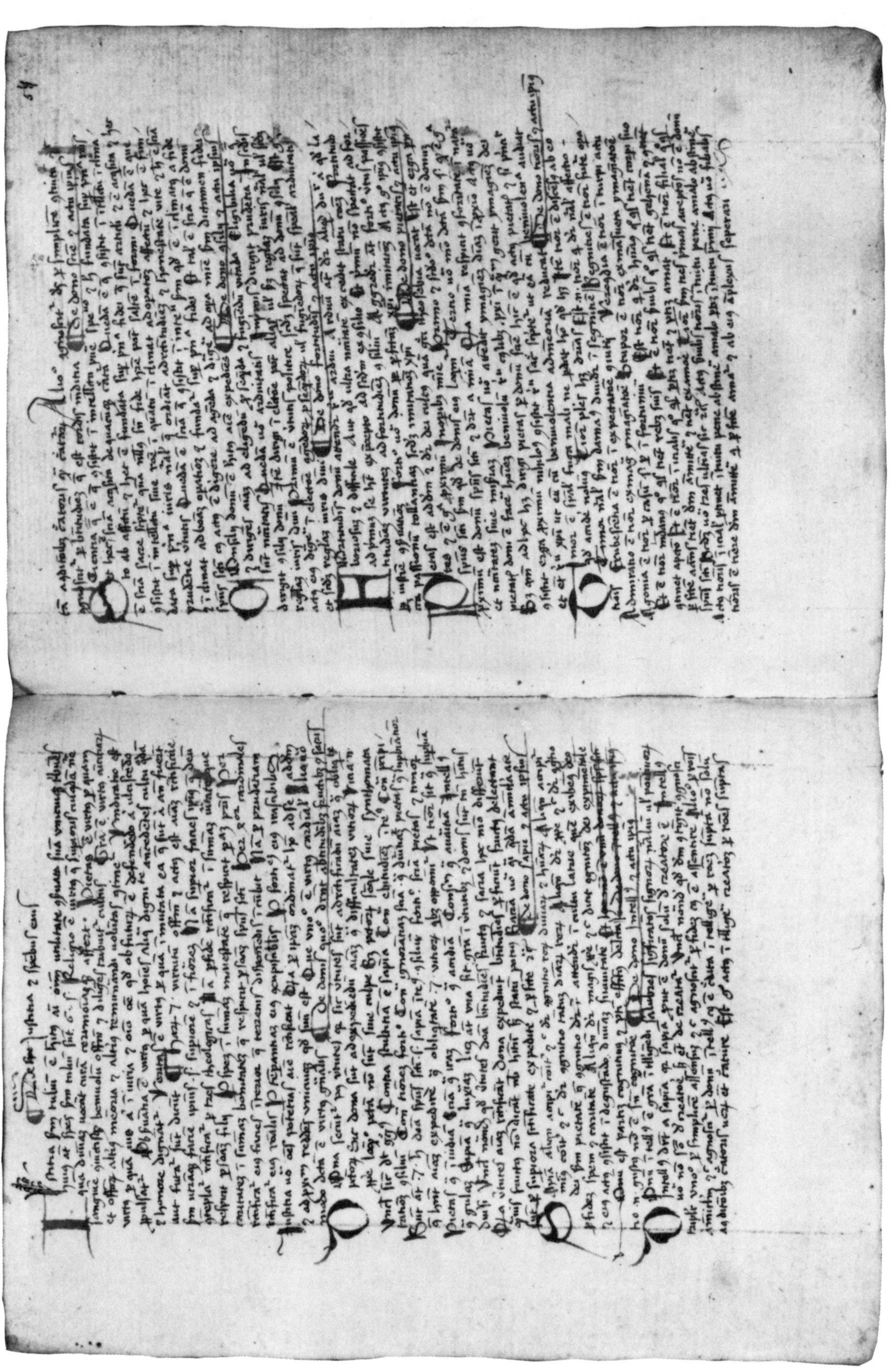

MS 90.1, fols. 53v–54

Leonoram sanguine et moribus inclitam: hic ut diximus Romam uenit et Diadema a Nicolao quinto suscepit Deinde uisitauit Alphonsum regem Aragonum et Sicilie uxoris auunculum a quo honorifice apud Neapolim receptus: tandem Almaniam foeliciter rediit. Demum anno domini M CCCC lxix deuotionis et peregrinationis gratia Romam et Apostolorum sacra Limina uisitauit qui ab eodem Sanctissimo paulo secundo summo pontifice solennissime receptus est: illumque in suo Apostolico palatio humanissime et curialissime locauit et quamdiu rome fuit sibi et gentibus suis Lautissime expensas ministrauit: et in recessu spiritualibus et temporalibus muneribus eum magnifice donauit: Agimus iam huius historie finem sub eodem Herrico quarto Verum quia septies in die cadit homo Exorandus est Altissimus per quem reges regnant ut hunc Herricum quartum custodiat protegat et defendat: ut que foeliciter incoepit foelicius expleat: illique intellectum vires et conatum tribuat: quatenus se et subditos in viam pacis et salutis eterne dirigat eo prestante Qui est benedictus in secula Amen.

De Mandato R.P.D. Roderici Episcopi Palentini auctoris huius Libri Ego Udalricus Gallus sine calamo aut pennis eundem Librum impressi.

.De Bello Ciuili Sille & Marij./

b Bello Sociali nundum consumato Rome
q̃ noxiu̅ ciuile et mitridaticu̅ q̃d alij
triginta: alij quadraginta annis gestu̅
comemorant bella funesta comota sunt
Anno sexcentesimo sexagesimo secundo./
Sila igitur cum contra mitridatem rege̅
consul cum exercitu esset accessurus: Marius contra eundem Mitridatem. septimu̅
sibi consulatum dari postulauit: quod Sila
egre ferens uel p̃cipiens ut erat iuuenis
impatiens atq̃ sup̃bus cum quatuor legionib̃
ante urbem consedit: quam cu̅ intrasset
mariu̅ cum multis sibi adherentibus
curia foro atq̃ capitolio uulgo necatis p̃se-
cutus est: Marius u̅o fugiens in minturne-
sibus paludibus se abdidit Deinde comptus
& Minturnas ductus incarceratusq̃ demu̅
uinculis liberatus in Africam transfugit:
& inde continuo Roma̅ regressus est: Vbi
se Cinne consuli Senatorio & Gneo car-
boni coniunxit. Nan ad profligandam

uniuersam rem publicam tres legiones Marius, et unam exercitus Gneus carbo, alia̅
u̅o Sertorius & terciam Cinna partes
sortiti sunt. Igitur marius Colonia̅ hostiensem ingressus omnia genera libidinis
auaricie et crudelitatis exercuit. Pompe-
ius qui hor̃ erat inimicus et paulo ante
cum Sartorio su̅ pugnauerat fulmine per-
cussus interijt: eius u̅o exercitus pestile̅-
tia consumptus est. de quo quadraginta
uiror̃ mortua fuisse: Sex u̅o milia ab
Octauio consule oblata dicuntur. Postea
marius ip̃e Antium et Aritiu̅ ciuitates
hostiliter capit: Singulor̃q̃ bona diripi-
pit. postea cum fugitiuis et Cinna consul cum legionibus urbem ingressi q̃sq̃
nobilissimos Senatus et plurimos consu-
lares uiros interfecerut: Quor̃ tantus
fuit numerus ut pocius libeat subtice̅
q̃ dolendo comemorare. Nan capita in-
terfector̃ conuiuiis capitolijs et rostris

Facing page: MS 93.6, fols. 33v–34

MS –94, fols. 63v–64

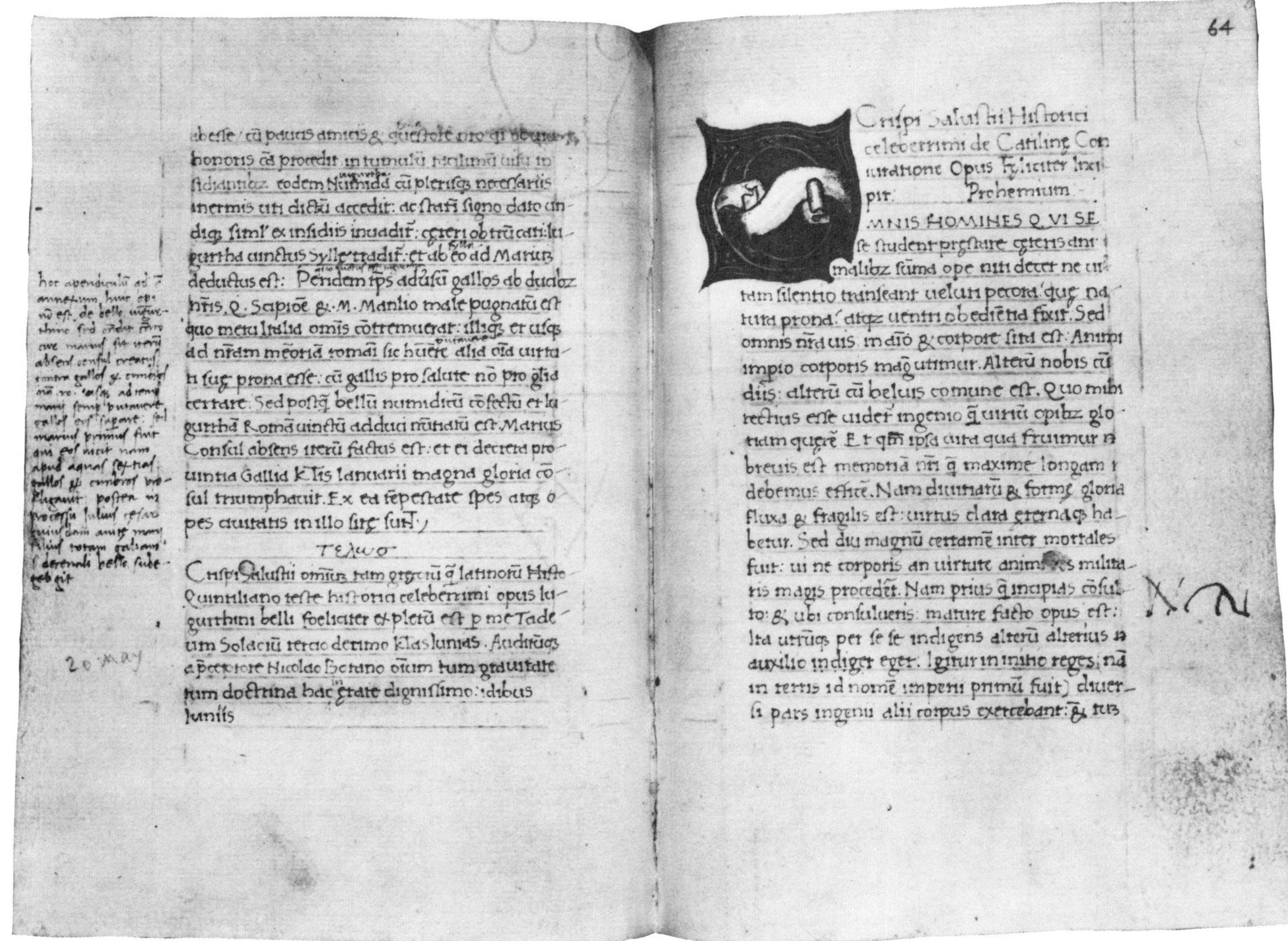

Following page: MS f95, fol. 74

sibi unum dari optabat. Cum omnibus praeesset
solum hoc solio suo altius uidebat.
AT quod augustus optauerat dioclitianus impleuit. Ille qui primus ex nris imperatoribus
adorari se: ut deum iusserat: quiq; calciamentis
ac uestibus inserens margaritas & honustus gemis incedens habitum caesareum ex romano atq;
humano persicum: seu diuinum fecisse uidebatur
qui captiuis insignibus ante currum actis praelataq;
parthorum praeda paulo ante triumpharat. postq
frementis aulae praeciosaeq; sarcinae ac satellitum
actici & seruitutis publicae pertesum e: mutauit
repente aium: ut solus & pauper & liber esse concupisceret
interq; fluctus imperialium curarum in portum uitae humilioris quasi gubernator nudus ex
magno naufragio enataret. & miramur celestinum. Cum tamen qd propter aeternam uitam sanctus
ille uir fecit: tantus iste peccator propter breuissimas & incertas senectutis reliquias iam fecisset
Qui quietis extremae desyderio priuatae fortunae
redditus no sibi mutatae sedem uitae Romam statuit
nequis uanam requiem dimissi fumus aut
odor imperij turbaret: sed antiquam patriam
Salonas dalmaciae repetijt. Illic quoq; non intra
sed prope muros patrios in uilla propria moriens
quam id ipsum praecogitans forte construxerat: ut
multum tranquillitatis senio additum: sic summis
honoribus nil detractum p solitariam atq; humilem
uitam sensit. solus omnium priuatus Eutropio
atq; Eusebio testibus relatus in numerum deorum
Sane quod post imperium dioclitianus fecit id
ante imperium Antonius primus fecerat quem
Julius capitolinus historicus omni priuata uita

in eorum negociis benignitatem tuam expectant.

Cum tua benignitas nemini unquam defuerit nihil est igitur quod mireris si quam plurimum eorum causis te sibi asistant.

Quia tua apud omnes officiosos beneficentia nota est nulla igitur te moveat admiratio si multi se tibi commendant.

Cum te omnes liberalissimum cognoscant non est quod aliqua tenearis admiratione si omnes tuum requirant officium.

Io me alegro molto de la conservatione de la tua fama

Letor plurimum te in columem conservasse.

Non parva afficior leticia tuam nominis existimationem te integram deffendisse.

Non dici posset quantum gaudeam honorem tuum illesum retinuisse.

Io desidero molto da podere essere insiema

Quam optarem ut multis ex causis una esse possemus.

Desiderarem vehementissime ut cum pluribus de rebus presentiam nostram collere possemus.

Quam vellem ut multis ac magnis rerum accessionibus ad utriusque nostrum pertinentibus sermone coram conferre valeremus.

Se tu valesse per desiderare valeti hoi io voria chi tu fosse semper ne li mei consilii

Si te arbitratu meo possiderem possem numquam a tuis consiliis discrepare

Si ex sententia mea te frui valere tu eras ducem consiliorum meorum mo

Si ex voto michi data esset tui possidendi facultas omnia mea consilia tibi gubernanda committerem. [Moderator]

Io ho grande pietad de la nostra compagnia

Maxima afficior iocunditate ex familiaritate nostra.

Non mediocri afficior voluptate ex nostra affinitate.

Non parva afficior utilitate ex consilio tuo.

Io oldendo parlare catone me pare de odire ti

Cum catonem loquentem audio te audire videor

Cum tuum sermonem tuo ad me nomine venientem video te videre existimo.

Quoties fabricius tuas michi litteras obsignat toties tecum sermonem meditari videor

Non se poria dire quanto io desideri la salute de la re publica

Non posset verbis explicari quantopere rei publice faveam.

Non posset oratione declarari quanta amoris caritate rem publicam contemplatur

Non posset aliquo nutu exprimi quantum rem publicam carissimam semper habuerim.

Non posset aliqua signe describi quam verus communis salutis patrius atque deffensor extiterim.

Io me alegro molto de la salute di boni

Ego salute bonorum maxiopere letor.

Ego officiosorum hominum incolumitatis sum vehementissime cupidus.

Ego virtuosorum felicitatis sedulo sum curiosus

Tulio non poria esser stado piu diligente a la tua laude commo luy e stado.

Cato gravior dignitati tue quam extitit gravior esse non potuisset.

Milo constantior tue salutis esse non esse valuisset quam fuit.

Lentulus amicior tuis commodis esse non potuisset quam extiterit.

La tua dignita si fa che le molto nota ogni tua causa

Tua dignitas facit ut animadvertatur quicquid facias.

Clarissima tue auctoritatis excelentia efficit ut quicquid agas vehementer denotentur.

Tuarum virtutum splendor homines commonet ut quecumque facias ponderet

Sulpicio non sara inganato in quelle cose chi se pono vedere

Sulpicius in rebus illis que humano ingenio evitari possunt non decipitur.

Cato in his que aliquo consilio rafelli possunt non capiatur

MS 97.2,
fol. 115v

poeta laureato et sepellito infirençe nel
la chiesa di sancta croce in una sepoltu
ra marmorea bellissima et ornatissima
allato alla porta che va ne chiostri di det
ta chiesa finis amē finis amen —
Sono le predette battaglie di maggiore
numero et quantita di gēte et dinari che
mai fussi interra · finis amē finis amen —
laus tibi domine rex etterne glorie —
Io Jachopo di francescho di lorenço
di niccolo da soci di casentino al presen
te infirençe ho transcripto e chopiato que
sto libro di mia propria mano et chomi
cialo a scriuere il sichondo di di quaresima
cioe adi sedici di março 1463 et finilo
oggi questo di sei di março prossimo pu
re nel 1463 in detta quaresima et scrip
silo i chasa di domenicho di bel frale di
firēçe nel popolo di sancta trinita il qua
le libro ho scripto A bartolomeo di det
to domenicho di bel frale finito amen

Preceding page: MS 97.1, fols. 22v–23

MS 97.3, fols. 21v–22

cui coniuratorum. Itaque partim simulta-
te: partim beneficio accusatoris: et mer
cede provinciarum inducti clodio favebant.
ciceroni adversabantur. Mutavit veste
cum ipso universus equestris ordo: et ad xx.
milia hominum mutato habitu eum seque
bantur. Senatus etiam convenerat decre
turus: ut omnes cives veluti in publica
moestitia vestem mutarent: quod tamen
Senatusconsultum impedientibus consulibus:
et clodio armatis hominibus curiam obsi
dente: fieri non potuit. Tantum enim terro
rem clodiana arma iniecerat: ut non
nulli senatores laceratis togis e curia
fugerent. Postquam igitur manifestum
erat: neque senatus auctoritatem: neque
commiserationem habitus quicquam prodesse:
ad pompeium pro veteri amicitia conver
sus: ut sibi opem ferret adversus tribu
nicium furorem rogabat. At ille iam
inde ab initio huius contentionis: ro
gatu caesaris e medio se abstulerat:

Per hunc modum undique oppugnatus Cicero: vestem mutavit. et sordidatus circumiens: homines pro salute precabatur

et in albanum secesserat. Venientem
autem ad eum ciceronem hominem de se be
ne meritum: videre non sustinuit: sed
pudore perductus: quando caesari
socero nihil illius gratia se facturum
promiserat: per aliam portam villae
egressus: longius abiit. reliquum ergo
erat: aut in exilium abire: aut ferro
dimicare. L. lucullus vir clarissimus:
et magnae auctoritatis: arma capere
et ferro decernere suadebat. Alius
cedere satius videbatur: in aliud tem
pus reditum expectare: hec tandem
sententia ciceroni placuit. Itaque per mediam
noctem urbe egressus: terrestri iti
nere lucaniam petiit ea mente: ut
in siciliam inde traiceret. Clodius:
ut eius fugam intellexit: ad populum tu
lit de eius exilio: rogationemque pro
posuit: per quam infra cccc. ab italia mi
liarium aqua: et igni ciceroni interdi
cebatur: Si quis reciperet: poena adu-

22

no generat n[on] q[uia] p[ro]p[te]r e[s]t agn[iti]o sensi[bilium] q[uod] i[n]de apud i[n]de et de m[u]ltis aliis h[ab]es habundanter scr[ip]t[u]m i[n] q[uesti]o[n]e quadam i[n] q[ua] d[icitur] q[uod] sunt grat[ia] sensi[bilium] tam[en] m[...] q[uo]d i[n]tell[igi]t[ur] fantasmata spe[cierum] h[ab]it[ibus] q[uo]d destinant n[on] s[unt] nobiliores sunt xl q[ue]o p[er] [illegible] d[i]ff[i]c[u]ltate tollendam s[ecundu]m s[...] de a[n]i[m]a

[...] hi[c] pre dit aliam s[ecundu]m d[icitu]r q[uo]d p[ro]ponat[ur] hi[c] tu[n]c alire mone[n]dum d[i]ff[icultate]s ut ad ignorandum p[ri]us ut ad speculandum seu speculationem aliam i[n] tali[bus] q[ui]d ad sunt dimittenda q[uia] sunt alterius specu[lationis] n[on] s[...] et theo[logi]e i[n] i[m]ponimus hiis scr[ipt]is p[ri]mi et 2[i] p[er]ier[mene]ias analeticorum questiunculis e[xi]mii [...]

Expliciunt q[uesti]o[n]es sup[er] p[rim]o et 2[o] p[er]ier[mene]ias edit[e] p[er] reverendissimum d[omi]n[u]m Antonium quondam archiep[iscop]um amalfitanum scripte p[er] me petrum anno d[omi]ni Mill[esim]o cccc° Lxviii mensis aug[us]ti co[m]plete in nat[ivitate] s[an]c[t]i martini

Scripsit has q[uesti]o[n]es petrus de afelatro de [...] anno [...] studii i[n] hiis artib[us]

Incipit tabula questionum sup[er] p[ri]mo

a 1 Utrum demonstr[ati]o sit subiectum i[n] libro p[er]ier[menei]as
a 2 Utrum o[mn]is doctrina et o[mn]is disciplina fiat et c[etera]
a 3 Utrum sint tres due p[ro]gnitiones
a 4 Utrum a et b p[ro]gnostica[n]t[ur] an [...]
a 5 Utrum sci[enti]a sit b[e]n[e] diffinitum
a 6 Utrum 1a diffi[niti]o demonstr[ati]onis sit bona
a 7 Utrum o[mn]is demonstr[ati]o sit de ente
a 8 Utrum o[mn]is demonstr[ati]o sit ex p[ri]mis
a 9 Utrum sit n[ecessari]e mag[is] adherere p[ri]n[cipi]is q[uam] [con]clusionib[us]
a 10 Utrum semp[er] p[ro]pt[er] q[uod] unumq[uo]dq[ue] tale et i[psum] magis
a 11 Utrum dicti demonstr[ati]o a[n]i[m]alis
a 12 Utrum dici de o[mn]i b[e]n[e] diffiniat[ur]
a 13 Utrum b[e]n[e] assignet[ur] ordo q[ui] modi p[er]seitatis
a 14 Utrum [...] et q[ua]rt[us] modus b[e]n[e] ponat[ur]
a 15 Utrum diffi[niti]o u[niversa]lis sit ab a[ris]t[otele] b[e]n[e] assignata
a 16 Utrum demonstr[ati]o sit semp[er] ex n[ecessari]is
a 17 Utrum demonstr[ati]o possit e[ss]e ex p[ri]n[cipi]is [con]ven[ienti]b[u]s
a 18 Utrum b[e]n[e] assignet[ur] p[ri]n[cipiu]m [con]plexa demonstr[ati]onis
a 19 Utrum [...] p[ri]n[cipiu]m n[on] [...] sit aff[irmativ]e et [...] demonstr[ati]o[n]em
a 20 Utrum sc[ienti]e m[athemati]ca sint certissime
a 21 Utrum gene[r]e diversi demonstr[ati]o i[n] q[ui]a et p[ro]pt[er] q[ui]d
a 22 Utrum gene[r]e assignet[ur] ab a[ris]t[otele] d[istin]ctiones sc[ienti]e subalternantis
a 23 Utrum desinet[ur] sc[ienti]a sit n[ecessari]e sc[ienti]a[m] deferre et subalternatis
a 24 Utrum [...] i[n] remo ge ab a[ris]t[otele] sit i[n] m[ediat]e
a 25 Utrum iter [...] ex possint e[ss]e m[edi]e i[n]finita
a 26 Utrum demonstr[ati]o u[niversa]lis sit potior p[articula]ri
a 27 Utrum demonstr[ati]o aff[irmativ]a sit potior neg[ativa]
a 28 Utrum demonstr[ati]o ostensiva sit potior ducente ad impo[ssibi]le
a 29 Utrum u[n]itas sc[ienti]e s[...] ex u[n]i[tate] subi[ecti]
a 30 Utrum sc[ienti]a et s[ci]re d[iffer]ant ab op[inio]ne et op[in]a[ri]

2 p[er]ier[menei]as tabula

a 1 Utrum q[uesti]o[n]es sint tm q[ua]t[uor] et equales n[umer]o hiis et c[etera]
a 2 Utrum o[mn]is q[uesti]o sit q[uesti]o medii
a 3 Utrum u[nu]m et eadem possit e[ss]e diffi[niti]o et demonstr[ati]o
a 4 Utrum diffi[niti]o possit demonstrari de suo diffi[ni]to
a 5 Utrum diffi[niti]o possit demonstrari de suo diffi[ni]to a sillo[gismo]
a 6 Utrum diffi[niti]o possit de diffi[ni]to p[er] sill[ogismum] distinctum demonstrari
a 7 Utrum sillo[gismu]m demonstr[ati]o declarat e[ss]e
a 8 Utrum m[edi]um i[n] demonstr[ati]one p[otissi]ma sit diffi[niti]o subi[ecti]
a 9 Utrum [...] ge[...] possit demonstrari effectus
a 10 Utrum [...] diversis i[n] d[iffe]r[enti]a s[...] [...]
a 11 Utrum plurium [...] possit e[ss]e idem m[edi]um
a 12 Utrum [...] n[on] [...] nob[ilissim]a natura

Explicit tabula questionum

Facing page: MS 97.5, fol. 47v (*bottom margin trimmed*)

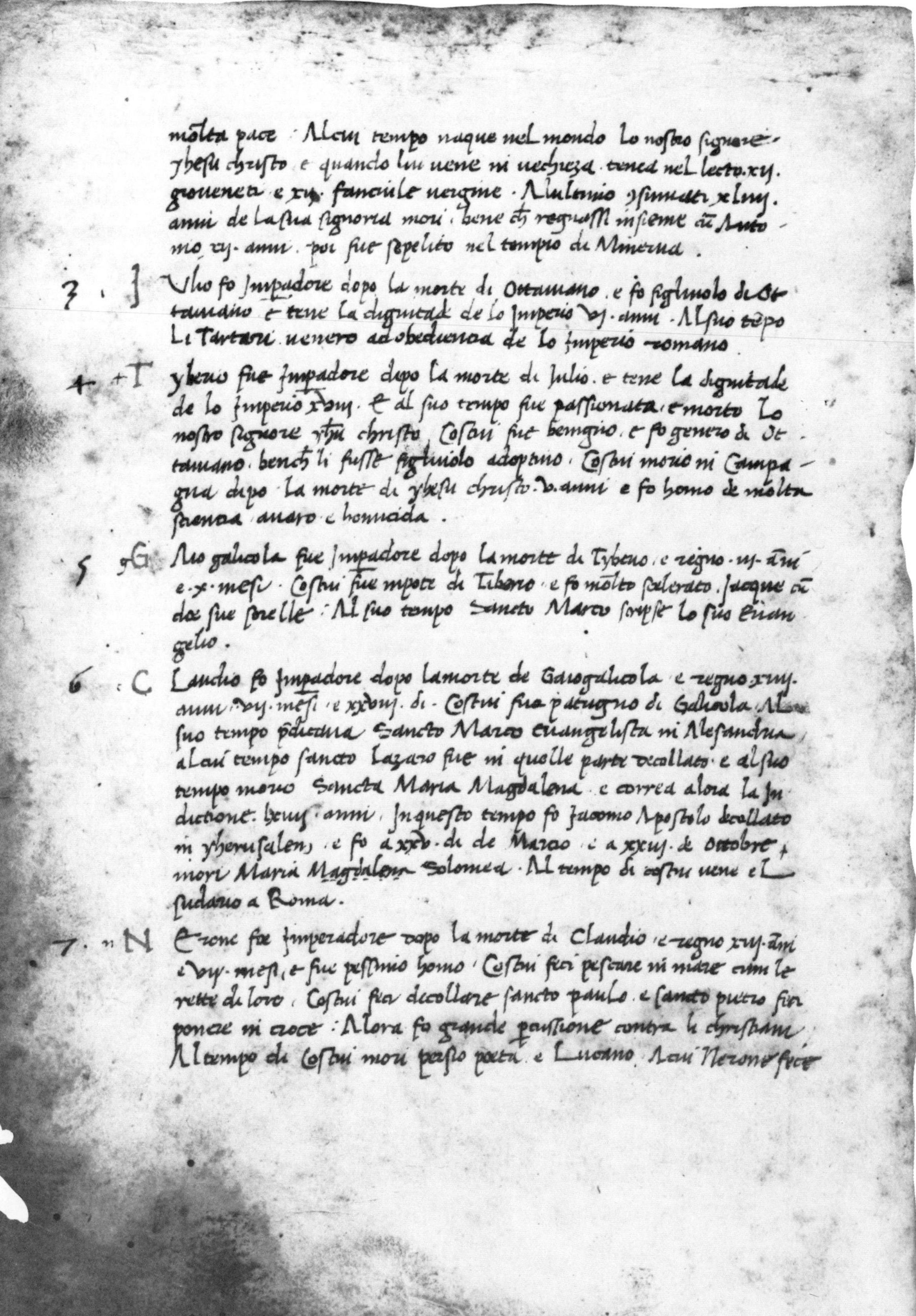

molta pace · Al cui tempo naque nel mondo lo nostro signore
yhesu christo e quando lui uene in uechieza tenea nel lecto .xij.
giouenecti e xij. fanciulle uergine · Al ultimo consumati xlviij.
anni de la sua signoria mori · bene che regnassi insieme cum Antonio xij. anni · poi fue sepelito nel tempio de Minerua .

3 · J Ulio fo Jmpadore dopo la morte di Ottauiano · e fo figliuolo de Ottauiano e tene la dignitade de lo Jmperio vij. anni · Al suo tempo
Li Tartari uenero ad obedientia de lo Jmperio romano .

4 · T yberio fue Jmpadore dopo la morte di Julio · e tene la dignitade
de lo Jmperio xxiij · E al suo tempo fue passionato · e morto Lo
nostro signore yhu christo · Costui fue benignio · e fo genero de Ottauiano · benche li fusse figliuolo adoptiuo · Costui morio in Campa-
gna dopo la morte di yhesu christo v. anni e fo homo de molta
scientia auaro e homicida .

5 · G Aio galicola fue Jmpadore dopo la morte di Tyberio · e regno · iij · anni
e · x · mesi · Costui fue nepote di Tiberio · e fo molto scelerato · Jacque cum
doe sue sorelle · Al suo tempo Sancto Marco scripse lo suo Euangelio .

6 · C Laudio fo Jmpadore dopo la morte de Gaio galicola e regno xiiij.
anni vij · mesi · e xxviij · di · Costui fue patrigno di Galicola · Al
suo tempo predicaua Sancto Marco euangelista in Alesandria
al cui tempo sancto Lazaro fue in quelle parte decollato · e al suo
tempo morio Sancta Maria Magdalena · e correa alora la Jn-
dictione · lxviij · anni · Jn questo tempo fo Jacomo Apostolo decollato
in yherusalem · e fo a xxv · di de Marzo · e a xxiij · de ottobre
mori Maria Magdalena Salomea · Al tempo di costui uene el
sudario a Roma .

7 · N Erone fue Jmperadore dopo la morte di Claudio · e regno xiij · anni
e vij · mesi · e fue pessimo homo · Costui fecie pescare in mare cum le
rette de loro · Costui fece decollare sancto paulo · e sancto pietro fici
poncere in croce · Alora fo grande passione contra li christiani
Al tempo di costui mori persio poeta · e Lucano · Al cui Nerone fece

MS 98.1, fol. 53v

dam obuiamus. amor ergo christi est cui seruiamus credentes quod nos sine operibus ad [illegible]
qui ad saluatorem nostrum sanctam infantiam puram obedientiam potuerunt peruenire.

Epistola hieronimi ad theophilum exhortatiua ut heresim quam pe titur extirpet.

Beatissimo pape theophilo hyeronimus salutem.

Meminit beatitudo tua quod eo tempore quo tacebam numquam a bonis officiis mea [illegible] cessauit. Nec consideraui quid tu nunc pro dispensatione faceres. Sed quid me facere conueniret. et nunc suscepta dignatione tue epistole fructum aliquem cepisse me video euangelice lectionis. Si enim duri iudicis sententiam crebra uidue flexit petitio. quanto magis paterna uiscera interpellatione sedula molliuit. Et de canonibus ecclesiasticis quod commonemus gratias agimus. quem enim diligit dominus corripit et flagellat omnem filium quem recepit. Sed scito nobis nihil esse antiquius quam christi iura seruare nec patrum transferre terminos semperque meminisse romanam fidem apostolico ore laudatam cuius esse participem alexandrina ecclesia gloriatur. Super nepharia heresi quod multam patientiam geris et putas ecclesie uisceribus incubantes tua posse corrigi lenitate multis sanctis displicet ne dum paucorum penitentiam prestolaris nutrias audatiam perditorum et factio robustior fiat.

Epistola theophili ad ieronimum responsiua super eadem heresi.

Dilectissimo et amantissimo fratri hieronimo. Theophilus episcopus. Sanctus episcopus agato cum dilectissimo dyacono athanasio in ecclesiastica directus est causa. quos cum uideris non ambigo quin nostrum studium probes. et in ecclesie uictoria glorieris. Nam origenis heresim in monasteriis nitentes quidam et furiosi homines serere et fundare. impietates prophetica falce succisi sunt qui recordati sunt commonentis apostoli. Argue eos seuere. festina igitur et tu partem huius primum recipere deceptos quosque emendare sermonibus. Optamus si fieri potest in diebus nostris catholicam fidem. et ecclesie regulas subiectis nobis populis custodire et omnes nouas sopire doctrinas.

Epistola hieronimi ad theophilum responsiua superiori super eadem heresi.

Beatissimo pape Theophilo. hieronimus. duplicem mihi gratiam beatitudinis tue littere prestiterunt quod et sanctos et uenerabiles agatonem episcopum et dyaconum athanasium habuerunt portitorem et aduersum sceleratissimam heresim zelum fidei demonstrarunt. Vox beatitudinis tue in toto orbe personuit. et cunctis christi ecclesiis letantibus dyaboli. dyaboli uenena siluere. nequaquam antiquus serpens sibilat. Sed contortus et euisceratus in cauernarum tenebris delitescit. Solem clarum ferre non sustinet. Cui quidem super hac re et antequam scriberes ad occidentem epistolas missas. expertem hereticorum strophas mee lingue [illegible] indicans. Ex dispensatione dei factum puto ut eo tempore tu quoque ad papam anastasium scriberes et nostram dum ignoras sententiam roborares. Verum ante [illegible]

Facing page: MS 102.2, fol. 238v (*top and bottom margins trimmed*)

Wing
MS ZW 1.467,
fols. 2v–3

S ic hominum mundiq; diu moderat⁹ habenas
Candidus excuperes serius astra pie;
Explicit elegia.

INCIPIT. PREFATIO

IOGENIS.

philosophi epistolas nuper a
me e greco in latinum tra
ductas: cui potius dicare pos
sum et debeo q̄ sanctissimo
nomini tuo beatissime pater pie. Non q exi
guum munus: et tua indignum maiestate
et ingenioli mei uires non intelligam. Sed
pro suis erga me et studiosos omnes immor
talib; meritis omne meum studium quã
tulumcunq; est laborem uigilias iure op
timo sibi uendicat clementia tua. Verum
si recto iudicio quae te digna sunt uellem
dum taxat intueri: uix unus aut alter: ne
dicam nemo hac nostra etate meritas Sancti
tatis tuae laudes animo: nedum oratione
unq̄ assequi: complectiq; posset. Nam ut id

quod maximum est in presentia taceam Te
summum pontificem: christi uicarium:
alteru deum in terris: quo nihil admirabili⁹
nihil sanctius uidet. Quanti existiman
dum est q tam amplissimam dignitatem
innumeris: maximisq; uirtutib; prestan
tissimo ingenio: clarissimis artib; summo
studio et labore comperatis; exornas auges
illustras. Quae non opinione quadam: sed
certitudine. Non auditu: sed uisu ipso: nõ
unius aut alterius predicatione: sed totius
orbis testimonio luce clariora in te appare
ant. Quid admiramur: q ex tanto et tam
clarissimo reuerendissimorum patrũ ordi
ne: et uere uniuersi orbis cardinũ: omnes
uno ore te summum pont. iampridem fo
re augurabant. Siue enim religionem:
siue clementiam: siue animi magnitudinẽ:
siue bonarum artium studia intueri ueli
mus: ad hunc te summi pontificatus apicẽ
iure ipso quiuis ascendisse profiteatur ne
cesse est. Sed longius q̄ instituetam stu
dio utinam non audatiore prouectus

ra inutanda. sed cō cupiscencia finienda; Nā beatus
augustinus hanc questionē in suis tractatib. uersās.
melius mihi ait sapere uidentur. qui utrūq; sexū
resurrecturū ee. nō dubitant; Non enī libido ibi
erit. que confusionis ē. causa; Nā priusquā peccas
sent. nudi erant & nō cōfundebātur uir & femina;
Corporibus ergo illis uicia detrahentur. natura seruabi
tur; Nō ē aut uiciū sexus femineus. sed natura. que tūc
quidē a cō cubitu. & a partu inmunis erit; Quibus ita
ap̄ dicto uiro digestis. erit ut p̄ceptor nr̄ sacer euge
nius doc&. tanta ac talis glorificati corporis pulcri
tudo. ut ob lec t&ur intuitu. & cor nulla tenus inflec
tat ad uicium; CURA SOLLICITE. QUOD NULLA RESUR
GENTES CIBI AC POTUS. CP̄. XXVI.
Necessitatē cibi ac potus natura nr̄a quā diu corrup
tibilis in hoc sub est corpore patitur. cū merito cor
ruptionis ac mortalitatis sue languenti. eidē
uelut quedā medicamina p̄bentur; Cū aut fac
ta fuerit resurreccio corporū. in sūmi di ibi cibi ac po
tus necessitas nulla erit. que corruptioni tantū
in hac uita tribuit. nō incorruptioni. ut inmor
talitati que post hanc uitā ē. futura uidetur; Deni
que iuxta qd iulianus pomerius ait. omni corruptio
ni ac mortalitate cōsūpta. nō ibi erit ulla carnis
infirmitas. sed natura; hic ergo ubi potest caro
mori. cibo ac potu iuuanda est ne moriatur sub cibat;
Illa aut uita ubi mori nō poterit. nihil requir&
alimonię. quia inmortalē nec famis potest. nec sitis

MS f2, fol. 39v
(80% of actual size)

quentatione mysterii crescat nre salutis effect'. ℟
Deus q nos redeptionis nre In viglia natl' dni.
annua expectatione letificas. pra ut unige
nitu tuum que redeptore leti suscipim'. uenien
tem quoq; iudicem securi uideamus. ℟ eunde.
Da nobis qs omnpe ds. ut sic adoranda filii tui Scr
natalicia preuenim'. sic ei munera capiam' sempitna
Da nobis dne qs unigeniti filii P co gaudentes. Cr
tui recensita natiuitate respirare. cuius celesti
mysterio pascimur et potam. ℟ eunde. Missa de
nocte ad scam Mariam maiore. Ad hac
missam n dr n una colla. Gla in ex
celsis do. et Credo in unum. dicit.
Deus. Qui. hanc Colla
sacratissimam noctem.
ueri luminis fecisti illustratione
clarescere. da qs ut cui lucis myste
ria in tra cognouim'. ei quoq; gaudi
is in celo pfruamur. Cr tecu. v. Scra
Accepta t sit dne qs hodierne festiuitatis ob
latio. ut tua gra largiente phec sacro sca com
mertia. in illius inueniam forma in quo tecu
e nra substantia. Cr tecu. u. Prefacio.
Aeterne ds. Quia pincarnati uerbi
mysteriu. n. Infra act. Communican
tes et noctem sacratissima celebrantes in qua
beate Marie intemerata uirginitas huic mun
do edidit saluatore. Sed et memoria ueneran
tes eide gl'ose semp uirginis Marie. genitricis di
et dni nri ihu xp. Sed et beator aplor. Post co

MS +7, fol. 146v

(50% of actual size)

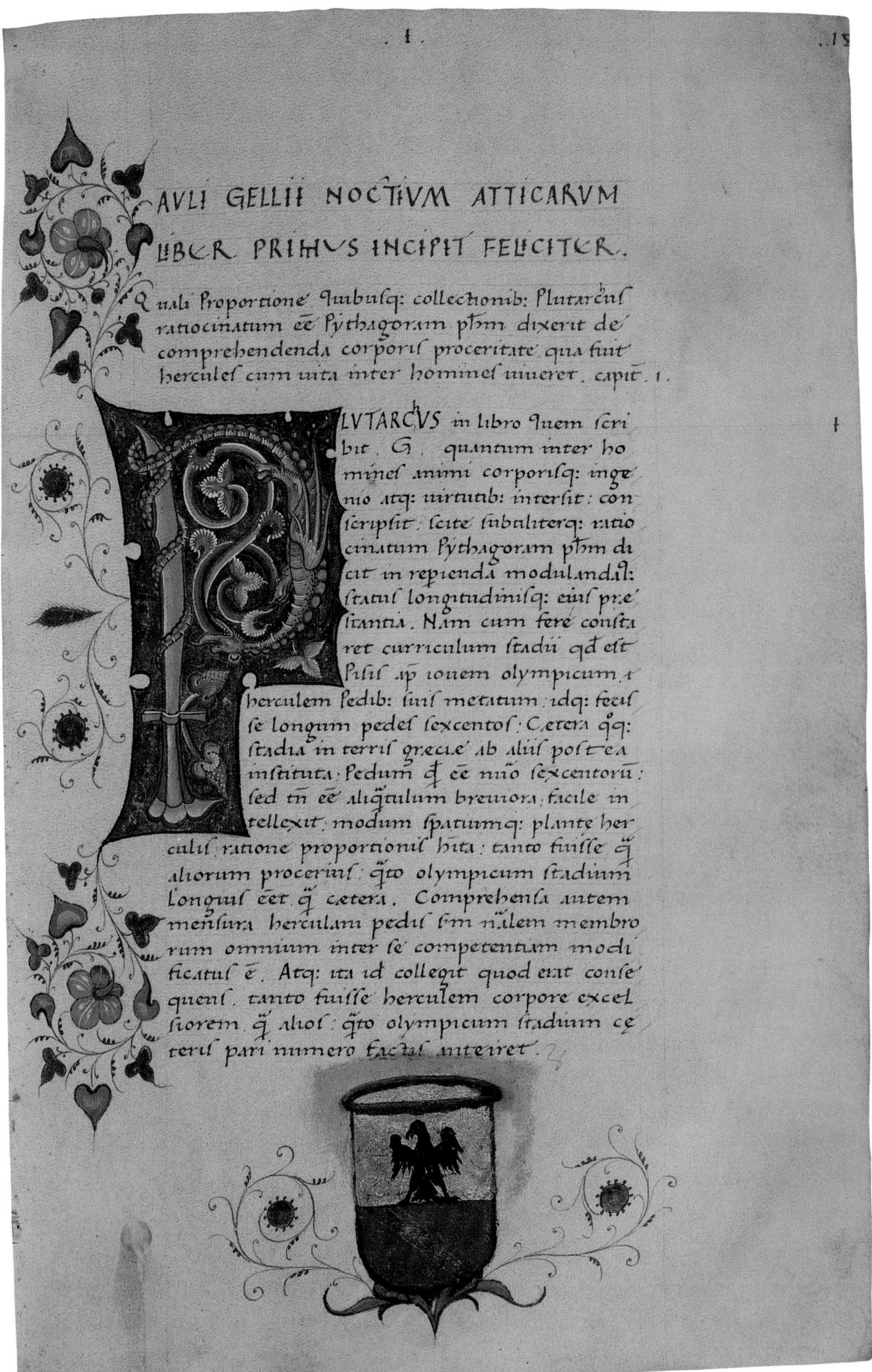

. I . ..15

AVLI GELLII NOCTIVM ATTICARVM
LIBER PRIMVS INCIPIT FELICITER.

Quali proportione quibusq: collectionib: Plutarcus ratiocinatum ee Pythagoram phm dixerit de comprehendenda corporis proceritate qua fuit hercules cum uita inter homines uiueret. capit. I.

PLVTARCVS in libro quem scribit. G. quantum inter homines animi corporisq: ingenio atq: uirtutib: intersit: conscripsit: scite subtiliterq: ratiocinatum Pythagoram phm dicit in repienda modulandaq: status longitudinisq: eius prestantia. Nam cum fere constaret curriculum stadii qd est pisis ap iouem olympicum, herculem pedib: suis metatum: idq: fecisse longum pedes sexcentos: Cetera qq: stadia in terris grecie ab aliis postea instituta: pedum qdem ee nuo sexcentorum: sed tn ee aliqtulum breuiora: facile intellexit: modum spatiumq: plante herculis ratione proportionis hita: tanto fuisse qm aliorum procerius: qto olympicum stadium longius eet q cetera. Comprehensa autem mensura herculani pedis sm nalem membrorum omnium inter se competentiam modificatus e. Atq: ita id collegit quod erat consequens. tanto fuisse herculem corpore excelsiorem q alios: qto olympicum stadium ceteris pari numero factis anteiret.

MS f90, fol. 18

MS −53, fol. 13v

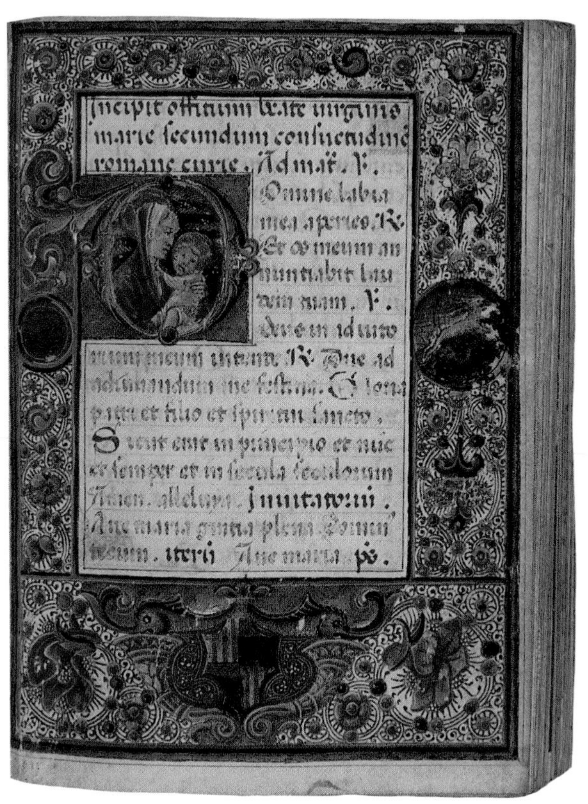

MS 84, fol. 13

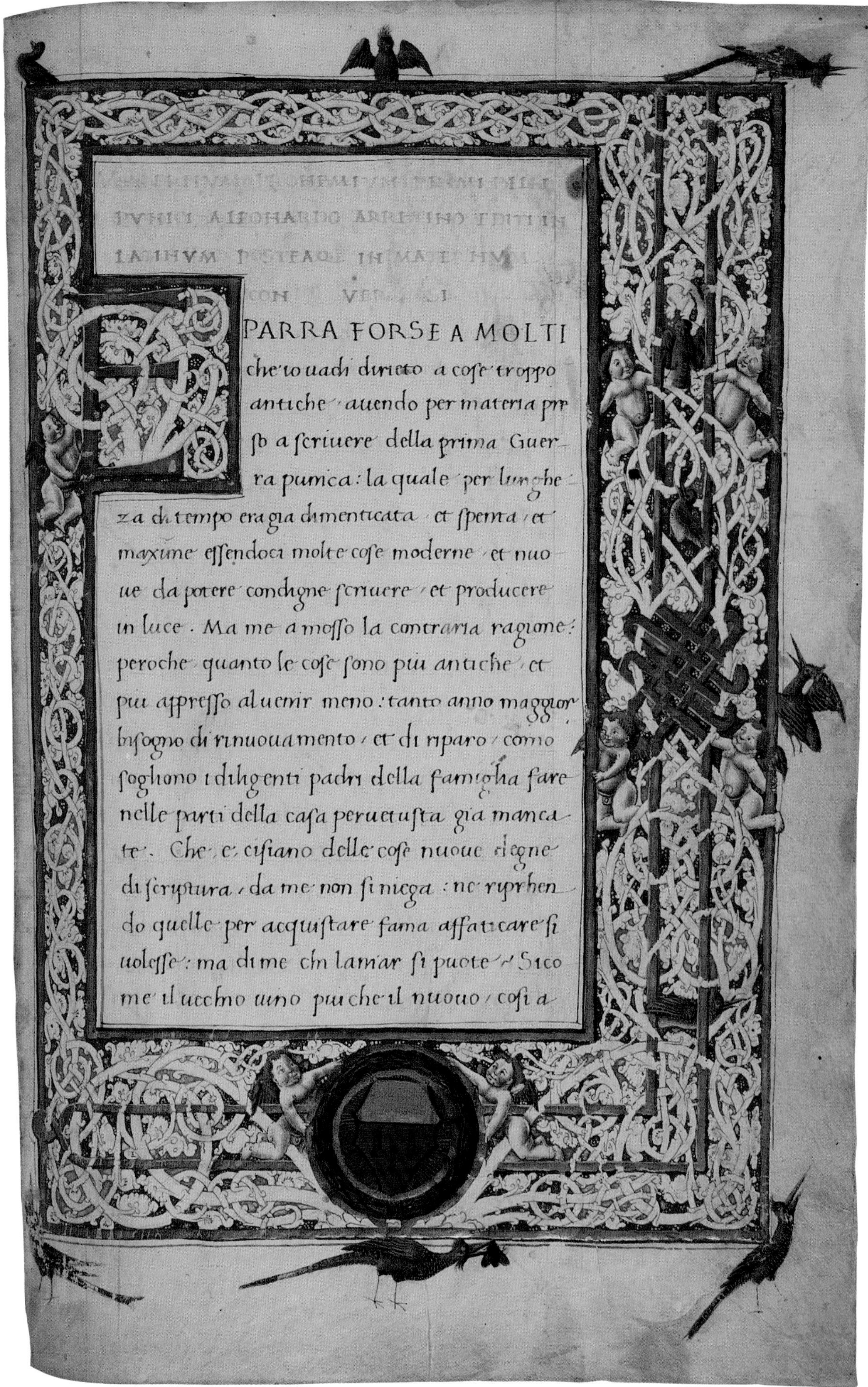

PARRA FORSE A MOLTI che io uadi dirieto a cose troppo antiche auendo per materia pre so a scriuere della prima Guerra punica: la quale per lungheza di tempo era gia dimenticata et spenta, et maxime essendoci molte cose moderne et nuoue da potere condigne scriuere, et producere in luce. Ma me a mosso la contraria ragione: peroche quanto le cose sono piu antiche, et piu appresso al uenir meno: tanto anno maggior bisogno di rinuouamento, et di riparo, como sogliono i diligenti padri della famiglia fare nelle parti della casa peruetusta gia mancate. Che e cisiano delle cose nuoue degne di scriptura, da me non si niega: ne riprhendo quelle per acquistare fama affaticare si uolesse: ma di me ch'n lamar si puote. Sicome il uecchio uino piu che il nuouo, cosi a

MS f93, fol. 1

MS 99.1, fol. 1
(Detail)

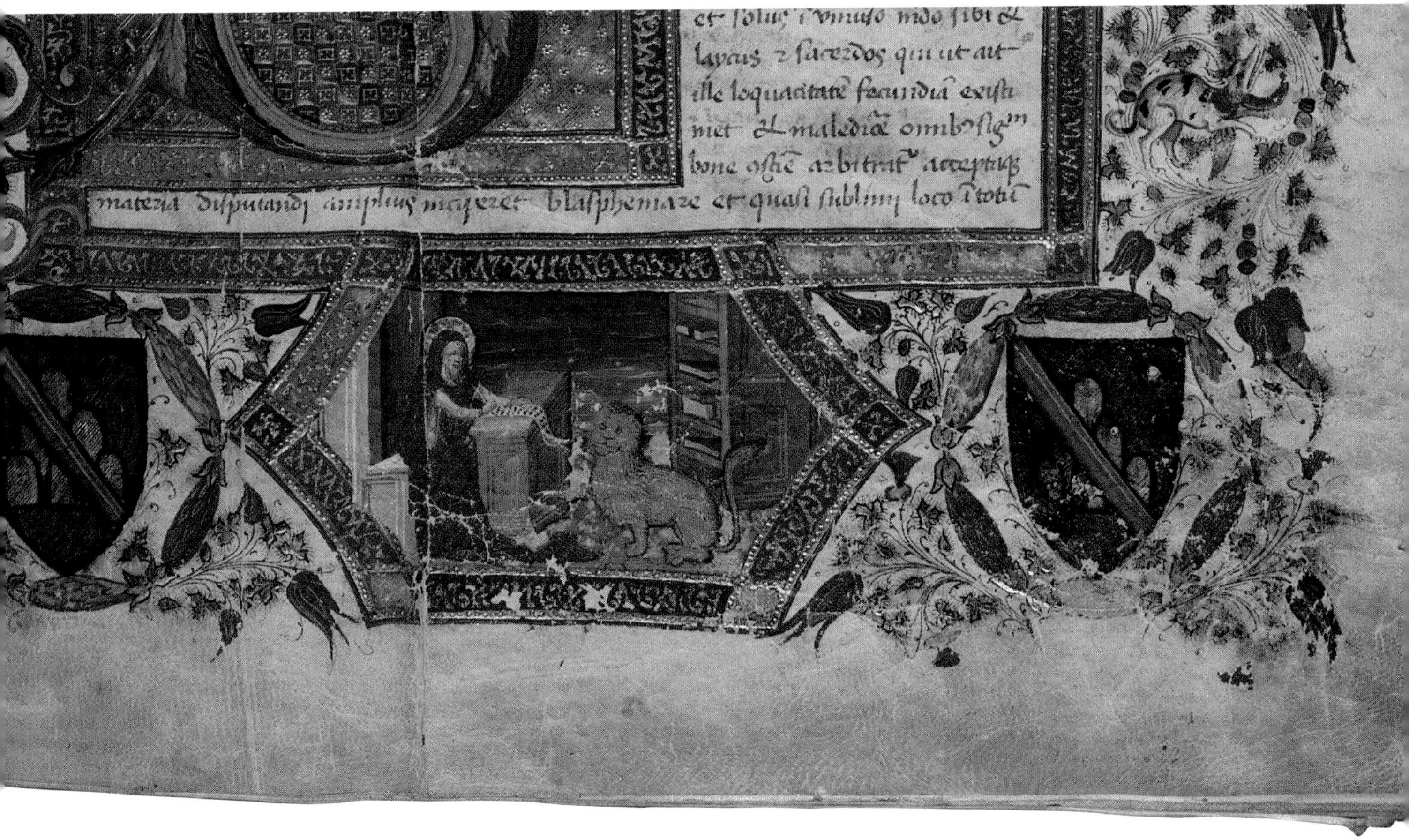

MS 102.2, fol. 3
(Detail)

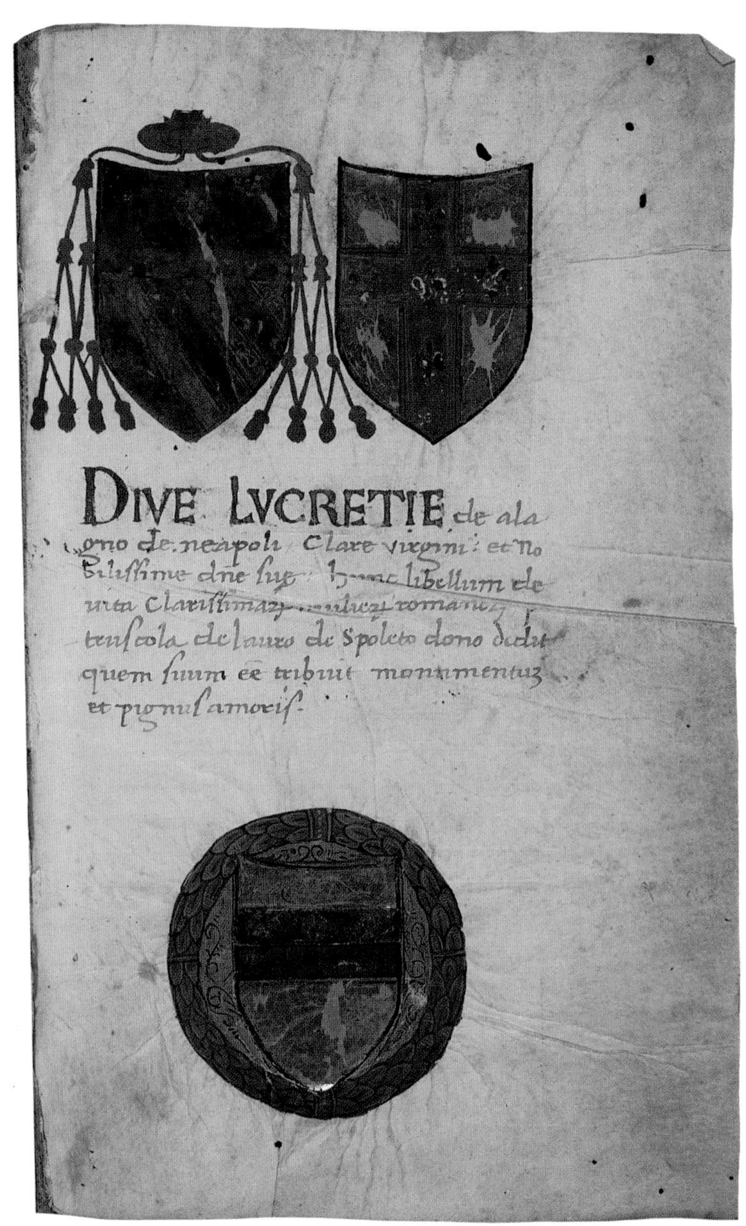

MS 105, fol. 1